Programming Languages

An Interpreter-Based Approach

Samuel N. Kamin

University of Illinois at Urbana-Champaign

Addison-Wesley Publishing Company, Inc.

Reading, Massachusetts • Menlo Park, California • New York
Don Mills, Ontario • Wokingham, England • Amsterdam
Bonn • Sydney • Singapore • Tokyo • Madrid • San Juan

The APLitalic font was designed by Joey Tuttle and copyrighted by I.P. Sharp Associates.

Library of Congress Cataloging-in-Publication Data

Kamin, Samuel N.
  Programming Languges.

  Bibliography: P.
  Includes index.
  1. Programming languages (electronic computers). 2. Interpreters (computer programs).
  I. Title.
  QA76.7.K35   1990   005.13'3   88-34998
  ISBN 0-201-06824-9

Reprinted with corrections May, 1990.

3 4 5 6 7 8 9-MA-97 96 95 94 93

For Judy and Rebecca

Preface

> The chief goal of my work as educator and author is to help
> people learn to write *beautiful programs*.
>
> Donald E. Knuth, *Computer Programming as an Art*,
> 1974 ACM Turing Award Lecture

Beauty in programs, as in poetry, is not language-independent. There is an aesthetic dimension in programming that is visible only to the multi-lingual programmer. My purpose in writing this book has been to present that dimension in the plainest possible way.

My focus in this endeavor has been on non-imperative languages, since they present a stark aesthetic contrast with what the reader is assumed already to know — namely, PASCAL. A study of the comparatively subtle differences among more traditional languages would be less likely to make a strong impression. My specific choice, reflecting the principal concepts underlying non-imperative languages generally, is: LISP, APL, SCHEME, SASL, CLU, SMALLTALK, and PROLOG.

The beauty in these languages reveals itself slowly. Not only are the conceptual difficulties great, but they are compounded by the usual problems of learning new syntax, memorizing function and procedure names, dealing with a compiler, and other such minutiae. The challenge is to present clearly what is aesthetically interesting, and to avoid what is not.

I have tried to meet this challenge directly, in this way: Each language is presented in a syntactically and semantically simplified form, and for each we provide an interpreter, written in PASCAL. The more educated reader will be struck by this immediately, as the sample programs appear quite different from those in the real languages. No doubt some will think too much has been omitted, but it is my hope and intention that the central concepts in each language have been preserved.

The use of interpreters for simplified language subsets contributes to the overall pedagogical style, which is characterized by these principles:

Concreteness. I have emphasized the presentation of specific programs in each language. (If I were attempting to instill an appreciation of poetry, I would do it not with abstract principles or history, but with poems, and the same principle applies here, albeit on a more prosaic level.) Moreover, the languages can be described very specifically, and can be *completely understood.*

Multiple presentations of concepts. Each language is described both "top-down," by syntactic and semantic descriptions and sample programs, and "bottom-up" by the language's interpreter. Each chapter has a section documenting its interpreter, which is then listed in an Appendix.

Exploiting prior knowledge. The use of interpreters is a way of building on the reader's knowledge of PASCAL to teach him new languages. PASCAL is also used to illustrate concepts such as type-checking and scope.

Generalities emerge from specifics. Readers will learn about recursion by seeing many examples of LISP functions, about higher-order functions by seeing them used in SCHEME, and so on. (The exercises aim at making the concepts still more concrete.) Furthermore, the use of interpreters tends to wash out many nonessential distinctions among the languages covered, allowing unifying principles to reveal themselves.

Overview

The ACM Curriculum 78 recommendations (Austing, et.al. [1979]) describe the course CS8, *Organization of Programming Languages*, as "an applied course in programming language concepts." The current book is intended as a text for CS8, as well as for self-study. It takes a "comparative" approach, which is to say that it covers specific languages, teaching general concepts only as they arise in particular languages. Each of the first eight chapters covers a different language; this coverage includes a complete context-free syntax (easy because the languages are highly simplified), an interpreter written in PASCAL, and, of course, many sample programs. Chapters 9 and 10 cover, respectively, compilation and memory management.

Chapter 1 discusses the design of a simple interpreter for a language with LISP-like syntax (though without LISP data structures), with the complete PASCAL code given in Appendix B. The principal design criterion of this and all the interpreters is simplicity. The student is assumed to have a good knowledge of PASCAL. The only warning to be given is that our code makes heavy use of recursive procedures; the student whose knowledge of recursion is weak will need to spend extra time studying the Appendix. On the other hand, it is not expected that students have had much experience *writing* recursive procedures; the study of LISP is largely intended to provide such experience.

The languages covered in Chapters 2 through 8 are, in order, LISP, APL, SCHEME, SASL, CLU, SMALLTALK, and PROLOG. Each of these chapters has roughly the same structure:

- General introduction to the language, its history, and its influence.
- Discussion of the basic ideas of the language, its syntax and semantics, and simple examples.

- The design of the interpreter for the language; some code is listed here, some in the Appendix.

- One or more larger (several page) examples.

- Aspects of the language as it is in real life, including its true syntax and interesting language features not included in our version. This section is not intended for use as a reference, nor to give a complete definition of the language, but merely to provide the student with a "reading knowledge" of the language.

- A brief summary, suggestions for further study, and a glossary of terms commonly associated with the language.

- Exercises, divided in two parts: programs in the language, and modifications to the interpreter.

Some chapters have additional sections exploring concepts pertinent to that language or describing different languages based on similar concepts.

Listings of all the interpreters, in PASCAL, are available in machine-readable form from the author (see below). The individual instructor may wish to use them in different ways. Some possibilities are:

- Have students study interpreters for, and write programs in, all or a subset of the languages covered. Studying the interpreters will most likely take the form of assigning some of the interpreter-modification exercises.

- Have each student study an interpreter for only one or two of the languages, and write programs in some or all of the remaining languages.

- Use the interpreters as "black boxes;" that is, do not study the interpreters *per se*. In that case, this book has the advantage of maintaining some syntactic uniformity across languages, thereby focusing more attention on the essential features of each language, less on their syntax or other idiosyncracies.

The "prerequisite structure" of the chapters is summarized in this chart:

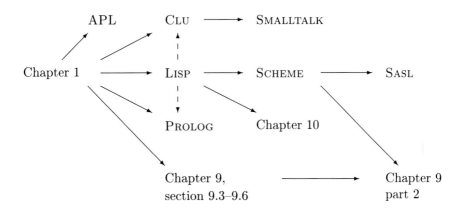

LISP is a "weak prerequisite" for CLU and PROLOG, in that some examples in those chapters use lists and recursion in LISP-like ways.

Obtaining the Interpreters

The interpreter code, and all the code appearing in this book, can be obtained by "anonymous ftp": `ftp` to node `uihub.cs.uiuc.edu`, sign on as `anonymous`, giving your own name as the password, then `cd` to directory `uiuc/kamin.distr`. You may either copy the compressed tar file `distr.tar.Z` (then uncompress and de-tar to get the `distr` directory), or simply copy the `distr` directory. For questions or comments, contact the author at: Computer Science Dept., Univ. of Illinois, 1304 W. Springfield, Urbana, IL 61801, or by electronic mail at: `kamin@cs.uiuc.edu`.

Acknowledgments

I have benefited from the comments and criticisms of many colleagues and students at the University of Illinois. The comments of Luddy Harrison, Tim Kraus, and Vipin Swarup have affected virtually every page. Ralph Johnson gave the manuscript a thorough reading. Others here whose help has been highly appreciated are (in alphabetical order) Subutai Ahmad, Nachum Dershowitz, Ken Forbus, Alan Frisch, Simon Kaplan, Kyung Min, Uday Reddy, Ed Reingold, Hal Render, Vince Russo, and Dong Tang.

Among the outside reviewers, I would especially like to thank Andrew Appel and Ryan Stansifer for their useful feedback and their continuing interest in the project. Other helpful reviews were provided by Neta Amit, Myla Archer, Ray Ford, Takayuki Dan Kimura, William J. Pervin, and Clifford Walinsky. Thanks also to Dave Jackson, Jim DeWolf, and Helen Wythe of Addison-Wesley and Lori Pickert of Archetype Publishing.

Writing a book is a strange mixture of pain and pleasure. For easing the pain and enhancing the pleasure, I thank my wife Judy.

S.N.K.

Contents

Part I
Starting Off

The idea of this book is to learn about programming languages both by programming in them and by studying interpreters for them.

In Part I, then, we present the language and interpreter which will be used as the basis for the languages and interpreters in the remainder of the book. The language we interpret here is intended to be about the minimal language, using the simplest syntax, which contains enough features to be called a programming language. The programming environment is, likewise, skeletal, providing only the ability to enter programs (no editing) and run them. Finally, the interpreter is built for simplicity, and to this goal all concerns of efficiency have been sacrificed.

My fondest hope is that the student will feel moved to correct these various deficiencies, in both this and subsequent chapters. Suggestions for improvement are made throughout the book, especially in the programming exercises that end each chapter.

Chapter 1

The Basic Evaluator

This chapter describes a simple language whose constructs should be regarded as simplified versions of the constructs of PASCAL, written in a syntax designed for ease of parsing. We then present the interpreter for that language, giving the code in PASCAL in Appendix B. The chapter ends with an outline of what this book is about and why.

1.1 The Language

Our interpreter is interactive. The user will enter two kinds of inputs: function definitions, such as:

$$\text{(define double (x) (+ x x))}$$

and expressions, such as:

$$\text{(double 5)}.$$

Function definitions are simply "remembered" by the interpreter, and expressions are evaluated. "Evaluating an expression" in this language corresponds to "running a program" in most other languages.

The subsections of this section present the language's syntax, its semantics, and examples. It is to be hoped that the reader will soon find the syntax, if not elegant, at least not a major hindrance.

1.1.1 SYNTAX

The syntax of our language is like that of LISP, and can be very simply defined:[1]

| input | $\longrightarrow$ | expression \| fundef |
| fundef | $\longrightarrow$ | (define function arglist expression) |

---

[1]Appendix A gives an explanation of this notation.

arglist	$\longrightarrow$	(variable*)
expression	$\longrightarrow$	value
	$\mid$	variable
	$\mid$	(if expression expression expression)
	$\mid$	(while expression expression)
	$\mid$	(set variable expression)
	$\mid$	(begin expression$^+$)
	$\mid$	(optr expression*)
optr	$\longrightarrow$	function $\mid$ value-op
value	$\longrightarrow$	integer
value-op	$\longrightarrow$	+ $\mid$ - $\mid$ * $\mid$ / $\mid$ = $\mid$ < $\mid$ > $\mid$ print
function	$\longrightarrow$	name
variable	$\longrightarrow$	name
integer	$\longrightarrow$	sequence of digits, possibly preceded by minus sign
name	$\longrightarrow$	any sequence of characters not an integer, and not containing a blank or any of the following characters: ( ) ;.

A function cannot be one of the "keywords" define, if, while, begin, or set, or any of the value-op's. Aside from this, names can use any characters on the keyboard. Comments are introduced by the character ';' and continue to the end of the line; this is why ';' cannot occur within a name. A session is terminated by entering "quit"; thus, it is highly inadvisable to use this name for a variable.

Expressions are fully parenthesized. Our purpose is to simplify the syntax by eliminating such syntactic recognition problems as operator precedence. Thus, the PASCAL assignment

$$i := 2*j + i - k/3;$$

becomes

$$(\text{set } i \ (- \ (+ \ (* \ 2 \ j) \ i) \ (/ \ k \ 3))).$$

The advantage is that the latter is quite trivial to parse, where the former is not. Our form may be unattractive, but then most PASCAL programmers will agree that assignments of even this much complexity occur rarely.

1.1.2 SEMANTICS

The meanings of expression's are presented informally here (and more formally in Section 1.2.8). Note first that integers are the only values; when used in conditionals (if or while), zero represents false and one (or any other nonzero value) represents true.

(if e_1 e_2 e_3) — If e_1 evaluates to zero, then evaluate e_3; otherwise evaluate e_2.

(while e_1 e_2) — Evaluate e_1; if it evaluates to zero, return zero; otherwise, evaluate e_2 and then re-evaluate e_1; continue this until e_1 evaluates to zero. (A while expression always returns the same value, but that really doesn't matter since it is being evaluated only for its side-effects.)

(set x e) — Evaluate e, assign its value to variable x, and return its value.

(begin e_1 ... e_n) — Evaluate each of e_1 ... e_n, in that order, and return the value of e_n.

(f e_1 ... e_n) — Evaluate each of e_1 ... e_n, and apply function f to those values. f may be a value-op or a user-defined function; if the latter, its definition is found and the expression defining its body is evaluated with the variables of its arglist associated with the values of e_1 ... e_n.

if, while, set, and begin are called *control operations.*

All the value-op's take two arguments, except print, which takes one. The arithmetic operators +, -, *, and / do the obvious. The comparison operators do the indicated comparison and return either zero (for false) or one (for true). print evaluates its argument, prints its value, and returns its value.

As in PASCAL, there are global variables and formal parameters. When a variable reference occurs in an expression at the top level (as opposed to a function definition), it is necessarily global. If it occurs within a function definition, then if the function has a formal parameter of that name, the variable is that parameter, otherwise it is a global variable. This corresponds to the *static scope* of PASCAL, in the (relatively uninteresting) case where there are no nested procedure or function declarations.[2] There are no local variables *per se*, only formal parameters.

1.1.3 EXAMPLES

As indicated earlier, the user enters function definitions and expressions interactively. Function definitions are stored; expressions are evaluated and their values are printed. Our first examples involve no function definitions. "->" is the interpreter's prompt; an expression following a prompt is the user's input, and everything else is the interpreter's response:

```
-> 3
3
-> (+ 4 7)
11
-> (set x 4)
4
```

---

[2] For more on static scope, see Section 4.7 (the chapter on SCHEME), and also Chapter 9.

```
-> (+ x x)
8
-> (print x)
4
4
```

Notice that (print x) first prints the value of x, then returns the value; the interpreter always prints the value of an expression, so in this case 4 is printed twice.

```
-> (set y 5)
5
-> (begin (print x) (print y) (* x y))
4
5
20
-> (if (> y 0) 5 10)
5
```

The body of a while expression (that is, its second argument) will almost always be a begin expression.

```
-> (while (> y 0)
>        (begin (set x (+ x x)) (set y (- y 1)))))
0
-> x
128
```

Note that the interpreter allows expressions to be entered on more than one line; if an incomplete expression is entered, the interpreter gives a different prompt and waits for more input.

User-defined functions work very much as in PASCAL: The arguments to the function are evaluated first, then the function body is evaluated with its *formal parameters* (i.e., variables occurring in the function's arglist) "bound" to the *actual parameters* (i.e., evaluated arguments of the application). When a function is entered, the interpreter responds by echoing the name of the function.

```
-> (define +1 (x) (+ x 1))
+1
-> (+1 4)
5

-> (define double (x) (+ x x))
double
```

```
-> (double 4)
8
```

It is important to realize that the variable "x" occurring as the function's formal parameter is distinct from the "x" used earlier as a global variable. This is again similar to PASCAL, where a global variable may have the same name as a formal parameter and the two occurrences represent distinct variables. A reference to x *within* the function refers to the formal parameter; a reference outside the function refers to the global variable. Unlike PASCAL, our language uses call-by-value parameter-passing exclusively (no **var** parameters); this means that a global variable can never have its value altered by an assignment to a formal parameter within a function.

```
-> x
128
-> (define setx (x y) (begin (set x (+ x y)) x))
setx
-> (setx x 1)
129

-> x
128
```

Most function definitions use either iteration or recursion. Here is a PASCAL version of the gcd function:

$$
\begin{aligned}
&\textbf{function } gcd\ (m,\ n\text{: } integer)\text{: } integer;\\
&\textbf{var } r\text{: } integer;\\
&\textbf{begin}\\
&\quad r := m \textbf{ mod } n;\\
&\quad \textbf{while } r <> 0 \textbf{ do begin}\\
&\qquad m := n;\\
&\qquad n := r;\\
&\qquad r := m \textbf{ mod } n\\
&\quad \textbf{end};\\
&\quad gcd := n\\
&\textbf{end};
\end{aligned}
$$

and here it is in our language:[3]

```
-> (define not (boolval) (if boolval 0 1))

-> (define <> (x y) (not (= x y)))
```

---

[3] From now on, and throughout the rest of the book, when presenting an interpreter session, both the echoing of function names and the secondary prompts (">") will be elided.

```
-> (define mod (m n) (- m (* n (/ m n))))
-> (define gcd (m n)
       (begin
          (set r (mod m n))
          (while (<> r 0)
             (begin
                (set m n)
                (set n r)
                (set r (mod m n))))
          n))
-> (gcd 6 15)
3
```

A recursive version in PASCAL is:

> **function** *gcd* (*m*, *n*: *integer*): *integer*;
> **begin**
>   **if** $n = 0$
>   **then** *gcd* := *m*
>   **else** *gcd* := *gcd*(*n*, *m* **mod** *n*)
> **end**;

which would be rendered in our language as:

```
-> (define gcd (m n)
       (if (= n 0) m (gcd n (mod m n)))))
```

The reader should work some of the problems in the "Learning about the Language" section of the exercises before going on to the next section.

1.2   The Structure of the Interpreter

The code for our interpreter, written in PASCAL, appears in Appendix B. This section is essentially the documentation of that program. The listing is divided into eight sections, and this documentation is structured likewise. The most important function is *eval* in Section *EVALUATION*, which evaluates an expression; it is explained in Section 1.2.8 in great detail.

1.2.1   DECLARATIONS

This section contains the declarations of the records *EXPREC*, *EXPLISTREC*, and *FUNDEFREC*, and their associated pointer types *EXP*, *EXPLIST*, and

FUNDEF (we will often use these shorter names when referring to the corresponding records):

$$EXP = \uparrow EXPREC;$$
$$EXPLIST = \uparrow EXPLISTREC;$$
$$NAMELIST = \uparrow NAMELISTREC;$$
$$FUNDEF = \uparrow FUNDEFREC;$$

$$NUMBER = integer;$$

$$EXPTYPE = (VALEXP, VAREXP, APEXP);$$
$EXPREC$ = **record**
      case *etype*: *EXPTYPE* **of**
         VALEXP: (*num*: *NUMBER*);
         VAREXP: (*varble*: *NAME*);
         APEXP: (*optr*: *NAME*; *args*: *EXPLIST*)
  end;

$EXPLISTREC$ = **record**
     head: *EXP*;
     tail: *EXPLIST*;
  end;

$FUNDEFREC$ = **record**
     funname: *NAME*;
     formals: *NAMELIST*;
     body: *EXP*;
     nextfundef: *FUNDEF*
  end;

$NAMELISTREC$ = **record**
     head: *NAME*;
     tail: *NAMELIST*;
  end;

As given in the syntactic description of the language, an expression can be either a *value* (integer), a *variable* (formal parameter or global variable), or an *application* (function call). These correspond to *EXP*'s of types *VALEXP*, *VAREXP*, and *APEXP*, respectively. (*NAME* is declared as an integer subrange, as explained under *NAME MANAGEMENT*.) A user-defined function is stored internally as a record containing the name of the function (*funname*), its formal parameters (*formals*), and its body (*body*); the *nextfundef* field in *FUNDEFREC* is used to chain together all the function definitions the user has entered. The *INPUT* section contains functions that translate the user's input into its internal representation as an *EXP* or *FUNDEF*.

Types containing the word "*LIST*" all have the same form: a *head* field and a *tail* field, defining a linked list of whatever type.

Environments (*ENV*'s) are used to hold the values of variables, whether global variables or formal parameters. Note that the value of every variable is an integer.

$$ENV = \uparrow ENVREC;$$
$$VALUELIST = \uparrow VALUELISTREC;$$

$ENVREC = $ **record**
        vars: *NAMELIST*;
        values: *VALUELIST*
    end;

$VALUELISTREC = $ **record**
        head: *NUMBER*;
        tail: *VALUELIST*
    end;

Operations on *ENV* records are given in section *ENVIRONMENTS*.

The values of scalar type *BUILTINOP* correspond to the built-in operations of the language. (All end with the characters "*OP*" to avoid collisions with PASCAL keywords.)

$BUILTINOP = (IFOP, WHILEOP, SETOP, BEGINOP, PLUSOP, MINUSOP,$
          $TIMESOP, DIVOP, EQOP, LTOP, GTOP, PRINTOP);$
$VALUEOP = PLUSOP \;..\; PRINTOP;$
$CONTROLOP = IFOP \;..\; BEGINOP;$

1.2.2 DATA STRUCTURE OP'S

This section gives operations for constructing expressions, environments, and various kinds of lists, and for computing the lengths of lists.

1.2.3 NAME MANAGEMENT

All function names and variables are translated to integers by the input routines. This is accomplished by calling *install* (from *parseName* in *INPUT*), which installs new names and recognizes previously installed ones. From then on, all references to that name use that integer (which is why the type *NAME* is an integer subrange). This is just an optimization to avoid having to store multiple copies of each name and to save some time in looking up variables.

initNames is called at the beginning of each session; it places the built-in names into the array *printNames* and initializes the global variables *numBuiltins* and *numNames* to contain the highest occupied index in *printNames* (i.e., the number of built-in operations).

primOp translates *NAME*'s corresponding to built-in operations (more precisely, those in the range 1 to *numBuiltins*) to the corresponding element of *BUILTINOP*.

1.2.4 INPUT

There are three important routines in this section — *reader*, *parseExp*, and *parseDef* — plus various supporting functions.

The procedure *reader* reads characters from the terminal and places them into the array *userinput*. It reads a single line, unless that line contains an unmatched left parenthesis, in which case it reads until all parentheses are balanced. It places a sentinel value (namely, a semicolon) after the last input character in *userinput*, and sets the variable *pos* to the index of the first nonblank character in *userinput*.

At the top level (*READ-EVAL-PRINT LOOP*), *reader* is called, and then the input is examined to determine if it is an expression or a function definition, calling either *parseExp* or *parseDef* accordingly.

parseExp and *parseDef* use a "recursive-descent" approach to parsing. Each syntactic category has a function which recognizes inputs in that category and translates them to internal form. Thus, *parseDef* is for function definitions, *parseExp* for expressions, *parseEL* for expression lists, *parseNL* for name lists, *parseVal* for integers, and *parseName* for names. These functions are mutually recursive.

For example, if the user enters the expression (f x (* y 3)), *reader* will place these characters in *userinput*. The read-eval-print loop will recognize that this is an expression (because it doesn't start with the word "define"), so will call *parseExp*, which will construct, and return a pointer to, the following structure:

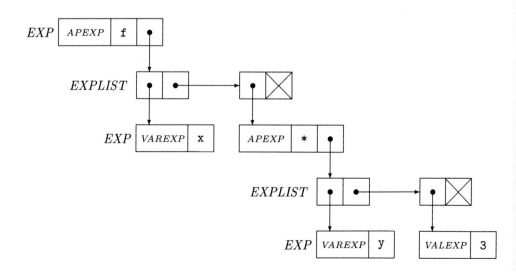

Whenever a *parse····* function is called, *pos* — the current location in the input string *userinput* — points to the first nonblank character of the corresponding syntactic item; when it is finished, it has produced a structure of its particular kind and has updated *pos* to point to the first nonblank character after the end of that item. (In the case of parenthesized lists, *pos* starts out pointing to the first nonblank character after the opening parenthesis and ends up at the first nonblank after the closing parenthesis.) These details must be borne in mind when adding new syntax to the language, that is, when modifying these parsing routines.

1.2.5   ENVIRONMENTS

The values of variables must be stored in symbol tables. The structure of symbol tables is defined by the *ENVREC* record. Each table is a pair, containing a *NAMELIST* and a *VALUELIST*. The *NAMELIST* contains the variables' names and the *VALUELIST* the corresponding values; of course, these two lists must be of the same length.

There are two types of variables, global variables and formal parameters of functions. Global variables are contained in the environment *globalEnv*, which is initialized before the read-eval-print loop and updated in *eval* (see case *SETOP*). The environments giving bindings for formal parameters are different for each function call, so these are passed as parameters to *eval*; they are constructed in *applyUserFun* in *EVALUATION*.

1.2.6   NUMBERS

The only kinds of values in this language are integers. However, this should not be expected to hold true in the future. On the contrary, the principal changes in the languages of Part II will be in replacing integers by other values, such as matrices. The operations defined here are: *prValue* (called from the top level and from *applyValueOp*); *isTrueVal* (called from *eval*); and *applyValueOp* (called from *eval*). The latter gets a *VALUEOP* and a *VALUELIST* as its arguments and, after checking that the right number of arguments has been provided, applies the *VALUEOP* and returns the result.

There is another value-dependent function, *parseVal*, in *INPUT*, which will change when there are values other than integers.

1.2.7   READ-EVAL-PRINT LOOP

The body of the program is a *read-eval-print loop*. It *reads* an expression or function definition from the terminal; if it reads an expression, it *evaluates* it by calling the function *eval*, and *prints* the value.

When a function definition is entered, it is stored in an unordered linked list of *FUNDEFREC*'s, whose beginning is given by the global variable *fundefs*.

Each *FUNDEFREC* contains a function's name, formal parameter list, and body.

1.2.8 EVALUATION

eval is the heart of the interpreter. Indeed, it is not too much to say that all the rest is just bookkeeping for *eval*. Accordingly, we will study it in some detail, quoting extensively from the code, which appears in Appendix B.

An expression is evaluated in a context in which the global variables have certain values, and, if the expression occurs within a function definition, the formal parameters likewise have values. Evaluation of an expression leads eventually to its value, and may also change the values of global variables or formal parameters. To explain the computation process, we need a definition:

Definition 1.1 An *environment* is an association of values (that is, integers) with variables. For environment ρ and variable x, $\rho(x)$ denotes the value associated with x in ρ; we will say x is *bound* to $\rho(x)$ in ρ, or that $\rho(x)$ is the *binding* of x in ρ. $\{x_1 \mapsto n_1, \ldots, x_m \mapsto n_m\}$ denotes the environment that associates value n_i with variable x_i, for $1 \leq i \leq m$.

So, to restate the preceding paragraph, an expression is evaluated with respect to an environment giving bindings for global variables — the *global* environment — and an environment giving bindings for the formal parameters of the function in which the expression occurs — the *local* environment. Note that set can be used to assign a new value to either a global variable or formal parameter; thus, an expression evaluation can result in a change to either environment. The global environment is given by the variable *globalEnv*, which is initialized in *READ-EVAL-PRINT LOOP*. The local environment passed to *eval* from *READ-EVAL-PRINT LOOP* is empty, but new local environments are created during the evaluation process, as we will see; the formal parameter *rho* of *eval* contains the local environment for the evaluation of *e*:

function eval (e: EXP; rho: ENV): NUMBER;

The action of *eval* depends upon the type of the expression *e* (integer constant, variable, or application) and, if it is an application, the type of its operator (user-defined, vaiue-op, or control). Thus, the body of *eval* is a **case** statement:

```
begin (* eval *)
    with e↑ do
        case etype of
            VALEXP:
                eval := num;
            VAREXP:
                if isBound(varble, rho)
```

```
                then eval := fetch(varble, rho)
                else if isBound(varble, globalEnv)
                    then eval := fetch(varble, globalEnv)
                    else ... undefined variable error ...;
          APEXP:
              if optr > numBuiltins
              then eval := applyUserFun(optr, evalList(args))
              else begin
                      op := primOp(optr);
                      if op in [IFOP .. BEGINOP]
                      then eval := applyCtrlOp(op, args)
                      else eval := applyValueOp(op, evalList(args))
                  end
        end (* case and with *)
  end; (* eval *)
```

Thus, if e is an integer constant, the integer is returned; if it is a variable, it is looked up first in the local, and then in the global, environment; and if it is an application, one of the functions *applyUserFun, applyValueOp,* or *applyCtrlOp* is called. To elaborate further on the *APEXP* case:

- *applyUserFun* is called to apply a user-defined function. Before it is called, all the arguments are recursively evaluated by *evalList*, yielding a list of values, say $n_1, \ldots, n_m$ (and also possibly modifying the local and global environments). Then, if the function was defined as:

$$\texttt{(define f (x}_1 \ \ldots \ \texttt{x}_m\texttt{) e),}$$

  e is evaluated in environment $\{\texttt{x}_1 \mapsto n_1, \ldots, \texttt{x}_m \mapsto n_m\}$:

```
function applyUserFun (nm: NAME; actuals: VALUELIST): NUMBER;
var
      f: FUNDEF;
      rho: ENV;
begin
      f := fetchFun(nm);
      ... check if f defined ...
      with f↑ do begin
          ... check number of arguments ...
          rho := mkEnv (formals, actuals);
          applyUserFun := eval(body, rho)
          end
  end; (* applyUserFun *)
```

- *applyValueOp* is called to apply a *VALUEOP*. Before it is called, all its arguments are (recursively) evaluated by calling *evalList. applyValueOp* was described under *NUMBERS*.

- *applyCtrlOp* applies *CONTROLOP*'s, which correspond to control structures in PASCAL. Unlike user-defined functions and *VALUEOP*'s, the arguments to *CONTROLOP*'s are not evaluated. For instance, consider the expression (set x e); its arguments are x and e, but clearly it would be wrong to evaluate x. The body of *applyCtrlOp* is a **case** statement:

$$
\begin{array}{l}
\textbf{function } applyCtrlOp \ (op: \ CONTROLOP; \\
\qquad\qquad\qquad args: \ EXPLIST): \ NUMBER; \\
\textbf{var } n: \ NUMBER; \\
\textbf{begin} \\
\quad \textbf{with } args{\uparrow} \ \textbf{do} \\
\quad\quad \textbf{case } op \ \textbf{of} \\
\quad\quad\quad IFOP: \cdots \\
\quad\quad\quad WHILEOP: \cdots \\
\quad\quad\quad SETOP: \cdots \\
\quad\quad\quad BEGINOP: \cdots \\
\quad\quad \textbf{end } (* \ \textbf{case and with } *) \\
\textbf{end}; \ (* \ applyCtrlOp \ *)
\end{array}
$$

The processing of these operators is straightforward:

IFOP: Evaluate argument one; if it evaluates to a true (nonzero) value, then evaluate and return the value of argument two; otherwise, evaluate and return the value of argument three:

$$
\begin{array}{l}
IFOP: \\
\quad \textbf{if } isTrueVal(eval(head, \ rho)) \\
\quad \textbf{then } applyCtrlOp := eval(tail{\uparrow}.head, \ rho) \\
\quad \textbf{else } applyCtrlOp := eval(tail{\uparrow}.tail{\uparrow}.head, \ rho);
\end{array}
$$

WHILEOP: Repeatedly evaluate argument one and argument two in turn, until argument one evaluates to false (zero):

$$
\begin{array}{l}
WHILEOP: \\
\quad \textbf{begin} \\
\quad\quad n := eval(head, \ rho); \\
\quad\quad \textbf{while } isTrueVal(n) \\
\quad\quad \textbf{do begin} \\
\quad\quad\quad n := eval(tail{\uparrow}.head, \ rho); \\
\quad\quad\quad n := eval(head, \ rho) \\
\quad\quad \textbf{end}; \\
\quad\quad applyCtrlOp := n \\
\quad \textbf{end};
\end{array}
$$

SETOP: Evaluate argument two and assign it to argument one, after determining whether the latter is a global variable or formal parameter:

> *SETOP:*
> **begin**
>> $n := eval(tail{\uparrow}.head, rho)$;
>> **if** $isBound(head{\uparrow}.varble, rho)$
>> **then** $assign(head{\uparrow}.varble, n, rho)$
>> **else if** $isBound(head{\uparrow}.varble, globalEnv)$
>>> **then** $assign(head{\uparrow}.varble, n, globalEnv)$
>>> **else** $bindVar(head{\uparrow}.varble, n, globalEnv)$;
>>
>> $applyCtrlOp := n$
> **end**;

BEGINOP: Evaluate all arguments and return the last value. (*BEGINOP* could have been treated as a *VALUEOP*, since it evaluates all its arguments, but it fits better with the control structures.)

> *BEGINOP:*
> **begin**
>> **while** $args{\uparrow}.tail <>$ **nil do**
>> **begin**
>>> $n := eval(args{\uparrow}.head, rho)$;
>>> $args := args{\uparrow}.tail$
>> **end**;
>> $applyCtrlOp := eval(args{\uparrow}.head, rho)$
> **end**

1.3   Where We Go from Here

PASCAL is a representative of the class of *imperative programming languages*. This class includes such languages as FORTRAN, COBOL, ALGOL-60, and C, among many others. Indeed, these languages — often called "conventional," usually in a sense denoting mild exasperation — account for the vast majority of programming done in the real world.

Since the reader knows PASCAL well, she or he knows about imperative programming languages, or at least about *imperative programming*, the prevailing programming style associated with these languages. Some of the characteristics of this style and of these languages are:

- "Word-at-a-time" processing. A computation consists of many individual movements and computations of small items of data.

- Programming by side-effect. The computation proceeds by continually changing the "state" of the machine — the values contained in the various machine words — by assignment.

- Iteration is the predominant control structure. Whether by explicit control structures (**while, repeat**) or **goto**, iteration is the primary method of control. Procedures, and particularly recursion, take a back seat.

- The language structures, both data and control, are fairly close to the underlying machine architecture. **goto**'s are unconditional jumps (**if**s and **while**s are bundled conditional and unconditional jumps), arrays are contiguous blocks of memory, pointers are pointers, assignment is data movement, and so on. For example, debuggers for imperative languages are often simple adaptations of machine-level debuggers.

Of course, knowing no alternatives, the reader may not realize that he has been programming in a particular style — he's just been programming! It is precisely the purpose of this book to acquaint the reader with the principal alternatives.

Our presentation of them is structured thusly:

Part II. The languages LISP and APL differ from the language of this chapter in a conceptually small way: Instead of manipulating (that is, assigning, passing as arguments, returning as results) integers, they manipulate larger values. LISP manipulates lists, and APL manipulates arrays. It transpires that this conceptually small change has a deep effect on one's programming habits. One result is that in LISP, recursion is the predominant control structure; where recursion in PASCAL is rather exotic, in LISP it is iteration that is rare.

Part III. The *functional languages* are characterized by their treating functions as "first-class" (i.e., assignable, passable, returnable) values. A highly distinctive programming style emerges from this feature. The best-known functional language is SCHEME, a dialect of LISP. The language SASL incorporates *lazy evaluation*, which even more strongly supports the functional programming style. (λ-calculus, a mathematical system that inspired these languages, is covered in Chapter 5.)

Part IV. The *object-oriented languages* share the feature that they allow users to add to the set of data types. The first one presented is CLU, which adds this capability in a very clean and simple way. SMALLTALK represents a more radical departure based on the same idea; here, the ability of a data type to *inherit* properties from a previously defined type allows for effective code reuse. (Also briefly covered in these chapters are ADA and C++.)

Part V. The concept of *logic programming*, whereby the principles of mathematical logic are adapted to programming, is represented by PROLOG. Also discussed in this part is the subject of *mechanical theorem-proving*, to which PROLOG traces its origins.

Part VI. As far as these languages may take us from the world of imperative
programming, eventually programs must run on computers. This part
discusses compilation in general, and an implementation issue especially
important to non-imperative languages, that of *memory management*.
(Note that the interpreters provided for the languages are little more
than existence proofs and bear little relation to how the languages are
actually implemented.)

For each of the principal languages covered — LISP, APL, SCHEME, SASL,
CLU, SMALLTALK, and PROLOG — we present a simplified subset, giving its
syntax (formally, as in this chapter) and semantics (informally) and many examples. In addition, we present an interpreter, adapted from the one presented
in this chapter, which the reader can use to run programs in the language.
That interpreter is documented in the chapter and listed in an Appendix.

The presentation of these languages, and of the other topics covered along
the way, has ultimately one goal: to foster an appreciation of the range of
programming languages and styles that are possible.

1.4 Exercises

1.4.1 LEARNING ABOUT THE LANGUAGE

The first six exercises define some number-theoretic functions for you to program. Try to use recursion; it will be good practice for Chapter 2.

1. $(\texttt{sigma } m\ n) = m + (m+1) + \cdots + n$.

2. $(\texttt{exp } m\ n) = m^n$ $(m, n \geq 0)$. $(\texttt{log } m\ n) =$ the least integer l such
   that $m^{l+1} > n$ $(m > 1, n > 0)$.

3. $(\texttt{choose } n\ k)$ is the number of ways of selecting k items from a collection of n items, without repetitions, n and k nonnegative integers. This
   quantity is called a *binomial coefficient*, and is notated $\binom{n}{k}$. It can be
   defined as $\frac{n!}{k!(n-k)!}$, but the following identities are more helpful compu-
   tationally: $\binom{n}{0} = 1$ $(n \geq 0)$, $\binom{n}{n} = 1$ $(n \geq 0)$, and $\binom{n}{k} = \binom{n-1}{k} + \binom{n-1}{k-1}$
   $(n, k > 0)$.

4. $(\texttt{fib } m)$ is the mth Fibonacci number. The Fibonacci numbers are defined by the identities: $(\texttt{fib } 0) = 0$, $(\texttt{fib } 1) = 1$, and for $m > 1$, $(\texttt{fib }
   m) = (\texttt{fib } m-1) + (\texttt{fib } m-2)$.

5. $(\texttt{prime } n) =$ true (1) if n is prime, false (0) otherwise. $(\texttt{nthprime } n) =$
   the nth prime number. $(\texttt{sumprimes } n) =$ the sum of the first n primes.
   $(\texttt{relprime } m\ n) =$ true if m and n are relatively prime (have no common
   divisors except 1), false otherwise.

6. (binary m) = the number whose decimal representation is the binary representation of m. For example, (binary 12) = 1100, since $1100_2 = 12_{10}$.

7. The scope rule of our language is identical to that of PASCAL, when we consider a PASCAL without nested function definitions. Consider this PASCAL program:

> **program** P (*input, output*);
>
> **var** x: *integer*;
>
>> **procedure** R (y: *integer*);
>> **begin** $x := y$ **end**;
>>
>> **procedure** Q (x: *integer*);
>> **begin** $R(x+1)$; *writeln*(x) **end**;
>
> **begin**
>> $x := 2$; $Q(4)$; *writeln*(x)
>
> **end**.

What is its output? Give the analogous program in the language of this chapter.

1.4.2 LEARNING ABOUT THE INTERPRETER

8. Add the function **read** to the language; **read** is a function of no arguments, which reads a number from the terminal and returns it. It should be added as a value-op. (When adding value-op's, make sure that *primOp* still works and that the *APEXP* case in *eval* still properly tests for control operations.)

9. Add the function **for** as a control operation, with syntax:

   (for variable expression expression expression).

   (for x e_1 e_2 e_3) first evaluates e_1 and e_2, yielding values n_1 and n_2, then proceeds to evaluate e_3 $n_2 - n_1 + 1$ times, with x bound to values $n_1, n_1 + 1, \ldots, n_2$. Like **while**, the value it returns is unimportant, since a **for** expression is evaluated for its side-effects; you may choose any final value you find convenient.

10. Change the parameter-passing mechanism to use **var** parameters (also called *reference* parameters) instead of value parameters. No change in the syntax of the language is needed. To implement this, let the type

NUMBER be a pointer type to a one-field record called NUMBERREC:

$$NUMBER = \uparrow NUMBERREC;$$
$$NUMBERREC = \textbf{record}$$
$$ival: integer$$
$$\textbf{end};$$

applyValueOp allocates these records dynamically and returns pointers to them. Write a function that makes use of this feature (e.g., **var** parameters can be used to return multiple values from a function). How does it affect the truth of the assertion (page 7) that "a global variable can never have its value altered by an assignment to a formal parameter"? Discuss the advantages and disadvantages of **var** parameters; how would this discussion change if our language had arrays?

11. Enhance the "programming environment" by adding the function **load**. This function prompts the user for a filename and then reads input from that file until eof, after which it returns to normal terminal I/O. You may disallow nested **load**'s, i.e., not process **load**'s in files that are being loaded; this allows a considerable simplification of the implementation of **load**, but also significantly reduces its usefulness.

12. Add local variables to function definitions. That is, change the syntax of definitions to:

    fundef $\longrightarrow$ (define function arglist localvarlist expression),

    where localvarlist, having the same syntax as arglist, names those variables that are local to the function. The affected code is mainly in *INPUT* (more specifically, in *parseDef*) and *applyUserFun* in *EVALUATION*. When a user-defined function is applied, the local variables should be initialized to zero. Make sure to still check, in *applyUserFun*, that the number of actual parameters is correct.

13. Add real numbers to the language. Let *NUMBER* be a pointer type to a tagged variant record (a "discriminated type union") *REALORINT*, containing either an integer or a real number:

$$NUMBER = \uparrow REALORINT;$$
$$NUMBERTYPE = (REALNUM, INTNUM);$$
$$REALORINT = \textbf{record}$$
$$\textbf{case } numtype: NUMBERTYPE \textbf{ of}$$
$$REALNUM: (rval: real);$$
$$INTNUM: (ival: integer)$$
$$\textbf{end};$$

applyValueOp should apply the appropriate operation — integer or real — depending upon the types of its arguments, and it should return a pointer to a newly allocated record. Real constants should be allowed. You should have automatic coercions from integer to real, as in PASCAL, and should include functions `trunc` and `round` as new value-op's.

14. To elaborate further on Exercise 13, consider the problem of implementing static type-checking. First, you'll need to add variable declarations, so assume the syntax of function definitions is changed to:

fundef	$\longrightarrow$	(define function arglist : typename expression)
arglist	$\longrightarrow$	(var-decl*)
var-decl	$\longrightarrow$	variable : typename
typename	$\longrightarrow$	integer | real

You can also assume that global variables are declared before use:

input	$\longrightarrow$	expression | fundef | var-decl

The type-checking rules are:

- If `f` is a user-defined function or value-op, in any use the types of the actual parameters must match the types of the formals. Also, the type of the body of a user-defined function must match the declared type of the function's result.

- In (set x e), x and e must have the same type, unless x has type `real` and e type `integer`, in which case the automatic coercion should be applied.

- In (if e_1 e_2 e_3), e_1 must have type `integer`, and e_2 and e_3 must have the same type (which is the type of the expression as a whole).

- In (while e_1 e_2), e_1 must have type `integer`, which is also the type of the expression as a whole. e_2 must be type-correct, but it doesn't matter what its type is.

- In (begin e_1 ... e_n), all the expressions e_1, ..., e_n must be type-correct, and the type of e_n is the type of the expression as a whole.

You must find a way to handle mutually recursive functions. Explain how the type-checking process obviates the need for the tag in *REALORINT* records, permitting the use of an untagged variant, or "free type union:"

$$NUMBER = \uparrow REALORINT;$$
$$NUMBERTYPE = (REALNUM, INTNUM);$$
$$REALORINT = \textbf{record}$$
$$\textbf{case } NUMBERTYPE \textbf{ of}$$
$$REALNUM: (rval: real);$$
$$INTNUM: (ival: integer)$$
$$\textbf{end};$$

15. Continuing with Problem 14: Use type-checking to enforce a distinction between *statements* and *expressions* and a corresponding distinction between *procedures* and *functions* (as in PASCAL). Do this by adding a new type, called `void`, which is the result type of a statement. In particular, it is the result type of every `set`, `while`, and `begin` expression, and it must be the type of the body of a `while` and of all the expressions in a `begin`. For `if`, you can allow two forms, a conditional expression and a conditional statement; the type-checking rule for `if` is that the first argument should be of type `integer` and the second and third arguments should have the same type (possibly `void`). A function can be declared to have result type `void`, but a variable can never have this type.

One decision you will need to make is how to return a value from a function, since its body will be a statement and therefore have no value. You might try the PASCAL solution of assigning to the name of the function; you may use a special `return` statement; or you may add a new kind of expression, having the syntax:

(execute expression return expression) .

The type-checking rule for this new kind of expression is that the first expression must have type `void` and the expression as a whole takes its type from the type of the second expression.

Bearing in mind that the purpose of type-checking is to detect logical errors, discuss the value of thus distinguishing between statements and expressions. Assuming the distinction is useful, how does this type-checking approach compare with the PASCAL approach of making the distinction *syntactically?*

Part II
Using Larger Values

In an influential Turing Award lecture in 1977, John Backus argued that traditional imperative languages like PASCAL suffer from what he dubbed the "von Neumann bottleneck." Such languages, he said, tend to treat data primarily in small pieces, like characters, integers, and reals, mirroring the structure of a von Neumann computer with its narrow connection between memory and processor. Even when these small values are aggregated, as in arrays or records, their processing tends to be "word at a time." In PASCAL, for example, there are no array-valued functions. The reasons for this are technical but can be summed up by saying that these languages provide a conservative abstraction of the physical machine.

Our simple language suffers grievously from the von Neumann bottleneck, since the only values are integers. In Part II, we consider various methods of overcoming the bottleneck by treating aggregated values as "first-class." That is, instead of integers, we will use larger values, namely lists and arrays; section *NUMBERS* will be modified accordingly. However, *EVALUATION* will not change. Thus, the new values will still be assignable, printable, and passable to, and returnable from, functions.

What is meant by "larger values?" That is precisely the question that the languages we will be discussing answer differently:

LISP. The value space of LISP consists of "S-expressions" (for "symbolic expressions"), which are lists of numbers, symbols, and other lists. LISP was designed for the kinds of processing typical of artificial intelligence programming, and it is still the most widely used language, by far, in that field.

APL. The value space of APL consists of arrays of arbitrary dimension (limited to two dimensions in our version). So powerful are the operations provided by the language that APL programs are often dramatically shorter than equivalent programs in traditional languages. More interestingly, APL programs tend to have fewer loops and conditionals ("less control") than traditional programs, since array operations take their place.

Chapter 2

LISP

LISP is the prime example of the kind of language that computer scientists admire. They admire it for the same reason an engineer admires an especially elegant design: its combination of *power* and *simplicity.*

LISP was among the first, and was unquestionably the most important, of the languages developed for the needs of the artificial intelligence community. Inspired by ideas from mathematical logic, particularly the "λ-calculus," LISP was developed by John McCarthy as a language for symbolic computation (or "list-processing," as it was then called, whence its name). For the kinds of computations typical of artificial intelligence, LISP offers concise and natural programs, often close to mathematical definitions of the functions being computed. LISP has been used for most major AI programs in the last thirty years.

We have already seen three of the central ideas of LISP in the language of Chapter 1, namely:

- Applicative programming.[1] Instead of "writing a program," LISPers "define a function;" instead of "running a program," they "evaluate an expression," which is to say, apply a function to some arguments.

- Simplified syntax. In particular, operator precedence is eliminated.

- Recursion as the central control structure. This is, in combination with S-expressions (next section), the most important innovation of LISP.[2]

LISP continues to flourish. There are implementations available on almost every computer. In the past few years, a major effort has been undertaken to standardize LISP; implementations of the standard version, called COMMON

---

[1]This is sometimes called "functional programming," but we use that term in a different sense in Part III.

[2]Interestingly, although recursion has been used by mathematicians for centuries for defining functions, computer scientists did not at first recognize it as a *practical* method. In describing a meeting in 1960 of some of the world's leading computer scientists, to design the language ALGOL-60, Alan Perlis says, "We really did not understand the implications of recursion, or its value, ... McCarthy did, but the rest of us didn't." (Quoted by Peter Naur, in Wexelblat [1981, p. 160].)

LISP, are becoming widely available. With the portability problem solved, LISP should increase even more in popularity.

John McCarthy received the Turing Award of the ACM in 1971 for his work, primarily for the development of LISP. The importance of LISP goes beyond its various applications, to its influence on how computer scientists think about programming and programming languages. Since it was the first language to demonstrate how far language design could go beyond the imperative model, it is fitting that our study should begin with LISP.

2.1 The Language

The only difference between the language of Chapter 1 and LISP is, as has been mentioned, in the underlying space of values of LISP. These values are called "S-expressions" (for "symbolic expressions"), and it is really the marvelous match between the recursive structure of S-expressions and recursion as a control structure that gives LISP its special power and appeal.

2.1.1 S-EXPRESSIONS

Definition 2.1 An *S-expression* is either a *symbol*, a *number*, or a *list* $(S_1 \ldots S_n)$ of zero or more S-expressions. The list of zero elements, (), is called the *nil list*, or just *nil*. (*"Symbol"* is the LISP term for what was called a name in Chapter 1.)

The value space of LISP is S-expressions in precisely the same sense that the value space of the language of Chapter 1 is integers. *nil* is the false value, and any non-*nil* value represents true (our comparison functions use the symbol T). The operations are:

car: If S is the list $(S_1 \ldots S_n)$, $n > 0$, then (car S) is S_1; if S is *nil*, it is erroneous to apply car to it.

cdr: If S is the list $(S_1 \ldots S_n)$, $n > 0$, then (cdr S) is $(S_2 \ldots S_n)$; if S is *nil*, cdr may not be applied. Note that n may equal 1, in which case (cdr S) is *nil*.

cons: If S is the list $(S_1 \ldots S_n)$, then (cons S' S) is the list $(S' S_1 \ldots S_n)$; if S is not a list, (cons S' S) is erroneous.[3]

=: (= S_1 S_2) returns the symbol T if S_1 and S_2 are both the same number or both the same symbol or both *nil*, and returns *nil* otherwise. (Comparison of nonempty lists can be programmed, as will be seen below.)

---

[3]The function name cons stands for "construct," which makes sense, but the names car and cdr stand for, respectively, "contents of the address register" and "contents of the decrement register," which don't. These names are historical; they refer to the machine language implementation of LISP on the IBM 704.

number?, symbol?, list?, null?: These return T if their argument is of the
indicated type, *nil* otherwise. (list? returns *nil* if its argument is *nil*,
although, technically, *nil* is a list.)

+: If S_1 and S_2 are numbers, (+ S_1 S_2) is their sum; otherwise (+ S_1 S_2) is
erroneous.

-, *, /: Similar to +.

<, >: These return T if their arguments are both numbers and the indicated
condition holds; they return *nil* otherwise.

Note that these functions have no side-effects. That is, applying a function
like car to a list does not change the list. This is again analogous to the
value-op's of Chapter 1.

2.1.2 SYNTAX

We would be ready to look at some LISP function definitions except for one
thing: we have not stated how to write S-expression *constants* in LISP programs. Clearly, they cannot simply be written in programs as they are on
paper, because, for example, the list (a b) would be interpreted as the *application* of a function a to an argument b, rather than the list containing symbols
a and b. The solution is to precede S-expression constants by a single quote
('). For example, the symbol a is written 'a, and the list (a b 3) is written
'(a b 3). Integer constants will still be written directly, without the single
quote. The most common S-expression constant is '(), for *nil*.

The syntax of LISP is the same as that of Chapter 1, except for these
changes:

value	$\longrightarrow$	integer | quoted-const
value-op	$\longrightarrow$	+ | - | * | / | = | < | > | cons | car | cdr
	|	number? | symbol? | list? | null? | print
quoted-const	$\longrightarrow$	'S-expression
S-expression	$\longrightarrow$	integer | symbol | (S-expression*)
symbol	$\longrightarrow$	name

2.1.3 EXAMPLES

The reader will no doubt begin writing programs in LISP by imitating the
code in this and subsequent sections. One aspect of this code that the reader
should particularly note is that it rarely uses assignment or iteration; almost
everything is done with recursion. This is partly because that is typical of
LISP code, and partly because the reader already knows how to program using
assignment and iteration.

The functions defined in Chapter 1, such as gcd, still work. To get some practice with the basic list operations, consider these examples:

```
-> (cons 'a '())
(a)

-> (cons 'a '(b))
(a b)

-> (cons '(a) '(b))
((a) b)

-> (cdr '(a (b (c d))))
((b (c d)))

-> (null? '())
T

-> (null? '(()))
()
```

These examples do nothing more than illustrate the definitions of the value-op's. These definitions must be applied carefully, which is not as easy as it looks. For instance, (a (b (c d))) is a list of two elements, the symbol a and the list (b (c d)). Its cdr, therefore, is a list of one element, the just-named list, and is written ((b (c d))).

This may be easier to understand by picturing any non-*nil* list as a box — called a *cons cell* — with two pointers, one to its car and the other to its cdr; if its cdr is *nil*, the second box will just be filled with a big "x". For example, picture the list (a b c) as:

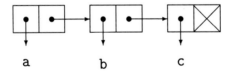

Using this graphical notation, find the car or cdr of a list by following its left or right arrow, and cons x and y by creating a cons cell with pointers to x and y. More examples:

(cons 'a '()) = '(a)

(cons 'a '(b)) = '(a b)

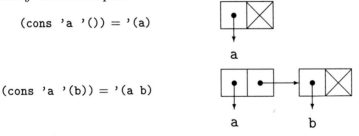

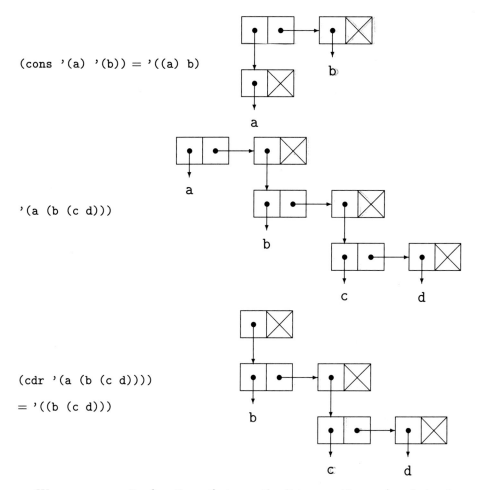

```
(cons '(a) '(b)) = '((a) b)
```

```
'(a (b (c d)))
```

```
(cdr '(a (b (c d))))
= '((b (c d)))
```

We can now write functions that use the list operations. An obviously desirable function is the one to find the length of a list:[4]

```
-> (define length (l) (if (null? l) 0 (+1 (length (cdr l)))))
```

Let's go over how this one works by following the evaluation of (length '(a b)):

- (a b) is not *nil*, so (null? l) returns *nil*, or false.

- (+1 (length (cdr l))) is evaluated, where l = (a b). (cdr l) evaluates to the list (b). Let us follow the application of length to (b):

    − (b) is not *nil*, so (null? l) returns *nil*.

---

[4]+1 is defined in Chapter 1. Throughout the book, we freely use functions defined in earlier chapters, provided the earlier definition remains appropriate.

       — (+1 (length (cdr l))) is evaluated. (cdr l) is *nil*. We follow the application of length to *nil*:

           * (null? l) returns T.
           * length returns 0.

       — (length (cdr l)) returned 0, so return 1.

- (length (cdr l)) returned 1, so return 2.

The following functions are quite useful:

```
-> (define caar (l) (car (car l)))
-> (define cadr (l) (car (cdr l)))
```

In fact, most LISP's provide many, or all, of the functions of the form c{a,d}$^+$r (i.e., c and r with any nonempty sequence of a's and d's in between), with definitions analogous to these. From now on, we will assume all such functions have been defined.

Another set of simple but useful functions are those that put their arguments into lists:

```
-> (define list1 (x) (cons x '()))
-> (define list2 (x y) (cons x (cons y '())))
-> (define list3 (x y z) (cons x (cons y (cons z '()))))
-> (list2 (list1 'a) 'b)
((a) b)
```

Real LISP's have a single function, list, that puts any number of arguments into a list; see Exercise 7.

A basic list operation is testing for equality. Our value-op = tests for equality only of *atoms*, i.e., numbers, symbols, and *nil*; this one tests for equality of any two S-expressions:

```
-> (define or (x y) (if x x y))[5]
```

---

   [5]or returns its first argument if it is non-*nil*, otherwise it returns its second argument; thus, it returns a true (non-*nil*) value if either of its arguments is true. Note that, like **or** in PASCAL, or *evaluates both its arguments*, even if its first argument is true. This is because or is a user-defined function, and arguments of user-defined functions are always evaluated.

   We will also use the function **and**, defined by:

```
(define and (x y) (if x y x)).
```

The definition of **not** is slightly different from Chapter 1:

```
(define not (x) (if x '() 'T)).
```

```
-> (define atom? (x) (or (null? x) (or (number? x) (symbol? x))))
-> (define equal (l1 l2)
       (if (atom? l1) (= l1 l2)
           (if (atom? l2) '()
               (if (equal (car l1) (car l2))
                   (equal (cdr l1) (cdr l2))
                   '()))))
-> (equal 'a 'b)
()
-> (equal '(a (1 3) c) '(a (1 3) c))
T
-> (equal '(a (1 3) d) '(a (1 3) c))
()
```

Prime Numbers.   Here is a LISP version of the well-known Sieve of Eratos-
thenes algorithm. The function divides tests if its first argument divides its
second; (interval-list m n) returns the list (m m+1 ... n); remove-multiples removes all multiples of n from l.

```
-> (define divides (m n) (= (mod n m) 0))
-> (define interval-list (m n)
       (if (> m n) '() (cons m (interval-list (+1 m) n))))
-> (interval-list 3 7)
(3 4 5 6 7)
-> (define remove-multiples (n l)
       (if (null? l) '()
           (if (divides n (car l))
               (remove-multiples n (cdr l))
               (cons (car l) (remove-multiples n (cdr l))))))
-> (remove-multiples 2 '(2 3 4 5 6 7))
(3 5 7)
-> (define sieve (l)
       (if (null? l) '()
           (cons (car l)
                 (sieve (remove-multiples (car l) (cdr l))))))
-> (define primes<= (n) (sieve (interval-list 2 n)))
-> (primes<= 10)
(2 3 5 7)
```

Sorting. The next example is a LISP version of the sorting algorithm *insertion sort*. This sort has a very simple recursive structure: given a list of n elements, first sort the last $n - 1$ recursively, then insert the first in its proper position.

```
-> (define insert (x l)
       (if (null? l) (list1 x)
           (if (< x (car l)) (cons x l)
               (cons (car l)(insert x (cdr l))))))
-> (define insertion-sort (l)
      (if (null? l) '()
          (insert (car l) (insertion-sort (cdr l)))))
-> (insertion-sort '(4 3 2 6 8 5))
(2 3 4 5 6 8)
```

Association Lists. The greatest strength of LISP is in dealing with symbolic information, and one of the most basic data types for such information is the *table*. A commonly-used table representation is the *association list*, or *a-list*, a list of the form

$$((k_1 \; a_1), \dots, (k_m \; a_m)),$$

where the k_i are symbols (called *keys*) and the a_i are *attributes*. The functions assoc and mkassoc respectively retrieve data from, and add it to, a-lists:

```
-> (define assoc (x alist)
       (if (null? alist) '()
           (if (= x (caar alist)) (cadar alist)
               (assoc x (cdr alist)))))
-> (assoc 'U '((E coli)(I Ching)(U Thant)))
Thant
-> (define mkassoc (x y alist)
       (if (null? alist)
           (list1 (list2 x y))
           (if (= x (caar alist)) (cons (list2 x y) (cdr alist))
               (cons (car alist) (mkassoc x y (cdr alist))))))
-> (set al (mkassoc 'I 'Ching '()))
((I Ching))
-> (set al (mkassoc 'E 'coli al))
((I Ching)(E coli))
-> (set al (mkassoc 'I 'Magnin al))
((I Magnin)(E coli))
-> (assoc 'I al)
Magnin
```

A-lists are not unlike the environments used in the interpreter; indeed, they will be used to represent environments in Section 2.4.

More generally, one may want to associate a variety of attributes with a given key. In effect, we need an a-list in which the attribute of any key is itself an a-list. We will call such a structure a *property list*.[6] For example, a property list for fruits might be:

```
(set fruits '((apple ((texture crunchy)))
              (banana ((color yellow)))))
```

Functions to retrieve and add properties to a property list can be written easily by making use of the nested a-list structure:

```
-> (define getprop (x p plist)
        ; find property p of individual x in plist
        (assoc p (assoc x plist)))

-> (getprop 'apple 'texture fruits)
crunchy

-> (define putprop (x p y plist)
        ; give individual x value y for property p
        (mkassoc x (mkassoc p y (assoc x plist)) plist))

-> (set fruits (putprop 'apple 'color 'red fruits))
((apple ((texture crunchy)(color red)))(banana ((color yellow)))))

-> (getprop 'apple 'color fruits)
red
```

Next the problem is to find all names that have a given value for a given property, for example, all yellow things.

```
-> (define hasprop? (p y alist) (= (assoc p alist) y))

-> (define gatherprop (p y plist)
        ; get all individuals having value y for property p
        (if (null? plist) '()
            (if (hasprop? p y (cadar plist))
                (cons (caar plist) (gatherprop p y (cdr plist)))
                (gatherprop p y (cdr plist)))))

-> (set fruits (putprop 'lemon 'color 'yellow fruits))
((apple ((texture crunchy) ...  (lemon ((color yellow))))

-> (gatherprop 'color 'yellow fruits)
(banana lemon)
```

---

[6] But see Section 2.6.1: Glossary.

Sets. Sets can be represented easily in LISP, using lists without repeated elements. Adding a new element is like `cons`, except that the element must first be tested for membership. Here is the code for some of the operations on sets.

```
-> (set nullset '())
()
-> (define addelt (x s) (if (member? x s) s (cons x s)))
-> (define member? (x s)
     (if (null? s) '()
         (if (equal x (car s)) 'T (member? x (cdr s)))))
-> (define size (s) (length s))
-> (define union (s1 s2)
     (if (null? s1) s2
         (if (member? (car s1) s2)
             (union (cdr s1) s2)
             (cons (car s1) (union (cdr s1) s2)))))
-> (set s (addelt 3 (addelt 'a nullset)))
(3 a)
-> (member? 'a s)
T
-> (union s (addelt 2 (addelt 3 nullset)))
(a 2 3)
```

The use of `equal` in `member?` allows us to construct sets of lists:

```
-> (set t (addelt '(a b) (addelt 1 nullset)))
((a b) 1)
-> (member? '(a b) t)
T
```

If = had been used instead of `equal`, this would not have worked. Other useful operations are given in Section 2.3 and in Exercise 2 at the end of the chapter.

Global Variables in Recursively-Defined Functions. There are occasions when one wants to use a temporary variable within a function definition. Since functions have no local variables, the obvious alternative is to use global variables for such temporaries. It is time to caution the reader about these.

Consider this function:

```
(define sum (l)
    (if (null? l) 0
        (if (number? l) l
            (+ (sum (car l)) (sum (cdr l))))))
```

Now consider:

```
(define wrong-sum (l)
    (if (null? l) 0
        (if (number? l) l
            (begin
                (set tmp (wrong-sum (car l)))
                (+ (wrong-sum (cdr l)) tmp)))))
```

wrong-sum is wrong:

```
-> (sum '(1 2 3 4))
10

-> (wrong-sum '(1 2 3 4))
16
```

We leave it to the reader to discover why this result is obtained (Exercise 3).

This one example should not be taken to mean that using global variables as temporaries never works. One must just be very careful that the value assigned to a global variable is consumed before a subsequent recursive call reassigns it.

Note that the effect of local temporaries can be achieved by defining auxiliary functions having extra formal parameters. For example, here is a fix to wrong-sum which still uses a temporary variable in the same way:

```
(define right-sum (l) (right-sum-aux l 0))
(define right-sum-aux (l tmp)
    (if (null? l) 0
        (if (number? l) l
            (begin
                (set tmp (right-sum (car l)))
                (+ (right-sum (cdr l)) tmp)))))
```

This technique is quite useful, and such auxiliary functions are frequently seen.

Trees.   Trees are very simple to manipulate in LISP. We will present programs for pre-order and level-order traversal of binary trees, defined to be trees whose nodes have either zero or two children.

Binary trees will be represented as follows: A node with no children is represented by an atom, which is the node's label, and a node with children is represented as a triple (three-element list) containing an atom (the label) and two sub-trees. For example, the list

$$\text{'(A (B C D) (E (F G H) I))}$$

represents the tree:

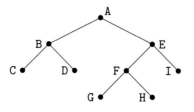

We illustrate the use of this representation by programming a pre-order traversal; the function **pre-ord** is applied as:

```
-> (pre-ord '(A (B C D) (E (F G H) I)))
A
B
C
D
E
F
G
H
I
```

pre-ord is given in Figure 2.1. (Actually, this function gives the result indicated, followed by another **I** after the last line, that being the *value* of the function call. Since the function is being called for its side-effect — the printing of the pre-order traversal — its *value* is of no interest and hence is omitted here.)

Level-order, or breadth-first, traversal — where the tree is visited one level at a time, producing the traversal **A B E C D F I G H** for our example — is

---

```
(define pre-ord (tree)
    (if (atom? tree) (print tree)
        (begin
            (print (car tree))
            (pre-ord (cadr tree))
            (pre-ord (caddr tree)))))
```

Figure 2.1: Function **pre-ord**

```
; Queue operations
(set empty-queue '())
(define front (q) (car q))
(define rm-front (q) (cdr q))
(define enqueue (t q)
    (if (null? q) (list1 t) (cons (car q) (enqueue t (cdr q)))))
(define empty? (q) (null? q))
; Level-order traversal
(define level-ord (tree) (level-ord* (enqueue tree empty-queue)))
(define level-ord* (node-q)
    (if (empty? node-q) '()
      (begin
        (set this-node (front node-q))
        (if (atom? this-node)
          (begin
            (print this-node)
            (level-ord* (rm-front node-q)))
          (begin
            (print (car this-node))
            (level-ord*
              (enqueue (caddr this-node)
                (enqueue (cadr this-node) (rm-front node-q)))))))))
```

Figure 2.2: Function `level-ord`

trickier. The basic method is to keep a queue of nodes which are yet to be visited. When the queue is empty, the traversal is finished. Otherwise, the node at the front of the queue is visited, and its children are placed at the end of the queue. The code for level-order traversal is given in Figure 2.2. The function `level-ord` performs the traversal by calling the auxiliary function `level-ord*`, passing it a queue whose one entry is the entire tree.

2.2 Implementation

To further solidify the reader's understanding of LISP, we present here — as we will do at this point in every chapter — a brief discussion of the LISP interpreter. In this case, most of the code has not changed from that of Chapter 1; Appendix C contains listings of those functions that are new or significantly changed with respect to the listings in Appendix B.

The principal changes from the interpreter of Chapter 1, explained further below, are:

- In *DECLARATIONS*, *NUMBER* is replaced by *SEXP*, which is the pointer type for *SEXPREC* records.

- In *INPUT*, *parseVal* is modified to parse list (i.e., quoted) constants.

- Section *NUMBERS* is replaced by *S-EXPRESSIONS*, in which all **value-op**'s are defined.

SEXP replaces *NUMBER* throughout the code. Aside from this, sections *EVALUATION* and *ENVIRONMENTS* do not change at all, and *DATA STRUCTURE OP'S*, *NAME MANAGEMENT*, and *READ-EVAL-PRINT LOOP* have only minor changes.

2.2.1 DECLARATIONS

In place of the type *NUMBER*, LISP uses *SEXP*:

$$SEXP = \uparrow SEXPREC;$$
$$SEXPTYPE = (NILSXP, NUMSXP, SYMSXP, LISTSXP);$$

$$SEXPREC = \textbf{record}$$
$$\qquad \textbf{case } sxptype: SEXPTYPE \textbf{ of}$$
$$\qquad\qquad NILSXP: ();$$
$$\qquad\qquad NUMSXP: (intval: integer);$$
$$\qquad\qquad SYMSXP: (symval: NAME);$$
$$\qquad\qquad LISTSXP: (carval, cdrval: SEXP)$$
$$\qquad \textbf{end};$$

Of course, *SEXP* replaces *NUMBER* in the declaration of types *VALUELISTREC* and *EXPREC*, and throughout the interpreter.

Type *BUILTINOP* is changed:[7]

$$BUILTINOP = (IFOP, WHILEOP, SETOP, BEGINOP, PLUSOP, MINUSOP,$$
$$\qquad TIMESOP, DIVOP, EQOP, LTOP, GTOP, CONSOP,$$
$$\qquad CAROP, CDROP, NUMBERPOP, SYMBOLPOP,$$
$$\qquad LISTPOP, NULLPOP, PRINTOP);$$

Finally, variables *nilValue* and *trueValue* of type *SEXP* are declared; they are initialized in *READ-EVAL-PRINT LOOP* to contain, respectively, an S-expression of type *NILSXP* and an S-expression of type *SYMSXP* with *symval* T; they are used in *S-EXPRESSIONS*.

2.2.2 DATA STRUCTURE OP'S

The function *mkSExp*, analogous in function to the other *mk·· ·* functions, is added.

---

[7]Operation **number?** is called *NUMBERPOP*, the middle "*P*" standing for "predicate;" similarly for **symbol?**, **list?**, and **null?**.

2.2.3 NAME MANAGEMENT

The new operator names are installed in *initNames*.

2.2.4 INPUT

parseVal, which translates the input string to an *SEXP*, is completely different from the old *parseVal*, which translated only numbers.

2.2.5 ENVIRONMENTS

No changes here.

2.2.6 S-EXPRESSIONS

As did the old *NUMBERS* section, *S-EXPRESSIONS* defines the three functions:

> **procedure** *prValue* (*s*: *SEXP*);
> **function** *isTrueVal* (*s*: *SEXP*): *Boolean*;
> **function** *applyValueOp* (*op*: *VALUEOP*; *vl*: *VALUELIST*): *SEXP*;

Each is, of course, completely new. The value returned by *applyValueOp* when a comparison operation is applied is obtained from either *nilValue* or *trueValue*.

2.2.7 EVALUATION

Aside from replacing *NUMBER* by *SEXP*, there are no changes.

2.2.8 READ-EVAL-PRINT LOOP

The only change is the initialization of variables *nilValue* and *trueValue*.

2.3 Example — Relational Data Bases

In an influential 1970 paper, E. F. Codd [1970] introduced the concept of *relational data bases*. His idea was to simplify the overall conception of data bases by, in effect, treating the individual tables in a data base as first-class values. He gave a list of operations on tables sufficient to formulate many data base queries. He also proved a kind of "completeness" of this set of operations. In this section, we will give a simple representation of relational data bases in LISP and give LISP code for the principal operations. First, we give an informal introduction to relational data bases by way of an example.

2.3.1   AN EXAMPLE OF A RELATIONAL DATA BASE

A *relational data base* is a set of rectangular *tables*. Each table has a list of *attribute names*, which are headings for the table's columns. Here are two examples; table CRIMES has attributes *Victim, Crime, Criminal,* and *Location,* and table MURDERS has attributes *Victim, Weapon,* and *Motive.*

CRIMES

Victim	Crime	Criminal	Location
Phelps	robbery	Harrison	London
Drebber	murder	Hope	London
Sir Charles	murder	Stapleton	Devonshire
Lady Eva	blackmail	Milverton	London
Brunton	murder	Howells	West Sussex

MURDERS

Victim	Weapon	Motive
Drebber	poison	revenge
Sir Charles	hound	greed
Brunton	burial-alive	passion

Note that each column in a table has a different attribute name, but different tables may share attribute names.

2.3.2   R. D. B. OPERATIONS

The purpose of having a data base is to be able to answer *queries* about the data. It turns out that such queries can be formulated as expressions formed from a small set of operations on tables. We now describe and exemplify these operations.

Selection.   The operation *SELECT* takes a subset of the rows of a table, determined by testing the value of a given attribute. For example, *SELECT*(*Crime*, murder, CRIMES) is the table

MURDER-CRIMES

Victim	Crime	Criminal	Location
Drebber	murder	Hope	London
Sir Charles	murder	Stapleton	Devonshire
Brunton	murder	Howells	West Sussex

and *SELECT*(*Location*, London, MURDER-CRIMES) is the table

LONDON-MURDER-CRIMES

Victim	Crime	Criminal	Location
Drebber	murder	Hope	London

In effect, we have answered the query, *"What murders occurred in London?"*

Projection. *PROJECT* takes a subset of the *columns* of a table, chosen by giving the attribute names that are to be retained. So, *PROJECT*({*Victim*, *Criminal*}, LONDON-MURDER-CRIMES) is the table

LONDON-MURDER-VICTIMS

Victim	Criminal
Drebber	Hope

Join. *JOIN* puts two tables together. The set of attribute names of the new table is the union of the attributes of the two tables being joined. The rows of the new table are determined as follows: For any pair of rows, one from each table, if their attribute values match on every attribute that the two tables have in common, then a new row in the new table is formed by concatenating these two rows, identifying the common values. Thus, *JOIN*(MURDERS, LONDON-MURDER-VICTIMS) is the table

LONDON-MURDERS

Victim	Weapon	Motive	Criminal
Drebber	poison	revenge	Hope

Set Operations. *UNION*, *INTERSECT*, and *DIFF* can be applied to two tables having the same attributes (in the same order).

What our examples show is that the expression:

> *JOIN*(MURDERS,
>   *PROJECT*({*Victim*, *Criminal*},
>   *SELECT*(*Location*, London,
>   *SELECT*(*Crime*, murder, CRIMES)))))

expresses the query

> *Name the victims, criminals, weapons, and motives of murders that occurred in London.*

As another example:

> *PROJECT*({*Criminal*},
>   *UNION*(
>   *JOIN*(*PROJECT*({*Victim*},
>   *SELECT*(*Weapon*, poison,
>   MURDERS)),
>   CRIMES),
>   *DIFF*(CRIMES, *SELECT*(*Crime*, murder, CRIMES)))))

returns the table

It corresponds to the query:

> *Name all criminals who either committed a murder by poisoning,*
> *or committed a nonmurder.*

2.3.3   R. D. B. OPERATIONS IN LISP

In our implementation of relational data bases, each table is represented as a
list of lists, the first list containing the attribute names, and the remaining lists
the rows of the table. Thus, the table MURDERS is entered as:

```
(set MURDERS '((Victim Weapon Motive)
               (Drebber poison revenge)
               (Sir-Charles hound greed)
               (Brunton burial-alive passion)))
```

In programming the r.d.b. operations in LISP, the operations on sets defined in Section 2.1.3 are used. We also need two new set operations, namely,
intersection and set difference. The definitions of these, and of the set-theoretic
relational data base operations, are given in Figure 2.3.

(SELECT A v r) (Figure 2.4) works by first finding which column of r corresponds to attribute A (this is the purpose of the call (col-num A (car r));
recall that (car r) is the list of attribute names of r), then iterating over the
rows of r ((cdr r)) selecting those rows that have value v in that position.

(PROJECT X r) (Figure 2.5), where X is a list of attribute names occurring
in r, first finds the list of positions in (car r) at which the attributes in X occur.
It then iterates over the rows of r, selecting just the columns of each row that
correspond to positions in X, and forming a list of these smaller rows. Note that
when it adds a new row to the set of rows it is forming (in include-cols*),
it uses the set operation addelt. To understand this, note that the new table
may have *fewer* rows than the old one, because rows that differed in the old
table may have differed only on columns that have been removed. To make
sure that rows aren't duplicated, we use addelt.

(JOIN r s) (Figure 2.6) iterates over all pairs of rows, one each from r and
s, joining them and adding them to the result if they are equal on the attributes
they have in common. What makes this complicated is that the common attributes occupy different columns in r and s. Thus, JOIN first determines which
attribute names are shared, then determines the column numbers of those at-

```
(define inter (s1 s2)
    (if (null? s1) s1
        (if (member? (car s1) s2)
            (cons (car s1) (inter (cdr s1) s2))
            (inter (cdr s1) s2))))
(define diff (s1 s2)
    (if (null? s1) s1
        (if (null? s2) s1
            (if (member? (car s1) s2)
                (diff (cdr s1) s2)
                (cons (car s1) (diff (cdr s1) s2))))))
(define UNION (r s)
    (if (not (equal (car r) (car s)))
        (print 'error)
        (cons (car r) (union (cdr r) (cdr s)))))
(define INTER (r s)
    (if (not (equal (car r) (car s)))
        (print 'error)
        (cons (car r) (inter (cdr r) (cdr s)))))
(define DIFF (r s)
    (if (not (equal (car r) (car s)))
        (print 'error)
        (cons (car r) (diff (cdr r) (cdr s)))))
```

Figure 2.3: Functions UNION, INTER, and DIFF

```
(define SELECT (A v r)
    (cons (car r) (include-rows v (col-num A (car r)) (cdr r))))
(define col-num (A A-list)
    (if (= A (car A-list)) 0
        (+1 (col-num A (cdr A-list)))))
(define include-rows (v n rows)
    (if (null? rows) '()
        (if (= v (nth n (car rows)))
            (cons (car rows) (include-rows v n (cdr rows)))
            (include-rows v n (cdr rows)))))
(define nth (n l)
    (if (= n 0) (car l) (nth (- n 1) (cdr l))))
```

Figure 2.4: Function SELECT

```
(define PROJECT (X r)
    (cons X (include-cols* (col-num* X (car r)) (cdr r))))
(define col-num* (X A-list)
    (if (null? X) '()
        (cons (col-num (car X) A-list) (col-num* (cdr X) A-list))))
(define include-cols* (col-nums rows)
    (if (null? rows) nullset
        (addelt (include-cols col-nums (car rows))
            (include-cols* col-nums (cdr rows)))))
(define include-cols (col-nums row)
    (if (null? col-nums) '()
        (cons (nth (car col-nums) row)
            (include-cols (cdr col-nums) row))))
```

Figure 2.5: Function PROJECT

tribute names in both r and s, and the column numbers of the nonshared
attribute names in r and s. The arguments to join-cols* give the column
numbers of shared and nonshared attributes in r (X-r and r-cols), the corresponding values for s (X-s and s-cols), and the rows from the two tables
(r-rows and s-rows). join-cols* iteratively looks at every pair of rows, determines if they have equal values on the shared attributes, and if so joins the
two rows and adds them to the list of rows it is building (new-rows). Note that
addelt is not needed here, since the joined rows cannot be duplicated (exercise
for the reader). The auxiliary function append concatenates the elements of
its arguments (both lists) into a single list; for example, (append '(a b) '(c
d)) equals (a b c d).

We can now run the following session in the interpreter:

```
-> (set CRIMES
    '((Victim Crime Criminal Location)
      (Phelps robbery Harrison London)
      (Drebber murder Hope London)
      (Sir-Charles murder Stapleton Devonshire)
      (Lady-Eva blackmail Milverton London)
      (Brunton murder Howells West-Sussex)))
-> (set MURDERS
    '((Victim Weapon Motive)
      (Drebber poison revenge)
      (Sir-Charles hound greed)
      (Brunton burial-alive passion)))
-> (JOIN MURDERS
        (PROJECT '(Victim Criminal)
            (SELECT 'Location 'London
```

```
               (SELECT 'Crime 'murder CRIMES))))
((Victim Weapon Motive Criminal) (Drebber poison revenge Hope))
```

```
(define append (x y)
    (if (null? x) y (cons (car x) (append (cdr x) y))))
(define JOIN (r s)
    (begin
        (set intersection (inter (car r) (car s)))
        (set r-intersection (col-num* intersection (car r)))
        (set s-intersection (col-num* intersection (car s)))
        (set r-diff-s (diff (car r) intersection))
        (set r-diff-s-cols (col-num* r-diff-s (car r)))
        (set s-diff-r (diff (car s) intersection))
        (set s-diff-r-cols (col-num* s-diff-r (car s)))
    (cons (append intersection (append r-diff-s s-diff-r))
        (join-cols* r-intersection r-diff-s-cols s-intersection
            s-diff-r-cols (cdr r) (cdr s)))))
(define join-cols* (X-r r-cols X-s s-cols r-rows s-rows)
    (begin
        (set new-rows '())
        (while (not (null? r-rows))
            (begin
                (set s-tmp s-rows)
                (while (not (null? s-tmp))
                    (begin
                        (if (equal (include-cols X-r (car r-rows))
                                   (include-cols X-s (car s-tmp)))
                            (set new-rows (cons (join-cols X-r r-cols s-cols
                                                    (car r-rows) (car s-tmp))
                                               new-rows))
                            '())
                        (set s-tmp (cdr s-tmp))))
                (set r-rows (cdr r-rows))))
        new-rows))
(define join-cols (X-r r-cols s-cols r-row s-row)
    (append (include-cols X-r r-row)
        (append (include-cols r-cols r-row)
            (include-cols s-cols s-row))))
```

Figure 2.6: Function JOIN

2.4 Example — eval in LISP

One of the most intriguing features of LISP is that programs can be represented
very naturally as S-expressions, so that other programs can operate upon them.
This allows LISP programmers to extend their programming environment more
readily than with almost any other language. This extensibility[8] accounts in
part for the great power and variety of the programming environments in which
LISP is often embedded (which, however, are beyond the scope of this book).

The treatment of programs as data was illustrated by McCarthy [1962] in
a particularly neat way, namely by programming a "meta-circular" interpreter
for LISP, that is, a LISP interpreter written in LISP. In this section, we will
follow McCarthy's lead.

The first question is: how will programs, i.e., expressions, be represented
as S-expressions? The answer is simple: exactly as they would be represented
if they were read in as S-expression constants. Thus, expression (+ x 4) will
be represented by the S-expression '(+ x 4), which is the same as (cons '+
(cons 'x (cons 4 '()))).

We will begin by writing an evaluator for arithmetic expressions. The function eval will be passed, as an argument, the S-expression version of an expression containing only arithmetic operations and integer constants, and will
return its value:

```
-> (eval '(+ 3 (* 4 5)))
23
```

Its operation is simple: a case analysis on the type of expression (integer
constant or application), with recursive calls to evaluate sub-expressions:

```
-> (define eval (exp)
       (if (number? exp) exp
          (apply-op
             (car exp)
             (eval (cadr exp))
             (eval (caddr exp)))))

-> (define apply-op (f x y)
       (if (= f '+) (+ x y)
       (if (= f '-) (- x y)
       (if (= f '*) (* x y)
       (if (= f '/) (/ x y) 'error!)))))
```

---

[8]Another language with which the reader is familiar and which shares this property —
that programs are represented in the same form as data — is machine language. This analogy
is well worth thinking about.

```
-> (eval '(+ 3 4))
7
-> (eval '(+ (* 4 (/ 10 2)) (- 7 3)))
24
```

We now go a bit further, by allowing the interpreted language to include variables. eval now has two arguments, the expression and an *environment* assigning values to variables. The environment is represented as an a-list:

```
-> (define eval (exp rho)
       (if (number? exp) exp
          (if (symbol? exp) (assoc exp rho)
             (apply-op
                (car exp)
                (eval (cadr exp) rho)
                (eval (caddr exp) rho)))))
-> (eval '(+ i (/ 9 i)) (mkassoc 'i 3 '()))
6
```

Before going all the way to LISP eval, let us write an evaluator for expressions involving S-expression operators. To do this, a problem not mentioned earlier must be confronted. To see the problem, consider this call to eval:

(eval '(car (cdr '(a b c))) '()).

This call is incorrect, because *parseVal* doesn't know how to handle a quoted constant *within* a quoted constant. In saying S-expressions would be represented as if they were read in as S-expression constants, we overlooked this problem. Our solution is to add a new operator, called quote, to the interpreted language. The above would be entered as:

(eval '(car (cdr (quote (a b c)))) '())

The new eval is:

```
-> (define eval (exp rho)
       (if (number? exp) exp
       (if (symbol? exp) (assoc exp rho)
       (if (= (car exp) 'quote) (cadr exp)
       (if (= (length exp) 2)
          (apply-unary-op (car exp) (eval (cadr exp) rho))
          (apply-binary-op (car exp)
             (eval (cadr exp) rho)
             (eval (caddr exp) rho))
       )))))
```

```
-> (define apply-binary-op (f x y)
    (if (= f 'cons) (cons x y)
    (if (= f '+) (+ x y)
    (if (= f '-) (- x y)
    (if (= f '*) (* x y)
    (if (= f '/) (/ x y)
    (if (= f '<) (< x y)
    (if (= f '>) (> x y)
    (if (= f '=) (= x y) 'error!)))))))))
-> (define apply-unary-op (f x)
    (if (= f 'car) (car x)
    (if (= f 'cdr) (cdr x)
    (if (= f 'number?) (number? x)
    (if (= f 'list?) (list? x)
    (if (= f 'symbol?) (symbol? x)
    (if (= f 'null?) (null? x) 'error!)))))))
-> (eval '(car (quote (a b))) '())
a

-> (eval '(cons 3 (cons (+ 4 5) (quote ()))) '())
(3 9)
```

We can now give our meta-circular interpreter for LISP. As a simplification, we omit set, begin, while, and global variables. eval has three arguments, the third being for function definitions. eval and all auxiliary operations are given in Figure 2.7. A session using it would look like this:

```
-> (set E (mkassoc 'double '((a) (+ a a)) '()))
((double ((a) (+ a a))))

-> (eval '(double (car (quote (4 5)))) '() E)
8

-> (set E (mkassoc 'exp
              '((m n) (if (= n 0) 1 (* m (exp m (- n 1)))))
              '()))
((exp ((m n) (if (= n 0) 1 (* m (exp m (- n 1)))))))

-> (eval '(exp 4 3) '() E)
64
```

The only thing preventing us from defining our own read-eval-print loop is the absence of an input capability. This could be remedied by adding a **read** function to the language, but that will be left for the reader (Exercise 10). Instead, we'll fake it by defining our "read-eval-print loop" to be a function from lists of inputs to lists of outputs. Thus, the function **r-e-p-loop** will be

```
(define eval (exp rho fundefs)
    (if (number? exp) exp
    (if (symbol? exp) (assoc exp rho)
    (if (= (car exp) 'quote) (cadr exp)
    (if (= (car exp) 'if)
       (if (null? (eval (cadr exp) rho fundefs))
           (eval (cadddr exp) rho fundefs)
           (eval (caddr exp) rho fundefs))
    (if (userfun? (car exp) fundefs)
       (apply-userfun (assoc (car exp) fundefs)
           (evallist (cdr exp) rho fundefs)
           fundefs)
    (if (= (length exp) 2)
       (apply-unary-op (car exp)
           (eval (cadr exp) rho fundefs))
       (apply-binary-op (car exp)
           (eval (cadr exp) rho fundefs)
             (eval (caddr exp) rho fundefs)))))))))))
(define userfun? (f fundefs) (assoc f fundefs))
(define apply-userfun (fundef args fundefs)
    (eval (cadr fundef) ; body of function
       (mkassoc* (car fundef) args '()) ; local env
       fundefs))
(define evallist (el rho fundefs)
    (if (null? el) '()
       (cons (eval (car el) rho fundefs)
           (evallist (cdr el) rho fundefs))))
(define mkassoc* (keys values al)
    (if (null? keys) al
       (mkassoc* (cdr keys) (cdr values)
           (mkassoc (car keys) (car values) al))))
```

Figure 2.7: Function eval

```
(define r-e-p-loop (inputs) (r-e-p-loop* inputs '()))
(define r-e-p-loop* (inputs fundefs)
    (if (null? inputs) '() ; session done
        (if (atom? (car inputs)) ; input is variable or number
            (process-exp (car inputs) (cdr inputs) fundefs)
            (if (= (caar inputs) 'define) ; input is function definition
                (process-def (car inputs) (cdr inputs) fundefs)
                (process-exp (car inputs) (cdr inputs) fundefs)))))
(define process-def (e inputs fundefs)
    (cons (cadr e) ; echo function name
        (r-e-p-loop* inputs
            (mkassoc (cadr e) (cddr e) fundefs))))
(define process-exp (e inputs fundefs)
    (cons (eval e '() fundefs) ; print value of expression
        (r-e-p-loop* inputs fundefs)))
```

Figure 2.8: Function `r-e-p-loop`

used as follows:

```
-> (r-e-p-loop '(
        (define double (a) (+ a a))
        (double (car (quote (4 5))))
        (define exp (m n) (if (= n 0) 1 (* m (exp m (- n 1)))))
        (exp 4 3)
        ))
(double 8 exp 64)
```

The list returned by the call contains just what the LISP interpreter would return for the four inputs. `r-e-p-loop` is defined in Figure 2.8.

The point has at last been reached where the adjective "meta-circular" begins to take on significance. Observe that *our evaluator evaluates all of* LISP *that is used in the evaluator itself.* Thus, it can evaluate itself! The only change to make to `eval` in order to input it to itself is the one mentioned earlier of replacing "'···" by "(quote ···)" everywhere. Even the definition of `r-e-p-loop` is interpreted "meta-circularly:"

```
-> (r-e-p-loop '(
        (define cadr (exp) (car (cdr exp)))
        (define cddr (exp) (cdr (cdr exp)))
        (define caar (exp) (car (car exp)))
        (define caddr (exp) (car (cdr (cdr exp))))
        (define cadddr (exp) (car (cdr (cdr (cdr exp))))) 
```

```
(define cadar (exp) (car (cdr (car exp))))
(define list2 (x y) (cons x (cons y (quote ()))))
(define +1 (x) (+ x 1))
(define length (l) (if (null? l) 0 (+1 (length (cdr l)))))
(define assoc (x alist) ... )
(define mkassoc (x y alist) ... )
(define mkassoc* (keys values al) ... )
(define eval (exp rho fundefs)
    (if (number? exp) exp
    (if (symbol? exp) (assoc exp rho)
    (if (= (car exp) (quote quote)) (cadr exp)
    (if (= (car exp) (quote if))
        (if (null? (eval (cadr exp) rho fundefs))
           (eval (cadddr exp) rho fundefs)
           (eval (caddr exp) rho fundefs))
    ⋮
(define apply-unary-op (f x fundefs) ... )
(define apply-binary-op (f x y) ... )
(define userfun? (f fundefs) (assoc f fundefs))
(define apply-userfun (fundef args fundefs) ... )
(define evallist (el rho fundefs) ... )
(define r-e-p-loop (inputs) (r-e-p-loop* inputs (quote ())))
(define r-e-p-loop* (inputs fundefs) ... )
(define process-def (e inputs fundefs) ... )
(define process-exp (e inputs fundefs) ... )
(r-e-p-loop (quote (
        (define double (a) (+ a a))
        (double (car (quote (4 5))))
        )))
))
(cadr cddr ... process-exp (double 8))
```

For further developments of this evaluator, see Exercise 6.

2.5   LISP as It Really Is

It must be understood that there really is no one language called LISP. The
language we have called LISP is contained, with minor variations, in all "real"
LISP's, but it is extended in many different ways. Recently, a kind of standard
version has been promulgated under the name COMMON LISP. To give an idea
of the difference in complexity from our language, the COMMON LISP manual
lists about 1000 built-in functions.

Our language corresponds to the subset of LISP known as "Pure LISP" (except for assignment, which is absent from pure LISP), which accounts for a large percentage of the LISP code that is written in real life. It is fair to say that the LISP code presented in this chapter is representative of real LISP.

In this section, we will first discuss two ways in which our LISP differs from the standard form of pure LISP, then some of the ways in which real LISP's extend pure LISP.

2.5.1 STANDARD "PURE LISP"

As just mentioned, every version of LISP contains a subset corresponding to our language. There are, however, two differences between the standard versions of pure LISP and our language.

cond.   A minor difference is the form of the conditional expression. The standard and traditional conditional expression construct is `cond`, which has the form:

$$\text{(cond } (e_1 \ e_1') \ \ldots \ (e_n \ e_n')).$$

This expression is evaluated by evaluating e_1, e_2, and so on, until some e_i evaluates to a non-*nil* value. Then, e_i' is evaluated and its value returned as the value of the conditional expression.

As an example, (if e_1 e_2 e_3) would be rendered using `cond` as:

$$\text{(cond } (e_1 \ e_2) \ (\text{'T } e_3)).$$

Another example, showing the advantage of `cond` in avoiding parenthesis overload, is our `apply-binary-op` from page 48:

```
(define apply-binary-op (f x y)
    (cond
        ((= f 'cons) (cons x y))
        ((= f '+) (+ x y))
        ((= f '-) (- x y))
              ⋮
        ((= f '=) (= x y))
        ('T 'error!)))
```

S-Expressions.   Our definition of S-expression is nonstandard. The real definition is:

Definition 2.2 An *S-expression* is either a *symbol*, a *number*, or a *pair* of S-expressions.

This definition permits the consing of two non-lists. For example, in standard LISP, (cdr (cons 2 3)) is legal and evaluates to 3. "Dot notation" is provided for both input and output. With it, one writes '(2 . 3) for (cons 2 3), or

2   3

and '((a . b) . c) for (cons (cons 'a 'b) 'c), or

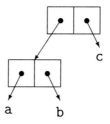

Note that a "." corresponds precisely to a cons cell.

What about lists and list notation? List notation is still supported. A list is considered to be a special kind of S-expression, one having the property that, if you follow all the cdr's out to the end, you hit the symbol nil (nil is no longer a distinct type of S-expression, but simply a symbol used, by convention, to terminate lists). Thus, list '(a b c) corresponds to '(a . (b . (c . nil))), or

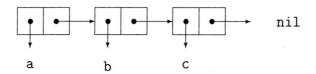

a   b   c

In fact, our interpreter nearly uses this definition of S-expression. For example, (cdr (cons 3 4)) actually does evaluate to 4. On the other hand, (cons 3 4) does not print correctly (since *prValue* knows only how to print lists, and this is not one); and, of course, dot notation is not provided on either input or output (see Exercise 11).

2.5.2 DATA TYPES

The S-expression is the basic type of data of any LISP, but other types of data are usually included as well.

Numbers. Although LISP was never intended as a language for doing numerical processing, its implementations have extremely elaborate and general numerical data types. COMMON LISP, for example, has `complex` as well as `real` numbers. It also has `bignum`'s, meaning infinite-precision integers; integer operations are thereby guaranteed not to overflow (unless the computer runs out of memory).

Arrays. Arrays are, of course, also provided, often in great generality. In COMMON LISP, arrays can be created dynamically (e.g., `(setq A (make-array '(3 4)))` assigns to A an uninitialized 3×4 array[9]), can share parts, and can sometimes change shape dynamically. Character strings are a special case of arrays, for which some additional functions are provided (e.g., `string<` compares strings lexicographically).

2.5.3   FUNCTIONS WITH SIDE-EFFECTS

A *side-effect* of a function call is any action of the function that affects the state of the world *after* the function has returned, beyond simply returning a value. The most common type of side-effect — and one which is possible in our language — is an assignment to a global variable. Side-effects are generally to be avoided, because they can make programs difficult to understand. For example, here is a session in our language:

```
-> (define f (x) (begin (set a (+ a x)) a))
-> (set a 0)
0
-> (f 4)
4
-> (f 4)
8
```

What is confusing is that the same expression can yield two different answers. This can also make debugging difficult, because expression evaluations are not perfectly reproducible.

Although our version of LISP does admit this kind of side-effect, it excludes a still more dangerous kind: the direct alteration of list structures. In our version of LISP, if a variable x has been assigned a list structure (whether by `set` or by being bound in a function call), no subsequent expression evaluation can change that value *unless* it has the form (set x $\cdots$). The binding of x can be changed, but the *list* assigned to x is inviolate ("immutable," in jargon).

In real LISP's, this is not the case. S-expressions *can* be mutated. This is made possible by two new functions: `rplaca` (for "replace the car") and `rplacd`

---

[9]Another minor difference: `setq` is used instead of `set`.

(for "replace the cdr"). (rplaca L M) actually modifies the list L, making M its first element; rplacd similarly modifies the cdr of its argument. For example:

```
-> (set x '(a b c))
(a b c)

-> (set y x)
(a b c)

-> (rplaca y 'd)
(d b c)

-> y
(d b c)

-> x
(d b c)
```

Furthermore, this alteration of lists can lead to *circular* S-expressions, as in:

```
-> (set x '(a b))
(a b)

-> (rplacd x x)
(a a a a a a ...
```

rplaca and rplacd are included in all LISP's, in one form or another. They have two major purposes. First, they can allow for more efficient code by minimizing consing. For example, the function rplac-assoc modifies an a-list so as to add a new association or change an existing one. Unlike mkassoc, which returns a new a-list with the modified association, rplac-assoc actually changes the a-list. Also unlike mkassoc, rplac-assoc does either one cons (if the key is already present in the a-list) or three (if it is not); mkassoc can perform as many conses as the length of the a-list.

```
(define rplac-assoc (x y alist)
    (if (null? alist) '()
       (if (= x (caar alist))
          (rplacd (car alist) (list1 y))
             (if (null? (cdr alist))
                 (rplacd alist (list1 (list2 x y)))
                 (rplac-assoc x y (cdr alist)))))))
```

Note that rplac-assoc does not *return* the modified a-list.

There is some reason to argue that cons is an expensive operation and that this efficiency gain is therefore significant, but informed discussion of this question will have to await Chapter 10.

The other, and more compelling, use for rplac is to allow the construction of circular lists (as we have seen) and thereby the direct representation of arbitrary graphs.

2.5.4 MACROS

A *macro* is a function that transforms expressions. Since programs are naturally represented as data in LISP (as shown in Section 2.4), LISP systems always provide macro facilities. Macros provide a simple way to extend the language without modifying the underlying evaluation mechanism. Furthermore, they permit the individual programmer to customize the language for a particular application.

To be more specific, suppose m is an n-argument macro, and we find it used in the application (m e_1 ... e_n). To evaluate this application, apply m to the *expressions* e_1 ... e_n (this is crucial: m is applied to the expressions, not to their values); the result is a new expression e. Then, e is evaluated, its value being returned as the value of the expression (m e_1 ... e_n).

The macro we present provides a simple version of a `for` statement. For example, `(for x 1 10 (print x))` will behave more or less like the PASCAL statement

$$\textbf{for } x := 1 \textbf{ to } 10 \textbf{ do } write(x).$$

The `for` macro is defined like any other LISP function, except for the key-word `define-macro`:

```
(define-macro for (indexvar lower upper body)
    (list 'begin
        (list 'set indexvar lower)
        (list 'while
            (list '<= indexvar upper)
            (list 'begin body
                (list 'set indexvar (list '+ indexvar 1))))))
```

When invoked as `(for x 1 10 (print x))`, `for` is applied to expressions x, 1, 10, and `(print x)`, to produce the expression:[10]

```
(begin (set x 1)
    (while (<= x 10)
        (begin (print x)
            (set x (+ x 1)))))
```

This expression is then evaluated, and its value is returned as the value of the original expression.

It is important to notice that the `for` macro could *not* have been programmed as a function, because functions always evaluate their arguments,

---

[10] Assuming `<=` has been defined; for future reference, we also define `>=`:

```
(define <= (x y) (or (< x y) (= x y)))
(define >= (x y) (or (> x y) (= x y)))
```

and the arguments x and (print x) could not have been sensibly evaluated before the call. Thus, macros involve a kind of "delayed evaluation" of their arguments, which can be invaluable in programming language extensions like for.

Macros are sometimes used in cases where functions would also work, because they offer a different kind of time/space tradeoff than functions do. Macro "expansion" can be performed before evaluation (at compile-time), so it is like a function that is compiled "in-line;" it imposes no function-call penalty at run-time. On the other hand, the code resulting from the macro expansion is usually larger than it would have been with function calls.

2.5.5 GARBAGE COLLECTION

LISP would not exist without the facility of dynamic storage allocation. Whenever cons is applied, memory must be allocated for the cons cell. Our interpreter does this by invoking the PASCAL procedure *new*.

But our use of the *new* procedure would not be acceptable in any real LISP system. All we do is continue allocating memory until there's none left, and then "dump core" (perhaps the reader has experienced this). Real LISP systems take advantage of the fact that, generally speaking, many previously allocated cons cells are no longer in use; these "garbage" cells can be reclaimed and reallocated, thus giving the illusion of having much more memory than actually exists. In this way, the LISP system can continue to run indefinitely, so long as the total number of non-garbage cons cells never exceeds the size of memory. In practice, this usually means forever.

There are many methods for doing "garbage collection." Chapter 10 discusses some of those methods, producing in the process several garbage-collecting versions of the LISP interpreter.

Garbage collection is, in fact, a feature of all the languages covered in this book. In purely operational terms, it is one of the major differences between these languages and more traditional languages like PASCAL.

2.6 Summary

LISP has dominated the world of artificial intelligence programming almost from its inception. It introduced several concepts whose importance seem only to grow the more is learned about programming languages: recursion, recursively-defined data structures, dynamic memory allocation and garbage collection, and simplified syntax. The influence of LISP is nowhere more apparent than in the book you are holding in your hands: in the syntax we have chosen for our languages; in the evaluation method (which reflects McCarthy's eval); and, most especially, in the programming techniques employed in the interpreters.

2.6.1 GLOSSARY

a-list, or association list. A simple representation of symbol tables as a list of pairs, easily programmed and commonly used in LISP.

applicative, or functional, programming. A style of programming characterized by the (usually recursive) definition of functions over recursively-defined data, avoiding iteration and side-effects. The more modern use of these terms extends this meaning by adding an emphasis on the use of *higher-order functions*; see Part III.

atom. A "simple" item of data, generally either a number or symbol.

car, cdr, cons. The basic operations on S-expressions. If not for the historical factor, `car` would probably be called `head` or `first`, `cdr` would be `tail` or `rest`, and `cons` `join` or `pair`.

imperative programming. Traditional programming, as in PASCAL, characterized by many small changes of state, i.e., heavy use of assignment. Taking the more general definition of "side-effect" (see below), this could also be called "programming by side-effect."

macro. A function that operates on expressions to produce other expressions. Macros are used both as a language-extension facility and as a more time-efficient substitute for ordinary functions.

meta-circular interpreter. An interpreter whose object language (the language it interprets) is the same as its source language (the language in which it is written), so that it can, in principle, interpret itself.

property list. (1) An a-list the attributes of which are a-lists. (2) (*Standard definition*) In LISP systems, *every* symbol has an associated a-list, called the *property list* of that symbol. Operations with names like `getprop` and `putprop` are provided for retrieving data from, and adding data to, these property lists.

pure LISP. The language defined in Chapter 1 of McCarthy [1962] and in McCarthy [1960]; basically, it is our LISP minus all imperative features (`while`, `begin`, `set`, and `print`).

recursion. Self-referential definition. In LISP, recursion is seen both in the definition of S-expressions and in user-defined functions. Recursion is closely associated with the mathematical proof method called **induction**.

S-expression, or symbolic-expression. The basic unit of data in LISP. S-expressions are tree-structured, the leaves containing atoms.

side-effect. Any change in state beyond the simple returning of a value. In this general sense, programmers are using side-effects whenever they use assignment. The term is sometimes used in a narrower sense, referring to changes of state which are in some sense unexpected, such as assignment to global variables inside a function, or changes to data structures made without explicit assignment. In LISP, such changes can be made to lists by use of the functions `rplaca` and `rplacd`. Side-effects in the narrower sense are generally considered a Bad Thing.

special form. A type of function, like `set` or `if`, that does not evaluate its arguments, or more precisely, that evaluates its arguments *selectively*. Such functions are necessarily built into the LISP interpreter, since all user-defined functions evaluate their arguments. Macros provide a way to, in effect, add new special forms.

2.6.2   FURTHER READING

It is always fun to go to the source, which in this case means a paper and a book by John McCarthy ([1960] and [1962]). Still, it cannot be denied that there are modern treatments of LISP which are clearer and more complete; examples are Friedman [1974], Touretzky [1984], Wilensky [1986], and Winston [1984]. The COMMON LISP manual (Steele [1984]) is an invaluable *reference* book for the real LISPer, the more so as COMMON LISP becomes more widely available.

Tree traversals are covered in depth in Reingold and Hansen [1986].

The original article on relational data bases by Codd is [1970]. Maier [1983] is a thorough treatment of the subject. More information on the topic of Section 2.3 can also be found in Baring-Gould [1967].

Our major emphasis in this chapter has been on the use of recursion. Two books dealing specifically with recursion in the context of imperative languages are Rohl [1984] and Roberts [1986]. Also interesting is the chapter on recursion in Reingold and Reingold [1988].

2.7   Exercises

2.7.1   LEARNING ABOUT THE LANGUAGE

1. Code the following LISP functions:

   (a) `(count x l)` counts the number of occurrences of `x` at the top level of `l`, and `(countall x l)` counts the number of occurrences throughout `l`.

   ```
   -> (count 'a '(1 b a (c a)))
   1
   -> (countall 'a '(1 b a (c a)))
   2
   ```

(b) (reverse 1) returns a list containing the elements of 1 in reverse order. (*Hint:* you will probably want to use the **append** function.)

```
-> (reverse '(a b (c d) e))
(e (c d) b a)
```

(c) (twist 1) reverses the top level of 1 and recursively twists all the items in 1.

```
-> (twist '((a (b 5)) (c d) e))
(e (d c) ((5 b) a))
```

(d) (flatten 1) constructs a list having the same atoms as 1 in the same order but in a flat list.

```
-> (flatten '((a b) ((c d) e)))
(a b c d e)
```

(e) (sublist 11 12) and (contig-sublist 11 12) determine whether the elements of 11 are contained, and contiguously contained, respectively, in the same order in 12.

```
-> (sublist '(a b c) '(x a y b z c))
T
-> (contig-sublist '(a b c) '(x a y b z c))
()
-> (contig-sublist '(a y) '(x a y b z c))
T
```

2. Program the following set functions:

   (a) (remove x s) returns a set having the same elements as set **s** with element **x** removed.

   (b) (subset s1 s2) determines if **s1** is a subset of **s2**.

   (c) (=set s1 s2) determines if **s1** and **s2** are the same set.

3. Explain why **wrong-sum** (page 2.1.3) doesn't work. Then explain why it works when the last line is changed to:

$$(+ \ \text{tmp} \ (\text{wrong-sum} \ (\text{cdr} \ 1))).$$

4. This set of questions concerns tree traversal.

   (a) Program post-order and in-order traversal for binary trees.

   (b) Modify the pre-order and level-order traversals so that, instead of the node labels being printed, they are placed in a list, which is returned as the value of the call.

(c) Extend the pre-order and level-order traversals to trees of arbitrary degree, represented in such a way that binary trees have the same representation given them in the text. For example, '(a b c d) represents a ternary tree whose root is labeled with a and which has three children, labeled b, c, and d, respectively, all leaf nodes. Note that there are two ways to represent leaf nodes: 'a and '(a) both represent a leaf node labeled a.

5. These problems relate to the relational data base example.

(a) Program AND-SELECT, whose first two arguments are lists (of the same length) and which selects only those rows that have all the given values for the given attributes. For example, (AND-SELECT '(Crime Location) '(murder London) CRIMES) would select only rows representing murders in London.

(b) Program OR-SELECT, whose first argument is an attribute name, whose second argument is a list of values, and which selects those rows which have any of the values for the given attribute.

(c) Lift the restriction on UNION, INTER, and DIFF that the attributes of their two arguments must occur *in the same order*. These operations should check that their arguments have the same set of attributes and then choose an order of those attributes for the result.

(d) REMOVE has the same arguments as PROJECT, but projects onto those attribute *not* in its first argument.

6. Modify the last version of eval in Section 2.4 as follows:

(a) Add begin and print.

(b) Add set and global variables.

(c) Add local variables, as described in Exercise 12 of Chapter 1.

2.7.2 LEARNING ABOUT THE INTERPRETER

7. Add the function list as a value-op.

8. Implement rplaca and rplacd. Test them first using rplac-assoc, then define nreverse, which reverses a list *in place*, that is, with no conses. (Code nreverse using only rplacd.)

9. Add a trace facility to the language. This feature should permit users to name the functions that are to be traced, so that whenever they are called, their arguments and result are printed to the terminal. The trace output should be clearly labeled and should use indentation to indicate calls and returns. Trace length (as we did on page 29), then sieve and remove-multiples.

10. Add a `read` function (as in Exercise 8 of Chapter 1) and use it to program an interactive version of the meta-circular interpreter. The new version of the meta-circular interpreter should both read and print interactively; you will find it necessary to add `print` as a unary operation and `begin` as a control operation.

11. Modify the interpreter to have it use the standard definition of S-expressions as given in Section 2.5.1, which is to say, allow for dot notation on input and output.

    To give some more explanation of this notation: First, on *output*, a dot can appear only before the *last number or symbol* in a list (this rule applying as well to sublists). The S-expression

    `(cons (cons 'a 'b) (cons 4 5))`

    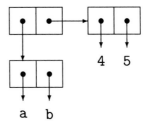

    would be written: `((a . b) 4 . 5)`. Another way to state this rule is that *dots should be minimized* on output.

    For *input*, a dot can appear only before the *last item* in a list (though this last item can be a list), so `'(a b . c d)` is illegal. The dot represents a cons cell pointing to the items before and after the dot. Thus, `'(a b c . d)` represents the list `(cons 'a (cons 'b (cons 'c 'd)))`, and `'(a b . (c d))` the list `(cons 'a (cons 'b '(c d)))`, which is the same as `'(a b c d)`.

12. Implement macros. The main part of the job is to write functions *EXPto-SEXP*, translating *EXP*'s to *SEXP*'s (use the `quote` trick from Section 2.4 to translate *VALEXP*'s), and *SEXPtoEXP*, going in the other direction. The keyword `define-macro` can be used to introduce macro definitions, their syntax being otherwise identical to ordinary function definitions. You'll need to add the function *applyMacro* to *eval*. To see how it works, assume macro m has been defined as:

    $$(\text{define-macro } m \ (x_1 \ \ldots \ x_n) \ e)$$

    and we are evaluating a call

    $$(m \ e_1 \ \ldots \ e_n)$$

    in environment ρ. Then *applyMacro* is passed the *unevaluated* arguments

$e_1 \ldots e_n$ and does the following:

(a) Constructs environment $\rho' = \{x_1 \mapsto \textit{EXPtoSEXP}(e_1), \ldots, x_n \mapsto \textit{EXPtoSEXP}(e_n)\}$.

(b) Recursively evaluates e in environment ρ', yielding *SEXP* s.

(c) Recursively evaluates $\textit{SEXPtoEXP}(s)$ in environment ρ.

Define `cond` as a macro.

Chapter 3

APL

The central insight on which APL is based is that by using certain operations on arrays, a good deal of what is normally computed by iteration can be expressed in a single expression ("in closed form," a mathematician would say). For example, suppose we want to sum the even elements of a one-dimensional array v, a process which would require both conditional and iterative control in most languages; in APL[1] we say: `(+/ (compress (even? v) v))`. In jargon, we have "traded control for data." The array operations provided in the language can be used in ways that are sometimes elegant, sometimes fiendishly clever, often impenetrable. Not surprisingly, APL has been a controversial language from the first.

Like LISP, APL is largely the product of one man's imagination. In 1962, Ken Iverson published a book entitled "A Programming Language." Several years later, an adaptation of that notation, bearing the book's initials as its name, appeared as the interactive programming system APL\360, developed by an IBM group led by Iverson and Adin Falkoff.

The group's efforts stand as a remarkable *tour-de-force*, since they not only refined and expanded Iverson's notation and developed an interactive programming system, but also designed a new type font and built the terminals to support it. The combination of the unique programming concepts on which the language is based and the character set in which programs are expressed makes APL programs probably the oddest-looking, and possibly the shortest, in any major language. (Our version of the language will, of course, use the regular ASCII characters.)

Ken Iverson won the Turing Award in 1979 for developing APL, a sign of the esteem in which his work is held. On the other hand, APL is more widely admired than imitated; it seems difficult to apply the concepts of APL to other languages. For us, APL is, above all, an excellent example of gaining power by using "large values."

---

[1] A reminder is in order here that, outside of Section 3.4, APL refers to the language we are interpreting. In some chapters (e.g., Chapter 2) the differences between the real language and our version thereof are not so striking, but here they are; hence, this reminder.

3.1 The Language

We again find ourselves discussing the *values* of the language and the *operations* over those values. The values in this case are familiar: integers (called *scalars*), one-dimensional arrays of integers (called *vectors*), and two-dimensional arrays of integers (called *matrices*). Each of these types has distinct values; for example, a 1-by-10 matrix is not the same as a 10-element vector. Indexing is from 1.

Some terminology will be helpful in the description of the operations. The *rank* of a value is its type — scalar, vector, or matrix. An n-vector is a vector of length n; [1 2 3 4] is a 4-vector. An m, n-matrix is one having m rows and n columns;

$$\begin{matrix} 1 & 2 & 3 \\ 4 & 5 & 6 \end{matrix}$$

is a $2, 3$-matrix. We will sometimes refer to the *shape* of a value, by which is meant its rank and dimensions.

3.1.1 OPERATIONS

The power of APL derives from its particular set of built-in operations (value-op's). There are many (twenty-six in our version). Before presenting them in detail, here is an overview of the main ones:

- The arithmetic operations are extended to vectors and matrices "naturally." For example, to add two matrices, add their corresponding elements; to add a scalar to a matrix, add it to each element of the matrix.

- Relational operations return zero for false and one for true; they are extended to vectors and matrices just as are arithmetic operations.

- To "reduce" a vector by an operation is to apply the operation "across" the vector; for example, +-reduction is the summation of the vector.

- To "compress" a vector A with respect to a vector B of zeros and ones is to remove those elements of A whose corresponding element of B is zero.

These are the most important concepts in understanding APL: extending scalar operations to values of higher rank, reduction, and compression.

Rather than have the descriptions of these and the other operations extended over many pages, we will define them all at once, without pausing for examples or motivation. Table 3.1 gives an example for each one, and there will be many more examples in Section 3.1.3. In the explanations that follow, V will be a typical n–vector, with elements $v_1, \ldots, v_n$, and A will be the m, n-matrix:

$$\begin{matrix} a_{11} & \cdots & a_{1n} \\ a_{21} & \cdots & a_{2n} \\ \vdots & \ddots & \vdots \\ a_{m1} & \cdots & a_{mn} \end{matrix}$$

Operation	Expression	Value
Sample data	A ; a 2,3-matrix	1 2 3 4 5 6
	V ; a 3-vector	2 4 6
	C ; a logical 2-vector	1 0
	D ; a logical 3-vector	1 0 1
Arithmetic	(* A A)	1 4 9 16 25 36
	(- V 1)	1 3 5
Relational	(> A 4)	0 0 0 0 1 1
Reduction	(+/ V)	12
	(max/ A)	3 6
Compression	(compress D V)	2 6
	(compress C A)	1 2 3 (a 1,3-matrix)
Shape	(shape A)	2 3
Raveling	(ravel A)	1 2 3 4 5 6
Restructuring	(restruct (shape A) V)	2 4 6 2 4 6
	(restruct (shape V) C)	1 0 1
Catenation	(cat A C)	1 2 3 4 5 6 1 0
Index generation	(indx 5)	1 2 3 4 5
Transposition	(trans A)	1 4 2 5 3 6
Subscripting	([] V (indx 2))	2 4
	([] A 1)	1 2 3 (a 1,3-matrix)
	([] (trans A) (indx 2))	1 4 2 5

Table 3.1: Examples of APL Operations

Finally, APL terminology calls one-argument functions *monadic* and two-argument functions *dyadic*.

+,-,*,/,max,or,and,=,>,<. When applied to scalars, these dyadic operations do exactly what they did in Chapter 1. max returns the larger of its two arguments; or and and are the same as the PASCAL operations, with integers zero and one representing false and true, respectively.

When exactly one of their arguments is a scalar, these operations are extended as follows: The operation is performed between the scalar and each element of the vector or matrix, the result having the same shape as the vector or matrix. (For this rule, a 1-vector is regarded as a scalar.)

When neither argument is a scalar, the two arguments must have the same shape. The operation is performed between corresponding components, returning a result of the same shape as the arguments.

+/,-/,*/,//,max/,or/,and/. These are the *reduction* operations. They are monadic. For a scalar argument, they do nothing and return the argument. For a vector argument, the binary operation is placed between the elements of the vector and the resulting expression is evaluated. More precisely, if $\oplus/$ is applied to vector V, where $\oplus$ is any primitive dyadic operation, the result is the *scalar*

$$(\oplus\ v_1\ (\oplus\ v_2\ (\ldots(\oplus\ v_{n-1}\ v_n)\ldots)))$$

(If V has just one element, it is returned.)

For a matrix argument, each *row* is reduced as a vector, and the result is the *vector* of the resulting values. More precisely, $\oplus$-reduction over A results in the m-vector

$$(\oplus/\ A_1)\ \ldots\ (\oplus/\ A_m),$$

where A_i is the ith row of A.

compress. *Compression* is a dyadic operation whose first argument is an m-vector of zeros and ones (a "logical vector"), and whose second is either an m-vector or an m,n-matrix.

If the second argument is a vector, the result is a vector whose elements are drawn from exactly those positions in the second argument where the first argument has a one. If it is a matrix, the result is a matrix whose rows are drawn from those positions in the second argument where the first argument has a one.

Note that compression can lead to vectors having no elements and matrices having no rows. These are called *null vectors* and *null matrices*.

shape. This monadic function returns a vector giving the shape of its argument: a null vector for a scalar argument, a 1-vector giving the length of a vector argument, and a 2-vector giving the numbers of rows and columns of a matrix argument.

ravel. *Raveling* means turning a value of any rank into a vector having the same elements. Thus, a vector argument is unchanged; a scalar argument is converted to a 1-vector; and an m,n-matrix is converted to an $m \times n$-vector. For example, the ravel of A is the vector

$$a_{11}\ a_{12}\ \ldots\ a_{1n}\ a_{21}\ \ldots\ a_{2n}\ \ldots\ a_{mn}.$$

restruct. *Restructuring* is a dyadic operation whose first argument is a "shape vector," i.e., a vector of length 0, 1, or 2. It returns a value having that shape, with elements drawn from the ravel of the second argument, repeated as often as necessary. (`restruct` aborts if its second argument is null. If its first argument is a scalar, it is regarded as a 1-vector.)

`cat`. *Catenation* is the joining of two values into a vector. More precisely, if the ravel of its two arguments are, respectively, an m-vector and an n-vector, its result is an $m + n$-vector containing the ravel of the first argument followed by the ravel of the second.

`indx`. The *index generation* operation has a single, scalar argument, x; it returns the vector consisting of the values $1\ 2\ \ldots\ x$. (If its argument is not a scalar, `indx` uses its first value.)

`trans`. *Transposition* is a monadic operation applying to matrices (it returns scalars and vectors unchanged). The transpose of the m, n-matrix A is the n, m-matrix:

$$\begin{matrix} a_{11} & \cdots & a_{m1} \\ a_{12} & \cdots & a_{m2} \\ \vdots & \ddots & \vdots \\ a_{1n} & \cdots & a_{mn} \end{matrix}$$

`[]`. The *subscripting* operation is dyadic. Its first argument is a vector or matrix; its result has the same rank. Its second argument is a vector (or a scalar, which is treated by this operation as a 1-vector).

Assume the second argument is a p-vector. If the first argument is a vector, the result is a p-vector, its values being drawn from the first argument at the positions given by the second argument. If the first argument is an m, n-matrix, the result is a p, n-matrix, its rows being drawn from the first argument at the positions given by the second argument.

Table 3.1 gives examples of each operation.

3.1.2 SYNTAX

A way to write constants is needed. There will be only scalar and vector constants; scalars are written as single integers, and vectors as single-quoted parenthesized lists of integers. (Matrix constants can be obtained easily by applying `restruct` to vector constants.)

Except for having different operations and constants, the syntax is the same as in Chapter 1:

```
value          ⟶   integer | vector-const
value-op       ⟶   + | - | * | / | max | or | and | = | < | >
               |   +/ | -/ | */ | // | max/ | or/ | and/
               |   compress | shape | ravel | restruct
               |   cat | indx | trans | [] | print
vector-const   ⟶   '( integer* )
```

3.1.3 EXAMPLES

All the ingredients are now in our hands, and it is only a matter of seeing how far our ingenuity can take us in mixing them. The factorial is a simple one:

```
-> (define fac (n) (*/ (indx n)))
```

Equally easy is finding the (integer) average of a vector:

```
-> (define avg (v) (/ (+/ v) (shape v)))
```

min and min/ were omitted from the set of value-op's because they are simple to define in terms of max and max/:

```
-> (define neg (v) (- 0 v))
-> (define min (v1 v2) (neg (max (neg v1) (neg v2))))
-> (define min/ (v) (neg (max/ (neg v))))
```

We can define the even-sum function discussed in the introductory paragraph of this chapter:

```
-> (define mod (m n) (- m (* n (/ m n))))
-> (define even? (n) (= (mod n 2) 0))
-> (define even-sum (v) (+/ (compress (even? v) v)))
```

The reader should note that the functions defined up to now, such as mod and even?, extend naturally to vectors and matrices:

```
-> (mod '(2 5 8 11) '(1 2 3 4))
    0 1 2 3
-> (mod 10 '(2 5 8 11))
    0 0 2 10
```

However, not every function you can define will work this way. In particular, functions that are defined using control operations usually will not. An example is not=:

```
-> (define not= (x y) (if (= x y) 0 1))
-> (not= 3 5)
    1
-> (not= '(1 3 5) '(1 4 8))
    0
```

What happened here is that only the first two elements of the two vectors were compared, though even something this reasonable may not always happen. In this case, we can get around the problem as follows:

```
-> (define not (x) (- 1 x))
-> (define <> (x y) (not (= x y)))
-> (<> '(1 3 5) '(1 4 8))
   0 1 1
```

Reversal. The next function reverses the elements of a vector. It works by constructing the index vector $n, n-1, \ldots 1$, where n is the length of the vector.

```
-> (define reverse (a)
     (begin
        (set size ([] (shape a) 1))
        ([] a (+1 (- size (indx size))))))
```

reverse has been written to apply to matrices as well as vectors. Here is an example; notice the trick for constructing the matrix m:

```
-> (set m (restruct '(4 4) '(1 1 0 0 0)))
   1   1   0   0
   0   1   1   0
   0   0   1   1
   0   0   0   1
-> (reverse m)
   0   0   0   1
   0   0   1   1
   0   1   1   0
   1   1   0   0
```

It is somewhat an aspect of the APL programming style to attempt to fit as much code on a single line as possible, and one way of accomplishing this is to place assignments *within* expressions, relying on the order of evaluation of expression arguments to ensure that the assignment gets done at the right time. Thus, reverse could have been written like this:

```
-> (define reverse (a)
     ([] a (+1 (- (set size ([] (shape a) 1)) (indx size)))))
```

find-closest. Given scalar x and vector v, (find-closest x v) finds the index in v of the value closest to x (or the first such value, if there is a tie). To define it, we first need to define abs and find.

The **signum** function gives the sign of its arguments — either -1, 0, or 1.

The absolute value function is defined using it:

```
-> (define signum (x) (+ (* (< x 0) -1)(> x 0)))
-> (define abs (x) (* x (signum x)))
```

The useful dyadic function find finds the index of the first occurrence of
its first argument within its second argument;

```
-> (define find (x v) ([] (compress (= x v) (indx (shape v))) 1))
-> (find 3 '(1 4 7 3 9 2))
   4
```

find assumes x occurs in v; otherwise it bombs. It should do something sensible, like returning 0; see Exercise 2.

find-closest works by first computing the absolute values of the differences between x and the elements of v, then finding the index of the smallest
difference:

```
(define find-closest (x v)
      (begin
         (set absdiffs (abs (- v x)))
         (find (min/ absdiffs) absdiffs)))
-> (find-closest 10 '(8 11 4 13 7))
   2
```

Variance.   As the avg example hints, APL is wonderfully well suited for
programming statistical functions. Lacking floating-point numbers, our version
is rather less so, but here is one example. The *variance* of a set of points is a
measure of the "spread-out-ness" of the points. It is defined as the average of
the squares of the differences between each point and the mean; symbolically,
if we let $\bar{a}$ represent the mean of the numbers $a_1, \ldots, a_n$, it is:

$$\frac{\sum_{i=1}^{n}(a_i - \bar{a})^2}{n}$$

The variance is a "one-liner:"

```
-> (define sqr (x) (* x x))
-> (define variance (v) (/ (+/ (sqr (- v (avg v)))) (shape v)))
```

By contrast, a PASCAL program for the variance is about eight lines long.

Binomial Coefficients.   The binomial coefficients were defined in Exercise 3
of Chapter 1. They are usually drawn in the form of a triangle, with $\binom{n}{k}$ being

the $(k + 1)$th number in the $(n + 1)$th row $(k, n \geq 0)$. The pattern is easy to see:

$$
\begin{array}{ccccc}
 & & 1 & & \\
 & 1 & & 1 & \\
1 & & 2 & & 1 \\
\end{array}
$$

```
            1
          1   1
        1   2   1
      1   3   3   1
    1   4   6   4   1
```

Here is an APL program to compute the first **n** rows of this triangle (though we cannot quite print it in triangular form):

```
-> (define binom (n)
     (begin (set l '(1))
        (print l)
        (while (< (shape l) n)
           (begin
              (set l (+ (cat 0 l)(cat l 0)))
              (print l)))))
```

Note the test (< (shape l) n). In APL, 1 is regarded as a true value. For convenience, our interpreter takes this to include the scalar 1, or any vector or matrix whose first element is 1 (see *isTrueVal* in Appendix D).

Primes. Primality testing is a good showpiece for APL, since it is always considered a naturally iterative process. In APL, we divide all the numbers less than **n** into **n** at once, and then check if any of the remainders is zero:

```
-> (define prime (n) (and/ (<> 0 (mod n (+1 (indx (- n 2)))))))
```

This one seems complicated enough to be worth tracing. Consider the computation of (prime 14):

```
(indx (- n 2))        =   1 2 3 4 5 6 7 8 9 10 11 12
(+1 (indx (- n 2)))   =   2 3 4 5 6 7 8 9 10 11 12 13
(mod n (+1 ···))      =   0 2 2 4 2 0 6 5 4 3 2 1
(<> 0 (mod n ···))    =   0 1 1 1 1 0 1 1 1 1 1 1
(and/ (<> 0 ···))     =   0
```

Sparse Vector Representation. The next problem is from Polivka and Pakin [1975, p. 173]. Solving it will lead us to define several generally useful functions. The input is a sparse representation of a logical vector, and the output is its expanded form. Specifically, for argument vector **v**, the result vector is to contain (shape v) ones, and the ith one is to be preceded by v_i zeros. Thus, we want:

```
-> (fillzeros '(2 0 3 1))
    0   0   1   1   0   0   0   1   0   1
```

First, define the function +\, a kind of generalization of +/, called "+-scan:"

```
-> (define dropend (v) ([] v (indx (- (shape v) 1))))
-> (define +\ (v)
      (if (= (shape v) 0) v
         (cat (+\ (dropend v)) (+/ v))))
-> (+\ '(1 3 5 7))
    1   4   9   16
```

The operation +\ , called "+-scan," is especially useful for generating indices of vectors, as we will see shortly.

```
-> (define assign (v i x)
      (cat ([] v (indx (- i 1)))
         (cat x ([] v (+ i (indx (- (shape v) i)))))))
-> (assign '(1 2 3 4 5) 3 6)
1 2 6 4 5
-> (define drop1 (v) ([] v (+1 (indx (- (shape v) 1)))))
-> (define vecassign (v i x)
      (if (= (shape i) 0) v
         (vecassign (assign v ([] i 1)([] x 1))
            (drop1 i) (drop1 x))))
-> (vecassign '(10 20 30 40 50) '(3 5 1) '(7 9 11))
11 20 7 40 9
```

Note that assign and vecassign do not actually change the v argument but merely return a new vector in which the indices given in i have been changed to the values given in x.

```
-> (define fillzeros (v)
      (vecassign (restruct (+/ (+ v 1)) 0)
         (+\ (+ v 1))
         (restruct (shape v) 1)))
```

Primes Revisited.   Our last example is another version of the primality test. In this one, all the primes less than some number will be found, with no looping.

The function `mod-outer-prod` applies the `mod` operation between every pair of elements from its two arguments.

```
-> (define mod-outer-prod (v1 v2)
       (mod (trans (restruct (cat (shape v2) (shape v1)) v1))
            (restruct (cat (shape v1) (shape v2)) v2)))
-> (mod-outer-prod (indx 4) (indx 7))
     0   1   1   1   1   1   1
     0   0   2   2   2   2   2
     0   1   0   3   3   3   3
     0   0   1   0   4   4   4
-> (define primes<= (n)
     (compress (= 2 (+/ (= 0 (mod-outer-prod (set s (indx n)) s))))
               s))
-> (primes<= 7)
     2   3   5   7
```

3.2 Implementation

As in Chapter 2: LISP, the APL interpreter will be described in terms of its deviation from the interpreter of Chapter 1. Indeed, the overall structure of these changes is very much as in LISP:

- In *DECLARATIONS*, *NUMBER* is replaced by *APLVALUE*, which is the pointer type for *APLVALUEREC*.

- In *INPUT*, *parseVal* is modified to parse APL vector constants.

- Section *NUMBERS* is replaced by *APL VALUES*, in which all value-op's are defined. This is, of course, the most significant change.

- There are minor changes in *NAME MANAGEMENT* (in *initNames*) and in *DATA STRUCTURE OP'S* (adding one new function). Aside from replacing *NUMBER* by *APLVALUE*, *EVALUATION*, *ENVIRONMENTS*, and *READ-EVAL-PRINT LOOP* are unchanged from Chapter 1.

3.2.1 DECLARATIONS

The declaration of type *NUMBER* is replaced by:

$$APLVALUE = \uparrow APLVALUEREC;$$
$$INTLIST = \uparrow INTLISTREC;$$

$RANK = (SCALAR, VECTOR, MATRIX);$
$APLVALUEREC = $ **record**
        intvals: *INTLIST*;
        case *rnk*: *RANK* **of**
            SCALAR: ();
            VECTOR: (*leng*: *integer*);
            MATRIX: (*rows*, *cols*: *integer*)
   end;

$INTLISTREC = $ **record**
        int: *integer*;
        nextint: *INTLIST*
   end;

Of course, *APLVALUE* replaces *NUMBER* in the declaration of types *VAL-UELISTREC* and *EXPREC*, as it does throughout the interpreter.

    BUILTINOP becomes:

$BUILTINOP = (IFOP, WHILEOP, SETOP, BEGINOP,$
        $PLUSOP, MINUSOP, TIMESOP, DIVOP, MAXOP,$
        $OROP, ANDOP, EQOP, LTOP, GTOP,$
        $REDPLUSOP, REDMINUSOP, REDTIMESOP,$
        $REDDIVOP, REDMAXOP, REDOROP, REDANDOP,$
        $COMPRESSOP, SHAPEOP, RAVELOP, RESTRUCTOP,$
        $CATOP, INDXOP, TRANSOP, SUBOP, PRINTOP);$

3.2.2   DATA STRUCTURE OP'S

Function *lengthIL*, analogous to *lengthVL*, is added.

3.2.3   NAME MANAGEMENT

The new **value-op** names are installed in *initNames*.

3.2.4   INPUT

parseVal translates inputs to *APLVALUE*'s.

3.2.5   ENVIRONMENTS

No changes here.

3.2.6   APL VALUES

The purpose of this section, like the *NUMBERS* section of Chapter 1, is to
define the three functions:

procedure *prValue* (*a*: *APLVALUE*);
function *isTrueVal* (*a*: *APLVALUE*): *Boolean*;
function *applyValueOp* (*op*: *VALUEOP*; *vl*: *VALUELIST*): *APLVALUE*;

The code for each is quite straightforward. *applyValueOp* is very much longer
than in either of the preceding chapters, coming to about 500 lines of code.
Still, there does not seem to be much need for explanation. Each operation
is represented by a function, and none of these functions is more than about
sixty lines. The most complicated are reduction, compression, and subscripting
applied to matrices. This section is listed in its entirety in Appendix D.

3.2.7   EVALUATION

Aside from replacing *NUMBER* by *APLVALUE*, there are no changes.

3.2.8   READ-EVAL-PRINT LOOP

No changes.

3.3   Example — Drawing a Histogram

We will develop a package of functions for the display of data, especially drawing
histograms and graphs. This is a typical data-processing activity, and one for
which APL is remarkably well suited.

The input data are given as a vector of integers (think of them as scores
on a test). Since our version of APL has no characters, all our graphs will
consist of 0's, and 1's; if you think of them as, respectively, blank and *, you
can imagine a much nicer looking graph (see Exercise 14).

Figure 3.1 gives a sample session using the functions written in this section.
If you don't understand all the output right now, don't worry — it is given
mainly for reference later in this section.

3.3.1   PREPROCESSING

Before doing anything else, the raw list of grades must be transformed into
a list of *frequencies* of occurrences of grades. For example, if the minimum and
maximum achievable scores on a test are −2 and 2, respectively, and the raw
scores are −2 1 −1 0 0 2 1 1, then the frequency vector will be 1 1 2 3 1,
meaning 1 person scored −2, 1 scored −1, 2 scored 0, etc.

```
-> (set SCORES '(-2 1 -1 0 0 2 1 1))
   -2 1 -1 0 0 2 1 1

-> (set FREQS (freqvec SCORES -2 2))
   1 1 2 3 1

-> (set CUMFREQS (cumfreqvec FREQS))
   1 2 4 7 8

-> (range SCORES)
   -2 2

-> (mode FREQS -2)
   1

-> (median CUMFREQS -2)
   0

-> (histo FREQS -2 2)
      -2   1   0   0
      -1   1   0   0
       0   1   1   0
       1   1   1   1
       2   1   0   0

-> (graph FREQS -2)
       0   0   0   1   0
       0   0   1   0   0
       1   1   0   0   1
      -2  -1   0   1   2

-> (graph CUMFREQS -2)
       0   0   0   0   1
       0   0   0   1   0
       0   0   0   0   0
       0   0   0   0   0
       0   0   1   0   0
       0   0   0   0   0
       0   1   0   0   0
       1   0   0   0   0
      -2  -1   0   1   2
```

Figure 3.1: A sample run

The function `freqvec` is given in Figure 3.2. Our method is typical APL: clever and inscrutable. Given the score vector above, we want to create two 8, 5-matrices (8 being the number of scores reported and 5 the number of possible

```
(define dup-cols (v n)
   (trans (restruct (cat n (shape v)) v)))
(define dup-rows (v n)
   ([] (restruct (cat 1 (shape v)) v) (restruct n 1)))
(define freqvec (scores lo hi)
   (begin
      (set width (+ (- hi lo) 1))
      (+/ (trans (=
            (dup-cols scores width)
            (dup-rows (+ (indx width) (- lo 1)) (shape scores)))))))))
(define cumfreqvec (freqs) (+\ freqs))
```

Figure 3.2: Functions `freqvec` and `cumfreqvec`

distinct grades, which is the length of the frequency vector) as follows:

$$
A = \begin{array}{ccccc}
-2 & -2 & -2 & -2 & -2 \\
1 & 1 & 1 & 1 & 1 \\
-1 & -1 & -1 & -1 & -1 \\
0 & 0 & 0 & 0 & 0 \\
0 & 0 & 0 & 0 & 0 \\
2 & 2 & 2 & 2 & 2 \\
1 & 1 & 1 & 1 & 1 \\
1 & 1 & 1 & 1 & 1
\end{array}, \quad
B = \begin{array}{ccccc}
-2 & -1 & 0 & 1 & 2 \\
-2 & -1 & 0 & 1 & 2 \\
-2 & -1 & 0 & 1 & 2 \\
-2 & -1 & 0 & 1 & 2 \\
-2 & -1 & 0 & 1 & 2 \\
-2 & -1 & 0 & 1 & 2 \\
-2 & -1 & 0 & 1 & 2 \\
-2 & -1 & 0 & 1 & 2
\end{array}
$$

Applying = to these two matrices yields the logical matrix:

$$
\begin{array}{ccccc}
1 & 0 & 0 & 0 & 0 \\
0 & 0 & 0 & 1 & 0 \\
0 & 1 & 0 & 0 & 0 \\
0 & 0 & 1 & 0 & 0 \\
0 & 0 & 1 & 0 & 0 \\
0 & 0 & 0 & 0 & 1 \\
0 & 0 & 0 & 1 & 0 \\
0 & 0 & 0 & 1 & 0
\end{array}
$$

The frequency vector is just what is obtained by summing the columns of this vector, so `freqvec` first transposes and then +-reduces. The reader is invited to think about how to construct A and B before continuing.

A and B are constructed using functions `dup-cols` and `dup-rows`, respectively. These names are appropriate, because A is a matrix whose columns are the score vector, and B is a matrix whose rows are the vector of distinct grades. Here are explanations of these two functions:

dup-cols: A can be obtained by taking the scores vector and restructuring it to a 5,8–matrix (i.e., a matrix of 5 rows and 8 columns); this will force the eight scores to be repeated five times to form the rows of this matrix. The result needs only to be transposed to give us A.

dup-rows: Subscripting is used in a clever way to construct B. To get this 8,5-matrix, we first construct the vector of possible scores, $-2 \ -1 \ 0 \ 1 \ 2$, then restructure it into a 1,5–matrix; the one row of this matrix is the vector just given. Subscripting the matrix by a vector of eight 1's causes this one row to be duplicated eight times.

We will also want the *cumulative frequencies*, giving, for each score, the number of occurrences of that score or a lower one. The cumulative frequency vector for our example is 1 2 4 7 8. This is obviously just the +-scan of the frequency vector; `cumfreqvec` is shown in Figure 3.2.

3.3.2   RANGE, MODE, AND MEDIAN

Before constructing the histogram, we compute some simple statistics (Figure 3.3). The *range* of the scores is simply the lowest and highest scores actually achieved (as opposed to the lowest and highest *possible* scores).

The *mode* is the score that was achieved most often. Our method is to use the function **find** to find the index of the first occurrence of the maximum value in the frequency vector; this number is then adjusted by the difference between 1 (the lowest index) and the lowest attainable score.

The *median* is that score at or below which half the scores fall. The algorithm used by **median** is to multiply each element in the cumulative frequency vector by two and find the one closest to the total number of scores reported (the maximum element in the cumulative frequency vector). **find-closest** again gives us an index value which must be adjusted to the actual scores.

3.3.3   HISTOGRAM

To construct the histogram, we will employ a method reminiscent of **freqvec**, in that it involves building two matrices and comparing them. The code appears in Figure 3.4.

Much of the code (including the functions **addelt**, **addrow**, and **addcol**) is used only to add the labels to the histogram — that is, the column of numbers on the left (see Figure 3.1). This code is not without interest, but we will first concentrate on the heart of the matter, the histogram itself, which is computed by the first three assignments in **histo**.

```
(define range (scores) (cat (min/ scores) (max/ scores)))
(define mode (freqs lo) (+ (find (max/ freqs) freqs) (- lo 1)))
(define median (cumfreqs lo)
    (+ (- lo 1) (find-closest (max/ cumfreqs) (* 2 cumfreqs))))
```

Figure 3.3: Functions range, mode, and median

The first two assignments just compute the dimensions of the histogram. It must have as many rows as there are possible scores, since each row represents the number of times that score is achieved; and it must have as many columns as the greatest number of occurrences of any score; these are the values of width and length. In our running example, these values are 5 and 3, respectively.

```
(define addelt (e i v)
    (cat ([] v (indx (- i 1)))
        (cat e ([] v (+ (indx (- (+1 (shape v)) i)) (- i 1))))))
(define addrow (v i m)
    ([] (restruct (+ '(1 0) (shape m)) (cat v m))
        (addelt 1 i (+1 (indx ([] (shape m) 1))))))
(define addcol (v i m)
    (trans (addrow v i (trans m))))
(define histo (freqs lo hi)
    (begin
        (set width (+1 (- hi lo)))
        (set length (max/ freqs))
        (set hist
            (<= (restruct (cat width length) (indx length))
                (dup-cols freqs length)))
        (addcol (- (indx width) (- 1 lo)) 1 hist)))
```

Figure 3.4: Functions histogram

We next construct the 5, 3-matrices

$$
\begin{array}{ccc}
1 & 2 & 3 \\
1 & 2 & 3 \\
1 & 2 & 3 \quad \text{and} \\
1 & 2 & 3 \\
1 & 2 & 3
\end{array}
\qquad
\begin{array}{ccc}
1 & 1 & 1 \\
1 & 1 & 1 \\
2 & 2 & 2 \\
3 & 3 & 3 \\
1 & 1 & 1
\end{array}
$$

Comparing them by `<=` produces the desired logical vector:

$$
\begin{array}{ccc}
1 & 0 & 0 \\
1 & 0 & 0 \\
1 & 1 & 0 \\
1 & 1 & 1 \\
1 & 0 & 0
\end{array}
$$

The labels are added to the histogram by `addcol`, which is derived from `addrow`. `addrow` has three arguments, an n-vector v, a scalar i, and a p, n-vector m; i must be between 1 and $p + 1$. It inserts v as the ith row of m, returning a $p + 1, n$-matrix. This is accomplished by first constructing a $p + 1, n$-matrix having v as its first row (this is the meaning of (`restruct (+ '(1 0) (shape m)) (cat v m)`)), and then subscripting this by a vector consisting of the vector 2 3 ... $p+1$, with a 1 added in position i (returned by the expression (`addelt 1 i (+1 ...)`)). For example, if i=1, this subscript vector is 1 2 3 ... $p + 1$; if i=$p + 1$, it is 2 3 ... $p + 1$ 1. Finally, (`addelt e i v`) inserts e as the ith element of p-vector v by splitting v into two vector $v_1 \ldots v_{i-1}$ and $v_i \ldots v_p$ (using subscripting) and then putting them back together with e in between (using catenation).

3.3.4 GRAPH

The graph is quite similar to the histogram, except that it is rotated 90° counterclockwise and includes only the top 1 in each column. The code is in Figure 3.5.

graph first constructs a graph whose orientation is the same as the histogram's and then rotates it. It uses a different method than was used for the histogram. The idea is to construct a matrix whose *rows* are all possible *columns* of the graph, and use the frequency vector to index that matrix.

The "possible columns" of the graph include the column of all zeros, the column with a 1 in the first position, the column with a 1 in the second position,

```
(define graph (freqs lo)
    (begin
        (set length (max/ freqs))
        (set lines (restruct (cat (+ length 1) length)
                             (cat (restruct length 0) 1)))
        (set thegraph (reverse (trans ([] lines (+ freqs 1)))))
        (addrow (- (indx (shape freqs)) (- 1 lo)) (+ length 1) thegraph)))
```

Figure 3.5: Function graph

and so on. For our example, then, this matrix is

$$\begin{matrix} 0 & 0 & 0 \\ 1 & 0 & 0 \\ 0 & 1 & 0 \\ 0 & 0 & 1 \end{matrix} .$$

This is the variable called lines; it is computed very simply by restructuring the vector 0 0 0 1 into a 4, 3-matrix. This matrix is indexed by the frequency vector (incremented by 1, since zeros may occur in it). Finally, it is rotated counterclockwise by transposing and then reversing. (To see that this works, consider the simple array

$$\begin{matrix} a & b \\ c & d \end{matrix} ;$$

its transpose is

$$\begin{matrix} a & c \\ b & d \end{matrix} ,$$

and

$$\begin{matrix} b & d \\ a & c \end{matrix}$$

is the reverse of that.) The labels are added as in the histogram, except that they now form a row instead of a column.

3.4 APL as It Really Is

As mentioned in the introduction to this chapter, real APL uses a specialized keyboard and font, which includes a number of Greek letters and mathematical symbols, and also allows for over-striking, so that the total number of symbols that can be formed is enormous. These symbols are used as the names of value-op's. Because most built-in operations are single characters, real APL programs are much shorter than ours. In fact, most of the programs in this chapter are "one-liners" in APL. This is one of the attractions of the language.

We'll discuss real APL syntax first, then some semantic issues (especially additional operations).

3.4.1 SYNTAX

The use of special symbols for value-op's has already been noted. Table 3.2 gives equivalences with our operations.

One point that shows up in Table 3.2 is that some of our operations share symbols. How is this possible? APL syntax distinguishes between the *monadic* and *dyadic* forms of operations, so that the same symbol can have different meanings when used as a monadic or dyadic operation. (APL syntax restricts *all* operations — even user-defined ones — to no more than two arguments.) These meanings are not necessarily related, though the APL designers have chosen them to be related (as the two meanings of ρ illustrate).

Aside from the many available operations, expression syntax is nearly traditional, basically conforming to the following syntax:

```
expression  ⟶   operand
            |   expression dyadic-op expression
            |   monadic-op expression
            |   ( expression )
operand     ⟶   variable | constant
```

Our syntax	*APL syntax*
Vector constants	
'(7 9 5)	7 9 5
Subscripting	
([] A B)	A[B]
Operations	
+, -, *, /	+, -, ×, ÷
max	⌈
or, and	∨, ∧
=, < , >	=, <, >
compress	/
shape, restruct	ρ
indx	ι
trans	⍉
ravel, cat	, (comma)
Reduction	
Any dyadic operation followed by / , e.g. or/ is ∨/	
Assignment	
(set A B)	A ← B

Table 3.2: Real APL Syntax

However, there are two *very unusual* aspects of APL syntax:

1. There is *no precedence* among operations.

2. Evaluation is uniformly *right* to *left*.

Thus, the expression $3×4+5$ evaluates[2] to 27.

As a full-fledged example, this is the **reverse** function:[3]

$$A[1+S-\iota S\leftarrow(\rho A)[1]]$$

To remind you of the order of evaluation, here is a fully-parenthesized version of this expression (which is also legal APL syntax):

$$A[1+(S-(\iota(S\leftarrow((\rho A)[1]))))]$$

3.4.2 SEMANTICS

The normal APL value space is somewhat different from ours. The basic values are either integers, reals, or characters (with coercions between real and integer being automatic), and the dimensionality of arrays is not limited to two.

There are also many more operations. Indeed, many of the operations for which we wrote user-defined functions, such as +-scan, are built-in. Table 3.3 gives the APL symbols for some of our user-defined operations, plus a few new ones.

Using these, many of our examples become extremely compact. Here is the function **prime**:

$$\wedge/0\neq(1+\iota N-2)|N$$

Much of what is done using conditional control and iteration in other languages can be done in APL using only expressions. However, some control is still necessary. APL includes a goto operation "→" that works as follows: The application of → to a vector v whose first element is m causes control to be transferred to line m of the current function (or out of the current function, if there is no line m); if v is the empty vector, control is not transferred at all, but simply passes to the next line of the function. Thus,

$$\rightarrow(X>0)/3$$

branches to line 3 if X is greater than 0; otherwise it goes to the next line. (Lines can be given symbolic labels which automatically get the right values, so using hard-coded line numbers is unnecessary.)

---

[2]These decisions have sometimes been criticized precisely because they violate the programmer's normal expectations, as this case shows. Still, it is difficult to see how any manageable precedence rules could have been established among so many operations.

[3]The APL keyboard has only upper-case letters.

APL *syntax*	*Explanation*
≠, ≤, ≥	`<>, <=, >=`
⌊, ⌊/	`min, min/`
!	`fact`
|	mod (abs in monadic form)
×X	`(signum X)`
X∗Y	X^Y
VιX	`(find X V)`
$A[B]$←C	`(set A (vecassign A B C))`
$A[B;C]$	Double subscripting; equivalent to `(trans ([] (trans ([] A B)) C))`
+\	`+\`
∘.|	`mod-outer-prod`
⌽	`reverse`
?X	Returns a randomly-chosen integer in the range $1 \ldots X$.
⍋V	"Grade up" returns a vector of indices of V such that $V[\text{⍋}V]$ is sorted in ascending order.
A⌹B	Matrix division of A by B. (This character is □ overstruck with ÷.)
C\V	"Expansion" is a kind of inverse of compression. C is a logical vector. The result has the same length as C, with zeros where C has zeros, and elements drawn from V where C has ones. For example, `1 0 1 0 1\2 4 8` evaluates to `2 0 4 0 8`. (See Exercise 9.)

Table 3.3: Additional APL Operations

3.4.3 *OPERATORS*

A special class of syntactic forms are those which act as "modifiers" on operations, producing new operations. In APL, these are called *operators*. Since these have the effect of *multiplying* the number of available operations, they add tremendous power to the language. We will discuss four: reduction, scan, outer product, and subscripting. (We omit discussion of a fifth, the inner product.)

Reduction and Scanning. If ⊕ is any primitive (not user-defined) dyadic operation, ⊕/ is the operation of "⊕-reduction" and ⊕\ is the operation of "⊕-scanning," as we have seen.

The restriction to primitive functions is unfortunate, as is the lack of user-defined operators. Operators have been the subject of much discussion in the APL community (see Iverson [1979]). Part III of this book gives another perspective on them.

Outer Product. If $\oplus$ is a primitive dyadic operation, then $\circ.\oplus$ is its *outer product*, a dyadic operation. When applied to an m-vector and an n-vector, it produces the m,n-matrix resulting from applying $\oplus$ between each pair of elements from the two arguments. For example, if V is 5 10 and W is 1 2 3, then $V \circ . \times W$ is

$$\begin{array}{ccc} 5 & 10 & 15 \\ 10 & 20 & 30 \end{array}$$

Subscripting. The dimension along which compression, reduction, and scan operate can be altered by subscripting. Suppose A is the 3, 3-matrix

$$\begin{array}{ccc} 1 & 2 & 3 \\ 4 & 5 & 6 \\ 7 & 8 & 9 \end{array}$$

(or, as a true APLer would say, 3 3$\rho\iota$9) and C is the logical vector 1 0 1. Then $C/[1]A$ is

$$\begin{array}{ccc} 1 & 2 & 3 \\ 7 & 8 & 9 \end{array}$$

and $C/[2]A$ is

$$\begin{array}{cc} 1 & 3 \\ 4 & 6 \\ 7 & 9 \end{array}$$

Similarly, $+/[1]A$ is 12 15 18, and $+/[2]A$ is 6 15 24.

Note that the subscripting operator, and the double subscripting operation of Table 3.3, obviate most uses of transposition. Therefore, in real APL, transposition is used much less frequently than in our version.

3.5 Summary

APL is an object lesson in the power of using large values. By providing functions which operate on entire arrays at once, APL allows for remarkably short programs. Furthermore, complicated testing and looping can be replaced by simple data operations, allowing the programmer to live in the "orderly world of expressions" instead of the "disorderly" one of statements (Backus [1978, p. 149]).

3.5.1 GLOSSARY

APL font. A character set specially designed for APL. You can, for example, purchase APL type-balls for IBM typewriters. Many APL systems have an alternate method of naming operations, such as using two-letter names, allowing the system to be used where APL terminals are not available. However, the resulting programs tend to be very ugly.

APL one-liner. That for which APL is most notorious. An example is given in Gilman and Rose [1974, pg. 55]; it is an expression for the correlation coefficient in statistics:

$$(+/X×Y)÷((+/(X←X-(+/X)÷\rho X)⋆2)×+/(Y←Y-(+/Y)÷\rho Y)⋆2)⋆.5$$

Why notorious? Because this compactness of code is often obtained at the cost of readability. Even the "proper" use of APL — and this example shows perfectly good APL style — leads to programs that are hard to understand. When it becomes a point of pride to squeeze the program into the smallest possible space, the problem is compounded.

compression. Applying a logical vector to another vector (or array) to select those elements (or rows) which have passed some test whose results are given by the logical vector.

monadic and dyadic operations. APL terminology for one-argument and two-argument functions, respectively. (More common terminology in programming languages would be *unary* and *binary*.) The term **niladic** is sometimes also used to refer to functions having no arguments.

operator. A syntactic form which applies to other operations to produce new operations. In Part III, we use the synonymous term **functional**.

reduction. Combining the elements of a vector by way of a dyadic operation.

3.5.2   FURTHER READING

Iverson's book [1962] is interesting and challenging reading; it contains all the basic concepts and long examples. However, the implemented language APL is quite different from this notation. Also challenging are Iverson's recent APL definition [1987] and his Turing Award lecture [1980]. The paper previously cited on operators [1979] is somewhat more accessible.

There are several introductory books on APL. Two of the best are Gilman and Rose [1974] and Polivka and Pakin [1975]. Wexelblat [1981] contains a historical overview of APL (as well as many other languages).

The ACM Special interest group SIGAPL publishes a quarterly newsletter, the APL Quote Quad, containing articles and announcements concerning APL.

3.6   Exercises

3.6.1   LEARNING ABOUT THE LANGUAGE

1. Define the function (count x M) which counts the number of occurrences of scalar x in matrix m.

2. Program **find** (page 72) so that (**find** x v) returns 0 if x does not occur in v. Try to do this without using **if**.

3. A possible sparse representation of a logical vector V is the vector containing, as its first element, the length of V, followed by the positions at which V contains a 1.

```
-> (expand-rep '(5 1 4))
   1 0  0 1  0
```

Program the function **expand-rep** which translates this representation back to V.

4. A possible sparse representation of an arbitrary vector V is the vector containing the length of V, followed by the positions at which V is non-zero, each followed by the non-zero value at that position.

```
-> (expand-rep '(5 1 23 4 15))
   23 0 0 15 0
```

Program **expand-rep** for this representation.

5. Form the following n, n-matrices, where n is an argument:

(a) The identity matrix
$$\begin{pmatrix} 1 & 0 & \cdots & 0 \\ 0 & 1 & \cdots & 0 \\ \vdots & & \ddots & \vdots \\ 0 & 0 & \cdots & 1 \end{pmatrix}$$

(b)
$$\begin{pmatrix} 0 & \cdots & 0 & 1 \\ 0 & \cdots & 1 & 0 \\ \vdots & & \ddots & \vdots \\ 1 & \cdots & 0 & 0 \end{pmatrix}$$

(c)
$$\begin{pmatrix} 1 & 1 & \cdots & 1 \\ 0 & 1 & \cdots & 1 \\ \vdots & & \ddots & \vdots \\ 0 & 0 & \cdots & 1 \end{pmatrix}$$

(d)
$$\begin{pmatrix} 1 & 0 & 0 & \cdots & 0 \\ 1 & 2 & 0 & \cdots & 0 \\ \vdots & \vdots & & \ddots & \vdots \\ 1 & 2 & 3 & \cdots & n \end{pmatrix}$$

Hint: This equals
$$\begin{pmatrix} 1 & 2 & \cdots & n \\ 1 & 2 & \cdots & n \\ \vdots & \vdots & \ddots & \vdots \\ 1 & 2 & \cdots & n \end{pmatrix} \times \begin{pmatrix} 1 & 0 & 0 & \cdots & 0 \\ 1 & 1 & 0 & \cdots & 0 \\ \vdots & \vdots & & \ddots & \vdots \\ 1 & 1 & 1 & \cdots & 1 \end{pmatrix}$$

$$
\text{(e)} \quad
\begin{matrix}
1 & 0 & 0 & \cdots & 0 \\
2 & 1 & 0 & \cdots & 0 \\
\vdots & \vdots & & \ddots & \vdots \\
n & n-1 & n-2 & \cdots & 1
\end{matrix}
\;.
$$

6. Program the function `diag-prod` which computes the product of the elements along the diagonal of a matrix.

7. Program +-scan (`+\`) using only **value-op**'s (no control operations). *Hint:* First do Exercise 5.

8. Code matrix multiplication. You may assume the arguments are conformable. Can this be done using only **value-op**'s?

9. Program expansion, as described in Table 3.3. Does your solution apply to matrices (in the second argument) as well as vectors? If not, write one that does.

10. These questions refer to the histogram example.

    (a) Re-code `freqvec` in such a way that it applies `trans` only once (it currently applies it twice, once in its own body and once in `dup-cols`).

    (b) Program the histogram using the method we used for the graph, and vice versa.

    (c) A *grouped histogram* divides the set of scores into intervals, giving the frequency of occurrence for each. Re-code the histogram to take one more argument — the size of each interval — and produce a grouped histogram. The labels should be the low points of each interval.

11. It has been suggested that APL be generalized to allow *nonhomogeneous* arrays, e.g., vectors containing both scalar and vector components. As an example of the power of this generalization, APL would immediately contain LISP S-expressions: A pair would be represented by a 2-vector, and each of its components could be either an atom (i.e., scalar) or another pair. Read and report on two papers concerning "array theory:" More [1979] presents the theory; Jenkins, et al. [1986] describes a new language, NIAL, based on it.

3.6.2 *LEARNING ABOUT THE INTERPRETER*

12. Add an assignment operation `:=` as a **value-op**, where (`:= v i x`) is equivalent to (`set v` (`vecassign v i x`)).

13. Add double-subscripting, as described in Table 3.3.

14. Add character data to the value space. You should make the restriction (which APL has) that vectors and matrices are *homogeneous*, i.e., consist of only numeric or only character data. Allow for writing character vector constants using double quotes; that is, input `"ABCD"` denotes a 4-vector of characters. Re-program `histo` using characters to form the histogram. *Hint:* You may as well represent characters by their ASCII codes, i.e., as integers, changing only the way these values are input and printed. Since arrays are to be homogeneous, put the type tag in the *APLVALUEREC* and leave the *INTLISTREC* as is.

15. Add reals to the value space. Coercions from integer to real should be handled automatically. As in the previous Exercise, insist on homogeneity. (As in that Exercise, put the type tag in the *APLVALUEREC*; you will, however, have to change the definition of *INTLISTREC* as well, using an untagged variant for it.)

Part III
Functional Programming

The central idea of functional programming is to expand the value space in a simple but crucial way: by including *functions* as values.

This idea first appeared among mathematical logicians in the 1930's in the form of a logical system called *λ-calculus*. It did not seem relevant to the programming community until John McCarthy incorporated some of the ideas of λ-calculus into LISP. However, the use of function values was never a major part of the LISP programming style, largely due to an unfortunate design decision, discussed in Chapter 4 (Section 4.7), which rendered function values much less useful than they can be.

Function values reappeared in force in the late 1970's. The renewed activity was fueled in part by theoretical studies in programming languages, which tended to make heavy use of λ-calculus. The major developments were:

- John Backus delivered his Turing Award lecture (mentioned in the introduction to Part II) in 1977. In it, he introduced a new language based upon a function-level view of programming; he called it FP, for "functional programming." Backus's strong stand against traditional languages, backed by his own great prestige,[4] had considerable influence.

- Guy Steele and Gerald Sussman defined a new dialect of LISP, called SCHEME, which fixed McCarthy's mistake. In a series of entertaining papers, they demonstrated the power of SCHEME, which has since become the best known language supporting functions as "first-class" values.

- SCHEME may be regarded as taking LISP *back* toward the λ-calculus. In a 1979 paper, David Turner argued in favor of a language even closer to λ-calculus, called SASL, and presented an interesting method of executing it (based, not coincidentally, on a mathematical technique developed by the logicians).

---

[4] Based in great measure, ironically, on his being the principal designer and first implementor of FORTRAN, the most traditional of languages.

- A parallel development was the language ML, which combines functional programming with static type-checking in an ingenious way.

In this part, we will discuss SCHEME and SASL as we did the languages in Part II, by building interpreters for them and giving many examples of their use. ML and λ-calculus are covered in sections of Chapters 4 and 5, respectively.

A note on terminology: "Functional programming" has traditionally referred to programming without side-effects; used in this sense, LISP and even APL can be regarded as functional programming languages.[5] Backus was thinking of this meaning when he named his language, but he also emphasized the construction of programs by applying special types of functions — called "higher-order" functions or "functionals" — to other functions to create new functions. It is this sense of "functional programming" that we are exploring in Part III. In the languages of this part, functionals tend to be used very heavily, giving quite a different flavor to programming.

---

[5]Of course, LISP and APL do have side-effects, and so, for that matter, does SCHEME, but let's not split hairs. The point is that the prevailing programming style in these languages, and a large percentage of the code that is written in them, is side-effect-free.

Chapter 4

SCHEME

SCHEME first appeared in a series of MIT technical reports by Guy Steele and Gerald Sussman in the late 1970's. It was presented as a dialect of LISP, extending LISP by adding functions as *first-class* values. This means that functions can not only be defined, they can be passed as arguments to, and returned as values from, other functions; assigned to variables; and even stored in lists.

SCHEME has already had considerable influence in the LISP community. (Guy Steele authored the COMMON LISP reference manual, and SCHEME ideas appear there.) At the same time, it has kept its own identity as a small, clean dialect. The publication of Abelson and Sussman's SCHEME-based textbook [1985], used in the introductory programming course at MIT, has increased its exposure still more. Though it is unlikely ever to replace LISP, it will undoubtedly see increasing use as an educational language, at both the introductory level and higher levels.

In addition to introducing SCHEME by our usual method — small examples, interpreter explanation, larger examples — this chapter includes a general discussion of *scope* and a "related language" section on the functional language ML.

4.1 lambda

The basic difference between LISP and SCHEME is the inclusion in SCHEME of one new type of expression:[1]

$$(\text{lambda (x y ... z) e})$$

This expression denotes the function which takes values x, y, ..., z to the value which e would have if the occurrences of x were replaced by x, y by y, etc.

---

[1]Real LISP's do have `lambda` expressions, but not in a very useful form; see Section 4.7.

For example,

$$\text{(lambda (x y) (+ (* x x) (* y y)))}$$

denotes the function that takes x and y to $x^2 + y^2$.

Note that this function is *anonymous*; we are allowing functions to be the values of expressions without their necessarily being tied to names as before. In fact, the **define** facility becomes superfluous; in place of

$$\text{(define f (x y ... z) e)}$$

we may write

$$\text{(set f (lambda (x y ... z) e))}$$

That is, since the function denoted by (lambda (x) e) is just a value like any other, it may be assigned to a variable, in this case f.

Functions may also be passed as arguments to other functions. Suppose we want a sorting routine that can sort any type of object. The main difficulty is that each type of object needs a different comparison function. To sort a list of numbers, the built-in function $<$ will probably suffice, but to sort a list of lists, this function no longer makes sense. Here is an example of what can be done in SCHEME, using, for simplicity, a function that sorts two objects:[2]

```
-> (set sort2 (lambda (x y comp)
       (if (comp x y) (list2 x y) (list2 y x))))
-> (sort2 7 5 <)
(5 7)
-> (set compare-pairs (lambda (p1 p2)
       (if (< (car p1) (car p2)) 'T
           (if (< (car p2) (car p1)) '()
               (< (cadr p1) (cadr p2)))))))
-> (sort2 '(4 5) '(2 9) compare-pairs)
((2 9)(4 5))
```

These features don't go very much beyond what is available in PASCAL, in which functions can be passed as arguments to other functions. What SCHEME adds is the ability to return a function as the result of another function call.

---

[2]SCHEME does not print the names of functions that are entered, as do our earlier interpreters. Rather, it prints the word <closure> (whose meaning will become clear before long). In any case, in the interpreter interactions presented in the text, this response is elided just as the echoing of function names was.

Consider the functions `add` and `add1`:

```
-> (set add (lambda (x) (lambda (y) (+ x y))))

-> (set add1 (add 1))

-> (add1 4)
5
```

In English: Given argument m, `add` returns a function which, given argument n, returns $m + n$. Thus, `add1` is a function which, given argument n, returns $1 + n$.

This is a natural result of the inclusion of `lambda`. (add 1) is computed by applying (lambda (x) (lambda (y) (+ x y))) to 1, which yields (lambda (y) (+ 1 y)). The latter is the function `add1`.

4.2 The Language

4.2.1 SYNTAX

Since functions can now be computed as the results of other functions, our insistence that applications have the form (optr expression*) is anachronistic; for example, ((add 3) 4) should be legal. It also becomes counter-productive to distinguish function names from other variables, since in the expression (set f (lambda (x) ...)), f is a *variable* (whose value happens to be a function). With these changes and the addition of `lambda`, the syntax of our language is the syntax of LISP modified as follows:

```
input       ⟶   expression
expression  ⟶   value
            |    variable
            |    ( if expression expression expression )
            |    ( while expression expression )
            |    ( set variable expression )
            |    ( begin expression⁺ )
            |    ( expression⁺ )
value-op    ⟶   + | - | * | / | = | < | >
            |    car | cdr | cons | number? | symbol? | list? | null?
            |    primop? | closure? | print
value       ⟶   integer | quoted-const | ( lambda arglist expression ) | value-op
```

The two new value-op's, `primop?` and `closure?`, are explained below.

4.2.2 SEMANTICS

The languages of Part II involved no changes to the basic semantics of the language, since they altered the meanings only of value-op's. For SCHEME, however, the evaluation mechanism itself is altered. In this section, the changes in the language are explained in more specific terms than the introduction has done; still more detail will be given in Section 4.3.

The first change is to the set of values. SCHEME being a variant of LISP, our basic data type is still S-expressions, but they are augmented with function values. There are two types of functions, those denoted by value-op's and those denoted by `lambda` expressions. The former will be represented by S-expressions giving the name of the built-in operation. The latter will be represented by a structure called a *closure*, which contains the `lambda` expression and an environment (page 13). Closures are denoted by using double angle brackets, $\langle\!\langle\rangle\!\rangle$. For example, the function `add1` is represented by the closure $\langle\!\langle(\texttt{lambda (y) (+ x y))}, \{x \mapsto 1\}\rangle\!\rangle$.

Thus, *S-expression* has a new definition:

Definition 4.1 An *S-expression* is either a *symbol*, a *number*, a *primitive operation*, a *closure*, or a *list* $(S_1, \ldots, S_n)$ of zero or more S-expressions.

The new operations `primop?` and `closure?` test for these new types of values:

```
-> (primop? +)
T

-> (closure? (lambda (x) (lambda (y) (+ x y))))
T

-> (closure? add1)
T
```

Evaluation is altered in two significant ways. First, there is a new type of expression to be evaluated, the `lambda` expression. When expression

$$(\texttt{lambda } (\texttt{x}_1 \ \ldots \ \texttt{x}_n) \ \texttt{e})$$

is evaluated in local environment ρ, it returns the closure

$$\langle\!\langle(\texttt{lambda } (\texttt{x}_1 \ \ldots \ \texttt{x}_n) \ \texttt{e}), \rho\rangle\!\rangle.$$

The difference between $(\texttt{lambda } (\vec{x}) \ \texttt{e})$ — an *expression* — and $\langle\!\langle(\texttt{lambda}$ $(\vec{x}) \ \texttt{e}), \rho\rangle\!\rangle$ — a *value* — is easy to miss but extremely important.

Second, although the evaluation of expressions with control operations is very little changed, the evaluation of other applications ($\texttt{e}_0 \ \texttt{e}_1 \ \ldots \ \texttt{e}_n$) is quite changed. First, $\texttt{e}_0$ may be an arbitrary expression, so it must be evaluated. If it evaluates to a value-op, things proceed pretty much as in previous interpreters, with *applyValueOp* being called. For example, in evaluating (+ 3 4), the "+" will be evaluated, yielding the value-op +; that value-op will then be applied to 3 and 4, yielding 7.

The other possibility is that e_0 evaluates to a closure, say

$$\langle\!\langle(\texttt{lambda } (\texttt{x}_1 \ \ldots \ \texttt{x}_n) \ \texttt{e}), \rho\rangle\!\rangle.$$

It is important to understand that e may contain variables which are neither any of the $\texttt{x}_i$ nor global; such variables are called *free*. (This contrasts with the previous languages, where the variables in the bodies of user-defined functions were either formal parameters or global variables.) It is precisely the purpose of ρ to supply the values of these free variables. For example, in $\langle\!\langle(\texttt{lambda } (\texttt{y}) \ (\texttt{+ x y})), \{\texttt{x} \mapsto 1\}\rangle\!\rangle$, x is free in $(\texttt{lambda } (\texttt{y}) \ (\texttt{+ x y}))$, and $\{\texttt{x} \mapsto 1\}$ supplies its value. It is clear, then, that it will at some point be necessary to create an environment which assigns values to both the formal parameters $(\texttt{x}_1 \ldots \texttt{x}_n)$ and the free variables. Accordingly, we make the following definition:

Definition 4.2 The environment $\rho\{\texttt{x}_1 \mapsto v_1, \ldots, \texttt{x}_n \mapsto v_n\}$ — ρ *extended by* $\{\texttt{x}_1 \mapsto v_1, \ldots, \texttt{x}_n \mapsto v_n\}$ — is the same as ρ, except that it associates with each $\texttt{x}_i$ the value v_i (regardless of whether $\texttt{x}_i$ was bound in ρ). The set of bindings $\{\texttt{x}_1 \mapsto v_1, \ldots, \texttt{x}_n \mapsto v_n\}$ for a single **arglist** is called an *environment frame*.

We continue with the evaluation of $(\texttt{e}_0 \ \texttt{e}_1 \ \ldots \ \texttt{e}_n)$. Having evaluated $\texttt{e}_0$ to a closure, evaluate $\texttt{e}_1 \ldots \texttt{e}_n$; let us suppose their values are $v_1, \ldots, v_n$. Finally, the environment $\rho\{\texttt{x}_1 \mapsto v_1, \ldots, \texttt{x}_n \mapsto v_n\}$ is constructed and used to evaluate e.

For example, consider the evaluation of

$$(\texttt{add1 } 2)$$

We have already seen that the value of **add1**, found by looking up variable **add1** in the global environment, is the closure $\langle\!\langle(\texttt{lambda } (\texttt{y}) \ (\texttt{+ x y})), \{\texttt{x} \mapsto 1\}\rangle\!\rangle$. To apply this closure to 2, the application process just described directs us to evaluate $(\texttt{+ x y})$ in an environment that extends $\{\texttt{x} \mapsto 1\}$ by $\{\texttt{y} \mapsto 2\}$, that is, the environment $\{\texttt{x} \mapsto 1, \texttt{y} \mapsto 2\}$.

To summarize: to apply a closure to some arguments, first evaluate the arguments, yielding the actual parameters, then *evaluate the body of the* **lambda** *expression contained in the closure, in an environment that extends the environment contained in the closure by binding the formal parameters of the* **lambda** *expression to the actual parameters.*

4.2.3 SCOPE IN SCHEME

The concept of *scope* is discussed in detail in Section 4.7, but a brief preview is in order here. For any *use* of a variable name, there must be a *declaration*, that is, an occurrence in the **arglist** of a **lambda** expression. The only exceptions are global variables, which are taken to be implicitly declared at the top level. The question is: Given a use, where is the associated declaration?

The answer we give for SCHEME is analogous to that for PASCAL: To find the declaration of a variable, look first in the arglist of the nearest enclosing lambda (in PASCAL: Look in the formal parameter list or local declarations of the enclosing procedure/function). If it is not there, look in the next enclosing lambda, and so on. Finally, if found nowhere else, it must be a global variable (in both SCHEME and PASCAL).

4.2.4 EXAMPLES

All the functions defined in Chapter 2 (LISP) chapter will still work in SCHEME (but be sure to write (set f (lambda (x) ···)) instead of (define f (x) ···)[3]). Our examples in this chapter are intended to demonstrate the use of functional values.

Mapcar. The real power of function values is the ability to abstract patterns of computation and reuse them in different, and sometimes unexpected, circumstances. Perhaps the classic example is mapcar, which abstracts the process of applying a single operation to each element of a list:

```
-> (set mapcar (lambda (f l)
       (if (null? l) '()
           (cons (f (car l)) (mapcar f (cdr l))))))
-> (mapcar number? '(3 a b (5 6)))
(T () () ())
-> (mapcar add1 '(3 4 5))
(4 5 6)
```

Note that both primitive functions (like number?) and closures (like add1) are first-class, so can be passed as arguments to mapcar.

Naming the list-extended function can be done as follows:

```
-> (set add1* (lambda (l) (mapcar add1 l)))

-> (add1* '(3 4 5))
(4 5 6)
```

A neater way to do this is to define function curry[4] and mapc:

```
-> (set curry (lambda (f) (lambda (x) (lambda (y) (f x y)))))

-> (((curry +) 3) 4)
7
```

---

[3]The use of set at the top level should not be taken as an endorsement of imperative programming. As in LISP, the use of set *within* functions is discouraged. The point is that define is no longer necessary, so in the interests of language purity has been omitted.

[4]curry is named for the logician H. B. Curry.

```
-> (set mapc (curry mapcar))
-> (set add1* (mapc add1))
-> (add1* '(3 4 5))
(4 5 6)
-> (set add1** (mapc add1*))
-> (add1** '((2 3)(4 5)))
((3 4)(5 6))
```

Admittedly, this is getting a bit confusing. Let's look at what happened up to the evaluation of (add1* '(3 4 5)):

- As discussed earlier, the global variable add1 is bound to the closure:

$$\kappa_{\text{add1}} = \langle\!\langle(\text{lambda (y) (+ x y))}, \{x \mapsto 1\}\rangle\!\rangle.$$

- mapcar is bound to the result of evaluating a lambda expression at the top level, which is the closure:

$$\kappa_{\text{mapcar}} = \langle\!\langle(\text{lambda (f l) (if (null? l) '() } \cdots)), \{\}\rangle\!\rangle.$$

- mapc is the result of applying curry to mapcar:

$$\langle\!\langle(\text{lambda (x) (lambda (y) (f x y)))}, \{f \mapsto \kappa_{\text{mapcar}}\}\rangle\!\rangle.$$

- add1* is the result of applying mapc to add1, which, according to the procedure for applying a closure, is the result of evaluating expression (lambda (y) (f x y)) in environment $\{f \mapsto \kappa_{\text{mapcar}}, x \mapsto \kappa_{\text{add1}}\}$, which is the closure:

$$\langle\!\langle(\text{lambda (y) (f x y))}, \{f \mapsto \kappa_{\text{mapcar}}, x \mapsto \kappa_{\text{add1}}\}\rangle\!\rangle.$$

- (add1* '(3 4 5)) is the application of the last-named closure to the list (3 4 5), which application is performed by evaluating the expression (f x y) in environment

$$\{f \mapsto \kappa_{\text{mapcar}}, x \mapsto \kappa_{\text{add1}}, y \mapsto (3\ 4\ 5)\}.$$

- To apply κ_{mapcar} to κ_{add1} and (3 4 5), evaluate the expression (if (null? l) $\cdots$) in the environment

$$\{f \mapsto \kappa_{\text{add1}}, l \mapsto (3\ 4\ 5)\}.$$

The rest of the computation is left to the reader.

There are many patterns of "iteration over a list," of which mapcar abstracts just one. A more general pattern is: Combine all the elements of a list using

a function sum, where "combine" may have meanings as different as "sum up"
or "put together into a list:"

```
-> (set combine (lambda (f sum zero)
       (lambda (l) (if (null? l) zero
           (sum (f (car l)) ((combine f sum zero) (cdr l)))))))
```

This abstract version of list iteration has many instances:[5]

```
-> (set sum-squares (combine (lambda (x) (* x x)) + 0))
```
```
-> (sum-squares '(1 2 3 4))
30
```
```
-> (set id (lambda (x) x))
```
```
-> (set +/ (combine id + 0))
```
```
-> (+/ '(1 2 3 4))
10
```
```
-> (set */ (combine id * 1))
```
```
-> (*/ '(1 2 3 4))
24
```
```
-> (set list-id (combine id cons '()))
```
```
-> (list-id '(3 4 5))
(3 4 5)
```
```
-> (set alternate-mapc (lambda (f) (combine f cons '())))
```

Functions that have functions as arguments or return functions as values,
are called *higher-order functions* or *functionals*. We have seen them in APL
as "operators," but APL had neither *user-defined* operators nor the ability to
apply operators to user-defined functions.

Orderings.   For another set of examples, let's go back to the sort2 function
and consider the question of *orderings*. The function compare-pairs compares
pairs of numbers by lexicographic, or alphabetical, ordering, where the first
elements of the pairs dominate the comparison and the second elements are
consulted only if the first are equal. To compare *pairs of pairs* lexicographically:

```
-> (set cmp-pairs-of-pairs (lambda (t1 t2)
       (if (compare-pairs (car t1) (car t2)) 'T
           (if (compare-pairs (car t2) (car t1)) '()
               (compare-pairs (cadr t1) (cadr t2))))))
```

---

[5]The symbols +/ and */, which appear as value-op's in APL (Chapter 3), are called +-
reduction and *-reduction.

We can now recognize that the process of extending `compare-pairs` to pairs of pairs is exactly the same as the extension of `<` to pairs of integers. By thinking of lexical ordering as *a function from orderings to orderings*, both can be coded far more neatly in SCHEME:

```
-> (set lex-order (lambda (<1 <2)
      (lambda (p1 p2)
        (if (<1 (car p1) (car p2)) 'T
          (if (<1 (car p2) (car p1)) '()
            (<2 (cadr p1) (cadr p2)))))))
```

```
-> (set compare-pairs (lex-order < <))
```

```
-> (set cmp-pairs-of-pairs
      (lex-order compare-pairs compare-pairs))
```

Why does `lex-order` have two arguments? Because it may be desired to order the `car`'s on a different basis than the `cadr`'s. Suppose that we have pairs of scores and student identification numbers, and they are to be sorted in *descending* order on scores and, within groups of equal scores, in *ascending* order on id numbers. We could write:

```
-> (set student-order (lex-order > <))
```

```
-> (sort2 '(85 1005) '(95 2170) student-order)
((95 2170) (85 1005))
```

```
-> (sort2 '(85 1005) '(85 2170) student-order)
((85 1005) (85 2170))
```

The notion of sorting in *descending* order makes sense for any ordering. Think of *inverting* an ordering as just another way of deriving a new ordering from an existing one:

```
-> (set invert-order (lambda (<) (lambda (x y) (< y x))))
```

```
-> (sort2 '(85 1005) '(95 2170) (invert-order student-order))
((85 1005) (95 2170))
```

We are, as yet, capable only of constructing orderings on numbers and on pairs, but usually one wants to sort entire lists, the ordering being based on a subset of the items. A real student record, for example, contains many more than two fields. What is needed is a way to extend an ordering to lists by selecting columns. `compare-cols` does just that. Its arguments are an ordering and two item (or column) numbers; it extracts those items from each list and compares records by applying the given ordering to the pairs so obtained. `select-cols` is the function that actually extracts the two columns (note that `nth` indexes from zero). `compose-binary` takes any function `f` (in this case, the function that extracts the columns from a list), applies it to two separate arguments, then applies the function `g` to the two results.

```
-> (set select-cols (lambda (c1 c2)
   (lambda (l) (list2 (nth c1 l) (nth c2 l)))))
-> (set compose-binary
      (lambda (f g) (lambda (x y) (g (f x) (f y)))))
-> (set compare-cols (lambda (< c1 c2)
   (compose-binary (select-cols c1 c2) <)))
```

Thus, if student records contain the student's name, id number, and scores
on two exams, it is possible to sort first in descending order on the first exam
and then in ascending order on id number as follows:

```
-> (set new-student-order (compare-cols student-order 2 1))
-> (sort2 '(Kaplan 1005 85 87) '(Reddy 2170 95 92)
          new-student-order)
((Reddy 2170 95 92) (Kaplan 1005 85 87))
```

More general transformations on the data to be compared are also possible.
Here we sort in descending order on the difference between each student's score
on the second and first exams, i.e. on the student's "improvement." compose
is used to first apply (select-cols 3 2) to each student record, producing a
list of the two exam scores, then subtract the first from the second.

```
-> (set compose (lambda (f g) (lambda (x) (g (f x)))))
-> (set apply-binary (lambda (f)
      (lambda (l) (f (car l) (cadr l)))))
-> (set improvement (compose (select-cols 3 2) (apply-binary -)))
-> (set comp-improvement (compose-binary improvement >))
-> (sort2 '(Kaplan 1005 85 87) '(Reddy 2170 95 92)
          comp-improvement)
((Kaplan 1005 85 87) (Reddy 2170 95 92))
```

In summary, SCHEME enables us to program functionals that can be applied
to create new orderings from existing ones. In this way, all sorts of orderings
can be created with comparative ease and great compactness of code.

Sets.   Consider again the representation of sets, as we did in LISP. The use of
functionals allows a slight shortening of the code given in Section 2.1.3:

```
-> (set find (lambda (pred lis)
   (if (null? lis) '()
       (if (pred (car lis)) 'T (find pred (cdr lis))))))
-> (set nullset '())
```

```
-> (set addelt (lambda (x s) (if (member? x s) s (cons x s))))

-> (set member? (lambda (x s) (find ((curry equal) x) s)))

-> (set union (lambda (s1 s2) ((combine id addelt s1) s2)))

-> (set s1 (addelt 'a (addelt 'b nullset)))
(a b)

-> (member? 'a s1)
T

-> (member? 'c s1)
()

-> (set s2 (addelt 'b (addelt 'c nullset)))
(b c)

-> (set s3 (union s1 s2))
(c a b)
```

The more interesting aspect of sets, however, is the problem of *polymorphism*, or *code genericity*. This is the need to treat different types of data *slightly* differently, but *mostly* the same. An example we have just seen is sorting: Sorting a list of numbers is only slightly different from sorting a list of pairs — a different comparison function is used, but otherwise everything is the same.

Sets raise this problem in an interesting form. Suppose we have the code for sets of lists but would like code for sets of some other type of data, for which the predicate `equal` is not adequate. We might, for example, want to have sets of association lists; a-lists are considered equal if they have all the same keys and attributes, regardless of their order; the function `=alist` compares a-lists for equality:

```
-> (set sub-alist (lambda (al1 al2)
     (not (find
             (lambda (pair)
               (not (equal (cadr pair) (assoc (car pair) al2))))
             al1))))

-> (set =alist (lambda (al1 al2)
     (if (sub-alist al1 al2) (sub-alist al2 al1) '())))

-> (=alist '((E coli)(I Magnin)(U Thant))
           '((E coli)(I Ching)(U Thant)))
()

-> (=alist '((U Thant)(I Ching)(E coli))
           '((E coli)(I Ching)(U Thant)))
T
```

The difficulty is that it is necessary to redefine `member?` using `=alist` in place of `equal`; call the new version `al-member?`. Then, of course, `addelt` must

be redefined to use `al-member?` — call it `al-addelt` — and then `union` must
be redefined to use `al-addelt`. The upshot is that nearly identical code will
have to be written for almost all the set operations. And it will have to be
done again for every new type of data using a different equality test.

There are a variety of ways to approach this problem in SCHEME:[6]

- Taking a solution analogous to the one used in `sort2`, make the equality
  test an argument to every function:

  ```
  -> (set member? (lambda (x s eqfun)
       (find ((curry eqfun) x) s)))

  -> (set addelt (lambda (x s eqfun)
       (if (member? x s eqfun) s (cons x s))))
  ```

  and so on. Uses of the set operations would look, for example, like
  `(member? x s equal)` or `(addelt x s =alist)`.

- The additional argument in every function is a disadvantage of the previous approach. It must be passed wherever the set is passed, since almost
  nothing can be done to the set without it. The equality function may as
  well be *part of the set*. Accordingly, represent a set by a pair consisting
  of an equality function and a list of elements (with no repetitions).

  ```
  -> (set nullset (lambda (eqfun) (list2 eqfun '())))

  -> (set member? (lambda (x s)
       (find ((curry (car s)) x) (cadr s))))

  -> (set addelt (lambda (x s)
       (if (member? x s) s (list2 (car s) (cons x (cadr s))))))
  ```

  These operations are used as follows for sets of a-lists: `(nullset =alist)`
  produces the empty set of a-lists. When performing an operation on a set
  of a-lists, no mention is made of the equality function: just write `(addelt
  al s)`, `(member? al s)`, etc.

- If there will be only a few different types of sets, but many sets of each
  type, then the last solution has the disadvantage that *each set* must contain the equality function, requiring one extra cons cell per set. Instead,
  make the equality function *part of the operations*. The memory loss becomes independent of the number of sets that are created. The idea is to
  have a function whose argument is an equality function, and whose result

---

[6]This is an example of the kind of problem the object-oriented languages of Part IV handle
extremely well.

is a list of set operations:

```
-> (set mk-set-ops (lambda (eqfun)
    (cons '() ; empty set
      (cons (lambda (x s) (find ((curry eqfun) x) s)) ; member?
        (cons (lambda (x s) ; addelt
                (if (find ((curry eqfun) x) s) s (cons x s)))
          ⋮
    )))))
```

To obtain the operations for a set of a-lists, write:

```
-> (set list-of-al-ops (mk-set-ops =alist))

-> (set al-nullset (car list-of-al-ops))

-> (set al-member? (cadr list-of-al-ops))

-> (set al-addelt (caddr list-of-al-ops))
```

and so on. The operations themselves would be used without mention of the equality function, as in (al-member? al s).

Continuations.   Another application of function values is for handling situations requiring "abnormal" flow of control. Consider the problem of computing the greatest common divisor of a list of positive, nonzero integers. Suppose the list is expected to be very long and, with high probability, to contain some 1's. Thus, it is profitable to check each element to see if it is 1, and, if so, terminate the loop early.

It is not immediately clear how to code this. The simple recursive version:

```
-> (set gcd* (lambda (l)
     (if (= (car l) 1) 1
       (if (null? (cdr l)) (car l)
         (gcd (car l) (gcd* (cdr l)))))))
```

won't quite answer. After finding a 1, it does end the recursion but computes all the gcd's while popping out of the recursion. Thus, the evaluation of:

```
-> (gcd* '(20 48 32 1))
```

calls gcd three times.

Here is another recursive version:

```
-> (set gcd* (lambda (l)
     (if (= (car l) 1) 1
       (gcd*-aux (car l) (cdr l)))))

-> (set gcd*-aux (lambda (n l)
     (if (null? l) n
       (if (= (car l) 1) 1
         (gcd*-aux (gcd n (car l)) (cdr l))))))
```

This version does exit immediately, but by then it may have already computed many gcd's. For example, the above expression calls `gcd` two times.

What we want is for the recursion to *abort*, in the same sense that this PASCAL version does; that is what we mean by an "abnormal" exit:

function *gcdstar* (*l*: *LISTPTR*): *integer*;

label 99;

    function *recgcdstar* (*l*: *LISTPTR*): *integer*;
    begin
        if *l*↑.*head* = 1
        then goto 99
        else if *l*↑.*tail* = **nil**
            then *recgcdstar* := *l*↑.*head*
            else *recgcdstar* := *gcd*(*l*↑.*head*, *recgcdstar*(*l*↑.*tail*))
    end; (* *recgcdstar* *)

begin (* *gcdstar* *)
    gcdstar := 1;
    gcdstar := *recgcdstar*(*l*);
99:
end; (* *gcdstar* *)

The property of this code that we are after is that, if a 1 is present in the list *l*, then *gcd* is *never* called.

The following version accomplishes this, using *continuation-passing style*. Rather than calling `gcd`, it builds up the *capability* of doing so, and then does so only when it has gone through the entire list and found no 1's:

```
-> (set gcd* (lambda (1) (gcd*-aux 1 id)))
-> (set gcd*-aux (lambda (1 f)
     (if (= (car 1) 1) 1
        (if (null? (cdr 1)) (f (car 1))
           (gcd*-aux (cdr 1)
              (lambda (n) (f (gcd (car 1) n)))))))))
```

The basic rule governing computation in `gcd*-aux` is that whenever it is called, `f` applied to the gcd of `1` is the gcd of the original list (the argument of `gcd*`). This is guaranteed at two points:

- It is established when `gcd*-aux` is called, since `f` is the identity function and `1` is the original list; thus, `f` applied to the gcd of `1` is, trivially, the gcd of the original list.

- When `gcd*-aux` calls itself recursively, it passes `(cdr l)` and the function `f' = (lambda (n) (f (gcd (car l) n)))`. If n is the gcd of `(cdr l)`, then `(gcd (car l) n)` is the gcd of l, and, according to the rule, `(f (gcd (car l) n))` is therefore the gcd of the original list. Thus, `f'` applied to the gcd of `(cdr l)` gives the gcd of the original list, so the rule obtains on the recursive call.

`gcd*-aux` takes advantage of this fact when it is called with `(cdr l)` being *nil*. In this case, `(car l)` is, trivially, the gcd of l, so applying `f` gives us the gcd of the original list. The more interesting case, however, is when `(car l)` is 1. Since certainly the gcd of the *entire* list will be 1, we can *ignore* `f` and simply return 1. This is, in effect, an abnormal exit. `gcd` will never be called.

`f` is called a *continuation* because it embodies, in some sense, the *future* of the computation; on any call of `gcd*-aux`, `f` says what to do *after* computing the gcd of `(cdr l)`. The power of using continuations is that several futures can be established and selectively followed. In this way, any conceivable flow of control can be handled.

To give a slightly more complex example, alter the problem so that instead of a *list* of integers the input is an S-expression of arbitrary shape, containing only integer atoms. Again, what we want is to abort when a 1 is found. The continuation-passing version is:

```
-> (set gcds (lambda (s) (gcds-aux s id)))

-> (set gcds-aux (lambda (s f)
     (if (number? s) (if (= s 1) 1 (f s))
        (if (null? (cdr s))
           (gcds-aux (car s) f)
           (gcds-aux (car s)
              (lambda (n) (gcds-aux (cdr s)
                    (lambda (p) (f (gcd n p)))))))))))
```

Own Variables. Yet another application of function values is to implement what are known as *own variables*. These are variables which are local to a function but are preserved across calls of the function. A good example is the seed of a random number generator.

A random number generator, call it `rand`, will ordinarily be applied to a random number to produce a new one; at the next call, this new one will be passed to it and another returned; and so on:

```
-> (set rand (lambda (seed) (··· seed ···)))
```

A serious drawback of this is that any procedure wishing to call `rand` must know the last random number it generated. This can be accomplished by passing this number as an argument to any function which may eventually call `rand`, or which may eventually call a function which will call `rand`; the effect is to add the new argument to the argument list of virtually every function in the program, an impractical proposal. The only alternative is to make the seed a global variable.

It must be borne in mind that this number can be extremely important in a program; its corruption can undermine the validity of the program's results and do so in the worst possible way, by producing *plausible* results. Making it global is too dangerous.

Own variables can solve this problem. They allow `rand` to save its own version of the seed, to which no other function has access. Some languages (notably ALGOL-60) include own variables as a special feature, but in SCHEME they are obtained directly from the capabilities already present in the language. The following code generates random numbers in the range 0 to 1023 using the *linear congruential* method (Knuth [1981, pp. 9–25]):

```
-> (set init-rand (lambda (seed)
        (lambda () (set seed (mod (+ (* seed 9) 5) 1024))))))

-> (set rand (init-rand 1))
<closure>

-> (rand)
14

-> (rand)
131
```

Thus, the value of `seed` is updated at each call to `rand`, but it is protected from access by anyone except `rand`.

4.3 Implementation

The SCHEME interpreter is based upon the LISP interpreter (Appendix C). Unlike the interpreters of Part II, the SCHEME interpreter requires a change in *eval*. In overview, here are the changes from LISP:

- In *DECLARATIONS*, the new types of expressions and S-expressions are declared. The structure *ENVREC* has a new field added to allow for environment extension. Since functions are no longer distinguished from other values, type *FUNDEF* and variable *fundefs* are removed.

- There are minor changes in *DATA STRUCTURE OP'S*, among which is the alteration of *mkEnv* to a three-argument function.

- *INPUT* is changed to allow for `lambda` expressions, and to remove `define`.

- In *ENVIRONMENTS*, the changes are the addition of the function *extend-Env* and the modification of *findVar* (the function that does the actual searching in environments) to accommodate the new *ENVREC* structure.

- The only changes in *S-EXPRESSIONS* are that *prValue* knows about the two new types of *SEXP*'s, and *applyValueOp* knows about the two new operations `primop?` and `closure?`.

- In *EVALUATION*, *applyUserFun* is replaced by *applyClosure*. Also, in the body of *eval*, the application case is changed and a case is added to handle `lambda`'s.

- The check for `define` is removed from *READ-EVAL-PRINT LOOP*, and the function *initGlobalEnv* is added. The latter defines the built-in operations by placing them into *globalEnv*. *globalEnv* is passed to *eval* as its environment argument, instead of passing in an empty environment. This entails small changes in the processing of *VAREXP*'s and in the processing of *SETOP* in *applyCtrlOp*, since *globalEnv* is no longer to be treated as a special case.

The parts of the interpreter that have changed from LISP are listed in Appendix E. As usual, we now go through the changes in detail.

4.3.1 DECLARATIONS

The declaration of *SEXPREC* changes to allow the two new types of values, called *PRIMSXP*'s and *CLOSXP*'s:

$$SEXPTYPE = (NILSXP, NUMSXP, SYMSXP, LISTSXP, CLOSXP, PRIMSXP);$$

SEXPREC = **record**
      case *sxptype*: *SEXPTYPE* **of**
          NILSXP: ();
          NUMSXP: (*intval*: *integer*);
          SYMSXP: (*symval*: *NAME*);
          LISTSXP: (*carval, cdrval*: *SEXP*);
          CLOSXP: (*clofun*: *EXP*; *cloenv*: *ENV*);
          PRIMSXP: (*primval*: *BUILTINOP*)
   end;

There is also a new type of expression:

      EXPTYPE = (*VALEXP, VAREXP, APEXP, LAMEXP*);
      EXPREC = **record**
          case *etype*: *EXPTYPE* **of**
             VALEXP: (*sxp*: *SEXP*);
             VAREXP: (*varble*: *NAME*);
             APEXP: (*optr*: *EXP*; *args*: *EXPLIST*);
             LAMEXP: (*formals*: *NAMELIST*; *lambdabody*: *EXP*)
          end;

Environments may be chained together (this is discussed further under *ENVIRONMENTS*), so *ENVREC* is changed:

$$ENVREC = \textbf{record}$$
$$vars\text{: } NAMELIST;$$
$$values\text{: } VALUELIST;$$
$$enclosing\text{: } ENV$$
$$\textbf{end};$$

FUNDEF, *FUNDEFREC*, and *fundefs* are removed.

4.3.2   DATA STRUCTURE OP'S

Functions *mkLAMEXP*, *mkPRIMSXP* (to make an *SEXP* of type *PRIMSXP*), and *mkCLOSXP* (to make an *SEXP* of type *CLOSXP*) are added. *mkEnv* has a new third argument of type *ENV*.

4.3.3   NAME MANAGEMENT

fetchFun and *newFunDef* are removed. *primOp*, which was formerly used to find the *BUILTINOP* for a given *NAME*, is not needed; since function names are now just variables, this is handled by initializing *globalEnv* (see *READ-EVAL-PRINT LOOP*).

4.3.4   INPUT

The changes here are in *parseExp*, where `lambda` expressions are translated to *EXP*'s of type *LAMEXP*, and in the removal of *parseDef*.

4.3.5   ENVIRONMENTS

The new representation of environments needs to be explained. What used to be an environment (namely, a record containing a *NAMELIST* and a *VALUELIST*) is now just one environment frame; an environment is a linked list of frames. For example, if the following expression is evaluated:

```
(((lambda (x) (lambda (y z) (+ x (* y z)))) 3) 4 5)
```

then the inner expression, `(+ x (* y z))`, is evaluated in an environment that looks like this:

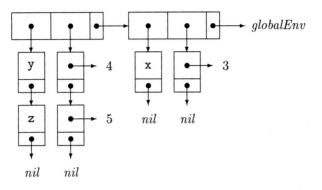

Notice that the last environment frame is *globalEnv*. The top level can be regarded as defining an "enclosing environment" for top-level expressions in the same sense that a `lambda` defines an environment for the expressions it contains. (This is also why *globalEnv* is passed as an argument to *eval*: The principle is to pass to *eval* the environment within which the expression is to be evaluated.)

The searching function, *findVar*, which is called from *assign*, *fetch*, and *isBound*, is more complicated. Notice that *findVarInFrame* does what *findVar* did in previous interpreters:

function *findVar* (*nm*: *NAME*; *rho*: *ENV*): *VALUELIST*;

var *vl* : *VALUELIST*;

```
    function findVarInFrame (nl: NAMELIST;
                            vl: VALUELIST): VALUELIST;
    var found: Boolean;
    begin
        found := false;
        while (nl <> nil) and not found do
            if nl↑.head = nm
            then found := true
            else begin
                    nl := nl↑.tail;
                    vl := vl↑.tail
                end; (* while *)
        findVarInFrame := vl
    end; (* findVarInFrame *)
```

begin (* *findVar* *)
    repeat
        vl := *findVarInFrame*(*rho*↑.*vars*, *rho*↑.*values*);
        rho := *rho*↑.*enclosing*
    until (*vl* <> **nil**) **or** (*rho* = **nil**);
    findVar := *vl*
end; (* *findVar* *)

extendEnv is called when an environment saved in a closure is to be extended with the actual parameters for an application of that closure (see *EVALUA-TION*):

    function *extendEnv* (*rho*: *ENV*;
                    vars: *NAMELIST*;
                    vals: *VALUELIST*): *ENV*;
    begin
        extendEnv := *mkEnv*(*vars*, *vals*, *rho*)
    end; (* *extendEnv* *)

4.3.6   S-EXPRESSIONS

prValue is modified to print *CLOSXP*'s (though it does it stupidly) and *PRIM-SXP*'s. *applyValueOp* defines cases for `primop?` (*PRIMOPPOP*) and for `closure?` (*CLOSUREPOP*).

4.3.7   EVALUATION

The principal change here is the replacement of *applyUserFun* by *applyClosure*, which does what was described in Section 4.2.2. Namely, it "opens" a closure and evaluates the body of the `lambda` expression therein in an environment formed by extending the environment of the closure by bindings for the formal parameters:

    function *applyClosure* (*op*: *SEXP*; *actuals*: *VALUELIST*): *SEXP*;
    var
        fun, body: *EXP*;
        forms: *NAMELIST*;
        savedrho, newrho: *ENV*;
    begin
        fun := *op*↑.*clofun*;
        savedrho := *op*↑.*cloenv*;
        forms := *fun*↑.*formals*;
        body := *fun*↑.*lambdabody*;
        ... check for correct number of arguments ...
        newrho := *extendEnv*(*savedrho*, *forms*, *actuals*);
        applyClosure := *eval*(*body*, *newrho*)
    end; (* *applyClosure* *)

Also, the body of *eval* handles *LAMEXP*'s, treats *APEXP*'s quite differently, and treats *VAREXP*'s slightly differently:

```
begin (* eval *)
    with e↑ do
        case etype of
            VALEXP:
                eval := sxp;
            VAREXP:
                if isBound(varble, rho)
                then eval := fetch(varble, rho)
                else ... undefined variable error ...
            APEXP:
                begin
                    op := eval(optr, rho);
                    if op↑.sxptype = PRIMSXP
                    then begin
                            primname := op↑.primval;
                            if primname in [IFOP .. BEGINOP]
                            then eval := applyCtrlOp(primname, args)
                            else eval := applyValueOp(primname, evalList(args))
                        end
                    else eval := applyClosure(op, evalList(args))
                end;
            LAMEXP:
                eval := mkCLOSXP(e, rho)
        end (* case and with *)
end; (* eval *)
```

The *SETOP* case in *applyCtrlOp* is modified in a way analogous to the *VAREXP* code above.

The reader may notice that control operations are treated as values, the same as value-op's, although we had not mentioned this in describing the language. In fact, control operations are rather useless as values; they are treated as such only for convenience, particularly in *parseExp*.

4.3.8   READ-EVAL-PRINT LOOP

As mentioned earlier, *globalEnv* is initialized to assign *PRIMSXP*'s to each of the built-in operators:

```
     procedure initGlobalEnv;
     var op: BUILTINOP;
     begin
          globalEnv := emptyEnv;
          for op := IFOP to PRINTOP do
               bindVar(ord(op)+1, mkPRMSXP(op), globalEnv)
     end; (* initGlobalEnv *)
```

Also, the check for "`define`" is eliminated, and *globalEnv* is passed to *eval*.

4.4 Example — Term-Rewriting Systems

It is often convenient to represent data by *expressions* over a set of operations
appropriate to that type of data. For example, integers can be represented by
expressions over the constant 0 and the unary operations `succ` (for `successor`
or +1) and `pred` (for `predecessor` or −1).

The advantage of such a representation is that computations can be viewed
as transformations of expressions, and these transformations can be expressed
simply in a set of "rewrite rules," allowing for a kind of "table-driven" symbolic
computation. Such a set of rules is called a *term-rewriting system*, or *TRS*.

These rules have the form "*lhs* → *rhs*," where *lhs* is a pattern which may
match an expression, and *rhs* is the expression to which an expression matched
by *lhs* is transformed. In fact, both *lhs* and *rhs* are just expressions themselves, but with the additional feature of *pattern variables* which can match
any subexpression.

Figure 4.1 presents two examples of useful term-rewriting systems, the first
a simple arithmetic system, and the second a symbolic differentiation scheme.
The pattern variables are the upper-case letters X and Y.

Our goal is to "compile" such rules into functions which, when applied to
expressions of the appropriate form, will transform them repeatedly according
to the given rules, until no more transformations are possible. Thus, we would
like to define function `compile-trs` which can be applied as follows:

```
-> (set diff-rules '(
       ((Dx x) 1)
       ((Dx c) 0)
       ((Dx (+ X Y)) (+ (Dx X) (Dx Y)))
       ((Dx (- X Y)) (- (Dx X) (Dx Y)))
       ((Dx (* X Y)) (+ (* Y (Dx X)) (* X (Dx Y))))
       ((Dx (/ X Y)) (/ (- (* Y (Dx X)) (* X (Dx Y))) (* Y Y)))))

-> (set differentiate (compile-trs diff-rules))

-> (differentiate '(Dx (+ x c)))
(+ 1 0)
```

Hopefully, the intuition is clear. It will be helpful, nonetheless, to have some precise definitions before proceeding further. These are supplied in Section 4.4.1, and Section 4.4.2 explains our code.

A term-rewriting system for simple arithmetic (addition and subtraction of integers):

- (succ (pred X)) → X

- (pred (succ X)) → X

- (+ (succ X) Y) → (succ (+ X Y))

- (+ (pred X) Y) → (pred (+ X Y))

- (+ 0 X) → X

- (- (succ X) Y) → (succ (- X Y))

- (- (pred X) Y) → (pred (- X Y))

- (- X X) → 0

- (- 0 (succ X)) → (pred (- 0 X))

- (- 0 (pred X)) → (succ (- 0 X))

A term-rewriting system for symbolic differentiation. The function Dx represents differentiation with respect to x, so that (Dx e) represents $\frac{de}{dx}$. c represents a constant:

- (Dx x) → 1

- (Dx c) → 0

- (Dx (+ X Y)) → (+ (Dx X) (Dx Y))

- (Dx (- X Y)) → (- (Dx X) (Dx Y))

- (Dx (* X Y)) → (+ (* Y (Dx X)) (* X (Dx Y)))

- (Dx (/ X Y)) → (/ (- (* Y (Dx X)) (* X (Dx Y))) (* Y Y))

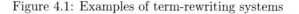

Figure 4.1: Examples of term-rewriting systems

4.4.1 DEFINITIONS FOR TERM-REWRITING SYSTEMS

Definition 4.3 A *pattern variable* is simply an atom designated as such. In the following definitions, we assume a set $\{X, Y, X_1, X_2, \ldots\}$ of pattern variables. In our code, there are just two pattern variables, X and Y.

Definition 4.4 A *pattern* is either a pattern variable, an atom (other than a pattern variable), or a list containing an operator symbol and zero or more patterns as its arguments.

Definition 4.5 An *expression* is a pattern that contains no pattern variables.

Assume that a given operator symbol always has the same number of arguments.

Note that the lower-case "x" in our differentiation rules is not a pattern variable. As far as these definitions are concerned, it is simply an atom.

In using a TRS, the idea is to apply any of the rules anywhere within the expression to be transformed, and continue transforming until nothing more can be done. For the moment, consider only the effect of applying a *single rule* at the *top level* of an expression.

Definition 4.6 A pattern P *matches* an expression e if either:

- P is a pattern variable, or

- P is an atom and P = e, or

- P is (f P_1 ... P_n), e is (f e_1 ... e_n), and each P_i matches e_i.

Furthermore, if a pattern variable occurs more than once in P, each occurrence must match the same expression.

Definition 4.7 A *substitution* σ is a mapping from pattern variables to expressions, written $\{X_1 \mapsto e_1, \ldots, X_n \mapsto e_n\}$. The *substitution induced by* P *and* e, where P is a pattern that matches expression e, is the one mapping each pattern variable in P to the subexpression of e that it matches.

For example, (+ (succ X) Y) matches (+ (succ (succ 0)) 0), and induces substitution { X $\mapsto$ (succ 0), Y $\mapsto$ 0 }. (- X X) does not match (- (succ (pred 0)) (pred (succ 0))), but it does match (- 0 0), with induced substitution { X $\mapsto$ 0 }.

Definition 4.8 Given a substitution $\sigma = \{X_1 \mapsto e_1, \ldots, X_n \mapsto e_n\}$, the function $\widehat{\sigma}$ maps patterns to expressions as follows:

- $\widehat{\sigma}(X) = \sigma(X)$, if X is among the X_i; $\widehat{\sigma}(X) = X$, if X is any other pattern variable.

- $\widehat{\sigma}(a) = a$, if a is an atom.

- $\widehat{\sigma}((\texttt{f } P_1 \ \ldots \ P_n)) = (\texttt{f } \widehat{\sigma}(P_1) \ \ldots \ \widehat{\sigma}(P_n)).$

Thus, given $\sigma = \{\texttt{X} \mapsto \texttt{(succ 0)}, \texttt{Y} \mapsto 0\}$, $\widehat{\sigma}(\texttt{(succ (+ X Y))}) = \texttt{(succ (+ (succ 0) 0))}$.

Definition 4.9 A *rewrite rule* R is a pair of patterns, written as either (*lhs rhs*) or *lhs* $\longrightarrow$ *rhs*, such that any pattern variable occurring in *rhs* also occurs in *lhs*.

If *lhs* matches expression e, then the *top-level rewriting of* e *by* R is the expression $\widehat{\sigma}(rhs)$, where σ is the substitution induced by *lhs* and e.

An *inner rewriting of* e *by* R is any replacement of a subexpression of e (possibly e itself) by its rewriting. That is, if $e = (\cdots e' \cdots)$ is an expression with subexpression e', and e'' is the top-level rewriting of e' by R, then $e = (\cdots e'' \cdots)$ is an inner rewriting of e by R. Note that any top-level rewriting is also an inner rewriting.

Thus, given rule $R = \texttt{(+ (succ X) Y)} \rightarrow \texttt{(succ (+ X Y))}$ and expression $e = \texttt{(+ (succ (succ 0)) 0)}$, the top-level rewriting of e by R is $\texttt{(succ (+ (succ 0) 0))}$. Given $R' = \texttt{(+ 0 X)} \rightarrow \texttt{X}$ and $e' = \texttt{(+ (succ 0) (+ 0 (succ (+ 0 (succ 0)))))}$, then $\texttt{(+ (succ 0) (succ (+ 0 (succ 0))))}$ and $\texttt{(+ (succ 0) (+ 0 (succ (succ 0))))}$ are both inner rewritings of e' by R'.

Definition 4.10 A *term-rewriting system* (*TRS*) is a list of rewrite rules. A *computation* of a TRS on an expression e is a sequence of expression $e_1, e_2, \ldots, e_n$, where $e = e_1$ and for all $1 \leq i < n$, e_{i+1} is an inner rewriting of e_i by some rule in the TRS. A *completed computation* is a computation in which no inner rewriting of e_n is possible.

4.4.2 PROGRAMMING TERM-REWRITING SYSTEMS IN SCHEME

The beauty of the SCHEME code for `compile-trs` is that it closely follows the mathematical definitions just given. The code in Figure 4.2 corresponds to Definitions 4.6, 4.7, and 4.8, Figure 4.3 implements top-level rewriting; Figure 4.4, inner rewriting; and Figure 4.5, computations.

The functions in Figure 4.2 deal with matching and substitutions. Substitutions are represented as ordinary SCHEME functions. Any pattern variable not bound in the substitution is mapped to the symbol **unbound**. Thus, `empty-subst` is a function that returns **unbound** for all arguments. `fun-mod` is a general-purpose functional that modifies a given function at a single point. `mk-subst-fn` takes a left-hand side of a rule (which is to say, a pattern) **lhs**, an expression e to be matched, and a substitution **sigma** (initially empty), and returns the substitution induced by **lhs** and e (as per Definition 4.7); `mk-subst-fn*` is an auxiliary function that matches a list of patterns to a list of expressions. Note in `mk-subst-fn` that, when a variable is to be bound to an expression, the code first checks whether that variable has already been bound;

```
(set fun-mod (lambda (f x y) (lambda (z) (if (= x z) y (f z)))))
(set variable? (lambda (x) (member? x '(X Y))))
(set empty-subst (lambda (x) 'unbound))
(set mk-subst-fn
    (lambda (lhs e sigma)
       (if (variable? lhs)
          (if (= (sigma lhs) 'unbound)
             (fun-mod sigma lhs e)
             (if (equal (sigma lhs) e) sigma 'nomatch))
          (if (atom? lhs)
             (if (= lhs e) sigma 'nomatch)
             (if (atom? e) 'nomatch
                (if (= (car lhs) (car e))
                   (mk-subst-fn* (cdr lhs) (cdr e) sigma)
                   'nomatch))))))
(set mk-subst-fn*
    (lambda (lhs-lis exp-lis sigma)
       (if (null? lhs-lis) sigma
          (begin
             (set car-match
                  (mk-subst-fn (car lhs-lis) (car exp-lis) sigma))
             (if (= car-match 'nomatch) 'nomatch
                (mk-subst-fn* (cdr lhs-lis) (cdr exp-lis) car-match))))))
(set extend-to-pat
    (lambda (sigma)
       (lambda (p)
          (if (variable? p) (if (= (sigma p) 'unbound) p (sigma p))
             (if (atom? p) p
                (cons (car p)
                     (mapcar (extend-to-pat sigma) (cdr p))))))))
```

Figure 4.2: Functions `mk-subst-fn` and `extend-to-pat`

if so, the expression it matched earlier must be identical to the expression it matches now. If `lhs` does not match `e`, then `mk-subst-fn` returns the symbol `nomatch`.

The value returned by `mk-subst-fn` is just a substitution, i.e., a function from *pattern variables* to expressions. What we need to do is extend this to a function from *patterns* to expressions. The function `extend-to-pat` follows Definition 4.8 very closely.

Define a *rewriting function* to be a function that, when applied to an expression, either returns a rewriting of that expression or returns *nil* (indicating that no rewriting was possible). From now on, we will be dealing primarily with functionals whose arguments and/or results are such rewriting functions.

`mk-toplvl-rw-fn` (Figure 4.3) takes a single rewriting rule and transforms

```
(set mk-toplvl-rw-fn
   (lambda (rule)
      (lambda (e)
         (begin
            (set induced-subst (mk-subst-fn (car rule) e empty-subst))
            (if (= induced-subst 'nomatch) '()
               ((extend-to-pat induced-subst) (cadr rule)))))))
```

Figure 4.3: Function `mk-toplvl-rw-fn`

it to a rewriting function. That function attempts to apply the rewriting rule at the top level of an expression; if it can (that is, if the left-hand side of the rule matches), it returns the rewritten expression (that is, applies the induced substitution to the right-hand side of the rule); otherwise, it returns *nil*.

`mk-toplvl-rw-fn` implements *top-level* rewriting (Definition 4.9). The function `apply-inside-exp` (Figure 4.4) implements *inner* rewriting. Its argument is a rewriting function `f`, and it returns a new rewriting function. The new rewriting function applies `f` *anywhere* within `e`; if it succeeds anywhere, it returns the rewritten version of `e`; otherwise, it returns *nil*. `apply-inside-exp*` is an auxiliary function that does an analogous thing to lists of expressions: It applies a rewriting function to the first expression in the list which can be matched, and then returns the entire list with the matched expression rewritten.

It is important to note that `apply-inside-exp` applies to *any* rewriting function — it does not matter that it is being applied to rewriting functions that are obtained from `mk-toplvl-rw-fn`. Thus, it represents the idea of taking a function from expressions to expressions and extending it to operate on subexpressions.

`mk-rw-fn` (Figure 4.4) puts `mk-toplvl-rw-fn` and `apply-inside-exp` together, thereby obtaining, for any rule, a rewriting function that attempts to apply the rule anywhere within an expression.

So far, we can take a single rewriting rule and produce a rewriting function. `mk-rw-fn*` (Figure 4.5) extends this to a list of rules by mapping `mk-rw-fn` across the list of rules and combining the results by `compose-rewrites`. The latter takes two rewriting functions as arguments, applies the first and, if that fails, applies the second. (Notice the trick used to avoid evaluating (f x) twice.)

We are nearly done. The rewriting function obtained from `mk-rw-fn*` has to be repeated until it fails. This is the purpose of `repeat-fn`, which takes a rewriting function as its argument and returns a function from expressions to expressions. `compile-trs` is the composition of `repeat-fn` and `mk-rw-fn*`.

```
(set apply-inside-exp
    (lambda (f)
        (lambda (e)
            (begin
                (set newe (f e))
                (if newe newe
                    (if (atom? e) '()
                        (begin
                            (set newargs ((apply-inside-exp* f) (cdr e)))
                            (if newargs (cons (car e) newargs) '())))))))))
(set apply-inside-exp*
    (lambda (f)
        (lambda (l)
            (if (null? l) '()
                (begin
                    (set newfirstarg ((apply-inside-exp f) (car l)))
                    (if newfirstarg
                        (cons newfirstarg (cdr l))
                        (begin
                            (set newrestofargs ((apply-inside-exp* f) (cdr l)))
                            (if newrestofargs
                                (cons (car l) newrestofargs) '())))))))))
(set mk-rw-fn (compose mk-toplvl-rw-fn apply-inside-exp))
```

Figure 4.4: Functions `apply-inside-exp` and `mk-rw-fn`

```
(set failure (lambda (e) '()))
(set compose-rewrites (lambda (f g)
    (lambda (x)
        ( (lambda (fx) (if fx fx (g x))) (f x)))))
(set mk-rw-fn* (combine mk-rw-fn compose-rewrites failure))
(set repeat-fn
    (lambda (f)
        (lambda (e)
            (begin
                (set tmp (f e))
                (if tmp ((repeat-fn f) tmp) e)))))
(set compile-trs (compose mk-rw-fn* repeat-fn))
```

Figure 4.5: Functions `mk-rw-fn*` and `compile-trs`

4.5   Example — eval in SCHEME

The meta-circular interpreter for SCHEME is similar to the one for LISP. After
reviewing Section 2.4, the reader should have no trouble understanding this,
and it is presented in Figure 4.6 with little commentary.

The following auxiliary functions define the structure of closures and lambda
expressions:

```
(set formals (lambda (lamexp) (cadr lamexp)))
(set body (lambda (lamexp) (caddr lamexp)))
(set funpart (lambda (clo) (cadr clo)))
(set envpart (lambda (clo) (caddr clo)))
```

lambda expressions are triples, containing the atom lambda, the formal parameter list, and the body. Closures are also triples, in which the first item is
the atom closure, followed by the lambda expression and the environment.
Primitive operation values are represented by pairs, the car being the symbol
primop and the cadr being the name of the operation.

The functions apply-binary-op and apply-unary-op (except for the new
operations closure? and primop?) are as in LISP eval, and are omitted. The
other functions are given in Figure 4.6.

This interpreter can be used as follows:

```
-> (set E (mkassoc 'double (eval '(lambda (a) (+ a a)) valueops)
                   valueops))
((+ (primop +)) (- (primop -)) ... (double (closure (lambda (a) (+
(a a)) ... ))))
-> (eval '(double 4) E)
8
```

There is a problem here that did not arise in LISP. Because functions
and variables are handled by different mechanisms in LISP, our eval could deal
with function definitions even though it did not handle either global variables or
set. This SCHEME eval still does not have those features, but now that implies
that it cannot have top-level function definitions either. This means there is
no obvious way to program r-e-p-loop so as to allow for function definitions,
which makes it impossible to tie the meta-circular knot. This problem is left
for the Exercises (Exercise 17).

4.6   SCHEME as It Really Is

Many of the comments about real LISP apply to SCHEME as well. Real SCHEME
is very much like our version, only bigger and better.

```
(set eval (lambda (exp env)
    (if (number? exp) exp
    (if (symbol? exp) (assoc exp env)
    (if (= (car exp) 'quote) (cadr exp)
    (if (= (car exp) 'lambda) (list3 'closure exp env)
    (if (= (car exp) 'if)
        (if (null? (eval (cadr exp) env))
            (eval (cadddr exp) env)
            (eval (caddr exp) env))
        (apply (evallist exp env) env)))))))))
(set evallist (lambda (el env)
    (if (null? el) '()
        (cons (eval (car el) env)
            (evallist (cdr el) env)))))
(set apply (lambda (el env)
    (if (closure? (car el))
        (apply-closure (car el) (cdr el))
        (apply-value-op (car el) (cdr el)))))
(set apply-closure (lambda (clo args)
    (eval (body (funpart clo))
        (mkassoc* (formals (funpart clo)) args (envpart clo)))))
(set apply-value-op (lambda (primop args)
    (if (= (length args) 1)
        (apply-unary-op (cadr primop) (car args))
        (apply-binary-op (cadr primop) (car args) (cadr args)))))
(set closure? (lambda (f) (= (car f) 'closure)))
(set primop? (lambda (f) (= (car f) 'primop)))
(set valueops '(
    (+ (primop +))
    (- (primop -))
    (cons (primop cons))
    (* (primop *))
    (/ (primop /))
    (< (primop <))
    (> (primop >))
    (= (primop =))
    (cdr (primop cdr))
    (car (primop car))
    (number? (primop number?))
    (list? (primop list?))
    (symbol? (primop symbol?))
    (null? (primop null?))
    (closure? (primop closure?))
    (primop? (primop primop?))))
```

Figure 4.6: eval in SCHEME

4.6.1 *let, let*, AND letrec*

One frequently used feature not included in our version of SCHEME is the variety of "binding forms" — ways of introducing new variables. We have `set` (on global variables; `set` can never introduce a new local variable) and `lambda`. The most useful additional binding constructs[7] are `let`, `let*`, and `letrec`.[8] The form of the `let` expression is:

$$\texttt{(let ((x}_1 \texttt{ e}_1\texttt{) ... (x}_n \texttt{ e}_n\texttt{)) e)}.$$

`let*` and `letrec` expressions have the same form, changing only the word `let`.

The `let` expression above is evaluated, in an environment ρ, as follows:

1. Evaluate $\texttt{e}_1$, ..., $\texttt{e}_n$ in ρ, obtaining values $v_1, \ldots, v_n$.

2. Evaluate `e` in the environment $\rho\{\texttt{x}_1 \mapsto v_1,\ \texttt{x}_2 \mapsto v_2, \ldots,\ \texttt{x}_n \mapsto v_n\}$.

A more concise way of explaining `let` is to say that the `let` expression above is equivalent to:

$$\texttt{((lambda (x}_1 \texttt{ ... x}_n\texttt{) e) e}_1 \texttt{ ... e}_n\texttt{)}.$$

`let`, you will observe, is not even an abbreviation, since it is no shorter than this equivalent expression, but it is more natural and so is used often.[9] (This equivalence permits `let` to be defined as a macro, which it usually is, as are `let*` and `letrec`.)

`let*` adds the bindings to ρ sequentially:

1. Evaluate $\texttt{e}_1$ in ρ obtaining v_1, and extend ρ to $\rho' = \rho\{\texttt{x}_1 \mapsto v_1\}$.

2. Evaluate $\texttt{e}_2$ in ρ' obtaining v_2, and extend ρ' to $\rho'' = \rho'\{\texttt{x}_2 \mapsto v_2\}$.

3. Continue in this way, obtaining eventually environment $\rho^{(n)}$.

4. Evaluate `e` in $\rho^{(n)}$.

Thus, the `let*` version of the expression above is equivalent to:

```
((lambda (x₁)
   ((lambda (x₂)
       ...
          ((lambda (xₙ) e) eₙ) ...  ) e₂)) e₁).
```

---

[7]Technically, `set`, called `set!` in SCHEME, is not a binding construct in real SCHEME. Rather, `define` is used to introduce new global variables, and either `lambda`, `define`, or one of the forms of `let` is used to introduce local variables. `set!` is used only to modify the value of an existing (global or local) variable.

[8]These binding forms are also available in LISP. They are somewhat easier to explain in the context of SCHEME.

[9]Note the use of this form in `compose-rewrites` in Figure 4.5.

This differs from `let` when one of the expressions e_i contains a variable x_j, for $j < i$. For example,

```
((lambda (x) (let ((x 3)(y x)) (+ x y))) 4)
```

evaluates to 7, while

```
((lambda (x) (let* ((x 3)(y x)) (+ x y))) 4)
```

evaluates to 6.

`letrec` is used for defining recursively defined functions locally. For example, this expression:

```
(letrec
       ((countones (lambda (l)
            (if (null? l) 0
                (if (= (car l) 1) (+ 1 (countones (cdr l)))
                    (countones (cdr l)))))))
    (countones '(1 2 3 1 0 1 1 5)))
```

evaluates to 4.

Here is another example of the use of `letrec`.

```
(set combine (lambda (f sum zero)
        (letrec
            ((loop (lambda (l) (if (null? l) zero
                     (sum (f (car l)) (loop (cdr l)))))))
    loop)))
```

Note how the use of `f`, `sum`, and `zero` as global variables within the definition of `loop` allows a less cluttered definition than the one on page 102.

`letrec` also has an equivalent form in SCHEME, but it uses `set`. The expression:

$$(\text{letrec } ((f \ e)) \ e'),$$

where `e` is a `lambda` expression, is equivalent to:

```
(let ((f '()))
     (begin (set f e) e')).
```

To understand this, note first that the `begin` expression is evaluated in the following environment, established by the `let`:

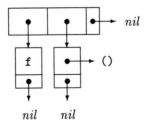

Since e is a lambda expression, it evaluates to a closure:

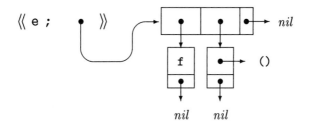

The assignment (set f e) alters the value of f in this environment, giving:

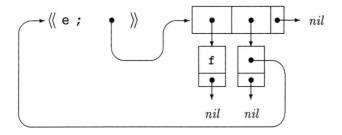

Thus, this form sets up a *circular* environment in which to evaluate e'. Since any use of f within e will refer to this same closure, this gives the effect of recursion.

4.6.2 call/cc

Another interesting feature of SCHEME is the function call-with-current-continuation, or call/cc, which gives the user access to the interpreter's underlying continuation, thereby allowing for a wide range of control structures to be programmed cleanly.

To understand call/cc, you must first understand the idea of the "current continuation." This refers to "whatever the evaluator is planning to do with the value of the current expression." Thus, it is a function of one argument, taking the value of the current expression to some ultimate answer.

For example, consider the expression (+ 3 4). It contains three subexpressions, +, 3, and 4, which are evaluated in order. The "current continuation" during the evaluation of each is:

+: "What the evaluator is planning to do" with the value of this expression is to apply it to the values obtained from evaluating 3 and 4. In other words, its continuation is the function (lambda (f) (f 3 4)).

3: The evaluator is going to evaluate 4 and then add its value to the value of this expression; i.e., (lambda (x) (+ x 4)).

4: Add 3 to the value of this expression; i.e., `(lambda (x) (+ 3 x))`.

`call/cc` is a function of one argument, which is itself a one-argument function. It applies this function to the current continuation. For example, suppose `f` is the function `(lambda (k) (k 5))`. Then,

$$(+ \ (call/cc \ f) \ 4)$$

evaluates to 9. To see this, recall that the continuation for the middle expression (3 in the example above) is `(lambda (x) (+ x 4))`, so `(call/cc f)` is `(f (lambda (x) (+ x 4)))`, which evaluates to 9.

Again, the utility of `call/cc` is in programming abnormal control flows. A good example is our `gcd*` function (for which using `letrec` is also particularly convenient):

```
(set gcd* (lambda (l)
    (call/cc (lambda (exit)
        (letrec ((gcd*-aux (lambda (l)
                (if (= (car l) 1) (exit 1)
                    (if (null? (cdr l)) (car l)
                        (gcd (car l) (gcd*-aux (cdr l)))))))))
            (gcd-aux* l)))))))
```

This is far neater than our previous continuation-passing version. Note, in particular, that in this version the continuation is applied only in the *abnormal termination* case, leaving the normal termination case uncluttered.

4.7   SCHEME vs. LISP, or Lexical Scope vs. Dynamic Scope

Some of what is done in this chapter can be done in (real) LISP. For example, the *name* of a function — if it has one — is just a symbol, so it can be passed as an argument, stored in lists, etc. The function can be applied using the built-in function `funcall`, as in:

```
-> (set f '+)
+

-> (funcall f 3 4)
7
```

Using this feature, our set representation problem could be solved according to the first suggested method by writing:

```
(define member? (x s eqfun)
    (if (null? s) '()
        (if (funcall eqfun x (car s)) 'T
            (member? x (cdr s) eqfun))))
```

This ability to pass *named* functions would account for some of the things done in this chapter, but not very many.

What is really needed is `lambda`. As a matter of fact, LISP has `lambda` expressions (despite our previous denials). However, as traditionally implemented, their semantics are essentially different from those of `lambda` expressions in SCHEME — different and far less useful. Since the technical difficulty here — *static*, or *lexical, scope* (used by SCHEME) vs. *dynamic scope* (traditionally used by LISP) — is an important concept in programming languages, we are devoting this section to its explanation.[10]

4.7.1 WHAT IS SCOPE?

In all programming languages, a single name can be used in more than one way, for example, both as a global variable and as a formal parameter. The various occurrences of the name are, intuitively, unrelated, each having its own declaration. The question that arises is: For any *use* of a name, where is its *declaration*? What makes the question important is that its answer determines in what environment frame the value of the name will be found.

Consider the case of PASCAL in a simplified version, having no nested function[11] definitions. The following picture gives a PASCAL program with each *use* of a variable (circled) connected to the associated *declaration* (boxed). Although we consider only variable names here, the same question arises for type names, function names, etc.:

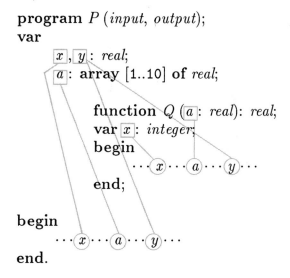

---

[10] However, COMMON LISP has lexical scope and, therefore, essentially the power of SCHEME. We refer here to older versions of LISP (including most dialects currently in use).

[11] Throughout this section, when discussing PASCAL, "function" means "function or procedure."

The rules telling us how to draw these lines are called the *scope rules* of PASCAL. As applied to this subset of the language, they are:

- If the use is in the program body, the declaration is global; there is either a (unique) declaration of that variable at the top level, or the program is erroneous.

- If the use is in a function body, and the variable is declared locally, that is the declaration associated with this use; otherwise, there must be a global declaration.

One significant fact these rules tell us is that the declaration of a variable used in the body of a function is never given in a different function. That is, a picture like this will never be seen:

$$
\begin{aligned}
&\textbf{function } Q \cdots; \\
&\textbf{var } \boxed{x}: \cdots; \\
&\textbf{begin} \cdots \textbf{end}; \\
\\
&\textbf{function } R \cdots; \\
&\textbf{begin} \cdots \widehat{x} \cdots \textbf{end};
\end{aligned}
$$

How does this relate to finding the variable's value at run-time? Very simply: The environment frame which contains the variable's binding is the one created for the applicable declaration. Specifically:

- If the use is in the program body, then its value is in the global environment frame.

- If the use is in a function body, then if the variable is local, its value is in the environment frame created for the invocation of this function; otherwise, it is in the global environment frame.

These observations are also directly applicable to our version of LISP, about which more in the next section.

Each language has its own scope rules (also called scope *policy* or *regime*). There are two broad categories of scope regimes:

Static, or lexical, scope. The connection between *uses* and *declarations* can be made statically, based on the text of the program. The scope regime just described for the subset of PASCAL is static.

Dynamic scope. The declaration of a variable is not determined, in general, until run-time, and may even change as the program executes.

All the languages in this book use static scope, with the single exception of SMALLTALK. It may, indeed, be difficult for the reader to visualize what a dynamic scope rule might be. However, there are several languages — APL and LISP are the best known — that have traditionally used dynamic scope regimes, and this is what causes the difficulty with `lambda` in LISP. Dynamic scope is widely regarded as a mistake in the original design of LISP. We are presenting it — after a fuller discussion of static scope — for historical perspective and to provide, by contrast, a greater appreciation for static scope.

Scope policies also have an important impact on compilation and efficiency, static scope generally being superior in this regard. Compilation is the subject of Chapter 9.

Finally, a point of terminology: A program construct in which new names are introduced — such as a function in PASCAL or a `lambda` expression in SCHEME — is called a *block* or *scope*. There is a global scope as well, corresponding to the program itself in PASCAL, or to the top level in LISP or SCHEME. Whenever a scope is entered, an environment frame is created.[12]

4.7.2 SCOPE IN OUR VERSION OF LISP

Our LISP (as well as our APL and the language of Chapter 1) is analogous to this simplified version of PASCAL. To make the analogy complete, we need only assert that global variables are *implicitly* declared at the top level. Then the following picture is analogous to the previous one (here representing the implicit declarations of global variables by top-level assignments):

```
-> (set  y  0)
-> (set  a  0)
-> (set  x  0)
-> (define Q ( a x )
           (··· x ··· a ··· y ··· ))
-> (··· x ··· a ··· y ··· )
```

With respect to environments, the same situation obtains as in PASCAL. Variables in top-level expressions (analogous to the program body) can only be global, while variables occurring in function bodies are either formal parameters or, if not, then global variables. The interpreter enforces this by having the local environment passed as an argument to *eval*, and a separate global environment, *globalEnv*, which is consulted only if the local environment lacks a binding for the variable in question.

---

[12]Prior to this chapter, we have regarded the global environment in our interpreter, *globalEnv*, as an *environment*, with new *environments* being created for each function call. The term *environment frame* is now more appropriate for these things. Operationally, just consider that a single *ENVREC* structure corresponds to an environment frame. With the linking of these structures that occurs in SCHEME, an environment is made up of a linked list of environment frames.

4.7.3   SCOPE IN PASCAL

With nested function definitions, the scope rule for PASCAL is a generalization of
the idea used in the simplified version: Starting at the use, look for a declaration
in the nearest enclosing block (i.e., function or program). Here is an example:

program P (*input, output*);
var x, y: $\cdots$;

   function Q (z: $\cdots$): $\cdots$;
   var x: $\cdots$;

      function R (y: $\cdots$): $\cdots$;
      var z: $\cdots$;
      begin $\cdots$ x $\cdots$ y $\cdots$ z $\cdots$ **end**;

      function S: $\cdots$;
      begin $\cdots$ x $\cdots$ y $\cdots$ z $\cdots$ **end**;

   begin (* Q *)
      $\cdots$ x $\cdots$ y $\cdots$ z $\cdots$
   end (* Q *)

begin
   $\cdots$ x $\cdots$ y $\cdots$
end.

   As for environments, the same rule applies: The binding of a name is found
in the environment frame created when the block containing the name's declaration was entered. In the example, when executing in the body of S, the value
of z is found in the environment frame created when Q was called, while the
value of y is found in the global environment frame. Note that S is not visible
outside of Q (as a result of the scope rules for function names, which we have
not stated), so that if S has been called, it has been called from within Q; this
guarantees that an environment frame for Q exists when S is executing.

   Passing functions as arguments raises interesting questions of scope, but
the answers are those already given. As an example, the function *multiplesOf*
counts the number of elements of A that are multiples of integer i, where A
is declared as **array** $[1..Amax]$ **of** *integer*. The auxiliary function *countPred*
counts the number of elements of A that satisfy P:

```
function countPred (function P (x: integer): Boolean): integer;
var i, cnt: integer;
begin
     cnt := 0;
     for i := 1 to Amax do
        if P(A[i]) then cnt := cnt+1;
     countPred := cnt
end; (* countPred *)

function multiplesOf (i: integer): integer;

     function iDivides (y: integer): Boolean;
     begin
        iDivides := (y mod i) = 0
     end; (* iDivides *)

begin
     multiplesOf := countPred(iDivides)
end; (* multiplesOf *)
```

References to i in *iDivides* can be found (according to the scope rule already given) only in the environment frame created when *multiplesOf* was invoked. This is true even when *iDivides* is called from *countPred*, and that is crucial, because *countPred* has a local variable also called i.

4.7.4 SCOPE IN SCHEME

Although SCHEME is more powerful than PASCAL in having "upward funargs" — function values returned from function calls — its scope policy is substantially identical. Here are some familiar SCHEME functions with the scope policy illustrated as previously. Note that each **lambda** expression is a scope, and the top level is a scope that implicitly declares global variables, though for purposes of illustration we are pretending that the assignment to a global variable is its declaration.

```
-> (set add (lambda ( x ) (lambda ( y ) (+ x y ))))
-> (set add1 (add 1))
-> (set incr-all (lambda ( x )
       (if (null? x) '()
          (cons ( add1 (car x ) ( incr-all (cdr x )))))))
```

Whenever **add1** is applied, the binding for **x** in its body is found in the environment frame created when **add** was applied to 1, regardless of the existence of another, more recent, binding for x.

4.7.5 SCOPE IN REAL LISP

LISP has traditionally used a dynamic scope policy. This was apparently a mistake on the part of McCarthy,[13] but one not considered worth fixing at the time, nor, for that matter, for many years after. SCHEME's contribution was to show that the mistake was indeed worth fixing.

Specifically, the scope rule for LISP is this: The declaration associated with a variable — and, consequently, the environment frame in which its value is found — is not known until the moment that the variable is evaluated, and it may vary from one evaluation to another. At that point, the declaration is whatever is the most recently elaborated, and still active, declaration of that variable. In other words, *the environment frame in which the variable's value is found is the most recently created, and still surviving, frame containing a binding for that variable.* "Still surviving" means that the scope for which the environment frame was created has not exited. As one simple case of this rule, the declaration of any use of a formal parameter of a *nonnested function* is its declaration as a formal parameter, the same as for lexical scope.

On the other hand, when nonlocal variables are involved, the results can be different from static scope. Consider this session in LISP:

```
-> (set s 10)
-> (define f (x) (+ x s))
-> (define g (s) (f (+ s 11)))
-> (g 5)
??
```

In our (static scope) version of LISP, (g 5) would evaluate to 26. The crucial point to note in that case is that the s in the body of f is the *global* s.

In dynamically scoped LISP, here is what happens: (g 5) creates the environment frame $\{s \mapsto 5\}$, then calls (f 16), which creates $\{x \mapsto 16\}$. The reference to x in f is resolved in the latter (just as for static scope), but the reference to s is resolved in the environment frame created for g, because it is the *most recently created* frame that has a binding for s, and it is *still surviving* (since the call to g has not terminated). Thus, f returns $16 + 5 = 21$, and that is what g returns.

This example shows that dynamic scope is *different* from static scope, but it should not, in itself, convince the reader that static scope is *better*. One argument against dynamic scope is that it violates what logicians call the principle of α-*conversion*, which states that changing the name of a formal parameter of

---

[13]McCarthy writes in Wexelblat [1981, p. 180], "I must confess that I regarded this difficulty [with lambda expressions] as just a bug [in the LISP interpreter]," indicating that he had expected lambda to work correctly and hadn't recognized the problem with dynamic scope.

a function should never change the meaning of the function.[14] To see how this is violated, just consider:

```
-> (set s 10)
-> (define f (x) (+ x s))
-> (define g (s1) (f (+ s1 11)))
-> (g 5)
??
```

Here, (g 5) evaluates to 26, even under dynamic scope. Thus, changing the local variable s to s1 changed the outcome. Under lexical scope, the answer is 26 in both cases.

Still, the problem illustrated here — name clashes between local and global variables — can be solved easily enough in practice by adopting a policy of giving distinctive names to global variables. A more severe problem arises with the use of lambda. Though present in all versions of LISP, it is of extremely limited usefulness under a dynamic scope regime. Indeed, virtually none of the examples given in this chapter would work. To see this, just look at the simplest example, add. Reverting to SCHEME syntax:

```
-> (set add (lambda (x) (lambda (y) (+ x y))))
-> (set add1 (add 1))
-> (set f (lambda (x) (add1 x)))
-> (f 5)
??
```

Of course, in SCHEME, (f 5) evaluates to 6. But consider the dynamic scope case: When f is applied to 5, it creates the frame $\{x \mapsto 5\}$. add1 is then applied to 5, creating $\{y \mapsto 5\}$, and then (+ x y) is evaluated. The value of x is obtained from the *most recently created, still surviving* environment frame that binds x, namely $\{x \mapsto 5\}$. Then, y evaluates to 5 and the value 10 is returned.

What happened to the environment frame $\{x \mapsto 1\}$, created when add was applied to 1? It is gone. That application is completed, so $\{x \mapsto 1\}$ is not a surviving environment frame. According to the dynamic scope policy, therefore, it will *never* be consulted. As another example, under this regime we would see:

```
-> (set x 17)
-> (add1 5)
22
```

---

[14]Though this principle should be intuitively obvious, some care is needed to define it precisely. For example, (define f (x) (+ x s)) is equivalent to (define f (y) (+ y s)) by α-conversion, but (define f (s) (+ s s)) is plainly not. Formal definitions can be found in any book on the λ-calculus; see the references at the end of the next chapter.

```
(set eval (lambda (exp env)
    (if (number? exp) exp
    (if (symbol? exp) (assoc exp env)
    (if (= (car exp) 'quote) (cadr exp)
    (if (= (car exp) 'lambda) exp ; closure is not formed
    (if (= (car exp) 'if)
        (if (null? (eval (cadr exp) env))
            (eval (cadddr exp) env)
            (eval (caddr exp) env))
        (apply (evallist exp env) env)))))))))
(set apply (lambda (el env)
    (if (lambda? (car el))
        (apply-lambda (car el) (cdr el) env)
        (apply-value-op (car el) (cdr el)))))
(set apply-lambda (lambda (lam args env)
    (eval (body lam)
        (mkassoc* (formals lam) args env))))
(set lambda? (lambda (f) (= (car f) 'lambda)))
```

Figure 4.7: Dynamic scope LISP `eval`, in SCHEME

In short, closures are not formed.

There can be no question that what dynamic scope is doing in these cases is simply wrong. The intent of the programmer in defining **add1** could not have been clearer. Dynamic scope virtually eliminates **lambda**. In the end, the only uses of **lambda** that always work as expected are those containing no nonlocal variables. In **add**, for example, the inner **lambda** violates this restriction, since **x** is nonlocal to it, and that is why **add1** does not work.

4.7.6   LISP eval WITH lambda

Finally, we present an **eval** written in SCHEME for a dynamically scoped LISP (or SCHEME) with **lambda**. This **eval** may in part explain why dynamic scope was invented to begin with. Unlike our LISP **eval** (Section 2.4), this one allows global variables (without additional machinery), and unlike SCHEME **eval** (Section 4.5), it avoids the expensive operation of forming closures.

The code is in Figure 4.7 (omitted functions **evallist** and **apply-value-op** are as in Section 4.5). Here are two examples previously given to illustrate dynamic scope:

```
-> (set E (mkassoc 's (eval 10 valueops) valueops))
-> (set E (mkassoc 'f (eval '(lambda (x) (+ x s)) E) E))
-> (set E (mkassoc 'g (eval '(lambda (s) (f (+ s 11))) E) E))
-> (eval '(g 5) E)
21
```

```
-> (set E
    (mkassoc 'add (eval '(lambda (x) (lambda (y) (+ x y))) E) E))
-> (set E (mkassoc 'add1 (eval '(add 1) E) E))
-> (set E (mkassoc 'f (eval '(lambda (x) (add1 x)) E) E))
-> (eval '(f 5) E)
10
```

4.7.7 CONCLUSION

The languages of this book use static scope regimes, except for SMALLTALK, which uses a mixed regime (static scope for variables, dynamic scope for functions). LISP's dynamic scope policy is, for the most part, history; it has never seen widespread use outside of LISP and has now been substantially abandoned by the LISP community.

Along with its effect on the semantics of a language, scope also has an important effect on compilation. Static scope allows for more efficient code. In fact, most LISP systems simply assume static scope when compiling. Thus, code that has been fully checked out using a LISP interpreter can break when compiled. Compilation of lexically scoped languages is the subject of Chapter 9.

4.8 Related Language — ML

A feature of many modern programming languages, including PASCAL, that is absent from SCHEME and LISP, is *compile-time* (or *static*) *type-checking*. The advantages of type-checking are well-known: it allows the compiler to catch certain logical errors and imposes a discipline that promotes better "programming hygiene." There is every reason to expect that these advantages might accrue as well to SCHEME as to PASCAL, if SCHEME were type-checked. ML is a functional language which, in its essence, is SCHEME with type-checking. This section is mainly a discussion of type-checking in ML, but using SCHEME syntax; following that is a brief introduction to ML syntax and to a particular ML feature appearing in many new functional languages: functions defined using pattern-matching.

Consider this incorrect definition of the functional find:

```
(set find (lambda (pred lis)
    (if (null? lis) '()
        (if (pred (car lis)) 'T
            (find pred (cadr lis))))))
```

The error here is not especially subtle, but it is a common kind of error and one which we might hope a type-checker could discover. How would it do so? It could reason as follows:

> Since null? is applied to lis, lis must be a list. Therefore, the second argument to find is a list; let's say it's a list of values of

type τ. But in the last line, `find` is called with its second argument
an *element* of `lis`, that is, a value of type τ. This is the wrong type
of argument for `find`.

In the correct version of `find`, the type-checker would not find such an incon-
sistency in the arguments to `find`. We will see later how the ML type-checker
behaves when presented with the ML version of this definition.

The reasoning used above already makes certain assumptions that are not
true in SCHEME and which point to an essential difference between languages
like ML and PASCAL having static type-checking, and SCHEME. Namely, we
assumed that a function cannot apply both to values of a type τ and to lists
containing values of type τ; for example, it could not apply to integers and
lists of integers. In effect, the set of all values in the language is assumed to be
partitioned neatly into types, and functions to be applicable to just one type.
This view is familiar to the reader from PASCAL; there are exceptions — for
example, "+" applies to integers, reals, and integer subranges, all distinct types
— but for the most part it holds, especially as regards user-defined functions.
In SCHEME, by contrast, the world is not partitioned nearly so neatly. Indeed,
there is really just one type — S-expressions — and the only "partitioning"
of this type arises from the inability of certain primitive operations to apply
to all S-expressions: `car` can apply only to nonempty lists, + to numbers, etc.
Moreover, in SCHEME there are primitive functions to distinguish these cases.
In PASCAL, there are no built-in functions to determine, for instance, whether
a value is real or integer; such a function would be superfluous.

The kind of rigid partitioning of the value space exemplified by PASCAL is
needed to allow compile-time type-checking. In SCHEME, the only proper notion
of a "type-correct" function is one which does not apply `car` to a non-list, +
to non-numbers, and so on; but such "dynamic" properties are impossible to
check. Discipline must be imposed on the use of values, and in ML it is imposed
by restricting values to the following:

- Primitive values of types integer (called *int*), real (*real*), Boolean (*bool*),
  and string (*string*). In keeping with the idea of partitioning the space
  of values into disjoint types, type *bool* has its own values *true* and *false*,
  rather than sharing values with other types, as in LISP and SCHEME.

- *Lists* containing an arbitrary number of elements of a single type, written
  $[v_1, v_2, \ldots, v_n]$. The type of a list containing values of type τ is "τ *list*."
  Thus, [2, 3, 5, 7] is a constant of type *int list* and [*true, true, false*] is a
  constant of type *bool list*, but [2, *true*, 3] is a type error. There can be
  lists of any type; for example, [[1, 2], [3]] has type *(int list) list*, but [[1,
  2], 3] is again a type error, since the types *int list* and *int* are distinct.

- *Tuples* contain a fixed number of elements of possibly different types; the
  type of a tuple containing values of type τ_1, τ_2, ..., τ_n is denoted $\tau_1 * \tau_2$
  $* \ldots * \tau_n$. For example, ("abc", 3, 9) is a constant of type *string * int *
  int*.

- *Functions* have a fixed number of arguments of fixed type and a result of fixed type. The type of functions taking arguments of type τ_1 and returning values of type τ_2 is denoted $\tau_1 \to \tau_2$. For example, +1 has type $int \to int$, and a function taking an integer and a string to a list of strings would have type $int * string \to string\ list$. (In the latter case, the function may be regarded as having a single argument of tuple type.) To give one more example (several more are given below), add has type $int \to (int \to int)$.

These types are essentially the two major structured types of PASCAL — homogeneous collections are represented in PASCAL by arrays and here by lists; and heterogeneous ones are represented by records in PASCAL and by tuples here — plus the function types. This is entirely to be expected. ML provides the usual operations on all these types (though in a form syntactically distinct from either PASCAL or SCHEME, as we shall see), the only operation on functions being application. Missing are the type distinguishers like number? and list?, which would be equally superfluous here as in PASCAL.

Armed with the ML system of types, let us venture forth to assign types to some of the functions defined in this chapter, or rather to the analogous ML functions. We've already seen:

$$
\begin{array}{ll}
\text{+:} & int * int \to int \\
\text{+1:} & int \to int \\
\text{add:} & int \to (int \to int)
\end{array}
$$

What about find? This presents a problem. One possible type is:

$$(int \to bool) * int\ list \to bool.$$

But that is just one; another equally good one is:

$$(int\ list \to bool) * (int\ list)\ list \to bool.$$

Indeed, for any type α, find could have type:

$$(\alpha \to bool) * \alpha\ list \to bool.$$

In truth, our primitive types and type constructors didn't get us very far. What is to be done with functions like find that are applicable to a variety of types — *polymorphic* functions? To eliminate them — that is, to require that the user define separate versions of find for each type, changing only the function's name and formal parameter declarations — is not acceptable. Though this is the approach taken by PASCAL — note the functions *lengthNL* and *lengthVL* used in our interpreters — it would not work for functional languages. The whole idea of functional programming — the construction of programs by application of general-purpose functionals — would be defeated, in that the "general-purpose functionals" would have to be redefined for each specific type of argument.

ML supports polymorphism in the following way: If a function is defined so that it could have type "$\cdots \alpha \cdots$" for any type α, then that function is said to have *polymorphic type* "$\forall \alpha. \cdots \alpha \cdots$." Such a function is considered an abbreviation for all its nonpolymorphic instances, that is, all the functions that look exactly like this one except that the formal parameters are declared as having a specific, nonpolymorphic type. For example, find has type

$$\forall \alpha. \ (\alpha \rightarrow bool) \rightarrow \alpha \ list \rightarrow bool.$$

For each application of such a function, the type-checking process determines which instance of the function is being used in that particular application. Of course, the idea is extended to allow for polymorphism with respect to multiple types α, β, ...

We can now assign types to virtually every function defined in this chapter. Here are a few examples:

$$
\begin{array}{ll}
\texttt{length:} & \forall \alpha. \ \alpha \ list \rightarrow int \\
\texttt{mapcar:} & \forall \alpha, \beta. \ (\alpha \rightarrow \beta) * \alpha \ list \rightarrow \beta \ list \\
\texttt{lex-order:} & \forall \alpha, \beta. \ (\alpha * \alpha \rightarrow bool) * (\beta * \beta \rightarrow bool) \\
& \qquad\qquad \rightarrow (\alpha * \beta) * (\alpha * \beta) \rightarrow bool
\end{array}
$$

The basics of ML's type system have now been covered. What ML is best known for is its ability to type-check functions without the programmer supplying any declarations at all. This process, more properly called "type inference" than "type-checking," is our next topic.

4.8.1   TYPE INFERENCE

The functional style of programming encourages the use of many small functions, and higher-order functions tend to have rather long types. To relieve the programmer of the burden of declaring these types, ML *infers* them. *Type inference* is, of course, a much harder job than type-checking, but the beauty of it is that the programmer gets the benefits of type-checking without the pain. Indeed, as long as the programmer enters type-correct expressions — and "type-correct" is almost a synonym for "sensible" — he or she is nearly unaware that type-checking is being done.

In this section, an intuitive description of the method of type inference is given, based on that in one of the earliest ML papers (Gordon, et al. [1978]). Consider the function combine:

```
(set combine (lambda (f sum zero)
       (lambda (l) (if (null? l) zero
            (sum (f (car l)) ((combine f sum zero) (cdr l)))))))
```

Let us write down everything we know about the types of the names appearing in this definition. The types will be denoted σ_f, σ_{sum}, $\sigma_{null?}$, and so on. The built-in functions have polymorphic types:

$$
\begin{aligned}
\sigma_{null?} &= \forall\alpha.\ \alpha\ list \rightarrow bool \\
\sigma_{car} &= \forall\alpha.\ \alpha\ list \rightarrow \alpha \\
\sigma_{cdr} &= \forall\alpha.\ \alpha\ list \rightarrow \alpha\ list \\
\sigma_{if} &= \forall\alpha.\ bool * \alpha * \alpha \rightarrow \alpha
\end{aligned}
$$

Concerning the types of the bound variables, we can only say, at this point:

$$
\sigma_{combine} = \sigma_f * \sigma_{sum} * \sigma_{zero} \rightarrow \sigma_1 \rightarrow \tau_1
$$

Note that the "τ_1" in this type is *not* quantified. In following the method here, it is crucial to distinguish between *polymorphic type variables* (the α's), which are used to indicate that the function can have any type obtained by replacing the α's by any nonpolymorphic type, and the *unknowns* (the τ_i), which are simply types about which nothing is known. At this point, we know that ((combine f sum zero) l) has *some* type, so we call it τ_1, but we have no idea that combine is polymorphic; that determination will have to wait until we know more.

The method is to begin generating type constraints — equations between types — on the following basis: (1) Whenever a polymorphic function is applied, the type of that occurrence is obtained by uniformly substituting for the polymorphic type variables; for example, this ensures that the branches of an if have the same type. (2) In any function application (e$_0$ e$_1$ ... e$_n$), e$_0$ must have a type of the form $\tau_1 * \cdots * \tau_n \rightarrow \tau_0$, and each expression e$_i$ must have type τ_i. (3) In a definition (set f e), any occurrence of f within e has the same type as e itself. In generating the constraints, a given type may be constrained to be a list, function, or tuple type without its component types being known; in this case, new unknowns τ_i are created and used for the components.

All possible constraints are generated. If no absurd constraint — say, $int = bool$, or $\tau_1\ list = \tau_2 \rightarrow \tau_3$ — is generated, then the function is well typed and its type can be extracted from the generated constraints. Furthermore, if its type contains an unknown that is unconstrained, it can be taken as a polymorphic type variable.

The constraints generated in this case are:

(1) $\sigma_1 = \tau_2\ list$ (since null? is applied to l)

(2) $\sigma_f = \tau_2 \rightarrow \tau_3$ (f is applied to (car l), which has type τ_2 by (1))

(3) $\sigma_{sum} = \tau_3 * \tau_1 \rightarrow \tau_4$ (sum is applied to the result of f and of combine)

(4) $\sigma_{zero} = \tau_4$ (the branches of an if have the same type)

(5) $\sigma_{zero} = \tau_1$ (zero can be the value of

                          ((combine f sum zero) l))

(6) $\sigma_{sum} = \tau_3 * \tau_1 \rightarrow \tau_1$ ((3), (4), and (5))

(7) $\sigma_{combine} = (\tau_2 \rightarrow \tau_3) * (\tau_3 * \tau_1 \rightarrow \tau_1) * \tau_1 \rightarrow (\tau_2\ list \rightarrow \tau_1)$

This, it turns out, is as far as we need to go. The variables τ_1, τ_2, and τ_3 will not be further constrained and so may be regarded as polymorphic. The result, replacing the τ_i for uniformity with earlier practice, is:

$$\texttt{combine: } \forall \alpha, \beta, \gamma. \; (\alpha \to \beta) * (\beta * \gamma \to \gamma) * \gamma \to (\alpha \; list \to \gamma).$$

Then, for example, the definition (`set */ (combine id + 0)`) has its type inferred by the same method. The types of built-in and previously defined names are:

$$
\begin{aligned}
\sigma_+ &= int * int \to int \\
\sigma_0 &= int \\
\sigma_{\texttt{id}} &= \forall \alpha. \; \alpha \to \alpha \\
\sigma_{\texttt{combine}} &= \forall \alpha, \beta, \gamma. \; (\alpha \to \beta) * (\beta * \gamma \to \gamma) * \gamma \to (\alpha \; list \to \gamma)
\end{aligned}
$$

The constraints generated are:

(1) $\sigma_{\texttt{combine}} = (\tau_1 \to int) * (int * int \to int) * int \to (\tau_1 \; list \to int)$
   (β and γ replaced by int because of the types of + and 0)

(2) $\sigma_{\texttt{id}} = int \to int$ (since α in $\sigma_{\texttt{id}}$ must be replaced uniformly)

(3) $\sigma_{\texttt{combine}} = (int \to int) * (int * int \to int) * int \to (int \; list \to int)$
   ((1) and (2))

(4) $\sigma_{+/} = int \; list \to int$ (3)

On the other hand, the expression (`combine id + '()`) would generate a constraint of the form "$int = \tau \; list$," which is absurd.

This is all very vague, and it may seem that this "algorithm" is too nondeterministic to be of much help. In fact, the algorithm used by ML is acceptably efficient but a bit too complicated to present here.

4.8.2 ML SYNTAX

Unlike LISP and SCHEME, ML has a fairly complex syntax. To begin with, arithmetic and comparison operations are written in ordinary PASCAL-like notation, with normal precedence rules applying:

$$\textbf{val } add = \textbf{fn } x\text{: } int \Rightarrow (\textbf{fn } y \Rightarrow x + y);$$

"**fn** x: int => ..." corresponds to SCHEME's "(`lambda (x) ...`)" with the type of x declared, and **val** is just a keyword used to introduce definitions. The reason the type of x must be given in this definition is that there is otherwise no way for the type-inference algorithm to determine if it is int or $real$, the operation + being applicable to either. This is an exception to the rule that types needn't be declared. Note that the type of y isn't declared; since x is of type int, + is of type $int * int \to int$, so y is of type int.

Lists have operations *hd*, *tl*, [], and *isnull*, corresponding to `car`, `cdr`, `'()`, and `null?`, respectively. The list constructor is the infix operator "::". If-then-else is written in infix notation. Thus, *mapcar* is:

> **val rec** *mapcar* =
> **fn** (*f*, *l*) => **if** *isnull l* **then** [] **else** *f* (*hd l*) :: *mapcar*(*f*, *tl l*);

The type of *mapcar* is $\forall \alpha, \beta.\ (\alpha \rightarrow \beta) * \alpha\ list \rightarrow \beta\ list$.

Note the keyword **rec**. ML does not allow for *implicit recursion* (where a function is recursive simply by virtue of referring to itself by name). Rather, the intent to define a function (or group of functions) recursively is signalled explicitly by the keyword **rec**; it is as if the only way to define functions recursively in SCHEME were to use `letrec`.

Constructor Algebras. Users can define their own data types by way of either an **abstype** or **datatype** declaration. **abstype** declarations are used to define abstract data types in the sense of Chapter 6, and we will not discuss them.

The **datatype** declarations introduce *constructor algebras*, a feature becoming common in functional languages. Combined with *pattern-matching* function definitions, these provide a high level of convenience in manipulating some symbolic data. (PROLOG has a similar feature, without the type declarations, that forms the basis for almost all data in that language.)

The idea of constructor algebras can be explained by analogy with PASCAL, where they correspond roughly to "variant records." For example,

> **datatype** *SEXP* = *NILSXP*
> | *NUMSXP* **of** *int*
> | *SYMSXP* **of** *NAME*
> | *LISTSXP* **of** *SEXP * SEXP*
> | *CLOSXP* **of** *EXP * ENV*
> | *PRIMSXP* **of** *BUILTINOP*;

is analogous to our PASCAL declaration of *SEXP* given on page 111. However, the ML declaration provides additional power in two ways. First, each variant — called a *constructor* — becomes a function producing a new element of the type:

NILSXP:	*SEXP*
NUMSXP:	*int* $\rightarrow$ *SEXP*
SYMSXP:	*NAME* $\rightarrow$ *SEXP*
LISTSXP:	*SEXP * SEXP* $\rightarrow$ *SEXP*
CLOSXP:	*EXP * ENV* $\rightarrow$ *SEXP*
PRIMSXP:	*BUILTINOP* $\rightarrow$ *SEXP*

For example, the function *NUMSXP* corresponds to what might be written in
PASCAL as:

> **function** *mkNUMSXP* (*i*: *integer*): *SEXP*;
> **var** *s*: *SEXP*:
> **begin**
>> *new*(*s*);
>> *s↑.sxptype* := *NUMSXP*;
>> *s↑.intval* := *i*;
>> *mkNUMSXP* := *s*
> **end**;

The ML declaration provides nothing analogous to the component selectors
of the PASCAL declaration, but these can be defined easily — and in fact are
substantially obviated — by the second feature of constructor algebras: function definition by pattern-matching. The idea is to have the form of a value
(i.e., its constructor) determine the action to take, just as a **case** statement is
used in PASCAL. For example a definition of the form:

> **val** *f* = **fn** *NILSXP* => ...
>> | *NUMSXP i* => ... *i* ...
>> | *SYMSXP nm* => ... *nm* ...
>> | *LISTSXP*(*car*, *cdr*) => ... *car* ... *cdr* ...
>> | *CLOSXP*(*e*, *rho*) => ... *e* ... *rho* ...
>> | *PRIMSXP optr* => ... *optr* ... ;

is analogous to the PASCAL:

> **function** *f* (*s*: *SEXP*): ···;
> **begin**
>> **case** *s↑.sxptype* **of**
>>> *NILSXP*: ...;
>>> *NUMSXP*: ... *s↑.intval* ...;
>>> *SYMSXP*: ... *s↑.symval* ...;
>>> *LISTSXP*: ... *s↑.carval* ... *s↑.cdrval* ...;
>>> *CLOSXP*: ... *s↑.clofun* ... *s↑.cloenv* ...;
>>> *PRIMSXP*: ... *s↑.primval* ...
>> **end** (* **case** *)
> **end**;

Pattern-matching has more power than this, as the pattern may include not
only the constructor but the constructors of its arguments. For example, the
function *applyClosure* might be:

> **val** *applyClosure* =
>> **fn** (*CLOSXP*(*LAMEXP*(*vars*, *body*), *rho*), *actuals*) =>
>> *eval*(*body*, *extend*(*rho*, *vars*, *actuals*));

which is quite neat compared to the PASCAL definition. Applying *applyClosure* to a non-closure would result in failure of the pattern-match and the reporting of an error by the program.

Lists are actually a predefined constructor algebra, based on constructors [ ] and ::. The "destructor" operations are defined by pattern-matching:

> **val** *hd* = **fn** *a*::*d* => *a*;
> **val** *tl* = **fn** *a*::*d* => *d*;
> **val** *isnull* = **fn** [ ] => *true* | *a*::*d* => *false*;

mapcar can be defined as:

> **val rec** *mapcar* =
>   **fn** (*f*, [ ]) => [ ]
> | (*f*, *a*::*d*) => *f a* :: *mapcar*(*f*, *d*);

A more idiomatic ML definition would use the more direct but equivalent pattern-matching form introduced by the keyword **fun**:

> **fun** *mapcar* (*f*, [ ]) = [ ]
> | *mapcar* (*f*, *a*::*d*) = *f a* :: *mapcar*(*f*, *d*);

Furthermore, the ML programmer would most likely use the curried version, having type:

$$\forall\, \alpha, \beta.\ (\alpha \rightarrow \beta) \rightarrow \alpha\ list \rightarrow \beta\ list,$$

defining it as:

> **fun** *mapcar f* [ ] = [ ]
> | *mapcar f* (*a*::*d*) = *f a* :: *mapcar f d*;

Another use of constructor algebras is to obtain "heterogeneous" lists:

> **datatype** *int_or_string* = *intv* **of** *int* | *stringv* **of** *string*;

A mixed list could be entered as:

> **val** *mixedlist* = [*intv* 3, *stringv* "abc", *stringv* "def"];

and the type-checker would infer its type as *int_or_string list*.

As a final example, here is an ML definition of *find*:

> **fun** *find pred* [ ] = *false*
> | *find pred* (*a*::*d*) = **if** *pred a* **then** *true* **else** *find pred d*;

Here is the ML version of the incorrect definition:

> **fun** *find pred* [ ] = *false*
> | *find pred* (*a*::*d*) = **if** *pred a* **then** *true* **else** *find pred* (*hd d*);

ML indeed finds a type error in this definition, being unable to reconcile the types $(\tau \rightarrow bool) \rightarrow \tau \rightarrow bool$ and $(\tau \rightarrow bool) \rightarrow \tau\ list \rightarrow bool$, which is exactly what we would have expected.

4.9 Summary

SCHEME is LISP with `lambda` and lexical scope. Functions are first-class values; they can be assigned to variables, stored in lists, and returned from functions. This feature encourages a programming style quite different from that of LISP. High-level abstractions are programmed and then specialized for each particular task; much of the effort of programming is finding the proper abstractions.

4.9.1 GLOSSARY

block, or scope. An area of the program which introduces new variables, and upon entering which, therefore, an environment frame is created. In PASCAL, the program itself is one block (introducing the global variables), and each function and procedure is a block. In SCHEME, the top level is a scope, and each `lambda` expression is one also.

closure. A type of S-expression in SCHEME that represents a function value. It contains a `lambda` expression and an environment.

continuation. A function that is passed into another function, which, in effect, tells the latter what to do with its result. Programming in *continuation-passing style* allows for more sequential-looking code and permits abnormal control flows to be programmed cleanly. SCHEME also permits access to the interpreter's continuation, via the function `call-with-current-continuation`, which often allows for even cleaner coding of unusual control flows.

downward or upward funarg. A downward funarg is a function passed as an argument to another function, and an upward funarg is one that is returned as the value of a function call. Many traditional languages — notably PASCAL — handle downward funargs correctly (although older versions of LISP, with dynamic scope, do not). SCHEME handles both downward and upward funargs correctly; it is sometimes described as a "full funarg" language.

dynamic scope. In the broad sense, this refers to scope regimes in which it is not known in what environment frame the value of a variable will be found until the moment that the variable is evaluated. A specific dynamic scope rule, traditionally employed in LISP, is: Find the value of the variable in the *most recently constructed, still surviving, environment frame* that has a binding for that variable.

functional. A function which has either arguments or results that are functions. A synonym is **higher-order function**.

functional programming. A style of programming characterized by the use of functionals to abstract patterns of computation, and the application of such functionals to produce the desired functions. An alternative meaning of this term is "programming without side-effects." This meaning encompasses pure LISP and possibly also APL. It is shown in Chapter 5 how the combination of these two meanings — using functionals and avoiding side-effects — leads to a powerful programming paradigm.

lambda. The word used to introduce a function value in SCHEME.

lexical, or static, scope. In the broad sense, scope regimes enabling one to determine at compile-time what environment frame will have the value of a variable. In the static scope regime of SCHEME, the value of a variable is found in the environment frame created for the invocation of the declaring scope, which is the closest enclosing scope that declares the variable.

polymorphism. The ability to apply the same code to differing types of data. In PASCAL, there is almost no polymorphism; it is not even possible, for example, to have a single procedure that can sort arrays of different lengths. LISP and SCHEME admit a good deal of polymorphism by virtue of having no type-checking (or rather, only *run-time* type-checking). For example, `mapcar` applies to any arbitrary function and list, so long as the function is applicable to the elements of the list. ML allows polymorphism without sacrificing type-checking.

4.9.2 FURTHER READING

Abelson and Sussman [1985] is an introductory book on SCHEME, noted for its many interesting examples and difficult problems. Dybvig [1987] is more like an expanded reference manual, but as such it is clear and well organized. Slade's book [1987] on T, a SCHEME-like dialect of LISP, is longer and has more examples. The series of articles by Steele and Sussman [1975,1976,1978] introducing SCHEME make entertaining reading (especially recommended is [1978]). There is also a "revised report" (Rees and Clinger [1986]) giving the official definition of the language.

SCHEME is not the first language to use lexical scope and support functions as first-class values. In fact, there is a long tradition, mainly European, of such languages, which predates SCHEME. Examples are ISWIM (Landin [1966]), POP-2 (Burstall, et al. [1971]), and HOPE (Burstall, et al. [1980]). The book by Henderson [1980] is from this school. Also highly recommended is the short but very interesting book by Burge [1975].

ML comes from this tradition. There is, at present, no full-length introduction to ML aimed at the experienced programmer. The language definition (Milner [1984,1987]) is too concise to be useful as an introduction and contains very few examples. Wikström [1987] is an ML-based introduction to programming, so is not pitched at the right level for readers of this book, but it appears to be, as of this writing, the only place to see a lot of ML programs.

Be it noted that our entire discussion of ML was based on the dialect called "Standard ML," which is comparatively new. The original version of ML used essentially the same type-inference ideas, first expressed in theoretical form by Milner [1978], but lacked some features, notably constructor algebras and pattern-matching, and differed from Standard ML syntactically. It is described in Gordon, et al. [1979b, Chapter 2], but again this is more of a language definition than a programmer's introduction. An excellent and detailed treatment of both type inference and pattern-matching is in Peyton Jones [1987]; though directed at lazy evaluation languages (Chapter 5), most of the discussion of these two topics applies equally to ML. The ML examples in this chapter were tested using the "Standard ML of New Jersey" compiler, described by Appel and MacQueen [1987].

A detailed discussion of scope rules will be found in any textbook on programming languages, such as MacLennan [1987], Marcotty and Ledgard [1986], Ghezzi and Jazayeri [1987], and Sethi [1989], as well as compiler books such as Aho, et al. [1986] and Barrett, et al. [1986]. The classic paper by Johnston [1971] gives a graphical interpretation of static scope. The principle of α-conversion comes — as, indeed, do many of the basic ideas of functional programming — from the λ-calculus, to which a section of the next chapter is devoted; see the end of that chapter for references.

The theory of term-rewriting systems has yet to receive a book length treatment, although that theory is quite advanced. Bundy [1983] has one chapter on it. Dershowitz and Jouannaud [1988] is a survey of the field, written for theoreticians. Aside from that, the student must consult the research literature. Recommended papers are Huet and Oppen [1980], Futatsugi, et al. [1985], and Dershowitz [1985].

4.10 Exercises

4.10.1 *LEARNING ABOUT THE LANGUAGE*

1. Use `mapcar`, `mapc`, or `combine` to define the following functions (those not defined here were defined in Chapter 2):

   (a) `cdr*` takes the `cdr`'s of each element of a list of lists:

   ```
   -> (cdr* '((a b c) (d e) (f)))
   ((b c) (e) ())
   ```

   (b) `max*` finds the maximum of a list of nonnegative integers.

   (c) `append`.

   (d) `addtoend` adds its first argument (an arbitrary S-expression) as the last element of its second argument (a list):

   ```
   -> (addtoend 'a '(b c d))
   (b c d a)
   ```

    (e) `reverse` (use `addtoend`).

    (f) `insertion-sort` (you may take `insert` as given).

    (g) `(mkpairfn x)` is a function which, given a list, places `x` in front of each element:

```
-> ((mkpairfn 'a) '(() (b c) (d) ((e f))))
((a) (a b c) (a d) (a (e f)))
```

2. `lex-order*` extends `lex-order` to apply to lists of differing length, as in normal alphabetical ordering:

```
-> (set alpha-order (lex-order* <))

-> (alpha-order '(4 15 7) '(4 15 7 5))
T

-> (alpha-order '(4 15 7) '(4 15 6 6))
()
```

    To relate this to normal alphabetical ordering, just translate the numbers to letters: These two results say DOG < DOGE and DOG $\not<$ DOFF. Program `lex-order*`.

3. An alternate representation for sets in SCHEME is as Boolean-valued functions, called "characteristic functions." In particular, the null set is represented by a function that always returns *nil*, and the membership test is just application:

```
-> (set nullset (lambda (x) '()))

-> (set member? (lambda (x s) (s x)))
```

    (a) Program `addelt`, `union`, `inter`, and `diff` using this new representation.

    (b) Code the third approach to polymorphism (page 106) using this representation.

4. Our continuation-passing versions of `gcd*` and `gcds` did not handle another case where premature termination is desirable: when the gcd's that have been computed at some point degenerate to 1 (even if the list itself contains no 1's). For example, our last version of `gcd*`, when applied as in `(gcd* '(3 5 7 9 11))`, will call `gcd` four times, even though the result is guaranteed to be 1 as soon as the first call, `(gcd 9 11)`, is made. Modify both functions to abort and return 1 as soon as it is known that the answer will be 1.

5. The following problems refer to the term-rewriting system code of Section 4.1.

(a) In our code, the overall approach is to extend a single rule to operate inside expressions (using `mk-rw-fn`), then process the entire list of rewrite rules (using `mk-rw-fn*`). Do this in the opposite order; i.e., first produce a rewriting function that applies any of the rules at the top level of an expression, and then extend this to operate inside expressions.

(b) `apply-inside-exp` has the property that it applies the function *once*, at the first place within the expression that the function is applicable. Modify it so that it applies the function to as many subexpressions as it can on a single traversal of the expression. (After it applies the function somewhere, it should *not* attempt to apply it *within* the newly created subexpression.)

6. Extend the equivalence given for `letrec` in Section 4.6 to allow for multiple recursive definitions, i.e., to allow for the general form of `letrec`, as in this version of `eval`, which evaluates expressions having operations `+` and `*`, of arbitrary arity:

```
(set eval (lambda (e)
    (letrec
        ((ev (lambda (exp)
                (if (number? exp) exp
                    (if (= (car exp) '+)
                        (+/ (evlis (cdr exp)))
                        (*/ (evlis (cdr exp)))))))
         (evlis (mapc ev)))
        (ev e))))
```

(a) Give the extension on paper.

(b) Translate `eval` by hand, and run it to test the translation.

(c) Write the SCHEME functions `trans-let`, `trans-letrec`, and `trans-let*` that do the translations of each type of expression into SCHEME; for example:

```
-> (trans-letrec '(letrec ((f e1)) e2))
((lambda (f) (begin (set f e1) e2)) (quote ()))
```

(d) Add `let` and `let*` to SCHEME `eval` (Section 4.5). (Note that adding `letrec` is much more difficult, because it requires implementing `set` in SCHEME `eval`.)

7. Consider the PASCAL program given in Exercise 7 in Chapter 1. What would its output be if PASCAL used dynamic scope? Discuss the implications of dynamic scope for type-checking in PASCAL.

8. The discussion in Section 4.6.2 only hinted at the power of `call/cc`. Read and report on the paper by Friedman, et al. [1984], which contains many more examples.

9. Steele [1978] argues that, while static scope should certainly be the default scope rule, dynamically scoped — or *fluid* — variables have their uses, as in this example: Suppose there is a function `print-num` to print integers, and you would like to make it possible to change the radix of printing. One way to accomplish this is to have `print-num` consult the global variable `RADIX`, so that a user who wants to print in base 8 does so in this way:

$$\vdots$$

```
(set saveradix RADIX)
(set RADIX 8)
(print-num N)
(set RADIX saveradix)
```

$$\vdots$$

Note the need to save and reset `RADIX` in order that later users of `print-num` will not be surprised. If `RADIX` were a dynamically-bound variable, the same effect could be obtained by defining:

```
(set print-8 (lambda (n) ( (lambda (RADIX) (print-num n)) 8)))
```

and replacing the code above by:

$$\vdots$$

```
(print-8 N)
```

$$\vdots$$

Convinced by this and other examples of the usefulness of dynamically scoped variables, some versions of SCHEME include them in addition to ordinary, lexically scoped ones. Explain this example and discuss whether you think the introduction of fluid variables into SCHEME is justified. (See Abelson and Sussman [1985, pp. 321–325] for more on fluid variables.)

4.10.2 *LEARNING ABOUT THE INTERPRETER*

10. Call "environment depth" the length of a chain of *enclosing* pointers. Argue that there is a fixed maximum environment depth of any environment created during a computation, and that it can be determined from the text of the SCHEME program. (Instrumenting the interpreter to compute this value may help you answer this question.)

11. Create a trace facility that will print the closure and arguments for any closure application. The biggest part of this problem is the printing of closures, which includes the printing of expressions and environments. (Furthermore, you will probably want some means of limiting the amount of data printed for a closure, which could otherwise be enormous. One possibility is to make sure the global environment is not printed in its entirety, which can be accomplished by pointer comparison.) Trace the application (add1* '(3 4 5)), and compare your results to the trace given on page 101.

12. Add let to the language. There are two ways this can be done: (1) In *parseExp*, translate any let expression to its equivalent lambda form; no changes are needed in *eval* itself. (2) Define a new type of expression, *LETEXP*, to represent let expressions; modify *parseExp* to create such *EXP*'s, and modify *eval* to process them. These two alternatives apply to the next two exercises as well.

13. Add let*.

14. Add letrec. Either of the methods used for adding let can be used for adding letrec. However, if the second alternative is taken, you will find that the example given in Exercise 6 will not work; can you see why?

15. Add macros, as in Exercise 12. Then use them to solve the previous three problems.

16. Change the interpreter to use dynamic scope.

17. Add rplaca and rplacd. Use these to add set to the SCHEME interpreter of Section 4.5, and then program r-e-p-loop as we did in LISP (Section 2.4).

Chapter 5

SASL

The term "functional programming" refers to a programming style in which functions are manipulated as first-class values. Especially characteristic of this style is the construction of functions by applying general-purpose functionals (such as `combine`, `lex-order`, and `extend-to-exp`) to other functions.

In SASL, this style is supported even more strongly than in SCHEME, by way of a more general evaluation method known as *lazy evaluation*. More on that later, but first let's look at an example showing the difference between imperative programming and functional programming.

Consider the following function in PASCAL:

> **function** *srch* (*n*: *integer*): *integer*;
> **var** *i*: *integer*;
> **begin**
>   *i* := 1;
>   **while** (*i* <= *n*) **and not** *pred*(*i*)
>   **do** *i* := *i*+1;
>   *srch* := *i*
> **end**; (* *srch* *)

What this code does, of course, is to test all i, $1 \leq i \leq n$, until it finds one for which *pred* holds. A direct translation into SCHEME using `while` is straightforward:

```
(set iter-srch-for (lambda (n)
    (begin
      (set i 1)
      (while (and (<= i n) (not (pred i)))
        (set i (+1 i)))
      i)))
```

A more "functional"-looking version is:

```
(set fun-srch-for (lambda (n)
    (find-val pred (interval 1 n) (+1 n))))
(set find-val (lambda (pred lis failure-value)
    (if (null? lis) failure-value
        (if (pred (car lis)) (car lis)
            (find-val pred (cdr lis) failure-value)))))
(set interval (lambda (i j)
    (if (> i j) '() (cons i (interval (+1 i) j)))))
```

Is "functional" better? It would not appear so, since `fun-srch-for` is longer than `iter-srch-for`, and not conspicuously clearer. But it really is better code because it is *more general*. To see this, consider this variant of the problem, namely to search for the first perfect square less than n^2 that satisfies `pred`:

```
(set iter-srch-for-sqr (lambda (n)
    (begin
        (set i 1)
        (while (and (<= i n) (not (pred (sqr i))))
            (set i (+1 i)))
        (sqr i))))
```

`iter-srch-for` may serve as a model in programming `iter-srch-for-sqr`, but it offers no *tangible* help; despite the similarity of the two functions, they *share no code*. On the other hand, the functional version, `fun-srch-for-sqr`, is obtained by combining the parts already written in a different way:

```
(set fun-srch-for-sqr (lambda (n)
    (find-val pred (mapcar sqr (interval 1 n)) (sqr (+1 n)))))
```

Thus, *given* the tools in the form of functionals like `find-val`, programs can be built more quickly in the functional style. *Using the functional style, code is highly reusable.*

`fun-srch-for` has a serious flaw, however. It can be inefficient in that it *always* runs in time proportional to n, even when (`pred 1`) is true! We appear to be on the horns of a classic dilemma: the need to choose between well-structured but inefficient, and efficient but awkward, code.

In fact, the problem is even worse. Consider this variant of `iter-srch-for`, which looks for i satisfying `pred`, but without the *a priori* bound on i:

```
(set iter-srch-while (lambda ()
    (begin
        (set i 1)
        (while (not (pred i))
            (set i (+1 i)))
        i)))
```

There seems to be *no* definition of `fun-srch-while` *having the same structure as* `fun-srch-for` for this case. This is because there is no way to create a list of *all i* that might possibly satisfy `pred`; since that list is infinite, any attempt to construct it is hopeless.

The inefficiency of `fun-srch-for` and the apparent impossibility of coding `fun-srch-while` are in fact symptoms of the same problem, and they are both solved in SASL. SASL achieves this by changing, in a subtle but crucial way, the evaluation method of SCHEME, employing instead *lazy evaluation*.[1] Lazy evaluation was first proposed by Friedman and Wise [1976] and Henderson and Morris [1976], but both those papers are quite theoretical. Its implications for practical programming were explored by David Turner [1979a], who designed the language SASL and also presented an ingenious method of implementing it.

We start this chapter with a discussion of lazy evaluation, then present our version of SASL, as usual, by giving a variety of small examples, an exegesis of the interpreter, and two longer examples. Turner's implementation method — called *combinator-reduction* or *graph-reduction* — is discussed in Section 5.9. Also included in this chapter is a section on λ-calculus, a simple language that can be regarded as the "core" of SASL.

5.1 Lazy Evaluation

The principle of lazy evaluation is this:

> *Don't evaluate an expression until its value is needed.*

This may sound like plain common sense, but it has far-reaching semantic consequences.

There are two different places where SCHEME violates the lazy evaluation principle:

1. In calls to user-defined functions, all actual parameters are evaluated. It may be that some formal parameters are never referenced in that call, in which case the evaluation of the corresponding actuals was unnecessary.

2. In applying `cons`, there is no immediate need to evaluate its arguments until the `car` or `cdr` of the list is requested. If either part of the list is never requested, then the evaluation of that part will have been needless.

To show how laziness affects evaluation, consider the execution of (`fun-srch-for` 100). Lazy evaluation allows this to be done without constructing

---

[1]or *normal-order* or *delayed* evaluation; SCHEME's strategy is called *eager* or *applicative-order* evaluation.

the entire list (`interval 1 100`). Suppose, for example, that (`pred 1`) is true:

```
(fun-srch-for 100)
    ⟹  (find-val pred (interval 1 100) (+1 100))
    ⟹  (if (null? ilis) (+1 100)
            (if (pred (car ilis)) (car ilis)
                (find-val pred (cdr ilis) (+1 100))))
```

where *ilis* = (`interval 1 100`). Since we are asked to evaluate (`null?` *ilis*), we have no choice but to evaluate *ilis*, but, *by the principle of lazy evaluation, it should be evaluated only far enough to determine if it is nil.* So,

```
ilis = (interval 1 100)
    ⟹  (if (> 1 100) '() (cons 1 (interval 2 100)))
    ⟹  (cons 1 (interval 2 100))
```

This is as far as we need to go. It is now certainly safe to say that *ilis* is not *nil.* Returning to the main computation:

```
(if (null? ilis) (+1 100)
        (if (pred (car ilis)) (car ilis)
            (find-val pred (cdr ilis) (+1 100))))
    ⟹  (if (pred (car ilis)) (car ilis)
            (find-val pred (cdr ilis) (+1 100))))
```

We are asked for (`car` *ilis*). If *ilis* had not already been partially evaluated, it would be now. In fact, the `car` of *ilis* is already known to be 1, so:

```
    ⟹  (if (pred 1) 1 (find-val pred (cdr ilis) (+1 100)))
```

By assumption, (`pred 1`) is true, so the result is 1. The remainder of *ilis* is never needed, so it is never evaluated.

This exercise makes it clear that the bound on the length of *ilis* is not really relevant to the computation. Consider the `fun-srch-while` problem. The special difficulty here is that there is no way to bound the value of *i* at which `pred` may first hold. This is why we gave up on the idea of coding it in a way similar to `fun-srch-for`. But now consider this solution:

```
(set fun-srch-while (lambda ()
    (find-val pred (ints-from 1) '())))
(set ints-from (lambda (i) (cons i (ints-from (+1 i)))))
```

Impossible though this may look, *the exact same execution sequence takes place as for* `fun-srch-for`. Thus, if (`pred 1`) is true, (`fun-srch-while`) will return 1, and very quickly at that.

Before leaving this example, let us discuss the notion of "unevaluated expression" in more depth. In the example, *ilis* was the expression (`interval 1 100`). Was this expression actually constructed? The answer is no. What was constructed was a structure containing all the information necessary to evaluate *ilis* when needed. That information is just the expression (interval 1 n), and the value of the variable n (namely, 100).

This structure should remind you of a closure. Indeed, like a closure, it contains an expression and an environment; it is different from a closure only in the way it is used. By tradition, it is called a *thunk*; the thunk containing expression e and environment ρ is denoted by $\triangleleft e, \rho \triangleright$.

ilis, then, is actually the thunk $\triangleleft$ (interval 1 n), $\{n \mapsto 100\} \triangleright$. A thunk can be created very quickly, and when it is time to evaluate it, it is simply opened up and its two parts are passed to *eval*. (More details are given in Section 5.2.2.)

In the following sections, there are many examples of the power of lazy evaluation. We will see that it permits a functional-style coding of many problems for which such a coding in SCHEME would be either extremely inefficient or impossible.

However, before we do, there is one important point to be made: *lazy evaluation is inconsistent with side-effects*. This is so in two senses:

1. Side-effects are inherently time-dependent. To set a variable, for example, can be sensible only if you can tell what references to that variable will occur *after* the set — hence, time. However, lazy evaluation is inherently disrespectful of time, in that no perusal of an expression can determine in general when its various subexpressions will be evaluated. Thus, the interaction of side-effects and lazy evaluation leads to incomprehensible and usually erroneous code. For this reason, SASL omits side-effects. Our version, accordingly, omits set (except at the top level), print, begin (because (begin e_1 ... e_n) is distinguished from e_n only by the side-effects of e_1 ... e_{n-1}), and while (because it is substantially useless without side-effects).

2. In the absence of side-effects, expressions have the very interesting property that they always return the same value whenever they are evaluated. (This is another way of stating the point about time.) This in turn leads to an important optimization in the evaluation process: When a thunk is finally evaluated, it is *replaced in memory* by its value. Future references to the value automatically get the benefit of this evaluation. For example, in evaluating fun-srch-for, *ilis* — which was the thunk $\triangleleft$ (interval 1 n), $\{n \mapsto 100\} \triangleright$ — was evaluated for the null? test, and it evaluated to (cons 1 $\cdots$). The subsequent application (car *ilis*) *immediately* found the car of *ilis* to be 1, without having to re-evaluate the thunk, because it had already been *replaced* by (cons 1 $\cdots$). To allow this optimization, also, SASL omits side-effects.

5.2 The Language

5.2.1 SYNTAX

The syntax of our version of SASL is almost the same as the syntax of SCHEME.
The major differences are the omissions to eliminate side-effects and the rein-
sertion of `set` at the top level.

```
input         ⟶    expression | ( set variable expression )
expression    ⟶    value
              |     variable
              |     ( if expression expression expression )
              |     ( expression⁺ )
value         ⟶    integer | quoted-const | ( lambda arglist expression ) | value-op
value-op      ⟶    + | - | ⋯ | closure?
```

5.2.2 SEMANTICS

The difference between SCHEME and SASL can be explained as follows. Call
a function *strict* if all of its arguments must be evaluated before it is applied.
Numerical value-op's are naturally strict — it is impossible to add two numbers
without knowing what they are. `if` is naturally strict in its first argument, but
not in its second and third. SCHEME and SASL differ in this way: In SCHEME,
function application is performed in such a way that all functions except control
operations are strict; in particular, all closures — which is to say, all user-
defined functions — define strict functions. In SASL, the only strict functions
are those that are *naturally* strict, such as numerical value-op's; `cons` is not
strict, and closures do not necessarily define strict functions.

Thus, the evaluation of function arguments will be delayed as long as possible. To accomplish this, a new kind of value, called a *thunk*, or *suspension*, is
introduced. As previously discussed, a thunk represents a subexpression whose
evaluation has been suspended because it was not needed (but may be needed
later). It is very much like a closure, in that it contains an expression and an
environment — everything necessary to carry out the evaluation of the expression whenever that is indicated. Thunks will occur either bound to variables
in environments or as elements of lists.

There are two major differences between a thunk and a closure. First, the
expression in a closure is always a `lambda` expression, whereas in a thunk it
can be anything. Second, a closure is "opened up" and evaluated only when it
is applied, whereas a thunk is evaluated whenever the variable it is bound to is
referenced, or whenever the list position it occupies is accessed.

A thunk, then, is like a "promissory note" for the value of an expression.
However, when the value of an expression is requested, we want to be sure to
get paid in cash. Thus, the evaluator must never return a thunk as its value.
It may return a list *containing* a thunk, but not just a thunk.

We need to explain exactly how function application is done. Consider that the expression

$$(e_0 \ e_1 \ \ldots \ e_n)$$

is to be evaluated in local environment ρ. First, e_0 must be evaluated; call its value v_0. Next, no matter what v_0 is — a value-op, a closure, or if — its arguments are turned into thunks; so the argument list is $\triangleleft e_1, \rho \triangleright$, $\triangleleft e_2, \rho \triangleright$, ..., $\triangleleft e_n, \rho \triangleright$. Our next action depends upon v_0:

- $v_0 = $ if: This is exactly as in SCHEME: Evaluate e_1 in environment ρ; if it evaluates to *nil* (remember that *eval* will necessarily return a nonthunk), evaluate e_3; otherwise, evaluate e_2.

- $v_0 = $ a strict value-op, which is any value-op except cons: Evaluate each of the arguments recursively (that is, evaluate each e_i in ρ), perform the operation, and return the result. There is a slight exception: Since a list can contain a thunk, car and cdr run the danger of returning one; so after applying car or cdr, if a thunk results, it must be evaluated.

- $v_0 = $ cons: A list is returned having $\triangleleft e_1, \rho \triangleright$ as its car and $\triangleleft e_2, \rho \triangleright$ as its cdr.

- $v_0 = \langle\!\langle (\text{lambda } (x_1 \ \ldots \ x_n) \ e), \rho' \rangle\!\rangle$. Evaluate e in environment

$$\rho'\{x_1 \mapsto \triangleleft e_1, \rho \triangleright, \ldots, x_n \mapsto \triangleleft e_n, \rho \triangleright\}.$$

The important point to note in the last case is that the actual parameters are not evaluated. When a local variable is referenced, if it is bound to a thunk, that thunk is opened up and evaluated.

Note the phrase "if it is bound to a thunk;" the rule for applying closures shows *all* actual parameters being thunks, so why the "if?" When a thunk is evaluated, it is *overwritten* by the resulting value. Thus, when a local variable is first referenced, the thunk it is bound to is evaluated, but all future references to that variable see only the value.

As an example, consider the evaluation of ((lambda (x) (+ x x)) 3):

- The operator position is evaluated, yielding the closure:

$$\langle\!\langle (\text{lambda } (x) \ (+ \ x \ x)), \{\} \rangle\!\rangle,$$

and its actual parameter is $\triangleleft 3, \{\} \triangleright$.

- The application rule directs us to evaluate (+ x x) in environment $\rho_0 = \{x \mapsto \triangleleft 3, \{\} \triangleright\}$. + is given two arguments, both the same thunk, $\triangleleft x, \rho_0 \triangleright$.

- + being a strict function, it evaluates its arguments:

— x is evaluated in ρ_0. Its value is a thunk, $\triangleleft 3, \{\} \triangleright$, so it is in turn evaluated.

 * 3, evaluated in environment $\{\}$, returns 3. This value overwrites the thunk, so that $\triangleleft 3, \{\} \triangleright$ becomes 3, and ρ_0 becomes $\{x \mapsto 3\}$.

— x is evaluated again, this time in the new ρ_0. It is bound to 3, so 3 is returned.

- \+ returns 6.

5.2.3 EXAMPLES

As usual, we'll first try some simple examples. To begin with, note that all side-effect-free SCHEME programs work in SASL subject to one caveat: Since list components are not evaluated, lists will rarely be printed in their entirety. Instead, they will usually print as "(...   ...)", "..." being our way of printing thunks. On the other hand, as the list is "interrogated," it will improve itself, so that it will afterwards print in a more complete form. Here is an example of this:

```
-> (set x (mapcar +1 '(2 3)))
(...   ...)
-> (car x)
3
-> (cadr x)
4
-> x
(3 4 ...)
-> (cddr x)
()
-> x
(3 4)
```

This printing of ellipses can be pretty annoying when you want to see what's in a list. We will shortly see a way around it. The reader might ask why the evaluator doesn't just evaluate the entire list when it is time to print it. The reason it cannot do this is that the list may be infinite:

```
-> (set ints-from (lambda (i) (cons i (ints-from (+1 i)))))

-> (set ints (ints-from 0))
(...   ...)
```

Note that `cons` did not evaluate either of its arguments. Its first argument was just a variable (`i`), but it is quite stubborn about not evaluating arguments, even when they are as simple as this. Thus, both its arguments are thunks, so both print as ellipses. (Really, it is *too* stubborn; see Exercise 6.)

```
-> (car ints)
0

-> (cadr ints)
1

-> ints
(0 1 ...)
```

Such infinite lists are called *lazy lists*. It is possible for a language to have lazy lists but not lazy evaluation (see Abelson and Sussman [1985] and Friedman and Wise [1976]), though the two are usually associated (see Section 5.7).

Despite the existence of infinite lists, the majority of lists are still finite, and it would be pleasant to be able to print them whole. There are various ways to alter the language to side-step the problem, but we prefer to keep it pure. An approach that works, if a bit awkwardly, is to write a function that applies a value-op (other than cons) to every component of the list; since value-op's always evaluate their arguments, this forces evaluation of the list:

```
-> (set force (lambda (x)
    (if (list? x) ; apply list? to every component
       (if (force (car x)) (force (cdr x)) '())
       'T)))
-> (set x (mapcar +1 '(2 3)))
(...  ...)
-> (force x)
'T

-> x
(3 4)
```

This is a useful trick to keep in mind, but be careful never to apply force to an infinite list! If you want to see some initial segment of an infinite list, use first-n:

```
-> (set first-n (lambda (n l)
    (if (null? l) '()
       (if (= n 0) '()
          (cons (car l) (first-n (- n 1) (cdr l)))))))
-> (set ints5 (first-n 5 ints))
(...  ...)
```

```
-> (force ints5)
'T

-> ints5
(0 1 2 3 4)
```

Newton–Raphson Square Root Computation.   A simple but telling example in SASL is from Hughes [1984]. The problem is the computation of the square root by the Newton–Raphson method. (Lacking real numbers, this example is necessarily somewhat artificial, but the student will have no problem envisioning it in a more realistic setting; real SASL, of course, has real numbers.) For input n, the algorithm works by assuming the initial approximation $x_0 = 1$ and improving it at step i, $i \geq 0$, by computing:

$$x_{i+1} = (x_i + n/x_i)/2.$$

Here is the SASL function to generate the x_i:

```
-> (set next (lambda (n xi) (/ (+ xi (/ n xi)) 2)))

-> (set xlist (lambda (xi n) (cons xi (xlist (next n xi) n))))

-> (set mk-xlist (lambda (n) (xlist 1 n)))
```

There is some "convergence condition," a predicate on x_i and x_{i-1} indicating when they are close enough to accept x_i as the answer.[2] One possibility is *absolute distance* (between x_i and x_{i-1}):

```
-> (set abs-conv (lambda (epsilon)
    (lambda (l) (< (abs (- (cadr l) (car l))) epsilon))))
```

These parts are now easily put together:

```
-> (set abs-sqrt (lambda (n)
    (find-list (abs-conv 3) cadr (mk-xlist n))))

-> (set find-list (lambda (pred extract l)
    (if (null? l) '() (if (pred l) (extract l)
        (find-list pred extract (cdr l))))))

-> (abs-sqrt 100)
10
```

The beauty of the lazy evaluation solution is that the generation of the x_i can be separated from the convergence condition, permitting different sequences and different convergence conditions to be put together easily.

---

[2]the idea being that if $x_i \approx x_{i-1}$,

$$x_i = (x_{i-1} + n/x_{i-1})/2 \approx (x_i + n/x_i)/2,$$

so $x_i \approx \sqrt{n}$.

For example, by changing the function **next**, a program for cube roots is obtained:

```
-> (set next (lambda (n xi) (/ (+ xi (/ n (* xi xi))) 2)))
-> (set abs-cbrt (lambda (n)
      (find-list (abs-conv 2) cadr (mk-xlist n))))
-> (abs-cbrt 100)
5
```

Generating Primes.   Another problem along the same lines is a variant of the function **primes<=** (page 31). That function returned a list of all the primes less than a given number. Here is its definition in SCHEME or SASL:

```
-> (set remove-multiples (lambda (n l)
      (if (null? l) '()
         (if (divides n (car l))
            (remove-multiples n (cdr l))
            (cons (car l) (remove-multiples n (cdr l)))))))
-> (set sieve (lambda (l)
      (if (null? l) '()
         (cons (car l)
               (sieve (remove-multiples (car l) (cdr l)))))))
-> (set primes<= (lambda (n) (sieve (interval 2 n))))
```

The variant is **first-n-primes**, with the obvious meaning. Although it is not really hard to code in SCHEME, the structure of **first-n-primes** is necessarily quite different from that of **primes<=**. This is an example of the difference between the **for** loop and **while** loop problems in the introduction: There is no way to generate all candidates for membership in (**first-n-primes** n) except by creating an infinite list. Of course, in SASL that is exactly what is done:

```
-> (set primes (sieve (ints-from 2)))
-> (set first-n-primes (lambda (n) (first-n n primes)))
```

This is a clear example of the advantage of lazy evaluation. The two functions **primes<=** and **first-n-primes** share almost all their code; this is difficult to achieve in an eager evaluation language like SCHEME.

Why It Can't Be Done in SCHEME.   We need to tie up an end left loose in the introduction to this chapter. There is, in fact, a true functional solution for `fun-srch-while` in SCHEME that avoids the problems discussed there. It is:

```
-> (set next-int +1)
-> (set repeat-until (lambda (init next pred)
     (if (pred init) init
         (repeat-until (next init) next pred)))))
-> (set new-fun-srch-while (lambda ()
     (repeat-until 1 next-int pred)))
```

It is hard to find fault with this SCHEME solution, as compared with **fun-srch-while** in SASL. Our point in mentioning it is to argue that such a solution is not always available. Even when it is possible to compute a list of all candidate solutions, it may be very difficult — even impossible — to write a **next** function to generate, from any element of the list, the next element of the list. This may sound paradoxical, but we will present two examples: atoms of an S-expression and permutations of a list.

The first problem, then, is to find the first atom satisfying predicate **pred** in a pre-order traversal of an S-expression. The SASL solution is:

```
-> (set find-atom (lambda (s) (find-val pred (flatten s) '())))
```

`flatten` is a function that returns the list of atoms in a pre-order traversal of its argument. It was given as an exercise in Chapter 2; here is its definition in SCHEME or SASL:

```
-> (set flatten (lambda (x)
     (if (null? x) '()
         (if (atom? x) (list1 x)
             (append (flatten (car x)) (flatten (cdr x)))))))
```

Again, the problem is how to program `find-atom` in a *functional style* in SCHEME without having to flatten the entire tree (considering that **pred** may be true of the very first atom). And again, the SCHEME solution calls for us to write a function **next-atom**. This is impossible. Really, the best solution in SCHEME is to, in effect, have it imitate SASL; see Section 5.7.

A well-known application of flatten is the **samefringe** problem (Henderson and Morris [1976]), which compares the pre-order traversals of two S-expressions. The SASL solution is as simple as could be:

```
-> (set samefringe (lambda (x y) (equal (flatten x) (flatten y))))
```

x and y will be flattened just enough to tell whether they differ.

The next problem is, given a list 1, to find some permutation of the elements of 1 satisfying a predicate **pred**. Given a function to generate all permutations of 1, we will write as before:

```
-> (set find-perm
     (lambda (1) (find-val pred (permutations 1) '())))
```

Here is a definition of **permutations**:

```
-> (set append* (lambda (1)
     (if (null? 1) '() (append (car 1) (append* (cdr 1))))))
-> (set filter (lambda (pred 1)
     (if (null? 1) '()
         (if (pred (car 1)) (cons (car 1) (filter pred (cdr 1)))
             (filter pred (cdr 1))))))
-> (set remove (lambda (item 1)
     (filter (lambda (x) (not (= x item))) 1)))
-> (set permutations (lambda (1)
     (if (= (length 1) 1) (list1 1)
         (append* (mapcar (lambda (x)
                     (mapcar (lambda (z) (cons x z))
                         (permutations (remove x 1)))) 1)))))
```

This may not be the world's simplest code, but the question is: how easy would it be to write **next-permutation**? The answer is that it is extremely difficult. The reader should try it first for the case of lists of the form (**interval** 1 n), which is comparatively easy, since arithmetic can be used to compute the next permutation from a given one. For arbitrary lists, it is certainly impossible, but it can be done if **next-permutation** can take the original list as a second argument in each call. In short, as difficult as **permutations** may be, **next-permutation** is far more difficult, even impossible.

To summarize the previous discussion: We first noticed that a perfectly well structured functional solution to the **while** search problem could be found in SCHEME, using **next-int**, which is also efficient in that it avoids generating more candidates than necessary. However, we then argued that the **next-int** approach could not always be generalized, and we offered two examples: **find-atom** and **find-permutation**. In each case, the SASL approach generalizes easily. The SCHEME approach calls for functions **next-atom** and **next-permutation**, which are extremely difficult or impossible to code.

Sequences Defined by Recursion Schemes. One more nifty coding technique made possible by lazy evaluation is constructing infinite sequences of values defined by recursion schemes. Suppose the sequence $\vec{x} = x_0, x_1, \ldots$ is defined by the conditions:

$$x_0 = \text{some initial value}$$
$$x_{i+1} = f(x_i)$$

Then the list $\vec{x}$ can be produced in SASL this way:

```
(set X (cons x0 (mapcar f X)))
```

For example, the sequence of all nonnegative integers — which is also (ints-from 0) — can be obtained as:

```
(set ints (cons 0 (mapcar +1 ints)))
```

and the list of all powers of 2 by:

```
(set powersof2 (cons 1 (mapcar double powersof2)))
```

This idea can be extended further. Suppose a sequence $\vec{x}$ is defined by:

$$x_0 = \text{some initial value}$$
$$x_{i+1} = f(x_i, i + 1)$$

$\vec{x}$ can be computed in this way:

```
(set mapcar2 (lambda (f l1 l2)
     (cons (f (car l1) (car l2))
          (mapcar2 f (cdr l1) (cdr l2)))))
(set posints (cdr ints))
(set X (cons x0 (mapcar2 f X posints)))
```

The standard example here would be factorial:

```
-> (set facs (cons 1 (mapcar2 * facs posints)))

-> (cadddr facs)
6
```

Notice that nothing analogous can be done in an eager evaluation language like SCHEME. More examples are given in Exercise 1.

5.3   Implementation

The SASL interpreter is derived from the SCHEME interpreter (Appendix E). The changes are quite small, affecting only about fifty lines of code overall.

- The control operations begin, while, and set, and the operation print, are removed from *BUILTINOP* in *DECLARATIONS* (and from *init-Names* in *NAME MANAGEMENT*). Also, *THUNK* is a new type of *SEXP*, whose values look much like closures.

- **set** is handled at the top level (just as **define** was in Chapter 1). This requires a new function, *parseSet* in *INPUTS* and, of course, a change in *READ-EVAL-PRINT LOOP*.

- In *S-EXPRESSIONS*, all functions must deal with thunks. Most importantly, *applyValueOp* must usually "open up" and evaluate thunks it gets as arguments (it does this by calling *evalThunk* in *EVALUATION*), and **car** and **cdr** have to evaluate thunks before returning them.

- In *EVALUATION*, *evalList* is changed to a function that simply turns a list of expressions into a list of thunks. Furthermore, there is now only one control operation, **if**. Finally, the function *evalThunk*, whose job is to open up a thunk, evaluate it, and replace it by its value, is added.

It is important to remember that *eval* is obliged never to return a thunk; this is to ensure that progress is made in the computation.

5.3.1 *DECLARATIONS*

S-expressions are now declared as:

$$SEXPTYPE = (NILSXP, NUMSXP, SYMSXP, LISTSXP,$$
$$CLOSXP, PRIMSXP, THUNK);$$

$$SEXPREC = \textbf{record}$$
   case *sxptype*: *SEXPTYPE* **of**
     NILSXP: ();
     NUMSXP: (*intval*: *integer*);
     SYMSXP: (*symval*: *NAME*);
     LISTSXP: (*carval, cdrval*: *SEXP*);
     CLOSXP, THUNK: (*clofun*: *EXP*; *cloenv*: *ENV*);
     PRIMSXP: (*primval*: *BUILTINOP*)
       end;

Note that the difference between closures and thunks is that the *clofun* component of a closure is a **lambda** expression, whereas for a thunk it can be anything.

5.3.2 *DATA STRUCTURE OP'S*

The function *mkThunk* has two arguments, an *EXP* and an *ENV*, and creates an S-expression of type *THUNK*.

5.3.3 *NAME MANAGEMENT*

The only change here is to remove **begin**, **while**, **set**, and **print** from *init-Names*.

5.3.4 INPUT

parseSet is called from *READ-EVAL-PRINT LOOP* when an input of the form
"(set x e)" is read. It assigns the name ("x") to the global variable *setName*,
and returns the expression ("e").

5.3.5 ENVIRONMENTS

There are no changes here.

5.3.6 S-EXPRESSIONS

prValue prints S-expressions of type *THUNK* as ellipses ("...").
    The arguments to *applyValueOp* are thunks (since they are produced by
evalList; see below). In most cases, these must be evaluated — in fact, only
cons is nonstrict. Also, just as *eval* is expected never to return a thunk, so it
expects *applyValueOp* not to return one. For this reason, *applyValueOp* calls
evalThunk before returning the car or cdr of a list.

5.3.7 EVALUATION

evalList is altered so that, instead of evaluating the actual parameters, it makes
thunks out of them:

```
        function evalList (el: EXPLIST): VALUELIST;
        var
            h: SEXP;
            t: VALUELIST;
        begin
            if el = nil then evalList := nil
            else begin
                    h := mkThunk(el↑.head, rho);
                    t := evalList(el↑.tail);
                    evalList := mkValuelist(h, t)
                end
        end; (* evalList *)
```

    applyCtrlOp is down to one function, if; its treatment is no different from
in SCHEME.
    In the body of *eval*, the *VAREXP* case must consider the possibility that the
stored value is a thunk; since *eval* does not want to return a thunk, *evalThunk*
is called in this case.
    evalThunk is called whenever it is necessary to ensure that a value is not a
thunk. It first checks if its argument is a thunk, and if not, it returns without
doing anything at all. If it is a thunk, it opens it up and evaluates it, then
copies the value into the *SEXP* node which formerly had the thunk.

```
procedure evalThunk (s: SEXP);

var result: SEXP;

    procedure copyValue (s1, s2: SEXP);
    begin
      with s1↑ do begin
        s2↑.sxptype := sxptype;
        case sxptype of
          NILSXP: ;
          NUMSXP: s2↑.intval := intval;
          SYMSXP: s2↑.symval := symval;
          PRIMSXP: s2↑.primval := primval;
          LISTSXP:
            begin
              s2↑.carval := carval;
              s2↑.cdrval := cdrval
            end;
          CLOSXP, THUNK:
            begin
              s2↑.clofun := clofun;
              s2↑.cloenv := cloenv
            end
        end (* case *)
      end (* with *)
    end; (* copyValue *)

begin (* evalThunk *)
  with s↑ do
    if sxptype = THUNK
    then begin
      result := eval(clofun, cloenv);
      copyValue(result, s)
    end
end; (* evalThunk *)
```

5.3.8   READ-EVAL-PRINT LOOP

"set" is processed here. *parseSet* is called; it assigns the variable name to *setName* and returns the expression. The latter is evaluated and its value placed in *globalEnv*.

5.4   Example — Satisfiability of Boolean Expressions

Consider PASCAL-style Boolean expressions over the operators **not**, **or**, and **and**, and containing only Boolean variables, e.g.,

$$\textbf{not } (p \textbf{ or } ((\textbf{not } p \textbf{ or } q) \textbf{ and } (\textbf{not } p \textbf{ or not } q))).$$

It is natural to ask about this expression: Are there truth values for the variables p and q such that the expression evaluates to true? In the terminology of mathematical logic, is this expression *satisfiable*? In this section, we will write a program to answer that question for any such Boolean expression.

5.4.1   REPRESENTATION OF BOOLEAN EXPRESSIONS

We will use a LISP-style (prefix) representation for expressions, writing "(or p q)" instead of "p **or** q," and similarly for **not** and **and**. The expression above becomes:

```
(not (or p (and (or (not p) q) (or (not p) (not q))))).
```

5.4.2   THE ALGORITHM

We use the obvious solution of just trying all possible assignments of truth values to the variables of the expression. The function evalBool in Figure 5.1 produces the truth value of an expression e under a given assignment a. (This code works as well in SCHEME as in SASL.)

The code in Figure 5.1 leaves open the question of how assignments are represented; the code that deals with assignments is in Figure 5.2. Our decision

---

```
(set evalBoolexp (lambda (e a)
   (if (symbol? e) (isTrue? e a)
   (if (= (car e) 'not)
      (not (evalBoolexp (cadr e) a))
   (if (= (car e) 'or)
      (or (evalBoolexp (cadr e) a)
          (evalBoolexp (caddr e) a))
   (and (evalBoolexp (cadr e) a)
        (evalBoolexp (caddr e) a)))))))
```

Figure 5.1: Function evalBool

```
(set mapaddx (lambda (x l) ; add x to each list in l, then append to l
    (append l (mapcar (lambda (y) (cons x y)) l))))
(set gensubsets (lambda (l) ; create a list containing all subsets of l
    (if (null? (cdr l)) (list2 l '())
        (mapaddx (car l) (gensubsets (cdr l))))))
(set variables (lambda (e) ; All variables occurring in e
    (if (symbol? e) (cons e '())
        (if (= (car e) 'not) (variables (cadr e))
            (union (variables (cadr e)) (variables (caddr e)))))))
(set assignments (lambda (e) (gensubsets (variables e))))
(set isTrue? member?)
```

Figure 5.2: Functions `assignments` and `isTrue?`

is to represent them as subsets of the set of variables in the given expression; a variable is taken to be true if it is in the set and false otherwise (as can be seen in the function `isTrue?`). The function `assignments` generates the list of all assignments of the variables occurring in an expression.

Finally, `SAT` in Figure 5.3 puts these functions together.

We have written nothing that couldn't be run in SCHEME. Why, then, regard this as an example of SASL? The reader must realize that the list (`assignments e`) is quite large — exactly 2^n, if n is the number of variables

```
(set findTruth (lambda (e alist)
    ; Find if any assignment on alist satisfies e
    (if (null? alist) '() ; No assignments left to try
        (if (evalBoolexp e (car alist)) 'T
            (findTruth e (cdr alist))))))
(set SAT (lambda (e)
    (if (findTruth e (assignments e))
        'Satisfiable
        'Unsatisfiable)))
```

Figure 5.3: Function `SAT`

in e. In SCHEME, SAT would invariably take this much time, even if the very first assignment in (assignments e) made e true. This is the behavior that is avoided in SASL. However, even in SASL, this code runs in exponential time if e is unsatisfiable; for this reason, a naive technique like this cannot replace a more sophisticated method, regardless of the language in which it is programmed. (On the other hand, this is a basic example of an NP-complete problem; no subexponential algorithm is known for any problem in this class. Thus, no *good* solution is known, but there are *better* solutions than the one we've given.)

5.5   Example — The Reachability Problem

The reachability problem for vector addition systems is to determine whether a given point can be reached by composing vectors from a given finite set, under the constraint that the composed path remains always within the first quadrant. We will solve a simplified version, the *reachability problem for positive two-dimensional vector addition systems*:

> We are given a point $p_0 = (x_0, y_0)$ and a set of points $\mathcal{P} = \{(x_1, y_1),$
> $\ldots, (x_n, y_n)\}$, all x_i, y_i nonnegative integers, for $i \geq 0$; we may
> assume none of the (x_i, y_i) is $(0, 0)$. Define $(x, y) \oplus (x', y') = (x +$
> $x', y + y')$. A *path* is an arbitrary sequence of points from $\mathcal{P}$. The
> reachability problem is: Is there a path $p, p', \ldots, p^{(k)}$ such that $p \oplus$
> $p' \oplus \ldots \oplus p^{(k)} = p_0$?

For example, let $\mathcal{P} = \{(2, 2), (0, 1), (3, 0)\}$. Then $(4, 6)$ is reachable by the path $(2, 2)(2, 2)(0, 1)(0, 1)$, as illustrated here:

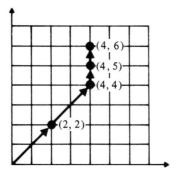

However, $(4, 3)$ is not reachable.

The problem is not difficult to solve. Go ahead and enumerate all the paths from $(0, 0)$; on each path, either (x_0, y_0) is reached, so terminate with success,

```
(set add-points (lambda (p q)
    (list2 (+ (car p) (car q)) (+ (cadr p) (cadr q)))))
(set gen-paths (lambda (p points)
    (cons p
      (mapcar (lambda (r) (gen-paths r points))
        (mapcar (lambda (q) (add-points q p)) points)))))
```

Figure 5.4: Function `gen-paths`

or it is overshot, so terminate the search along this path and try the next. This enumeration of paths is the kind of very costly operation that lazy evaluation allows us to handle neatly.

The paths naturally present themselves as a tree. The nodes of this tree are labeled with points. The root label is $(0, 0)$, and a node labeled with point (x, y) has n children labeled with points $(x, y) \oplus (x_1, y_1)$, ..., $(x, y) \oplus (x_n, y_n)$. This tree is, of course, infinite, but we are used to that by now. Given the code in Figure 5.4, this tree is produced by entering:

```
-> (set P '((2 2)(0 1)(3 0)))
((2 2)(0 1)(3 0))

-> (set PATHS (gen-paths '(0 0) P))
```

`gen-paths` works as follows: Starting from a point p, it creates a list containing each of the n points that can be reached from p in one step; this is the function of the expression `(mapcar (lambda (q) (add-points q p)) points)`. Then it applies `gen-paths` to each point in this list, creating a list of trees. Consing p to the front of this list gives the entire search tree starting from p.

The problem of searching this tree for an occurrence of (x_0, y_0) remains. This can be done in either a breadth-first or a depth-first manner. The beauty of the SASL code is that the choice can be made independently of the `gen-paths` code. Figure 5.5 contains the code for both kinds of search. To solve the reachability problem, enter either:

```
-> (reaches-dfs p0 PATHS)
```

or

```
-> (reaches-bfs p0 PATHS)
```

where p0 is the pair representing point p_0.

`reaches-dfs` uses a depth-first search strategy, which is coded in the function `dfs`. The arguments to `dfs` are a search tree, a predicate `pred` indicating when the search is successful, and a predicate `term` indicating when the search

```
(set == (lambda (p q) (and (= (car p) (car q)) (= (cadr p) (cadr q)))))
(set << (lambda (p q) (or (< (car p) (car q)) (< (cadr p) (cadr q)))))
(set dfs (lambda (t pred term)
    (if (pred (car t)) 'T ; success
        (if (term (car t)) '() ; failure on this branch
            (dfs* (cdr t) pred term)))))
(set dfs* (lambda (l pred term)
    (if (null? l) '() ; failure
        (if (dfs (car l) pred term) 'T
            (dfs* (cdr l) pred term)))))
(set reaches-dfs (lambda (p0 paths)
    (dfs paths
        (lambda (q) (== p0 q))
        (lambda (q) (<< p0 q)))))
;
(set enqueue* (lambda (q items)
    (if (null? items) q (enqueue* (enqueue (car items) q) (cdr items)))))
;
(set bfs (lambda (t pred term)
    (bfs-queue (enqueue t empty-queue) pred term)))
(set bfs-queue (lambda (q pred term)
    (if (empty? q) '()
        (if (pred (car (front q))) 'T
            (if (term (car (front q))) (bfs-queue (rm-front q) pred term)
                (bfs-queue (enqueue* (rm-front q) (cdr (front q)))
                           pred term))))))
(set reaches-bfs (lambda (p0 paths)
    (bfs paths
        (lambda (q) (== p0 q))
        (lambda (q) (<< p0 q)))))
```

Figure 5.5: Functions `reaches-dfs` and `reaches-bfs`

should be terminated (along a particular path of the search tree). Its coding is quite simple; `dfs*` is the extension of `dfs` to a list of trees. The arguments that `reaches-dfs` passes to `dfs` show that success occurs when point p0 is reached, and failure occurs along any path when p0 is passed.

`reaches-bfs` calls `bfs` to perform a breadth-first search. Since breadth-first search is just another word for level-order traversal, the student should review Section 2.1.3 where level-order tree traversal was done in LISP. After that, the coding of `bfs` should present no problems. (The function `enqueue*` enqueues a list of items onto a queue; it was not needed in Section 2.1.3 because the code there handled only binary trees.)

5.6 SASL as It Really Is

Real SASL has a non-LISP-like syntax, which we will briefly describe. It also has a feature called *ZF-expressions*, which is remarkably powerful as well as being easy to implement under a lazy evaluation regime. The evaluation strategy employed by Turner for SASL is discussed in Section 5.9.

5.6.1 SYNTAX

Unlike LISP, SASL uses a syntax which includes infix operators and operator precedence. Here is the absolute value function in SASL:

$$\text{abs } x = x{<}0 \text{ -> } -x; \ x$$

Function application for noninfix functions like abs is indicated by simple juxtaposition and associates to the left; thus, "f x y" instead of "((f x) y)". The notation e_1 -> e_2 ; e_3 corresponds to our (if e_1 e_2 e_3). *nil* is represented by () (no apostrophe), (cons e_1 e_2) by e_1 : e_2, and car and cdr by hd and tl, respectively. Thus:

$$\text{mapcar f } x = \text{null } x \text{ -> } (); \ f \text{ (hd } x) : \text{mapcar f (tl } x)$$

Furthermore, SASL provides a kind of pattern-matching in function definitions similar to that of ML (but lacking *user-defined* data types), exemplified by this equivalent definition of mapcar:

$$\text{mapcar f } () = ()$$
$$\text{mapcar f (h:t)} = \text{f h : mapcar f t}$$

A SASL programmer would never define mapcar the first way. In fact, the null test is so rarely used that it is not even built into the language. Of course, it is easily defined using pattern-matching:

$$\text{null } () = \text{true}$$
$$\text{null (h:t)} = \text{false}$$

(SASL does not use *nil* to represent falsehood but has distinct Boolean values true and false.)

One operator we will see again is ".."; "m .. n" corresponds to (interval m n).

5.6.2 ZF-EXPRESSIONS

The expression:

$$\{ \text{ m; m <- 1 .. 50; divides m 100 } \}$$

denotes the list of all factors of 100. It should be read: "the list of all m drawn
from the list 1 .. 50 that divide 100."

Such expressions are called ZF-expressions after the mathematicians E. Zer-
melo and A. Fraenkel, who developed a well-known version of the theory of sets.
They often allow for concise and natural expressions for complex lists. As another example,

$$\{ \ \texttt{a, b; a <- 1..n; b <- 1..n; prime (a+b)} \ \}$$

is the list of all pairs of numbers less than or equal to n whose sum is prime.

A more complex example is:

```
gensubsets () = (())
gensubsets (h:t) = (gensubsets t) ++ { h:s; s <- subsets t }
```

++ is what we call **append**. The first case says that the only subset of the empty
set is the empty set.

It will come as no surprise to the reader to discover that the lists denoted
by ZF-expressions may be infinite, and that, in any event, the elements of the
list are not created all at once but only as needed. It may not be obvious
that ZF-expressions are purely syntactic sugar, and can always be translated
to ordinary SASL. Exercise 2 discusses this translation, while introducing more
complex types of ZF-expressions.

5.7 SASL vs. SCHEME

In the interest of purity of presentation, we have exaggerated the differences
between SASL and SCHEME. In fact, much of what is done in this chapter can
be done in SCHEME, for two reasons: (1) Some versions of SCHEME have lazy
lists, and (2) closures can often be used to stand in for thunks. We'll explore
these two points in this section.

Some versions of SCHEME (TI SCHEME [1985], Abelson and Sussman [1985])
provide lazy lists under the name **streams**.[3] Streams are *separate from* and *in
addition to* regular lists. They come with their own operations; in Abelson and
Sussman [1985], these operations are **cons-stream**, **head**, **tail**, **empty-stream?**,
and **the-empty-stream**. Much of the code in this chapter can be written using
these operations. For example, this rewritten version of **find-val** would work
in SCHEME:

```
(set find-val (lambda (pred str failure-value)
    (if (empty-stream? str) failure-value
        (if (pred (head str)) (head str)
            (find-val pred (tail str) failure-value)))))
```

---

[3]However, the term **stream** is also sometimes used in a different sense in both the LISP
and SCHEME communities, referring to a data type associated with I/O operations, so care
should be taken in using it.

Nonetheless, the combination of *eager* evaluation and *lazy* lists is somewhat anomalous. For example, this seemingly innocent variation, intended to avoid the repetition of "(head str)" in the above, goes into an infinite loop if its argument is an infinite stream:

```
(set if2 (lambda (pred x y) (if (pred x) x y)))

(set find-val (lambda (pred str failure-value)
    (if (empty-stream? str) failure-value
        (if2 pred (head str)
            (find-val pred (tail str) failure-value)))))
```

Although the stream operations are used throughout, the function as a whole loops because the eager evaluation mechanism calls for all arguments of if2 — a user-defined function — to be evaluated. Thus, as long as (empty-stream? str) is never true, find-val will be recursively called *ad infinitum*. Such behavior can be confusing. Of course, no such problem arises in SASL.

Another approach to writing SASL-style code in SCHEME is simply to use closures to accomplish what lazy evaluation does automatically: delay evaluation. Here is a simple example, an infinite list of 1's:

```
-> (set ones (cons 1 (lambda () ones)))
(1 <closure>)

-> (car ((cdr ones)))
1
```

This use of closures is quite powerful and requires no special stream primitives to be built into the language. Here is the find-atom example:

```
(set flatten (lambda (l)
    (if (null? l) '()
        (if (atom? l) (list2 l (lambda () '()))
            (append-str (flatten (car l))
                        (lambda () (flatten (cdr l))))))))
(set append-str (lambda (s1 s2)
    (if (null? s1) (s2)
        (list2 (car s1) (lambda () (append-str ((cadr s1)) s2))))))
(set find-str (lambda (pred s)
    (if (null? s) '()
        (if (pred (car s)) (car s)
            (find-str pred ((cadr s)))))))
(set find-atom (lambda (pred l) (find-str pred (flatten l))))
```

The idea is to represent a stream of atoms by a pair (i.e., a two-element list) containing an atom and a function of no arguments, which produces a stream when applied; *nil* is also a stream. `flatten` takes a list as its argument and returns a stream, while `append-str` takes two streams and returns a stream. `find-atom` takes a list and applies `find-str` to the stream containing its atoms.

In the end, `find-atom` does the trick: it finds the first atom in a list that satisfies `pred`, without flattening the entire list. But clearly this code cannot bear comparison with the SASL code on page 164; it is far more subtle and difficult to understand.

5.8 Related Language — λ-Calculus

At this point, the reader may feel SASL is as small a language as it can be, but this is not so. On the contrary, it is fairly bloated with unneeded features. The λ-calculus, a small subset of SASL long studied by logicians (who like their languages small) is, in a direct and practical sense, equally powerful. In this section, we study the λ-calculus *as a programming language*. Its study *as a logic* has produced a theory of great richness and beauty, which is also one of the principal tools in the theoretical study of programming languages, but that theory is beyond the scope of this book. The "Further Reading" section gives some pointers into the area. Section 5.9 contains some desultory discussion of λ-calculus topics pertinent to graph reduction.

For our purposes, the λ-calculus is the subset of SASL defined by the grammar:

```
input        ⟶    expression | ( set variable expression )
expression   ⟶    value
             |     variable
             |     ( expression⁺ )
             |     ( lambda arglist expr )
value        ⟶    'name | EQ
```

`if` has been removed, as well as integer constants and all **value-op**'s. The new **value-op** EQ is a slightly different version of =, as explained shortly. There is another restriction, not stated in the grammar: Top-level functions cannot be defined by *implicit recursion*, that is, by calling themselves. Rather, an expression bound to a global variable via `set` can refer only to *previously defined* variables. Thus, a top-level definition merely gives an abbreviation, which could be removed at the cost of inputting larger expressions. Clearly, this is a severe restriction; that it can be overcome is one of the most remarkable facts about the λ-calculus.

To account for the removed features — conditionals, lists, integers, recursion — we proceed to show how to remove each one in turn, so that by the end of this section our programs will be in pure λ-calculus. The new primitives will be written in capitals (e.g., IF for `if`). All our examples will run in the SASL interpreter.

5.8.1 IF

Not only is `if` gone, but we don't even have a way to express *falsehood*, since there are no lists and therefore no null list. The representations of true and false are tied in with the definition of IF:

```
-> (set TRUE (lambda (t f) t))
-> (set FALSE (lambda (t f) f))
-> (set IF (lambda (c t f) (c t f)))
-> (IF TRUE 'a 'b)
a
```

EQ is an operation that compares symbols or numbers for equality and returns TRUE or FALSE.[4] Thus,

```
-> (set fac (lambda (x) (IF (EQ x 0) 1 (* x (fac (- x 1))))))
-> (fac 4)
24
```

Boolean operations AND, OR, and NOT can be defined exactly as before, for example:

```
-> (set AND (lambda (x y) (IF x y x)))
```

5.8.2 LISTS

The ability to store values is shared by lists and closures. In fact, lists are redundant:

```
-> (set CONS (lambda (a d) (lambda (f) (f a d FALSE))))
-> (set NIL (lambda (f) (f NIL NIL TRUE)))
-> (set CAR (lambda (l) (l (lambda (car cdr null?)  car))))
-> (set CDR (lambda (l) (l (lambda (car cdr null?)  cdr))))
-> (set NULL? (lambda (l) (l (lambda (car cdr null?)  null?))))
```

Thus, (CONS 3 NIL) is the closure:

$$\langle\!\langle \ \text{(lambda (f) (f a d FALSE))}, \\ \{a \mapsto 3,\ d \mapsto \langle\!\langle(\text{lambda (f) (f NIL NIL TRUE)}), \{\}\rangle\!\rangle\} \ \rangle\!\rangle,$$

and (CONS 'abc (CONS 3 NIL)) is the closure:

$$\langle\!\langle \quad \text{(lambda (f) (f a d FALSE))}, \\ \{ a \mapsto abc,\ d \mapsto \langle\!\langle \ \text{(lambda (f) (f a d FALSE))}, \\ \{a \mapsto 3, d \mapsto \langle\!\langle(\text{lambda (f) (f NIL NIL TRUE)}), \{\}\rangle\!\rangle\} \\ \rangle\!\rangle\} \quad \rangle\!\rangle.$$

---

[4] As compared with =, which returns T or (). EQ can be defined in SASL as:

```
(set EQ (lambda (x y) (if (= x y) TRUE FALSE)))
```

We will later see how to define equality on integers separately, using EQ only for symbols.

Thus,

```
-> (CADR (CONS 'abc (CONS 3 NIL)))
3
-> (set 11 (CONS 4 (CONS 5 (CONS 6 NIL))))
-> (set +/ (lambda (1)
        (IF (NULL? 1) 0 (+ (CAR 1) (+/ (CDR 1))))))
-> (+/ 11)
15
```

(CADR is the capitalized version of cadr.)

5.8.3 NATURAL NUMBERS

We now show how to recover the natural numbers (nonnegative integers). (The integers themselves can be represented by signed-magnitude, but this extension is left to the reader.) One way to represent natural numbers would be as lists, any list of length n representing n. All the integer operations could be defined using recursion. However, we will use instead a classical representation known as *Church numerals*, for which the basic arithmetic operations are definable without recursion.

The Church numerals are lambda-expressions of the form (lambda (f) f^n), that is,

$$(\text{lambda (f) (lambda (x)} \underbrace{\text{(f (f} \cdots \text{(f x)} \cdots \text{))))}}_{n \text{ times}}.$$

This expression represents the number n. For future reference, here are a few specific examples:

```
-> (set ZERO (lambda (f) (lambda (x) x)))
-> (set ONE (lambda (f) (lambda (x) (f x))))
-> (set TWO (lambda (f) (lambda (x) (f (f x)))))
```

To enable us to "see" the answers, it is helpful to define a printing function, though this requires us to go briefly outside the λ-calculus (as in defining EQ; here, +1 is defined using a SASL value-op):

```
-> (set print-int (lambda (n) ((n +1) 0)))
-> (print-int TWO)
2
```

Since n is represented by (lambda (f) f^n), ((n +1) 0) = (+1^n 0) = $\underbrace{(\text{+1 (+1} \cdots \text{(+1}}_{n \text{ times}}$ 0) $\cdots$)), which explains how print-int works.

A simple function to define is +ONE. If n is represented by `(lambda (f) `f^n`)` and $n+1$ by `(lambda (f) `f^{n+1}`)`, +ONE is:

```
-> (set +ONE (lambda (n) (lambda (g) (compose g (n g)))))
```

Then `(+ONE `n`)` = `(lambda (g) (compose g (`n` g)))` = `(lambda (g) (com-`
`pose g `g^n`))` = `(lambda (g) `g^{n+1}`)`.

Of course, +ONE is just a particular case of addition:

```
-> (set PLUS (lambda (m n) (lambda (g) (compose (m g) (n g)))))
```

Since `(`m` g)` = g^m and `(`n` g)` = g^n, their composition is g^{m+n}.

```
-> (set THREE (PLUS ONE TWO))
-> (print-int THREE)
3
```

Multiplication has an even briefer definition:

```
-> (set MULT (lambda (m n) (compose m n)))
```

`((compose `m` $n$`) g)` = `(`$n$` (`$m$` g))` = $(g^m)^n$ = g^{mn}.

```
-> (set SIX (MULT THREE TWO))
-> (print-int SIX)
6
```

Subtraction is very much trickier to define. Instead, we'll define the predecessor function, after which subtraction will be easy. -ONE itself is far from simple. The idea is this: To find $n-1$, initialize a to ZERO, then repeat the following two statements n times:

$$m \;:=\; a$$
$$a \;:=\; (\texttt{+ONE}\; a)$$

m is now equal to $n-1$. Of course, we have no assignment statement, so instead define:

```
-> (set STEP (lambda (m-a) (LIST2 (CADR m-a) (+ONE (CADR m-a))))),
```

where LIST2 is the capitalized version of list2. If m-a is the list containing m and a, (STEP m-a) contains a and (+ONE a), giving the effect of the two assignment statements. The next problem is to execute STEP n times; how can this be done? Very easily: apply n. Thus:

```
-> (set -ONE (lambda (n) (CAR ((n STEP) (LIST2 ZERO ZERO)))))
```

For example, if n=THREE, this gives (using quoted list notation for illustrative purposes):

```
    (CAR (STEP (STEP (STEP '(ZERO ZERO)))))
  = (CAR (STEP (STEP '(ZERO ONE))))
  = (CAR (STEP '(ONE TWO)))
  = (CAR '(TWO THREE))
  = TWO
```

As advertised, subtraction is now very easy:

```
-> (set SUB (lambda (m n) ((n -ONE) m)))
-> (set FOUR (SUB SIX TWO))
-> (print-int FOUR)
4
```

$((n$ -ONE) $m)$ is, of course, just $(\text{-ONE}^n\ m)$. Note that (-ONE ZERO) is ZERO, so that (SUB m n) is ZERO whenever $n \geq m$. This allows the numeric comparison functions to be defined, assuming the function =ZERO? is available:

```
-> (set GT (lambda (m n) (NOT (=ZERO? (SUB m n)))))
-> (set GE (lambda (m n) (=ZERO? (SUB n m))))
-> (set EQUAL (lambda (m n)
         (AND (=ZERO? (SUB m n)) (=ZERO? (SUB n m)))))
```

=ZERO? is the most difficult function we'll define. Our definition is based on this idea: Define F to be (lambda (x) (lambda (y) y)). Then $(n\ F)$ is equal to id (that is, ONE) if $n = 0$, and equal to (lambda (x) id) (that is, ZERO) otherwise (exercise for the reader). But observe:

- (lambda (y) (ONE (lambda (x) y))) = (lambda (y) (lambda (x) y))
- (lambda (y) (ZERO (lambda (x) y))) = (lambda (y) (lambda (x) x)

Thus, inserting ONE or ZERO into the expression (lambda (y) (● (lambda (x) y))) leads to results that are very close to TRUE and FALSE, respectively; in fact, they are "curried" versions of them; that is, they are obtained by applying curry to each. It is easy to undo the effect of curry, so we arrive at last at:

```
-> (set uncurry (lambda (f) (lambda (x y) ((f x) y))))
-> (set F (curry FALSE))
-> (set =ZERO? (lambda (n)
       (uncurry (lambda (y) ((n F) (lambda (x) y))))))
-> (IF (=ZERO? ZERO) 'yes 'no)
yes

-> (IF (=ZERO? FOUR) 'yes 'no)
no
```

With that, we are in a position to define numeric functions almost entirely in λ-calculus:

```
-> (set fac (lambda (n)
   (IF (EQUAL n ZERO) ONE (MULT n (fac (SUB n ONE)))))))
-> (print-int (fac FOUR))
24
```

This definition is exactly as in SASL, except for the names of the primitive functions. Aside from the use of `print-int`, which cannot be eliminated, it departs from λ-calculus in just one way: It uses implicit recursion. This we now set out to eliminate.

5.8.4 RECURSIVE DEFINITIONS

One way to eliminate the recursion in the definition of FAC is to use the trick we used in defining -ONE:

```
-> (set FAC-STEP (lambda (x-y)
   (LIST2 (-ONE (CAR x-y)) (MULT (CAR x-y) (CADR x-y)))))
-> (set FAC (lambda (n) (CADR ((n FAC-STEP) (LIST2 n ONE)))))
-> (print-int (FAC FOUR))
24
```

However, this works only when the number of iterations can be bounded beforehand. This type of recursion accounts for very little of what has been done in this chapter.

Moreover, in saying that λ-calculus is equipollent with SASL, we did not mean to refer to power in some abstract sense. We meant that one could write essentially the same programs in both. Aside from local changes — specifically, name changes — the previous λ-calculus definition of `fac` is identical to the SASL definition. Our goal would not be accomplished if SASL programs could be translated to λ-calculus only with major structural changes. For this reason, we should be satisfied only when the effect of recursion can be obtained in a very direct way.

Consider this simple, implicitly recursive definition:

```
(set ones (CONS ONE ones)).
```

A good way to think of the recursion is that it tells us that the occurrence of `ones` in the definition (inside the `CONS`) can be replaced by the definition itself. In other words, this definition of `ones` is exactly the same as:

```
(set ones (CONS ONE (CONS ONE ones))),
```

which, in turn, is equivalent to

```
(set ones (CONS ONE (CONS ONE (CONS ONE ones)))).
```

Furthermore, this "macro expansion" view of ones is a complete explanation of its behavior. All we can do with ones, since it is a list, is to ask for its CAR or CDR. Consider the expression

$$(\text{CAR } \underbrace{(\text{CDR } (\text{CDR } (\cdots (\text{CDR }}_{i \text{ times}} \text{ones})\cdots))))$$

Our view of recursion tells us this is ONE, because it tells us that ones is equivalent to:

$$\underbrace{(\text{CONS ONE } (\text{CONS ONE } (\cdots (\text{CONS ONE }}_{i \text{ times}} (\text{CONS ONE ones}))\cdots))),$$

from which the answer follows.

The same view works for recursively defined functions:

```
-> (set fac (lambda (n)
     (IF (EQUAL n ZERO) ONE (MULT n (fac (SUB n ONE))))))
```

This definition is equivalent to:

```
-> (set fac (lambda (n)
     (IF (EQUAL n ZERO) ONE
        (MULT n
           ((lambda (n) (IF (EQUAL n ZERO) ONE
                            (MULT n (fac (SUB n ONE)))))
            (SUB n ONE))))))
```

which was obtained by replacing the occurrence of fac in the definition of fac by that definition. To make this clearer, apply the inner lambda to its argument symbolically, giving:

```
-> (set fac (lambda (n)
     (IF (EQUAL n ZERO) ONE
        (MULT n
           (IF (EQUAL (SUB n ONE) ZERO) ONE
              (MULT (SUB n ONE) (fac (SUB (SUB n ONE) ONE))))))))
```

which can be simplified to:

```
-> (set fac (lambda (n)
     (IF (EQUAL n ZERO) ONE
        (IF (EQUAL n ONE) ONE
           (MULT n (MULT (SUB n ONE) (fac (SUB n TWO))))))))
```

Substituting for `fac` one more time and simplifying, we would find at the next step:

```
-> (set fac (lambda (n)
     (IF (EQUAL n ZERO) ONE
        (IF (EQUAL n ONE) ONE
           (IF (EQUAL n TWO) TWO
              (MULT n
                 (MULT (SUB n ONE) (MULT (SUB n TWO)
                                   (fac (SUB n THREE))))))))))))
```

By substituting, the definition is turning into a sort of table, giving more and more of the answers without recursion. Thus the substitution approach to recursion is again sufficient to answer any question about the value of (`fac` n) for any n.

If the reader is convinced that the substitution approach is a reasonable way to interpret recursion, we can proceed. Again consider `ones`. We need to find an expression e such that e is equivalent to (`CONS ONE e`); then this e will be equivalent to (`CONS ONE (CONS ONE e)`), and so on. Another way of stating this requirement on e is to say that e is equivalent to ((`lambda (ones) (CONS ONE ones)`) e). In fact, for any τ, the following expression has the property that e is equivalent to (τ e):

$$e = ((\texttt{lambda (x) } (\tau \ (\texttt{x x}))) \ (\texttt{lambda (x) } (\tau \ (\texttt{x x})))).$$

By applying the `lambda` expression to its argument,[5] we get:

$$e = (\tau \ ((\texttt{lambda (x) } (\tau \ (\texttt{x x}))) \ (\texttt{lambda (x) } (\tau \ (\texttt{x x}))))) = (\tau \ e).$$

Thus, we can define:

```
-> (set W (lambda (F) (lambda (f) (F (f f)))))
-> (set Y (lambda (F) ((W F) (W F))))
```

The effect of implicit recursion in any definition:

```
        (set f e) ; f occurs in e
```

can be obtained by:

```
        (set f (Y (lambda (f) e))).
```

---

[5] Formally, this is *β-reduction*, defined in Section 5.9.

Note that neither W nor Y nor this definition of f is implicitly recursive. It is truly amazing that all of this works, but it does:

```
-> (set ONES (Y (lambda (ones) (CONS ONE ones))))
-> (print-int (CAR (CDR (CDR ONES))))
1

-> (set FAC (Y (lambda (fac)
   (lambda (n)
       (IF (EQUAL n ZERO) ONE (MULT n (fac (SUB n ONE)))))))))
-> (print-int (FAC FOUR))
24
```

The only significant remaining differences between λ-calculus and SASL are in those features related to I/O, namely integer and list constants, and printing of integers and lists. These could not be restored without having the I/O routines know the internal representation of numbers and lists. But those routines could easily be rewritten to incorporate that knowledge. So there remains just one reason for SASL to provide separate representations of integers and lists, to define if as a built-in operation, and to allow implicit recursion: efficiency.

5.9   Graph Reduction

In 1979, David Turner proposed a method of evaluating SASL programs. The roots of this method go back to the λ-calculus and, more specifically, to its variant, the theory of combinators (a programming language in some ways even simpler than λ-calculus). In this section, a formal semantics is given to SASL, which is then used to explain the translation from SASL to the language of combinators, called SKI; finally, we show how SKI is implemented by graph reduction.

To simplifiy the notation in this chapter — and to be consistent both with Turner [1979a] and with the classical treatment of the λ-calculus — SASL is restricted to one-argument functions. Note that this is not a real restriction of programming power. Any expression (lambda (x y) e) can be replaced by:

$$(lambda \ (x) \ (lambda \ (y) \ e)),$$

and any expression of the form (e$_0$ e$_1$ e$_2$) by ((e$_0$ e$_1$) e$_2$). (This transformation is called *currying*; see page 100.)

A further simplification is that we restrict primitive values to be integers — no lists. With that, and treating if as a value-op (see Exercise 5), we arrive at this syntax for simplified SASL expressions:

expression	$\longrightarrow$	value
	|	variable
	|	(expression expression)

value $\longrightarrow$ integer | (lambda (variable) expression) | value-op
value-op $\longrightarrow$ + | - | $\cdots$ | if

5.9.1 A FORMAL SEMANTICS FOR SASL

The spareness of SASL — and, in particular, its freedom from side-effects — allows us to present its semantics in a very simple, yet formal, way. This definition, developed for the λ-calculus, is based on a process of rewriting expressions to equivalent ones. Rules will be given which can be used to find the value of an expression by repeatedly rewriting it to equivalent expressions, until no more rewritings are applicable.

The most basic rule is the one telling us how to apply a lambda expression to its argument:

Definition 5.1 (β-reduction) The expression $e_1 = ((\text{lambda (x) e) e}')$ can be rewritten to $e_2 = e|_x^{e'}$, which is the result of substituting e' for free occurrences of x in e (defined precisely below). Say e_1 β-reduces to e_2, and write $e_1 \xrightarrow{\beta} e_2$.

A computation consists mainly of a sequence of such β-reductions. For example,

$$(((\text{lambda } (\underline{x}) \ (\text{lambda } (y) \ (x \ y))) \ \underline{(\text{lambda } (z) \ z)}) \ 2)$$
$$\xrightarrow{\beta} ((\text{lambda } (\underline{y}) \ ((\text{lambda } (z) \ z) \ y)) \ \underline{2})$$
$$\xrightarrow{\beta} ((\text{lambda } (\underline{z}) \ z) \ \underline{2})$$
$$\xrightarrow{\beta} 2$$

We have underlined in each expression the bound variable (corresponding to "x" in the definition) and the argument (e'). Note that, at the second step, there was a choice between two "redexes" to β-reduce, i.e., two subexpressions which could have been β-reduced. That is, the computation might have been:

$$((\text{lambda } (y) \ ((\text{lambda } (\underline{z}) \ z) \ \underline{y})) \ 2)$$
$$\xrightarrow{\beta} ((\text{lambda } (\underline{y}) \ y) \ \underline{2})$$
$$\xrightarrow{\beta} 2$$

The choice of redexes to reduce may be significant in some circumstances (unlike this example); more will be said about it later. For now, we give the promised definition of the substitution operation $e|_x^{e'}$, following two preliminary definitions.

For technical reasons, the variables bound in lambda expressions must be assumed to be distinct from value-op's and from user-defined names (i.e., those defined at the top level using set).

Definition 5.2 The *free variables* of e, FV(e), are those variables x which do not occur within a subexpression of the form (lambda (x) e′). More precisely, the set FV(e) is defined recursively by:

$\text{FV}(n) = \emptyset$, n an integer constant

$\text{FV}(f) = \emptyset$, f a value-op or user-defined name

$\text{FV}(x) = \{x\}$, x a variable

$\text{FV}((e_1 \ e_2)) = \text{FV}(e_1) \cup \text{FV}(e_2)$

$\text{FV}((\texttt{lambda (x) e})) = \text{FV}(e) - \{x\}$

Definition 5.3 An expression e is *closed* if $\text{FV}(e) = \emptyset$.

For example, if e = (lambda (x) (y (lambda (y) (y (+ x 1))))), FV(e) = $\{y\}$.

Definition 5.4 $e|_x^{e'}$, the *substitution* of e′ for free occurrences of x in e, *where e′ is closed*, is defined recursively as follows:

- $n|_x^{e'} = n$

- $f|_x^{e'} = f$

- $y|_x^{e'} = \begin{cases} e' & \text{if } y = x \\ y & \text{otherwise} \end{cases}$

- $(e_1 \ e_1)|_x^{e'} = (e_1|_x^{e'} \ e_2|_x^{e'})$

- $(\texttt{lambda (y) e})|_x^{e'} = \begin{cases} (\texttt{lambda (y) e}) & \text{if } y = x \\ (\texttt{lambda (y) } e|_x^{e'}) & \text{otherwise} \end{cases}$

The definition of $e|_x^{e'}$ when e′ is not closed is a good deal more subtle and is not needed for the purposes of this chapter. For the definition in the general case, see any of the references named at the end of the chapter.

β-reduction tells us how to handle applications of lambda expressions. Applications of value-op's and references to user-defined names must still be handled. As a simplification, we will not consider lists; so all value-op's are numerical operations and user-defined names are bound to either numbers or lambda expressions.

Definition 5.5 (δ-*reduction*) The expression $e_1 = (f \ n_1 \ n_2)$ can be rewritten to $e_2 = n_1 \ \bar{f} \ n_2$ if f is a value-op corresponding to function $\bar{f}$, and n_1 and n_2 are integers. Say e_1 δ-*reduces* to e_2, and write $e_1 \xrightarrow{\delta} e_2$.

For example, (* 4 5) $\xrightarrow{\delta}$ 20.

Definition 5.6 (μ-*reduction*) If user-defined name f has been set to expression e via set, then expression f can be rewritten to e. Write f $\overset{\mu}{\longrightarrow}$ e.

Intuitively, a computation consists of a sequence of rewritings, via either $\overset{\beta}{\longrightarrow}$, $\overset{\mu}{\longrightarrow}$, or $\overset{\delta}{\longrightarrow}$, at subexpressions of the object expression:

$$((\text{lambda } (y) \ (y \ 3)) \ \text{+1})$$
$$\overset{\beta}{\longrightarrow} \ (\text{+1 } 3)$$
$$\overset{\mu}{\longrightarrow} \ ((\text{lambda } (x) \ (+ \ x \ 1)) \ 3)$$
$$\overset{\beta}{\longrightarrow} \ (+ \ 3 \ 1)$$
$$\overset{\delta}{\longrightarrow} \ 4$$

Finally, a decision must be made on the order in which subexpressions are chosen for reduction. To show what can happen, suppose we have defined:

$$(\text{set self-apply (lambda } (x) \ (x \ x)))$$

and consider the expression:

$$((\text{lambda } (y) \ 0) \ (\text{self-apply self-apply})).$$

If we were silly enough to choose our redex from the argument position, there would be trouble:

$$((\text{lambda } (y) \ 0) \ (\text{self-apply self-apply}))$$
$$\overset{\mu}{\longrightarrow} \ ((\text{lambda } (y) \ 0) \ ((\text{lambda } (x) \ (x \ x)) \ \text{self-apply}))$$
$$\overset{\beta}{\longrightarrow} \ ((\text{lambda } (y) \ 0) \ (\text{self-apply self-apply}))$$
$$\overset{\mu}{\longrightarrow} \ \dots \ ad \ infinitum.$$

On the other hand, being smarter:

$$((\text{lambda } (y) \ 0) \ (\text{self-apply self-apply}))$$
$$\overset{\beta}{\longrightarrow} \ 0$$

Getting into trouble by evaluating arguments first is something we are quite familiar with: It is eager evaluation. In this context, the solution is always to pick *outermost* redexes. That is, never reduce in a subexpression if it is possible to reduce in a containing expression. Furthermore, since the operator of an application is always evaluated before the arguments, a stipulation should be added that *leftmost* reducible arguments should be reduced first. Finally, there is never a need to reduce *within* a lambda expression. Thus, we arrive at our operational semantics:

Definition 5.7 A *computation* is a sequence of β-, δ-, and μ-reductions in which all reductions are applied to the leftmost-outermost redex not contained within a lambda expression, ending either with an integer, a value-op, or a lambda expression.

5.9.2   SKI

The work of the previous section was done to help explain the translation of SASL to a new language called SKI, a language based upon the theory of combinators. The syntax of SKI is (compare to SASL syntax on page 186):

input	$\longrightarrow$	expression | (set variable expression)
expression	$\longrightarrow$	value
	|	variable
	|	(expression expression)
value	$\longrightarrow$	integer | value-op
value-op	$\longrightarrow$	+ | - | $\cdots$ | if | S | K | I

The essential differences from SASL are: (1) there are no `lambda` expressions (any variable occurring in an expression is a user-defined name); and (2) there are new value-op's called S, K, and I.

The operational semantics of this language is not unlike that given in the previous section, in that it consists of repeated applications of three kinds of rewriting rules. One kind is δ-reduction, another is μ-reduction, and the third is a new one called κ-reduction. What makes SKI interesting is that κ-reduction is much simpler than β-reduction; in particular, β-reduction is defined recursively (in that $e|_x^{e'}$ is), while κ-reduction is not.

Definition 5.8 κ-*reduction*, written $\overset{\kappa}{\longrightarrow}$, is defined by three rules:

- (I e) $\overset{\kappa}{\longrightarrow}$ e

- ((K e_1) e_2) $\overset{\kappa}{\longrightarrow}$ e_1

- (((S e_1) e_2) e_3) $\overset{\kappa}{\longrightarrow}$ ((e_1 e_3)(e_2 e_3))

Definition 5.9 A *computation* in SKI is a sequence of κ-, δ-, and μ-reductions, reductions always being performed at the leftmost-outermost redex, terminating with either an integer, a value-op, or a functional expression. A *functional expression* is one of the form (($\cdots$ ((f e_1) e_2) $\cdots$) e_n), where f is either S, K, I, or a value-op, but in which n is less than the number of arguments required by f; e.g., f is S and $n < 3$, or f is + and $n < 2$. It is to be understood that, just as reductions in SASL are not done inside `lambda` expressions, so in SKI they are not done inside functional expressions.

SKI could be considered as simply a subset of SASL, in which only the following `lambda` expressions can be written:

- (lambda (x) x)

- (lambda (x) (lambda (y) x))

- (lambda (x) (lambda (y) (lambda (z) ((x z) (y z)))))

It is a remarkable result that the language SKI is of precisely equivalent power to SASL. The immediate importance of that fact lies in the simplicity of the operational semantics of SKI. The proof of this equivalence, which is presented in this subsection, consists of a translation from SASL to SKI. Turner's method of evaluating SASL expressions consists of performing this translation and then using the method of *graph reduction*, covered in the next subsection, to evaluate SKI programs.

To get us going, here is an example of a SKI computation. The function double would be written in SASL as:

$$\text{(set double (lambda (x) ((* x) 2))).}$$

In SKI, it is:[6]

$$\text{(set double ((S ((S (K *)) I)) (K 2)))}$$

The SKI computation of (double 5) is as follows (the arguments for each application of κ-reduction are underlined):

$$
\begin{aligned}
&\text{(double 5)}\\
&\xrightarrow{\mu} \text{(((S \underline{((S (K *)) I))} \underline{(K 2)}) \underline{5})}\\
&\xrightarrow{\kappa} \text{((((S \underline{(K *)}) \underline{I}) \underline{5}) ((K 2) 5))}\\
&\xrightarrow{\kappa} \text{((((K \underline{*}) \underline{5}) (I 5)) ((K 2) 5))}\\
&\xrightarrow{\kappa} \text{((* (I \underline{5})) ((K 2) 5))}\\
&\xrightarrow{\kappa} \text{((* 5) ((K \underline{2}) \underline{5}))}\\
&\xrightarrow{\kappa} \text{((* 5) 2)}\\
&\xrightarrow{\delta} 10
\end{aligned}
$$

Since S, K, and I correspond to specific lambda expressions, obviously SASL is as powerful as SKI.

For the other direction, we need to translate an arbitrary lambda expression, say (lambda (x) e), from SASL into SKI. Assume that e contains no lambda expressions; this assumption entails no loss of generality, because the translation can first be applied to any inner lambda expressions.

Call the translation of (lambda (x) e) the *abstraction of* x *from* e, and denote it [x]e. The essential point is that for any e', ([x]e e') must reduce, by $\xrightarrow{\kappa}$, to the same value that ((lambda (x) e) e') reduces to by $\xrightarrow{\beta}$. Thus, the translation will be correct so long as it satisfies:

$$\text{([x]e e')} \xrightarrow{\kappa}{}^{*} \text{e}|_x^{e'} ,$$

where $\xrightarrow{\kappa}{}^{*}$ denotes any number of rewritings via $\xrightarrow{\kappa}$. Given this requirement,

---

[6]The reader may get the impression that SKI is not very user-friendly. This impression is entirely accurate. It should be regarded as a kind of machine language for functional programming.

we go back to the definition of $e|_x^{e'}$ and consider the cases:

- $[x]n = (K\ n)$, for constant n, by the following reasoning:

  We require $([x]n\ e') \xrightarrow{\kappa}^* n|_x^{e'} = n$; but $((K\ n)\ e') \xrightarrow{\kappa} n$ by the definition of $\xrightarrow{\kappa}$.

- $[x]y = (K\ y)$ if y is a value-op, a user-defined name, or a variable other than x, by identical reasoning.

- $[x]x = I$.

  We require $([x]x\ e') \xrightarrow{\kappa}^* x|_x^{e'} = e'$; but $(I\ e') \xrightarrow{\kappa} e'$ by the definition of $\xrightarrow{\kappa}$.

- $[x](e_1\ e_2) = ((S\ [x]e_1)\ [x]e_2)$.

  We require $([x](e_1\ e_2)\ e') \xrightarrow{\kappa}^* (e_1\ e_2)|_x^{e'} = (e_1|_x^{e'}\ e_2|_x^{e'})$. But $(((S\ [x]e_1)\ [x]e_2)\ e') \xrightarrow{\kappa} (([x]e_1\ e')\ ([x]e_2\ e'))$. By induction, we may assume that $([x]e_1\ e') \xrightarrow{\kappa}^* e_1|_x^{e'}$ and $([x]e_2\ e') \xrightarrow{\kappa}^* e_2|_x^{e'}$, which gives the conclusion.

Here is the translation of `double` to SKI:

$$[x]((*\ x)\ 2)$$
$$= ((S\ [x](*\ x))\ [x]2)$$
$$= ((S\ ((S\ [x]*)\ [x]x))\ [x]2)$$
$$= ((S\ ((S\ (K\ *))\ I))\ (K\ 2))$$

5.9.3   IMPLEMENTING SKI

Turner's method of evaluating SASL programs is to first curry, then translate to SKI. His implementation of SKI, which is the topic of this subsection, is based upon a representation of SKI expressions as graphs, which are continually transformed according to $\xrightarrow{\kappa}$, $\xrightarrow{\mu}$, and $\xrightarrow{\delta}$, each node being *replaced in memory* by its transformed version. We need to first describe this internal graph representation and then discuss the overall evaluation process, including the choice of redexes and the termination conditions.

The graph structure precisely mirrors the structure of SKI expressions. It is a directed acyclic graph,[7] with two kinds of nodes:

- Atomic nodes, containing constants, user-defined names, and value-op's, including the symbols S, K, and I. These nodes have no children.

---

[7] Actually, recursion can be implemented by introducing cycles into the graph; in this presentation, the only recursion is that obtained by functions referring to user-defined names, i.e., implicit recursion.

- Application nodes, having two children, the operator and the argument.

The only difficulty in understanding this representation is that the graphs tend to look upside-down to the human reader. For example, the expression

$$((S ((S (K *)) I)) (K 2))$$

is represented as:

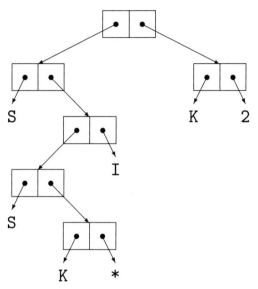

(Double boxes represent application nodes, and unboxed names and numbers represent atomic nodes.)

κ-reduction, then, corresponds to graph transformation. Here are the κ-reduction rules in graph form:

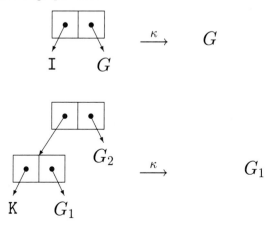

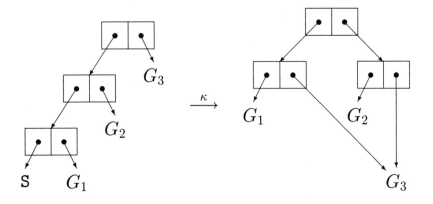

Note that S introduces sharing in the graph, so that these graphs are not all trees.

δ-reduction occurs when a value-op is found with integer arguments; it is transformed to an atomic node with the appropriate value:

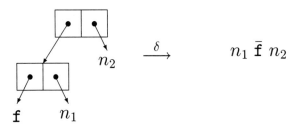

($\bar{f}$ is the function named by value-op f.)

Finally, an application of a user-defined function f is transformed by replacing the atomic node containing the name f by the function's body, which has previously been translated to SKI form as graph G_f and stored in a table:

$$ f \quad \stackrel{\mu}{\longrightarrow} \quad G_f $$

Figure 5.6 gives the graph-reduction procedure itself, called *reduce*, in PASCAL-like pseudo-code. This corresponds to our *eval*; it is called from the read-eval-print loop, after the input expression has been transformed to SKI and then represented in graph form. It should be called with the root of the graph as its argument.

The real work is done in the *perform* procedures. We give pseudo-code for *performS* and *performValueOp* (Figure 5.7), and leave the others as exercises.

There is one fact about graph reduction that can be gleaned from the PASCAL code but that did not show up in the graphs. It is that when a graph is

---

procedure *reduce* (*n* : *NODE*);

var
      done: *Boolean*;
      nsave: *NODE*;
      args: stack of *NODE*;

begin
      done := *false*;
      nsave := *n*;
      while not *done* **do begin**
          n := *nsave*;
          args := empty stack;
          while (*n* an application node) **do begin**
              push (*n*, *args*);
              n := left child of *n*
              end;
          (* *n* is an atomic node *)
          if (*n* an integer node)
          then *done* := *true*
          else if (*n* a user-defined name)
              then replace *n* by its definition
              else (* *n* is a value-op, including **if**, S, K, or I *)
                  if (size of *args* < number of arguments required by *n*)
                  then *done* := *true*
                  else begin
                     n1 := top of *args*; *n2* := second from top of *args*; etc.
                     case (type of *n*) **of**
                        if: *performIF* (*n1*, *n2*, *n3*);
                        value-op other than **if**: *performValueOp*(*n*, *n1*, *n2*);
                        S: *performS*(*n1*, *n2*, *n3*);
                        K: *performK*(*n1*, *n2*);
                        I: *performI*(*n1*)
                    end (* **case** *)
                end
      end (* **while** *)
end; (* *reduce* *)

Figure 5.6: Procedure *reduce*

---

procedure *performS* (*n1, n2, n3* : *NODE*);
begin
      left child of *n3* :=
          mkAppNode(right child of *n1*, right child of *n3*);
      right child of *n3* :=
          mkAppNode(right child of *n2*, right child of *n3*)
end;

procedure *performValueOp*(*n, n1, n2* : *NODE*);
begin
      reduce(right child of *n1*); *i1* := value of right child of *n1*;
      reduce(right child of *n2*); *i2* := value of right child of *n2*;
      i := *applyValueOp*(*n, i1, i2*);
      replace *n2* by *i*
end;

Figure 5.7: Procedures *performS* and *performValueOp*

changed, its top node is *replaced in memory* by its κ-reduced form. This is precisely analogous to the replacement of thunks in our SASL implementation. This is an extremely important aspect of the graph reduction approach.

5.9.4 ALTERNATIVE COMBINATOR TRANSLATIONS

As the `double` example shows, the translation of a SASL function to SKI can — and usually does — entail an enormous growth in its size. One of Turner's contributions was to show that by introducing a few additional combinators, this expansion could be substantially nullified. His approach was to start from the SKI translation given above and then *optimize* the SKI expression by introducing new combinators where certain patterns occurred.

For example, Turner's combinators B and C are defined by these rules:

- $(((B\ e_1)\ e_2)\ e_3) \xrightarrow{\kappa} (e_1\ (e_2\ e_3))$

- $(((C\ e_1)\ e_2)\ e_3) \xrightarrow{\kappa} ((e_1\ e_3)\ e_2)$

Turner optimizes SKI expressions by replacing expressions of the form (S (K e_1)) by (B e_1), and expressions of the form ((S e_1) (K e_2)) by ((C e_1) e_2). To see why these expressions are equivalent, just consider the operational semantics of SKI:

$$(((S\ (K\ e_1))\ e_2)\ e_3)$$
$$\xrightarrow{\kappa} ((K\ e_1)\ e_3)(e_2\ e_3))$$
$$\xrightarrow{\kappa} (e_1\ (e_2\ e_3))$$

This shows that the introduction of B is correct; the correctness of the C optimization is equally easy.

Using these optimizations, the expression for `double` can be shortened to:

$$((S \ ((S \ (K \ *)) \ I)) \ (K \ 2))$$
$$\equiv ((S \ ((B \ *) \ I)) \ (K \ 2))$$
$$\equiv ((C \ ((B \ *) \ I)) \ 2)$$

Turner lists several such optimizations in [1979a,1979b].

5.9.5 POSTSCRIPT

Graph reduction is the subject of continuing research, of which we have presented only the first step (c. 1979). There is considerable controversy surrounding the implementation of lazy evaluation languages like SASL, over whether graph reduction is the way to go and, if so, whether SKI is the right form of graph reduction. Furthermore, one of the main arguments in favor of graph reduction is that it allows for parallel implementation (since different parts of a graph can be evaluated separately); the study of parallel evaluation being in its infancy, this argument may not be settled for some time.

What can be said without fear of contradiction is that the SKI approach is marvelous in its elegance and simplicity, and it is well worth studying for that reason alone.

5.10 Summary

By generalizing the evaluation mechanism of SCHEME to lazy evaluation and removing side-effects, we arrive at SASL. SASL supports functional-style programming in ways that SCHEME cannot, by permitting the manipulation of very long, and even infinite, lists, without unacceptable inefficiencies.

5.10.1 GLOSSARY

eager evaluation. An evaluation regime in which the arguments to functions are evaluated before the function begins execution. Eager evaluation is the rule in programming languages and is used in PASCAL as well as all the languages previously covered in this book. It can be argued on both practical and mathematical grounds that a *pure* eager evaluation strategy is inadmissible: There must always be *at least one function* whose arguments are not evaluated (a *nonstrict* function). In LISP and SCHEME, such functions were called *special forms*; the most important special form is `if`. **Applicative-order evaluation** is a synonym for eager evaluation.

graph reduction. A method of evaluating SASL by translating expressions to combinator form, then representing the combinator form by a graph, and repeatedly performing in-place transformations of the graph. **Combinator reduction** is a synonym. By contrast, the evaluation mechanism used in our interpreter is called the "SECD machine" approach, after Landin [1964].

lazy evaluation. An evaluation regime in which the arguments to functions are not evaluated until the corresponding formal parameters are actually used. **Delayed evaluation**, **normal-order evaluation**, and **call-by-need** are synonyms.

lazy list. An infinite list. Lazy lists are made possible by having `cons` be nonstrict.

strict function. A function which must evaluate all its arguments. An example of a function which is naturally strict is `+`. A function which is nonstrict is `if`. The difference between lazy evaluation and eager evaluation is that in eager evaluation certain functions — namely, `cons` and all user-defined functions — are *artificially* turned into strict functions.

thunk. A closure-like object which contains all the information necessary to evaluate an actual parameter or list component (namely, the expression and the environment) if and when such evaluation is indicated. The differences between a thunk and a closure are (1) a closure always represents a function, whereas a thunk can represent any type of value; and (2) a closure is evaluated when it is applied, whereas a thunk is evaluated when the formal parameter with which it is associated is referenced, or when the list position it occupies is accessed. **Suspension** is a synonym.

5.10.2   *FURTHER READING*

The literature on lazy evaluation is scattered, with no book-length treatment for the noninitiate. The discussion of streams in Abelson and Sussman [1985, Chapter 3] is excellent, and the articles by Hughes [1984] and Turner [1985a] are also recommended. Turner [1983] is the most recent manual for SASL. Kahn and MacQueen [1977] is a classic paper in which streams are used as a model for parallel processing.

It should be mentioned that SASL itself is now obsolete, having been superseded by the language MIRANDA, which can be described as SASL with type inference and pattern-matching (as in ML). Turner [1985b,1985c] are introductory papers on MIRANDA.

For further reading on graph reduction, we refer the reader to Turner [1979a], and especially to the recent book by Peyton Jones [1987], which will lead the interested reader to a wealth of research in this area.

λ-calculus is a language of enormous importance in the theoretical study of programming languages, which has for years been studied by mathematical logicians. Church [1941] is an accessible treatment from this school; Barendregt

[1981] is the standard reference but is highly mathematical. λ-calculus has been revitalized in recent years by its applications in computer science, particularly in the formal definition of programming languages (what is known as *denotational semantics*). Gordon [1979] is a pragmatic treatment; Stoy [1977] and Schmidt [1986] cover the theory as well as the applications. Discussions that are less formal and emphasize λ-calculus as a programming language can be found in Burge [1975], Peyton Jones [1987], and Wegner [1968].

Vector addition systems were introduced in Karp and Miller [1969]. Our definition is simpler than the one given there in our requirement that the points in $\mathcal{P}$ have nonnegative coordinates. This makes it simple for us to decide when (x_0, y_0) is *not* reachable. If $\mathcal{P}$ is permitted to include points with negative coordinates, our method of finding paths still works when a path exists, but we can't know when to stop looking for a path. Furthermore, if we restore the restriction that the path remain entirely within the first quadrant, nobody knows if this problem is *decidable*, that is, if any computer program can be written which infallibly determines when (x_0, y_0) is *not* reachable.

5.11 Exercises

5.11.1 LEARNING ABOUT THE LANGUAGE

1. Construct the following lists by the method of recursion schemes (page 165).

   (a) The list **evens** containing all even numbers.

   (b) The list **xlist** from Section 5.2.3.

   (c) The list of all lists of binomial coefficients (see page 72).

   (d) The list of all Fibonacci numbers, that is, the list $0, 1, 1, 2, 3, 5, 8, \ldots$.
   Give the general solution for recursion schemes of the form:

   $$
   \begin{aligned}
   x_0 &= \text{some initial value} \\
   x_1 &= \text{some initial value} \\
   x_{i+2} &= f(x_{i+1}, x_i).
   \end{aligned}
   $$

2. These questions relate to the implementation of ZF-expressions. You are to code the functions described in each part. Note first that the function **filter** (defined on page 165) implements the simplest kind of ZF-expression; namely, (**filter pred lis**) is equivalent to the ZF-expression:

   ```
   { a; a <- lis; pred a }.
   ```

   (a) (**filter-fun f pred lis**) corresponds to the ZF-expression

   ```
   { f a; a <- lis; pred a }
   ```

   (b) (**mkfinitepairs l1 l2**) forms all pairs of elements from l1 and l2, assuming 11 and 12 are finite. It implements the ZF-expression

$$\{ \ a, \ b; \ a <- \ 11; \ b <- \ 12 \ \}$$

for finite 11, 12.

(c) Actually, ZF-expressions are more general than we have indicated, in that 12 can be a function of a:

$$\{ \ a, \ b; \ a <- \ 11; \ b <- \ (12 \ a) \ \}$$

denotes the list of all pairs (a, b) such that b is in the list (12 a). For example,

$$\{ \ m, \ n; \ m <- \ 1..5; \ n <- \ m..m+1 \ \}$$

returns the list of pairs (1,1), (1,2), (2,2), (2,3), and so on (not necessarily in that order).

(mkfinitepairs* 11 12) should implement this ZF-expression, assuming that 11 is a finite list and that (12 a) is a finite list for all a.

(d) (mkpairs 11 12) extends the ZF-expression from part (b) to *arbitrary* (finite or infinite) 11 and 12. (Since this case is much trickier than for finite lists, it is most unlikely that your solution to part (b) works for infinite lists.) Here is an approach to this problem. Suppose $11 = (x_1 \ x_2 \ ...)$, and $12 = (y_1 \ y_2 \ ...)$. Then: (1) generate the list

$$(((x_1 \ y_1) \ (x_1 \ y_2) \ ...) \ ((x_2 \ y_1) \ (x_2 \ y_2) \ ...) \ ...).$$

(2) Write a function merge, which merges two lists, finite or infinite, into a single list. (3) Use merge to write a function interleave which flattens a list of the form

$$((a_1 \ a_2 \ ...) \ (b_1 \ b_2 \ ...) \ ...),$$

where the sublists may be infinite. (Note that flatten does not work in this case.)

(e) Program mkpairs*, which implements ZF-expressions of the form

$$\{ \ a, \ b; \ a <- \ 11; \ b <- \ (12 \ a) \ \}$$

in the case that 11 can be infinite and each (12 a) can be infinite.

(f) (filter-pair pred 11 12) implements

$$\{ \ a, \ b; \ a <- \ 11; \ b <- \ 12; \ pred \ a \ b \ \}$$

Use it to construct the list `relative-primes` containing every pair of integers greater than 2 which are relatively prime (have no common factors). Then program `filter-pair*`, which bears the same relation to `filter-pair` that `mkpairs*` does to `mkpairs`. Specifically, it implements the ZF-expression

$$\{ \ a, \ b; \ a \ <- \ l1; \ b \ <- \ (l2 \ a); \ pred \ a \ b \ \}.$$

(g) `(filter-pair-fun f pred l1 l2)` implements

$$\{ \ f \ a \ b; \ a \ <- \ l1; \ b \ <- \ l2; \ pred \ a \ b \ \}$$

Program `filter-pair-fun` and `filter-pair-fun*`. The latter can be used to code a nice version of `permutations`, given in Turner [1983]:

```
perms () = (())
perms x = { a:p; a <- x; p <- perms (x -- a) },
```

where "`(x -- a)`" is the list obtained by removing `a` from the list `x`.

3. These questions relate to the reachability problem (Section 5.5).

(a) Our `reach-dfs` and `reach-bfs` return only a truth value indicating the existence or nonexistence of a path. Modify them to return the path itself.

(b) The reachability problem in n dimensions deals with points in n-space; i.e., instead of points it uses lists of nonnegative integers of length n. Code `reach-dfs` and `reach-bfs` so that they can be applied to a reachability problem of any dimension.

(c) `(reach-dfs p0 PATHS k)` searches for a path to p0 of length not greater than k; it returns either `T` if it finds it, `()` if it can determine, by searching the tree to k levels, that no path exists, or `Dunno` if it determines that no path of length k or less exists but does not know whether a longer path might exist. It searches the k levels in depth-first order.

4. These problems relate to the λ-calculus (Section 5.8).

(a) Define `FIB` in λ-calculus, using the same technique as for `FAC`.

(b) Modify the definition of integers to allow for negative numbers, using a "signed-magnitude" representation.

(c) Show how `Y` can be extended to an arbitrarily long list of mutually-recursive functions, i.e., a `letrec`.

(d) Which of the definitions given in Section 5.8 would work in SCHEME? Can you write a Y in SCHEME for the single-function case? (This is a difficult problem. *Hint:* make use of the rule of "η-equivalence": e $\equiv$ (lambda (x) (e x)), if x does not occur in e.) What about the multiple-function case?

5.11.2   *LEARNING ABOUT THE INTERPRETER*

5. *applyCtrlOp* can be removed from the interpreter. What mainly distinguished control operations from value-op's in the past was that they did not evaluate their arguments. Since even value-op's do not necessarily evaluate their arguments anymore, if may as well be considered a value-op. Make this change, removing all code relating to control operations.

6. *evalList* is too simple-minded. The evaluator would run a bit faster if it only made thunks out of applications (*APEXP*'s) and evaluated other types of expressions. Explain this statement and implement the change.

7. Implement letrec. Consult Exercise 14 in Chapter 4. Note that the restriction on letrec's in SCHEME, where only functions can be defined recursively, can be eased in SASL. Also unlike SCHEME, letrec cannot be defined by translating it to an equivalent already existing expression, since SASL has no assignment. The other alternative — defining a new type of *EXP* — must be followed. To illustrate how this new type of expression is evaluated, this is how to evaluate (letrec ((f e)) e') in environment ρ:

(a) Create environment $\rho' = \rho\{f \mapsto \triangleleft e, \rho \triangleright\}$.

(b) Change the environment pointer in the thunk just created to ρ', obtaining the circular environment $\rho' = \rho\{f \mapsto \triangleleft e, \rho' \triangleright\}$.

(c) Evaluate e' in ρ'.

Your implementation should, of course, handle letrec's with more than one variable being defined.

8. Implement streams in the SCHEME interpreter. That is, without changing the eager evaluation semantics of SCHEME, add the new data type of streams, with operations cons-stream, head, tail, and empty-stream?, and constant the-empty-stream. The difference between list operations and these stream operations is that cons-stream evaluates only its first argument (creating a thunk for the second), and tail, in turn, evaluates the thunk, if it has not already been evaluated and replaced. (Note that replacement still is done for thunks, even though it is not really mathematically justified in SCHEME because the presence of side-effects makes the time at which an expression is evaluated significant.) Which examples given in this chapter work when translated to this version of SCHEME?

5.11.3 LEARNING ABOUT GRAPH REDUCTION

9. Translate the following SASL expressions to SKI, then show the computations as they are applied to the given arguments:

   (a) `(lambda (x) (lambda (y) x))` ; apply to 3 and 4.

   (b) `(lambda (x) (lambda (y) y))` ; apply to 3 and 4.

   (c) `(lambda (x) (lambda (y) ((+ x) y)))` ; apply to 3 and 4.

   (d) `(lambda (x) (lambda (y) (y x)))` ; apply to 4 and `(* 3)`.

10. In addition to the introduction of combinators B and C, Turner [1979a]
    gives the following optimizations, which are to be performed before B-
    and C-introduction:

    $$((S \ (K \ e_1)) \ (K \ e_2)) \equiv (K \ (e_1 \ e_2))$$

    $$((S \ (K \ e)) \ I) \equiv e$$

    Prove these equivalences.

11. Implement the abstraction operation [x]e. For extra credit, implement
    Turner's optimizations. For more extra credit, implement the optimiza-
    tions given in Turner [1979b].

12. Give pseudo-code for procedures *performK*, *performI*, and *performIF*.

13. One way that our graph-reduction code in Figure 5.6 is unnecessarily
    inefficient is that it rebuilds the argument stack, *args*, from scratch on
    each iteration. Each of the graph transformations has a very local and
    predictable effect on the stack, so it would be far more efficient to have the
    perform procedures adjust *args* themselves. Implement this improvement
    to the code.

14. Implement graph reduction. You will need to choose a representation for
    graph nodes, implement abstraction, and complete the code for *reduce*
    and the *perform* procedures.

Part IV
Object-Oriented Programming

What makes programming difficult? An answer that has gained currency during that last twenty years is that what makes it difficult is that *computer representations of data are unnatural.* There is such a wide gap between a table and a binary search tree implemented as a record with two pointer fields, or between a picture and the bit string used to represent its pixels, that the programmer is in a continual state of tension between what he wants to do in the abstract and what he must do with the concrete data with which he has to work. A central question in language design has become: how can we reduce this tension?

The two languages covered in this Part exemplify different answers to this question. Both were strongly influenced by SIMULA 67 (Birtwhistle et. al. [1973]), a language of the late 1960's designed for doing computer simulations, though they seem to have drawn quite different lessons from it. (It is perhaps not surprising that a simulation language, being designed specifically for the representation of real-world objects and their actions, should provide an answer to the natural representation of data.)

- CLU reduces the unnaturalness of computer representations by giving the programmer the power to hide, or *encapsulate*, representation-dependent code. The syntactic capsule is called a *cluster*. Aside from this feature, CLU is quite a traditional language, very much in the PASCAL family[8]. Our discussion of CLU — a language designed with the expressed goal of reliable programming — leads naturally to the topic of *program verification*, which we survey in Chapter 6.

- SMALLTALK is one of the "hottest" programming languages around at the present time. It was developed over a period of about fifteen years,

---

[8]though it is more radical than the language MODULA-2, which is a legitimate successor to PASCAL (being the work of the same language designer, Niklaus Wirth) based also on the idea of encapsulating data representations.

by a group at Xerox Palo Alto Research Center led by Alan Kay. In SMALLTALK, data items are viewed as representations of real world objects, which interact with other objects by sending and receiving messages. It is really this view of data as active agents that goes by the name *object-oriented programming.*

The concept of data encapsulation, exemplified by CLU, was strongly represented in language designs of the 1970's; in the late 1980's, object-oriented programming in the SMALLTALK sense shows signs of having nearly as great an influence.

Chapter 6

CLU

Procedures are an important tool that every language provides in some form. Why are they valuable? By *hiding the details of a computation*, making a complex set of instructions accessible to the programmer at the mere mention of a name, they free him or her from thinking about *how* the computation is performed. The programmer needn't be concerned about clashes between the variables he or she is using for other things and the variables used in that computation. If changes must be made in that code, the programmer doesn't worry that those changes will affect the rest of the program in unforeseen ways. In short, the interactions between the procedure and its clients — the procedures that call it — are limited to just what the procedure is *expected* to do, with no gratuitous side-effects. These are inestimable benefits, as has been realized from the earliest programming languages.

Arguably the most important advance in the understanding of programming during the past twenty years has been the realization that the same advantages obtain from *hiding the details of data representations*, or, as it is called, *data abstraction*. PASCAL was part of the movement in this direction in the late 1960's, and the 1970's saw a spate of new languages based upon data abstraction. In addition to CLU, the list includes SIMULA 67, ALPHARD, MODULA-2, and more recently ADA, as well as many others. We have chosen CLU as a representative of these languages because of its particularly clean design, although our dialect could be taken as representative of any of them.

This chapter is more *serious* than most of the other chapters in this book. Data abstraction is not a feature that encourages clever and inscrutable code, and CLU is not designed to help the programmer show off. On the contrary, the intention is to encourage the writing of programs that are correct, reliable, maintainable, and readable. Indeed, CLU has a number of features in addition to data abstraction to aid in writing such programs; these will be discussed in Section 6.5.

Data abstraction has also come to be a central notion in the study of *program verification*, the mathematical proof of program correctness. Section 6.7 is devoted to it.

207

Among the languages emphasizing data abstraction, ADA may well come to be the most widely used. Its use is being strongly supported by the U. S. Department of Defense, which is said to spend more on software development than any other organization in the free world. Thus, its technical merits aside, the well-educated multi-lingual programmer should have at least some knowledge of it. For this reason, Section 6.6 is devoted to ADA, especially to the ways in which it supports data abstraction.

6.1 Data Abstraction

What do we mean by "hiding the details of data representations?" We mean thinking more in terms of the *abstract* data that we would like to be manipulating in a program and less in terms of the *concrete* data that actually are being manipulated. Here are some examples:

Integers

Concrete view: Bit strings.

Abstract view: Mathematical integers.

This may seem like an odd example. After all, programmers are quite comfortable thinking of integers in the abstract; they are rarely concerned about their concrete representation as bit strings. It would be very surprising, for example, to see this code in a program:

> **if** $hiOrderBit(i) = 1$
> > **then** *writeln*('i is negative')
> > **else** *writeln*('i is non-negative');

But that is precisely the point: integers are one data type about which programmers have learned to think abstractly. We would all reject this sign-testing code as confusing and nonportable (in that it can be guaranteed to work right only on a computer that uses a 2's-complement representation for integers). What it does wrong can be summarized so: It makes an unnecessary assumption about the representation of integers.

Binary Tree

Concrete view: Record containing a `label` field and two pointer fields to binary trees, `leftchild` and `rightchild`.

Abstract view: An object which can be queried for its label and for its left and right children.

Every programmer would recognize our concrete version of binary trees as just one possible representation among many. Yet, it would not be surprising to see a program containing this code:

$$r := t{\uparrow}.rightchild;$$
$$writeln(r{\uparrow}.label);$$

This code looks quite innocent, but it is really guilty of precisely the same crime as the sign-testing code: It makes unnecessary assumptions about the representation of binary trees. It would not survive a change of representation from records to parallel arrays or linked lists, should such a change become desirable, just as the sign-testing code would not survive a change to a 1's-complement machine. By building in assumptions about data representations, we make our code more obscure and more difficult to modify.

Points on the Plane

Concrete view: Record with two fields, giving the x and y coordinates.

Abstract view: A position on the plane, which can be determined in several ways: by its x and y coordinates; by its x coordinate, distance from the origin, and quadrant; by "polar coordinates," i.e., angle and distance; and so on.

Again, code that assumes the stated concrete representation and contains expressions like "$p{\uparrow}.xcoord$" is assuming too much; many representations of points are possible.

These examples are tending to the conclusion that programs should insulate themselves from the specific representation of data they use. The benefits of doing so will show up, perhaps not immediately, but when the program is to be modified, as all useful programs eventually are.

How can a programming language help and encourage programmers to maintain an abstract view of data? Ultimately, data must be represented concretely in arrays, records, and so on; there is certainly no way around that. What can be done is to provide a syntactic "capsule" containing both the representation of a data type and all functions that need to know that representation. This capsule hides the representation from all outside programs. A program wishing to use this data type — a *client* of the data type — is given access only to the operations of the type. For example, a Tree capsule defines functions *label(t)*, *mkTree(l, t1, t2)*, *leftchild(t)*, and so on; a client of Tree can create and use trees via these operations but can never discover how they are represented. In CLU, such a capsule is called a *cluster*.

In the LISP chapter, we mentioned that the influence of the language could be seen easily in our interpreter code. The same can be said of the data abstraction languages like CLU. For example, the only functions that know about the concrete representation of *ENV* structures are *mkEnv* and the functions contained in the *ENVIRONMENTS* section. Of course, in PASCAL this discipline is strictly self-imposed.

6.2 The Language

The idea of CLU is to allow users to define their own *data types*. They do so by
giving a *cluster*, which defines how elements of the type are to be represented
and what functions are provided by that type. A value created by cluster
operations will be referred to as an *instance* (of the cluster).

A cluster, then, consists of a data type representation — which is a list
of data items, i.e., a record — and a collection of functions operating on that
representation. All the functions that need to know how the data are being
represented are included. In particular, clients cannot directly access the record
that represents an instance because they are not permitted to apply the record
selectors to the instance.

As an example, Figure 6.1 contains a cluster representing points in the
plane with integer coordinates. The cluster starts by listing, in a comment, the
operations that the cluster defines and makes available to the outside world,
called the "exported" functions. These functions are to present an "abstract"
picture of `Point` to the outside world (i.e., the clients). They need not make
available each component of the representation (though in this case they do),
because that kind of information is not inherent to point-hood, only to the
specific representation chosen. Similarly, they need not allow each component
to be altered individually (as in this case they don't), because such an operation
can be done only with knowledge of the representation of values. Here are the
functions `Point` exports; we are not intending to explain the code itself, just
give the "abstract" meaning of each function (i.e., the client's view):

new: Create a new `Point`, given its x and y coordinates.

abscissa and ordinate: Return the x and y coordinates, respectively, of the
argument.

reflect and rotate: Change the point to its reflection or rotation, respectively; these operations are illustrated in Figure 6.2.

compare: Test if the first argument is closer to the origin than the second.

quadrant: Return the quadrant number (also shown in Figure 6.2) of the point.

The function `sqrdist` is used by `compare`, but is not exported.[1]

The important point to note is that our discussion thus far has made no
mention of the representation of points. The operations of the cluster `Point`
are operations that make sense for points in the plane, independent of any
particular concrete representation. In the following session, the variables `p1`
and `p2` contain instances of `Point`; though we know (from reading the code
of `Point`) that these each contain two integers, we are not allowed to access

---

[1]Since the export list appears only in a comment, it is not binding but is simply an
indication that clients *should not* use nonexported functions. In real CLU, the export list is
a *bona fide* part of the cluster, as we will see; see also Exercise 8.

```
(cluster Point
    ; Export:  new, abscissa, ordinate, reflect, rotate, compare, quadrant
    (rep x-coord y-coord)
    (define new (x y) (Point x y))
    (define abscissa (p) (x-coord p))
    (define ordinate (p) (y-coord p))
    (define reflect (p)
       (begin
          (set-x-coord p (- 0 (x-coord p)))
          (set-y-coord p (- 0 (y-coord p)))))
    (define rotate (p)
       (begin
          (set temp (x-coord p))
          (set-x-coord p (y-coord p))
          (set-y-coord p (- 0 temp))))
    (define compare (p1 p2) (< (sqrdist p1) (sqrdist p2)))
    (define quadrant (p)
       (if (>= (x-coord p) 0)
          (if (>= (y-coord p) 0) 1 2)
          (if (< (y-coord p) 0) 3 4)))
    ; sqrdist is not exported
    (define sqrdist (p) (+ (sqr (x-coord p)) (sqr (y-coord p))))
)
```

Figure 6.1: Cluster Point

those integers except as specifically permitted by the operations defined in the cluster. The function enclosed-area computes the area of a rectangle, given the locations of opposite corners:

```
-> (set p1 (Point$new 3 4))
-> (Point$rotate p1)
-> (Point$abscissa p1)
4

-> (Point$ordinate p1)
-3

-> (Point$reflect p1)
-> (Point$abscissa p1)
-4

-> (Point$ordinate p1)
3

-> (set p2 (Point$new 1 5))
```

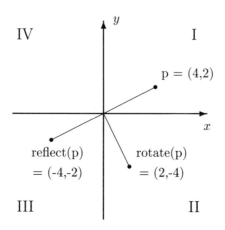

Figure 6.2: The operations of `Point`

```
-> (Point$compare p1 p2)
1

-> (define enclosed-area (p1 p2)
      (abs (* (- (Point$abscissa p1) (Point$abscissa p2))
         (- (Point$ordinate p1) (Point$ordinate p2))))))

-> (enclosed-area p1 p2)
10
```

The functions defined in cluster `Point` are always referenced, by its clients, via their *two-part names*, consisting of the cluster name and the function name, separated by "$".

Let's take a look at the cluster itself. As clients, we needed to know only the name of the cluster and the name and purpose of the functions it exports. We could think of the instances of the cluster as points in a perfectly abstract sense. Now we are placing ourselves in the role of the programmer of the cluster and are going to look inside it.

The first thing that we see after the export list is the line "(rep x-coord y-coord)", which is followed by a sequence of function definitions. The "rep" line says that points are to be represented by their x and y coordinates (that is, by two integers, though the fact that they are integers is not stated). Again, this representation is of no interest to clients, but it is of central importance to the cluster's programmer. These operations are quite simple, once some basic facts about the language are explained:

- **new** creates a new instance of `Point`, by applying the function `Point`. The latter is an *implicitly defined* function available within the cluster, which takes two arguments and creates a `Point`. In effect, it puts these two values into a package to which clients have access only via the cluster operations.

- `abscissa` and `ordinate` return the x and y coordinates of their argument, respectively, which also happen to be the two components of the point's representation. To get at these representation components, these functions apply the *selector* functions, which are also implicitly defined and have the same names as the corresponding components. Thus, *within the cluster*, `x-coord` is defined to be a function that returns the `x-coord` component of any `Point`; outside the cluster, `x-coord` is undefined; and similarly for `y-coord`. Again, the idea is to deny clients access to the representation of points, so they are forced to think of points in the abstract.

- Another capability provided by implicitly-defined functions within the cluster, used by `reflect` and `rotate`, is modification of the representation of an instance. `set-x-coord` modifies the `x-coord` component of its first argument to be equal to its second argument. Note that this *modifies the first argument* and does not return a new `Point` instance.

The importance of hiding the representation from clients can best be illustrated by presenting an alternative representation, given in Figure 6.3. There, a point is represented by three values, the *absolute values* of its x and y coordinates and its quadrant number. Abstractly, the operations work in exactly the same way, and the session given above has identical results. If, however, clients had been allowed to use selectors, that fact could no longer be guaranteed, since the selectors of the two versions of `Point` are different. The situation is precisely analogous to the examples given in the introduction, where troublesome things happened when the user of a data type wrote representation-specific code. The whole idea of clusters is to discourage the writing of such code.

6.2.1 SYNTAX

The syntax of CLU is the same as that of Chapter 1 except for cluster definitions and two-part names.

input	$\longrightarrow$	expression | fundef | clusterdef
clusterdef	$\longrightarrow$	(cluster cluster rep fundef$^+$)
rep	$\longrightarrow$	(rep variable$^+$)
fundef	$\longrightarrow$	*same as in Chapter 1*
expression	$\longrightarrow$	*same as in Chapter 1*
optr	$\longrightarrow$	value-op | one-part-name | two-part-name
value-op	$\longrightarrow$	+ | ... | > | print
one-part-name	$\longrightarrow$	name
two-part-name	$\longrightarrow$	cluster$name
cluster	$\longrightarrow$	name

```
(cluster Point
    ; Exports: new, abscissa, ordinate, reflect, rotate, compare, quadrant
    (rep x-mag y-mag quad)
    (define new (x y) (Point (abs x) (abs y) (compute-quad x y)))
    (define abscissa (p) (if (> (quad p) 2) (- 0 (x-mag p)) (x-mag p)))
    (define ordinate (p)
        (if (or (= (quad p) 2) (= (quad p) 3))
            (- 0 (y-mag p))
            (y-mag p)))
    (define reflect (p)
        (set-quad p (+1 (mod (+1 (quad p)) 4))))
    (define rotate (p)
        (begin
            (set temp (x-mag p))
            (set-x-mag p (y-mag p))
            (set-y-mag p temp)
            (set-quad p (+1 (mod (quad p) 4)))))
    (define compare (p1 p2) (< (sqrdist p1) (sqrdist p2)))
    (define quadrant (p) (quad p))
    ; compute-quad, sqrdist are not exported
    (define compute-quad (x y)
        (if (>= x 0)
            (if (>= y 0) 1 2)
            (if (< y 0) 3 4)))
    (define sqrdist (p) (+ (sqr (x-mag p)) (sqr (y-mag p)))))
)
```

Figure 6.3: Cluster `Point`

In addition, there is a convention that the second line of every cluster definition be a comment naming the exported functions.

6.2.2 SEMANTICS

Functions defined inside a cluster have access to certain functions that cannot be used outside the cluster, to wit:

- The names used in the representation (x-coord and y-coord in the first `Point` cluster, x-mag, y-mag, and quad in the second) can be used as functions which, when applied to an instance of the cluster, return the corresponding component of its representation. These functions are called *selectors*.

- For each selector, the name formed by prefixing its name by "set-" (set-x-coord, etc.) is a function of two arguments; when applied to an instance v_1 of the cluster and another value v_2, it sets the selected component of v_1 to v_2. These functions are *settors*.

- The name of the type (`Point`) is itself a function, called a *constructor*, which has as many arguments as the number of selectors. It forms a new instance of the type, having the given representation components.

- Each function defined in the cluster can be called by the other functions defined there, using its *one-part* name.

By contrast, access to the functions defined in a cluster from outside the cluster is strictly limited:

- Selectors, settors, and constructors cannot be used. This is to be expected, since these three types of functions cannot sensibly be used without knowledge about the type's representation.

- Functions defined in a cluster are referred to by two-part-names.[2] Furthermore, only those functions named in the cluster's export list should be used; others are private to the cluster.

6.2.3 SCOPE IN CLU

The scope rules for variables are exactly as in Chapter 1. Variables are either formal parameters or global variables. This is equally true for functions defined within clusters as for functions defined at the top level.

For function names, the scope rules are an elaboration of those in Chapter 1, where all functions had global scope.[3] A cluster defines a scope, making names available globally and also making some names visible within the cluster which are not visible outside it. In particular, the cluster exports the two-part names of the functions it defines. Internally, it defines both the one-part and two-part names of those functions, and also the constructor, selectors, and settors, as previously described.

6.2.4 EXAMPLES

CLU contains the language of Chapter 1 as a subset, so everything done there still works. Our examples involve only what is unique to CLU, namely, clusters.

Lists. The cluster `List` (Figure 6.4) implements lists of values. The exported functions are:

`nil:` The list of zero items.

---

[2]This is easy to forget, but doing so usually leads to an "undefined function" error very quickly.

[3]We are assuming some familiarity with the discussion of scope in Chapter 4 (Section 4.7); the first few subsections of that section can be read independently of the rest of Chapter 4.

```
(cluster List
    ; Exports:  nil, null?, cons, car, cdr, rplaca, rplacd
    (rep type a d)
    (define nil () (List 0 0 0))
    (define null? (l) (= (type l) 0))
    (define cons (item l) (List 1 item l))
    (define car (l) (a l)) ; apply selector a to l
    (define cdr (l) (d l)) ; apply selector d to l
    (define rplaca (l a) (set-a l a))
    (define rplacd (l d) (set-d l d))
)
```

Figure 6.4: Cluster `List`

null?: The test for an empty list.

cons: The function to add a new item to the front of a list. If x is the list $(3, 4, 5)$, then (List$cons 2 x) is $(2, 3, 4, 5)$. Note that x is not changed, but rather a new instance is returned.

car: Return the first item in a list. Given x above, (List$car x) is 3.

cdr: Return the list consisting of all items in the argument except the first. (List$cdr x) is $(4, 5)$.

rplaca: "Replace the car;" i.e., modify the first argument, a list, by making its first element equal to the second argument. This function actually changes its first argument. So, after calling (List$rplaca x 8), x is $(8, 4, 5)$.

rplacd: "Replace the cdr;" i.e., modify the first argument, a list, by making its cdr equal to the second argument. This function also changes its first argument. If x is $(3, 4, 5)$ and y is $(7, 8, 9)$, then after calling (List$rplacd x y), x is $(3, 7, 8, 9)$.

Here is a session using `List`:

```
-> (set x (List$cons 1 (List$cons 2 (List$nil)))) ; x is (1, 2)
-> (set y x) ; y is (1, 2)
-> (List$car x)
1

-> (List$car y)
1

-> (List$car (List$cdr x))
2
```

```
-> (List$rplaca y 3) ; y is (3, 2), and so is x
-> (List$car x)
3

-> (List$car y)
3

-> (define length (l)
     (if (List$null? l) 0 (+1 (length (List$cdr l)))))
-> (length x)
2
```

Another point to be made from this session is that the assignment (set y x) sets y and x to be the *exact same list*, so that subsequent changes to y via rplaca are at the same time changes to x.

Having seen what List's are in the abstract, let us look at how they are represented. The three components of the representation are:

type: 0 if the list is empty, 1 otherwise.

a, d: The first item and the remaining items, if type = 1. If type = 0, the values of a and d are irrelevant.

Note that the d component of any List instance (that represents a nonempty list) is itself a List instance. This kind of recursive representation is perfectly legal in CLU.

Arrays. A cluster that is frequently used, both for itself and to represent other types of data, is **Array** (Figure 6.5), implementing one-dimensional arrays with integer indices and arbitrary components. Unlike **Array** in real CLU, our arrays are not built-in and do not enjoy constant-time access to all components, but aside from that they provide the programmer with basically the same capability. The operation **new** is a kind of "declaration" of an array, creating a new array with given base index and size; **index** and **assign** perform subscripting and assignment, respectively.

Arrays are represented by lists of integers, together with the base address and the size of the array (though the latter is redundant, since it is just the length of the list). When (new b s) is called, it forms the new **Array** instance by creating a list of s zeros and packaging it together with b and s. Subscripting is a straightforward process of cdr'ing down the list the correct number of times. (assign A i x) modifies the array A. That is, A is, in effect, a **var** parameter; note the use of rplaca in changenth.

The operations **zerolist**, **nth**, and **changenth** are not really operations on arrays but are instead operations on lists which are auxiliary to the array operations. **zerolist** is included as a nonexported function in the cluster, but **nth** and **changenth** are defined globally; this decision is discussed further below.

```
(define nth (n l)
    (if (= n 0) (List$car l) (nth (- n 1) (List$cdr l))))
(define changenth (n x l)
    (if (= n 0) (List$rplaca l x) (changenth (- n 1) x (List$cdr l)))))
;
(cluster Array
    ; Exports:  new, index, assign
    ; Indexing is from base, array has length size,
    ; and elements are in list elts.
    (rep base size elts)
    (define new (b s) (Array b s (zerolist s)))
    (define index (A i)
       (if (out-of-bounds A i) 0 (nth (- i (base A)) (elts A))))
    (define assign (A i x)
       (if (out-of-bounds A i) A (changenth (- i (base A)) x (elts A))))
    ; zerolist, out-of-bounds not exported
    (define zerolist (n)
       (if (= n 0) (List$nil) (List$cons 0 (zerolist (- n 1)))))
    (define out-of-bounds (A i)
       (or (< i (base A)) (> i (- (+ (base A) (size A)) 1))))
)
```

Figure 6.5: Cluster `Array`

Sparse Arrays. When an array is expected to be filled mostly with zero entries, the normal array representation may be considered too wasteful of memory. Here we present a cluster for sparse arrays, in which an array is represented by a list of pairs. The cluster `Pair` is shown in Figure 6.6 and `SpArray` in Figure 6.7.

```
(cluster Pair
    ; Exports:  fst, snd, mkPair
    (rep f s)
    (define fst (p) (f p))
    (define snd (p) (s p))
    (define mkPair (x y) (Pair x y))
)
```

Figure 6.6: Cluster `Pair`

```
(define assoc (i l)
    (if (List$null? l) l
        (if (= (Pair$fst (List$car l)) i)
            l
            (assoc i (List$cdr l)))))
;
(cluster SpArray
    ; Exports:  new, index, assign
    (rep base size elts)
    (define new (b s) (SpArray b s (List$nil)))
    (define index (A i)
        (begin
            (set found (assoc i (elts A)))
            (if (List$null? found) 0 (Pair$snd (List$car found)))))
    (define assign (A i x)
        (if (out-of-bounds A i) A
            (begin
                (set found (assoc i (elts A)))
                (if (List$null? found)
                    (set-elts A (List$cons (Pair$mkPair i x) (elts A)))
                    (List$rplaca found (Pair$mkPair i x)))
                A)))
    ; out-of-bounds not exported
    (define out-of-bounds (A i)
        (or (< i (base A)) (> i (- (+ (base A) (size A)) 1)))))
)
```

Figure 6.7: Cluster SpArray

In SpArray, arrays are represented by lists of pairs of integers, $((i_1, x_1),$ $\ldots, (i_n, x_n))$, such that no two i_j, $i_{j'}$ are equal. The function assoc is the basic searching function; (assoc i l) returns either the empty list or a suffix $((i_j, x_j), \ldots, (i_n, x_n))$ of the list l such that $i = i_j$. Note that SpArray is mutable; in assign, A itself is changed either by consing on a new pair (i, x), or, if $i = i_j$ for some j, changing the jth pair to (i, x).

Sparse arrays are a standard example of a change of data representations that should be transparent to the client. Any client of Array can be readily modified to be a client of SpArray simply by changing function calls of the form "Array$$\cdots$" to "SpArray$$\cdots$."

Mutable Types vs. Immutable Types   Clusters whose instances can be changed by cluster operations are called *mutable*;[4] Point (both versions), List, and Array are examples. Otherwise, a cluster is *immutable*; Pair is our only immutable cluster thus far. Note that mutability is an "abstract" property of clusters, one which must be appreciated by a client. Another way to say this is that it is a property of *data types*, not of the *clusters* that implement them.

It seems to be very natural to distinguish between mutable and immutable types. In ordinary programming languages, "small" values are generally immutable, e.g., integers, characters, enumerated constants. By contrast, structured values like arrays and records can be changed.

In Section 2.5.3 of Chapter 2, when discussing rplaca and rplacd, we observed that mutable values are dangerous. Furthermore, LISP and APL are case studies in the power of languages without mutable values.[5] Nonetheless, it is hard to argue that arrays should not be mutable. We only exhort the programmer to be careful when using mutable types.

Where Should Functions be Defined?   Consider the function nth, used in cluster Array. There are three places in which it could plausibly be defined:

- In the List cluster, since it is a list operation. However, it does not need to know the representation used by List, so that it *can* be defined as a client. If we were to follow the principle of including in each cluster all the operations naturally associated with that type, even those which *could* be defined outside it, several bad things might occur in the long run:

  - Clusters would get unmanageably large.

  - If there were more than one cluster representing a type, these definitions would have to be repeated in each one, expanding the total volume of code and presenting a severe version control problem.

  - Most importantly, this policy implies making the cluster effectively public, to allow for new functions to be added. Having clusters be so public invites programmers to write representation-dependent code, and thus mitigates the benefits of representation-independence.

  According to these arguments, a cluster should be limited to those operations having a legitimate need to know the representation.

---

[4]This is almost the same thing as saying that the cluster operations use settors, except that an operation may create a new instance and then apply settors to it rather than to any argument; the later example Poly does exactly this.

[5]In fact, real LISP has mutable lists, as we have seen, and real APL has mutable arrays; however, the examples in those chapters show how much can be done with immutable data.

- At the top level. Succumbing to the arguments just given, the choice was made to define `nth` globally. However, this approach is not without disadvantages. Mainly, with `List`-oriented code spread all over, the programmer cannot easily determine whether a certain function has previously been written; reuse of code is hindered.

- As a nonexported function in `Array`. This approach would have the advantage of maintaining the independence and "territorial integrity" of `Array`. For `zerolist`, the decision was made that there is so little likelihood of outside interest that defining it within `Array` was justified. However, for a function of general interest like `nth`, it would end up being defined locally in many clusters, again leading to a problem of code bulk and version control.

Deciding where to define functions — like deciding what data types to use in a given program — is not a scientific process. There are a variety of principles of function placement — keep the cluster itself simple, including only truly representation-dependent code; keep all functions associated with a given data type together; maintain the independence of a cluster, by having it define what it needs — that are mutually contradictory. The decisions made in the code in this chapter simply tried to balance these principles in particular cases, and no attempt to justify each has been made.

6.3 Implementation

The principal changes in the interpreter (Appendix G), as compared with the interpreter of Chapter 1, are in the *INPUT* section, and in the function *applyUserFun* in *eval*, plus the supporting declarations for these changes.

6.3.1 DECLARATIONS

The following declaration supports the notion of two-part names:

$$FNAMETYPE = (ONEPART, TWOPART);$$
$$FUNNAME = \textbf{record}$$
$$funpart\text{: } NAME;$$
$$\textbf{case } nametype\text{: } FNAMETYPE \textbf{ of}$$
$$ONEPART\text{: } ();$$
$$TWOPART\text{: } (clpart\text{: } NAME)$$
$$\textbf{end};$$

The *APEXP* case in the definition of *EXPREC* is changed to allow for two-part names.

Values can be either primitive (that is, integers) or user-defined, that is, cluster instances. The latter are represented by environments giving bindings for the representation variables:

$$CLUVALUE = \uparrow CLUVALUEREC;$$
$$CLUVALUETYPE = (PRIM, USER);$$
$$CLUVALUEREC = \textbf{record}$$

$$\textbf{case } vtype: \ CLUVALUETYPE \ \textbf{of}$$
$$PRIM: \ (intval: \ integer);$$
$$USER: \ (userval: \ ENV)$$

$$\textbf{end};$$

There are three new types of user-defined functions — constructors, selectors, and settors:

$$FUNTYPE = (NORMAL, CONSTRUCTOR, SELECTOR, SETTOR);$$
$$FUNDEFREC = \textbf{record}$$
$$funname: \ NAME;$$
$$nextfundef: \ FUNDEF;$$
$$\textbf{case } ftype: \ FUNTYPE \ \textbf{of}$$
$$NORMAL: \ (formals: \ NAMELIST; \ body: \ EXP);$$
$$CONSTRUCTOR, \ SELECTOR: \ ();$$
$$SETTOR: \ (selname: \ NAME)$$

$$\textbf{end};$$

Finally, each cluster is represented by a structure giving its name, the names of its selectors, and the functions it defines. These cluster structures are linked together just as function definitions are:

$$CLUSTER = \uparrow CLUSTERREC;$$
$$CLUSTERREC = \textbf{record}$$
$$clname: \ NAME;$$
$$clrep: \ NAMELIST;$$
$$exported: \ FUNDEF;$$
$$nonexported: \ FUNDEF;$$
$$nextcluster: \ CLUSTER$$

$$\textbf{end};$$

A new variable, *clusters*, is added, whose function is precisely analogous to that of *fundefs*; namely, it is the beginning of the linked list of cluster records.

6.3.2 DATA STRUCTURE OP'S

The only significant change in this section is the addition of functions *mkPRIM* and *mkUSER*, which construct new *CLUVALUE*'s. *mkAPEXP* is modified to create applications whose operators are either one-part or two-part names.

6.3.3 NAME MANAGEMENT

Functions *fetchCluster* and *newCluster* have been added whose purpose is analogous to that of *fetchFun* and *newFunDef*. On the other hand, *fetchFun* and *newFunDef* must be modified to take a second argument, which is the function environment (a *FUNDEF* pointer) in which the function is to be looked up or into which it is to be added.

6.3.4 INPUT

The main change here is the addition of *parseCluster*, whose action is fairly straightforward. One problem is that the names `set-`··· must be created. The functions defined by the cluster are placed on two lists which are placed into a new *CLUSTERREC* structure (user-defined functions in the *exported* field, constructor, selector, and settor functions in the *nonexported* field). This *CLUSTERREC* structure in turn is placed on the global list of cluster records (the one pointed to by *clusters*).

    parseExp is modified to allow for two-part names in applications.

6.3.5 ENVIRONMENTS

There are no changes here.

6.3.6 VALUES

The only changes here are to check that values passed as arguments to arithmetic operations are integers and not cluster instances. The only false value is the integer zero; any user value or any other integer is considered true.

6.3.7 EVALUATION

eval has one new argument, the cluster in which the currently evaluated function was defined:

    function *eval* (*e*: *EXP*; *rho*: *ENV*; *c*: *CLUSTER*): *CLUVALUE*;

(*eval* is called with a nil third argument from the top level.) This is needed for two reasons:

- When executing within a function defined in *c*, there are names defined that are not defined globally, namely, the constructor, selectors, and settors. These names are found by looking in the *nonexported* field of *c*. Thus, the cluster argument is used to support the nested function name scope defined by the cluster, just as the environment argument supports the nested variable scopes defined by functions.

- A constructor operation forms a *CLUVALUE* of type *USER* by constructing an environment the *vars* component of which is the list of the cluster's
  selector names. The latter is obtained from the *clrep* field of *c*.

These uses of *c* both appear in the new version of *applyUserFun*, which
has changed more than any other function in the interpreter. First, its *nm*
argument is of type *FUNNAME*, as shown in its new header:

> **function** *applyUserFun* (*nm*: *FUNNAME*;
>   *actuals*: *VALUELIST*): *CLUVALUE*;

applyUserFun has no way of knowing immediately whether *nm* is defined globally or in the current cluster; or it may be a two-part name, in which case it
has to be looked up in a different cluster. This is the purpose of the first part
of *applyUserFun*. Variable *cl* is set to either the cluster in which the function
is found or **nil** if it turns out to be a top-level function; note that in the case
of implicitly defined functions, *cl* will be the same as *c*:

> **begin** (* *applyUserFun* *)
>   **if** *nm.nametype* = *TWOPART*
>   **then begin**
>   *cl* := *fetchCluster*(*nm.clpart*);
>   **if** *cl* = **nil**
>   **then** ... undefined cluster error ...;
>   *f* := *fetchFun*(*nm.funpart*, *cl*↑.*exported*)
>   **end**
>   **else begin** (* one-part name *)
>   *cl* := *c*;
>   **if** *cl* = **nil** (* called from top level *)
>   **then** *f* := *fetchFun*(*nm.funpart*, *fundefs*)
>   **else begin** (* try exported function first *)
>   *f* := *fetchFun*(*nm.funpart*, *cl*↑.*exported*);
>   **if** *f* = **nil**
>   **then begin** (* else non-exported *)
>   *f* := *fetchFun*(*nm.funpart*, *cl*↑.*nonexported*);
>   **if** *f* = **nil**
>   **then begin** (* else top-level *)
>   *cl* := **nil**;
>   *f* := *fetchFun*(*nm.funpart*, *fundefs*);
>   **end**
>   **end**
>   **end**
>   **end**;
>   **if** *f* = **nil**
>   **then** ... undefined function error ...;
>   *checkArgs*(*nm*, *f*, *cl*);

checkArgs is a local procedure, not shown here, that does various kinds of checks on the arguments to *f*, such as that the number of arguments is correct. It does a sort of "type-checking" for selectors and settors, testing, for example, that when a settor **s** is applied, its argument is a *USER* value that has a binding for **s**.

applyUserFun continues with a case statement that handles the four types of functions. The *NORMAL* case should be familiar:

```
with f↑ do
    case ftype of
        NORMAL:
            begin
                rho := mkEnv(formals, actuals);
                applyUserFun := eval(body, rho, cl)
            end;
        CONSTRUCTOR:
            applyUserFun := mkUSER(mkEnv(cl↑.clrep, actuals));
        SELECTOR:
            begin
                valrho := actuals↑.head↑.userval;
                applyUserFun := fetch(nm.funpart, valrho)
            end;
        SETTOR:
            begin
                valrho := actuals↑.head↑.userval;
                v := actuals↑.tail↑.head;
                assign(selname, v, valrho);
                applyUserFun := v
            end
    end (* case and with *)
end; (* applyUserFun *)
```

6.3.8 READ-EVAL-PRINT LOOP

The only change here is to recognize cluster definitions and print the cluster names, just as is done for function definitions.

6.4 Example — Polynomials

This example is from Liskov and Guttag [1986, p. 68]. It is the cluster **Poly** (Figures 6.8 and 6.9), an immutable type whose elements are polynomials over a single variable, which we will refer to as x. In our version, their degree is limited to 19.

```
(cluster Poly
    ; Export:  create, degree, coeff, zero?, add, minus, sub, mul, prnt
    (rep coeffs lo hi)
    (define create (c n)
        (begin
            (set A (Array$new 0 20))
            (Array$assign A n c)
            (Poly A n n)))
    (define degree (p) (hi p))
    (define coeff (p n)
        (if (or (< n (lo p)) (> n (hi p))) 0 (Array$index (coeffs p) n)))
    (define zero? (p) (= 0 (coeff p (lo p))))
    (define add (p q)
        (begin
            (set result (create 0 0))
            (set-lo result (min (lo p) (lo q)))
            (set-hi result (max (hi p) (hi q)))
            (set i (lo result))
            (while (<= i (hi result))
                (begin
                    (set-coeff result i (+ (coeff p i) (coeff q i)))
                    (set i (+1 i))))
            (remove-zeros result)
            result))
    (define minus (p)
        (begin
            (set result (create 0 0))
            (set-lo result (lo p))
            (set-hi result (hi p))
            (set i (lo p))
            (while (<= i (hi p))
                (begin
                    (set-coeff result i (- 0 (coeff p i)))
                    (set i (+1 i))))
            result))
    (define sub (p q)
        (add p (minus q)))
```

Figure 6.8: Cluster Poly (part 1)

```
(define mul (p q)
   (begin
      (set result (create 0 0))
      (if (> (+ (hi p) (hi q)) 19) result ; error!
         (if (or (zero? p) (zero? q)) result
            (begin
               (set-lo result (+ (lo p) (lo q)))
               (set-hi result (+ (hi p) (hi q)))
               (set p-hi (hi p))
               (set q-hi (hi q))
               (set q-lo (lo q))
               (set i (lo p))
               (while (<= i p-hi)
                  (begin
                     (set j q-lo)
                     (while (<= j q-hi)
                        (begin
                           (set-coeff result (+ i j)
                              (+ (coeff result (+ i j))
                                 (* (coeff p i) (coeff q j))))
                     (set j (+1 j))))
                  (set i (+1 i))))
               result)))))
(define prnt (p)
   (if (zero? p) (begin (print 0) (print 0))
      (begin
         (set expon (hi p))
         (while (>= expon (lo p))
            (if (= (coeff p expon) 0)
               (set expon (- expon 1))
               (begin (print (coeff p expon)) (print expon)
                  (set expon (- expon 1)))))))))
; set-coeff, remove-zeros not exported
(define set-coeff (p n c) (Array$assign (coeffs p) n c))
(define remove-zeros (p) ; (lo p) is too low, and/or (hi p) too high
   (begin
      (while (and (= 0 (coeff p (lo p))) (<= (lo p) (hi p)))
         (set-lo p (+1 (lo p))))
      (if (> (lo p) (hi p)) ; p a zero polynomial
         (begin (set-lo p 0) (set-hi p 0))
         (while (= 0 (coeff p (hi p))) (set-hi p (- (hi p) 1))))))
)
```

Figure 6.9: Cluster Poly (part 2)

```
(define diff (p)
    (begin
       (set n 1)
       (set pdx (Poly$create 0 0))
       (while (<= n (Poly$degree p))
          (begin
             (set pdx (Poly$add pdx
                     (Poly$create (* n (Poly$coeff p n)) (- n 1))))
             (set n (+1 n))))
       pdx))
```

Figure 6.10: Function `diff`

Polynomials have the following operations:

create: Given arguments c and n, return the polynomial cx^n.

degree: The highest power of x that has a nonzero coefficient.

coeff: The coefficient of a given power of x.

zero?: Test if a polynomial is zero.

add: Add two polynomials.

minus: Negate a polynomial.

sub: Subtract two polynomials.

mul: Multiply two polynomials.

prnt:[6] Print the nonzero coefficients and corresponding exponents. Polynomial $5x^2 + 7$ prints as:

5

2

7

0.

Here, then, is a use of `Poly`. The client function `diff`, given in Figure 6.10,

---

[6]Why "prnt" instead of "print"? Because `print` is called from within `prnt`, to print integers, and if the cluster had a function called `print`, then, by the scope rules, it would be the one invoked. In short, if a cluster function has the same name as a built-in (or any other globally defined) function, it is impossible to call that built-in function from within the cluster.

does differentiation:

```
-> (set p (Poly$create 5 2)) ; represents polynomial 5x²
<userval>

-> (set q (Poly$create 3 1)) ; represents 3x
<userval>

-> (set r (Poly$add p q)) ; represents 5x² + 3x
<userval>

-> (Poly$prnt (diff r)) ; derivative of 5x² + 3x is 10x + 3
10
1
3
0
```

Polynomials are represented by three items of data: the 20-element array `coeffs`, giving the coefficients, and the integers `lo` and `hi`, $0 \leq lo, hi < 20$, giving the exponents corresponding to the lowest and highest nonzero coefficients. A polynomial is zero if (`Array$index coeffs lo`) is zero. The coding of the functions is generally straightforward. `mul` determines the coefficient of x^n by adding the products of all coefficients of x^i in p and x^j in q for which $i + j = n$. `add` adds the coefficients of x^i in p and q for all i; when done, it calls `remove-zeros`, which adjusts `lo` higher and/or `hi` lower, if their coefficients are zero.

`Poly` is an immutable data type. The exported functions that return polynomials — `add`, `minus`, `sub`, and `mul` — return new instances of `Poly` and do not modify their arguments. Although the function `set-coeff` does mutate its argument, it is not exported and is applied only to new instances.

6.5 CLU as It Really Is

CLU is a language for building reliable programs. Data abstraction via clusters is the principal feature supporting this goal. It is not the only one, however. One of the most crucial is *compile-time type-checking*, as in PASCAL. Another is *exception-handling*. Following a brief discussion of real CLU syntax and some aspects of clusters which are absent from our version of CLU, these other CLU features are discussed.

6.5.1 SYNTAX

CLU syntax is traditional and rather PASCAL-like. References to cluster operations use two-part names just as in our version, but several data types we have defined are built in and use special syntax; for example, arrays use PASCAL syntax for indexing and assignment.

Here is our differentiation function (Figure 6.10) in real CLU:

```
diff = proc (p: Poly) returns (Poly)
        n: int := 1
        pdx: Poly := Poly$create(0,0)
        while (n <= Poly$degree(p))
                pdx := Poly$add(pdx, Poly$create(n*Poly$coeff(p, n), n−1))
                n := n+1
        end
        return (pdx)
    end diff
```

6.5.2   CLUSTERS IN REAL CLU

Syntax.   Figure 6.11 contains part of the code for the `Poly` cluster, as it would appear in real CLU. Some points may require explanation:

- A record with three components is used for the representation, introduced by the keyword **rep**. The notation for record types and record selection

---

```
Poly = cluster is create, degree, coeff, iszero, add, minus, sub, mul, prnt

        rep = record[coeffs: array[int], lo, hi: int]

        create = proc (c, n: int) returns (Poly)
                A: array[int] := array[int]$create(0)
                A[n] := c
                return (up(rep${coeffs: A, lo: n, hi: n}))
            end create

        degree = proc (p: Poly) returns (int)
                return (down(p).hi)
            end degree

        coeff = proc (p: Poly, n: int) returns (int)
                r: rep := down(p)
                if (n < r.lo) | (n > r.hi)
                then return (0)
                else return (r.coeffs[n])
                end
            end coeff
                ⋮
end Poly
```

Figure 6.11: Cluster *Poly* in real CLU

is close to that of PASCAL.

- The *coeffs* component is declared to be of type *array*[*int*]. This is the type of arrays with integer entries. The index type of arrays is always *int*.

- In *create*:

  – Variables may be declared and initialized in the same statement.

  – The *create* operation on arrays has only one argument. It gives the lower index bound; the upper index bound is initially set to one less than this value (giving an empty array), but it can be increased dynamically.

  – The keyword **rep** is used in cluster operations as an abbreviation for the representation type. Record constants can be written by writing the type of the record (here, **rep** abbreviates it), a "$", then the value of each field, enclosed in curly braces.

  – The keyword **up** is used similarly to our constructor functions: it turns an element of the representation type into an instance of the cluster.

- In *degree*:

  – **down** is the inverse of **up**: it turns an instance of the cluster into an instance of the representation type. This permits record selection to be applied to *p*.

There is one other syntactic abbreviation that should be mentioned because it occurs frequently. Note that **up** and **down** are used in very stereotyped ways: **down** is applied to instances of the cluster when they are passed in as arguments, and **up** is applied before instances are returned as results. To handle these situations more conveniently, the keyword **cvt** can appear in an argument list of a cluster function or as the return type; it causes **up** or **down** to be applied at the appropriate time. Thus, *create* and *degree* become:

$$create = \textbf{proc } (c,\ n:\ int)\ \textbf{returns } (\textbf{cvt})$$

$$\vdots$$

$$\qquad \textbf{return } (\textbf{rep}\${\text{coeffs}:\ A,\ lo:\ n,\ hi:\ n\})$$
$$\textbf{end } create$$

$$degree = \textbf{proc } (p:\ \textbf{cvt})\ \textbf{returns } (int)$$
$$\qquad \textbf{return } (p.hi)$$
$$\textbf{end } degree$$

Poly = **cluster** [*t*: **type**] **is** *create, degree, coeff, iszero, add, minus, sub, mul, prnt*
    where *t* **has**
        add, mul, sub: **proctype** (*t,t*) **returns** (*t*)
        zero: **proctype** () **returns** (*t*)
        iszero: **proctype** (*t*) **returns** (*bool*)

    rep = **record**[*coeffs*: *array*[*t*], *lo, hi*: *int*]
       ⋮

    add = **proc** (*p, q*: **cvt**) **returns** (**cvt**)
        result: **rep** := **rep**$*create*(*array*[*t*]$*create*(0),0,0)
        result.lo := *min*(*p.lo, q.lo*)
        result.hi := *max*(*p.hi, q.hi*)
        i: *int* := *result.lo*
        while (*i* <= *result.hi*)
            result.coeffs[*i*] := *t*$*add*(*p.coeffs*[*i*], *q.coeffs*[*i*])
            i := *i*+1
        end
        removezeros(*result*)
        return *result*
    end *add*
       ⋮

    end *Poly*

Figure 6.12: Cluster *Poly*, polymorphic version

Parameterized Clusters. Our version of *Poly* allows only polynomials with integer coefficients. There is no real reason for this, since addition and multiplication of polynomials is the same regardless of the type of coefficient; the only requirement is that it be possible to add, negate, and multiply coefficients and test if they equal zero. In real CLU, *Poly* could be written to permit different types of coefficients by using *type parameters*. Such clusters are called *generic*, or *polymorphic*.[7] Figure 6.12 gives part of the polymorphic version of *Poly*. With it, we can write:

        intpoly: *Poly*[*int*]
        realpoly: *Poly*[*real*]
        polypoly: *Poly*[*Poly*[*int*]]

Iterators. One frequently wants to iterate over all the elements of a list, a set, or an array, the coefficients of a polynomial, or the labels in a tree. To aid in such iteration, CLU has a feature called *iterators*, which involves both the

---

[7]We discussed a similar problem in the SCHEME chapter, where we had two different types of sets; see page 104.

cluster feature and the control structures of the language. Within a cluster, the programmer can define a special kind of function, called an *iterator*, which, in effect, produces a list of values; a client of the cluster can invoke this iterator within a special type of iterative statement, executing its body for each value yielded by the iterator.

We use *List* for our example. Here is an iterator which produces a list of all the elements in a list; it would appear within the cluster, like a cluster operation. Assume lists are represented by records having a *car* and a *cdr* field (much as in our version); "˜" is the logical "**not**" operator:

$$elements = \textbf{iter} \ (l \text{: } \textbf{cvt}) \ \textbf{yields} \ (int)$$
$$\textbf{while} \ (\tilde{\ } isnull(l))$$
$$\textbf{yield} \ (l.car)$$
$$l := l.cdr$$
$$\textbf{end}$$
$$\textbf{end} \ elements$$

When *elements* is invoked, the **while** loop is executed as usual, but whenever the **yield** statement is encountered, execution of the loop is suspended and the argument of **yield** is returned. The client calls this iterator within a statement which is a kind of generalization of the traditional **for** statement:

$$sum \text{: } int := 0$$
$$\textbf{for} \ i \text{: } int \ \textbf{in} \ List\$elements \ (l) \ \textbf{do}$$
$$sum := sum + i$$
$$\textbf{end}$$

Each time another value in *List$elements*(*l*) is requested (that is, on each iteration of the **for** loop), the iterator is resumed from just after the last-executed **yield**. When the iterator terminates (in this example, when *isnull*(*l*)), the **for** loop does likewise.

6.5.3   TYPE-CHECKING

All the languages covered in this book thus far, except ML, are *dynamically type-checked*. What this means is that, for example, if you enter (+ (car '(a b c)) 2) in LISP, the interpreter (in real LISP as well as our version) will consider this quite normal, will go ahead and evaluate (car '(a b c)), and only when it is about to try to add 'b to 2 will it realize there is a problem.

Such languages are sometimes called "untyped," but that is a misnomer. Every value *has* a type (integer, symbol, nil, or list, in the case of LISP), but these types are not used in any way until run-time.

There is a broad consensus among language designers and theoreticians that type information should be used to catch program errors *at compile-time*. Furthermore, the more detailed the user's description of his or her data types is, the more such errors can be found. The reader may have found this type-checking in PASCAL to be occasionally burdensome and may even know some language, such as C (Kernighan and Ritchie [1978]), in which type-checking is not so strict. Nonetheless, expert opinion is nearly unanimous that compile-time type-checking is a great boon to programmers and well worth the inconvenience it may sometimes cause.

CLU extends and improves PASCAL's type system in several ways. For one thing, it is *stricter*. PASCAL has a "type insecurity" in its untagged variants:

$$r: \textbf{record}$$
$$\quad \textbf{case } CASETYPE \textbf{ of}$$
$$\quad\quad INTCASE: (icase: integer);$$
$$\quad\quad REALCASE: (rcase: real)$$
$$\quad \textbf{end}$$

$$\vdots$$

$$r.icase := 3;$$
$$write\ (r.rcase);$$

The value that will be written will be the representation of the integer 3, *regarded as floating-point*. Thus, the value that will be printed depends upon the representation of integers and reals. In CLU, this cannot be done. All variants are tagged, and no operation can be performed on the value without first checking the tag.

The major improvement is the introduction of polymorphism. We have mentioned that clusters can have type parameters. Procedures can have them also. A classic problem in PASCAL is the inability to write a procedure *sort* that can be applied to arrays having different element types. Figure 6.13 contains a generic sort routine written in CLU.

In short, by employing an elaborate system of types, CLU provides both convenience of use and strict compile-time type-checking.

6.5.4   EXCEPTION-HANDLING

Many bugs in software can be traced to the programmer's failure to handle a case considered unlikely to occur. In effect, the programmer makes some assumptions about the input data or the operating environment that turn out to be wrong. Even if they are anticipated, these cases can be difficult to deal with; by the time the unusual situation arises, the program may be in a state from which it can find no good way to extricate itself. For example, it might be many levels deep in a recursion and not be able to exit gracefully; or it may have to undo a long series of assignments to restore the state before aborting. This is perhaps why programmers find it easy to convince themselves that *unlikely* cases are in fact *impossible*.

```
sort = proc [t: type] (a: array[t], lo, hi: int) returns (array[t])
        where t has lt: proctype (t,t) returns (bool)
        i: int := lo
        j: int := i+1
        while (i < hi)
                while (j <= hi)
                        if (t$lt(a[j], a[i]))
                        then
                                tmp: t := a[i]
                                a[i] := a[j]
                                a[j] := tmp
                        end
                        j := j+1
                end
                i := i+1
        end
end sort
```

Figure 6.13: Polymorphic procedure *sort*

The CLU designers looked at how exceptional cases could be handled with minimum inconvenience to the programmer (Liskov and Snyder [1979]). This was a signal contribution of the language, because few language designers had confronted the issue. We will describe a subset of CLU's exception-handling mechanism.

Three new statements are added to CLU to implement this feature. In what follows, *e-name* is an arbitrary identifer chosen (by the programmer) to represent some type of exception:

signal *e-name*: This statement causes the current procedure to terminate abruptly; *e-name* determines what *exception handler* will be invoked. A procedure that wants to signal an exception must declare the exception name. Here is an example:

```
car = proc (l: cvt) returns (int) signals (nil_error)
        if (l.type = nil)
        then signal nil_error
        else return (l.carval)
        end
end car
```

statement$_1$ **except when** *e-name*: *statement*$_2$ **end:** This compound statement defines the handler for exception *e-name* in the context of *statement*$_1$. *statement*$_1$ is executed; if, during its execution, *e-name* is signalled by a procedure that it has called, then *statement₂* is immediately executed. An example is:

$$v := \mathit{List\$car(l)}$$
$$\textbf{except when } \mathit{nil\_error}\colon \ v := 0 \textbf{ end}$$

statement **resignal** *e-name***:** If *statement* may receive a signal *e-name* from a procedure that it calls, but it does not wish to handle the exception itself, it may signal the exception to its caller. This is equivalent to:

$$\mathit{statement} \textbf{ except when } \mathit{e\text{-}name}\colon \textbf{ signal } \mathit{e\text{-}name} \textbf{ end}$$

Note that a statement always signals an exception to the calling routine. Thus, if the **signal** is executed in this statement:

$$\cdots \textbf{ signal } \mathit{e\text{-}name} \ \cdots \textbf{ except when } \mathit{e\text{-}name}\colon \ \mathit{statement} \textbf{ end}$$

statement is *not* executed. Rather, the procedure containing this entire statement is terminated, and *e-name* is signalled to its caller.

If a procedure fails to provide a handler for an exception, and if it receives a signal for that exception, the exception is automatically handled by signalling the special exception *failure*, which is implicitly declared globally in every CLU program.

6.6 Related Language — ADA

The ADA programming language grew out of concern within the United States Department of Defense over the proliferation of programming languages being used for DOD software development. Of particular moment was the problem of "embedded systems," in which computers are installed in other equipment and used to control or monitor that equipment. These applications often involve difficult programming problems, such as multiple processes and processors, real-time constraints, and unreliable or vulnerable components. The mainstream languages used for ordinary data-processing and scientific work — mainly COBOL and FORTRAN — had not been applicable for various reasons, so a variety of high-level and machine languages had filled the gap. Around 1974, the DOD decided it could not let this chaotic situation continue and solicited proposals for a new language design, which was to become the standard language for programming embedded systems for the Department. To clarify its needs, the DOD published a series of five documents — called, respectively, Strawman, Woodenman, Tinman, Ironman, and Steelman — giving, in increasingly refined form, the requirements for this new language.

In 1979, the DOD announced its choice to be the language design submitted by CII Honeywell Bull, designed by a team led by Jean Ichbiah. It also announced that the language would be called ADA, after Augusta Ada Byron, daughter of Lord Byron and the world's first programmer, who worked with Charles Babbage, the visionary computer designer. Ichbiah's team then undertook an intensive effort, with input from around the world, to finalize the language design. This was substantially accomplished with publication of the ADA Reference Manual in 1980 (Department of Defense [1983] is a revised version thereof).

The language is in the PASCAL family, in the sense that it supports primarily imperative-style programming. However, it is a much larger language than PASCAL, with many features reflecting advances in language design during the 1970's. The centerpiece of the language is its support for data encapsulation via the *package* feature, a scope-control mechanism. Other features are an exception-handling construct for improved reliability and a "generics" feature for polymorphism. Interprocess communication is supported by a rendezvous mechanism called *tasks*.

ADA appears to be flourishing. There are now many compilers available — after a slow start owing to the size of the language — and DOD continues to support the language with a vast research and education effort. Moreover, increasing numbers of schools are teaching ADA in their computer science curricula.

This section provides an overview of the most significant features of ADA:

- The PASCAL-like base of ADA includes such additional features as aggregate initialization, subtypes, and overloading of function and procedure names. Examples are used to give the flavor of these features.

- Support for "programming in the large" — that is, for large-scale program organization — is provided by the *package*. A package is a separately-compilable program unit in which a number of names can be defined and selectively exported. One application is data encapsulation.

- An exception-handler can be attached to any function or procedure body.

- An entire program unit can be parameterized with respect to types, functions, and constants. Such a parameterized program unit is called a *generic*. Generics are analogous to the polymorphic procedures and clusters of CLU.

A major feature we will not cover is ADA's support for concurrent programming *via* the *tasking* feature, using which the programmer can define separate processes and their communication protocols.[8] An adequate discussion of the problem of concurrent programming would be a major digression from the theme of this chapter.

---

[8]Support for concurrent programming is actually somewhat characteristic of this entire class of languages. The connection between data abstraction and concurrency is made in a classic paper by Hoare [1974].

6.6.1 *"PROGRAMMING IN THE SMALL" IN ADA*

At the level of individual statements, type declarations, and function and procedure definitions, ADA is similar enough to PASCAL to allow us to present it by example. Here, for example, is the ADA version of the nonrecursive *gcd* function from page 9:

```
— — Non-recursive gcd in ADA
function gcd (m, n: integer) return integer is
      r: integer := m mod n;
      m1: integer := m;
      n1: integer := n;
begin
      while r /= 0 loop
          m1 := n1;
          n1 := r;
          r := m1 mod n1;
          end loop;
      return n1;
end gcd;
```

Comments are opened by double hyphens and extend to the end of the line. Like CLU, ADA allows variables to be declared and initialized on one line. It does not permit assignment to value parameters, which is why the new variables *m1* and *n1* are introduced. (*m* and *n* could be declared as the equivalent of PASCAL **var** parameters, by declaring them as "*m, n*: **in out** *integer*," but that hardly seems the thing to do in this case.) The **while** loop is just as in PASCAL, except that "/=" is used instead of "<>" and the loop is terminated by **end loop**, rather than having its body be a **begin** block. The **return** statement is as in CLU.

Array and record declarations are similar to PASCAL's:

```
type EXPTYPE is (VALEXP,VAREXP,APEXP);

type EXPREC (etype: EXPTYPE);
type EXPLISTREC;
type EXP is access EXPREC;
type EXPLIST is access EXPLISTREC;

type EXPREC (etype: EXPTYPE) is
      record
          case etype is
              when VALEXP => num: NUMBER;
              when VAREXP => varble: NAME;
              when APEXP => optr: NAME; args: EXPLIST;
          end case;
      end record;
```

> **type** *EXPLISTREC* **is record**
> > *head*: *EXP*;
> > *tail*: *EXPLIST*;
> > **end record**;

NAMESIZE: **constant** *integer* := 10;
type *NAMESTRING* **is array** (*integer* **range** 1..*NAMESIZE*) **of** *character*;

The keyword "**access**" is used in declarations in place of the "↑" of PASCAL.
The discriminant of a variant record appears just after the name of the record
in its declaration. Declarations of constants, variables, and types can be freely
interspersed, provided they are declared before use. Unlike PASCAL, pointer
(that is, access) types cannot be declared until the type to which they point is,
which causes a circularity. To get around it, the referent type (e.g., *EXPREC*)
is declared first, but just as a stub; the access type can then be declared,
followed by the full declaration of the referent. The index type "*integer* **range**
1..*NAMESIZE*" is the same as the PASCAL subrange "1..*NAMESIZE*".

Arrays and records are called *composite* types, and ADA allows for writing
constants of composite types, which are called *aggregates*. For example,

> (1=>'a', 2=>'b', 3=>'c', 4..*NAMESIZE*=>'.');

is an aggregate of type *NAMESTRING*, which could be used either in an initialization, for example:

> *name1*: *NAMESTRING* := (1=>'a', 2=>'b', 3=>'c', 4..*NAMESIZE*=>'.');

or in an assignment statement.

In ADA, a subtype of a type *T* is a type having the same operations as *T*
but fewer elements. To put it another way, it is the same as *T* but with certain
constraints imposed on its values. The simplest kind of constraint is a *range*
constraint, as in:

> **subtype** *NAME* **is** *integer* **range** 1..*MAXNAMES*;

which is precisely analogous to the PASCAL declaration "*NAME* = 1..*MAX-NAMES*;" The ADA concept of subtype, however, is more general than this.
For example, this type:

> **type** *NAMESARRAY* **is array** (*integer* **range** <>) **of** *NAMESTRING*;

has subtypes:

> **subtype** *NAMES* **is** *NAMESARRAY*(*NAME*);
> **subtype** *FEWNAMES* **is** *NAMESARRAY*(1..5);

The beauty of this feature is that a function can be declared with parameters of type *NAMESARRAY* and applied to values of type *NAMES* or *FEWNAMES*:

> **procedure** *sort* (*A*: **in out** *NAMESARRAY*; *size*: *integer*) **is**
> **begin**
>   **for** *i* **in** 1..*size* **loop**
>   **for** *j* **in** 1..*i*+1 **loop**
>   **if** *compare_string*(*A*(*i*),*A*(*j*))
>   **then** *swap_string*(*A*(*i*),*A*(*j*));
>   **end if**;
>   **end loop**;
>   **end loop**;
> **end** *sort*;

This solves a well-known problem with PASCAL's type system, alluded to in Section 6.5.3.[9]

To end this section, we mention the feature of *overloading*, whereby the same name can have different meanings depending upon the context of its usage. In ADA, the programmer can define two different procedures called *P*, but having a different number or different types of arguments. The compiler will determine which one is referred to in any call from the number and types of the actual parameters of that call.

6.6.2 SCOPE CONTROL AND PACKAGES

Encapsulated data types as presented in CLU are largely a matter of visibility of names, i.e., scope: In one part of the program — the part in which the operations are defined — the names of representation components, as well as both exported and nonexported operations, are known, and elsewhere in the program only the operations are known. In ADA, data encapsulation is supported entirely by a scope-control construct called the *package*.

A package is a set of declarations divided into two parts, the *specification* and the *body*. The specification contains variable, constant, and type declarations and procedure headers, while the body contains the definitions of those procedures plus auxiliary (nonexported) declarations of all kinds. The names declared in the specification are exported from the package, and the others are not. For example, in our interpreter it would be helpful to isolate those declarations related to names, such as the constants *NAMELENG*

---

[9]Actually, there are two distinct problems here, the problem of polymorphism with respect to the *index* type and with respect to the *component* type. In PASCAL, a sort procedure can sort only arrays of exactly one range and component type — no polymorphism is admitted. The subtype feature of ADA solves the first problem (which is not a problem at all in CLU, because array indices are never declared but instead are determined at run time). For the other part of the problem, the routine in Figure 6.13 gives the CLU solution, and the ADA solution is given in Section 6.6.4.

and *MAXNAMES*, types *NAME*, *NAMESIZE*, and *NAMESTRING*, variables *printNames* and *numNames*, procedures *initNames* and *prName*, and function *install*. Note that the array *printNames*, in which the names are actually stored, is never mentioned outside of *NAME MANAGEMENT*, so it need not be exported from the package that defines these names. Figure 6.14 gives the specification of the package *NameManagement*, and Figure 6.15 gives its body (with the actual definitions of the procedures omitted).

The package specification and body are *separate program units* which may even be compiled separately. Clients of the package need to see only the specification, since they can use only names declared there. This clean separation of specification from implementation is one of the important contributions of ADA to language design.

This example is a useful application of packages to control the visibility of the name *printNames* and as a general organizing unit of a program, but it is not really an encapsulated data type because it is missing the notion of *protection*. The idea of an encapsulated data type is that the user is provided a new type name *T* and can declare variables of type *T* but can do *nothing else* with those variables aside from passing them as arguments and assigning values (of type *T*) to them. By contrast, the types declared in the *NameManagement* package are not protected in any way: A client could declare *nm* to be a *NAME* and then add 1 to it, or declare *word* to be of type *NAMESTRING* and subscript it. This was intentional because there are, in fact, procedures in the interpreter which do just that (e.g., *match* in *INPUT*). However, what we have seen so far affords no way to create this protection should it be needed.

To better appreciate the problem — and its solution — consider another

---

package *NameManagement* **is** — — specification

    NAMELENG : *integer* := 20;
    MAXNAMES : *integer* := 100;

    subtype *NAMESIZE* **is** *integer* **range** 0..*NAMELENG*;
    subtype *NAME* **is** *integer* **range** 1 .. *MAXNAMES*;
    type *NAMESTRING* **is array** (1..*NAMELENG*) **of** *character*;

    numNames: *NAME*;

    procedure *initNames*;
    function *install* (*nm*: *NAMESTRING*) **return** *NAME*;
    procedure *prName* (*nm*: *NAME*);

end *NameManagement*;

Figure 6.14: Specification of package *NameManagement*

---

package body *NameManagement* **is** — — body

> *printNames*: **array** (*NAME*) **of** *NAMESTRING*;
>
> **procedure** *initNames* **is**
>   ... body of *initNames* ...
> **end** *initNames*;
>
> **function** *install* (*nm*: *NAMESTRING*) **return** *NAME* **is**
>   ... body of *install* ...
> **end** *install*;
>
> **procedure** *prName* (*nm*: *NAME*) **is**
>   ... body of *prName* ...
> **end** *prName*;
>
> **end** *NameManagement*;

Figure 6.15: Body of package *NameManagement*

data type in the interpreter which might more naturally be encapsulated, namely environments. Types *ENV* and *ENVREC* are declared globally, and variables of type *ENV* are declared in various places. However, all functions that refer to components of *ENV* records — that is, all those that know how environments are represented — are isolated in the *ENVIRONMENTS* section, with the single exception of *mkEnv* in *DATA STRUCTURE OP's*. Moving *mkEnv* into *ENVIRONMENTS*, this lends itself naturally to being an ADA package, whose specification is given in Figure 6.16.

The body of the *Environments* package (not shown) contains the definitions of all the functions declared in the specification, as well as functions *mkEnv* and *findVar*, which are auxiliary. However, again this specification offers no protection against unwarranted uses of types *ENV* and *ENVREC*; it does not guarantee that environments will only be created by *mkEnv* or that bindings will only be added by *bindVar*. These types must be in the package's specification, since clients need to declare variables of those types (or at least of type *ENV*), but their placement there leaves them unprotected. What is needed is the ability to declare that *ENV* is a type but not say *what* type it is. This is the purpose of *private* types, exemplified in the specification of *Environments* in Figure 6.17.

Clients of this package can declare variables of type *ENV*, assign values to those variables, compare two values of that type for equality, and pass *ENV*'s as arguments to functions and procedures. That is all they can do. Thus, by limiting the scope of names in a particular way, ADA has provided the equivalent of CLU's cluster mechanism. The major difference is that in CLU, a

package *Environments* **is** — — specification

    type *ENVREC*;
    type *ENV* **is access** *ENVREC*;

    type *ENVREC* **is record**
           vars: *NAMELIST*;
           values: *VALUELIST*;
      end record;

    function *emptyEnv* **return** *ENV*;
    procedure *bindVar* (*nm*: *NAME*; *n*: *integer*; *rho*: *ENV*);
    procedure *assign* (*nm*: *NAME*; *n*: *integer*; *rho*: *ENV*);
    function *fetch* (*nm*: *NAME*; *rho*: *ENV*) *return integer*;
    function *isBound* (*nm*: *NAME*; *rho*: *ENV*) *return boolean*;

end *Environments*;

Figure 6.16: Specification of package *Environments*

package *Environments* **is** — — *specification*

    type *ENV* **is private**;

    procedure *bindVar* (*nm*: *NAME*; *n*: *integer*; *rho*: *ENV*);
    procedure *assign* (*nm*: *NAME*; *n*: *integer*; *rho*: *ENV*);
    function *fetch* (*nm*: *NAME*; *rho*: *ENV*) **return** *integer*;
    function *isBound* (*nm*: *NAME*; *rho*: *ENV*) **return** *boolean*;

    private

        type *ENVREC*;
        type *ENV* **is access** *ENVREC*;

        type *ENVREC* **is record**
            vars: *NAMELIST*;
            values: *VALUELIST*;
          end record;

end *Environments*;

Figure 6.17: Better specification of package *Environments*

cluster always corresponds to a new type, whereas in ADA a package is not the same as a type. Rather, it is just a general-purpose construct for controlling name visibility. When used as in Figure 6.17, it corresponds to an encapsulated data type definition, but it is more general in that it can declare more than one type, or none at all (as in our *NameManagement* example).

Packages are usually placed into *libraries*. A program becomes a client of a library package by including a **with** declaration, as in:

with *Environments*;

⋮

client of *Environments*

⋮

However, any use of the names declared in the package must be qualified by the package name. For example, the code in *eval* might be:

with *Environments*;

function *eval* (*e*: *EXP*; *rho*: *Environments.ENV*) **return** *integer*;

    ⋮

    when VAREXP =>
      if *Environments.isBound*(*v, rho*)
      then return *Environments.fetch*(*v, rho*)

    ⋮

This is analogous to CLU's two-part names. However, it can get cumbersome, so ADA provides a way to avoid it, the **use** declaration:

with *Environments*;
use *Environments*;

function *eval* (*e*: *EXP*; *rho*: *ENV*) **return** *integer*;

    ⋮

    when VAREXP =>
      if *isBound*(*v, rho*)
      then return *fetch*(*v, rho*)

    ⋮

Of course, *within* the package, names declared in the package are used in their unqualified form. (The **use** declaration is somewhat analogous to PASCAL's **with** statement, in that both permit components — of a package in ADA or a record in PASCAL — to be accessed via unqualified names.)

6.6.3 EXCEPTIONS

ADA's exception-handling mechanism is not unlike CLU's. Handlers may be attached to procedure or function bodies by adding an **exception** clause analogous to CLU's **except when** (which, in CLU, can be added to *any* statement). Exceptions are declared like constants and are raised by a **raise** statement (like CLU's **signal**). Thus, the *car* example which we used to illustrate CLU's exception-handling looks similar in ADA:

```
package Lists is — — specification

    NIL_ERROR: exception;
    type Listtype is (NILLIST,PAIR);
    type List is private;
    function car (l: List) return integer;
       ⋮
    private
       type List is record
          ⋮
          end record;
end Lists;

package body Lists is — — body

    function car (l: List) return integer is
    begin
       if l.ltype = NILLIST
       then raise NIL_ERROR;
       else return l.carval;
       end if;
    end car;
       ⋮
end Lists;
```

and a client might be:

```
with Lists;
use Lists;
procedure client_proc is
begin
       ⋮
    exception
       when NIL_ERROR => return;
end client_proc;
```

ADA provides several built-in exceptions, such as *CONSTRAINT_ERROR*, which is raised when a constrained value goes out of range, and *NUMERIC_ERROR*, raised for such errors as division by zero. A procedure can include exception-handlers for these exceptions. Exceptions can be handled anonymously by a **when others** clause in the handler and can be propagated by a **raise** statement with no arguments. Thus, this client:

> **with** *Lists*;
> **use** *Lists*;
> **procedure** *client_proc* **is**
> **begin**
>
> > .
> > .
> > .
>
> > **exception**
> > > **when** *NIL_ERROR* => **return**;
> > > **when others** => **raise**;
> > **end** *client_proc*;

returns if a *NIL_ERROR* occurs, and it propagates all other errors.

6.6.4   GENERICS

Figure 6.13 gives a polymorphic sort procedure in CLU that can sort any array regardless of the type of its components. It requires only a comparison function, *lt*, for that type. In ADA, this kind of polymorphism is provided by a macro-like facility called *generics*. A generic unit (whether procedure, function, or package), like a macro, defines certain parameters which are to be provided *at compile-time*. These can be constants, types, procedures, or functions. Here is a generic procedure whose one generic parameter is a type:

> **generic**
> > **type** *ITEM* **is private**;
> **procedure** *gen_swap* (*x*, *y*: **in out** *ITEM*);
>
> **procedure** *gen_swap* (*x*, *y*: **in out** *ITEM*) **is**
> > *temp*: *ITEM*;
> **begin**
> > *temp* := *x*; *x* := *y*; *y* := *temp*;
> **end** *gen_swap*;

The type *ITEM* is the generic parameter. *gen_swap* is the generic procedure; ADA syntax requires that its header be given just after the generic parameter and that its definition be given just after that.

New swap routines can be obtained by "generic instantiation," as in:

> **procedure** *int_swap* **is new** *gen_swap*(*integer*);
> **procedure** *float_swap* **is new** *gen_swap*(*float*);

---

generic
>   **type** *ITEM* **is private**;
>   **with function** *lt* (*x, y*: *ITEM*) **return** *boolean*;
>   **type** *ITEMARRAY* **is array** (*integer* **range** <>) **of** *ITEM*;
procedure *gen_sort* (*A*: **in out** *ITEMARRAY*; *size*: *integer*);

procedure *gen_sort* (*A*: **in out** *ITEMARRAY*; *size*: *integer*) **is**
>   **procedure** *swap* **is new** *gen_swap*(*ITEM*);
begin
>   **for** *i* **in** 1..*size* **loop**
>>   **for** *j* **in** 1..*i*+1 **loop**
>>>   **if** *lt*(*A*(*i*),*A*(*j*))
>>>   **then** *swap*(*A*(*i*),*A*(*j*));
>>>   **end if**;
>>   **end loop**;
>   **end loop**;
end *gen_sort*;

Figure 6.18: Generic sort in ADA

In fact, the overloading feature permits us to write:

>   **procedure** *swap* **is new** *gen_swap*(*integer*);
>   **procedure** *swap* **is new** *gen_swap*(*float*);

Generics allow us to define a sort procedure that is polymorphic with respect to the types of the components of the array being sorted; Figure 6.18 contains such a procedure. The generic parameters are *ITEM*, the type of the array components; *lt*, the comparison function; and *ITEMARRAY*, the type of the array to be sorted. The generic sort procedure is called *gen_sort*. In its definition, it uses a swap procedure obtained from the generic *gen_swap* and, of course, compares elements using *lt*.

Here is one use of *gen_sort*. The parameter ""<"" is called an *operator*, which is just a function whose name is composed of special characters. This is how the normal comparison function on integers is passed as a generic actual parameter:

>   **type** *INTARRAY* **is array** (*integer* **range** <>) **of** *integer*;
>   **procedure** *sort* **is** *new gen_sort*(*integer*, "<", *INTARRAY*);

Now, if a variable is declared of type *INTARRAY*, or more precisely, of a subtype of *INTARRAY*, it can be sorted:

$$AA:\ INTARRAY(1..100);$$
$$\vdots$$
$$sort(AA,\ 10);$$

Packages can also be generic. A generic package defining sets might have a specification like this:

> **generic**
> > **type** *ITEM* **is private**;
> > **with function** *eq* (*x*, *y*: *ITEM*) **return** *boolean*;
>
> **package** *gen_Set* **is**
>
> > **type** *ITEMSET* **is private**;
> > **function** *addelt* (*i*: *ITEM*; *s*: *ITEMSET*) **return** *ITEMSET*;
> > $$\vdots$$
>
> > **private**
>
> > > **type** *ITEMSET* **is** ...
>
> **end** *gen_Set*;

and a set of integers could subsequently be declared as:

> > **package** *INTSET* **is new** *gen_Set* (*integer*, "=");
> > **use** *INTSET*;
>
> > *set1*: *ITEMSET*;

6.6.5 SUMMARY

We cannot pass over ADA without some mention of the controversy that has attended it since the DOD announced its selection in 1979. The computer science community has been skeptical about it from the beginning, with many experienced language designers voicing strong objections either about specific features or about its overall unwieldiness. Perhaps the best known of these is C.A.R. Hoare, who stated in his 1980 Turing Award lecture (Hoare [1981, pg. 82]):

> The mistakes which have [been] made in the last twenty years are being repeated today on an even grander scale. I refer to ... ADA.
> ...

> It is not too late! I believe that by careful pruning of the ADA language, it is still possible to select a very powerful subset that would be reliable and efficient in implementation and safe and economic in use.

That was written in 1980. It is now 1989 and decidedly too late. However, perhaps Professor Hoare was overly pessimistic. Ada does have many features that can lead to better organized programs, and it has certainly garnered a following (though due perhaps as much to the economic clout of the DOD as to its own merits). While these facts cannot, in principle, ever answer Hoare's objections, they do open the possibility that reliable compilers can be developed and that programmers can, in fact, learn to understand the language despite itself.

6.7 Program Verification

Since CLU is the only language covered in this book the overriding goal of whose design is program correctness, this seems an appropriate place to discuss *program verification*, the mathematical proof of the correctness of programs. We will study first the verification problem for the language of Chapter 1, then show how the use of data abstraction allows the basic method to scale up cleanly to larger programs.

6.7.1 PROOFS OF INTEGER PROGRAMS

The central idea of program proofs is to make statements — called *inductive assertions* — about the relationship among the program's variables before and after each statement in the program. It must then be shown that, assuming the assertion made before a statement actually holds, the assertion after the statement will hold.

Thus, we will be looking at *correctness formulas*, written $P\{S\}Q$, where S is a statement in the programming language, and P and Q are inductive assertions. $P\{S\}Q$ means: If P correctly describes the relationship among the program variables before S executes, then after S executes — if it ever finishes — Q will be true.

Some examples follow. For now, we are working in the language of Chapter 1, so that all variables are integers. A combination of English and ordinary mathematical notation is used in the assertions,[10] while the statements will be in the programming language.

$$x \geq 0 \ \{(\text{set x (+1 x))}\} \ x > 0$$

---

[10]In particular, $|\, x\,|$ denotes the absolute value of x. In assertions, $\Rightarrow$ should be read as "implies," $\&$ as "and," $\vee$ as "or," $\sim$ as "not," $\exists$ as "there exists," $\not\exists$ as "there does not exist," and "$\forall$" as "for all."

$$\text{x} > \text{y} \ \{(\text{set x } (\text{- x } 1))\} \ \text{x} \geq \text{y}$$

$$\text{x} = \text{x}' \ \& \ \text{y} = \text{y}' \ \{(\text{begin } (\text{set t x}) \ (\text{set x y}) \ (\text{set y t}))\}$$
$$\text{x} = \text{y}' \ \& \ \text{y} = \text{x}'$$

$$\text{x} = \text{x}' \ \{(\text{if } (\text{>= x } 0) \ (\text{set y x}) \ (\text{set y } (\text{- } 0 \text{ x})))\} \ \text{y} = |\,\text{x}'\,|$$

To understand these formulas, a distinction needs to be made between *program variables* — those occurring in S — and *assertion variables* — those occurring in P or Q but not in S. The assertion variables can have any value, as long as it is the same for every occurrence in the correctness formula. The last correctness formula, for example, says that if x has some value, call it x′, then after executing the if statement, y has the value $|\,\text{x}'\,|$.

Of course, it is not just a matter of *stating* correctness formulas, but of *proving* them. Two kinds of knowledge are used in doing this:

Programming knowledge, that is, knowledge about the programming language. This is what allows us to say $\text{x} = \text{x}' \ \{(\text{set y x})\} \ \text{y} = \text{x} = \text{x}'$, and to assert the correctness of the swap example. However, in and of itself it does not suffice to prove any of the other examples.

Domain knowledge, that is, knowledge about the set of values being manipulated, the integers in this case. The use of domain knowledge is pervasive, and it is often applied unconsciously. The proof of the first example above relies upon the fact that for any integer x, $x \geq 0 \Rightarrow x+1 > 0$. The second uses the fact that for any x and y, $x > y \Rightarrow x - 1 \geq y$. These may seem obvious, but the former is false, for example, in modulo arithmetic, and the latter is false in the real numbers, so that it is really the properties of the domain of integers that are being relied upon.

A crucial discovery of Floyd [1967] and Hoare [1969] was that, although programming knowledge and domain knowledge are both needed in proving program correctness, the proof process can be structured in such a way that their uses are separated. What we will do is to give a rule for each type of statement, which embodies only programming knowledge about that statement. A single rule will be introduced whose purpose is to tie statements together by using domain knowledge.

The rule for the assignment statement, to be given first, requires a preliminary definition:

Definition 6.1 Given an assertion about some variables including x, and given an expression e, the assertion denoted $P|_{\text{x}}^{\text{e}}$ is P with occurrences of x replaced by e; that is, the assertion P is made about the value of e rather than the value of x.

This definition is, of course, very loose, since we haven't even said exactly what an "assertion" is. We prefer to keep things at this level and trust the reader will get the idea from examples, of which we now present two:

- If P is the assertion "x is odd," then $P|_x^{(* \ 2 \ x)}$ is the assertion "x $\times$ 2 is odd" (which is a false assertion for any x, of course, but still an assertion).

- If P is the assertion "x < y," then $P|_x^{(- \ x \ 1)}$ is "x $-$ 1 < y."

Here, then, is the rule that summarizes our programming knowledge about assignment statements, allowing us to deduce correctness formulas involving them:

Assignment Rule. If P is an assertion, and e is an expression that has no side-effects, then the following correctness formula is necessarily true:

$$P|_x^e \ \{ \ (\text{set x e}) \ \} \ P$$

The rule simply says this: If P is going to be true after the assignment to x, and if P talks about the value of x, then it must be true of the value that is being assigned to x. Two examples:

- y = y' {(set x y)} x = y', where P is x = y', so $P|_x^y$ is y = y'.

- x $-$ 1 $\geq$ y {(set x (- x 1))} x $\geq$ y, where P is x $\geq$ y, so $P|_x^{(- \ x \ 1)}$ is x $-$ 1 $\geq$ y.

This last example illustrates what is meant by saying that the assignment rule is devoid of domain knowledge. It does not allow us to assert

$$x > y \ \{(\text{set x (- x 1)})\} \ x \geq y \tag{6.1}$$

because it provides no way to apply our knowledge that $x - 1 \geq y$ and $x > y$ are equivalent. To draw conclusions like this, a rule that applies domain knowledge is needed. Here is such a rule; it will be followed by rules for the **begin**, **if**, and **while** statements.

Rule of consequence. Suppose we know (by whatever means) that $P\{S\}Q$, and we know by domain knowledge that $P' \Rightarrow P$ and that $Q \Rightarrow Q'$. Then we can conclude $P'\{S\}Q'$.

Again, the rule is not hard to understand. $P\{S\}Q$ means that, if P is true, then Q will be true after executing S. But if P' is true, then, since $P' \Rightarrow P$, P is also true, so after executing S, Q will be true; but since $Q \Rightarrow Q'$, Q' will be true. Thus, if P' is true, then Q' will be true after executing S; that is, $P'\{S\}Q'$.

The rule of consequence applies to (6.1) as follows: We learned (from programming knowledge, or more specifically, from the assignment rule) that

$$x - 1 \geq y \ \{(\text{set x (- x 1)})\} \ x \geq y.$$

By domain knowledge, we know $x > y \Rightarrow x - 1 \geq y$, so let P' be $x > y$. Of course, any assertion implies itself, so let both Q and Q' be $x \geq y$. The rule of consequence gives (6.1).

We can now complete our set of rules. The rules for begin and if are given first; the while rule requires somewhat more explanation.

Composition rule. If we know $P\{S_1\}R_1$, $R_1\{S_2\}R_2$, ..., $R_{n-1}\{S_n\}Q$, we can conclude

$$P\{(\text{begin } S_1 \ldots S_n)\}Q.$$

Alternation rule. From $P \& e\{S_1\}Q$ and $P \& \sim e\{S_2\}Q$, we can conclude

$$P\{(\text{if } e \ S_1 \ S_2)\}Q.$$

The proof of the swap routine uses the composition rule: First, the following conclusions are obtained from the assignment rule:

$$x = x' \ \& \ y = y' \ \{(\text{set } t \ x)\} \ t = x' \ \& \ y = y'$$
$$t = x' \ \& \ y = y' \ \{(\text{set } x \ y)\} \ t = x' \ \& \ x = y'$$
$$t = x' \ \& \ x = y' \ \{(\text{set } y \ t)\} \ y = x' \ \& \ x = y'$$

The rule of composition allows us to conclude

$$x = x' \ \& \ y = y' \ \{(\text{begin } \cdots)\} \ y = x' \ \& \ x = y'$$

The absolute value function serves as an example of the alternation rule. We obtain from the assignment rule:

$$x = x' \ \& \ x \geq 0 \ \{(\text{set } y \ x)\} \ y = x' \ \& \ y \geq 0$$
$$-x = -x' \ \& \ -x \geq 0 \ \{(\text{set } y \ (\text{- } 0 \ x))\} \ y = -x' \ \& \ y \geq 0$$

The rule of consequence gives:

$$x = x' \ \& \ x \geq 0 \ \{(\text{set } y \ x)\} \ y = \mid x' \mid$$
$$x = x' \ \& \ x \not\geq 0 \ \{(\text{set } y \ (\text{- } 0 \ x))\} \ y = \mid x' \mid$$

The alternation rule is now applicable:

$$x = x' \ \{(\text{if } (\text{>= } x \ 0) \ (\text{set } y \ x) \ (\text{set } y \ (\text{- } 0 \ x)))\} \ y = \mid x' \mid.$$

The rule for the while statement is more subtle than either of these rules. Since there is no way to know how many times the body of the while will be executed, we must make some assertion which will *always* be true when the body of the loop is begun, no matter how many iterations have occurred. In other words, it must be true whenever the body is executed, and *its truth must be preserved by the execution of the body*; such an assertion is called a *loop invariant*. The definition may sound difficult to satisfy, but in fact loop invariants always exist.

Consider this statement:

```
(begin
    (set y 1)
    (while (<> x 0)
        (begin
            (set y (* 2 y))
            (set x (- x 1)))))
```

What relation between x and y invariably holds both *before* and *after* the execution of the body of the loop? It is: $y = 2^{x'-x}$, where x' is the initial value of x (assuming that $x' \geq 0$).

Note two points about this invariant: First, it must hold only when the body actually *is* executed, which is to say, only when $x \neq 0$, and it is only in this case that the body preserves its truth. Second, it holds before and after execution of the body, but not necessarily *during*.

The rule for the while statement is:

Iteration Rule. Suppose P is a loop invariant for the statement (while e S); in other words, P & e$\{S\}P$. Then we can conclude

$$P\{(\text{while e } S)\}P \ \& \ \sim e.$$

For the exponentiation example, P is the assertion $y = 2^{x'-x}$ & $x \geq 0$, since

$$y = 2^{x'-x} \ \& \ x \geq 0 \ \& \ x \neq 0$$
$$\{(\text{begin (set y (* 2 y)) (set x (- x 1)))}\}$$
$$y = 2^{x'-x} \ \& \ x \geq 0$$

can be shown by use of the rules of assignment, composition, and consequence (exercise for the reader). From this, we conclude, from the iteration rule:

$$y = 2^{x'-x} \ \& \ x \geq 0 \ \{(\text{while (<> x 0) (begin } \cdots))\} \ y = 2^{x'-x} \ \& \ x = 0,$$

from which we infer, by the rule of consequence,

$$y = 2^{x'-x} \ \& \ x \geq 0 \ \{(\text{while (<> x 0) (begin } \cdots))\} \ y = 2^{x'}.$$

We can now prove

$$x = x' \ \& \ x \geq 0 \ \{(\text{begin (set y 1) (while } \cdots))\} \ y = 2^{x'}.$$

by the rules of assignment, composition, and consequence (exercise for the reader), the central use of domain knowledge being the use of the fact that $y = 1$ & $x = x' \Rightarrow y = 2^{x-x'}$.

6.7.2 PROOFS OF PROGRAMS WITH FUNCTION CALLS

The direct treatment of function calls in the context of Floyd–Hoare verification is problematic simply because there is no way to refer to the value returned from a function call. So we will assume that functions assign their values to global variables and these global variables are then used. This brings the entire program into the imperative programming style, for which this verification approach is suited. As an example, instead of writing:

```
(define listsum (l)
    (if (List$null? l) 0
        (+ (List$car l) (listsum (List$cdr l))))),
```

we will write:

```
(define listsum (l)
    (if (List$null? l) (set result 0)
        (begin
            (listsum (List$cdr l))
            (set result (+ (List$car l) result)))))
```

The verification of the uses of a function is not really difficult; it is a matter of verifying the body of the function and then adapting the correctness formula so obtained to a specific call. However, when the function is defined recursively it adds a slight twist to the problem. We present first three rules that together allow for the verification of calls of nonrecursive functions, and then we show how to verify recursive functions.

Suppose, then, that we have a function[11]

$$\text{(define f } (\vec{x}) \; S).$$

Throughout this section, we make two simplifying assumptions about f: (a) S contains no assignment to any of the x_i; and (b) in any call $(f \; \vec{u})$, S contains no assignment to any variable occurring in $\vec{u}$. (The result of these assumptions is that calling $(f \; \vec{u})$ is exactly the same as executing S after first substituting the u_i for all occurrences of the x_i.)

The function definition rule allows us to assert that a single correctness formula summarizes the action of f, and the function application rule then specializes that correctness formula for particular calls.

Function Definition Rule. From $P\{S\}Q$, we can conclude $P\{(f \; \vec{x})\}Q$.

---

[11]$\vec{x}$ is shorthand for $x_1 \ldots x_n$, and likewise for $\vec{u}$.

Function Application Rule. From $P\{(\text{f } \vec{x})\}Q$, we can conclude[12] $P|^{\vec{\text{u}}}_{\vec{x}}\{(\text{f } \vec{\text{u}})\}Q|^{\vec{\text{u}}}_{\vec{x}}$.

For example, define

```
(define abs (x) (if (>= x 0) (set y x) (set y (- 0 x))))
```

Rules given in earlier subsections allow us to prove easily:

$$\text{true} \quad \{(\text{if } (\text{>= x 0}) \cdots)\} \quad (x < 0 \,\&\, y = -x) \lor (x \geq 0 \,\&\, y = x)$$

where P's being "true" indicates that there are no special preconditions on x. The function definition rule implies:

$$\text{true} \quad \{(\text{abs x})\} \quad (x < 0 \,\&\, y = -x) \lor (x \geq 0 \,\&\, y = x)$$

Then, for the call (abs -7), the function application rule allows us to conclude:

$$\text{true} \quad \{(\text{abs -7})\} \quad (-7 < 0 \,\&\, y = 7) \lor (-7 \geq 0 \,\&\, y = -7),$$

from which the rule of consequence gives:

$$\text{true} \quad \{(\text{abs -7})\} \quad y = 7.$$

Our preference is to apply the function definition rule *once*, then use it for all calls of f. In other words, we want to prove one formula $P\{(\text{f } \vec{x})\}Q$ that completely summarizes the action of f. There is, however, a slight glitch. A function call may occur within another function, and any knowledge about the values of the calling function's variables must be preserved across the call. So we add a new rule, not specific to function calls, that allows the application rule to be more readily adapted to specific calls:

Frame Rule. If R is an assertion that does not mention any variables that can be modified during the execution of S, then if we can prove $P\{S\}Q$, we can conclude $R \,\&\, P\{S\}R \,\&\, Q$.

What is missing up to now is a way of proving properties of recursively defined functions. Conclusions about an application of a function f can be drawn only from a proof about the body of f. So if that body itself contains calls to f, we are in a cycle and can get nowhere. The following rule is rather surprising, because it seems circular. It is beyond the scope of this treatment to explain why it is valid, but we will, as usual, depend upon examples to build the reader's intuition.

---

[12]The notation $P|^{\vec{\text{u}}}_{\vec{x}}$ denotes the *simultaneous* substitution of all u_i for x_i. That is, the substitutions are not done sequentially, but all at once. This is significant if some u_i contains some x_j, which is possible if the calling function has a local variable called x_j.

Recursive Function Rule. Suppose that by *assuming* $P\{(\text{f } \vec{x})\}Q$, we can prove $P\{S\}Q$. Then we can conclude $P\{(\text{f } \vec{x})\}Q$.

In other words, roughly speaking, if f can be proven to work by assuming all recursive calls work, then f works.

One source of confusion, related to the apparent circularity of this rule, shows up in a function like this:

```
(define loop (x) (loop x)).
```

Clearly, loop does nothing but run forever, yet the recursive function rule allows us to prove $P\{(\text{loop } 0)\}Q$ for *any* P and Q! This is no contradiction, however, because according to the definition of correctness formulas, $P\{S\}Q$ is necessarily true if S does not terminate.

For a legitimate application of this rule, consider the function listsum given earlier:

```
(define listsum (l)
    (if (List$null? l) (set result 0)
      (begin
        (listsum (List$cdr l))
        (set result (+ (List$car l) result)))))
```

Letting $|\,\text{l}\,|$ denote the length of list l, omitting the "List$" on each function, and letting $(\text{cdr}^i \text{ l})$ denote i applications of cdr to l, our goal is to prove:

$$\text{true } \{(\text{listsum l})\} \text{ result} = \sum_{i=0}^{|\text{l}|-1} (\text{car } (\text{cdr}^i \text{ l})) \qquad (6.2)$$

The recursive function rule directs us to *assume* (6.2), and use it to prove:

$$\text{true } \{(\text{if } (\text{null? l}) \cdots)\} \text{ result} = \sum_{i=0}^{|\text{l}|-1} (\text{car } (\text{cdr}^i \text{ l})) \qquad (6.3)$$

Obviously, we need to apply the alternation rule, for which two correctness formulas must be proved:

$$\text{l} = \text{nil } \{(\text{set result 0})\} \text{ result} = \sum_{i=0}^{|\text{l}|-1} (\text{car } (\text{cdr}^i \text{ l})) \qquad (6.4)$$

$$\text{l} \neq \text{nil } \{(\text{begin } (\text{listsum } (\text{cdr l})) \cdots)\} \text{ result} = \sum_{i=0}^{|\text{l}|-1} (\text{car } (\text{cdr}^i \text{ l})) \qquad (6.5)$$

Formula (6.4) is true, because l=nil $\Rightarrow$ $|\,\text{l}\,|$=0, so $\sum_{i=0}^{|\text{l}|-1}(\cdots) = 0$. To prove (6.5), use the application rule on the assumption (6.2) to get:

$$\text{true } \{(\text{listsum } (\text{cdr l}))\} \text{ result} = \sum_{i=0}^{|(\text{cdr l})|-1} (\text{car } (\text{cdr}^i \text{ (cdr l)}))$$

Furthermore, the assignment rule gives:

$$\texttt{(car 1) + result} = \sum_{i=0}^{|1|-1} \texttt{(car (cdr}^i \texttt{ 1))}$$
$$\texttt{\{ (set result (+ (car 1) result)) \}}$$
$$\texttt{result} = \sum_{i=0}^{|1|-1} \texttt{(car (cdr}^i \texttt{ 1))}$$

We need only prove

$$\texttt{result} = \sum_{i=0}^{|\texttt{(cdr 1)}|-1} \texttt{(car (cdr}^i \texttt{ (cdr 1)))}$$
$$\Rightarrow \texttt{(car 1) + result} = \sum_{i=0}^{|1|-1} \texttt{(car (cdr}^i \texttt{ 1))},$$

which is straightforward, in order to obtain (6.5) by the composition rule, the rule of consequence, and the frame rule.

The alternation rule now gives (6.3), and the recursive function rule leads to (6.2).

6.7.3 PROOFS OF CLIENT PROGRAMS

The reason we have placed so much emphasis on the distinction between *programming knowledge* and *domain knowledge* in proving program correctness is that this is the distinction that allows us to extend the method to proofs of programs using user-defined data abstractions.

Indeed, there is little to say about proving such programs. The only difference from proving integer programs is that, in applying the rule of consequence, we can use our knowledge about the user-defined data abstraction (as well as about the integers, if they are also used in the program).

Consider the program `reverse` in Figure 6.19, a client of `SpArray`. The claim is that when this function is called it reverses the elements of `A`. That is, if `A` starts as the array $a_0, a_1, \ldots, a_{100}$, then it ends as $a_{100}, a_{99}, \ldots, a_0$.

To prove this, we will need to apply domain knowledge about arrays. In particular, we know that if $\texttt{A} = a_0, a_1, \ldots, a_{100}$, then $(\texttt{SpArray\$index A i}) = a_i$, and after executing $(\texttt{SpArray\$assign A i v})$, $\texttt{A} = a_0, \ldots, a_{i-1}, v, a_{i+1}, \ldots, a_{100}$.

The loop invariant here is somewhat complicated to express. What it says is that elements $a_0, \ldots, a_{\texttt{lo}-1}$ and $a_{\texttt{hi}+1}, \ldots, a_{100}$ have been swapped, in reverse order. More precisely, assuming the starting value of `A` was $a_0, a_1, \ldots, a_{100}$, then whenever execution of the body of the loop commences, we have:

$$\texttt{A} = a_{100}, \ldots, a_{\texttt{hi}+1}, a_{\texttt{lo}}, a_{\texttt{lo}+1}, \ldots, a_{\texttt{hi}}, a_{\texttt{lo}-1}, a_{\texttt{lo}-2}, \ldots, a_0.$$

When the loop terminates, `lo=hi`, so we can conclude:

$$\texttt{A} = a_{100}, \ldots, a_{\texttt{lo}}, \ldots, a_0.$$

It is in proving that the loop invariant is an invariant that our domain knowledge about arrays is applied. We will not go into the same kind of detail as

```
(define reverse (A)
    (begin
        (set lo 0)
        (set hi 100)
        (while (<> lo hi)
            (begin
                (set vlo (SpArray$index A lo))
                (set vhi (SpArray$index A hi))
                (if (or (<> vlo 0) (<> vhi 0))
                    (begin
                        (SpArray$assign A lo vhi)
                        (SpArray$assign A hi vlo))
                    0) ; no else branch
                (set lo (+1 lo))
                (set hi (- hi 1)))))))
```

Figure 6.19: Function `reverse`

in the last section, but the crucial step is to notice that, after the `if` statement, we have:

$$\mathtt{A} = a_{100}, \ldots, a_{hi+1}, a_{hi}, a_{lo+1}, \ldots, a_{hi-1}, a_{lo}, a_{lo-1}, \ldots, a_0;$$

that is, the values of a_{lo} and a_{hi} have been swapped. The assignments to `lo` and `hi` then restore the invariant.

Note that this client of `SpArray` could just as easily be a client of `Array` simply by changing the two-part names it uses. This fact gives a good handle on the value of data abstraction: Client programs are correct for reasons relating only to the abstract properties of the data types they use, independent of their representations. Whether or not you use formal verification techniques as in this section, this statement effectively summarizes the motivation behind the use of data abstraction in programming.

The student may well ask where this domain knowledge comes from. It is fine to assume an understanding of arrays, which are very familiar, but there is an infinite variety of data types definable in CLU: How can we know about all of them? One answer is, to find out about a data type, look inside the (or rather, a) cluster that defines it; but this goes rather against the philosophy of data abstraction. In fact, there has been a lot of research on *data type specification*, the study of how to present the abstract properties of data types in a representation-independent way.[13] The references at the end of the chapter will lead the student to this literature.

---

[13]The term "data type specification" should not be confused with the ADA term "package specification." The latter refers only to the specification of *syntactic* aspects of the operations of a package, such as the types of the arguments of each operation. Data type specification refers to the *semantics* of those operations — what they actually do.

6.7.4 PROOFS OF CLUSTERS

To summarize the previous subsections, the correctness of programs can be proven, assuming knowledge about the data types they use. What has not yet been done is to prove that we actually have correct implementations of those data types. In other words, it must be proven that the clusters that implement our data abstractions properly represent the abstractions we have in mind. Without this, of course, our domain knowledge is useless, since it does not correspond to what the cluster operations actually do. Different — or rather, additional — methods are needed for proofs of clusters, and we will be forced to be a bit more mathematical than we have been thus far.

The idea of these proofs is to relate the concrete cluster in question to an abstract, idealized cluster for the same data abstraction. The idealized cluster will be chosen so as to fit the abstraction perfectly. We will then look for a *homomorphism* from the concrete to the abstract. In this section, we will follow the SpArray example in detail.

For SpArray, then, the idealized cluster has, as its instance, "arrays in the abstract;" we'll call this cluster $\mathcal{A}$. To be precise, its elements are finite lists of integers labeled by some sequence of consecutive integers. When we are referring to the array operations as defined in $\mathcal{A}$, their names will be subscripted by $\mathcal{A}$. Here are the definitions; A is the array $a_b, a_{b+1}, \ldots, a_{b+s-1}$:

- $\text{new}_{\mathcal{A}}(b, s) = \underbrace{0, \ldots, 0}_{s \text{ times}}$

- $\text{index}_{\mathcal{A}}(A, i) = \begin{cases} a_i & \text{if } b \le i \le b + s - 1 \\ 0 & \text{otherwise} \end{cases}$

- $\text{assign}_{\mathcal{A}}(A, i, x) = \begin{cases} a_b, \ldots, a_{i-1}, x, a_{i+1}, \ldots, a_{b+s-1} & \text{if } b \le i \le b + s - 1 \\ A & \text{otherwise} \end{cases}$

The concrete cluster SpArray has, as its instances, triples $T = <b, s, ((i_1, x_1), \ldots, (i_n, x_n)) >$, $n \ge 0$. Its operations will be subscripted by $\mathcal{C}$ to emphasize that this is a concrete representation of arrays. The operations are as follows:

- $\text{new}_{\mathcal{C}}(b, s) = < b, s, () >$.

- $\text{index}_{\mathcal{C}}(T, i) = \begin{cases} x_j & \text{if } i = i_j \\ 0 & \text{if } \not\exists j \text{ such that } i = i_j \end{cases}$

- $\text{assign}_{\mathcal{C}}(T, i, x) = \begin{cases} < b, s, ((i_1, x_1), \ldots, (i_j, x), \ldots, (i_n, x_n)) > \\ \qquad \text{if } i = i_j \\ < b, s, ((i, x), (i_1, x_1), \ldots, (i_n, x_n)) > \\ \qquad \text{if } \not\exists j \text{ such that } i = i_j \\ \qquad \text{but } b \le i \le b + s - 1 \\ T \\ \qquad \text{otherwise} \end{cases}$

Notice that all the functions of `SpArray` have been treated *as* functions, including `assign`, ignoring the fact that `SpArray` is a mutable type. It is generally easier to formulate the correctness of immutable types, so this simplifying assumption is usually made.

In what sense is `SpArray` a "correct" representation of $\mathcal{A}$? C. A. R. Hoare gave the answer in [1972]. There is a *homomorphism* from `SpArray` to $\mathcal{A}$:

Definition 6.2 A *homomorphism* from `SpArray` to $\mathcal{A}$ is a map

$$\textbf{abs: triples} \rightarrow \text{finite, integer-labeled lists,}$$

such that, for any integers i and x, and any triple $T = \ <\ b, s, ((i_1, x_1),\ \ldots,$ $(i_n, x_n)) >$, the following hold:

- $\textbf{abs}(\text{new}_\mathcal{C}(b, s)) = \text{new}_\mathcal{A}(b, s)$.

- $\textbf{abs}(\text{assign}_\mathcal{C}(T, i, x)) = \text{assign}_\mathcal{A}(\textbf{abs}(T), i, x)$.

- $\text{index}_\mathcal{C}(T, i) = \text{index}_\mathcal{A}(\textbf{abs}(T), i)$.

More precisely, these conditions need not hold for *any* triple, but only for those triples that are used in `SpArray`, namely, those in which all i_j are distinct integers between b and $b + s - 1$. This condition is called the *representation invariant* of `SpArray` and is denoted $\mathcal{I}$. Technically, then, the homomorphism conditions for `assign` and `index` should be preceded by "$\mathcal{I}(T) \Rightarrow$".

Before proving that the homomorphism conditions hold, let us explain what they mean. The fundamental idea is that `SpArray` has instances that represent abstract arrays, and it may have (and does have) more than one instance representing each abstract array. The function **abs** takes any instance of `SpArray` to the abstract array it represents.

The homomorphism conditions require that `SpArray` consistently represent abstract arrays. More specifically,

- $\textbf{abs}(\text{new}_\mathcal{C}(b, s)) = \text{new}_\mathcal{A}(b, s)$ requires that $\text{new}_\mathcal{C}(b, s)$ represent $\text{new}_\mathcal{A}(b, s)$.

- $\textbf{abs}(\text{assign}_\mathcal{C}(T, i, x)) = \text{assign}_\mathcal{A}(\textbf{abs}(T), i, x)$ requires that if T is one of the instances of `SpArray` that represent array $A = \textbf{abs}(T)$, then $\text{assign}_\mathcal{C}(T, i, x)$ must be one of the instances that represent $\text{assign}_\mathcal{A}$ (A, i, x).

- $\text{index}_\mathcal{C}(T, i) = \text{index}_\mathcal{A}(\textbf{abs}(T), i)$ requires that if T represents $A = \textbf{abs}(T)$, it must return the same values as A when indexed.

The upshot of these homomorphism conditions is that a client of `SpArray` has the impression of using abstract arrays. If a sequence of operations were performed using $\mathcal{A}$ (if $\mathcal{A}$ were somehow made available to the program), leading to an element A, the same sequence of operations in `SpArray` would produce an instance T which represents A in the sense that $\mathbf{abs}(T) = A$ (this can be proven by an easy induction). Since the last homomorphism condition states that indexing of A or T always returns the same value, the client program cannot tell them apart. Thus, having a homomorphism guarantees that the concrete representation of the data type faithfully reproduces the behavior of the data abstraction.

Here, then, is the proof, consisting of the definition of $\mathbf{abs}$ followed by the proofs of the three homomorphism conditions:

- $\mathbf{abs}(< b, s, ((i_1, x_1), \ldots, (i_n, x_n)) >) = a_b, \ldots, a_{b+s-1}$, where $a_k = x_j$ if $k = i_j$ for some j, and $a_k = 0$ otherwise.

- $\mathbf{abs}(\mathbf{new}_C(b, s)) = \mathbf{new}_A(b, s)$; that is, $\mathbf{abs}(< b, s, () >) = \underbrace{0, \ldots, 0}_{s \text{ times}}$. This is

  immediate from the definition of $\mathbf{abs}$.

- $\mathcal{I}(T) \Rightarrow \mathbf{abs}(\mathbf{assign}_C(T, i, x)) = \mathbf{assign}_A(\mathbf{abs}(T), i, x)$. This splits into three cases. If $i < b$ or $i > b + s - 1$, then the result is easy, since $\mathbf{assign}_C(T, i, x) = T$, and $\mathbf{assign}_A(\mathbf{abs}(T), i, x) = \mathbf{abs}(T)$. If $i = i_j$ for some j, then we must prove

  $$\mathbf{abs}(< b, s, ((i_1, x_1), \ldots, (i_j, x), \ldots, (i_n, x_n)) >) = \mathbf{assign}_A(\mathbf{abs}(T), i, x).$$

  Otherwise, we must prove

  $$\mathbf{abs}(< b, s, ((i, x), (i_1, x_1), \ldots, (i_n, x_n)) >) = \mathbf{assign}_A(\mathbf{abs}(T), i, x).$$

  Both proofs are easy.

- $\mathcal{I}(T) \Rightarrow \mathbf{index}_C(T, i) = \mathbf{index}_A(\mathbf{abs}(T), i)$. Again there are three cases. If i is out of range, both sides have value 0. If $i = i_j$ for some j, then $\mathbf{index}_C(T, i) = x_j$ and, by definition of $\mathbf{abs}$, so is $\mathbf{index}_A(\mathbf{abs}(T), i)$. Otherwise, both are zero.

Note the tacit use of the representation invariant in the proofs of $\mathbf{assign}$ and $\mathbf{index}$ for the case that i is out of range. For example, the definition of $\mathbf{index}_C$ indicates that it returns whatever value is associated with i in the list $((i_1, x_1), \ldots, (i_n, x_n))$; only the fact that $\mathcal{I}(T)$ holds ensures that, if i is out of range ($i < \mathbf{b}$ or $i > \mathbf{b} + \mathbf{s} - 1$), it will not equal i_j for any j, so that $\mathbf{index}_C$ will return 0.

The proof is now complete, except for a step that should have been done earlier: proving that the functions in SpArray do what has been claimed. We said, for example, that $\mathbf{index}_C$ is this function:

- $\mathbf{index}_C(T, i) = \begin{cases} x_j & \text{if } i = i_j \\ 0 & \text{if } \not\exists j \text{ such that } i = i_j \end{cases}$

The code itself, on the other hand, is (from Figure 6.7):

```
(define index (A i)
    (begin
        (set found (assoc i (elts A)))
        (if (List$null? found) 0 (Pair$snd (List$car found)))))
```

There is something of a gap here. It can be rectified by treating the definition of index as a client of List and proving its correctness as in the previous section. To do this, index is modified as in Section 6.7.2:

```
(define index (A i)
    (begin
        (set found (assoc i (elts A)))
        (if (List$null? found)
            (set result 0)
            (set result (Pair$snd (List$car found))))))
```

What we want to prove, then, is:

$$\text{(elts A)} = ((i_1, x_1), \ldots, (i_n, x_n))$$
$$\{(\text{begin (set found } \cdots) \; \cdots)\}$$
$$\text{result} = x_j \text{ if } i = i_j, \; 0 \text{ otherwise}$$

Since index calls assoc, the correctness of assoc must also be established, but we will simply assume this has been done and that the following is known:

$$\text{(elts A)} = ((i_1, x_1), \ldots, (i_n, x_n))$$
$$\{(\text{set found (assoc (elts A) i)})\}$$
$$\text{found} = ((i_j, x_j), \ldots, (i_n, x_n)) \text{ if } i = i_j, \; \text{nil otherwise}$$

The rules of assignment and consequence give:

$$(\text{found} = ((i_j, x_j), \ldots, (i_n, x_n)) \text{ if } i = i_j, \; \text{nil otherwise}) \; \& \; \text{found} = \text{nil}$$
$$\{(\text{set result 0})\}$$
$$\text{result} = 0 \; \& \; \forall j. i \neq i_j$$

$$(\text{found} = ((i_j, x_j), \ldots, (i_n, x_n)) \text{ if } i = i_j, \; \text{nil otherwise}) \; \& \; \text{found} \neq \text{nil}$$
$$\{(\text{set result found})\}$$
$$\text{result} = x_j \; \& \; i = i_j$$

Applying the conditional and function application rules, we conclude with the desired result.

This proof of index did not, as a matter of fact, use the representation invariant, although proving the homomorphism condition for index did. In general, proofs of correctness of concrete implementations of cluster operations do use the invariant. It follows that the functions which return instances of a cluster must be shown to respect this invariant. So there is yet another set of facts to be proved:

- $\mathcal{I}(\text{new}_{\mathcal{C}}(b, s))$

- $\mathcal{I}(T) \Rightarrow \mathcal{I}(\text{assign}_{\mathcal{C}}(T, i, x))$

Thus, no instance of the cluster can ever be constructed that fails to satisfy the invariant, and the proofs of the implementations of each operation can rely on it.

Summary of Verification of Clusters. The steps in verifying a CLU cluster C, which have just been exemplified, are:

1. Prove the correctness of each operation in the cluster as a client of the types used in its representation. (This is logically the first step, although we did it last in our example.) Also, define the representation invariant $\mathcal{I}$ and prove it is preserved by the operations. Thus, for each function f, if f returns an instance of C, prove a correctness formula of the form:

$$T = \text{generic instance of C } \& \mathcal{I}(T)$$
$$\{(\mathtt{f} \ \cdots T \cdots)\} \text{ result} = f_{\mathcal{C}}(\cdots, T, \cdots) \& \mathcal{I}(\text{result})$$

where $f_{\mathcal{C}}$ is some expression describing the function computed by f. If f does not return an instance of C, prove:

$$T = \text{generic instance of C } \& \mathcal{I}(T)$$
$$\{(\mathtt{f} \ \cdots T \cdots)\} \text{ result} = f_{\mathcal{C}}(\cdots, T, \cdots)$$

The rule is: for each argument of f of type C (if any), assume it satisfies $\mathcal{I}$; if the result is of type C, then prove it satisfies $\mathcal{I}$.

2. Pick an abstract representation of the data abstraction which the cluster is representing. Call it $\mathcal{A}$, and denote its definition of function f by $f_{\mathcal{A}}$.

3. Define a map **abs** from the representation of C to $\mathcal{A}$.

4. Prove that **abs** is a homomorphism by proving the homomorphism conditions, defined as follows:

   - If the result of f is an instance of C, then the homomorphism condition for f is:

     $$\mathcal{I}(T) \Rightarrow \textbf{abs}(f_{\mathcal{C}}(\cdots, T, \cdots)) = \mathbf{f}_{\mathcal{A}}(\cdots, \textbf{abs}(T), \cdots).$$

   - If f has a result of type other than C, the homomorphism condition is:

     $$\mathcal{I}(T) \Rightarrow f_{\mathcal{C}}(\cdots, T, \cdots) = \mathbf{f}_{\mathcal{A}}(\cdots, \textbf{abs}(T), \cdots).$$

If f has no arguments of type C, or more than one, the homomorphism condition is adjusted accordingly. The rule is: assume $\mathcal{I}$ is true of each argument of type C, apply **abs** on the left-hand side of the = sign if the result is of type C, and apply **abs** on the right-hand side to each argument of type C.

6.8   Summary

In Liskov, et al. [1977, p. 565], the designers of CLU write:

> The motivation for the design of the CLU programming language was to provide programmers with a tool that would enhance their effectiveness in constructing programs of high quality — programs that are reliable and reasonably easy to understand, modify, and maintain.

Their principal method of achieving this was to provide for encapsulating data representations in *clusters*. Clusters enhance the readability of programs by allowing their division into logical units larger than procedures; they enhance their maintainability by restricting knowledge of data representations to those with a "need to know," thereby limiting the effects of code modifications; they also enhance their provability, by allowing the structuring of program proofs along data abstraction lines. In addition, CLU has strict type-checking and an exception-handling feature.

6.8.1   GLOSSARY

cluster. A syntactic "capsule" in which all information concerning the representation of a data type is contained. By supporting the separation of the code that implements a data abstraction from the code that uses it, clusters promote well-structured code.

The idea of supporting data abstraction in this way appears in several languages, and different names are used. Although many details differ, the constructs serve basically the same purpose in each language. Some of the names are **class** (SIMULA 67, SMALLTALK), **module** (MODULA-2), **form** (ALPHARD), and **package** (ADA). Parnas [1972b] uses the term **information-hiding module**.

data abstraction. An abstract data type, conceived of independently of any particular representation.

data type specification. A specification of the properties of a data abstraction independent of its representation. A completely formal method of proving cluster correctness would require such a specification.

Floyd–Hoare proof rules. A set of rules embodying the programming knowledge pertaining to a particular language and permitting proofs of programs in that language, like our proof rules for the language of Chapter 1. Such proof systems have been developed for a variety of programming languages (see McGettrick [1982] for one example), mainly of the traditional, imperative type. They do not exist, however, for most of the languages discussed in this book.

homomorphism. A map from the instances of a cluster to the abstract values they represent. The homomorphism is the basis of a proof of correctness of the cluster. **Abstraction function** is a synonym.

inductive assertion. An assertion about the relationships among the variables in a program. The basic method of program proving is to place inductive assertions around each statement in a program and then prove that these assertions are necessarily true when control reaches that point in the program.

iterator. A procedure-like construct in CLU that produces a *list* of values instead of a single value. A **for** statement is used to iterate over the elements of this list. As with lazy lists (Chapter 5), the elements are not produced all at once but rather as they are requested.

loop invariant. An assertion P whose truth is preserved by the body of a loop. P is a loop invariant for the loop (**while e** S) if, whenever both P and **e** are true before executing S, P is still true afterwards.

representation invariant. The condition that defines the instances of a cluster as a subset of the representing type. For example, instances of `SpArray` are represented by triples $< b, s, ((i_1, x_1), \ldots, (i_n, x_n)) >$, satisfying the representation invariant that the i_j are distinct integers between b and $b+s-1$. Representation invariants are needed for proving the correctness of clusters.

6.8.2 FURTHER READING

Liskov and Guttag [1986] is an excellent book containing an introduction to CLU and a concise reference manual, and explaining how CLU fits into the process of writing reliable software. Liskov, et al. [1977] is an introduction to the CLU approach to programming, and Liskov [1981] is a complete reference manual. Liskov and Snyder [1977] concerns CLU's exception mechanism.

The general topic of data abstraction as a useful concept for program development is discussed in classic papers by Wirth [1971], Parnas [1972b], and Hoare and Dahl [1972b]. Data abstraction is the centerpiece of several languages aside from CLU, including SIMULA 67 (Birtwistle, et al., [1973], Dahl and Hoare [1972b]), ALPHARD (Wulf, et al. [1976]), MODULA-2 (Wirth [1982]), and ADA. Abelson and Sussman [1985, Chapter 2] contains a most interesting discussion about data abstraction in SCHEME.

The basic reference for ADA is the Reference Manual (Department of Defense [1983]). Barnes [1983] is an excellent introduction to the language, and Cohen [1986] is a very complete and detailed one; but these are just two among many introductory books on the language. Bishop [1986] covers general data abstraction concepts in an ADA context.

Program verification is among the most heavily researched topics in computer science over the past twenty years. Loeckx [1984] gives a good overview. McGettrick [1982] is also introductory and gives a full set of rules for verification of ADA programs. Manna [1974, Chapter 3] is an excellent introduction to verification of programs using integers and arrays. Hoare [1972] was the first to discuss the verification of data representations. The subarea of *data type specification* is surveyed in Liskov and Zilles [1975] and is also discussed in Liskov and Guttag [1986]; other papers on this topic are Guttag, et al. [1978], Goguen, et al. [1979], Futatsugi, et al. [1985], Parnas [1972a], and Kamin [1983]. Gries [1981], Reynolds [1981], and Jones [1980] are excellent books on *formal program development*, in which program verification methods are applied to program construction.

6.9 Exercises

6.9.1 *LEARNING ABOUT THE LANGUAGE*

1. The data type `BinTree` has as its values binary trees with labeled nodes and as operations:

   `mkNode:` Create a single-node tree, given its label.

   `mkTree:` Create a new tree, given its label and two subtrees.

   `children?:` Test if a tree has children.

   `label:` Return the label of a tree.

   `leftchild:` Return the left child of a tree.

   `rightchild:` Return the right child of a tree.

   Implement `BinTree` using two different representations:

   (a) A recursive representation, such as we gave for `List`.

   (b) Represent a tree by a single list, which has either one element (for single-node trees) or three elements (the label and the two subtrees).

2. Implement a `Queue` cluster, with operations: `empty-queue, empty?, enqueue, front, rm-front`. Use it to define a function to traverse a `BinTree` in level order.

3. A mutable version of `BinTree` might have operations `change-label`, `add-leftchild`, and `add-rightchild`. `add-leftchild` and `add-right-child` have as arguments *labels* (not trees), so they add only a single node, replacing whatever subtree might have existed before. Make mutable versions of the two `BinTree` clusters previously given.

   Then define a new mutable representation of `BinTree`, based upon the tree representation used in the heap-sort algorithm. Namely, a tree is represented by an array `A`, indexed from 1, the label of the root being at `A[1]` and the children of node i at `A[2i]` and `A[2i + 1]`. (A special value needs to be reserved to indicate that a node is not present.)

4. Implement both immutable and mutable versions of cluster `Tree`, containing trees of arbitrary degree. You must choose appropriate operations in each case. Note that the `mkTree` approach to constructing trees does not work here, because every operation must have a fixed number of arguments. Program level-order traversal for these new clusters.

5. Implement a cluster `RatNum` of rational numbers; you should include the major arithmetic operations (addition, subtraction, multiplication, division) as well as comparisons (`<<` and `==`). Rational numbers can be represented simply by pairs of integers, representing numerator and denominator; it is a good idea to keep these integers in *reduced* form, meaning that the numerator and denominator should have no common factors. Implement a square root function based upon the Newton–Raphson method (page 162).

6. Implement a cluster `Matrix` that represents two-dimensional matrices; then implement `SpMatrix`, using a sparse representation of your own choosing. As a client, write function `rotate`, which performs a 90-degree clockwise *in-place* rotation of a matrix.

7. Using either of the `Point` clusters, define a cluster `Window`, which contains rectangles with integer vertices, with operations:

   new: Given any two opposing corners of a window, create the window.

   lower-left: Return the lower left corner of a window. (Note that this need not have been the first argument to `new`.)

   upper-right: Return the upper right corner of a window.

   intersect?: Check if two windows overlap.

   intersection: Return the window that is the intersection of two intersecting windows.

Then make this a mutable data type, adding operations:

horizontal-move: Move the first argument, a window, horizontally either to the right or the left, according as the second argument is positive or negative.

vertical-move: analogously.

grow: Given a window and two integers, grow or shrink in the horizontal and vertical directions based upon the second and third arguments, respectively, growing for positive integers and shrinking for negative ones. In all cases, the lower left corner of the window does not move.

6.9.2 *LEARNING ABOUT THE INTERPRETER*

8. Add export lists to the language. The new syntax for cluster definitions is:

$$
\begin{aligned}
\text{clusterdef} \quad &\longrightarrow \quad \text{(cluster cluster export-list rep fundef}^+ \text{)} \\
\text{export-list} \quad &\longrightarrow \quad \text{(export name}^+ \text{)}
\end{aligned}
$$

Clients should be able to call only the functions named in the export-list (using, of course, their two-part names), while cluster functions can call any function defined in the cluster (using its one-part name).

9. Implement type-checking. Refer to Exercise 14 in Chapter 1 for a syntax for declarations of global variables and formal parameters. In addition, each selector must have its type declared:

$$
\begin{aligned}
\text{clusterdef} \quad &\longrightarrow \quad \text{(cluster cluster rep fundef}^+ \text{)} \\
\text{rep} \quad &\longrightarrow \quad \text{(rep var-decl}^+ \text{)} \\
\text{var-decl} \quad &\longrightarrow \quad \text{variable : typename} \\
\text{typename} \quad &\longrightarrow \quad \text{integer | cluster}
\end{aligned}
$$

Note that however you choose to deal with mutual recursion at the top level, within clusters it should be possible to refer to functions that appear later in the cluster without special declarations.

The typename's are integer and the names of any clusters previously defined. There are no automatic coercions. The type-checking rules for the implicitly defined operations, assuming a cluster of the form:

```
(cluster C
    (rep r₁: T₁ ... rₙ: Tₙ)
        ⋮
    )
```

are:

Selectors: r_i has an argument of type C and result of type T_i.

Settors: set-r_i has arguments of type C and T_i and a result of type T_i.

Constructor: C has n arguments of types T_1, ..., T_n and a result of type C.

10. If you have solved the previous problem, you will undoubtedly have run into the problem of *polymorphism*, as discussed in Section 6.5. What, for example, should be the type of the selector a in the List cluster (Figure 6.4)? The answer in CLU is to give it as a *type variable*, which is filled in when a variable of the cluster is declared.

Consider only parameterized clusters (forget parameterized functions), and allow only one type parameter per cluster. Add a new field in the cluster definitions:

```
clusterdef        ⟶    ( cluster cluster type-variable-list rep fundef⁺ )
type-variable-list ⟶   () | ( type-variable )
type-variable     ⟶    name
```

and change the syntax of types:

```
typename ⟶ integer | cluster | type-variable | ( cluster typename )
```

This syntax allows for types of the form (List integer), or even (List (List integer)). The use of type-variable's in typename's is restricted to declarations within clusters declared with that type variable; in other words, the scope of a type variable is the cluster in which that variable is declared.

Formulate and implement the type-checking rules for this case.

6.9.3   *LEARNING ABOUT PROGRAM VERIFICATION*

11. Verify the body of the exponentiation loop (page 253).

12. We give two versions of the factorial function, the first purely iterative and the second recursive:

```
(define fac (x)
    (begin
        (set result 1)
        (while (<> x 0)
            (begin
                (set result (* result x))
                (set x (- x 1))))))

(define recfac (x)
    (if (= x 0) 1 (* x (recfac (- x 1)))))
```

Prove: $x > 0$ {(fac x)} `result` $= x!$. Then prove the corresponding result for `recfac`, after transforming it as per Section 6.7.2.

13. Transform the `listsum` function to iterative form and prove it using the iteration rule. Comment on the relation between the iteration rule and the recursive function rule.

14. Transform the exponentiation function from page 253 to recursive form, and prove it using the recursive function rule.

15. Prove the correctness of the second `Point` cluster. In this case, the first `Point` cluster can serve as the "abstract" cluster. As a first step, you may assume that all the operations in the second `Point` cluster are correct, but you should then prove each of them.

16. Prove the correctness of the `Poly` cluster. You will need to define a cluster of abstract polynomials. As a first step, you may assume that all `Poly` operations are correct, but you should then prove each of them.

Chapter 7

SMALLTALK

In 1971 a group of researchers at Xerox Palo Alto Research Center, led by Alan Kay, began to develop a programming language and environment. Their programming language ideas were largely derived from SIMULA 67. The programming environment ideas, based on powerful single-user machines with bit-mapped displays, were developed by them and other research groups at PARC; many of them — windows, menus, the mouse — have since been widely adopted. The group worked in relative isolation, developing several versions of their SMALLTALK system, culminating in SMALLTALK-80. In 1981, they published a collection of articles on SMALLTALK-80 in a special issue of *Byte Magazine* which aroused a great deal of interest; however, few readers could gain access to a SMALLTALK system at that time. SMALLTALK-80 is now becoming more widely available, and it — as well as the object-oriented concepts it represents — is growing enormously in popularity.

SMALLTALK ideas about both languages and environments have been extremely influential. We will, needless to say, be concentrating on the programming language. It is based upon the idea of user-defined data types, as is CLU, but its philosophy is very different. The instances of a *class* (the SMALLTALK word for cluster), called *objects*, represent individuals in the world. These individuals can send *messages* to other individuals, who can react to the receipt of a message by doing some computation and/or sending other messages to other individuals. The set of messages to which an object can respond is determined by the class of the object; this set of messages is called the *protocol* of the class. Each message is associated with a *method* (the SMALLTALK word for function). Objects are represented by sets of values, as in CLU, named by *instance variables*. A rough correspondence between these SMALLTALK terms and corresponding CLU terms is given in Table 7.1.

It is the emphasis on individuals, represented by class instances, as independent, communicating agents that justifies the term "object-oriented." Our first example is a class called `FinancialHistory`,[1] whose objects are records

---

[1]This class is from Goldberg and Robson [1983], where it is also used as an introductory example.

SMALLTALK term	CLU term	SMALLTALK meaning
Class	Cluster	Encapsulates the representation of a type of data
Object	Instance	A datum of a particular class
Method	Function	An operation defined in a class
Message	Function name	
Message send	Function application	
Instance variables	Selectors	The names of the values representing objects of a class
Protocol	Operations of a cluster	The messages to which an object of a given class can respond

Table 7.1: Correspondence between SMALLTALK and CLU terminology

of financial transactions and whose protocol contains the following messages:

receive:from: Sending this message to a `FinancialHistory` object `account`, with arguments `amount` and `source`, causes `account` to record that `amount` dollars were received from `source`. `account` actually changes itself to reflect this transaction; in CLU terminology, `FinancialHistory` is a mutable type.

spend:for: Sending this message to `account`, with arguments `amount` and `reason`, causes `account` to record that `amount` dollars were spent for `reason`.

cashOnHand `account` responds to this message by returning the total cash on hand; this message has no arguments.

totalReceivedFrom: With argument `source`, `account` responds to this message by returning the total amount received from `source`.

totalSpentFor: With argument `reason`, `account` responds to this message by returning the total amount spent for `reason`.

For example, if `account` has been initialized to have a 1000 dollar balance (we will see how to do this later), we can do the following (`#abc` denotes the symbol abc in SMALLTALK, analogous to `'abc` in LISP):

```
-> (spend:for: account 50 #plumber)
```

```
-> (receive:from: account 400 #salary)
```

```
-> (cashOnHand account)
1350
```

Note that a message always names the receiver and may have additional arguments as well. Throughout this chapter, being consistent with SMALLTALK terminology, *arguments* refers to arguments beside the receiver; this is why `cashOnHand` could be described above as having no arguments.

The essential feature that SMALLTALK adds to CLU, aside from the change of philosophy, is *inheritance*, and it will be the focus of our discussion in this chapter. All classes are placed in a hierarchy, the 'top of which is a class called simply `Object`. Each class definition must name another, pre-existing class which is its parent in the hierarchy. This establishes a *subclass–superclass* relationship between the new class and the parent class. Objects of the new class automatically know how to respond to messages defined in the superclass (or any of its ancestors); that is, a class *inherits* the methods defined in its ancestors.

Thus, a class can contain code that can be refined in different ways in different subclasses. This provides an effective way to *reuse code*; as this is a major goal of all programming languages, it is a major contribution of SMALLTALK. Indeed, the greatest effort in learning to program *efficiently* in SMALLTALK is learning what code is in the class hierarchy that is supplied with the system. The basic reference on the SMALLTALK-80 language (Goldberg and Robson [1983]) devotes about 90 pages to introducing the language, followed by 300 pages describing the class hierarchy.

7.1 The Language

7.1.1 TWO INTRODUCTORY EXAMPLES

Figure 7.1 contains the `FinancialHistory` class. It is different enough from the definition of a mutable cluster in CLU to require some explanation:

- This class is being added as a subclass of `Object`. It does not inherit any methods, because `Object` has none.

- A `FinancialHistory` object is represented by three instance variables, `cashOnHand`, `incomes`, and `expenditures`. `cashOnHand` is an integer, while `incomes` and `expenditures` are objects of the class `Dictionary`; this class is defined later, but in the meantime the reader should think of its objects as symbol tables, or association lists.

- Each method has an implicit first argument, an object of this class (or, as we shall see shortly, of a subclass). The special variable `self` refers to this object as a whole; to refer to any of its instance variables, we just use the instance variable, and the reference is implicitly to the `self` argument. (This obviates the selectors and settors of CLU.)

- Thus, `initFinancialHistory` actually has two arguments, a `Financial-History` object and an integer. The implicit, or `self`, argument is mod-

```
(class FinancialHistory Object
    (cashOnHand incomes expenditures)
    (define initFinancialHistory (amount)
        (begin
            (set cashOnHand amount)
            (set incomes (mkDictionary))
            (set expenditures (mkDictionary))
            self))
    (define receive:from: (amount source)
        (begin
            (at:put: incomes source (+ (totalReceivedFrom: self source) amount))
            (set cashOnHand (+ cashOnHand amount))))
    (define spend:for: (amount reason)
        (begin
            (at:put: expenditures reason (+ (totalSpentFor: self reason) amount))
            (set cashOnHand (- cashOnHand amount))))
    (define cashOnHand () cashOnHand)
    (define totalReceivedFrom: (source)
        (if (includesKey: incomes source)
            (at: incomes source)
            0))
    (define totalSpentFor: (reason)
        (if (includesKey: expenditures reason)
            (at: expenditures reason)
            0))
)
```

Figure 7.1: Class FinancialHistory

ified by setting its instance variables. This is done by simply assigning to those variables. incomes and expenditures are set to new, empty, Dictionary objects. The modified FinancialHistory object is returned.

- receive:from: has three arguments, one of which is the implicit self argument. (The funny form of this message name follows SMALLTALK notation, and actually makes sense in the context of real SMALLTALK syntax, as described in Section 7.5.) It modifies self as follows:

    1. incomes is modified using the at:put: message of Dictionary, analogous to mkassoc in LISP except that Dictionary is a mutable type. The value associated with source in incomes is changed to reflect the new amount received. The total previously received from this source is determined by sending the totalReceivedFrom: message to self, and then the new amount is added to it.

    2. cashOnHand is modified to reflect the windfall.

- `spend:for:` operates similarly to `receive:from:`.

- `cashOnHand` just returns the value of the instance variable `cashOnHand`. There is no necessary connection between messages and instance variables, but it is traditional for methods that just return the value of an instance variable to be given the same name as the instance variable (and for those that just set an instance variable to have the same name with a colon added).

- `totalReceivedFrom:` and `totalSpentFor:` use the `at:` message of Dictionary, analogous to `assoc` in LISP.

One gap needs to be filled in before using `FinancialHistory`. There is no way to create a new `FinancialHistory` object. Since *every* method in the class has an implicit argument, which *must* be a `FinancialHistory` object, no messages can be sent until such an object is created. To solve this problem, there is a function **new** which, when applied to a variable named `FinancialHistory`, returns a `FinancialHistory` object, which can then be initialized by sending it the `initFinancialHistory` message with an appropriate argument. We encapsulate this in a top-level function:

```
(define mkFinancialHistory (amount)
        (initFinancialHistory (new FinancialHistory) amount))
```

To summarize, the expression (`new C`) produces a new C object; *by convention*, C should define a message `initC`, and the user should define a top-level function having the form

$$(define\ mkC\ (\cdots\ args\ \cdots)\ (initC\ (new\ C)\ \cdots\ args\ \cdots))$$

We are now in a position to try out the `FinancialHistory` class:

```
-> (set myaccount (mkFinancialHistory 1000))
-> (spend:for: myaccount 50 #insurance)
-> (receive:from: myaccount 200 #salary)
-> (cashOnHand myaccount)
1150

-> (spend:for: myaccount 100 #books)
-> (cashOnHand myaccount)
1050
```

As mentioned earlier, a class can have *subclasses* which inherit the structure of the class. Subclasses can be used to *refine* the values of a class for more specific uses. This turns out to be a very effective way of reusing old code (the original class) by modifying it for new circumstances (the subclass).

Figure 7.2 contains a subclass of `FinancialHistory` called `Deductible-History`. Its objects are financial records which also record the amount of tax-deductible expenditures. Thus it represents an elaboration or refinement

```
(class DeductibleHistory FinancialHistory
   (deductible)
   (define initDeductibleHistory (amount)
      (begin
         (initFinancialHistory self amount)
         (set deductible 0)
         self))
   (define spend:Deduct: (amount reason)
      (begin
         (spend:for: self amount reason)
         (set deductible (+ deductible amount))))
   (define spend:for:deduct: (amount reason deduction)
      (begin
         (spend:for: self amount reason)
         (set deductible (+ deductible deduction))))
   (define totalDeductions () deductible))
```

Figure 7.2: Class `DeductibleHistory`

of the concept of financial records as given in `FinancialHistory`. To explain its definition:

- The first line indicates that `DeductibleHistory` is a subclass of `Financial History`. This means that it inherits instance variables and methods from `FinancialHistory` (details follow).

- `DeductibleHistory` has instance variable `deductible`, containing the total of deductible expenses. However, this is not the only instance variable used to represent `DeductibleHistory` objects. Because `DeductibleHistory` is a subclass of `FinancialHistory`, a `DeductibleHistory` object has all the instance variables associated with `FinancialHistory` *plus* instance variable `deductible`; this is what is meant by inheriting instance variables.

- A `DeductibleHistory` object can respond to any message defined in `FinancialHistory`. Since, as just explained, every instance variable of `FinancialHistory` is also an instance variable of `DeductibleHistory`, there is no trouble in applying `FinancialHistory` methods to `Deductible History` objects. This is what is meant by inheriting methods.

- A `DeductibleHistory` object can respond to some messages to which a `FinancialHistory` object cannot, namely `spend:Deduct:`, `spend:for:-deduct:`, and `totalDeductions`. Notice that in processing the message `spend:Deduct:`, `self` is sent the message `spend:for:`, defined in `FinancialHistory`.

- initDeductibleHistory appeals to initFinancialHistory to initialize the inherited instance variables, then sets the new instance variable and returns self.

To use DeductibleHistory, we follow the convention of defining mkDeductibleHistory. DeductibleHistory objects can respond to messages defined either in DeductibleHistory or FinancialHistory:

```
-> (define mkDeductibleHistory (amount)
        (initDeductibleHistory (new DeductibleHistory) amount))
-> (set myaccount (mkDeductibleHistory 1000))
-> (spend:for: myaccount 50 #insurance)
-> (receive:from: myaccount 200 #salary)
-> (cashOnHand myaccount)
1150

-> (totalDeductions myaccount)
0

-> (spend:Deduct: myaccount 100 #mortgage)
-> (cashOnHand myaccount)
1050

-> (totalDeductions myaccount)
100

-> (spend:for:deduct: myaccount 100 #3-martini-lunch 50)
-> (cashOnHand myaccount)
950

-> (totalDeductions myaccount)
150
```

7.1.2 SYNTAX

The principal syntactic changes from CLU are the inclusion of symbol values, the superclass name in class definitions, and the omission of two-part names:

input	$\longrightarrow$	expression | fundef | classdef
classdef	$\longrightarrow$	(class class class inst-vars methoddef$^+$)
inst-vars	$\longrightarrow$	(variable*)
methoddef	$\longrightarrow$	fundef
fundef	$\longrightarrow$	*same as in Chapter 1*
expression	$\longrightarrow$	*same as in Chapter 1*
value	$\longrightarrow$	integer | symbol
symbol	$\longrightarrow$	#name
value-op	$\longrightarrow$	+ | $\cdots$ | > | print (*same as in Chapter 1*)
class	$\longrightarrow$	name

The only operation that applies to symbol values is =, which can compare either numbers or symbols, but returns the false value (integer zero) for any other types of arguments.

inst-vars is analogous to rep in CLU. The rep keyword was removed only because a SMALLTALK class with no instance variables would have as its inst-vars "(rep)", which looks funny. In CLU, this was not a problem, because it could never make sense for a cluster to have no selectors.

7.1.3 SEMANTICS

There are a number of significant changes in the semantics, as compared with CLU. After listing these, we give an example illustrating a subtle but important point about inheritance:

Symbols: Values can now be either integers, symbols, or class instances (objects). The symbol #nil is used, by convention, to represent a "bad" or "undefined" value; for example, it is the value returned by (at: incomes source) when no income has been reported from that source. Note that this usage is somewhat different from the use of *nil* in LISP, which is a perfectly legitimate and well defined value.

self: The definition of a method always has one implicit argument, which can be referred to by the name **self**. Thus, when a message is sent, it appears to have one more argument than its definition gives it. Within a method definition, references to an instance variable implicitly refer to the **self** argument. Note that this obviates the use of specially named selectors and settors, as used in CLU.

new: This function creates a new object of class C when applied to the variable called C, initializing its instance variables to the integer zero. It replaces the constructors of CLU.

Redefinition of value-op's: A small extension not previously noted is that value-op's are allowed to be used as messages. The reason for this will become apparent in future examples.

Inheritance: The instance variables representing an object of class C are those named in C *or in any of its ancestors.* (Name conflicts should be avoided, though this is not enforced by the interpreter.) Objects of class C can respond to messages defined in an ancestor of C; here, in contrast to instance variables, C is free to redefine a message already defined in an ancestor. In that case, when this message is sent to an object of class C, C's definition is invoked (see below).

Method search: When a message m is sent to an object of class C, the interpreter first looks in C for a method named m; if that fails, C's superclass is consulted; and so on, until the top of the hierarchy is reached. Method search and inheritance are intimately connected.

The class Object: We start off with one class, called Object, which has one instance variable, self, and as its objects all the integers and symbols. All other classes inherit the instance variable self, which is initialized whenever a new object is created.

Inheritance can be tricky. Suppose C and D are defined as follows:

```
(class C Object ()
    (define m1 () (m2 self))
    (define m2 () #C))
(class D C ()
    (define m2 () #D))
```

Neither C nor D has instance variables, but that is not relevant to this discussion. Our goal is to understand what happens when message m1 or m2 is sent to an object of class C or D. The case of sending either to an object of class C is easy; in either case, the result is the symbol C. Furthermore, sending m2 to an object of class D is also easy; the method search will land on the definition of m2 within D, and the result will be symbol D. The most interesting case is sending message m1 to an object of class D. Let's try it:

```
-> (set x (new D))

-> (m1 x)
D
```

Here is what happened:

1. When m1 was sent to x, the method search revealed that m1 was defined in C.

2. m1 sent message m2 to self — which is to say, x. The method search for m2 began in x's class, namely D.

3. m2 was found in D, and it returned the symbol D.

This is very far from being a minor, technical point. On the contrary, this example emphasizes a crucial fact about SMALLTALK: *method search always begins in the class of the receiver.* We will see many examples of the importance of this principle in what follows.

7.1.4 SCOPE IN SMALLTALK

The rules connecting uses of names with their declarations in SMALLTALK are somewhat different from those of other languages. For variables, scope is static, and for functions it is dynamic. The rules for each are:

Variables: A variable occurring within a top-level expression is global, and
one occurring in a top-level function is either a formal parameter or is
global. These rules are identical to those of Chapter 1.

A variable occurring in a method (i.e., a function defined in a class), which
is not a formal parameter, follows different rules. It can be an instance
variable if it is declared as such either in the class of the method or in
an ancestor thereof. If not, it is global. In any case — formal parameter,
instance variable, global variable — its declaration can be determined
statically.

Functions and messages: There are two types of function applications, top-
level function calls and message sends.[2] If they could be distinguished
statically, they would be seen to follow different scope rules. Suppose the
call is (f x_1 ... x_n). Then

- If this is a call of a top-level function, then invoke the one top-level
  function called f. This is the same rule as in Chapter 1 and is, of
  course, a static rule.

- If it is a message send, then f is the method defined in the class of
  x_1 or an ancestor thereof, as determined by the method search. This
  is a dynamic rule.

In fact, there is no static way to make this determination — except if
$n = 0$, in which case this can only be a top-level function application
— so we follow the rule that if the method search succeeds, then it is a
message send; otherwise it is a top-level function application.

In summary, SMALLTALK follows a dynamic scope policy for message
sends, in which the receiver argument determines, via method search,
the method to be invoked. If the method search fails, the application is
considered to be a top-level function call.

7.1.5   THE COLLECTION HIERARCHY

In this section, we will present a single subhierarchy containing a variety of
useful auxiliary classes, including `Dictionary`. At the top of the subhierarchy
is the class `Collection`, which is a subclass of `Object`. Classes in this hierarchy
are those that *contain* things, in a sense presently to be made precise.

Real SMALLTALK has a Collection subhierarchy also, including similar classes,
though structured somewhat differently; it is discussed in Section 7.5.2. Our
version is inspired by the Collection hierarchy in Budd [1987].

---

[2]In real SMALLTALK, there are only message sends.

```
(set false 0)
(set true 1)
(define isNil (x) (= x #nil))
(define notNil (x) (<> x #nil))
```

Figure 7.3: Auxiliary functions and global variables

The overall shape of the `Collection` hierarchy is:

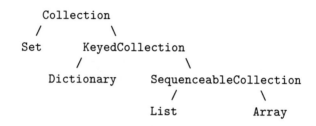

To give an intuitive description of each class:

`Collection:` objects that contain things.

`Set:` sets contain objects in no particular order, and provide no "random access."

`KeyedCollection:` the values contained in `KeyedCollection`'s can be retrieved by giving a key.

`Dictionary:` no assumptions are made about the keys except, of course, that they can be compared for equality.

`SequenceableCollection:` keys are integers.

`List:` objects can grow by having new items placed at the front.

`Array:` objects have fixed size.

In this hierarchy, every class uses `List` to represent its elements. Note that this does not entail that they be subclasses of `List`, only that their objects have instance variables containing `List`'s.[3]

Figure 7.3 contains a few auxiliary functions and global variables used throughout the remaining code.

---

[3]This locution is a shorthand for "`List` objects."

Collection. `Collection`'s contain things. This means, above all, that any `Collection` object can respond to the messages `first` and `next`. These must be defined so that, by sending `first` and then repeatedly sending `next`, we can cycle through all the items in the object; when no items are left, `next` must return `#nil`. (`first` and `next` are called *generators* by Budd [1987] because together they generate the elements of the object; compare CLU iterators.) In addition, a `Collection` object should respond to the message `add:` by adding the argument to itself. Every class in this subhierarchy is mutable.

Having spoken of "Collection objects," we hasten to point out that `Collection` itself is an *abstract class*, meaning it has no useful objects of its own. This is not an official designation but an intuitive one indicated by two facts: it has no instance variables, and many of its methods consist of only the symbol `#subclassResponsibility`. Moreover, those methods are used in other methods.

So of what use is `Collection`, and what is a "Collection object?" The sole and only purpose of `Collection` is to define methods that are inherited by subclasses. These subclasses must define the messages marked as `#subclassResponsibility`, at which time the methods containing real code become useful. A "Collection object" is any object of a subclass (or, more generally, any descendant) of `Collection`. To put it differently, it is any object that inherits the `Collection` protocol.

Figure 7.4 contains the `Collection` class. Let's look at the methods in more detail:

- `first`, `next`, and `add:` are subclass responsibilities. The remaining methods use `first` and `next`; the inheritance mechanism guarantees that when one of the messages is sent to an object of a subclass, the versions of `first` and `next` defined in that subclass will be invoked.

- `size` uses `first` and `next` to determine the number of items in a collection. This may not be a terribly efficient method of doing so, but keep in mind that a subclass can always *redefine* `size` if it can compute it more efficiently (see `Array`).

- `includes:` tests for membership of `item` in the `Collection` object that is its receiver, again using `first` and `next`.

Because `Collection` is an abstract class, no definition of `initCollection` or `mkCollection` is needed.

Set. The code for class `Set` is given in Figure 7.5. `Set` is a concrete class; i.e., it has objects. A `Set` object is represented by a `List`, contained in its instance variable `members`. Indeed, most of the `Set` methods just send the corresponding `List` message to `members`. Note again that `Set` is only a *client* of `List`, not a subclass or superclass; that both appear in the `Collection` subhierarchy is merely coincidental.

```
(class Collection Object
    () ; abstract class
    (define first () #subclassResponsibility)
    (define next () #subclassResponsibility)
    (define add: (item) #subclassResponsibility)
    (define size ()
       (begin
          (set tempitem (first self))
          (set tempsize 0)
          (while (notNil tempitem)
             (begin
                (set tempsize (+1 tempsize))
                (set tempitem (next self))))
          tempsize))
    (define isEmpty () (isNil (first self)))
    (define includes: (item)
       (begin
          (set tempitem (first self))
          (set found false)
          (while (and (notNil tempitem) (not found))
             (if (= tempitem item)
                (set found true)
                (set tempitem (next self))))
          found))
)
```

Figure 7.4: Class Collection

```
(class Set Collection
    (members) ; list of elements
    (define initSet () (begin (set members (mkList)) self))
    (define first () (first members))
    (define next () (next members))
    (define add: (item)
       (if (includes: members item) self (add: members item)))
)
(define mkSet () (initSet (new Set)))
```

Figure 7.5: Class Set

Reviewing the protocol of `Set`:

- `initSet` makes its receiver empty by setting `members` to the null list.

- `first` and `next` are delegated to `List`.

- `add:` cannot be delegated to `List`, because we want to be sure to avoid duplicates in `members`. Thus, membership of `item` is determined, by sending the `includes:` message to `members`, adding `item` to `members` only if it is not already present. Two points: (1) `add:` *could have* sent the `includes:` message to `self`; it sent it to `members` only in the hope that `List` may have defined a more efficient version of it. (2) `Set` is *mutable*; sending `add:` to a set actually *changes the set.*

- In addition, `Set` inherits `size`, `isEmpty`, and `includes:`; the latter corresponds to the function we used to call `member?` (but note the order of its arguments).

Being a concrete class, `Set` has a method `initSet`, and there is a global function `mkSet` which returns a null set. Here is a session using `Set`:[4]

```
-> (set S (mkSet))
-> (size S)
0
-> (add: S 2)
-> (add: S #abc)
-> (includes: S 2)
1
-> (add: S 2)
-> (size S)
2
-> (first S)
abc
-> (next S)
2
-> (next S)
nil
```

Remember that methods have one more argument than they appear to in their definition. For example, `add:` appears to have only one argument in its definition, that being the item to be added, but it actually has two, the first being the set to which the item is added.

---

[4]We omit the values returned from expressions when those values are of no interest. It does not matter to us here if, for example, `add:` returns the modified set, the value added to the set, or some other object altogether.

The definition of sets is very general, because sets can contain *any kind of object*, provided only that the object can respond to the = message (see the definition of `includes:`). With the ability to redefine value-op's in class definitions, it is always possible to define new classes that have = in their protocols. This *overloading* — giving several method definitions of the same message name — supports *polymorphism* — the ability of one function to be applied to data of different types — in SMALLTALK, which is another way SMALLTALK provides for reuse of code. We discussed this problem in the SCHEME chapter, and have also seen how (real) CLU clusters can have type parameters, providing for polymorphism by a different mechanism.

KeyedCollection. `KeyedCollection` is another abstract class, which represents objects that allow for "random access" to their elements. Such objects must still respond to `first` and `next` by returning the *values* they contain, but they also respond to `at:` by returning the value associated with a key, and to `currentKey` by returning the key associated with the value last returned by a call of `first` or `next`.

More precisely, the protocol of `KeyedCollection` (Figure 7.6) includes:

- `at:put:` and `currentKey`, to be defined in subclasses. (`at:put:` kc key value) will modify kc by associating `value` with `key`. `currentKey` is allied with `first` and `next`; the latter produce all the *values* in a collection, and `currentKey` can be used to find the key associated with each value.

- `at:`, defined using `first`, `next`, and `currentKey`. Intuitively, `at:` should be redefined for efficiency in most subclasses, but it turns out that there is little to be gained in our implementation by doing so; only `List` redefines it.

- `includesKey:`, to test whether a given key has a value. Note that `includes:` can be used to find whether a given *value* is in a collection.

- `indexOf:`, complementary to `at:`; it finds a key with which a given value is associated.

- Again, `size`, `isEmpty`, and `includes:`, inherited from `Collection`.

Dictionary. `Dictionary` is the basic `KeyedCollection` class, because it makes no assumptions about its keys, except that they respond to `=`. A `Dictionary` object contains a list of "associations" and a key; the key is used only to implement the generators. `Dictionary` is a concrete class, so has `initDictionary`, as well as `mkDictionary`, which returns an empty `Dictionary` object.

Specifically, a `Dictionary` object contains a list of `Association` objects. The class `Association` is not in the `Collection` hierarchy. It is given in

```
(class KeyedCollection Collection
    () ; abstract class
    (define at:put: (key value) #subclassResponsibility)
    (define currentKey () #subclassResponsibility)
    (define at: (key)
       (begin
          (set tempvalue (first self))
          (set found false)
          (while (and (notNil tempvalue) (not found))
             (if (= key (currentKey self))
                (set found true)
                (set tempvalue (next self))))
          tempvalue)) ; note:  nil if key out of range
    (define includesKey: (key) (notNil (at: self key)))
    (define indexOf: (value)
       (begin
          (set tempvalue (first self))
          (set found false)
          (while (and (notNil tempvalue) (not found))
             (if (= value tempvalue)
                (set found true)
                (set tempvalue (next self))))
          (if (isNil tempvalue) #nil (currentKey self)))))
)
```

Figure 7.6: Class KeyedCollection

```
(class Association Object
    (fst snd)
    (define initAssociation (x y) (begin (set fst x) (set snd y) self))
    (define fst () fst)
    (define snd () snd)
    (define fst: (x) (set fst x))
    (define snd: (y) (set snd y))
)
(define mkAssociation (a b) (initAssociation (new Association) a b))
```

Figure 7.7: Class Association

Figure 7.7. Its objects are arbitrary pairs, such that either component can be retrieved or changed.

`Dictionary` is defined in Figure 7.8. We have already seen it used, in `FinancialHistory`. To review its protocol:

- `currentKey` returns the instance variable of that name.

- `first` either returns `#nil`, or it retrieves the first `Association` in `tables`, sets `currentKey` to its key (first component), and returns its value (second component).

- `next` retrieves the next `Association` in `table`, then either returns `#nil` or sets `currentKey` to its key and returns its value.

- `associationAt:` returns the pair whose key matches the argument.

- `at:put:` first calls `associationAt:`. If it finds a pair whose key matches the `key` argument, then it changes the value in that pair to the `value` argument. If not, it puts a new pair into `table`.

- `Dictionary` inherits messages `at:` and `indexOf:` from `KeyedCollection`, and `size`, `isEmpty`, and `includes:` from `Collection`.

SequenceableCollection. This abstract class (Figure 7.9) represents `Keyed-Collection`'s whose keys are consecutive integers. The protocol defined here includes `firstKey` and `lastKey`, which are subclass responsibilities; `last`, which returns the last item; and `at:`. `at:` is a redefinition of the `at:` method inherited from `KeyedCollection`; using the fact that keys are consecutive integers, a more efficient version can be given.

List. This class, which has already been used often, is given in Figure 7.10. The `List` methods `car` and `cdr` correspond to the operations of the same name in LISP or in the `List` cluster in CLU; `car:` and `cdr:` correspond to `rplaca` and `rplacd`, respectively. `add:` corresponds to `cons`, but note that `List` is a mutable type: `add:`ing to the front of a `List` object actually modifies it; also, don't forget that the arguments are given in the reverse order from those of `cons`. The method `removeFirst` is a mutating version of `cdr`; that is, it modifies its receiver by removing its first element. `zerolist` adds `size` zeros to its receiver; it is called from the `Array` class.

A `List` object is represented by its car and its cdr, the current key, and the current cons cell. A list is considered empty if its car contains `#nil` (see `initList`).

```
(class Dictionary KeyedCollection
    (table currentKey)
    (define initDictionary ()
        (begin (set table (mkList)) self))
    (define currentkey () currentKey)
    (define first ()
        (if (isEmpty table) #nil
            (begin
                (set tempassoc (first table))
                (set currentKey (fst tempassoc))
                (snd tempassoc))))
    (define next ()
       (begin
           (set tempassoc (next table))
           (if (isNil tempassoc) #nil
               (begin
                   (set currentKey (fst tempassoc))
                   (snd tempassoc)))))
    (define at:put: (key value)
        (begin
            (set tempassoc (associationAt: self key))
            (if (isNil tempassoc)
                (add: table (mkAssociation key value))
                (snd: tempassoc value))))
    (define associationAt: (key)
       (begin
           (set temptable table)
           (set found false)
           (while (not (or (isEmpty temptable) found))
               (if (= (fst (car temptable)) key)
                   (set found true)
                   (set temptable (cdr temptable))))
           (if found (car temptable) #nil)))
)
(define mkDictionary () (initDictionary (new Dictionary)))
```

Figure 7.8: Class `Dictionary`

Several of the operations deserve explanation:

- Regarded as a `SequenceableCollection`, a `List` object must be indexable by integers. Indexing starts at 1. This fact is reflected in the definitions of `first`, `firstKey`, `lastKey`, and `at:put:`.

- `at:put:` uses a simple recursion, modifying the `car` after cdr'ing $n - 1$ times down the list. (It provides no protection against n's being out of range.)

- The idea of `add:` is to create a new `List` value and make it a copy of `self`, then assign it to `cdr` and assign `item` to `car`.

- A list contains within itself the index of the last item returned by `first` or `next` (`currentKey`) and a pointer to that item (`currentCell`). `first` initializes both instance variables (setting the `currentCell` point to the receiver itself), and `next` increments `currentKey` and `currentCell` and then returns the car of `currentCell`.

Here is how `List` is used:

```
-> (set L (mkList))
-> (add: L #a)
-> (add: L #b)
-> (first L)
b

-> (next L)
a

-> (next L)
nil

-> (at: L 2)
a
```

```
(class SequenceableCollection KeyedCollection
    () ; abstract class
    (define firstKey () #subclassResponsibility)
    (define lastKey () #subclassResponsibility)
    (define last () (at: self (lastKey self)))
    (define at: (index)
        (begin
           (set iterations (- index (firstKey self)))
           (set result (first self))
           (while (> iterations 0)
              (begin
                 (set result (next self))
                 (set iterations (- iterations 1))))
           result))
)
```

Figure 7.9: Class `SequenceableCollection`

```
(class List SequenceableCollection
    (car cdr currentKey currentCell)
    (define car () car)
    (define cdr () cdr)
    (define initList () (begin (set car #nil) self))
    (define add: (item)
        (begin
            (set temp (new List))
            (car: temp car)
            (cdr: temp cdr)
            (set cdr temp)
            (set car item)))
    (define car: (x) (set car x))
    (define cdr: (x) (set cdr x))
    (define first ()
        (begin
            (set currentKey 1)
            (set currentCell self)
            car))
    (define next ()
        (if (isNil (car currentCell)) #nil
            (begin
                (set currentKey (+1 currentKey))
                (set currentCell (cdr currentCell))
                (car currentCell))))
    (define firstKey () 1)
    (define lastKey () (size self))
    (define currentKey () currentKey)
    (define at:put: (n value)
        (if (= n 1) (set car value)
            (at:put: cdr (- n 1) value)))
    (define removeFirst ()
        (if (isEmpty self) self ; do nothing
            (begin
                (set car (car cdr))
                (set cdr (cdr cdr)))))
    (define zerolist (size)
        (while (> size 0)
            (begin
                (add: self 0)
                (set size (- size 1)))))
)
(define mkList () (initList (new List)))
```

Figure 7.10: Class List

```
(class Array SequenceableCollection
    (elements lobound hibound currentKey)
    (define initArray (lo size)
        (begin
            (set lobound lo)
            (set hibound (- (+ lo size) 1))
            (set elements (new List))
            (zerolist elements size)
            self))
    (define size () (+1 (- hibound lobound)))
    (define firstKey () lobound)
    (define lastKey () hibound)
    (define currentKey () currentKey)
    (define first ()
        (begin
            (set currentKey lobound)
            (first elements)))
    (define next ()
        (if (= currentKey hibound) #nil
            (begin
                (set currentKey (+1 currentKey))
                (next elements))))
    (define at:put: (n value)
        (if (> n hibound) #nil
            (if (< n lobound) #nil
                (at:put: elements (+1 (- n lobound)) value))))
)
(define mkArray (l s) (initArray (new Array) l s))
```

Figure 7.11: Class `Array`

Array.   Arrays (Figure 7.11) are one-dimensional and of fixed size and bounds, established by arguments to `mkArray` and, in turn, to `initArray`. They are represented by the list of their elements, integers `lobound` and `hibound`, and, as usual, `currentKey`.

`Array` employs the inherited definition of `at:` and defines `at:put:` by, in effect, delegating it to `List`. `firstKey` and `lastKey` return, of course, `lobound` and `hibound`, respectively. `first` and `next` work by setting `currentKey` and invoking `at:`. Finally, `initArray` sets `lobound` and `hibound` and sends `zerolist` to an empty list to obtain a list of the correct size. Note that `Array` objects never grow from their original size.

Admittedly, `Array` is not very useful in our language, because it has less real power than `List` with no compensating gain in efficiency. In real SMALLTALK, `Array`'s are represented by contiguous words in memory, so they enjoy constant-time random access.

7.2 Implementation

The listing of the SMALLTALK interpreter, insofar as it differs from that of CLU, is given in Appendix H. Here we briefly review the changes from CLU before proceeding with our usual section-by-section discussion.

- *All values are tagged with their class.* This is one of the most fundamental changes. In CLU, it is always possible, in any application ($f\ e_1\ \ldots\ e_n$), to determine, *by inspection of the program*, the definition of f; in short, CLU has static scope for functions. In SMALLTALK, on the other hand, it is impossible to make this determination, because the particular definition of f to be invoked depends upon the value (or, more precisely, the class) of e_1; SMALLTALK has dynamic scope for functions.

- The input routines must be changed to allow input of symbol constants and to accommodate the new syntax and semantics of classes. *parseClass* is generally simpler than *parseCluster*, in that it does not need to generate selectors, settors, or constructors. The only part that is more complicated is the construction of the *clrep*, the list of instance variables. In CLU this was obtained solely from the cluster definition, whereas in SMALLTALK it is obtained by finding the *clrep* of the superclass and appending it onto the list of instance variables given in the class definition. Note that the *clrep* component for `Object` contains the variable `self` (and nothing else), so `self` becomes an instance variable of every class; it is set when `new` is called.

- Application is somewhat complicated by the need to look in both the class hierarchy and the global function environment (*fundefs*) for a function's definition; by the ability to redefine `value-op`'s; and by the difference between applying a global function and a class method. Also, `new` needs to be processed. On the other hand, there are no selectors, settors, or constructors to handle, and no two-part names. On balance, application is about as complicated here as in CLU.

- At the top level, the initial hierarchy is established before the read-eval-print loop is entered, and some other new variables are initialized.

7.2.1 DECLARATIONS

`new` is treated as a control operation (see discussion under *EVALUATION*). Accordingly, *BUILTINOP* and *CONTROLOP* are changed slightly:

$$BUILTINOP = (IFOP, WHILEOP, SETOP, BEGINOP, NEWOP, PLUSOP,$$
$$\qquad\qquad MINUSOP, TIMESOP, DIVOP, EQOP, LTOP, GTOP, PRINTOP);$$
$$VALUEOP = PLUSOP\ ..\ PRINTOP;$$
$$CONTROLOP = IFOP\ ..\ NEWOP;$$

Symbols are a new type of value, and all values are tagged by their class, so the new space of values is:

$$STVALUE = \uparrow STVALUEREC;$$
$$STVALUETYPE = (INT,SYM,USER);$$
$$STVALUEREC = \textbf{record}$$
$$owner: CLASS;$$
$$\textbf{case } vtype: STVALUETYPE \textbf{ of}$$
$$INT: (intval: integer);$$
$$SYM: (symval: NAME);$$
$$USER: (userval: ENV)$$
$$\textbf{end};$$

With no implicitly defined functions, we can revert to the old definition of *FUNDEFREC* from Chapter 1:

$$FUNDEFREC = \textbf{record}$$
$$funname: NAME;$$
$$formals: NAMELIST;$$
$$body: EXP;$$
$$nextfundef: FUNDEF$$
$$\textbf{end};$$

CLASSREC (formerly *CLUSTERREC*) has one new field, giving the superclass, and dispenses with the "*nonexported*" field, which was used only for implicitly defined functions:

$$CLASSREC = \textbf{record}$$
$$clname: NAME;$$
$$clsuper: CLASS;$$
$$clrep: NAMELIST;$$
$$exported: FUNDEF;$$
$$nextclass: CLASS$$
$$\textbf{end};$$

There are also several new variables added:

numCtrlOps: *integer* will be explained later.

SELF: *NAME* gives the *NAME* of the string "`self`".

OBJECTCLASS: *CLASS* gives the *CLASS* record associated with the class `Object`.

objectInst: *STVALUE* will be explained under *READ-EVAL-PRINT LOOP*.

trueValue, falseValue: *STVALUE* will be initialized to contain the integers 1 and 0, respectively, and will be used as the results of comparison operations.

7.2.2 DATA STRUCTURE OP'S

mkPRIM is replaced by *mkINT* and *mkSYM*. *mkINT* and *mkSYM* also set the *owner* field to *OBJECTCLASS*.

7.2.3 NAME MANAGEMENT

In *initNames*, *numCtrlOps* and *SELF* are set, and **new** is included as a new name.

7.2.4 INPUT

parseVal handles both integers and symbols.

parseClass is simpler than *parseCluster* was in CLU, because there are no implicitly-defined operations to create. The changes are, first, that it must read the superclass name. More significantly, its *clrep* field is the *NAMELIST* constructed by appending the *clrep* field of the superclass to the list of instance variables given in this class. The code to do this follows; *rep* is the list of instance variables in this class, and *thisclass* and *superclass* are the *CLASS*es corresponding to the class being defined and its parent:

> **if** *rep* = **nil**
> **then** *thisclass*↑.*clrep* := *superclass*↑.*clrep*
> **else begin**
> $\qquad$ *thisclass*↑.*clrep* := *rep*;
> $\qquad$ **while** *rep*↑.*tail* <> **nil do** *rep* := *rep*↑.*tail*;
> $\qquad$ *rep*↑.*tail* := *superclass*↑.*clrep*
> $\quad$ **end**;

7.2.5 ENVIRONMENTS

No changes.

7.2.6 VALUES

The changes here are of two simple kinds:

- *prValue* and *applyValueOp* must handle symbol values. In particular, the treatment of *EQOP* in *applyValueOp* is changed.

- The occurrences of *mkPRIM* are changed to *mkINT*.

7.2.7 EVALUATION

Here we find the biggest changes. As in CLU, *eval* takes a third argument, but this time it is an *STVALUE*, the receiver of the message inside whose body *e* is contained:

function *eval* (*e*: *EXP*; *rho*: *ENV*; *rcvr*: *STVALUE*): *STVALUE*;

evalList is changed only to the extent of passing the *rcvr* argument in its recursive call of *eval*.

applyUserFun is removed and replaced by two functions, *applyGlobalFun* and *applyMethod*, used to invoke, respectively, functions defined at the top level and methods defined in classes. A function called *methodSearch* is also added. Before going into these, we look at the top level of *eval*.

The *VALEXP* case is unchanged. The *VAREXP* cases, however, is changed because a variable can be either a formal parameter, an instance variable, or a global variable. Precedence is given to these possiblities in just that order; thus:

> *VAREXP*:
>   **if** *isBound*(*varble*, *rho*)
>   **then** *eval* := *fetch*(*varble*, *rho*)
>   **else if** *isBound*(*varble*, *rcvr*↑.*userval*)
>   **then** *eval* := *fetch*(*varble*, *rcvr*↑.*userval*)
>   **else if** *isBound*(*varble*, *globalEnv*)
>   **then** *eval* := *fetch*(*varble*, *globalEnv*)
>   **else** . . . undefined variable error . . .

The *APEXP* case changes even more. In determining the binding of the operator of an application, the following considerations come into play:

- Control operations cannot be redefined. Thus, for these functions, call *applyCtrlOp*.

- If the function has no arguments, it is certainly not a method (since methods have at least one argument), nor is it a value-op, so it must be a top-level definition; therefore, look it up in *fundefs*.

- If the function has at least one argument, search for it in the class hierarchy, even if it has a built-in name.

- If the search succeeds, then the operator is a message. If it fails, then determine if it is a built-in operation or a function defined at the top level.

Taking all this into consideration, we arrive at the *APEXP* case:

```
APEXP:
      if optr <= numCtrlOps
      then eval := applyCtrlOp(primOp(optr), args)
      else begin
                vl := evalList(args);
                if lengthVL(vl) = 0
                then eval := applyGlobalFun(optr, vl)
                else begin
                        f := methodSearch(optr, vl↑.head↑.owner);
                        if f <> nil
                        then eval := applyMethod(f, vl)
                        else if optr <= numBuiltins
                            then eval := applyValueOp(primOp(optr), vl)
                            else eval := applyGlobalFun(optr, vl)
                    end
            end
```

The method search itself is very straightforward and hardly merits an explanation:

```
        function methodSearch (optr: NAME; cl: CLASS): FUNDEF;
        var f: FUNDEF;
        begin
            f := nil;
            while (f = nil) and (cl <> nil) do begin
                f := fetchFun(optr, cl↑.exported);
                if f = nil then cl := cl↑.clsuper
                end;
            methodSearch := f
        end; (* methodSearch *)
```

applyGlobalFun and *applyMethod* have these headers:

```
function applyGlobalFun (optr: NAME; actuals: VALUELIST): STVALUE;
function applyMethod ( f: FUNDEF; actuals: VALUELIST ): STVALUE;
```

applyGlobalFun is, in fact, identical to *applyUserFun* from Chapter 1. The main part of its body, you will recall, is:

```
            rho := mkEnv(formals, actuals);
            applyGlobalFun := eval(body, rho, rcvr)
```

applyMethod is only slightly different. Its first actual parameter is removed from the actual parameter list and assumes the role of the receiver. Thus, the corresponding part of its definition is:

$$rho := mkEnv(formals,\ actuals\uparrow.tail);$$
$$applyMethod := eval(body,\ rho,\ actuals\uparrow.head)$$

applyCtrlOp has a few minor changes, plus the code for **new**. The minor changes are adding the *rcvr* argument to all recursive calls of *eval* and modifying the *SETOP* case in parallel with the treatment of *VAREXP*'s in *eval*. The *NEWOP* case is rather subtle:

NEWOP:
>   **begin**
>>   (* Argument is a *VAREXP* with the name of a class *)
>> $cl := fetchClass(args\uparrow.head\uparrow.varble);$
>>   **if** $cl =$ **nil**
>>   **then** ... undefined class error ...
>> $newval := mkUSER(mkEnv(cl\uparrow.clrep,\ mkRepFor(cl\uparrow.clrep)),\ cl);$
>> $assign(SELF,\ newval,\ newval\uparrow.userval);$
>> $applyCtrlOp := newval$
>   **end**

Here, *cl* and *newval* are local variables of *applyCtrlOp* of type *CLASS* and *STVALUE*, respectively. *mkRepFor* (not shown) is a local function that, given a list of names (instance variables), produces a list of values (namely, zeros) of the same length. The argument to **new** is a variable whose name is the same as a class. This variable will never actually be bound to a value; it is only used for its name. The *NEWOP* code first looks for this class, setting *cl* to the corresponding *CLASS* value. It creates an object of that class by taking its *clrep* and constructing a value list of the same length. The call to *assign* is the trickiest part of this code. In English, it says "Bind the variable **self** to the value being created, in the environment contained in that value." The result is a circular data structure. This ensures that when a reference to **self** is made it will return the receiver itself as the value.

7.2.8   READ-EVAL-PRINT LOOP

The major change here is the addition of the procedure *initHierarchy*, which is called before the loop begins. It allocates a *CLASSREC* for class **Object**, makes **self** its sole instance variable, and creates a value of the class:

>   **procedure** *initHierarchy*;
>   **begin**
>> $classes :=$ **nil**;
>> $OBJECTCLASS := newClass(install('Object\ '),\ $**nil**$);$
>> $OBJECTCLASS\uparrow.exported :=$ **nil**;
>> $OBJECTCLASS\uparrow.clrep := mkNamelist(SELF,\ $**nil**$);$

$$objectInst := mkUSER(mkEnv(OBJECTCLASS\uparrow.clrep,$$
$$mkValuelist(mkINT(0), \textbf{nil})),$$
$$OBJECTCLASS);$$
end; (* *initHierarchy* *)

The only purpose of *objectInst* is to be passed to *eval* from the top level as its third argument; if **nil** were passed in, the interpreter would crash on an attempt to dereference it.

7.3 Example — Numbers

Our first large example for this chapter illustrates a natural use of inheritance: defining arithmetic operations over different numeric representations. The sub-hierarchy we present is:

```
            Object
              |
            Number
           /      \
      Fraction    Float
```

Objects of these new classes represent numbers with fractional parts. **Fraction** represents rational numbers by pairs of integers (a numerator and a denominator). **Float** uses a floating-point representation, giving as integers the mantissa and the exponent of 10. Eventually, we should be able to perform all the usual arithmetic operations on either kind of number. We will consider only *homogeneous* operations and not concern ourselves with coercions between **Fraction** and **Float**.

The question is how to structure the hierarchy, that is, what operations to define in the abstract class **Number** and which to define in the concrete classes. The protocol of **Number** lists as subclass responsibilities the following: **+**, *****, **=**, **<**, **negate** (additive inverse), **recip** (reciprocal), **zero** (to get the representation of 0 in the class of the receiver), and **one** (likewise for 1). Based on these operations, which can only be defined with knowledge of a particular representation, **Number** defines additional protocol, including **-**, **/**, **>**, **+1**, **sub1**, **isZero**, **isNegative**, **abs**, **sqr**, and **sqrt** (using the Newton–Raphson method; see page 162). The listing of class **Number** is in Figure 7.12.

7.3.1 FRACTION

Fraction (Figure 7.13) represents rationals as fractions (numerator and denominator) in reduced form, meaning: (1) the numerator and denominator have no common factors; (2) if the numerator is zero, the denominator is one; and (3) the denominator is positive. The virtue of reduced form is the simplic-

```
(class Number Object
    () ; abstract class
    (define + (x) #subclassResponsibility)
    (define negate () #subclassResponsibility)
    (define * (x) #subclassResponsibility)
    (define recip () #subclassResponsibility)
    (define = (x) #subclassResponsibility)
    (define < (x) #subclassResponsibility)
    (define zero () #subclassResponsibility)
    (define one () #subclassResponsibility)
    (define print () #subclassResponsibility)
    (define - (y) (+ self (negate y)))
    (define / (y) (* self (recip y)))
    (define > (y) (< y self))
    (define +1 () (+ self (one self)))
    (define sub1 () (- self (one self)))
    (define isZero () (= self (zero self)))
    (define isNegative () (< self (zero self)))
    (define abs () (if (isNegative self) (negate self) self))
    (define sqr () (* self self))
    (define sqrt (epsilon) ; find square root of receiver within epsilon
        (begin
            (set this-step (+1 (zero self)))
            (set two (+1 this-step))
            (set next-step (/ (+ this-step (/ self this-step)) two))
            (while (> (abs (- this-step next-step)) epsilon)
                (begin
                    (set this-step next-step)
                    (set next-step (/ (+ this-step (/ self this-step)) two))))
            next-step))
)
```

Figure 7.12: Class Number

ity of equality testing. The methods div-reduce and sign-reduce are used to enforce reduced form.

Before discussing the individual methods of this class, a point must be made which applies equally to Fraction and Float. Numerical data are naturally *immutable*: when adding 4 to 3, 3 should not change itself to 7; rather, it should return a new number. Yet the object-oriented programming style lends itself to defining *mutable* data, as in the Collection hierarchy. This remark is made to explain a certain awkwardness in Fraction and Float, where new objects have to be explicitly created and returned. The use of constructors in CLU, though no different in principle, seems more natural.

```
(class Fraction Number
    (x y)
    (define initFraction (a b)
        (begin
            (setFraction self a b)
            (sign-reduce self)
            (div-reduce self)))
    (define setFraction (a b) (begin (set x a) (set y b) self))
    (define x () x)
    (define y () y)
    (define + (f)
        (div-reduce
            (setFraction (new Fraction)
                (+ (* x (y f)) (* (x f) y))
                (* y (y f)))))
    (define negate () (setFraction (new Fraction) (- 0 x) y))
    (define * (f)
        (div-reduce
            (setFraction (new Fraction)
                (* x (x f))
                (* y (y f)))))
    (define recip () (sign-reduce (setFraction (new Fraction) y x)))
    (define = (f) (and (= x (x f)) (= y (y f))))
    (define < (f) (< (* x (y f)) (* (x f) y)))
    (define zero () (setFraction (new Fraction) 0 1))
    (define one () (setFraction (new Fraction) 1 1))
    (define print () (begin (print x) (print y)))
    ; div-reduce and sign-reduce should not be exported
    (define div-reduce ()
        (begin
            (if (= x 0)
                (set y 1)
                (begin
                    (set temp (gcd (abs x) y))
                    (set x (/ x temp))
                    (set y (/ y temp))))
            self))
    (define sign-reduce ()
        (begin
            (if (< y 0)
                (begin (set x (- 0 x))(set y (- 0 y)))
                0)
            self))
)
(define mkFraction (a b) (initFraction (new Fraction) a b))
```

Figure 7.13: Class Fraction

With that in mind, consider the methods of `Fraction`:

- `initFraction` sets the numerator and denominator of a fraction and reduces it (we will look at `sign-reduce` and `div-reduce` later).

- `setFraction` sets the numerator and denominator of a fraction without reducing it; this method is intended for internal use, not for export.

- `x` and `y` allow a client to see the numerator and denominator of a fraction.

- `+` adds fraction $\frac{x}{y}$ and $\frac{x'}{y'}$ by forming the new fraction $\frac{xy'+x'y}{yy'}$; this fraction may be in non-reduced form (e.g., $\frac{1}{2} + \frac{1}{2} = \frac{4}{4}$), so `div-reduce` is called.

- `negate` simply negates the numerator (allocating a new `Fraction` for the result).

- `*` multiplies $\frac{x}{y}$ and $\frac{x'}{y'}$, yielding the new fraction $\frac{xx'}{yy'}$, and reduces it.

- `recip` just inverts a fraction. This will leave the fraction in reduced form unless it was negative, in which case it will leave the denominator negative; `reduce-sign` is called to adjust this. (The reciprocal of zero will not be in reduced form, but of course there is nothing to be done in that case anyway.)

- `=` is very simple to define. `<` is also: $\frac{x}{y} < \frac{x'}{y'}$ if and only if $xy' < x'y$.

- `zero` returns $\frac{0}{1}$, and `one` returns $\frac{1}{1}$.

- `sign-reduce` and `div-reduce` enforce two aspects of reduced form: `sign-reduce` ensures that the denominator is positive, and `div-reduce` ensures both that zero is properly represented and that the numerator and denominator have no common divisors. Only `initFraction` calls both, since its arguments may be arbitrary integers. The other arithmetic operations call at most one, depending upon what kind of reduction might be needed for the result of that operation. For example, the result of `negate` is necessarily in reduced form if its argument is, so it needn't employ either function. In the result of `+`, the denominator will not be negative, since it is the product of two nonnegative denominators, but its numerator and denominator may have common factors, so `div-reduce` is called; likewise for `*`. The reader may verify that the proper reducing function is called in all cases.

Note that `setFraction`, `sign-reduce`, and `div-reduce` all return `self`. The arithmetic operations use this fact.

Here, then, is a session using `Fraction`'s. There is no good way of printing them; `print` just prints the numerator and denominator. The call (`sqrt f1 eps`) asks for the square root of 17. The result is the fraction $\frac{3437249}{833049}$, or 4.126; the square root of 17 is actually about 4.123.

```
-> (set eps (mkFraction 1 2))
-> (set f1 (mkFraction 17 1))
-> (set f2 (sqrt f1 eps))
-> (print f2)
3437249
833049
```

7.3.2 FLOAT

Numbers in floating-point form (Figure 7.14) are represented by a mantissa and exponent (of 10). That is, the `Float` having mantissa m and exponent e represents $m \times 10^e$; m and e can be negative. The mantissa is a number in the range 0–10,000.[5] When the mantissa exceeds this size, it is normalized by dividing by a power of 10 and incrementing the exponent accordingly.

Here is how the various methods are implemented in `Float`:

- Addition is based on the following idea: Assume $e \geq e'$ and let $\delta = e - e'$. Then
$$m \times 10^e = (m \times 10^\delta) \times 10^{e'},$$
so that
$$m \times 10^e + m' \times 10^{e'} = (m \times 10^\delta + m') \times 10^{e'}.$$

- Negation is accomplished by negating the mantissa.

- Multiplication follows the rule:
$$(m \times 10^e) \times (m' \times 10^{e'}) = (m \times m') \times 10^{e+e'}.$$
This may lead to a too large mantissa, as noted above, so the result must be normalized.

- `recip` is computed using the identity:
$$\frac{1}{m \times 10^e} = \frac{10^8}{m \times 10^8 \times 10^e} = \frac{10^8}{m} \times 10^{-e-8}.$$

- Zero is represented by a zero mantissa (the value of the exponent does not matter), and one by a mantissa of 1 and an exponent of 0.

- `Float` redefines `isZero` and `isNegative`, because = and < use them and the inherited versions of them use = and <, leading to a circularity.

`normalize` just adjusts the mantissa so that its magnitude is less than or equal to 10,000. Like the `reduce` operations in `Fraction`, `normalize` must return `self`.

---

[5]This is to ensure that when multiplying two `Float`'s, the mantissa does not overflow the machine word; this should be changed to 0–100 for machines using 16-bit integers.

```
(class Float Number
    (mant exp)
    (define initFloat (m e) (begin (set mant m) (set exp e) self))
    (define mant () mant)
    (define exp () exp)
    (define + (x)
       (begin
          (if (< exp (exp x))
             (begin
                (set min self)
                (set max x))
             (begin
                (set min x)
                (set max self)))
          (set delta (- (exp max) (exp min)))
          (set temp (+ (* (mant max) (powerof10 self delta)) (mant min)))
          (normalize
             (initFloat (new Float) temp (if (= temp 0) 0 (exp min))))))
    (define negate () (initFloat (new Float) (- 0 mant) exp))
    (define * (x)
       (normalize (initFloat (new Float)
          (* mant (mant x))
          (+ exp (exp x)))))
    (define recip ()
       (if (isZero self) self
          (normalize (initFloat (new Float)
             (/ 100000000 mant)
             (- (- 0 8) exp)))))
    (define zero () (initFloat (new Float) 0 0))
    (define one () (initFloat (new Float) 1 0))
    (define = (x) (isZero (- self x)))
    (define < (x) (isNegative (- self x)))
    (define print () (begin (print mant) (print exp)))
    (define isZero () (= mant 0))
    (define isNegative () (< mant 0))
    ; normalize and powerof10 should not be exported
    (define powerof10 (d) (if (= d 0) 1 (* 10 (powerof10 self (- d 1)))))
    (define normalize ()
       (begin
          (while (> (abs mant) 10000)
             (begin
                (set mant (/ mant 10))
                (set exp (+ exp 1))))
          self))
)
(define mkFloat (m e) (initFloat (new Float) m e))
```

Figure 7.14: Class Float

`Float` can now be used as follows:

```
-> (set eps (mkFloat 5 -1))
-> (set x1 (mkFloat 17 0))
-> (print (sqrt x1 eps))
4125
-3
```

The result is, of course, 4.125; recall that the correct answer is 4.123.

7.4   Example — Discrete-Event Simulation

We are presented with the following problem:

> The students at a small college for women do their programming
> assignments in a lab consisting of two computer terminals tied to a
> central computer. The procedure for sharing these two terminals is
> simple: Students are limited to using a terminal for t minutes at a
> time, after which they must go to the end of the waiting line. (The
> terminals are interchangeable to the students, so that a waiting
> student can always take the next available terminal, even if she was
> using a different one earlier.) The question is: What should t be?
> More specifically, what value of t will minimize the average amount
> of wasted time (time spent on line) per student?

One solution would be to run an experiment in the lab itself, trying different
values of t on successive weeks. There are some disadvantages to this, though:
The experiment is inconvenient and costly to run and, for poor choices of t,
possibly quite disruptive to the students. Worse, the results from one week
to another are not really comparable: That one value of t does better than
another can be attributed to any of a number of factors, such as the difficulty
of the two assignments, their due dates, other assignments due the same time,
etc. Without any control over these other factors, no definitive conclusions can
be drawn about the effect of changing the waiting times. In reality, these other
factors cannot be controlled.

The solution we explore here is to write a program to *simulate* the entire
system — students arriving, waiting on line, etc. — and run it several times
using different values of t. The disadvantages of running the experiment in the
real world are nullified: the experiment is not at all inconvenient or disruptive,
and it can be run under identical circumstances of lab use for the different
values of t. The only problem introduced — and it is a serious one — is to
ensure that the program accurately reflects, or *models*, the system.

Computer simulation is a very common method for exploring the effects of
changing conditions on real-world systems, when those effects are too complex
to compute directly, and when experiments on the system itself are expensive,

impractical, or dangerous. When the activities of interest in the system can be separated into discrete events, as in the computer lab, the method is called *discrete-event simulation*. Otherwise, as when simulating the movement of electrons in an integrated circuit, it is called *continuous-event simulation*; the techniques used there are very different from those we present in this section.

A discrete-event simulation runs like this:

> Maintain a variable CLOCK to hold the simulated time and a variable EVQUEUE, the *event queue*, to hold a list of pending events. At each iteration, the next event is taken off EVQUEUE, the clock is updated to the time of the event, and the event "occurs." The occurrence of the event usually results in placing new events on the event queue. Continue iterating until a predetermined time is reached in the simulation.

In our system, there are two types of events on the event queue:

1. The arrival of a student into the lab. When this event "occurs," either the student will get on line or, if a terminal is free, sit at the terminal, departing after t minutes or after finishing her work, whichever comes first. Also, the next arrival will be scheduled and put on the event queue.

2. The timing-out of a student on a terminal. There are several versions of this event: the student may (a) stay at the terminal (if her work is not done and noone is waiting), (b) leave the lab (if her work is done), or (c) go to the end of the line. In case (b) or (c), a new student may sit at the terminal, and that student's timing-out on the terminal will be scheduled on the event queue.

In the rest of this section, we present the details of the coding of this simulation in SMALLTALK and the results of some runs.

7.4.1 CODING THE LAB SIMULATION

The Class Simulation. All discrete-event simulations have the general form described in the last section. We assume CLOCK and EVQUEUE are global variables, and we define a class Simulation (Figure 7.15) which gives the main loop of a simulation in the method run.

Simulation is an abstract class. A specific simulation fills in the model-specific details by initializing global variables and reporting on the results when the simulation run ends.

The Class LabSimulation. This concrete class (Figure 7.16) provides initialization and reporting for the terminal lab model. Also, a LabSimulation object has a built-in terminal limit, provided when the object is initialized. The main

```
(class Simulation Object
    () ; abstract class
    (define initialize () #subclassResponsibility)
    (define report () #subclassResponsibility)
    (define run (timelimit)
       (begin
          (set CLOCK 0)
          (set EVQUEUE (mkEventQueue))
          (initialize self)
          (while (<= CLOCK timelimit) (doNextEvent EVQUEUE))
          (report self)))
)
```

Figure 7.15: Class Simulation

jobs of initialize and report are, respectively, to initialize and print certain global variables:

TERMINALLIMIT — the same as the instance variable termlimit, this gives the value of t.

THELAB — an object of class Lab, representing the state of the lab, i.e., the availability of the two terminals.

STUDENTNO — the number of the last student entering the lab; students are assigned consecutive numbers as they enter, for reporting purposes.

STUDENTSFINISHING — the number of students who have finished their work and left the lab.

TOTALTIMEWASTED — the total amount of time spent on line by all students who have finished.

TERMINALQUEUE — the waiting line, initially empty.

WAITTIMES, SERVICETIMES — explanation deferred.

The last line in initialize schedules the arrival of the first student; that is, it places an "arrival event" on EVQUEUE. The important question of *when* this first arrival is to occur — when, indeed, any arrival occurs — is related to the meaning of variables WAITTIMES and SERVICETIMES and will likewise be deferred.

The function of report will now be clear: It prints the total number of students who have finished their work, how many are left on line, and the total and average times wasted by the students who finished.

Several new classes have now been tacitly introduced: EventQueue, Lab, Queue, WaitTimeList, ServiceTimeList, and Student. Of these, Student is the longest and the one that gives the most detail about the model.

The Class Lab.   This class (Figure 7.17) represents the state of the lab in terms of the availability of its two terminals. Its protocol permits the lab to be initialized (`initLab`), making both terminals free, and allows clients to check if there is a free terminal (`terminals-free?`), choose a terminal (`pick-terminal`), and leave a terminal (`release-terminal`).

The Class Queue.   Queues are data structures with which we are quite familiar. Here we are using one to represent the waiting line in the lab, TERMINALQUEUE; it will contain objects of class `Student`. Because `Queue` will be defined as a subclass of `List`, we use different names for the operations than we have before: `enqueue:` for enqueue, `car` for front, `removeFirst` for rm-front, and `isEmpty` for empty?. Also, `enqueue:` and `removeFirst` are mutating operations.

```
(class LabSimulation Simulation
    (termlimit)
    (define initLabSimulation (t) (begin (set termlimit t) self))
    (define initialize ()
       (begin
          (set TERMINALLIMIT termlimit)
          (set THELAB (mkLab))
          (set STUDENTNO 0)
          (set STUDENTSFINISHING 0)
          (set TOTALTIMEWASTED 0)
          (set TERMINALQUEUE (mkQueue))
          (set WAITTIMES (mkWaitTimeList))
          (set SERVICETIMES (mkServiceTimeList))
          (scheduleNewArrival (new Student))))
    (define report ()
       (begin
          (print #simulation-done)
          (print #students-finishing)
          (print STUDENTSFINISHING)
          (print #left-on-queue)
          (print (size TERMINALQUEUE))
          (print #Total-time-wasted:)
          (print TOTALTIMEWASTED)
          (print #Average-time-wasted:)
          (print (/ TOTALTIMEWASTED STUDENTSFINISHING))))
)
(define mkLabSimulation (tl) (initLabSimulation (new LabSimulation) tl))
```

Figure 7.16: Class LabSimulation

```
(class Lab Object
    (term1free term2free)
    (define initLab ()
        (begin (set term1free true) (set term2free true) self))
    (define terminals-free? () (or term1free term2free))
    (define pick-terminal ()
        (if term1free
            (begin (set term1free false) 1)
            (begin (set term2free false) 2))))
    (define release-terminal (t)
        (if (= t 1) (set term1free true) (set term2free true))))
)
(define mkLab () (initLab (new Lab)))
```

Figure 7.17: Class Lab

List needs a subtle change in the definition of add: to allow Queue (as well as PriorityQueue, defined in the next subsection) to inherit from it. This change is given in Figure 7.18. As given in Figure 7.10, if we add Queue as a subclass of List, add: cannot be applied to Queue objects, because the cons cell it adds is always a List object. So, we change add: to create the new cons cell by sending the newEmptyCollection message to self, instead of just creating a new empty List object. By defining a newEmptyCollection message in Queue, which creates an empty Queue object, the inherited add: method works correctly on Queue's.

Queue can now be defined very briefly, as shown in Figure 7.19. enqueue: adds an item at the end of a queue.

The Class EventQueue. An event queue is a data structure which has the following protocol:

initEventQueue — make the queue empty.

```
(define add: (item)
    (begin
        (set temp (newEmptyCollection self))
        (car: temp car)
        (cdr: temp cdr)
        (set cdr temp)
        (set car item)))
(define newEmptyCollection () (initList (new List)))
```

Figure 7.18: Changes to class List for better inheritability

```
(class Queue List
    ()
    (define initQueue () (initList self))
    (define newEmptyCollection () (initList (new Queue)))
    (define enqueue: (item)
        (if (isEmpty self) (add: self item) (enqueue: cdr item)))
)
(define mkQueue () (initQueue (new Queue)))
```

Figure 7.19: Class `Queue`

scheduleEvent — add a new event, given the time and the "event object."

doNextEvent — perform the chronologically next event by sending it the take-Action message, remove it from the queue, and update CLOCK. Note that "chronologically next" has nothing to do with when the event was added to the event queue but only with the time that the event is scheduled to occur.

We will see that "event objects" will, in this simulation, just be the students themselves.

The EventQueue class is shown in Figure 7.20. An EventQueue object is represented by an object of the class PriorityQueue. A priority queue is a list-like data structure whose elements are pairs and which is sorted according to the first item in each pair. Thus, scheduleEvent constructs the pair containing the event and the time at which it is to occur and sends the message insert:

```
(class EventQueue Object
    (pqueue) ; a PriorityQueue
    (define initEventQueue ()
        (begin (set pqueue (mkPriorityQueue)) self))
    (define scheduleEvent (event time)
        (insert: pqueue (mkAssociation time event)))
    (define doNextEvent ()
        (begin
            (set pair (car pqueue))
            (removeFirst pqueue)
            (set CLOCK (fst pair))
            (takeAction (snd pair))))
)
(define mkEventQueue () (initEventQueue (new EventQueue)))
```

Figure 7.20: Class `EventQueue`

```
(class PriorityQueue List
    ()
    (define initPriorityQueue () (initList self))
    (define newEmptyCollection () (initList (new PriorityQueue)))
    (define insert: (pair)
        (if (isEmpty self) (add: self pair)
            (if (< (fst pair) (fst car)) (add: self pair)
                (insert: cdr pair)))))
)
(define mkPriorityQueue () (initPriorityQueue (new PriorityQueue)))
```

Figure 7.21: Class `PriorityQueue`

to the `PriorityQueue` object representing this event queue. `PriorityQueue` is another subclass of `List`, shown in Figure 7.21; the method `insert:` is analogous to the LISP function `insert`.

The Class Student.   The active agents in this model — the individuals that move into the lab, onto the waiting line, onto the terminals, and so on — are students. A student can be in one of five states as far as this simulation is concerned: scheduled to arrive but not yet there; waiting on line; using terminal 1; using terminal 2; or finished.

The `Student` class (Figures 7.22 and 7.23) represents a student by five instance variables:

status — a number between −1 and 3 representing the state of the student (−1 for scheduled to arrive; 0 for on the queue; 1 or 2 for on the corresponding terminal; and 3 for finished).

number — a number assigned to the student upon entering the lab, used for reporting purposes.

timeNeeded — the total amount of terminal connect time a student will need to complete her work. We assume there is no penalty for having this time broken into small chunks.

timeStillNeeded — the amount of terminal connect time still needed after whatever time has already been spent on the terminal.

arrivalTime — the time that this student arrived in the lab.

As can be seen in Figure 7.22, to initialize a `Student` object, one must provide the student's number, arrival time, and the amount of time that student will need on a terminal. Students are placed on `EVQUEUE` as "events," meaning

```
(class Student Object
    (status number timeNeeded timeStillNeeded arrivalTime)
    (define initStudent (n t a)
      (begin
         (set status -1)
         (set number n)
         (set timeNeeded t)
         (set timeStillNeeded t)
         (set arrivalTime a)
         self))
    (define takeAction ()
      (if (= status -1) (arrive self) (leaveTerminal self)))
    (define arrive ()
      (begin
         (if (terminals-free? THELAB)
            (grabTerminal self)
            (begin
               (set status 0)
               (enqueue: TERMINALQUEUE self)))
         (scheduleNewArrival (new Student))))
    (define leaveTerminal ()
      (if (= timeStillNeeded 0)
         (begin
            (release-terminal THELAB status)
            (set status 3)
            (set wasted (- (- CLOCK arrivalTime) timeNeeded))
            (set STUDENTSFINISHING (+1 STUDENTSFINISHING))
            (set TOTALTIMEWASTED (+ TOTALTIMEWASTED wasted))
            (if (not (isEmpty TERMINALQUEUE))
               (grabTerminal (car TERMINALQUEUE)) 0))
         (if (isEmpty TERMINALQUEUE)
            (scheduleLeaveTerminal self)
            (begin
               (release-terminal THELAB self)
               (set status 0)
               (enqueue: TERMINALQUEUE self)
               (grabTerminal (car TERMINALQUEUE))))))))
    (define grabTerminal ()
      (begin
         (if (= status 0) ; was on terminal queue
            (removeFirst TERMINALQUEUE)
            0) ; else do nothing
         (set status (pick-terminal THELAB))
         (scheduleLeaveTerminal self)))
```

Figure 7.22: Class Student, beginning

```
(define scheduleLeaveTerminal ()
  (if (<= timeStillNeeded TERMINALLIMIT)
      (begin
          (scheduleEvent EVQUEUE self (+ CLOCK timeStillNeeded))
          (set timeStillNeeded 0))
      (begin
          (scheduleEvent EVQUEUE self (+ CLOCK TERMINALLIMIT))
          (set timeStillNeeded (- timeStillNeeded TERMINALLIMIT)))))
(define scheduleNewArrival ()
  (begin
      (set wait (next WAITTIMES))
      (set service (next SERVICETIMES))
      (set STUDENTNO (+1 STUDENTNO))
      (set arrival (+ CLOCK wait))
      (initStudent self STUDENTNO service arrival)
      (scheduleEvent EVQUEUE self arrival)))
)
```

Figure 7.23: Class **Student**, conclusion

they can respond to the **takeAction** message. Students are scheduled to take
actions only if they are in one of three states:

Not arrived (status $= -1$) — If a student in this state receives the **takeAction** message, she responds by sending herself the **arrive** message. She
arrives, grabs a terminal if one is free (otherwise places herself on the
waiting line), and schedules the next arrival.

Using a terminal (status $= 1$ or 2) — If a student in this state receives the
takeAction message, she responds by sending herself the **leaveTerminal**
message. As indicated earlier, this has a variety of possible outcomes, depending upon whether the student is finished, whether there is anyone
waiting on line, etc. If this student retains use of the terminal, she schedules herself to leave the terminal by calling **scheduleLeaveTerminal**; if
a new student gets the terminal, she schedules that student's time-out in
the same way.

It is vitally important to understand the difference between *scheduling* an
event and that event's *occurring*. Messages **arrive** and **leaveTerminal** are sent
when an event is to *occur*; **scheduleLeaveTerminal** and **scheduleNewArrival**
are called to *schedule* events. Part of the action associated with an event's
occurrence may be the scheduling of some events for the future. Specifically:
when a student arrives, she schedules the next arrival, and if she gets on a
terminal immediately, she schedules her own departure from that terminal;
when a student's terminal time is up, but noone is waiting, she again schedules

her own departure from the terminal, and if someone is waiting, she schedules that student's departure from the terminal. *Scheduling* means simply placing an event on `EVQUEUE`, nothing more.

Let us look at `scheduleLeaveTerminal`. It is sent to a student to tell that student to schedule her timing-out on the terminal she is currently using. When will that departure occur? If the time the student needs on the terminal (`timeStillNeeded`) is less than `TERMINALLIMIT`, then it will occur `timeStillNeeded` minutes from now, otherwise `TERMINALLIMIT` minutes from now.

`scheduleNewArrival` is a bit more subtle. It is sent to a new `Student` object (even before that object has been initialized), telling that student to schedule her arrival. The student must determine *when* to arrive and *how much* terminal connect time ("service time") will be needed. This is done by sending the `next` message to variables `WAITTIMES` and `SERVICETIMES`, whose significance will be discussed next; note for now that `WAITTIMES` returns the number of minutes *from now* that the arrival will occur. The student determines her number and arrival time, initializes herself accordingly, and schedules her arrival.

The Classes WaitTimeList and ServiceTimeList. There are three parameters of any simulation of the lab:

- The length of time it will run. This is given by the `timelimit` parameter to the `Simulation` method `run`.

- The terminal time limit, given by instance variable `termlimit` of `LabSimulation`, and then assigned to global variable `TERMINALLIMIT` when a simulation run begins.

- The schedule of arrivals and service times.

The purpose of this section is to explain how the schedule of arrivals and service times is established and give several examples of simulation runs.

Consider arrival times first. We postulate a class `WaitTimeList`, whose protocol consists of `initWaitTimeList` and `next`. A `WaitTimeList` object responds to the `next` message by returning a number, which is the time interval (in minutes) before the next arrival. `WAITTIMES` is set (in `initialize`) to be a new `WaitTimeList` object. Thus, if sending `next` to `WAITTIMES` yields, on successive calls: 2, 13, 29, and 8, then there are arrivals at times: 2, 15, 44, and 52. Class `ServiceTimeList` has an analogous purpose, and `SERVICETIMES` is likewise initialized to a new `ServiceTimeList` object. If it were to respond to the first four `next` messages with numbers: 17, 46, 7, and 25, this would mean that the student arriving at time 2 will need 17 minutes of terminal time, the one arriving at time 15 will need 46 minutes, and so on. (Note again that these are *total* service times, independent of how many separate terminal sessions they are broken into.)

What do these classes look like? In a more elaborate and serious simulation, this would be among the most important and difficult questions to be confronted. Great care would be taken to ensure that the numbers used in the simulation faithfully reflect the actual activity in the lab. For our purposes, however, such scrupulousness would be overkill. Instead, we'll offer two versions of each of these classes, both manifestly unrealistic, and show the simulation results for each:

- In Figure 7.24, the two classes implement a very simple schedule: Twenty students arrive when the lab opens (at time 0), each needing 120 minutes of service. In other words, the arrival wait time is 0 for the first 20 arrivals, then goes up to a very large number (2000), ensuring that the 21st arrival does not occur until after the time period covered by the simulation run; the service times are all 120. We run the simulation four times, for 20 hours (1200 minutes) each time, with terminal limits of 30, 60, 90, and 120 minutes. For example, the first run goes like this:

```
-> (set sim30 (mkLabSimulation 30))
-> (run sim30 1200)
simulation-done
students-finishing
20
left-on-queue
0
Total-time-wasted:
18900
Average-time-wasted:
945
```

```
; Twenty arrivals at time zero
(class WaitTimeList Object
    (which)
    (define initWaitTimeList () (begin (set which 0) self))
    (define next ()
       (if (= which 20) 2000 (begin (set which (+1 which)) 0)))
)
(define mkWaitTimeList () (initWaitTimeList (new WaitTimeList)))
; All students need 120 minutes of terminal time
(class ServiceTimeList Object
    ()
    (define initServiceTimeList () self)
    (define next () 120)
)
(define mkServiceTimeList () (initServiceTimeList (new ServiceTimeList)))
```

Figure 7.24: Classes `WaitTimeList` and `ServiceTimeList`, first version

Note that there was enough time on the terminals to serve all 20 students, which is why there were none left on line at the end. The time limit of 30 minutes does not seem to have worked out well; the average student wasted 945 minutes, spending nearly eight times as much time on line as at a terminal. The results of all four runs are:

Terminal limit	Students finishing	Left on line	Average wasted time
30	20	0	945
60	20	0	810
90	20	0	945
120	20	0	540

Thus, according to the measure of "average wasted time," it is best to let students hold onto a terminal until their work is finished: it may not be fair, but it's efficient.

- The next schedule mixes up the arrivals and service times just a bit. Specifically, there is an arrival every 30 minutes; service times alternate between 120 and 30 minutes. The classes producing this schedule are shown in Figure 7.25. The results for the four runs are:

Terminal limit	Students finishing	Left on line	Average wasted time
30	30	8	103
60	30	8	114
90	29	9	125
120	31	7	109

This time, the shortest terminal limit seems the best.

7.4.2 SUMMARY

Our simulation omits many details. For example, in the real world, there is the phenomenon of *balking*, where a student entering the lab and finding too long a line leaves and tries again at another time. Another effect not considered is the "settling in" time needed when starting a session at a terminal, which effectively increases the required service time as the terminal limit decreases. Also, the single measure we have taken to compare terminal limits is not definitive. For one thing, it doesn't help answer the question of *fairness*, which dictates that we prefer a policy in which wasted time is proportional to service time over one in which everyone waits the same amount of time,

```
; Arrivals every 30 minutes
(class WaitTimeList Object
    ()
    (define initWaitTimeList () self)
    (define next () 30)
)
(define mkWaitTimeList () (initWaitTimeList (new WaitTimeList)))
; Service times alternating:  120, 30, 120, 30, ...
(class ServiceTimeList Object
    (which)
    (define initServiceTimeList () (begin (set which 1) self))
    (define next ()
       (begin
          (set which (- 1 which))
          (if (= which 0) 120 30)))
)
(define mkServiceTimeList () (initServiceTimeList (new ServiceTimeList)))
```

Figure 7.25: Classes `WaitTimeList` and `ServiceTimeList`, second version

regardless of how long a job they have.

Most importantly, our simulation runs were unrealistic in their assumptions about arrival and service times. What is seen clearly is that these assumptions can have a decisive effect on the results of the run. There are two ways to approach this: We can build into the simulation a list of arrival and service times, possibly obtained by monitoring the lab; or we can generate them randomly according to a distribution that we have reason to believe reflects the real situation.

Improvements to the model along the lines just discussed are suggested in the exercises.

7.5 SMALLTALK as It Really Is

SMALLTALK was developed in relative isolation on the basis of rather visionary ideas. To match the novelty of their philosophy, the Xerox PARC group created their own terminology.

The SMALLTALK language is unique in many ways as well. The goal of "simple but powerful" has been carried through to a remarkable degree, making the language itself quite small. Its power shows up in the class hierarchy that is delivered with the system. In this section, we will first discuss the language itself, both its syntax and certain features omitted from our version, and then briefly survey parts of the class hierarchy.

class name	FinancialHistory
superclass	Object
instance variable names	cashOnHand
	incomes
	expenditures

receive: amount from: source
      incomes at: source
            put: (self totalReceivedFrom: source) + amount.
      cashOnHand ← cashOnHand + amount

spend: amount for: reason
      expenditures at: reason
            put: (self totalSpentFor: reason) + amount.
      cashOnHand ← cashOnHand − amount

cashOnHand
      ↑cashOnHand

totalReceivedFrom: source
      (incomes includesKey: source)
          if True: [↑incomes at: source]
          if False: [↑0]

totalSpentFor: reason
      (expenditures includesKey: reason)
          if True: [↑expenditures at: reason]
          if False: [↑0]

setInitialBalance: amount
      cashOnHand ← amount.
      incomes ← Dictionary new.
      expenditures ← Dictionary new

Figure 7.26: Class FinancialHistory

7.5.1 THE LANGUAGE

Syntax. Because the programming environment provides for a kind of "menu-driven" input for classes, there is no official syntax for classes, so we use instead the publication format employed in Goldberg and Robson [1983]. Figure 7.26 gives the FinancialHistory class in this format, as obtained from that book (inside front cover).

The reader should compare this version of FinancialHistory to ours (page 274). The protocol is almost the same, except that it uses setInitialBalance instead of initFinancialHistory (which we used for uniformity with our other examples). Some points about the syntax merit explanation:

- The declarations at the top, giving the class name, superclass, and instance variables, are entirely analogous to the items of the same name in our version.

- The lines set in larger type are the headers for method definitions. Messages taking two arguments are split in half, with one argument name listed after each half. This matches the message-passing syntax, as we will see next. When talking about messages that have two or more arguments, we name them by concatenating the various parts (called *keywords*); each part must end with a colon. Thus, "receive:from:" is the official name of the first message.

- The most obvious oddity in the method definitions is that *the receiver of a message precedes the message*. Where we write, in the body of `receive:from:`,

$$(\texttt{totalReceivedFrom: self source}),$$

in real SMALLTALK it becomes

self totalReceivedFrom: source.

The idea is to have the syntax reflect the notion of sending messages to recipients.

In the case of two-argument messages, the receiver is listed first, then the first part of the message name followed by the first argument, then the second part of the message name and the second argument. The message send of at:put: in receive:from: is an example (the line breaks are not significant).

- Even + and − are messages; they are sent to integers and have one integer argument. They also have higher precedence than other messages. For example, in the spend:for: method, the at:put: message is sent to expenditures. The precedence of + requires the parentheses around self totalSpentFor: reason, and implies that the entire expression (self totalSpentFor: reason) + amount is the second argument to at:put:.

- The "←" symbol is used for assignment. Note also the unusual form of conditionals, with the conditional expression coming first; this is in fact just message-passing syntax, with message ifTrue:ifFalse: being sent to a Boolean value. The square brackets denote *blocks*, about which more later. Another new notation is "↑", which is used to return a value; methods that don't end with an "↑" expression are those which are evaluated for side-effects only. The difference is precisely the same as that between

functions and procedures in PASCAL. A period is used after each statement in a method except the last; it is analogous to the semicolon used
in PASCAL to separate statements in a **begin** block.

- In setInitialBalance (analogous to our `initFinancialHistory`), we find
  the expression "Dictionary new." This looks like a message send, but its
  receiver is a class, not an object. As we will see, in SMALLTALK, classes
  are objects (in fact, *everything* is an object), and this is indeed ordinary
  message-sending syntax.

Semantics.   SMALLTALK-80 has a number of specific features omitted from
our version. For one thing, it has several data types that are built-in in the sense
that the language provides constants (*literals*, in SMALLTALK terminology) of
those types. The types, and an example of a literal of each type, are:

Type	Literal
Integer	230
Character	$a
Float	3.39e-5
Symbol	#sameasours
String	's p a c e s'
Array	#($a $b $c)

Our language has only instance variables and global variables. SMALLTALK
has, in addition, *class variables*. These are variables which are shared by every
instance of a class, and can be referenced by any method in the class or in a
subclass. They can be useful when, for example, it is necessary to keep track
of all the objects of a class. (Actually, there are no global variables *per se*; the
class variables of class **Object** fill that role.)

Another type of message send is the "**super**" message, denoted by giving
the name **super** as the receiver of a message. What this indicates is that the
message is to be sent to **self**, but the method search is to start *in the superclass
of the class in which the* **super** *message appears*. That is, in contrast to normal
message sends, the starting place for method search is *statically determined* and
not dependent on the class of **self**. This is useful when one wants to be certain
that a particular piece of code will be executed.

By far the most significant difference between our language and real SMALL-
TALK is the use of *blocks*. Blocks are *functions* that are created using a special
notation and which can be stored in variables, passed to arguments, and so on.
A block is executed by sending it the message **value** or, if it takes an argument,
the message **value:** followed by the argument.

For example, Figure 7.26 contains the block

$$[\uparrow\text{incomes at: source}],$$

representing the function that sends the at: message to incomes, with argument source, and returns the result. The if True:if False: message is sent to a Boolean value, and its arguments are two blocks; it determines whether its receiver is true or false and, accordingly, sends the value message to one of the two blocks.

Blocks can also have arguments, which are indicated by naming them after the "[" and before a vertical bar "|", their names being preceded by colons. Thus,

$$\text{bindzero} \leftarrow [:x \mid D \text{ at: x put: 0}]$$

places into bindzero a block which,when invoked as:

$$\text{bindzero value: } \#\text{keyone}$$

associates symbol keyone with zero in the Dictionary object D.

Blocks are much like `lambda` expressions in SCHEME. What is so different about their use in SMALLTALK, however, is that they are used to implement control structures, somewhat as in the λ-calculus. We have already seen this in the case of conditionals. It is similar for loops; for example:

$$[\text{notNil item}] \text{ whileTrue: } [\text{item} \leftarrow \text{next D}]$$

is equivalent to our

```
(while (notNil item) (set item (next D))).
```

Note that in the case of whileTrue:, the receiver is a *block*, not a Boolean value. This is necessary because the conditional expression needs to be re-evaluated over and over. whileTrue: might be defined in the class Block as:

```
whileTrue: aBlock
    (self value)
        if True: [ aBlock value.
                self whileTrue: aBlock ]
        if False: [ ]
```

(The block "[ ]" is a no-op.)

More details on the treatment of control structures are given in the discussion of the class Boolean in the next section.

Another characteristic feature of SMALLTALK-80 is that *everything is an object*, even a class. This is important because, among other things, it allows for the programming of *instance creation methods*. Consider the expression "Dictionary new" that appears in setInitialBalance in Figure 7.26. The message new is being sent to the object called Dictionary. But what kind of object is that? That is, of what class is it an instance? The answer is: the Dictionary *metaclass*. Every class has a metaclass whose only object is that class. The metaclass defines so-called *class methods* like new. Thus, the expression "Dictionary new" represents sending the message new to the object of the metaclass of Dictionary; the method search begins in the metaclass and immediately succeeds, returning a new Dictionary object.

Thus, users can define new class methods and can even redefine new. This is useful when all objects of a class should be initialized, just as our `initList` initializes a list to be null. In fact, the FinancialHistory example in Goldberg and Robson [1983] includes two instance creation methods we omitted, which are given in Figure 7.27. Consider the expression

FinancialHistory initialBalance: 1000

"FinancialHistory" represents the one object of FinancialHistory's metaclass. Evaluating "super new" entails sending the message new to that object, but starting the method search in the superclass of the metaclass. That search eventually terminates in a class called simply Class, whose definition of new creates an uninitialized object of class FinancialHistory. That object is sent the setInitial-Balance: message with argument 1000, and finally the object is returned.

7.5.2 THE CLASS HIERARCHY IN SMALLTALK

SMALLTALK-80 is delivered with a large collection of class definitions. In this section, we will discuss the Boolean, Number, and Collection subhierarchies of

---

new
    ↑super new setInitialBalance: 0
initialBalance: amount
    ↑super new setInitialBalance: amount

Figure 7.27: Instance creation methods for FinancialHistory

the SMALLTALK hierarchy; these are classes that are used by all programmers, regardless of their specific application. There are many other classes in the hierarchy, including those related to graphics, compilation, and process scheduling, which are beyond the scope of our interests.

The Implementation of Control Structures. The SMALLTALK language is "pure" in the sense that it is close to minimal. For example, it has no built-in control structures except message-passing. Conditional execution is obtained with the help of several predefined classes. The classes UndefinedObject and Boolean, with its subclasses True and False, are both subclasses of Object:

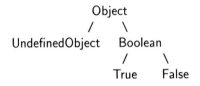

UndefinedObject. Rather than using the symbol #nil for undefined values, SMALLTALK defines this class, whose single instance is given the name nil. This object is used just as #nil has been used in this chapter, as a return value when no other value is appropriate.

The way the messages isNil and notNil are defined in SMALLTALK is an object lesson in the use of method search to implement a conditional operation. The technique used is to define each message *twice*, once in Object and once in UndefinedObject. The definitions in class Object are:

> isNil
> > ↑false
>
> notNil
> > ↑true

In UndefinedObject, they are:

> isNil
> > ↑true
>
> notNil
> > ↑false

It is assumed that no other class in the hierarchy will redefine these messages and that no subclasses will be added to UndefinedObject.

When the isNil message is sent to nil, the method search begins in the class of nil, which is UndefinedObject; it immediately succeeds and returns true. Similarly, notNil, when sent to nil, returns false. Thus, both messages respond correctly when sent to nil. On the other hand, when isNil is sent to *any other* object, the method search starts in the class of that object and goes all the way up to class Object, where it finally succeeds; the isNil method in Object, of course, returns false. Similarly, the notNil message, sent to any value other than nil, returns true. Thus, with no explicit conditional operation or equality test, but using only the conditional execution power of the method search itself, isNil and notNil have been programmed correctly.

Boolean, True, and False. A similar idea is used to implement if True:if False:. Classes True and False each have a single object; these objects are given the names true and false, respectively. Boolean-valued methods return one of these two objects. Thus, the if True:if False: message is always sent to one of these objects, its argument being a block. To implement conditional control, all that is needed is to define this message differently in the two classes. In True, it is defined as:

> if True: trueBlock if False: falseBlock
> ↑trueBlock value

whereas in False it is defined as:

> if True: trueBlock ifFalse: falseBlock
> ↑falseBlock value

So, in the expression:

> (incomes includesKey: reason)
>   if True: [↑incomes at: source]
>   if False: [↑0]

the expression on the first line evaluates to either true or false. If true, the search for method if True:if False: begins in class True and immediately succeeds, evaluating the block "[↑incomes at: source]"; if false, it begins in class False and again succeeds, evaluating "[↑0]".

The class Boolean is an abstract class that defines Boolean operations like & (and) and not, for example:

> & aBoolean
>   self if True: [↑aBoolean]
>   if False: [↑false]

Numbers.   The part of the class hierarchy that contains number classes looks
like this:

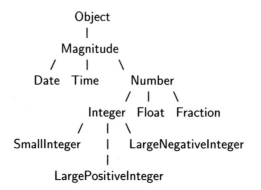

Magnitude objects (that is, objects of classes that are in the Magnitude
subhierarchy; Magnitude itself is an abstract class) are characterized by their
possessing a natural linear ordering; they respond to messages like < and <=.
Number objects respond, in addition, to all sorts of messages representing arithmetic operations, such as +, abs, and raisedTo:.

It must be remembered that numbers are objects like everything else. When
one writes "3 + 4" in SMALLTALK, this is an ordinary message send, the receiver being the number 3 and the argument 4. This is rather unnatural, but,
as we have noted, the object-oriented approach does not particularly lend itself
to natural definitions of *immutable* types. In any case, the syntax is designed
to make these message sends look like ordinary expressions, so the programmer does not pay a great penalty, while the system is able to stick to one
computational paradigm without exceptions.

The classes Float and Fraction are similar to our versions of same. Ordinary
floating-point notation is provided for literals of class Float, as previously noted.

Integer is an abstract class, providing for certain functions such as gcd which
do not apply to arbitrary numbers. SmallInteger objects are represented by machine words. LargePositiveInteger and LargeNegativeInteger provide for infinite
precision. Integer literals are provided, which are of arbitrary length; their class
is determined by their magnitude and sign.

The class of the result of an arithmetic operation may be different from the
class of its receiver or arguments, just as in Pascal (consider "3 / 4"). Unlike
Pascal, the class of the result may depend upon the *value* of the receiver or
argument, not just its type. For example, 10 raisedTo: 2 returns a SmallInteger,
but 10 raisedTo: 20 returns a LargePositiveInteger. The rule adopted is to return
an object of the *least general* class that can hold the result, where, for example,
SmallInteger is less general than LargePositiveInteger, which is less general than
Float. That is why 10 raisedTo: 20 does not return a Float. All these coercions
are handled within the Numbers hierarchy.

We should also mention how machine-level operations themselves can be invoked. There is a special kind of method, called a *primitive method,* having the following syntax:

> *method-header*
> <primitive *n*>
> *statements*

Primitive numbered *n* (e.g., 1 is addition of SmallInteger's) is invoked. If it fails for any reason (e.g., overflow) the *statements* are executed; if it succeeds, the result is returned and the *statements* bypassed. Thus, for example, the method + in SmallInteger can respond to overflow by coercing the receiver to be a Large···Integer and then sending the + message.

Users never need to write primitive methods, because the class hierarchy provides convenient user-level methods that perform any required operation, just as the Number hierarchy performs primitive operations while providing the programmer with a variety of number representations and transparent coercions among them.

Collection classes. SMALLTALK provides a Collection subhierarchy similar in purpose and, to an extent, in structure to ours (which is derived from that in Budd [1987]). Here is a part of it:

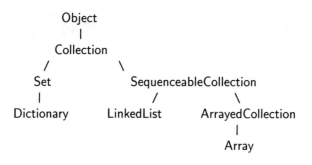

To understand the SMALLTALK Collection hierarchy, recall that the basic feature of all Collection's is the ability to enumerate elements. This was accomplished in our version of `Collection` by requiring all concrete `Collection` classes to provide generators `first` and `next`, but these were sometimes awkward to implement. In SMALLTALK, this enumerability requirement is asserted differently: each concrete Collection class is expected to define the message do:, whose single argument is a one-argument block; when do: is sent to collection aCollection with argument aBlock, aBlock is applied to each element of aCollection.

For instance, to sum the elements of a set S, one can write:

$$\text{sum} \leftarrow 0.$$
$$\text{S do: [:each | sum} \leftarrow \text{sum + each]}$$

Some enhancements of do: are also mandatory:

select: aBlock. Apply aBlock to each element of the receiver. Form a new collection from those elements for which aBlock returns true.

collect: aBlock. Form a new collection containing the values returned by aBlock when applied to each element of the receiver.

inject: thisValue into: binaryBlock. Repeatedly apply binaryBlock to two arguments, an element of the receiver and the result of the previous iterations (starting with thisValue). For example, another way to do the summation is:

$$\text{S inject: 0 into: [:sum :elt | sum + elt]}$$

7.6 Related Language — C++

C is the language in which the UNIX operating system, and much of its associated software, is written. It is PASCAL-like, though of somewhat lower level, and has gained popularity substantially in tandem with UNIX itself. Most UNIX programmers favor it over PASCAL due — aside from the UNIX tie-in itself — to its comparative conciseness, its low-level features (such as the ability to assign hard addresses to pointer variables), which allow the programming of operating system components normally written in machine language, and its more casual view of type-checking.

In 1984, Bjarne Stroustrup of Bell Labs published a paper entitled "Data Abstraction in C," describing an extension to C supporting data encapsulation and object-oriented programming. That extension is C++.[6] Among its features are class and subclass definitions, selective export of instance variables and class functions, and overloading of function names and operator symbols. Most importantly to us, the binding of function names is static (for the most part) and type-checking is strict, entailing some modification in the notion of "inheritance."

---

[6] Named for the C increment operator. In C, "$x{+}{+}$" is equivalent to the PASCAL statement "$x := x{+}1$".

Our presentation of C++ is organized as follows: Simple class and subclass definitions are discussed, using `FinancialHistory` and `DeductibleHistory`; for these examples, SMALLTALK and C++ are conceptually very similar. Further discussion of inheritance, using the "`C` and `D`" example (page 279) and the `Numbers` hierarchy, reveals the differences between the two languages in this area, differences resulting from C++'s type-checking and its emphasis on efficient compilation. Following this is a subsection on various other features of C++, such as overloading. Because C++ is an extension of C, when we say "in C, such-and-such," we can be taken to mean "in C++, such-and-such," whereas when we say "in C++, such-and-such," we will mean a feature of C++ not present in C.

7.6.1 CLASSES AND SUBCLASSES

C++ classes are given in two parts, first the *declaration* of the class, including its instance variables and functions (i.e., methods, but the term "method" is not used). Because C++ is a statically-typed language, the types of the variables and the types of the functions' arguments and results are all given here. Following this part are all the function definitions. (This is analogous to ADA's package specification/package body distinction.)

Here is the declaration part of the class *FinancialHistory*, which is quite close in spirit to its SMALLTALK version (Figure 7.1):

```
class FinancialHistory {
        int cashOnHand;
        Dictionary incomes, expenditures;
public:
        FinancialHistory (int);
        void receiveFrom (int, char*);
        void spendFor (int, char*);
        int cash ();
        int totalReceivedFrom (char*);
        int totalSpentFor (char*);
};
```

Several points may be noted:

- The name of the class is, of course, *FinancialHistory*, but no superclass name appears. Unlike SMALLTALK, C++ does not place all its classes in a single large hierarchy but instead can have many small hierarchies. Indeed, C++ is intended to support both object-oriented programming and simple data encapsulation as in CLU or ADA, so that classes often appear alone, with neither superclass nor subclasses. *FinancialHistory*, as declared, is such a class; later, a subclass will be added, but that requires no change in *FinancialHistory*'s declaration.

- The instance variables are the same as in the SMALLTALK version. In C, the type name in a variable declaration appears before the variable, so the declaration "**int** *cashOnHand*" is equivalent to the PASCAL declaration "*cashOnHand*: *integer*".[7] *Dictionary* is another class, whose definition we are omitting.

- The instance variables are in the *private* part of the class declaration, before the keyword **public**. This ensures that those variables cannot be used by clients of the class. The function names appear in the public part, so that clients can use them. (Auxiliary function declarations would be given in the private part, and instance variables could be made public by declaring them in the public part.) The names declared in the class are called *members*, so "member function" is the C++ term for "method;" we will continue to call the other members "instance variables." In C, there is no "**function**" keyword; a function declaration is distinguished from a variable declaration by the parentheses that follow its name.

  - The member functions are just as in the SMALLTALK class, with two exceptions: (1) `initFinancialHistory` is replaced by a function called simply *FinancialHistory* and having no return type; this is related to the C++ class instance intialization protocol, about which more later. (2) Because one cannot have two members with the same name — even if one is an instance variable and the other a function — the method `cashOnHand` has become the member function *cash*.

  - The arguments are of the same number as in the corresponding SMALLTALK methods. The type "**char***" is the type of a string (that is, an array) of characters, which we use in place of the symbol type of SMALLTALK.

  - The return types are given before the function name, as in variable declarations. Return type "**void**" means nothing is returned; in effect, this is the declaration of a procedure.

As in SMALLTALK, the member functions all have an implicit argument, which is an instance of this class. Before showing the definitions of these functions, here is a client of *FinancialHistory*:

```
void main ()
{
    FinancialHistory account = FinancialHistory(1000);

    account.spendFor(50, "plumber");
    account.receiveFrom(400, "salary");
    cout << "cash on hand = " << account.cash() << "\n";
}
```

---

[7] Minor point: in C, unlike in PASCAL, primitive typenames are keywords.

These lines are intended to be analogous to the session given on page 272. When procedure *main* is executed, it prints:

```
cash on hand = 1350
```

The points to note here are: (1) The declaration of variable *account* initializes the starting balance of the account (1000); this is done by the function *FinancialHistory* in a way that will be explained when that function is defined. (2) The "message-sending" syntax is to give the name of the instance (*account*) followed by a period and then the name of the member function with its explicit arguments. This is the same as record selection notation; indeed, in C++ there is no difference between a record and a class all of whose members are public. (3) The line starting with *cout* does the output, printing the string "`cash on hand = `", then the integer *account.cash*(), and finally the string "`\n`", which is just a newline character.[8]

The definitions of the member functions are given in Figure 7.28. Each definition starts with the function header, as given in the class declaration, except that the names are preceded by "*FinancialHistory*::" and the formal parameters are named; the types of the latter are, of course, just as in the class declaration. These definitions should be compared with those in Figure 7.1. The functions that return **int** contain **return** statements, like the CLU or ADA **return** statements or the SMALLTALK "↑". Those that return **void** (i.e., the procedures) do not. Aside from that, the definitions are very close. (Two points about syntax: The assignment operator in C is just "="; the equality comparison operator is "==". The **if** statement has no "then" keyword. Instead, the statement following the condition is the true branch; it can be a compound statement, formed by enclosing a list of statements in set braces "{" and "}". The false branch, if any, is introduced by the keyword "**else**".)

The keyword "**this**" has the same significance in C++ as does "**self**" in SMALLTALK. However, **this** actually refers to a *pointer* to the receiver rather than the receiver itself. Thus, before sending a message to the receiver, as is done in *receiveFrom* and *spendFor*, **this** must be dereferenced. For a pointer *v*, "**v*" is the C notation for PASCAL's "*v*↑", that is, pointer dereferencing. Thus, the expression "(***this**).*totalReceivedFrom*(···)" is evaluated by first dereferencing **this** — obtaining thereby the receiver itself — and then "sending a message," using the syntax already introduced. This idiom has a shorthand form, which we will use in subsequent examples; namely, "(**v*).···" can be written as "*v* − > ···".

---

[8]Note to C programmers: C++ is substantially downward compatible with C; almost everything not specifically related to the language extensions is the same as in C. In fact, the old *printf* function still works, but this form, using the **include** file **stream.h**, is more idiomatic for C++.

```
FinancialHistory::FinancialHistory (int amount)
{
     cashOnHand = amount;
}

void FinancialHistory::receiveFrom (int amount, char* source)
{
     incomes.atPut(source, (*this).totalReceivedFrom(source) + amount);
     cashOnHand = cashOnHand + amount;
}

void FinancialHistory::spendFor (int amount, char* reason)
{
     expenditures.atPut(reason, (*this).totalSpentFor(reason) + amount);
     cashOnHand = cashOnHand - amount;
}

int FinancialHistory::cash ()
{ return cashOnHand; }

int FinancialHistory::totalReceivedFrom (char* source)
{
     if (incomes.includesKey(source))
         return incomes.at(source);
     else return 0;
}

int FinancialHistory::totalSpentFor (char* reason)
{
     if (expenditures.includesKey(reason))
         return expenditures.at(reason);
     else return 0;
}
```

Figure 7.28: Member function definitions for *FinancialHistory*

Finally, a word about initialization of class instances. In C++, a function having the same name as the class of which it is a member is called a *constructor*. Whenever an instance is created, which occurs when a variable of the class is declared, this constructor is called with the new, uninitialized, instance as its receiver; it can then initialize its instance variables, as *FinancialHistory* does here for *cashOnHand*. Note that the creation of a *FinancialHistory* instance entails the creation of two *Dictionary* instances, whereupon the constructor for class *Dictionary* is called; that is why *FinancialHistory* doesn't have to explicitly initialize *incomes* and *expenditures*.

DeductibleHistory is a subclass — or *derived class*, in C++ terminology — of *FinancialHistory*; its SMALLTALK definition is in Figure 7.2. The C++ definition again comes in two parts and is generally very similar to the SMALLTALK version. This is its declaration:

```
class DeductibleHistory : public FinancialHistory {
    int deductible;
public:
    DeductibleHistory (int);
    void spendDeduct (int, char*);
    void spendForDeduct (int, char*, int);
    int totalDeductions ();
};
```

DeductibleHistory is a "public" derived class of *FinancialHistory*, meaning that public member functions of *FinancialHistory* can be applied to *DeductibleHistory* instances. Of course, it inherits all members of *FinancialHistory*, and it adds a new private instance variable, *deductible*. All of this is perfectly in accord with the SMALLTALK version. The procedure *DeductibleHistory* is a constructor, used in place of `initDeductibleHistory`.

This client represents the C++ version of the session given on page 277:

```
void main ()
{
    DeductibleHistory myaccount = DeductibleHistory(1000);

    myaccount.spendFor(50, "insurance");
    myaccount.receiveFrom(200, "salary");
    cout << "cash on hand = " << myaccount.cash() << "\n";
    cout << "total deductions = "
                    << myaccount.totalDeductions() << "\n";
    myaccount.spendDeduct(100, "mortgage");
    cout << "cash on hand = " << myaccount.cash() << "\n";
    cout << "total deductions = "
                    << myaccount.totalDeductions() << "\n";
    myaccount.spendForDeduct(100, "3 martini lunch", 50);
    cout << "cash on hand = " << myaccount.cash() << "\n";
    cout << "total deductions = "
                    << myaccount.totalDeductions() << "\n";
}
```

Its output is:

```
cash on hand = 1150
total deductions = 0
cash on hand = 1050
total deductions = 100
cash on hand = 950
total deductions = 150
```

As should be expected, member functions of both *FinancialHistory* and *DeductibleHistory* can be applied to instances of *DeductibleHistory*.

The definitions of the member functions are given in Figure 7.29. The correspondence with the method definitions in Figure 7.2 is again excellent. One new feature, in the constructor *DeductibleHistory*, is the notation ": (*amount*)" in the function header. As a constructor, *DeductibleHistory* will be called whenever a new instance of this class comes into existence. However, at that time, the *FinancialHistory* constructor should also be called, and indeed it will be. The problem is, where does that call get its argument? This is what the ": (*amount*)" is for. Thus, the declaration "*DeductibleHistory myaccount = DeductibleHistory*(1000)" causes *FinancialHistory* to be called with argument 1000; then the body of *DeductibleHistory* is called, setting *deductible* to zero.

DeductibleHistory::DeductibleHistory (**int** *amount*) : (*amount*)
{ *deductible* = 0; }

void *DeductibleHistory::spendDeduct* (**int** *amount*, **char*** *reason*)
{
    this− >*spendFor*(*amount, reason*);
    deductible = *deductible*+*amount*;
}

void *DeductibleHistory::spendForDeduct* (**int** *amount*, **char*** *reason*, **int** *deduction*)
{
    this− >*spendFor*(*amount, reason*);
    deductible = *deductible*+*deduction*;
}

int *DeductibleHistory::totalDeductions* ()
{ **return** *deductible*; }

Figure 7.29: Member function definitions for *DeductibleHistory*

These two examples have shown that many of the concepts of SMALLTALK — instances variables, message sending, inheritance — appear in very similar form — though with different syntax and under different names — in C++. However, there are important differences, which the next section will explore.

7.6.2   INHERITANCE IN C++

The *DeductibleHistory* example seems to indicate that inheritance in C++ and SMALLTALK work the same way, but that is not so. Consider the classes C and D defined in Figure 7.30. They are supposed to be analogous to classes C and D defined in SMALLTALK on page 278, where we said they illustrate a "crucial fact" about inheritance, that method search begins in the class of the receiver. The interesting case was, and is, when an instance of class D receives message *m1*, as in this client:

void *main* ()
{   *D x*;

x.m1(); }

In C++, this prints "C", whereas in SMALLTALK it printed "D". Thus, this "crucial fact" about inheritance is false in C++. What happened? In C++, there is (usually) no method search at all. Any member function of class C *assumes* its receiver will be of class C, even if C has derived classes. Thus, the call to *m1* in the body of *m2* in C is bound, *at compile-time*, to the *m1* defined in C. When *m1* is sent to *x*, the *m1* from C is invoked (having been inherited

---

```
class C {
public:
        void m1();
        void m2();
};

void C::m1 () { this– >m2(); }

void C::m2 () { cout << "C"; }

class D : public C {
public:
        void m2();
};

void D::m2 () { cout << "D"; }
```

Figure 7.30: Classes C and D

by *D*) and this *m1* calls the *m2* defined in *C*. This is quite a different, and more "static," notion of inheritance. Its justification seems to be the efficiency gained by eliminating the method search. However, the major examples given in this chapter — the `Collection` and `Number` hierarchies — make heavy use of SMALLTALK's version of inheritance, so that C++ does seem to suffer a real loss of programming power.

All is not lost, though. There is *usually* no method search, but the programmer can request that method search be performed[9] by declaring a member function "**virtual**". Such a function can then be redefined in derived classes and, when it is sent to an instance of the derived class, the derived class's version will be invoked. Thus, by simply changing the declaration of *m2* in *C* to:

$$\textbf{virtual void } m2();$$

the client given above will print "D".

This is, however, only a partial solution to the problem. To allow for static type-checking, a restriction is placed on virtual functions: All the definitions of a virtual function have the same type, that is, the same return type and the same types of explicit parameters. For function *m2* in this example, the restriction is no problem; both versions had return type **void** and no explicit arguments. For the other examples given in this chapter, the restriction is fatal.

Consider the class `Number`, with subclasses `Fraction` and `Float`, in Section 7.3. To get us into the spirit, a simplified version of `Fraction`, defined without using inheritance, is shown in Figure 7.31. One point to note, in comparing the code for *plus* with the definition of + in Figure 7.13, is that the instance variables of argument *f* are accessed directly; a more perfect correspondence with the SMALLTALK code would be obtained if "*f.y*" were replaced by "*f.gety*()", which is also perfectly legal C++. This class uses constructors to create temporary instances of a class. An expression "*Fraction* (· · ·)" creates a temporary *Fraction* instance, then calls *Fraction*'s constructor — that is, the function named *Fraction* — passing "· · ·" as arguments, and finally returns the new instance. (This value is temporary in the sense that it disappears when the function is done, just like any intermediate value in an expression; of course,

---

[9]That is, the effect will be *as if* method search were done. The implementation involves no real search. Rather, all the virtual members of a class, including inherited ones, are placed in a large array, and any reference to a virtual member is resolved by indexing this array, the index being computed at compile-time.

```
        class Fraction {
              int x, y;
              Fraction div_reduce();
        public:
              Fraction (int,int);
              int getx ();
              int gety ();
              Fraction plus (Fraction);
              Fraction minus (Fraction);
              Fraction negate ();
        };

        Fraction::Fraction (int a, int b)
        { x = a; y = b; }

        Fraction::getx ()
        { return x; }

        Fraction::gety ()
        { return y; }

        Fraction Fraction::plus (Fraction f)
        {
              return Fraction(x * f.y + y * f.x, y * f.y)− >div_reduce();
        }

        Fraction Fraction::minus (Fraction f)
        { return this− >plus(f.negate()); }

        Fraction Fraction::negate ()
        { return Fraction(−x, y); }

        Fraction Fraction::div_reduce ()
        {
              if (x == 0) y = 1;
              else {int temp = gcd (abs(x), y);
                    x = x/temp;
                    y = y/temp;}
              return *this;
        }
```

Figure 7.31: Class *Fraction*

when it is returned from a function call, as in *negate*, it survives long enough
to be consumed by the caller.) Thus, in this client, *f* is initialized to fraction $\frac{4}{9}$
and *g* to $\frac{2}{3}$:

> **void** *main* ()
> {
>   *Fraction f = Fraction*(4,9);
>   *Fraction g = Fraction*(2,3);
>
>   *f = f.plus*(*g*);
>   *cout* << *f.getx*() << " " << *f.gety*() << "\n";
> }

and the output is "10 9".

    How might the class *Number* be defined so that *Fraction* and *Float* could be
derived classes as in Section 7.3? First, it would declare all the functions defined
as methods in Figure 7.12; the ones defined as "`subclassResponsibility`"
would have to be virtual. Thus, the declaration of *Number* (confined to the
subset of operations that were defined for *Fraction*) would be:

> **class** *Number* {
> **public**:
>   **virtual** *Number plus* (*Number*);
>   **virtual** *Number negate* ();
>   **Number** *minus* (*Number*);
> };

plus and *negate* are **virtual** because they will have to be redefined in derived
classes (as in the SMALLTALK version), but *minus* is not. The types of the arguments and return values of these functions are *Number*; clearly, they cannot be
Fraction, since the class *Fraction* doesn't even exist yet. Furthermore, function
getx and *gety* are not declared here, because they are specific to *Fraction*. The
definitions of *plus* and *negate* are not interesting or useful, but *minus* is defined
as in SMALLTALK:

> *Number Number::minus* (*Number n*)
> { **return this**− >*plus*(*n.negate*()); }

    The idea now is to define *Fraction* as a derived class of *Number*, defining *plus*
and *negate*, but inheriting *minus*. However, there is no way to do this, given
the types of these functions, which may not be redeclared. Consider *plus*. It
will certainly need access to the *x* and *y* members of its receiver and argument.
But this is impossible, because the argument is declared to be a *Number*, and
Number has no members *x* or *y*. Furthermore, both functions are obliged to
return *Number*'s, and *Number*'s are almost totally useless, since they contain
no information at all.

Thus, the inheritance mechanism of C++ is strictly less powerful than that of SMALLTALK.[10] On the other hand, this example involves an immutable type, and it has already been suggested that immutable types don't fit into the object-oriented view very comfortably. Object-oriented programming usually makes heavier use of side-effects and procedures than of functions. For procedures, the prohibition against redeclaring virtual functions seems more supportable than the *Number* example implies. In any case, the designer of C++ apparently felt the added confidence gained from type-checking more than compensated for the loss of power.

7.6.3 OTHER FEATURES OF C++

Our main object in discussing C++ has been to demonstrate an alternative view of inheritance and to see how type-checking interacts with it. This accomplished, there remain two features of C++ that particularly merit attention: friend functions and overloading.

To understand the notion of a *friend*, consider how *Fraction* would be defined in CLU. The representation would be the same, but binary operations such as *add* would show no bias between receiver and argument:

```
(define add (f1 f2)
    (div-reduce
        (Fraction (+ (* (x f1) (y f2)) (* (y f1) (x f2)))
            (* (y f1) (y f2)))))
```

This is a more "detached" view of data abstraction, in which a data type operation is like any other, except that it is permitted access to the data type's selector functions.

C++ supports this kind of data abstraction by friend functions, functions which are declared as having access to class members, without themselves being members. Thus, they are invoked using ordinary function application notation, rather than the "message sending" notation used for member functions.

---

[10]There are ways to "fool" the type-checker which we are ignoring. These methods involve using pointers where they are otherwise unnecessary, and mucking up the code generally, but they can be used in a pinch.

Friends must be declared as such, as in this new version of *Fraction*:

```
class Fraction {
        int x, y;
        Fraction div_reduce();
public:
        Fraction (int,int);
        int getx ();
        int gety ();
        friend Fraction plus (Fraction, Fraction);
        friend Fraction minus (Fraction, Fraction);
        friend Fraction negate (Fraction);
};
```

The member functions — *getx*, *gety*, and *div_reduce* — and the constructor are unchanged, but the definitions of *add*, *minus*, and *negate* now appear as ordinary functions, the only difference being their access to private members of *Fraction* instances. Their definitions appear in Figure 7.32. Note that their names are not preceded by the "*Fraction::*" used for member functions. They have no implicit "receiver" argument, so they do not use the special name **this**, and they never refer to members x and y in unqualified form. A client with *Fraction* variables f and g would write simply "*plus(f, g)*", instead of "*f.plus(g)*".

Aside from "naturalness," there is little to choose between member functions and friends. Stroustrup [1986, page 187] states some criteria for deciding which to use, but these are rather too technical to go into here. Broadly speaking, friends support a "data abstraction" view of classes and members an "object-oriented" view, and each programmer must decide which view is appropriate in a particular situation.

```
Fraction plus (Fraction f1, Fraction f2)
{
        return Fraction(f1.x * f2.y + f1.y * f2.x, f1.y * f2.y).div_reduce();
}

Fraction minus (Fraction f1, Fraction f2)
{ return plus(f1, negate(f2)); }

Fraction negate (Fraction f)
{ return Fraction(-f.x, f.y); }
```

Figure 7.32: *plus*, *minus*, and *negate* as friends of *Fraction*

Overloading is the capability to have multiple definitions of a single function name. Both SMALLTALK and C++ have overloading, in that member functions can be redefined in subclasses. Another form of overloading, also present in ADA,[11] allows multiple definitions of a function provided that each has different types (and possibly a different number) of arguments. Any particular call can be resolved *at compile-time* to one of these definitions, based upon the types of the actual parameters.

One application of overloading in C++ is to define multiple constructors for a class. For instance, *Fraction* might have a constructor for creating a new instance whose value is an integer, that is, whose denominator is 1. It would have only one argument, so it could be distinguished from the existing constructor. Both constructors are given in the class declaration:

> **class** *Fraction* {
>
> $\vdots$
>
> **public**:
> > *Fraction*(**int**,**int**);
> > *Fraction*(**int**);
> >
> > $\vdots$
>
> };

and the new constructor is defined as follows (compare the definition of the other constructor in Figure 7.31):

> *Fraction::Fraction* (**int** *a*)
> { $x = a$; $y = 1$; }

Then a client can declare *Fraction*'s using either constructor:

> *Fraction f = Fraction*(4, 9);
> *Fraction g = Fraction*(2);

and the compiler will call the appropriate one in each case.

C++, like ADA, also allows for overloading of *operators*, the specially named, built-in operations like "+" and ">=". Defining a function called "*operator*$", where $ is an operator, has the effect of overloading $ with a new definition. When thus overloaded, operators retain their usual syntax, i.e., arity and precedence. Friend and member functions can be defined as overloaded operators. If "*operator*$" is defined as a member function of class *C*, and *x* is of type *C*, then the expression "*x* $ *y*" is equivalent to "*x.operator*$(*y*)". If it is a friend, the expression is equivalent to "*operator*$(*x, y*)".

---

[11] and, to some extent, even in PASCAL. Built-in operations like + and < apply to both integer and real operands, and the compiler determines which version to apply for a particular use, from the types of the operands.

With this feature, *Fraction* can be defined as in Figure 7.33. Note that "$-$" is overloaded twice, as a binary and a unary operation; since these two uses have different numbers of arguments, there is no problem with resolving the overloading. Notice also that the definition of binary "$-$" uses the overloaded operators "$+$" and (unary) "$-$".

```
class Fraction {
        int x, y;
        Fraction div_reduce ();
public:
        Fraction (int, int);
        int getx ();
        int gety ();
        Fraction operator+ (Fraction);
        Fraction operator- (Fraction);
        Fraction operator- ();
};

Fraction::Fraction (int a, int b)
        ... as before ...

Fraction::getx ()
        ... as before ...

Fraction::gety ()
        ... as before ...

Fraction Fraction::operator+ (Fraction f)
{
        return Fraction(x * f.y + y * f.x, y * f.y).div_reduce();
}

Fraction Fraction::operator- (Fraction f)
{ return (*this)+(-f); }

Fraction Fraction::operator- ()
{ return Fraction(-x, y); }

Fraction Fraction::div_reduce ()
        ... as before ...
```

Figure 7.33: *Fraction* using overloaded operators

Now, this client:

```
void main ()
{
        Fraction f = Fraction(8, 9);
        Fraction g = Fraction(2, 3);

        f = −f−g;
        cout << f.getx() << " " << f.gety() << "\n";
}
```

prints "−14 9".

7.7 Summary

SMALLTALK may well represent a revolution in programming languages. The object-oriented style seems to be very effective for certain types of programming problems, including simulation, graphics, and user interfaces; it is especially so when all three are combined. With the increasing use of single-user machines with graphics screens, these can only become more important. It is true that the basic ideas are due to the designers of SIMULA 67, but the SMALLTALK group has done so much to popularize them and make them convincing that they are now most often associated with SMALLTALK. The Apple Macintosh user interface uses many of the programming environment ideas developed for SMALLTALK and offers an object-oriented language for programming applications. A number of well-attended conferences on object-oriented programming have been held in the past few years, and the first edition of a *Journal of Object-Oriented Programming* has recently appeared (April, 1988).

7.7.1 GLOSSARY

abstract class. A class which has no instances. Abstract classes are defined in order to supply method definitions that can be inherited by subclasses.

block. A SMALLTALK object that represents a function. These values are "first class" in the sense that they can be passed as arguments to methods and returned as results, and can be assigned to variables. Blocks can have any number of arguments. To evaluate a zero-argument block, send it the value message; to evaluate a one-argument block, send it the value: message; to evaluate a two-argument block, send it the value:value: message; and so on. Blocks are used to implement control structures in SMALLTALK.

class. The basic programming unit in SMALLTALK. A class encapsulates the representation of a certain kind of object and defines the operations on objects of that kind.

class variable. A variable that has one occurrence in a class (regardless of the number of instances of that class). Subclasses can refer to a class's class variables.

inheritance. The feature of SMALLTALK whereby a class, being declared as a subclass of another, defines objects that have all the instance variables, and respond to all the messages, of that other class. New components can be added to the representation by the subclass, and new methods can be defined and inherited ones redefined. This is also known as **single inheritance**.

In **multiple inheritance**, a class can be declared as a subclass of *several* classes and inherit representation and methods from all of them.

instance variable. A variable of which each object of a class has its own version. The instance variables of a class define the representation of objects of that class.

message. The name of a method. Since SMALLTALK has **overloading** — the ability to define the same message in several places — it becomes important to distinguish between *message* and *method*.

method. The SMALLTALK term for a function defined within a class (and all functions in SMALLTALK are defined in classes). Methods always have at least one argument, called the **receiver** of the message. In SMALLTALK message-sending syntax, the message (i.e., method name) follows the expression defining the receiver.

method search. Inheritance is implemented by having the interpreter search for the method corresponding to a given message. This search begins in the class of the receiver of the message (with the exception of messages sent to **super**) and continues up the hierarchy until a definition for the message is found.

object. A value of a class; also called an **instance**. In SMALLTALK, everything is an object.

overloading. The defining of a single message name in more than one class, or, more generally, the use of a name in different ways. In this more general sense, many languages allow some form of overloading; for example, PASCAL overloads the name "+", using it for both integer and floating-point addition. In SMALLTALK, overloading is particularly important, as it permits the definition of polymorphic functions. C++

has both SMALLTALK-style overloading resolved by method-search and "static" overloading resolved by the compiler based on the types of the function's arguments.

polymorphism. The use of a single function for different types of data. Since in SMALLTALK the only notion of "type" is "protocol to which an object responds," any piece of code can be applied to any object that responds to the set of messages sent to it in that code; and since a message can be defined in more than one class, a piece of code can be applied to objects from different classes.

protocol. The set of messages to which objects of a given class can respond.

self. A special variable that can be used in method definitions to refer to the receiver of the message.

subclass. A class which is placed underneath another class in the inheritance hierarchy.

super. A special variable that can be used as the receiver of a message in an expression, with the following meaning: The object that receives the message is actually self, but the method search begins in the superclass of the class in which the expression occurs.

superclass. A class which is placed above another class in the inheritance hierarchy.

7.7.2 FURTHER READING

The "blue book," Goldberg and Robson [1983], is the basic reference on SMALL-TALK-80; it includes an introduction to the language and class hierarchy and also devotes a good deal of space to its implementation, especially the "virtual machine" on which it is based. Goldberg [1983] describes the programming environment and its implementation.

The August, 1981, edition of *Byte Magazine* [1981] contains several articles by members of the SMALLTALK group, presenting a fairly thorough introduction to the language and the programming environment. The paperback by Kaehler and Patterson [1986] is a simplified, concrete introduction, taking the user through a series of sessions with the SMALLTALK system, developing different solutions to the Towers of Hanoi problem. Another good next step for the student would be the book *Little Smalltalk* by Budd [1987], which describes a version of SMALLTALK which is nearly identical to SMALLTALK-80 but lacking some "bells and whistles," especially graphics; this book is rather more accessible than the blue book, and an interpreter, written in C, can be obtained from its author. A more recent book is Pinson and Wiener [1988].

In the end, there is no book that provides all the information necessary to become an effective SMALLTALK programmer. By definition, that requires the ability to use code in the existing class hierarchy, and that requires a familiarity with it which can be obtained only by reading the code.

Stroustrup [1986] is the basic reference for C++, written by its designer; see also Stroustrup [1988]. Wiener and Pinson [1988] is the most recent book on C++. The paper by Gorlen [1987] describes a class hierarchy written for C++ that provides similar functionality to that of SMALLTALK.

There are many other languages that follow the object-oriented approach. SIMULA 67 introduced many of the ideas in SMALLTALK, including classes and inheritance; references were given in the previous chapter. OBJECTIVE C is another object-oriented extension of C; it is described in Cox [1986]. Schmucker [1986] describes an object-oriented extension of PASCAL that runs on the Macintosh. Not all object-oriented languages are extensions of earlier languages; some are, like SMALLTALK, designed from scratch. Examples are OWL (Schaffert, et al. [1986]) and EIFFEL, described in the excellent book by Meyer [1988], which also gives an interesting defense of object-oriented programming in general; see also Meyer [1987]. All of the above, except OBJECTIVE C, share with C++ the feature of being statically typed.

The LISP community started getting on the object-oriented bandwagon quite early. The FLAVORS system (Moon [1986]) was first developed by the MIT Lisp Machine group in 1979; it includes multiple inheritance and takes a rather different view of the object-oriented paradigm. COMMONLOOPS and the COMMON LISP Object System (Bobrow, et al. [1986,1988]) are object-oriented extensions to COMMON LISP.

There are many books on computer simulation, running the gamut from highly theoretical to quite pragmatic. Among the latter are Payne [1982] and Schriber [1974], both of which also include introductions to the best-known special-purpose simulation languages. Goldberg and Robson [1983] and Budd [1987] include extended examples of simulations in SMALLTALK; Birtwistle, et al. [1973] does the same for SIMULA 67.

7.8   Exercises

7.8.1   *LEARNING ABOUT THE LANGUAGE*

1. Define a class `Rand` having the following protocol:

    - `initRand` sets the seed to the integer argument.

    - `nextRand` returns the next random number and updates the seed.

    Generate the random numbers as on page 110.

2. Define class `Interval` as a subclass of `SequenceableCollection`. This class represents finite subsets of the integers defined by arithmetic pro-

gressions. In other words, its objects are sets of the form $\{n, n+m, \ldots, n+km\}$ for some $n, k \geq 0$ and $m > 0$. An interval is initialized by giving n, m, and k and is immutable. Its protocol is the same as other `SequenceableCollection`'s, except that: (a) it lacks `add:`, and (b) instead of `initInterval`, there are two initializing methods `from:to:` and `from:to:by:`. (`from:to:by: n n + km m`) initializes its receiver to be the progression named above; (`from:to: n p`) is equivalent to (`from:to: by: n p 1`).

3. Add to `Collection` the following methods:

   (a) `asSet` — returns a set having the same elements as the receiver of the message.

   (b) `occurrencesOf:` — returns the number of times its argument occurs in its receiver.

   (c) `addAll:` — adds every value in its argument, which is a `Collection`, to its receiver.

4. Define the class `Bag`, whose objects are sets with multiple occurrences of elements (also called *multisets*). The protocol is the same as `Set`, but the generators should return as many occurrences of an element as have been added, and the method `count:` should give the number of occurrences of `item`. For example:

```
-> (set B (mkBag))
-> (add: B 1)
-> (add: B 1)
-> (first B)
1
-> (next B)
1
-> (next B)
nil
-> (count: B 1)
2
```

You should try to find a place in the `Collection` hierarchy to insert `Bag` so as to write as little new code as possible; do not change the existing hierarchy.

5. Define `TwoWayList` as a subclass of `List`. It is identical to `List` but for the addition of a method `prev`, which backs up the `currentKey` to the

previous item in the list and returns that item. Thus, if L is a `TwoWayList` containing 1 and 2, then:

```
-> (first L)
1
-> (next L)
2
-> (prev L)
1
-> (next L)
2
-> (prev L)
1
-> (prev L)
nil
```

6. In SMALLTALK-80, the `Number` hierarchy is found within the larger hierarchy `Magnitude`, as shown on page 324.

   (a) Define `Magnitude`, with protocol `>`, `>=`, `<=`, `min` (minimum of self and its argument), `max` (similarly), and `between` (determine if receiver is between the first and second arguments); messages `<` and `+1` are subclass responsibilities. Then redefine `Number` as a subclass of `Magnitude`, inheriting methods as appropriate.

   (b) Define `Date` as a subclass of `Magnitude`. A `Date` is given by a month, day, and year. Your `+1` message should properly account for the different lengths of the months and for leap years every fourth year.

   (c) Define `Time` as a subclass of `Magnitude`. `Time` objects represent time on a 24-hour clock.

7. These questions refer to the discrete-event simulation example:

   (a) Increase the number of terminals in the lab to five. Use an array to represent the state of the lab.

   (b) Print a message each time a student leaves the lab, giving the student's number and her time of arrival and departure. Accomplish this not by changing `Student` but by defining a subclass `VerboseStudent` which redefines the necessary message(s). (You will have to make a change in `Student` analogous to the change to `List` shown in Figure 7.18.) Discuss how the **super** facility would facilitate the coding of this subclass.

   (c) Modify the model to allow for balking (when a student arrives and finds the waiting line longer than five students, the student leaves immediately) and to account for context-switching time (each time a student sits down at a terminal, add five minutes to her total service time).

Chapter 8

PROLOG

In the early 1970's, several researchers in the area of mechanical theorem-proving observed that *proving* theorems by the method of *resolution* was closely related to *computing*; in particular, for theorems of the form "for every x there is a y such that $P(x, y)$," a proof might provide a method of *computing y* from given x. They further observed that a subset of first-order predicate logic called *Horn clause logic* was particularly useful for exploiting this relationship. On this basis, they designed PROLOG, which has gained great popularity as a language for artificial intelligence applications.

We will introduce the language in our usual way, first with a general discussion and two simple examples, then a formal presentation of its syntax and an informal one of its semantics, a longer list of examples, a discussion of our interpreter for it, and finally a larger example. A special section is devoted to logic and mechanical theorem-proving — especially the resolution method — and their relation to PROLOG. However, the reader will notice some differences between this chapter and others which arise from the great differences between PROLOG and all the other languages covered in this book. For one thing, the section on the semantics of the language is much longer than it has been in any other chapter. By the same token, the interpreter is almost completely different from our past interpreters. By contrast with all other interpreters except that of Chapter 1, the code for the PROLOG interpreter is given in full, in Appendix I.

8.1 Logic as a Programming Language

Consider the problem of *3-coloring of maps*. We are given three colors — red, yellow, blue — with which to color all the countries on a map. The colors must be chosen so that no two countries that share a border have the same color. The shapes of the countries are arbitrary, but a country must consist of a single piece. Countries that meet at a corner are not considered to share a border.

351

(d) For each student finishing, compute her *time-wasted ratio*: time in the lab divided by service time. At the end of the run, report on the maximum time-wasted ratio achieved during that run. Does this result contradict the average wasted time measure? (Use `Fraction` or `Float` to compute this ratio.)

(e) Define `WaitTimeList` and `ServiceTimeList` to use the random number generator from Exercise 1. Generate wait times as random numbers between 0 and 30 and service times between 10 and 120.

8. Here is a different approach to inheritance: Suppose D is a subclass of C, and let x be an object of class D. To send a message m to x, first look for a definition of m in D, and, if it is there, then invoke it. Otherwise, temporarily *coerce* x *to a* C and then repeat this process. (To clarify, you might implement this idea in the interpreter as follows: If m is not defined in D, then change the *owner* field of x to C and repeat this process; when the message send is finished, change the *owner* field of x back to D.) Compare this notion of inheritance to SMALLTALK's. If it will help you understand the difference, implement this approach and see what, if anything, still works.

9. As with any dynamic-scope mechanism, the message-sending discipline of SMALLTALK makes static type-checking difficult. Two of the most enlightening discussions of this problem are in Johnson [1988], which discusses a type-checking extension to SMALLTALK, and Meyer [1988, Sections 11.3 and 11.4], which describes the type-checking rules of EIFFEL. Read these and report on the type-checking problem in object-oriented languages as it relates to both efficiency and correctness.

7.8.2 LEARNING ABOUT THE INTERPRETER

10. Add class variables. The syntax for class definitions becomes:

classdef $\longrightarrow$ (class class class class-vars inst-vars methoddef$^+$)
class-vars $\longrightarrow$ (variable*)

A new field of type *ENV* should be added to the *CLASSREC* to hold the class variables. A "variable search," akin to method search, will need to be done when looking up a variable. In case of name conflicts, class variables should have priority just above global variables. That is, you should first look for a variable in the local environment (i.e., as a formal parameter), then in the receiver (instance variable), then try the variable search (class variable), and, if all else fails, look in *globalEnv* (global variable).

11. Add **super**. To do this, you should add a new argument, *C*, of type *CLASS*, to *eval*. *C* should give the class of the method definition in which expression *e* occurs (or **nil**, if *e* does not come from a method definition).

Then, messages sent to **super** can be recognized as such (it is important that the variable **super** be recognized before it is evaluated); the message is then sent to **self**, with method search beginning in the parent of C. Show how **super** can be used to rename all the init$\cdots$ messages to just init.

(An alternative version of **super** is this: When a message m is sent to **super**, send it to **self**, but start the method search in the superclass of **self**'s class. Compare this with the version of **super** you just implemented. You may find it expedient to implement this alternative version to better understand the difference; it so happens that this version is easier to implement in our interpreter than the correct one.)

12. One of the major efficiency problems in SMALLTALK is the cost of method search. Since all computation is done by message-sending in SMALLTALK — even integer arithmetic operations — the overhead is substantial. A method effective in reducing this overhead is *in-line caching of method addresses*, as described in Deutsch and Schiffman [1984]. The idea works like this: With each message send, associate two words of memory, one giving the class of the last object to receive that message, the other the address of the method that was invoked the last time the message was sent. Whenever the message is sent, this one-element cache is consulted; if the class of the current receiver is the same as the class of the last receiver (as stored in the cache), then the method stored in the cache is the one to be invoked, and the method search can be side-stepped. If the class of the current receiver is different, then undertake the usual method search and update the cache. This technique will save time if there is a high probability that the receiver of a message will be of the same class as the most recent receiver of that message. Researchers have placed the effectiveness of this cache at 95%. Instrument the interpreter with such caches and measure the hit ratio for a variety of programs. You will need to change the representation of expressions (to include the cache in each *APEXP*), and change **applyMethod**.

Part V

Logic Programming

Logic is the study of valid arguments. Long a part of the Western intellectual tradition, it began to assume new importance to mathematicians in the nineteenth century, when it was found that certain seemingly ordinary arguments led to clearly erroneous results. Mathematicians undertook a more rigorous and formal study of the reasoning used in mathematical proofs, creating in the end a new branch of mathematics called *mathematical logic*. Computer science has been a beneficiary of this study in many ways.[12]

Many systems of formalizing mathematical argument have been proposed, but the most popular is called *first-order predicate logic*. It is powerful enough to allow many arguments to be expressed and is at the same time weak enough to be mathematically tractable. In particular, a computer can be programmed to carry out all the reasoning used in this logic; if a theorem is provable at all, the program would, in principle, find a proof. The possibility of carrying this out in practice and thereby automating much of mathematical thinking has driven the computer science field known as *mechanical theorem-proving*, or *automated deduction*.

It was in studying this area that, in the early 1970's, several researchers — especially Alain Colmerauer and Robert Kowalski — had the insight that led to the development of PROLOG. They observed that when mechanical theorem-provers succeeded in proving a theorem, the proof very often had computational content. For example, the theorem-prover might be presented with (a formalized version of) the following:

Theorem. For any list of integers L, there exists a list M such that M contains exactly the same elements as L, and the elements of M are arranged in nondescending order.

---

[12]We have already come across it in two places. In Part III we discussed the λ-calculus; it was an attempt by logicians to capture aspects of mathematical reasoning related to the definition and use of names. In Chapter 6, we discussed program verification, which makes heavy use of first-order predicate logic, with which we are again concerned in Part V.

This theorem asserts that any list can be sorted. The proof of this theorem, discovered by a theorem-proving program, might implicitly give a method for *constructing* M from L. In short, in proving this theorem, a sort program may be obtained.

Thus was conceived *logic programming*. Among logic programming languages, PROLOG — the name is an abbreviation for "*pro*gramming in *log*ic" — is by far the best known and has achieved great popularity in the past ten years. Other logic programming languages exist but are nearly all confined to research labs. Nonetheless, it is well to keep separate in one's mind the idea of logic programming in general and its particular realization in PROLOG, and we will see how PROLOG, despite its virtues, fails in some ways to be all that one might hope for in a logic programming language.

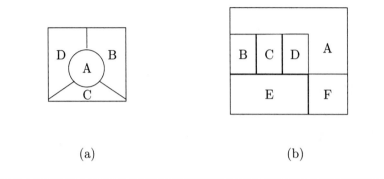

(a)   (b)

Figure 8.1: Maps

Is this possible? Not always, as the map in Figure 8.1(a) shows. On the other hand, some maps, such as that in Figure 8.1(b), can be 3-colored, and it is not necessarily obvious when it is or isn't possible. Our program should give us a 3-coloring when one exists and tell us if none does.

From the viewpoint of logic, it is easy to set down the parameters of the problem, that is, to assert what properties a solution, if it exists, must have. Take the map of Figure 8.1(b). Our solution should be a list of colors, A, B, ..., F, such that:

- A is different from B, C, D, and F.

- B is different from C and E.

- C is different from D and E.

- D is different from E.

- E is different from F.

To render this problem into PROLOG, we must first state the fact that the colors red, yellow, and blue are different, and then assert the conditions just stated about this particular map. Both types of assertions are given in Figure 8.2. There are seven assertions — called *clauses* — given. The first six assert the difference of all colors; note that it must be stated both that yellow is different from red *and* that red is different from yellow. The last, multiline, clause gives, in effect, the shape of the map. It should be read as:

The colors A, B, ..., F constitute a coloring of map b *if* A is different from B, and so on.

The symbols A through F are *logical variables*, to be filled in in such a way as to satisfy the clause. To make use of these clauses, we need to make a *query*,

```
(infer (different yellow blue))
(infer (different yellow red))
(infer (different blue yellow))
(infer (different blue red))
(infer (different red yellow))
(infer (different red blue))
;
(infer (mapb-coloring A B C D E F)
    from (different A B) (different A C) (different A D) (different A F)
        (different B C) (different B E) (different C E) (different C D)
        (different D E) (different E F))
```

Figure 8.2: Clauses for coloring of map of Figure 8.1(b)

asking the interpreter to attempt to prove a *goal* from the given clauses:

```
-> (infer? (mapb-coloring A B C D E F))
Satisfied
```

The interpreter has succeeded in assigning colors to the variables so as to constitute a coloring; it reported back that the query had been satisfied. If we wanted to know what colors it chose, a second goal would be added to the query:

```
-> (infer? (mapb-coloring A B C D E F) (print A B C D E F))
yellow blue red blue yellow blue
Satisfied
```

The second "goal" is just as it appears, a request to print the values of the variables; print goals are always satisfied.

Here is a more familiar example, checking membership of a value in a list. Lists are not built into PROLOG, but they can be represented using expressions formed from the operation cons and constant nil. We are attempting to define a predicate member such that (member x l) will be true if x occurs in the list l. The following assertions about member are certainly valid:

- (member x l) is true if l has the form (cons x m), for any list m.

- (member x l) is also true if l has the form (cons y m), for any y and m, provided that x occurs in m.

- (member x l) is false otherwise.

These facts are stated in PROLOG by way of the two clauses given in Figure 8.3. Note that those clauses state only the cases when the goal is true; it is considered to be false when none of these clauses apply.

```
(infer (member X (cons X L)))
(infer (member X (cons Y M)) from (member X M))
```

Figure 8.3: Clauses for member

Again, these clauses are used by making queries involving member:

```
-> (infer? (member 3 (cons 2 (cons 3 nil))))
Satisfied

-> (infer? (member 3 (cons 2 (cons 4 nil))))
Not satisfied
```

There is no need to print anything here, because we are just asking whether the goals are true or false.

This, then, is the idea behind PROLOG: the programmer describes the logical properties of the result of a computation, and the interpreter searches for a result having those properties.

8.2 The Language

8.2.1 SYNTAX

Our examples have shown most of what is in the language. Data structures are defined implicitly by introducing constructors like cons and constants like nil, which are called *functors* in PROLOG terminology. There are integers and just three built-in predicates to manipulate them.

input	$\longrightarrow$	clause | query
clause	$\longrightarrow$	(infer goal from goal$^+$) | (infer goal)
query	$\longrightarrow$	(infer? goal$^+$)
goal	$\longrightarrow$	predicate | (predicate expression*)
expression	$\longrightarrow$	integer | variable | functor | (functor expression*)
predicate	$\longrightarrow$	name
functor	$\longrightarrow$	name not beginning with capital letter
variable	$\longrightarrow$	name beginning with capital letter

For predicate p, the goals p and (p) are equivalent; similarly for expressions fun and (fun). Here are some examples of expressions:

```
(cons 14 (cons 7 nil))
(mktree 1 nil nil)
(ratnum 17 5)
```

It is important to understand that functor's like cons and mktree don't actually *do* anything; they are just a way of representing structured values. Expressions can also contain variables, which are distinguished as such by their starting with a capital letter, as in (cons X L).

The built-in predicates are print and, for numeric operations, plus, minus, and less. Their use is explained at the end of the next subsection (page 364).

Some terminology is needed to refer to the parts of a clause. The first goal will be called the *left-hand side* of the clause, or the *clause head*, the remaining goals the *right-hand side* or *subgoals* of the clause. expression's are also called *terms*. Finally, an expression or clause with no variables is called *ground*.

8.2.2 SEMANTICS

A typical PROLOG program consists of a list of clauses $C_1, \ldots, C_n$, of the form

$$(\text{infer } G \text{ from } H_1 \ldots H_m),$$

and a query, which for simplicity we will assume has just one goal:

$$(\text{infer? } g).$$

PROLOG semantics can be understood in two different ways, called the *logical interpretation* and the *procedural interpretation*. Of these, the former is simpler but occasionally misleading, and the latter is more accurate.

The Logical Interpretation. According to this view, the function of the PROLOG interpreter is to prove goals, and the clauses give the "rules of inference" to be used in doing proofs. The typical clause given above should be read in this way:

> If we can prove $H_1, \ldots, H_m$, then we can infer G. More generally, if G, $H_1, \ldots, H_m$ contain variables, then for all possible values for those variables, G is true if $H_1, \ldots, H_m$ are true. As a special case, the clause
>
> $$(\text{infer } G)$$
>
> means that G is true no matter what values are given to its variables.
>
> Thus, to satisfy the query (infer? g), we need to find values for the variables occurring in g such that it can be proven using the clauses as inference rules.

For example,

$$(\text{infer } (\text{member X } (\text{cons Y M})) \text{ from } (\text{member X M}))$$

is the assertion that for any values x, y, and m, if x occurs in m, then x occurs in (cons y m). Thus, from

$$\text{(member 3 (cons 4 (cons 3 nil))),}$$

we can infer

$$\text{(member 3 (cons 7 (cons 4 (cons 3 nil)))).}$$

Similarly,

$$\text{(infer (member X (cons X L)))}$$

states that (member x (cons x l)) is true no matter what the values of x and l.

Note that these two rules, regarded as assertions, are evidently true, each on its own and independent of the other and of any other assertions. This implies that the order of their occurrence or their position within the overall list of clauses has no affect on their meaning. Similarly, in a rule like:

```
(infer (mapb-coloring A B C D E F)
    from (different A B) (different A C) ... )
```

the order of the subgoals is immaterial;

```
(infer (mapb-coloring A B C D E F)
    from (different A C) (different A B) ... )
```

is precisely the same assertion.

One of the remarkable features of PROLOG, implicit in the logical interpretation, is that it permits programs to "run backwards." Although the obvious intention of the programmer of member was to be able to check whether a given value occurs in a given list, as in the examples given earlier, the same clauses can be used to choose an element from a list:

```
-> (infer? (member X (cons 4 (cons 3 nil))) (print X))
4
Satisfied
```

In this case, the system somehow "reasoned" that, if X were to equal 4, then the clause

$$\text{(infer (member X (cons X L)))}$$

could be used to infer that the query is true. It could also, by a longer chain of reasoning, have determined that X can equal 3. The logical interpretation doesn't tell us which value will be returned, only that it will be one of them.

The interpreter can even find a list that contains given values:

```
-> (infer? (member 3 L) (member 4 L) (print L))
(cons 3 (cons 4 L3))
Satisfied
```

Note that the result list contains a variable, L3, indicating that the rest of the list is undetermined. This is natural, since all we stated about L was that it contains 3 and 4, so there is no way to know what else it might contain.

The Procedural Interpretation. A logic program, like any program, ultimately instructs a computer to take certain actions. The procedural interpretation of PROLOG tells us what actions the interpreter takes in attempting to answer a query. In this section, we will present the procedural interpretation in three steps, first giving two preliminary versions of it and then a final, complete version. The first version applies only to *ground* clauses and goals. Recall that our "program" is the list of clauses $C_1, \ldots, C_n$.

Version 1. To satisfy g, we look through the clauses C_i in order; the first time a clause is found whose left-hand side equals g, say

$$(\text{infer } g \text{ from } H_1 \ldots H_m),$$

we attempt to satisfy $H_1, \ldots, H_m$, in that order, following the same procedure for each that was followed for g. When each of the H_j has been satisfied, g has been satisfied; if we are unable to satisfy any one of them, we fail to satisfy g. Also, if no clause exists whose left-hand side matches g, we fail to satisfy g.

Version 1 of the procedural interpretation is sufficient to explain the execution of some variable-free programs. Consider this example:

```
-> (infer imokay from youreokay hesokay) ; C₁
-> (infer youreokay from theyreokay) ; C₂
-> (infer hesokay) ; C₃
-> (infer theyreokay) ; C₄
-> (infer? imokay)
Satisfied
```

The procedural interpretation explains what happened:

1. The goal is imokay. The first (and only) matching clause is C_1. The new goals are youreokay and hesokay.

2. We attempt to satisfy youreokay first. Clause C_2 matches and requires that theyreokay be satisfied.

3. `theyreokay` is matched by clause C_4, which has no further goals. Thus, `theyreokay` is satisfied and therefore, so is `youreokay`.

4. `hesokay` is matched by C_3, with no further goals. Thus, `hesokay` is satisfied and so is `imokay`.

Note that the logical interpretation gives us the same result in this case. In fact, the logical interpretation can in general give us answers even when the procedural interpretation does not. Consider the program obtained by adding these clauses to the previous four:

```
-> (infer hesnotokay from imnotokay) ; C₅
-> (infer shesokay from hesnotokay) ; C₆
-> (infer shesokay from theyreokay) ; C₇
-> (infer? shesokay)
Satisfied
```

According to the logical interpretation, she is certainly okay, because they are. However, version 1 of the procedural interpretation does not lead us to that conclusion. Rather, it directs us to prove `shesokay` by applying C_6, which in turn requires us to prove `hesnotokay`, for which we apply C_5, which requires us to prove `imnotokay`, which cannot be proven.

What is missing is the notion of *backtracking*. There can be more than one clause that applies to a given goal, and not all applicable clauses necessarily lead to a solution. The next version of the procedural interpretation, again applicable only to programs containing only ground clauses, takes this into account:

Version 2. To satisfy g, look through the clauses C_i in order; the first time a clause is found whose left-hand side equals g, say

$$C_i = (\texttt{infer } g \texttt{ from } H_1 \ \ldots \ H_m),$$

we attempt to satisfy $H_1, \ldots, H_m$, in that order, following the same procedure for each that was followed for g. When each of the H_j has been satisfied, g has been satisfied. If we are unable to satisfy any one of them, we go back to the list of clauses, starting from C_{i+1}, and look for another clause whose left-hand side equals g. If the end of the list is reached without finding any matching clause, we fail to satisfy g.

Now we can prove `shesokay`:

1. Apply C_6, since it is the first clause that applies. Our new goal is `hesnotokay`.

2. Clause C_5 applies and calls for us to prove `imnotokay`.

3. `imnotokay` is not provable, since no clause applies to it.

4. Backtracking, we continue trying to satisfy `hesnotokay`, starting from C_6. C_6 and C_7 do not apply, so we fail.

5. Backtracking, we continue trying to satisfy `shesokay`, starting from C_7. C_7 applies, and our new goal is `theyreokay`.

6. C_4 applies, and we are done.

This brings the procedural interpretation more into line with the logical interpretation and better reflects what PROLOG actually does. However, it does not by any means reflect the logical interpretation exactly. Consider these two new clauses:

```
-> (infer hesnotokay from shesokay) ; C₈
-> (infer hesnotokay from imokay) ; C₉
-> (infer? shesokay)
```

Now, one fact about the logical interpretation that should be perfectly clear is that if something can be inferred from some set of clauses, it can still be inferred when new clauses are added. Therefore, `shesokay` is still provable after adding C_8 and C_9. But here is what happens according to version 2 of the procedural interpretation:

1. C_6 applies; the new goal is `hesnotokay`.

2. C_5 applies, leaving goal `imnotokay`, which still cannot be satisfied. Backtrack and continue trying to satisfy `hesnotokay`.

3. C_8 applies; the new goal is `shesokay`.

4. C_6 applies; the new goal is `hesnotokay`.

5. :

According to the procedural interpretation, we are in an infinite loop, and indeed PROLOG does go into a loop. Furthermore, if C_8 and C_9 had been reversed, `shesokay` would have been proven with no difficulty. This violates another feature of the logical interpretation, that the order of clauses does not affect the ability to satisfy a goal. Nonetheless, this is how PROLOG works.

Version 2 is accurate and sufficient for understanding how PROLOG executes *variable-free* programs but says nothing about variables. To rectify that will take a bit of work. First, we need several definitions:[1]

Definition 8.1 A *substitution* is a mapping from a finite set of variable's to expression's, written $\{X_1 \mapsto e_1, \ldots, X_n \mapsto e_n\}$, such that no e_i contains any X_j. The variables X_j are said to be *bound in* this substitution.

Definition 8.2 Given a substitution $\sigma = \{X_1 \mapsto e_1, \ldots, X_n \mapsto e_n\}$, and a goal g, the *application of σ to g*, denoted $\hat{\sigma}(g)$, is the goal obtained by replacing each occurrence of X_i by e_i in g.

For example, if

$$g = (\texttt{member X (cons Y L)}),$$

and

$$\sigma = \{X \mapsto 3, \, L \mapsto (\texttt{cons 4 M})\},$$

then

$$\hat{\sigma}(g) = (\texttt{member 3 (cons Y (cons 4 M))}).$$

Definition 8.3 Given substitutions σ_1 and σ_2, the *composition of σ_1 and σ_2*, denoted $\sigma_1 \diamond \sigma_2$, is that substitution such that, for any goal g, $\widehat{\sigma_1 \diamond \sigma_2}(g) = \widehat{\sigma_2}(\widehat{\sigma_1}(g))$.[2]

The next definition is of central importance in understanding PROLOG. It defines the conditions under which a clause is applicable to a goal.

Definition 8.4 *Unification* is the process of finding, for given goals g_1 and g_2, a substitution σ such that $\hat{\sigma}(g_1) = \hat{\sigma}(g_2)$. (Furthermore, σ should be minimal in the following sense: if $\hat{\sigma}'(g_1) = \hat{\sigma}'(g_2)$ for any σ', then there is a substitution σ'' such that $\sigma' = \sigma \diamond \sigma''$; we will not bother to verify this part of the definition in any of our examples.)

Some examples:

1. g_1 = (member 3 (cons 3 nil))
   g_2 = (member X (cons X L))
   σ = $\{X \mapsto 3, \, L \mapsto \text{nil}\}$

2. g_1 = (member Y (cons 3 nil))
   g_2 = (member X (cons X L))
   σ = $\{Y \mapsto 3, \, X \mapsto 3, \, L \mapsto \text{nil}\}$

---

[1] Some of these terms are also defined in the SCHEME chapter, in Section 4.1; the definitions here are not completely identical.

[2] Writing $\sigma_1 \circ \sigma_2$, with the usual meaning that $\sigma_1 \circ \sigma_2(X) = \sigma_2(\sigma_1(X))$, is tempting. However, it is wrong because $\sigma_1(X)$ is an expression and σ_2 applies only to variable's. What we want is some new substitution σ_3 such that $\hat{\sigma_3} = \hat{\sigma_1} \circ \hat{\sigma_2}$; it is that σ_3 that is being denoted $\sigma_1 \diamond \sigma_2$.

3. g_1 = (member 3 (cons 4 nil))
     g_2 = (member X (cons X L))

do not unify, since a substitution cannot map X to both 3 and 4.

4. g_1 = (length (cons 3 nil) N)
     g_2 = (member X (cons X L))

do not unify, since obviously no substitution can make them equal.

5. g_1 = (member X (cons X L))
     g_2 = (member Y (cons (mkTree Y nil nil) M))

do not unify. Since the X in g_1 and the Y in g_2 will be replaced by the same expression, say e, we will end up with goals

$$\widehat{\sigma}(g_1) = \text{(member } e \text{ (cons } e \text{ L))}$$
$$\widehat{\sigma}(g_2) = \text{(member } e \text{ (cons (mkTree } e \text{ nil nil) L))}$$

which are necessarily distinct because e can never equal (mkTree e nil nil).

A query in PROLOG is not simply satisfied, but at the same time it produces a substitution under which it is satisfied. That is, if the query (infer? g) contains variables, the interpreter must find expressions for those variables such that, after replacing each variable in g by its expression, the resulting goal is satisfiable. We can now state the procedural interpretation in full:

Final version. To satisfy g, look through the clauses C_i in order. If a clause is found, say

$$C_i = \text{(infer } G \text{ from } H_1 \ H_2 \ \dots \ H_m\text{),}$$

whose left-hand side unifies with g via substitution σ_0, attempt to satisfy $\widehat{\sigma_0}(H_1)$. If this attempt fails, continue from C_{i+1} looking for an applicable clause; if none is found, the attempt to satisfy g fails. On the other hand, if $\widehat{\sigma_0}(H_1)$ is satisfied, it yields a substitution σ_1; now, attempt to satisfy $\widehat{\sigma_1}(\widehat{\sigma_0}(H_2))$. Continue in this way, eventually satisfying goal $\widehat{\sigma_{m-1}}(\cdots(\widehat{\sigma_1}(\widehat{\sigma_0}(H_m)))\cdots)$, yielding substitution σ_m. The attempt to satisfy g has now succeeded, and it yields the substitution $\sigma_0 \diamond \sigma_1 \diamond \cdots \diamond \sigma_m$.

There is another kind of backtracking possible here that did not arise in version 2, namely backtracking *within right-hand sides*. Suppose the attempt to satisfy some $\widehat{\sigma_{j-1}}(\cdots(\widehat{\sigma_1}(\widehat{\sigma_0}(H_j)))\cdots)$ had failed. In version 2, this would imply the failure to satisfy g by this clause. Here, however, it may be only that H_{j-1} was satisfied *in the wrong way*. So, we backtrack and attempt to *resatisfy* $\widehat{\sigma_{j-2}}(\cdots(\widehat{\sigma_1}(\widehat{\sigma_0}(H_{j-1})))\cdots)$, hopefully yielding a different substitution σ'_{j-1}, and then we continue as before, trying to satisfy $\widehat{\sigma'_{j-1}}(\cdots(\widehat{\sigma_1}(\widehat{\sigma_0}(H_j)))\cdots)$. Failure occurs only when we backtrack to $\widehat{\sigma_0}(H_1)$ and have exhausted all ways of satisfying it.

One last note needs to be added about the unification of a left-hand side of a clause and a goal. The variables occurring in a clause are independent of all other variables occuring in other clauses of the program; that is, their names can always be changed without affecting the computation in any way. This implies that, when unifying g and G, any variables occurring in both do so purely by accident and it would be a mistake to let their common occurrence affect the unification process. Accordingly, before attempting the unification, all the variables in C_i should be renamed to variables not occurring in g.

We will go through three examples, two based upon member and then the coloring query. Recall the definition of member:

```
(infer (member X (cons X L)))  ;  C₁
(infer (member X (cons Y M)) from (member X M))  ;  C₂
```

To answer the query:

```
(infer? (member 3 (cons 4 (cons 3 nil))))
```

the procedural interpretation directs us to follow these steps:

1. The goal does not unify with C_1, but it does with C_2 via substitution

$$\{\texttt{X1} \mapsto 3,\ \texttt{Y1} \mapsto 4,\ \texttt{M1} \mapsto \texttt{(cons 3 nil)}\}$$

   (where X, Y, and M in C_2 have been renamed to X1, Y1, and M1).

2. We are now obliged to prove (member 3 (cons 3 nil)). C_1 applies, via $\{\texttt{X2} \mapsto 3,\ \texttt{L2} \mapsto \texttt{nil}\}$ (renaming X and L in C_1 to X2 and L2). As C_1 has no subgoals, we succeed without further ado.

That example did not return any substitution of interest, since the goal had no variables. Our next query involves "running the program backwards:"

```
(infer? (member 3 L) (member 4 L)).
```

1. We attempt first to satisfy (member 3 L). C_1 applies, yielding

$$\sigma_0 = \{\texttt{X1} \mapsto 3,\ \texttt{L} \mapsto \texttt{(cons 3 L1)}\}$$

   (renaming X and L in C_1 to X1 and L1).

2. The next subgoal to prove is

$$\widehat{\sigma_0}(\texttt{(member 4 L)}) = \texttt{(member 4 (cons 3 L1))}.$$

   C_1 does not apply, but C_2 does, via

$$\sigma_0' = \{\texttt{X2} \mapsto 4,\ \texttt{Y2} \mapsto 3,\ \texttt{M2} \mapsto \texttt{L1}\}.$$

   (renaming X, Y, and M in C_2 to X2, Y2, and M2).

3. We must now prove the right-hand side of C_2, which, applying the substitution, is:

$$\widehat{\sigma_0'}(\text{(member X2 M2)}) = \text{(member 4 L1)}.$$

C_1 applies, yielding[3] $\sigma_1' = \{\text{X3} \mapsto 4, \text{L1} \mapsto \text{(cons 4 L3)}\}$.

4. The attempt to satisfy (member 4 (cons 3 L1)) (step 2) has now succeeded with substitution

$$\sigma_1 \;=\; \sigma_1' \diamond \sigma_0' \;=\; \{\text{X3} \mapsto 4, \text{L1} \mapsto \text{(cons 4 L3)}, \text{X2} \mapsto 4,$$
$$\text{Y2} \mapsto 3, \text{M2} \mapsto \text{(cons 4 L3)}\}.$$

5. The original goal is satisfied with

$$\sigma_0 \diamond \sigma_1 \;=\; \{\text{X1} \mapsto 3, \text{X3} \mapsto 4, \text{L1} \mapsto \text{(cons 4 L3)},$$
$$\text{L} \mapsto \text{(cons 3 (cons 4 L3))}, \ldots\}.$$

The `mapb-coloring` query allows us to illustrate backtracking within right-hand sides, without complicated unification and variable renaming. The computation that solves the query

> (infer? (mapb-coloring A B C D E F))

is in fact quite long, so we will show only the first few steps. Of course, only one clause applies to this goal, and it leaves us with the subgoals (ignoring the renaming of variables):

> (different A B), (different A C), (different A D), ...

These are the steps to be followed according to the procedural interpretation:

1. (different A B) is immediately satisfied with $\sigma_1 = \{\text{A} \mapsto \text{yellow}, \text{B} \mapsto \text{blue}\}$.

2. $\widehat{\sigma_1}(\text{(different A C)}) = \text{(different yellow C)}$ is immediately satisfied with $\sigma_2 = \{\text{C} \mapsto \text{blue}\}$.

3. $\widehat{\sigma_2}(\widehat{\sigma_1}(\text{(different A D)})) = \text{(different yellow D)}$ yields $\sigma_3 = \{\text{D} \mapsto \text{blue}\}$.

4. $\widehat{\sigma_3}(\widehat{\sigma_2}(\widehat{\sigma_1}(\text{(different A F)}))) = \text{(different yellow F)}$ yields $\sigma_4 = \{\text{F} \mapsto \text{blue}\}$.

5. $\widehat{\sigma_4}(\widehat{\sigma_3}(\widehat{\sigma_2}(\widehat{\sigma_1}(\text{(different B C)})))) = \text{(different blue blue)}$ cannot be satisfied.

---

[3]Here and in subsequent examples, we tacitly rename the variables occurring in clauses, by concatenating successively higher integers to their original names.

6. Backtracking to the previous subgoal, (different yellow F) is resatisfied, yielding $\sigma_4' = \{\text{F} \mapsto \text{red}\}$.

7. $\widehat{\sigma_4'}(\widehat{\sigma_3}(\widehat{\sigma_2}(\widehat{\sigma_1}((\text{different B C}))))) $ still is (different blue blue).

8. Backtracking, (different yellow F) cannot be satisfied in any more ways, so we backtrack to the subgoal before that, (different yellow D), and resatisfy it via $\sigma_3' = \{\text{D} \mapsto \text{red}\}$.

9. analogous to 4.

10. analogous to 5.

11. analogous to 6.

12. analogous to 7.

13. Backtracking, (different yellow F) cannot be resatisfied. Backtracking further, (different yellow D) cannot be either. Finally, we backtrack to (different yellow C) and resatisfy it via $\sigma_2' = \{\text{C} \mapsto \text{red}\}$.

14. Satisfy $\widehat{\sigma_2'}(\widehat{\sigma_1}((\text{different A D}))) = (\text{different yellow D})$, yielding $\sigma_3 = \{\text{D} \mapsto \text{blue}\}$.

15. Satisfy (different yellow F) via $\sigma_4 = \{\text{F} \mapsto \text{blue}\}$.

16. Satisfy $\widehat{\sigma_4}(\widehat{\sigma_3}(\widehat{\sigma_2'}(\widehat{\sigma_1}((\text{different B C}))))) = (\text{different blue red})$.

The completion of this computation is left to the reader.

Primitive Predicates.   There are four primitive predicates, print, plus, minus, and less, which do the following:

print: Takes any number of expressions as arguments. Prints each of them and succeeds.

plus: Takes three arguments, the first two of which *must* be instantiated to integers, and the last of which must be either an integer or a variable; if any of these conditions is not met, the goal fails. If the third argument is an integer, the goal succeeds if the third argument is the sum of the first two and fails otherwise. If the third argument is a variable, the goal succeeds and returns the substitution mapping that variable to the sum of the first two arguments.

```
-> (infer? (plus 2 10 12))
Satisfied

-> (infer? (plus 2 5 X) (print X))
7
Satisfied
```

minus: Analogous to plus.

less: Its two arguments must be integers. It succeeds if and only if its first
argument is strictly less than its second.

The restrictions on the arguments of numeric predicates are to prevent
infinite backtracking. Suppose add were defined so that (add X Y 10) would
succeed, returning some substitution $\{X \mapsto a,\ Y \mapsto b\}$ such that $a + b = 10$.
Presumably, backtracking onto this goal would yield a different substitution
$\{X \mapsto a',\ Y \mapsto b'\}$ with $a' + b' = 10$. Since there are an infinite number of
such substitutions, add would be a very tricky predicate to use. In particular,
any right-hand side it appeared in would have to be *guaranteed* to succeed.
Otherwise, it would repeatedly backtrack into the add goal, which would always
be resatisfied. The result would be nontermination.

8.2.3 EXAMPLES

Lists. We have already seen how lists are represented by terms formed from
cons and nil, and we have seen an example of their manipulation in the predicate member. The reader will notice, in comparing this code with LISP code
for the same function:

```
(define member (x l)
    (if (null? l) '()
        (if (= x (car l)) 'T (member x (cdr l)))))
```

two striking differences: (1) there are no applications of car, cdr, or =, and (2)
there is no test for *nil*. These differences lead us to two general observations
about PROLOG:

Pattern-matching. In the LISP code, car and cdr are used to "destruct"
the list l, that is, to identify its components. In PROLOG, they are not
needed because, in unifying the goal with the left-hand side of the second
member goal, the two parts of the list are associated with variables Y and
M, respectively; the right-hand side of the rule then uses these variables
to refer to the two parts of the list. Similarly, the = test is implicit in the
unification used to invoke clauses.

Pattern-matching function invocation can be applied to functional programming languages as well — as in SASL (in a simpler form) and ML —
but PROLOG is, at the present time, the most widely available language
that uses it.

The closed-world assumption. In the LISP code, the null? test is used to
determine when to return false. In the PROLOG code, there seems to be
no clause that ever returns false. That is, the two clauses tell us only how
to infer when member is true, not how to infer when it is false.

Indeed, this is a general rule in PROLOG. The system assumes you have told it every possible way in which a goal can be proven; it therefore takes its inability to prove a goal as proof that the goal is false. Logically speaking, this conclusion is hardly justified: being unable to prove a theorem is not equivalent to disproving it. Nonetheless, this "closed-world assumption" is so pervasive that we will rarely take explicit note of it.

We will now present several familiar list operations, or rather list predicates. At first, the logical assertions will be stated in English before giving the code; afterwards, the translation will be left to the reader. The reader should keep uppermost in mind the logical interpretation; when the procedural interpretation is needed to understand a program, we will point it out.

The goal (`addtoend` l x m), for lists l and m and arbitrary expression x, is true if m is the list obtained by adding x to the end of l. For example,

```
(addtoend (cons 3 nil) 4 (cons 3 (cons 4 nil)))
```

is true. The following assertions describe `addtoend`:

- The result of adding x to the end of the empty list is (`cons` x `nil`), a list of one element.

- The result of adding x to the end of (`cons` y l) is (`cons` y m), where m is the result of adding x to the end of l.

These two assertions are codified in PROLOG in the clauses given in Figure 8.4. These clauses would normally be used to compute m from l and x, as in:

```
-> (infer? (addtoend (cons 3 nil) 4 L) (print L))
(cons 3 (cons 4 nil))
Satisfied
```

but they could also be used "backwards:"

```
-> (infer? (addtoend L 4 (cons 3 (cons 4 nil))) (print L))
(cons 3 nil)
Satisfied
```

`reverse` is defined so that goal (`reverse` l m) is true if m is the reverse of l. The code is given in Figure 8.5. It can be run either forward or backward;

```
(infer (addtoend nil X (cons X nil)))
(infer (addtoend (cons Y L) X (cons Y M)) from (addtoend L X M))
```

Figure 8.4: Clauses for `addtoend`

```
(infer (reverse nil nil))
(infer (reverse (cons X L) M) from (reverse L N) (addtoend N X M))
```

Figure 8.5: Clauses for **reverse**

indeed, it returns the same result in both directions:

```
-> (infer? (reverse (cons 1 (cons 2 nil)) L) (print L))
(cons 2 (cons 1 nil))
Satisfied
-> (infer? (reverse L (cons 1 (cons 2 nil))) (print L))
(cons 2 (cons 1 nil))
Satisfied
```

append is a standard PROLOG example that works out quite neatly. (append l m n) is true if n is the result of appending l to m, as in

$$(append\ (cons\ 3\ (cons\ 4\ nil))\ (cons\ 5\ nil)$$
$$(cons\ 3\ (cons\ 4\ (cons\ 5\ nil)))).$$

In the forward direction, it is used to find n given l and m; the backward direction, in which a given n is split into two pieces, also has interesting applications.

The clauses for append are given in Figure 8.6. Here are a forward and a backward example:

```
-> (infer? (append (cons 3 (cons 4 nil)) (cons 5 (cons 6 nil)) L)
           (print L))
(cons 3 (cons 4 (cons 5 (cons 6 nil))))
Satisfied

-> (infer? (append L (cons 6 (cons 7 nil))
                     (cons 5 (cons 6 (cons 7 nil))))
           (print L))
(cons 5 nil)
Satisfied
```

As an idea of what can be done using **append** in the backward direction, here is a one-clause definition of **member** that works exactly the same as our previous

```
(infer (append nil L L))
(infer (append (cons X L) M (cons X N)) from (append L M N))
```

Figure 8.6: Clauses for **append**

two-clause definition:

```
(infer (member X L) from (append L1 (cons X L2) L)).
```

Our last list example shows how PROLOG allows for code re-use in a novel way. The problem is to define the equivalent of assoc in LISP, which we call lookup. Association lists are represented as lists whose elements have the form (pair *key attribute*), e.g.,

```
(cons (pair chile santiago) (cons (pair peru lima) nil)).
```

The predicate (lookup *k a l*) is true if attribute *a* is paired with key *k* in association list *l*. It can be defined in a single clause:

```
-> (infer (lookup K A L) from (member (pair K A) L))
```

This example also shows how to permanently associate an expression with a name, i.e., assign it to the name; in this case, the name capitols is associated with the above list:

```
-> (infer (capitols (cons (pair chile santiago)
                          (cons (pair peru lima) nil))))
-> (infer? (capitols C) (lookup peru Capitol C) (print Capitol))
lima
Satisfied
```

Arithmetic.   We present two purely arithmetic predicates, mult and fac. For reasons to be explained, the definitions of these predicates can be fully understood only in relation to the procedural interpretation of PROLOG; more precisely, the clauses themselves can be interpreted logically, but to see why variations that are logically equivalent don't work, appeal to the procedural interpretation is unavoidable.

We give the mult predicate — defined so that (mult *x y z*) is true if $z = x \times y$ — for nonnegative integers only (see Exercise 3). Our definition of mult (Figure 8.7) is based upon two facts:

1. $0 \times y = 0$, for any y.

2. $x \times y = (x - 1) \times y + y$, for any $x > 0$ and y.

The second PROLOG clause in Figure 8.7 may not look very much like (2) above, but it can be read as: $x \times y = z$ if there are $v = x - 1$ and $w = v \times y$ such

---

```
(infer (mult 0 Y 0))
(infer (mult X Y Z) from (minus X 1 V) (mult V Y W) (plus W Y Z))
```

Figure 8.7: Clauses for mult

that $z = w + y$, which amounts to the same thing.

mult can be used in the forward direction:

```
-> (infer? (mult 3 5 X) (print X))
15
Satisfied
```

The logical interpretation certainly can explain this result, but the procedural interpretation is needed to explain why mult cannot (usually) be used in the backward direction. Consider:

```
-> (infer? (mult 3 X 12) (print X))
Not satisfied
```

What happened? The second mult clause matched, yielding subgoals (minus X1 1 V1) (renaming X and V), and so on. But according to the definition of minus, it fails if its first argument is not an integer.

Another consequence of the procedural interpretation and the definitions of plus and minus is that mult will not work, even in the forward direction, if its second clause is changed to:

```
(infer (mult X Y Z) from (minus X 1 V) (plus W Y Z) (mult V Y W)).
```

We leave it to the reader to explain this.

The definition of the factorial function via the predicate fac is based on the standard recursive definition thereof. The code is given in Figure 8.8. Like mult, it is nonreversible and the order of the subgoals is critical to its proper operation.

Sorting. In the introduction to Part V, our example of a theorem with computational content was a theorem asserting that any list can be sorted. It can be summarized in the PROLOG clause:

```
(infer (naive-sort L M) from (permutation L M) (ordered M)).
```

This can indeed be used as a sorting program in PROLOG, given clauses defining permutation and ordered. Those clauses are given in Figure 8.9.

```
(infer (fac 0 1))
(infer (fac N R) from (minus N 1 N1) (fac N1 R1) (mult R1 N R))
```

Figure 8.8: Clauses for fac

```
(infer (<= X X))
(infer (<= X Y) from (less X Y))
;
(infer (ordered nil))
(infer (ordered (cons A nil)))
(infer (ordered (cons A (cons B L))) from (<= A B) (ordered (cons B L)))
;
(infer (permutation nil nil))
(infer (permutation L (cons H T))
    from (append V (cons H U) L) (append V U W) (permutation W T))
;
(infer (naive-sort L M) from (permutation L M) (ordered M)).
```

Figure 8.9: Clauses for `naive-sort`

The definition of `ordered` is simple (the most interesting part is the definition of `<=`). As for `permutation`, the clauses say that:

- `nil` is a permutation of `nil`.

- (cons *h* *t*) is a permutation of *l* if *h* is an element of *l* and *t* is a permutation of the remaining elements; more precisely, if *l* can be split into two parts, *v* and (cons *h* *u*), such that *t* is a permutation of the list obtained by appending *u* to *v*. (This clause is another example of a backward use of `append`.)

It is remarkable that `naive-sort` works at all:

```
-> (infer? (naive-sort (cons 4 (cons 2 (cons 3 nil))) L)
          (print L))
(cons 2 (cons 3 (cons 4 nil)))
Satisfied
```

However, it is really an awful sorting algorithm. What it does is to try all permutations of its argument — as many as $n!$ for a list of length n — until it finds a sorted one. It is possible to define more efficient sorting algorithms in PROLOG. Our only example will be Quicksort (Figure 8.10).

The `quicksort` clauses are a very direct rendering of the algorithm. (partition H T A B) is true if A and B form a partition of T, with A containing all elements less than or equal to, and B all elements greater than, H. One feature of PROLOG that can be seen in the definition of `partition` is its ability to return multiple values from a single function. A use of `partition` in the forward direction has the form (partition *h* *t* *a* *b*), where *h* and *t* are instantiated to a specific list and value, respectively, and *a* and *b* are variables; satisfaction of this goal results in binding values to both *a* and *b*. In functional languages,

```
(infer (partition H (cons A X) (cons A Y) Z) from (<= A H) (partition H X Y Z))
(infer (partition H (cons A X) Y (cons A Z)) from (less H A) (partition H X Y Z))
(infer (partition H nil nil nil))
;
(infer (quicksort nil nil))
(infer (quicksort (cons H T) S)
    from
        (partition H T A B)
        (quicksort A A1)
        (quicksort B B1)
        (append A1 (cons H B1) S))
```

Figure 8.10: Clauses for `quicksort`

returning two values from a single function can be accomplished by returning a list containing those values, but it is a bit awkward.

`quicksort` can be used in the forward direction as:

```
-> (infer? (quicksort
              (cons 8 (cons 2 (cons 3 (cons 7 (cons 1 nil))))) S)
          (print S))
(cons 1 (cons 2 (cons 3 (cons 7 (cons 8 nil ) ) ) ) )
Satisfied
```

We leave it to the reader (Exercise 5) to determine why `quicksort` can't be used in the backward direction.

Difference Lists.   There is another representation of lists in PROLOG that has remarkable properties; it is called the *difference list*, or *diff-list*, representation. Diff-lists are expressions of the form (`diff` *l x*), where *x* is a variable and *l* is an ordinary list which contains as its last cdr the variable *x*. For example, the diff-list

$$(\text{diff (cons 3 (cons 4 X)) X})$$

represents the two-element list containing 3 and 4, i.e., the ordinary list (`cons` 3 (`cons` 4 `nil`)). (`diff X X`) represents the empty list.

Difference lists can be transformed to ordinary lists and vice versa. The relation (`simplify` *d l*) is true if *l* is the simple list representation of *d*; its PROLOG definition (Figure 8.11) is based on these facts:

- (`diff` *x x*), for any variable *x*, represents the empty list.

- (`diff` (`cons` *x y*) *z*) represents (`cons` *x w*), if (`diff` *y z*) represents *w*.

`simplify` is reversible, so it can be used to transform a simple list to a difference

---

```
(infer (simplify (diff X X) nil))
(infer (simplify (diff (cons X Y) Z) (cons X W)) from (simplify (diff Y Z) W))
```

Figure 8.11: Clauses for `simplify`

list. Here are examples of both kinds of uses:

```
-> (infer? (simplify (diff (cons 3 (cons 4 X)) X) L) (print L))
(cons 3 (cons 4 nil))
Satisfied
-> (infer? (simplify L (cons 3 (cons 4 nil))) (print L))
(diff (cons 3 (cons 4 Z1)) Z1)
Satisfied
```

What is remarkable about difference lists is that they allow us to code some
naturally recursive predicates without recursion. We give just one example here
(see Exercise 6), the difference list version of append, called `diffappend`. Here
is the entire definition:

```
    (infer (diffappend (diff L X) (diff X Y) (diff L Y))).
```

When used as in:

```
-> (infer? (diffappend (diff (cons 3 X) X) (diff (cons 4 Y) Y) Z)
           (print Z))
(diff (cons 3 (cons 4 Y)) Y)
Satisfied
```

the two goals to be unified, in order to apply the `diffappend` clause, are (after
variable renaming):

```
(diffappend (diff L1          X1) (diff X1          Y1) (diff L1 Y1))
(diffappend (diff (cons 3 X) X)   (diff (cons 4 Y) Y)   Z)
```

It is not hard to see that these unify via:

```
                { L1  ↦  (cons 3 (cons 4 Y)),
                  X1  ↦  (cons 4 Y),
                  Y1  ↦  Y,
                  Z   ↦  (diff (cons 3 (cons 4 Y)) Y)  },
```

which gives the result.

8.3 Implementation

The implementation of PROLOG is very different from that of all the other languages covered in this book. All that has been retained from Chapter 1 is some of the code related to I/O, namely sections *INPUT*, *NAME MANAGEMENT*, and *READ-EVAL-PRINT LOOP*, though most of it is in substantially altered form; *DATA STRUCTURE OP'S* has the same purpose, but the data types have all changed; and some of the code from *ENVIRONMENTS* has been retained in the new section *SUBSTITUTIONS*. Section *DECLARATIONS* is almost completely new; *VALUES* has been removed; *EVALUATION* is completely changed; and new sections *OUTPUT* and *UNIFICATION* have been added. The entire interpreter listing is given in Appendix I.

Here is a summary of the interpreter:

- In *DECLARATIONS*, types are declared to represent expressions, goals, substitutions, and clauses. The global list of clauses is given by a linked list pointed to by the variable *clauses*. Also, to make it easier to rename variables prior to unification, they are represented by a record type containing a *NAME* and an integer, instead of being represented simply as *NAME*'s.

- *DATA STRUCTURE OP'S* contains functions *mkGoal*, *mkVAREXP*, *mk-INTEXP*, *mkAPEXP*, *mkVariable*, and so on, as well as the Boolean-valued function *eqVar* to compare variables.

- *NAME MANAGEMENT* contains *newClause*, which adds a clause to the linked list *clauses*; unlike *newFunDef* in Chapter 1, *newClause* must place new clauses on the *end* of the list in order to preserve the ordering of clauses. *initNames* is largely as before, except that there are only four built-in names: **print**, **plus**, **minus**, and **less**. *install* and *prName* are unchanged.

- *INPUT* contains the same type of code as in all the interpreters. The new functions are *parseInt*, *parseExp*, *parseGoal*, *parseEL* (for expression lists), *parseGL* (for goal lists), *parseClause*, and *parseQuery*.

- *SUBSTITUTIONS* contains functions related to substitutions, which are represented just as environments have been in the past. *bindVar*, *findVar*, *fetch*, and *isBound* are similar to the like-named functions in previous interpreters. New functions *compose*, *applyToGoal*, *applyToGoallist*, *applyToExp*, and *applyToExplist* perform the operations described in Definitions 8.2 and 8.3.

- *OUTPUT* contains the function *prExplist*, called when predicate **print** is applied. It has local procedures *prExp* and *prVar*.

- *UNIFICATION* contains the single function *unify*.

- *EVALUATION* contains the function *prove*, which attempts to prove a list of goals. It attempts to prove the first one, call it *g*, using the first applicable clause. If no clause applies, it fails. If one does, producing substitution σ_0, *prove* calls itself recursively to prove the remaining goals (after applying $\widehat{\sigma_0}$ to them). If that call is successful, so is this one; if not, *prove* will attempt to re-prove *g* by looking for applicable clauses starting from where it left off before the recursive call. Also in this section are functions to copy (and possibly rename variables in) goals, and the function *applyPrim* to evaluate built-in predicates.

- The top level recognizes the "keywords" `infer` and `infer?`, calling, respectively, *parseClause* and *parseQuery*. In the latter case, *prove* is then called.

Sections *DECLARATIONS*, *SUBSTITUTIONS*, *UNIFICATION*, and *EVALUATION* receive further explanation here. The reader is assumed to have reviewed Section 8.2.2.

8.3.1   DECLARATIONS

Type declarations are given for clauses, goals, expressions, and variables. The declaration of *EXP* is very similar to its declaration in Chapter 1, and it is omitted here. *CLAUSE*'s contain, as should be expected, a left-hand side and a right-hand side; the *nextclause* field is used to link together all clauses:

$$CLAUSE = \uparrow CLAUSEREC;$$
$$CLAUSEREC = \textbf{record}$$
$$\qquad lhs: \ GOAL;$$
$$\qquad rhs: \ GOALLIST;$$
$$\qquad nextclause: \ CLAUSE$$
$$\textbf{end};$$

A *GOAL* contains a predicate and a list of arguments:

$$GOAL = \uparrow GOALREC;$$
$$GOALREC = \textbf{record}$$
$$\qquad pred: \ NAME;$$
$$\qquad args: \ EXPLIST$$
$$\textbf{end};$$

A *VARIABLE* is, as indicated above, a *NAME* and an integer, used to rename the variable easily:

$$VARIABLE = \uparrow VARIABLEREC;$$
$$VARIABLEREC = \textbf{record}$$
$$\qquad varname: \ NAME;$$
$$\qquad varindex: \ integer$$
$$\textbf{end};$$

GOALLIST, *VARLIST*, and *EXPLIST* are declared in the usual way, with *head* and *tail* fields. Finally, there is a type *SUBST*, to be described presently.

8.3.2 DATA STRUCTURE OP'S

Here, functions such as *mkGoal* and *mkINTEXP* are defined; these are low-level functions, most of which allocate new records via *new*.

8.3.3 SUBSTITUTIONS

Substitutions are represented in the interpreter just as environments were in the past. This declaration appears in *DECLARATIONS*:

$$SUBST = \uparrow SUBSTREC;$$
$$SUBSTREC = \textbf{record}$$
$$\quad domain: VARLIST;$$
$$\quad range: EXPLIST$$
$$\textbf{end};$$

These functions are analogous to their previous versions:

procedure *bindVar* (*v*: *VARIABLE*; *e*: *EXP*; *sigma*: *SUBST*);
function *findVar* (*v*: *VARIABLE*; *sigma*: *SUBST*): *EXPLIST*;
function *fetch* (*v*: *VARIABLE*; *sigma*: *SUBST*): *EXP*;
function *isBound* (*v*: *VARIABLE*; *sigma*: *SUBST*): *Boolean*;

The function *emptySubst* returns a *SUBST* both of whose fields contain **nil** (analogous to *emptyEnv*).

The procedures

procedure *applyToExplist* (*s*: *SUBST*; *el*: *EXPLIST*);
procedure *applyToExp* (*s*: *SUBST*; **var** *e*: *EXP*);
procedure *applyToGoal* (*s*: *SUBST*; *g*: *GOAL*);
procedure *applyToGoallist* (*s*: *SUBST*; *gl*: *GOALLIST*);

apply substitutions to expressions, goals, etc.; i.e., they apply $\hat{\sigma}$, where σ is the substitution represented by *s*. (Definition 8.2 spoke only of applying $\hat{\sigma}$ to goals, but it is obvious what is meant by applying it to expressions and so on.) These are coded to do the substitutions *in place*; i.e., the expression or goal argument is modified.

Finally,

procedure *compose* (*s1*, *s2*: *SUBST*);

computes the composition of *s1* and *s2*, $s1 \diamond s2$, modifying *s1* in the process.

$\sigma_1 \diamond \sigma_2$ can be defined explicitly by these two conditions:

- $\sigma_1 \diamond \sigma_2(v) = \widehat{\sigma_2}(\sigma_1(v))$, for all variables v that are bound in σ_1.

- $\sigma_1 \diamond \sigma_2(v) = \sigma_2(v)$, for all variables v that are bound in σ_2 but not in σ_1.

It is not obvious that $\sigma_1 \diamond \sigma_2$ defined in this way satisfies Definition 8.3, but it does. As an example, consider:

$$
\begin{array}{rcl}
\sigma_1 & = & \{\texttt{X} \mapsto \texttt{3, L} \mapsto \texttt{(cons 4 M)}\} \\
\sigma_2 & = & \{\texttt{Y} \mapsto \texttt{4, M} \mapsto \texttt{(cons Z nil)}\} \\
\texttt{e} & = & \texttt{(cons Y (cons X L))}
\end{array}
$$

Then, according to definition 8.3, $\sigma_1 \diamond \sigma_2$ must be such that

$$
\begin{array}{rcl}
\widehat{\sigma_1 \diamond \sigma_2}(\texttt{e}) & = & \widehat{\sigma_2}(\widehat{\sigma_1}(\texttt{e})) \\
& = & \widehat{\sigma_2}(\texttt{(cons Y (cons 3 (cons 4 M)))}) \\
& = & \texttt{(cons 4 (cons 3 (cons 4 (cons Z nil))))}
\end{array}
$$

On the other hand, the definition just given says:

$\sigma_1 \diamond \sigma_2 = \{\texttt{X} \mapsto \texttt{3, L} \mapsto \texttt{(cons 4 (cons Z nil)), Y} \mapsto \texttt{4, M} \mapsto \texttt{(cons Z nil)}\}$,

which gives:

$$\widehat{\sigma_1 \diamond \sigma_2}(\texttt{e}) = \texttt{(cons 4 (cons 3 (cons 4 (cons Z nil))))}.$$

As expected, the results are equal. This explicit definition is the one used by *compose*.

8.3.4   UNIFICATION

How can a unifying substitution for given goals g_1 and g_2 be found? The general approach will be to look for subexpressions where the goals differ; one of the subexpressions must be a variable; otherwise unification is impossible. We then replace the variable by the corresponding subexpression from the other goal, *and we also replace all other occurrences of that variable, in either goal, by that subexpression*. We then look for another place where they differ and continue in this way until no more differences are found.

For example, in the case of

$$
\begin{array}{rcl}
g_1 & = & \texttt{(member 3 (cons 3 nil))} \\
g_2 & = & \texttt{(member X (cons X L))}
\end{array}
$$

the first difference found is in the first argument of member, where g_1 has 3 and g_2 has X. Since one of these subexpressions is a variable, we can proceed. Letting $\sigma_1 = \{\texttt{X} \mapsto \texttt{3}\}$ and applying it to both g_1 and g_2, we obtain:

$$
\begin{array}{rclclcl}
g_1' & = & \widehat{\sigma_1}(g_1) & = & g_1 & = & \texttt{(member 3 (cons 3 nil))} \\
g_2' & = & \widehat{\sigma_1}(g_2) & = & & & \texttt{(member 3 (cons 3 L))}.
\end{array}
$$

g'_1 and g'_2 differ where g'_1 has `nil` and g'_2 has L, so letting $\sigma_2 = \{L \mapsto \texttt{nil}\}$:

$$
\begin{aligned}
g''_1 &= \widehat{\sigma_2}(g'_1) &= g_1 &= \texttt{(member 3 (cons 3 nil))} \\
g''_2 &= \widehat{\sigma_2}(g'_2) &&= \texttt{(member 3 (cons 3 nil))}.
\end{aligned}
$$

With no differences remaining, g_1 and g_2 have been unified by substitution

$$
\sigma = \sigma_1 \diamond \sigma_2 = \{X \mapsto 3, L \mapsto \texttt{nil}\}.
$$

Another example is

$$
\begin{aligned}
g_1 &= \texttt{(member Y (cons 3 nil))} \\
g_2 &= \texttt{(member X (cons X nil))}
\end{aligned}
$$

The first difference is between Y and X; since both are variables, either $\{Y \mapsto X\}$ or $\{X \mapsto Y\}$ can be used. So suppose we choose $\sigma_1 = \{X \mapsto Y\}$; it is then applied to both goals, obtaining:

$$
\begin{aligned}
g'_1 &= \widehat{\sigma_1}(g_1) &= \texttt{(member Y (cons 3 nil))} \\
g'_2 &= \widehat{\sigma_1}(g_2) &= \texttt{(member Y (cons Y nil))}.
\end{aligned}
$$

The next difference is between Y and 3, so defining $\sigma_2 = \{Y \mapsto 3\}$, we get:

$$
\begin{aligned}
g''_1 &= \widehat{\sigma_2}(g'_1) &= \texttt{(member 3 (cons 3 nil))} \\
g''_2 &= \widehat{\sigma_2}(g'_2) &= \texttt{(member 3 (cons 3 nil))}.
\end{aligned}
$$

We are done, and the unifying substitution is

$$
\sigma = \sigma_1 \diamond \sigma_2 = \{X \mapsto 3, Y \mapsto 3\}.
$$

How can unification fail? As already noted, if g_1 and g_2 differ at a position where neither has a variable, then it fails. The only other source of failure is when one subexpression is a variable x and the other is a nonvariable which *contains* x. For example, an attempt to unify (cons X L) with (cons 3 (cons 4 L)) would fail for this reason. This kind of failure is caught by searching the entire nonvariable expression for an occurrence of x. Many PROLOG implementations omit this so-called *occurs check*, holding that, because this situation is rare, its costs outweigh its benefits. However, our implementation includes it (see Exercise 4).

Assuming the occurs check is done, one observation that can be made is that after one step of unification, in which a variable x has been replaced by an expression, there are no longer any occurrences of x in either goal. This is a key point in proving that the unification algorithm is correct.

unify implements this algorithm. It is declared as:

function *unify* (*g1, g2*: *GOAL*): *SUBST*;

As the algorithm description implies, it modifies both its arguments. We make a few comments in the way of explanation of the code, which is in Appendix I:

- *unify* is called with two *GOAL* arguments and returns a unifying substitution; a **nil** return value indicates failure to unify. For efficiency, the
predicates of the two goals have been compared before calling *unify*, so
they are known to be equal; therefore, *unify* actually unifies the two argument lists, which are *EXPLIST*'s.

- The functions

    function *findExpDiff* (*e1, e2*: *EXP*): *Boolean*;
    function *findELDiff* (*el1, el2*: *EXPLIST*): *Boolean*;

    compare two expressions or expression lists, respectively, for differences,
    returning false if there are none and true otherwise. Furthermore, if a
    difference is found, global variables *diff1* and *diff2* are set to point to the
    differing subexpressions.

- *occursInExp* is called to do the occurs check.

- The body of *unify* repeatedly calls *findELDiff*. As long as it finds a
difference, it binds *diff1* to *diff2* (or vice versa, if *diff2* is the variable)
in *sigma*, after doing the occurs check. It replaces *diff1* by *diff2* (or vice
versa) in both goals, and then it repeats the loop.

8.3.5 EVALUATION

The function *prove* follows the procedural interpretation of PROLOG closely. It
is given a list of goals and attempts to satisfy them, returning the substitution
obtained if successful. Its method is this:

1. Look at the first goal. If its predicate is primitive, call *applyPrim*; no
further action is necessary or possible.

2. If the first goal's predicate is not primitive, begin looking through the
clauses of the program for one that matches the goal. If none is found,
fail by returning **nil**.

3. If a matching clause is found, call the unifying substitution *sigma0*.

4. Apply *sigma0* to each goal in the right-hand side of the clause and to each
of the remaining goals passed to *prove*; put these new goal lists together;
and call *prove* recursively.

5. If the recursive call fails, return to step 2, starting from just after the
clause that matched.

6. If the recursive call succeeds, it will return a substitution; call it *sigma1*.
Then this call succeeds and returns the composition of *sigma0* and *sigma1*.

Before looking at *prove* itself, note the auxiliary functions *applyPrim, copy-Goal*, and *copyGoallist*:

> **function** *applyPrim* (*g*: *GOAL*; **var** *sigma*: *SUBST*): *Boolean*;
> **function** *copyGoal* (*g*: *GOAL*; *id*: *integer*): *GOAL*;
> **function** *copyGoallist* (*gl*: *GOALLIST*; *id*: *integer*): *GOALLIST*;

applyPrim attempts to satisfy goal *g*, whose predicate is either `print`, `plus`, `minus`, or `less`. If it fails (which happens, for example, if the first two arguments of an arithmetic predicate are not both integers), it returns **false**. Otherwise, it returns **true** and modifies the *sigma* argument appropriately. *copyGoal* returns a copy of its argument, with all variables renamed if its second argument is nonzero; *copyGoallist* does likewise.

prove has two arguments, the list of goals to be proven and an integer used in renaming variables:

> **function** *prove* (*gl*: *GOALLIST*; *id*: *integer*): *SUBST*;

It returns **nil** if it fails to satisfy the goals and otherwise returns a proper *SUBST* (though possibly an empty one, if no substitution was required to satisfy the goal; note the difference between **nil** and an empty substitution).

prove handles only the first goal in *gl* (*gl↑.head*) directly, calling itself recursively to satisfy the remaining goals (*gl↑.tail*). It first checks if the first goal has a primitive predicate. If not, it goes through the global clauses data base *clauses* trying each clause; if the left-hand side of a clause matches the goal, then the right-hand side of that clause is added to *gl*, and an attempt is made to solve the resulting goal list. In any event, the result is two substitutions: *sigma0* is the one used to unify the first goal with the clause, and *sigma1* is the result of recursively satisfying the subgoals; if both processes succeeded, then the current call succeeds with substitution *sigma0*◇*sigma1*:

```
begin (* prove *)
    if gl = nil
    then prove := emptySubst
    else begin
            if gl↑.head↑.pred <= numBuiltins
            then if applyPrim(gl↑.head, sigma0)
                then begin
                        applyToGoallist(sigma0, gl↑.tail);
                        sigma1 := prove(gl↑.tail, id+1)
                    end
                else sigma1 := nil
```

```
            else begin
                    sigma1 := nil;
                    cl := clauses;
                    while (cl <> nil) and (sigma1 = nil) do begin
                            sigma0 := tryClause(cl↑.lhs, gl↑.head);
                            if sigma0 <> nil
                            then sigma1 := proveRest(cl↑.rhs, gl↑.tail);
                            cl := cl↑.nextclause
                            end (* while *)
                end;
        if sigma1 = nil
        then prove := nil
        else begin
                compose(sigma0, sigma1);
                prove := sigma0
            end
        end
    end; (* prove *)
```

tryClause tries to unify the head of *gl* with the first clause in *r*. If it fails, it returns **nil**; otherwise, it returns a substitution unifying the goal and the clause head:

```
        function tryClause (clgoal, g: GOAL): SUBST;
        begin
                tryClause := nil;
                if (clgoal↑.pred = g↑.pred)
                    and (lengthEL(clgoal↑.args) = lengthEL(g↑.args))
                then begin
                        clgoal := copyGoal(clgoal, id);
                        g := copyGoal(g, 0);
                        tryClause := unify(clgoal, g)
                    end
        end; (* tryClause *)
```

Note that *tryClause* must copy both the goal and the clause head. This is because *unify*, which it calls, is destructive, and neither argument is expendable: The clause head obviously must be preserved for future computations, and the goal must be preserved in case it needs to be re-satisfied after backtracking. Furthermore, the variables in the clause are renamed to avoid fortuitous collisions.

proveRest is called in case a clause matched with the first subgoal. It adds the subgoals of that clause to the remaining goals in *gl* (after applying the substitution to both), then calls *prove* recursively:

> **function** *proveRest* (*subgoals, restofgoals*: *GOALLIST*): *SUBST*;
> **begin**
>   *subgoals* := *copyGoallist*(*subgoals, id*);
>   *applyToGoallist*(*sigma0, subgoals*);
>   *restofgoals* := *copyGoallist*(*restofgoals*, 0);
>   *applyToGoallist*(*sigma0, restofgoals*);
>   *proveRest* := *prove*(*append*(*subgoals, restofgoals*), *id*+1)
> **end**; (* *proveRest* *)

proveRest copies subgoals for the same reasons that *tryClause* did.

8.4 Example — The Blocks World

The "blocks world" is a classic problem-solving domain in artificial intelligence. It is a simple test-bed for ideas in planning robot motions. The "world" consists of a table and three children's blocks. The important information about the state of the world is how the blocks are stacked. The problem is: Given an existing state and a desired new state, move the blocks to achieve that state. The allowable "moves" are those that move a single block from whatever it is on (another block or the table) to something else. Our approach to this problem closely follows that of Sterling and Shapiro [1986, p. 222].

The statement of the problem can be given quite easily in PROLOG. A state is represented by a list of the form

```
(cons (on a a) (cons (on b b) (cons (on c c) nil))),
```

where *a*, *b*, and *c* are either `table` or one of the blocks a, b, and c. Figure 8.12 contains some predicates outlining the basic parameters of the problem:

- `block` identifies the blocks a, b, and c. `block` is then used in the definition of `different` to distinguish blocks from the table.

- `(clear X State)` is true if `State` does not contain `(on B X)` for any B.

- `(on X Y State)` is true if `State` contains `(on X Y)`. (Here, `on` is being used both as a predicate and as a functor.)

- `update` defines how a move changes a state. Moves are represented as terms `(move X Y Z)`, indicating that X (which must be a block) is to be moved from Y to Z (which can be either blocks or `table`).

- `legal-move` defines when a move can be made in a state. The clauses treat the cases where a block is being moved onto the table and where it is being moved onto another block. In the first case, the move is legal if

```
(infer (block a))
(infer (block b))
(infer (block c))
;
(infer (different a b))
(infer (different a c))
(infer (different b a))
(infer (different b c))
(infer (different c a))
(infer (different c b))
(infer (different X table) from (block X))
(infer (different table Y) from (block Y))
;
(infer (clear X nil))
(infer (clear X (cons (on B Y) State))
    from (different X Y) (clear X State))
;
(infer (on X Y State) from (member (on X Y) State))
;
(infer (update (move X Y Z) (cons (on X Y) S) (cons (on X Z) S)))
(infer (update (move X Y Z) (cons (on U V) S1) (cons (on U V) S2))
    from (different X U) (update (move X Y Z) S1 S2))
;
(infer (legal-move (move B P1 table) State)
    from
        (on B P1 State)
        (different P1 table)
        (clear B State))
(infer (legal-move (move B1 P B2) State)
    from
        (block B2)
        (on B1 P State)
        (different P B2)
        (different B1 B2)
        (clear B1 State)
        (clear B2 State))
```

Figure 8.12: Clauses for blocks world

the block is indeed where the move claims it is, if it is not already on the table (in which case the move wouldn't do anything), and if the block to be moved has nothing on it. In the second case, we demand in addition that we are not trying to move a block onto itself and that the target block is clear. (Note that a block can hold only one other block, while the table can hold any number.)

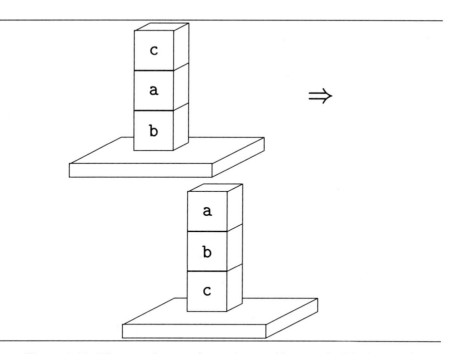

Figure 8.13: The sample transformation problem in the blocks world

The main predicate is `transform`. `(transform State1 State2 Plan)` is true if the sequence of moves in `Plan` leads from `State1` to `State2`. The simplest approach is to give the definition directly:

```
-> (infer (transform State1 State2 (cons Move Moves))
    from
        (legal-move Move State1)
        (update Move State1 State)
        (transform State State2 Moves))
```

However, this won't work. For example, the query:

```
-> (infer (state1 (cons (on a b)
                  (cons (on b table) (cons (on c a) nil))))))
-> (infer (state2 (cons (on a b)
                  (cons (on b c) (cons (on c table) nil))))))
-> (infer? (state1 S1) (state2 S2) (transform S1 S2 Plan))
```

asks us to make the transformation pictured in Figure 8.13. It does not terminate. To see why, change the second clause of `transform`:[4]

---

[4]N.B.: There is no direct way to simply *redefine* a predicate, since new clauses related to a predicate do not invalidate existing clauses. Hence, "change the second clause" means "terminate the session and re-enter the new clauses."

```
-> (infer (transform State1 State2 (cons Move Moves))
    from
        (legal-move Move State1)
        (update Move State1 State)
        (print State)
        (transform State State2 Moves))
```

Then,

```
-> (infer? (state1 S1) (state2 S2) (transform S1 S2 Plan))
(cons (on a b) (cons (on b table) (cons (on c table) nil)))
(cons (on a table) (cons (on b table) (cons (on c table) nil)))
(cons (on a table) (cons (on b a) (cons (on c table) nil)))

(cons (on a table) (cons (on b table) (cons (on c table) nil)))
(cons (on a table) (cons (on b a) (cons (on c table) nil)))
        ⋮
```

The problem is that states are repeating themselves. To protect against this, we need to keep a list of the states already visited. In Figure 8.14, a new version of **transform** is presented, which simply appeals to a new *four-argument* version of **transform**.[5] (transform State1 State2 Visited Plan) is true if **Plan** leads from **State1** to **State2**, while passing through the states in **Visited**. The new predicate **not-member** is needed to test membership of a state in the list **Visited** so as to avoid returning to that state, and **different** needs to be extended to states. With these new clauses, we get:

```
-> (infer?  (state1 S1) (state2 S2) (transform S1 S2 Plan)
            (print Plan))
(cons (move c a table) (cons (move a b table) (cons (move b table a)
    (cons (move b a c) (cons (move a table b) nil)))))
Satisfied
```

Note that this is not the best plan for this transformation, since it has five moves instead of the minimum, which is four. In particular, it has two consecutive moves of block **b**, something that is never sensible. This can be fixed very directly, but we prefer to leave that as an exercise. The overall problem is that the search for a solution is entirely "forward," that is, it starts from **State1** and tries every possible move until eventually, with luck, **State2** is reached. If the goal, **State2**, could be taken into account in looking for a plan, possibly a better plan could be found more quickly. A solution that attempts to do this is presented in Figure 8.15.

---

[5]The four-argument predicate is analogous to an auxiliary function. It is all right to use the same name for predicates with different numbers of arguments; since goals with different numbers of arguments can never unify, the name clash can never affect a computation.

```
(infer (different (cons (on A X) State1) (cons (on A Y) State2))
    from (different X Y))
(infer (different (cons (on A X) State1) (cons (on A X) State2))
    from (different State1 State2))
;
(infer (not-member X nil))
(infer (not-member X (cons Y L))
    from (different X Y) (not-member X L))
;
(infer (transform State1 State2 Plan)
    from (transform State1 State2 (cons State1 nil) Plan))
;
(infer (transform State State Visited nil))
(infer (transform State1 State2 Visited (cons Move Moves))
    from
        (legal-move Move State1)
        (update Move State1 State)
        (not-member State Visited)
        (transform State State2 (cons State Visited) Moves))
```

Figure 8.14: Clauses for transform, first version

```
(infer (transform State1 State2 Plan)
    from (transform State1 State2 (cons State1 nil) Plan))
;
(infer (transform State State Visited nil))
(infer (transform State1 State2 Visited (cons Move Moves))
    from
        (choose-move Move State1 State2)
        (update Move State1 State)
        (not-member State Visited)
        (transform State State2 (cons State Visited) Moves))
;
(infer (choose-move Move State1 State2)
    from (suggest Move State2) (legal-move Move State1))
(infer (choose-move Move State1 State2)
    from (legal-move Move State1))
(infer (suggest (move X Y Z) State)
    from (member (on X Z) State))
```

Figure 8.15: Clauses for transform, second version

Instead of just choosing any legal move to try next, this version of `transform`
takes a move chosen by `choose-move`, which in turn invokes `suggest`. `suggest`
looks at `State2`, and suggests a move that will result in achieving a placement
that occurs there. Thus, it is attempting to reason backward from the goal.
This program does result in a better plan:

```
-> (infer? (state1 S1) (state2 S2) (transform S1 S2 Plan)
           (print Plan))
(cons (move c a table) (cons (move a b table)
    (cons (move b table c) (cons (move a table b) nil))))
Satisfied
```

8.5   PROLOG as It Really Is

8.5.1   SYNTAX

There is no standard PROLOG syntax, but most versions are similar to one
another; our presentation is based upon DEC-10 PROLOG from the University
of Edinburgh, an early and well-known implementation.

PROLOG syntax is very simple. The clauses we write as

$$\text{(infer G)}$$
$$\text{and}\quad\text{(infer G from H ... I)}$$

are written in real PROLOG as

$$\text{G.}$$
$$\text{and}\quad\text{G :- H, ..., I.}$$

Furthermore, the goal (P e_1 ... e_n) is written as P(e_1, ..., e_n) and the
expression (f e_1 ... e_n) as f(e_1, ..., e_n). Variables are distinguished by
their starting with a capital letter, as in our version. Thus, the map coloring
code of Figure 8.2 is written:

```
different(yellow,red).
    ⋮
mapb-coloring(A,B,C,D,E,F) :- different(A,B), ... .
```

The goal we write as "(plus x y z)" is written in real PROLOG as "z is
$x+y$," so that our `fac` predicate becomes:

```
fac(0,1).
fac(N,R) :- N1 is N-1, fac(N1,R1), R is R1*N.
```

Special syntax is provided for lists, namely, "[]" for the empty list, [$x|l$] for
(cons x l), and [$a,b,...,z$] for (cons a (cons b ... (cons z nil)...)).

Thus, **append** is written as:

```
append([],L,L).
append([X - L],M,[X - N]) :- append(L,M,N).
```

8.5.2 SEMANTICS

The basic semantics of PROLOG is very much as we have presented it, except that most PROLOG's omit the occurs check in unification. There are some important embellishments, of which we present the most important: the "cut," **not**, and **assert** and **retract**. There are many more built-in predicates, for everything from I/O to arithmetic, which are not discussed here.

The cut is a way of giving the programmer additional control over the computation by allowing her to indicate places where backtracking is impermissible. Specifically, the cut is written as an exclamation mark (!) occurring as a goal in the right-hand side of a clause such as

$$G :- H, !, I.$$

Suppose this clause is chosen to satisfy a goal *g* with which G unifies. An attempt is made to satisfy H. If successful, I is proven. If the proof of I succeeds, then *g* is proven; in this case, the cut has no part to play. If, however, the proof of I fails, rather than backtrack and try to re-prove H, the presence of the cut causes the goal *g* to fail immediately; this occurs even if there are further clauses that might apply to *g*.

An example is the definition of **not-equal**:

```
not-equal(X,Y) :- equal(X,Y), !, fail.
not-equal(X,Y).
```

where the definition of **equal** is the single clause:

```
equal(X,X).
```

not-equal(X,Y) should succeed if X is not equal to Y, and fail if it is; X and Y should be bound to ground expressions when attempting to satisfy this goal. Here is what happens on query **not-equal(1,2)**:

1. The first clause matches, so we try to prove **equal(1,2)**. It fails, so we backtrack and look for another clause.

2. The second clause matches, and has no subgoals, so the original goal is proven. In other words, **not-equal(1,2)** succeeds, as it should.

On the other hand, if the query is **not-equal(2,2)**:

1. The first clause matches, so we try to prove **equal(2,2)**.

2. It succeeds, so we pass over the cut and try to prove `fail`.

3. `fail` is assumed to be a zero-argument predicate to which no clause applies. It fails.

4. We attempt to backtrack past the cut, which causes the original goal — `not-equal(2,2)` — to fail, as it should.

Another use of the cut is to prevent backtracking in cases where there are no variables, so that resatisfying the goal would be pointless. For example, if `member` is expected to be used only in the forward direction — i.e., as `member(`u`,`v`)`, where u and v are ground expressions — we might write its clauses like this:

```
member(X,[X - L]) :- !.
member(X,[Y - M]) :- member(X,M).
```

Now, suppose `member` is used in the subgoals of some clause. If it has been found to be true, it can only be because the first clause in its definition matched the goal. Suppose that some subgoal further along in the list of subgoals fails and control backtracks into the `member` goal. Assuming, to repeat, that its arguments are ground terms, then there is no point in trying to resatisfy it. In this case, the cut guarantees that the `member` goal will fail immediately, with no attempt to resatisfy it.

`not-equal` is just one example of negation of a predicate. In the blocks world there was another, the predicate `not-member`. In real PROLOG, `not-member` could have been defined by the same "cut fail" method:

```
not-member(X,Y) :- member(X,Y), !, fail.
not-member(X,Y).
```

As an abbreviation for this, PROLOG includes the predicate `not`, with which `not-member` could be written

```
not-member(X,Y) :- not(member(X,Y)).
```

`not` is no ordinary predicate, because its argument is a *goal* rather than an expression. What it does, as implied by the clauses it abbreviates, is to try to satisfy its argument, and to succeed if its argument fails. This is called "negation as failure," really just another name for the closed-world assumption.

`not` must be used with care, for it is different from the intuitive idea of negation. For example, suppose we wanted to satisfy the goal `not-member(X,[2,4, 6])`. The logical interpretation of this is that we want to find some `X` for which it holds. However, what will happen operationally is that the system will attempt to satisfy `member(X,[2,4,6])`, will *succeed*, and the goal will fail. Thus, `not` should never be applied to a goal whose variables have not been instantiated by ground terms.

Another significant addition to PROLOG are the predicates `assert` and `retract`, which allow a program to modify the data base of clauses. These take a clause as their argument and do the following:

- **assert**(*C*) places *C* into the global list of clauses at an undetermined position. (More commonly used are the variants **asserta** and **assertz**, which place the new clause at the beginning and end, respectively, of the clauses data base.)

- **retract**(*C*) removes the first clause that matches *C* from the clauses data base.

Any new clause can be added, or old clause removed, by these predicates, but they are most commonly used with ground predicates, to give the effect of global variables. The simplest example is using them to define a global counter, call it **ctr**. It can be set to zero by asserting:

$$\text{ctr(0).}$$

Then, the predicate **zeroCtr** resets it to zero, and **incrCtr** adds one to it:

```
zeroCtr :- retract(ctr(X)), assert(ctr(0)).
incrCtr :- retract(ctr(X)), Y is X+1, assert(ctr(Y)).
```

The extensions mentioned here, and many more in real implementations of PROLOG, can be understood only via the operational interpretation. Indeed, this is one of the major criticisms of the language: the logical interpretation often fails to explain real programs, which use nonlogical features like the cut heavily, yet at the same time the operational interpretation can be quite difficult to understand.

8.6 PROLOG and Mathematical Logic

Mathematical logic is the study of the meaning of "proof" in mathematics. It has been studied heavily since about the mid-nineteenth century, when mathematicians began to be concerned about the soundness of mathematical reasoning. Logicians have tried to formalize the language that mathematicians use and the reasoning processes by which theorems are deduced.

When computer scientists began to explore the limits of machine intelligence, one of their first goals was to develop programs that displayed mathematical reasoning. The formalizations developed by logicians were tailor-made for this kind of work. The creators of PROLOG were researchers in the field of *mechanical theorem-proving*. In this section, we will review some of the background knowledge possessed by those researchers, placing PROLOG into the overall framework of mechanized logic.

We will first discuss the simplest kind of logic, *propositional logic*, and then *first-order predicate logic*, probably the most studied of all logical systems and the one that forms the basis of almost all work in mechanical theorem-proving. PROLOG corresponds to a subset of first-order logic called *Horn clause logic*.

8.6.1 *PROPOSITIONAL LOGIC*

Propositional logic is the logic of *combinations* of elementary propositions, the truth of which are not considered to be at issue. Consider the following statements:

> Either the President or the Secretary of State prevails, but not both. When the President is sure, he prevails. When the President is unsure, the Secretary of State prevails. The Secretary of State prevailed. Therefore, the President was unsure.

Propositional logic tells us that the line of reasoning used here is proper, independent of whether the statements are actually true. In other words, if one accepts the truth of the first four statements (the *hypotheses*), then one is bound to accept the final statement (the *conclusion*). Indeed, suppose we make the following substitutions:

> p for "the President is sure."
> q for "the President prevails."
> $\sim p$ for "the President is unsure."
> r for "the Secretary of State prevails."

Then we can recast our argument in these terms:

> Either q or r, but not both. When p, q. When $\sim p$, r. r. Therefore, $\sim p$.

This reformulation points to the essential fact about propositional logic, and indeed about all formal logic: It concerns *arguments*, not *facts*. The argument just made is valid no matter what p, q, and r are, assuming only that $\sim p$ is the opposite of p. For example, the following is an equally valid argument; indeed, it is the identical argument:

> Either Hamlet is crazy, or he is pretending, but not both. If he's crazy, he will kill Polonius. If he's pretending, he will kill Claudius. He kills Polonius. Therefore, he is crazy.

Propositional logic was already discussed informally in Section 5.4 of Chapter 5, but the deeper study we are about to undertake calls for more formal definitions. The set of **propositions** is given by the grammar:

proposition	$\longrightarrow$	t | f | propositional-variable
	|	proposition & proposition
	|	proposition $\lor$ proposition
	|	proposition $\Rightarrow$ proposition
	|	$\sim$ proposition | (proposition)
propositional-variable	$\longrightarrow$	name (usually p, q, r, or s)

Here, " & " represents "and" or *conjunction*; " ∨ " is "or" or *disjunction*; " ⇒ " is *implication*; and "∼ " is *negation*. Our example becomes the proposition:

$$(((q \vee r) \mathbin{\&} \sim (q \mathbin{\&} r)) \mathbin{\&} (p \Rightarrow q) \mathbin{\&} (\sim p \Rightarrow r) \mathbin{\&} r) \Rightarrow \sim p.$$

Definition 8.5 A proposition containing no propositional-variable's is either true or false according to the following inductive definition:

- t is true.

- f is false.

- $P \mathbin{\&} Q$ is true *iff* P is true and Q is true.

- $P \vee Q$ is true *iff* P is true or Q is true, or both.

- $P \Rightarrow Q$ is true *iff* P is false or Q is true, or both.

- $\sim P$ is true *iff* P is false.

- (P) is true *iff* P is true.

A proposition containing variables is not simply true or false, since its truth may depend upon whether the variables it contains are true or false.

Definition 8.6 A *truth-value assignment* for proposition P is a substitution σ mapping each of its variables to t or f. $\widehat{\sigma}$ is defined in the obvious way (Definition 8.2) as a map from proposition's to proposition's. Say P *is true for* σ if $\widehat{\sigma}(P)$ is true. (Note that there are a finite number of truth-value assignments for any P; specifically, there are 2^n if P has n distinct variables.)

In our sample proposition, the variables are p, q, and r, so one truth-value assignment is $\sigma = \{p \mapsto \text{t}, q \mapsto \text{f}, r \mapsto \text{t}\}$; applying $\widehat{\sigma}$ yields:

$$(((\text{f} \vee \text{t}) \mathbin{\&} \sim (\text{f} \mathbin{\&} \text{t})) \mathbin{\&} (\text{t} \Rightarrow \text{f}) \mathbin{\&} (\sim \text{t} \Rightarrow \text{t}) \mathbin{\&} \text{t}) \Rightarrow \sim \text{t}.$$

Application of Definition 8.5 shows that this proposition is true. In fact, the sample proposition is true no matter what truth-value assignment is made:

Definition 8.7 A proposition P is *valid* if for any truth-value assignment σ for P, $\widehat{\sigma}(P)$ is true.

There is an obvious way to test the validity of a proposition: Check each of the 2^n truth-value assignments. This so-called *truth-table method* was used in Section 5.4. The main purpose of this section is to introduce another method to solve this problem, the method of *resolution*. First, some more definitions are needed.

Definition 8.8 A proposition P is *satisfiable* if there is some truth-value assignment making P true; otherwise, it is *unsatisfiable*.

Theorem 8.1 P is valid if and only if $\sim P$ is unsatisfiable.

Theorem 8.2 If $P \Rightarrow Q$ is valid, and Q is unsatisfiable, then P is unsatisfiable.

By Theorem 8.1, testing validity and unsatisfiability are problems of equivalent difficulty; if we can solve one, we can solve the other. An algorithm for proving unsatisfiability is called a *refutation procedure*. Resolution is a refutation procedure. It applies not to arbitrary propositions but only to the subset of propositions that are in *conjunctive normal form*. These can be defined by the grammar:

CNF-proposition	$\longrightarrow$	(clause) $\mid$ (clause) & CNF-proposition
clause	$\longrightarrow$	literal $\mid$ literal $\vee$ clause
literal	$\longrightarrow$	positive-literal $\mid$ negative-literal
positive-literal	$\longrightarrow$	propositional-variable
negative-literal	$\longrightarrow$	$\sim$ propositional-variable

It so happens that for every proposition P there is an *equivalent* CNF-proposition $\tau(P)$, equivalent in the sense that for any truth-value assignment σ, $\widehat{\sigma}(P)$ is true if and only if $\widehat{\sigma}(\tau(P))$ is true. We will not show how to do this translation (see any of the references on mechanical theorem-proving given at the end of the chapter). We will from now on assume we are looking at a CNF-proposition of the form

$$C_1 \,\&\, C_2 \,\&\, \ldots \,\&\, C_n.$$

Theorem 8.3 (*The resolution principle*) Given a CNF-proposition as above, suppose there are C_i and C_j, $i \neq j$, of the form:

$$
\begin{aligned}
C_i &= (p \vee l_1 \vee \ldots \vee l_m) \\
C_j &= (\sim p \vee l_1' \vee \ldots \vee l_{m'}')
\end{aligned}
$$

(possibly reordering the literals in C_i and C_j). Define a new clause:

$$C_i \square C_j = l_1 \vee \ldots \vee l_m \vee l_1' \vee \ldots \vee l_{m'}'.$$

Then

$$C_1 \,\&\, C_2 \,\&\, \ldots \,\&\, C_n \;\Rightarrow\; C_1 \,\&\, C_2 \,\&\, \ldots \,\&\, C_n \,\&\, (C_i \square C_j)$$

is valid.

$C_i \square C_j$ is called the *resolvent* of C_i and C_j; C_i and C_j are called its *parents*. In case $m = m' = 0$, so that $C_i \square C_j$ is empty, it is written as "$\square$".

Theorem 8.4 If the CNF-proposition above has $\square$ as a resolvent of any two clauses, then it is unsatisfiable.

These two theorems, together with Theorem 8.2, suggest a method for proving CNF-proposition's unsatisfiable:

Definition 8.9 (*The resolution method*) To prove a CNF-proposition P unsatisfiable, do as follows: Repeatedly apply the resolution principle (choosing the parent clauses from among the clauses in P as well as the resolvents produced in previous steps) until one of the following occurs:

1. $\square$ is derived. Stop and announce that P is unsatisfiable.

2. No new resolvents can be found. Stop and announce that P is satisfiable.

Theorem 8.5 The resolution method is *sound* in the sense that whatever result it announces is correct; it is also *complete* in the sense that if P is unsatisfiable, it is possible to derive "$\square$".

Resolution is the basis for computation in PROLOG (considering here only variable-free programs). To see this, observe first that a PROLOG clause

$$(\texttt{infer } P \texttt{ from } Q \ \ldots \ R),$$

which in propositional logic would be written

$$(Q \ \& \ \ldots \ \& \ R) \Rightarrow P,$$

is equivalent to the clause[6]

$$P \vee \sim Q \vee \ldots \vee \sim R.$$

Thus, PROLOG clauses can be regarded as the clause's of CNF-proposition's.

An entire PROLOG program consists of a list of such clauses, $C_1 \ \& \ C_2 \ \& \ \ldots \ \& \ C_n$, together with a query, $(\texttt{infer? } G_1 \ \ldots \ G_m)$. This program may be regarded as the proposition

$$(C_1 \ \& \ C_2 \ \& \ \ldots \ \& \ C_n) \Rightarrow (G_1 \ \& \ \ldots \ \& \ G_m).$$

To show this is valid is to show its negation unsatisfiable. Its negation is

$$\sim ((C_1 \ \& \ C_2 \ \& \ \ldots \ \& \ C_n) \Rightarrow (G_1 \ \& \ \ldots \ \& \ G_m)),$$

which can be shown equivalent to[7]

$$C_1 \ \& \ C_2 \ \& \ \ldots \ \& \ C_n \ \& \sim (G_1 \ \& \ \ldots \ \& \ G_m),$$

which is equivalent to

$$C_1 \ \& \ C_2 \ \& \ \ldots \ \& \ C_n \ \& \ (\sim G_1 \vee \ldots \vee \sim G_m).$$

We have already shown each of the PROLOG clauses to be equivalent to a CNF clause, so this is a CNF-proposition. The resolution method can therefore be applied to it.

As an example, let us return to the code of Section 8.2.2. Abbreviating

---

[6]In general, $Q \Rightarrow P$ is equivalent to $P \vee \sim Q$; the reader may want to use truth tables to prove this.

[7]Again, this is a simple fact of propositional logic which can be proven via truth tables.

goals by single letters ("i" for "imokay," etc.), the code was:

```
-> (infer i from y h)
-> (infer y from t)
-> (infer h)
-> (infer t)
-> (infer? i)
```

This program is equivalent to this CNF-proposition, obtained, as just explained, by negating the query and transforming each PROLOG clause to the equivalent CNF clause (and numbering each one):

$$
\begin{aligned}
(C_1) \quad & (i \vee \sim y \vee \sim h) \\
(C_2) \quad & \& \, (y \vee \sim t) \\
(C_3) \quad & \& \, h \\
(C_4) \quad & \& \, t \\
(C_5) \quad & \& \sim i
\end{aligned}
$$

The first step of resolution resolves C_1 and C_5:

$$
(C_6) \quad \& \, (\sim y \vee \sim h)
$$

Next, resolve C_6 and C_2:

$$
(C_7) \quad \& \, (\sim t \vee \sim h)
$$

Next, C_7 and C_4:

$$
(C_8) \quad \& \sim h
$$

Finally, C_8 and C_3:

$$
(C_9) \quad \& \, \square,
$$

refuting the proposition, and thereby showing the PROLOG program to be valid (i.e., showing that the query can be deduced from the clauses).

Resolution can be very inefficient, as there are in general many different resolvents available at each step. One way the PROLOG designers have attempted to deal with this potential inefficiency is by restricting the class of clauses that can be asserted:

Definition 8.10 A *Horn clause* is a clause containing no more than one positive-literal.

All CNF clause's derived from PROLOG clauses have a single positive-literal, and zero or more negative-literal's. The query contains only negative-literal's. Thus, PROLOG clauses are Horn clauses. Horn clauses are more amenable to resolution, because in each clause only one literal is a candidate to be cancelled by a negative literal.

8.6.2   FIRST-ORDER PREDICATE LOGIC

Propositional logic is concerned with how arguments are formed by combining basic propositions using logical connectives like disjunction and negation. However, these basic propositions are not *about* anything. First-order logic deals with assertions that describe properties of values drawn from some universe. These assertions, called *formulas*, are defined by the grammar:

formula	$\longrightarrow$	t | f | atomic-formula
	|	formula & formula | formula $\vee$ formula
	|	formula $\Rightarrow$ formula | $\sim$ formula | (formula)
	|	$\forall$ variable.formula | $\exists$ variable.formula
atomic-formula	$\longrightarrow$	predicate | (predicate expression*)
expression	$\longrightarrow$	variable | optr | (optr expression*)
predicate	$\longrightarrow$	name (usually p, q, r, or s)
variable	$\longrightarrow$	name (usually x, y, or z)
optr	$\longrightarrow$	name (usually f or g)

The symbols $\forall$ and $\exists$ are called the *universal* and *existential* quantifiers, respectively. Formula $\forall x.(p\ x)$ should be read: "For all x, $(p\ x)$ is true," and $\exists x.(p\ x)$ as: "There is at least one x such that $(p\ x)$ is true." Some typical statements in first-order logic are:

$$(\forall x.(p\ (f\ (g\ x)))) \Rightarrow \exists y.(p\ (f\ y))$$

$$(\forall x.(p\ x)) \Rightarrow \exists x.(p\ x)$$

$$(\exists x.(p\ x)) \Rightarrow \forall x.(p\ x).$$

The definition of *validity* here is not obvious and is somewhat too technical to present. Intuitively, the first two examples above are valid, while the third is not. In general, a formula is *valid* if it is true regardless of the meanings of the operations and predicates occurring in it. It is *satisfiable* if some meaning can be assigned to its operations and predicates so as to make it true; otherwise, it is *unsatisfiable*. It still holds true that a formula F is valid if and only if $\sim F$ is unsatisfiable.

It is also not obvious here how to prove validity or unsatisfiability, even disregarding questions of efficiency. It turns out that the notions of conjunctive normal form and resolution can be generalized to obtain a more general resolution method that is still sound and complete. First, here is the generalization of CNF to first-order logic:

CNF-formula	$\longrightarrow$	prefix matrix
prefix	$\longrightarrow$	quant*
quant	$\longrightarrow$	$\forall$ variable.
matrix	$\longrightarrow$	(clause) | (clause) & matrix
clause	$\longrightarrow$	literal | literal $\vee$ clause

literal $\longrightarrow$ positive-literal | negative-literal
positive-literal $\longrightarrow$ atomic-formula
negative-literal $\longrightarrow$ $\sim$ atomic-formula

The list of universally quantified variables in the prefix of a CNF-formula must include all variables occurring in the matrix. An important consequence of this is that we are allowed to rename the variables in individual clauses, because (writing $\equiv$ for "is equivalent to"):

$$\forall x.(C_1 \ \& \ C_2) \equiv (\forall x.C_1) \ \& \ (\forall x.C_2) \equiv (\forall x.C_1) \ \& \ (\forall y.C_2') \equiv \forall x.\forall y.(C_1 \ \& \ C_2'),$$

where C_2' is C_2 with all x's replaced by y's.

The resolution method for proving unsatisfiability of CNF-formula's is based on two theorems similar to those that justified resolution of CNF-proposition's. Again assume we are looking at a typical CNF-formula F of the form:

$$C_1 \ \& \ C_2 \ \& \ \ldots \ \& \ C_n.$$

Theorem 8.6 (*The resolution principle*[8]) Given F as above, suppose there are C_i and C_j, $i \neq j$, having no variables in common (renaming variables if necessary):

$$C_i = (p \lor l_1 \lor \ldots \lor l_m)$$
$$C_j = (\sim q \lor l_1' \lor \ldots \lor l_{m'}')$$

(possibly reordering the literals in C_i and C_j), and p and q are unifiable via σ. Define a new clause:

$$C_i \square C_j = (\hat{\sigma}(l_1) \lor \ldots \lor \hat{\sigma}(l_m) \lor \hat{\sigma}(l_1') \lor \ldots \lor \hat{\sigma}(l_{m'}')).$$

Then

$$F \Rightarrow F \ \& \ (C_i \square C_j).$$

Again, if $m = m' = 0$, write $C_i \square C_j$ as "$\square$".

Theorem 8.7 If F has $\square$ as a resolvent of any two clauses, then it is unsatisfiable.

As for CNF-propositions, these two theorems imply a method for proving unsatisfiability of CNF-formulas: Apply the resolution principle until $\square$ can be derived.

This method can in turn be applied to prove validity of arbitrary formula's. For any formula F, a CNF-formula $\tau(F)$ can be constructed such that F is

---

[8]Technically, what we define here is *binary* resolution. *Full* resolution is more complicated, especially notationally, though the idea is the same. Binary resolution is adequate for our purposes, but it is, in principle, strictly less powerful than full resolution; in particular, the analog of the completeness result of Theorem 8.5 is true only for full resolution.

(un)satisfiable if and only if $\tau(F)$ is (un)satisfiable.[9] To prove the validity of any F, apply the resolution method to $\tau(\sim F)$.

How does this relate to PROLOG? As in the propositional case, each PRO-LOG clause can be regarded as equivalent to a CNF-formula, or, more specifically, to a Horn clause (Definition 8.10). In particular,

$$(\text{infer } G \text{ from } H \ \dots \ I)$$

is interpreted as:

$$\forall \vec{x}.(H \ \& \ \dots \ \& \ I \Rightarrow G)$$

(where $\vec{x}$ includes all variables occurring in G, H, ..., I), which is equivalent to:

$$\forall \vec{x}.(\sim H \lor \dots \lor \sim I \lor G).$$

The program as a whole, consisting of clauses C_1, ..., C_n and query $(\text{infer?}$ $G_1 \ \dots \ G_m)$ is interpreted as the assertion:

$$C_1 \ \& \ \dots \ \& \ C_n \Rightarrow \exists \vec{z}.(G_1 \ \& \ \dots \ \& \ G_m)$$

($\vec{z}$ containing all the variables in the G_i). Negating this yields:

$$\begin{aligned} &\sim (C_1 \ \& \ \dots \ \& \ C_n \Rightarrow \exists \vec{z}.(G_1 \ \& \ \dots \ \& \ G_m)) \\ \equiv \ & C_1 \ \& \ \dots \ \& \ C_n \ \& \sim \exists \vec{z}.(G_1 \ \& \ \dots \ \& \ G_m) \\ \equiv \ & C_1 \ \& \ \dots \ \& \ C_n \ \& \ \forall \vec{z}.\sim (G_1 \ \& \ \dots \ \& \ G_m) \\ \equiv \ & C_1 \ \& \ \dots \ \& \ C_n \ \& \ \forall \vec{z}.(\sim G_1 \lor \dots \lor \sim G_m) \end{aligned}$$

This is not quite a CNF-formula, because it contains embedded quantifiers:

$$= \forall \vec{x}.C_1{}' \ \& \ \dots \ \& \ \forall \vec{y}.C_n{}' \ \& \ \forall \vec{z}.(\sim G_1 \lor \dots \lor \sim G_m)$$

But we are justified in pulling all the variables to the front, so:

$$\equiv \forall \vec{x}.\dots.\forall \vec{y}.\forall \vec{z}.(C_1{}' \ \& \ \dots \ \& \ C_n{}' \ \& \ (\sim G_1 \lor \dots \lor \sim G_m)),$$

which is a CNF-formula.

In summary, by simply negating the query, a PROLOG program can be regarded as the CNF-formula which is the negation of the assertion made implicitly by the program. Refuting this formula is equivalent to satisfying the query. Because it is a CNF-formula, the resolution method is directly applicable.

We now give several examples illustrating this. The reader should compare the resolution refutations to the PROLOG computations. All the examples are based on the member predicate, which we abbreviate as "mem" throughout. We start with a simple forward use of the predicate, the query:

$$(\text{infer? } (\text{mem } 3 \ (\text{cons } 4 \ (\text{cons } 3 \ \text{nil}))))$$

---

[9] Again, the complexity of the translation puts it beyond the scope of this presentation. Note that the translation is not as strong as for propositional logic: F and $\tau(F)$ are not, in general, equivalent.

The two clauses for member together with this query correspond to the formula:

$$\begin{aligned}
(\quad & \forall X. \ \forall L. \ (\text{mem X (cons X L)}) \\
\& \quad & \forall X. \forall Y. \forall M. \ (\text{mem X M}) \ \Rightarrow \ (\text{mem X (cons Y M))} \ ) \\
\Rightarrow \quad & (\text{mem 3 (cons 4 (cons 3 nil)))}
\end{aligned}$$

After negating the query and transforming to conjunctive normal form (and omitting the quantifiers as redundant):

$$\begin{aligned}
(1) \quad & & (\text{mem X (cons X L)))} \\
(2) \quad & \& & [(\text{mem X (cons Y M)}) \lor \sim (\text{mem X M))}] \\
(3) \quad & \& & \sim (\text{mem 3 (cons 4 (cons 3 nil)))}
\end{aligned}$$

We can now follow the refutation procedure:

$$\begin{aligned}
(4) \quad & \& & \sim (\text{mem 3 (cons 3 nil))} \ \ (= 3 \Box 2) \\
(5) \quad & \& & \Box \ \ (= 4 \Box 1)
\end{aligned}$$

Our next example is the refutation of the query:

$$(\text{infer? (mem 3 L) (mem 4 L)}).$$

The first three clauses give the translation of the program; variables are renamed when resolving with (1) or (2):

$$\begin{aligned}
(1) \quad & & (\text{mem X (cons X L)}) \\
(2) \quad & \& & [(\text{mem X (cons Y M)}) \lor \sim (\text{mem X M))}] \\
(3) \quad & \& & [\sim (\text{mem 3 L}) \lor \sim (\text{mem 4 L})] \\
(4) \quad & \& & \sim (\text{mem 4 (cons 3 L1))} \\
& & & (= 3 \Box 1 = \hat{\sigma}(\sim (\text{mem 4 L)}), \ \text{where} \ \sigma = \{X1 \mapsto 3, L \mapsto (\text{cons 3 L1})\}) \\
(5) \quad & \& & \sim (\text{mem 4 L1}) \\
& & & (= 4 \Box 2 = \hat{\sigma}(\sim (\text{mem X2 M2)}), \ \text{where} \ \sigma = \{X2 \mapsto 4, Y2 \mapsto 3, M2 \mapsto L1\}) \\
(6) \quad & \& & \Box \ (= 5 \Box 1, \ \text{where} \ \sigma = \{X3 \mapsto 4, L1 \mapsto (\text{cons 4 L3})\})
\end{aligned}$$

The goal has been satisfied, or rather its negation has been refuted. The "answer" — the list L — can now be computed by composing the unifying substitutions that were used in the refutation.

The resolution method does not prescribe any particular strategy for choosing clauses to resolve. Indeed, an implementation may incorrectly choose clauses so as to miss a proof that exists, as in this attempt to solve the same query:

$$\begin{aligned}
(1) \quad & & (\text{mem X (cons X L)))} \\
(2) \quad & \& & [(\text{mem X (cons Y M)}) \lor \sim (\text{mem X M})] \\
(3) \quad & \& & [\sim (\text{mem 3 L}) \lor \sim (\text{mem 4 L})] \\
(4) \quad & \& & [\sim (\text{mem 3 M1}) \lor \sim (\text{mem 4 (cons Y1 M1))}] \\
& & & (= 3 \Box 2, \ \text{where} \ \sigma = \{X1 \mapsto 3, L \mapsto (\text{cons Y1 M1})\}) \\
(5) \quad & \& & [\sim (\text{mem 3 M2}) \lor \sim (\text{mem 4 (cons Y1 (cons Y2 M2)))}] \\
& & & (= 4 \Box 2, \ \text{where} \ \sigma = \{X2 \mapsto 3, M1 \mapsto (\text{cons Y2 M2})\})
\end{aligned}$$

We can continue in this way, generating larger clauses *ad infinitum.* Thus, although resolution is in principle complete — any unsatisfiable CNF-formula can be proven so by a judicious choice of resolvents — any particular implementation may fail to be by repeatedly making injudicious choices. The PROLOG evaluation mechanism is an example. It is PROLOG's failure to provide a fully general strategy for performing resolution that accounts for the inconsistencies between the logical and procedural interpretations.

To better understand this, think of all possible resolutions as forming a tree. The root contains the original set of clauses, and the children of node N are labeled by the resolvents of clauses occurring at or above N. The completeness of resolution simply says that if the original set of clauses is unsatisfiable, $\square$ occurs somewhere in the tree. It remains the responsibility of the implementation to *search the tree* in such a way as to find the $\square$. A breadth-first (level-order) search would certainly suffice; a depth-first (pre-order) search might not, since it may get lost following an infinite branch.

PROLOG evaluation can be viewed in exactly this way. The tree in question is not precisely the one just described, but a smaller one:

Definition 8.11 A PROLOG *resolution search tree* for a CNF-formula C_1 & ... & C_n & Q (each C_i and Q Horn clauses) is defined as follows:

- The root is labeled with Q.

- The children of node N are labeled with resolvents of pairs of clauses (Q', C_i), Q' occurring in the tree at or above N, and C_i one of the clauses $C_1, \ldots, C_n$.

- The order of the children of N is determined by the parents of each resolvent. Children occurring to the left are those whose first parent is the most recently generated clause (i.e., lowest in the tree), whose second parent comes earliest in the list $C_1, \ldots, C_n$, and whose resolving literal occurs furthest to the left.

These trees are quite huge. A small part of the tree corresponding to the last resolution example is presented in Figure 8.16. In that tree, we have labeled each edge with the clauses resolved (it is possible to get two different resolvents from the same pair of clauses, by resolving on different literals). The ellipses are used to indicate places where not all the children of a node are presented. All nodes have children, even when none are shown, except, of course, the one node labeled "$\square$".

Despite the many restrictions on the form of this tree (especially the restriction on the parents of resolvents), it can be shown that it is also complete: if C_1 & ... & C_n & Q is unsatisfiable, the tree contains $\square$. PROLOG computation can be regarded as searching for $\square$ in this tree. However, its search is depth-first, and that is why it sometimes fails to find a solution when one exists. For example, in the middle of Figure 8.16 the beginning of an infinite branch can

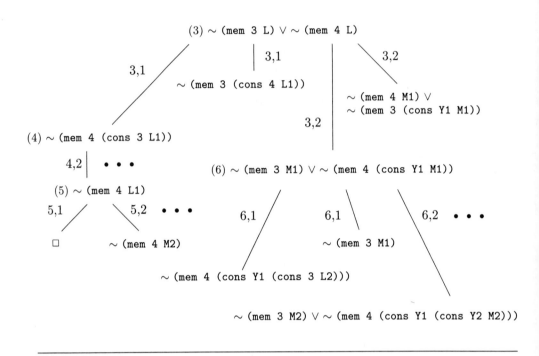

Figure 8.16: Part of a PROLOG resolution search tree

be seen; if clauses (1) and (2) (those defining mem) were exchanged, this would be the leftmost branch and a depth-first traversal would follow it into oblivion. The reader is invited to present these re-ordered clauses and the query to the PROLOG interpreter and observe that it does, indeed, go into an infinite loop; by instrumenting the interpreter, you can even see that the generated subgoals correspond exactly to those given along that branch of the tree.

8.7 Summary

PROLOG is the best known exemplar of the concept of logic programming. The PROLOG programmer programs by writing assertions, and the PROLOG interpreter attempts to validate those assertions, in the process computing values. PROLOG has attracted many avid proponents and is probably the leading language for artificial intelligence after LISP. It has also been the subject of research aimed at producing a more expressive logic programming language and at bringing the procedural interpretation more in line with the logical interpretation.

8.7.1 GLOSSARY

closed-world assumption. The assumption that the clauses in a PROLOG program constitute a complete picture of the world, insofar as the predicates it names are concerned. This justifies the rule of **negation as failure**, whereby a goal that cannot be proven is thereby assumed to be false, a central tenet of PROLOG programming.

conjunctive normal form, or clause form. The subset of first-order formulas of the form $\forall \vec{x}.C_1 \& \ldots \& C_m$, where the C_i are **clauses** of the form $l_1 \lor \ldots \lor l_p$, each l_j an atomic formula or the negation of an atomic formula. This is a "normal form" in the sense that any first-order formula can be translated to clause form in such a way that unsatisfiability is preserved.

the cut. A special PROLOG goal, written as an exclamation mark (!), which cannot be backtracked over. That is, if it appears in the goal list of a clause, and the goals that follow it are not satisfied, it causes the goal for which the clause was invoked to immediately fail. It is used to control backtracking, primarily for efficiency, but also to implement a kind of negation, as in the definition of `not-equal`.

difference lists. Lists represented in the form

```
(diff (cons a (cons b ( ··· (cons z X) ··· ))) X).
```

Such lists have many interesting uses; see Sterling and Shapiro [1986, Chapter 15] for a particularly good discussion.

first-order logic. A logic that subsumes propositional logic by permitting universal and existential quantification over the elements of some domain of values.

Horn clause. A clause $l_1 \lor l_2 \lor \ldots \lor l_n$ as in conjunctive normal form, with the additional restriction that at most one of the l_i is a "positive literal," i.e., an unnegated atomic proposition. The PROLOG clause (`infer` l_1 `from` $l_2 \ldots l_n$) is equivalent to the Horn clause $l_1 \lor \sim l_2 \lor \ldots \lor \sim l_n$.

Without the restriction on the presence of positive literals, such clauses would be equivalent in power to arbitrary first-order formulas, as explained for conjunctive normal form. The restriction makes the search for proofs much more efficient, at the cost of a loss of expressive power.

logic programming. A programming language concept in which programs are regarded as assertions in a logic, and computation corresponds to proving or satisfying the assertions. Logic programming languages differ in the logic on which they are based, and in the additional, non-logical, features they include. PROLOG is by far the best known logic programming language, based upon the logic of Horn clauses; its most prominent non-logical feature is the cut.

logical variable. The name sometimes used for PROLOG variables, to emphasize the difference between them and the variables in ordinary programming languages. Logical variables get bound to values by the unification process, whereas ordinary variables get their values by assignment or binding during function calls.

mechanical theorem-proving, or automated deduction. The study of how to program computers to solve mathematical problems, usually assuming those problems are stated in first-order logic. The resolution method is the best known, but by no means the only, method in this area.

occurs check. The test made, when unifying a variable with a nonvariable expression, that the variable does not occur in the expression. Technically, this test must be made for the unification process to be correct. However, because this test is expensive and the situation rarely occurs in practice, most real PROLOG implementations omit it.

propositional logic. The logic that deals with the combination, by way of *logical connectives* such as & and ∨, of assertions whose internal structure is not considered.

resolution. A method of proving the unsatisfiability of first-order formulas, presented as sets of clauses. It uses a single, easily programmed proof rule — the resolution principle — which can be stated in its simplest form as: from $(p \lor q)$ and $(\sim p \lor r)$, infer $(q \lor r)$. Resolution is a *complete* method in that any unsatisfiable first-order formula in conjunctive normal form can be refuted if the method is applied correctly, given enough time.

unification. The process whereby two expressions containing variables are "matched up." The result of unification is a substitution that, applied to the two expressions, makes them equal.

8.7.2 FURTHER READING

We often recommend going to the source, and in this case that would be the articles by Colmerauer, et al. [1973] and Kowalski [1974,1979a], as well as the book by Kowalski [1979b]. The very first description of PROLOG was given in the paper by Colmerauer, which describes a natural language processing system. (Three articles on the early history of PROLOG by Cohen [1988], Kowalski [1988], and Robinson [1983] name many more contributors and document the intimate connection between theorem-proving research and the development of PROLOG.)

For a general introduction to the language, the reader has a number of excellent books to choose from; the list given here is not exhaustive. The book by Kowalski, treating logic programming in general, is highly recommended. Clocksin and Mellish [1987], now in its third edition, has long been the standard introduction to PROLOG. More recent books are by Hogger [1984] and Sterling and Shapiro [1986]. The book by Maier and Warren [1988] is particularly recommended; it takes an approach similar to the present text, giving pseudo-PASCAL interpreters for various subsets of PROLOG. Rowe [1988] is a book on artificial intelligence using PROLOG; it assumes no prior knowledge of PROLOG.

Logic programming is an active research area, with frequent conferences and its own journal (the *Journal of Logic Programming*). Many PROLOG enhancements and alternative languages have been, and continue to be, proposed. The collections by Clark and Tarnlund [1982] and DeGroot and Lindstrom [1986] give the flavor of this activity. PROLOG has also been studied as a language for parallel processing; see Ringwood [1988] and the references cited there.

Automated deduction has been pursued almost as long as there have been computers; the two-volume collection edited by Siekmann and Wrightson [1983] includes the most important papers on the subject published between 1957 and 1970. The great breakthrough was the discovery of the resolution principle by Robinson [1965]; most mechanical theorem-proving programs developed since have been based on it. The books by Chang and Lee [1973], Gallier [1986] and Wos, et al. [1984] are highly recommended; the chapter on predicate calculus in Manna [1974] is also excellent. Maier and Warren [1988], cited above, contains an extensive introduction to this subject, especially as it relates to PROLOG. Along the same lines, Lloyd [1984] is an introduction to logic and theorem-proving written for the PROLOG programmer.

The blocks world is discussed in many books on artificial intelligence, including Nilsson [1980], an introductory book on AI with a strong logic orientation, Winston [1977], and Winograd [1972]. Kowalski [1979b] gives a complete discussion in the context of logic programming. As mentioned, our approach is derived from Sterling and Shapiro [1986].

8.8 Exercises

8.8.1 *LEARNING ABOUT THE LANGUAGE*

1. Finish the computation of the query for map b, begun on page 363. Give the clauses and query for map a in Figure 8.1. What happens when you evaluate the query? Give the steps of the computation.

2. Program the following predicates on lists:

   (a) `length` — (`length l n`) is true if list l has length n.

   (b) `remove` — (`remove x l m`) is true if list m is the result of removing all occurrences of x from l.

(c) `insert-sort` — (`insert-sort` l m) is true if list m is obtained from list l by insertion sorting.

(d) `flatten` — analogous to `flatten` in LISP.

3. These problems relate to the predicate `mult`:

   (a) Under exactly what circumstances will `mult` work in the backward direction?

   (b) Explain why the new version of `mult` on page 369 doesn't work.

   (c) Modify the clauses for `mult` to handle negative numbers.

4. What predicates given in the text, if any, depend upon the occurs check? (*Hint:* The easiest way to solve this is to modify the interpreter to report when the occurs check is true.)

5. Explain why `quicksort` can't be run backwards.

6. Program the following operations on difference lists; you are not allowed to simply transform them to ordinary lists:

   (a) `diffaddtoend`

   (b) `diffreverse`

   (c) `diffquicksort`

7. These problems concern the blocks world code:

   (a) Solve the problem of having two moves in a row that move the same block.

   (b) Change the representation of states to (`state` a b c), where a, b, and c are as in the current representation. Modify the program accordingly.

   (c) Represent moves by (`move` x y), meaning "move x to y," and modify the program accordingly.

   (d) How much backtracking is done by the two versions of `transform/4` (the four-argument `transform`) that work? In particular, how often do they attempt to satisfy a goal of the form (`transform` $\cdots$)?

8. The nonnegative integers can be represented as expressions of the form (`succ` (`succ` $\cdots$ (`succ` `zero`) $\cdots$)). Using this representation, and not using any built-in predicates, define: `equals`, `+`, `-` (assume `zero` minus anything is `zero`), `*`, and `/`. Use the built-in predicates to define `print-int`, which is satisfied for any such term and prints its value as an ordinary integer:

```
-> (infer? (print-int (succ (succ zero))))
2
Satisfied
```

8.8.2 LEARNING ABOUT THE INTERPRETER

9. Add a primitive predicate `not-equal`, which succeeds when it is applied to two identical integers or symbols, and fails otherwise. Incorporate it into the blocks world code, using it to replace the `different` predicate. How much of an efficiency improvement do you obtain?

Part VI

Implementation Issues

Our interpreters are slow and use far too much memory. That's okay — they were never intended to be realistic, production-quality language processors. In this section, we describe some ways they can be improved in these two areas.

To discuss the improvement of *execution speed*, we need to part from our interpreters, because the only solution is to *compile* code in the same way that PASCAL is compiled. References to variables are transformed from an environment search to just one or two machine instructions, and function calls from a search in the function environment and the creation of an environment record to just a few instructions. In Chapter 9, we discuss compilation, with particular emphasis on variable referencing and function calls. SCHEME turns out to be an especially interesting case, because of its nested scopes; PASCAL is, in turn, an interesting subcase of SCHEME, since it has nested scopes but not upward funargs.

We then look at *memory management*, returning to the interpreters in order to give a more concrete treatment. The problem is that they allocate memory (via *new*) continually throughout a computation, as if the available memory were infinite. Of course, it isn't, and eventually the interpreter will run out of memory and will crash (perhaps the reader has experienced this). We can go a long way toward solving this problem by realizing that many of the records that are dynamically allocated become *inactive* — or, in the lingo, *garbage* — at some time after their allocation and could be recycled. Thus, instead of calling *new* for a new record, the interpreter should first attempt to find a recycled record and reuse it. In Chapter 10, the LISP interpreter is modified to do this in three different ways.

It cannot be denied that users of the languages covered in this book will probably pay some penalty in both time and space as compared to PASCAL or other traditional languages. It will not be nearly as heavy a penalty as imposed by our interpreters, but it will be something. The compilation and memory management techniques described in this part, and others being studied by researchers and compiler developers, can greatly reduce and perhaps eliminate this penalty. Alternative, language-oriented, computer architectures show promise, as well. In any case, concerning questions of efficiency the well-educated programmer should always follow the advice to "avoid premature optimization," and that applies to choice of language as well as programming methods. Keep in mind that the definition of "acceptably efficient" depends upon the problem at hand; in many cases, programmer efficiency is a more important consideration than machine efficiency.

Chapter 9

Compilation

Efficient execution of any of the languages covered in this book demands that the programs be translated to machine language — or at least to some abstract machine language that can be efficiently interpreted — rather than having source programs directly interpreted as we have been doing. The techniques discussed in this chapter apply to all our languages, with exceptions as noted, excluding PROLOG. PROLOG compilation is a specialized topic beyond the scope of this book.

We present, more or less formally, several translations from languages we have studied to an invented machine language. Included are two translations of the language of Chapter 1, a translation of SCHEME, and a translation of a new language intermediate between these two. Following a brief description of the machine language, the presentation is structured in two large chunks, each consisting of two subchunks:

1. Translation to machine language, not using a stack:

   (a) Translation of the language of Chapter 1, including control operations and value-op's, variable references, and calls to user-defined functions. Here is introduced the very important notion of an *activation record*, essentially the machine language representation of an environment. Like environments (that is, *ENV*'s), activation records are allocated each time a user-defined function is called. We assume a machine language instruction, called ALLOC, that allocates memory, like *new* in PASCAL.

   (b) Translation of SCHEME. The nested scopes of SCHEME require a change in the representation of activation records (just as it did for *ENV*'s) and, accordingly, changes in variable referencing and function call (that is, closure application).

2. Translation to machine language, using a stack:

   (a) A very small change in the translation of Chapter 1 permits the elimination of the `ALLOC` instruction by placing all activation records on a stack.

(b) The same technique cannot be applied to SCHEME, not because it has nested scopes, but because it has first-class functions ("upward funargs"). PASCAL, for example, though it has nested scopes (and therefore has activation records similar to SCHEME's), can be executed using a stack for activation records. The structure of the PASCAL run-time stack is presented by way of a new language that extends the language of Chapter 1 with nested function definitions.

The translations of other languages not covered in this chapter (except PRO-LOG) are given as exercises. However, for the most part they are straightforward adaptations of Chapter 1 compilation (or, in the case of SASL, of SCHEME compilation). Indeed, the principal operational difference between Chapter 1 and these other languages is that they all use a heap to dynamically allocate data objects; Chapter 10 treats the management of heap memory.

9.1   Machine Language

We propose a simple machine language. It employs a stack for intermediate results; many instructions (especially arithmetic ones) have the top of stack as an implicit operand. The reader should have little difficulty rephrasing our treatment of compilation in her favorite machine language.

9.1.1   REGISTERS

Our machine has five registers, each a full word wide:

- **rv** ("return value") — *Every expression places its value into* **rv**.

- **sp** ("stack pointer") — A large area of memory is reserved for a stack, with **sp** pointing to the *next available location*.

- **scr** — a general-purpose "scratch" register.

- **ar** ("activation record") — to be explained in Section 9.2.

- **ds** ("display") — to be explained in Section 9.5.1.

There is also a program counter, of course, but there is no need to mention it explicitly.

9.1.2 INSTRUCTIONS

In the following list, c's represent integer constants, r's (possibly subscripted) registers, m's memory locations, and l's code labels. $C(r)$ (resp. $C(m)$) denotes the contents of register r (resp. memory location m). Take note of the order of operands, especially in arithmetic instructions.

LOAD	m,r	;	$r := C(m)$
LOADI	c,r	;	$r := c$
LOADL	l,r	;	$r :=$ address of code labeled l
STORE	r,m	;	$m := C(r)$
MOVE	r_1,r_2	;	$r_2 := C(r_1)$
ADD		;	$\mathbf{rv} :=$ top of stack $+ C(\mathbf{rv})$
SUB		;	$\mathbf{rv} :=$ top of stack $- C(\mathbf{rv})$
MULT		;	$\mathbf{rv} :=$ top of stack $\times C(\mathbf{rv})$
DIV		;	$\mathbf{rv} :=$ top of stack $\div C(\mathbf{rv})$
ADDI	c,r	;	$r := C(r) + c$
SUBI	c,r	;	$r := C(r) - c$
CMPEQ		;	if top of stack $= C(\mathbf{rv})$ then $\mathbf{rv} := 1$ else $\mathbf{rv} := 0$
CMPLT		;	if top of stack $< C(\mathbf{rv})$ then $\mathbf{rv} := 1$ else $\mathbf{rv} := 0$
JMP	l	;	goto l
JMPIFZ	l	;	if $C(\mathbf{rv}) = 0$ then goto l,
		;	else proceed to next instruction
PUSH	r	;	place $C(r)$ on top of stack
POP	r	;	pop top of stack into r
ALLOC	c	;	allocate a block of c words,
		;	and place its address in $\mathbf{rv}$

The zero-address arithmetic and comparison instructions also pop the stack.

The instruction ALLOC is analogous to PASCAL's *new* procedure. Admittedly, no real machine has such an instruction; instead the reader may prefer to think of it as a subroutine call. It will, in part, be eliminated in the second half of this chapter.

9.1.3 OPERANDS

To be more precise about the legal operands, the four types — constants, code labels, registers, and memory locations — are defined as follows:

Constants: Any integer constant, positive or negative.

Code labels: Instructions will be labeled with names beginning with upper-case letters and followed by colons.

Instructions whose operands are code labels can also use memory location operands.

Registers: The registers have been listed previously.

Memory locations: There are three forms of operands denoting memory locations:

> **Global variables:** We assume that each global variable has been assigned a memory location, and we will use the variable name to refer to that location in memory-referencing instructions.
>
> **Register-addressed:** The notation "$(r)\pm i$" denotes the address $C(r)\pm i$; if i=0, we will just write "(r)". (As an example, the operand "$(sp)-1$" denotes the address of the top item on the stack.)
>
> **Indirect:** If M is an operand of one of the two previous types, then "$(M)\pm i$" is the address obtained by adding (or subtracting) i to $C(M)$; again, i can be omitted if it is zero. (So, if the top item on the stack is an address, "$((sp)-1)$" denotes that address.)

The machine is word-addressable, and a word is large enough to hold an integer or a pointer.

9.2   Translation of Language of Chapter 1

Our intention is to explain how to translate any program in the language of Chapter 1 to machine language. The translation will be presented by giving the machine language corresponding to each syntactic structure. Machine language is given in a typewriter font, with the exception that code labels set in italics represent places where actual labels must be filled in by the compiler; this choice must be made, of course, so that each label in a program is unique. Phrases in Roman type, enclosed in angle brackets, denote code that cannot be given without more information, such as the translations of subexpressions.

There is a register called **rv**, for return value, in which the value of *every* expression is to be placed. We start with the simplest kind of expression, an integer constant:

c	$\Rightarrow$	LOADI	c,rv

References to global variables are equally simple; recall our assumption that they have been assigned locations:

x (x global)	$\Rightarrow$	LOAD	x,rv

To generate code for references to formal parameters, we must know about activation records. That discussion can be postponed briefly in favor of giving the translations of some control operations:

```
(begin e₁ ... eₙ)        ⇒        <code for e₁ >
                                  <code for e₂ >
                                       ⋮
                                  <code for eₙ >
```

```
(if e₁ e₂ e₃)            ⇒        <code for e₁ >
                                  JMPIFZ   l₁
                                  <code for e₂ >
                                  JMP      l₂
                         l₁:      <code for e₃ >
                         l₂:
```

```
(while e₁ e₂)            ⇒  l₁:   <code for e₁ >
                                  JMPIFZ   l₂
                                  <code for e₂ >
                                  JMP      l₁
                         l₂:
```

```
(set x e) (x global)     ⇒        <code for e >
                                  STORE    rv,x
```

Value-op's are easy to translate. We give three and leave the rest as exercises:

```
(+ e₁ e₂)                ⇒        <code for e₁ >
                                  PUSH     rv
                                  <code for e₂ >
                                  ADD      ; rv := top of stack + (rv)
```

```
(- e₁ e₂)                ⇒        <code for e₁ >
                                  PUSH     rv
                                  <code for e₂ >
                                  SUB      ; rv := top of stack - (rv)
```

```
(= e₁ e₂)                ⇒        <code for e₁ >
                                  PUSH     rv
                                  <code for e₂ >
                                  CMPEQ
```

As an example, the expression:

    (if (= x 2) (+ x 4) (begin (set y 5) (* x 7))),

where x and y are global variables, is translated to:

```
            LOAD      x,rv              ; x
            PUSH      rv
            LOADI     2,rv              ; 2
            CMPEQ                       ; (= x 2)
            JMPIFZ    L1
            LOAD      x,rv              ; x
            PUSH      rv
            LOADI     4,rv              ; 4
            ADD                        ; (+ x 4)
            JMP       L2
    L1:     LOADI     5,rv              ; 5
            STORE     rv,y              ; (set y 5)
            LOAD      x,rv              ; x
            PUSH      rv
            LOADI     7,rv              ; 7
            MULT                       ; (* x 7)
    L2:
```

Obviously, not much can be done without user-defined functions. To translate these, we need to describe the structure of *activation records*, or *AR*'s, which are, in effect, the machine language representations of environments. Assume the following definition has been given:

$$\text{(define f } (x_1 \ \ldots \ x_n) \text{ e)}$$

Generally, the AR for an invocation of f contains the actual parameters for that call. However, unlike an *ENV*, an AR is a *contiguous block of memory* — not a linked list — and contains no variable names. Modulo some information to be described shortly, the AR for f looks like this, each box representing a machine word:[1]

	Actual		Actual
to be explained	parameter	$\cdots$	parameter
	1		n

---

[1] All parameters occupy a single word. This is fine for Chapter 1, where the only values are integers. It also applies to our other languages, because the *values* that would be placed on the stack are actually *pointers*, e.g., *SEXP*'s in LISP, or *CLUVALUE*'s in CLU. It would not apply to PASCAL, where actual parameters can occupy more than one word, but neither is it hard to make the generalization to PASCAL. As long as the offset of each actual parameter within the AR can be determined at compile-time, as is the case for PASCAL, the kind of translation we give will work.

The address of the AR for the current function invocation will be maintained in the register ar (maintained, that is, by the action of function call and return). Thus, the address of variable x_i is $C(\text{ar}) + 2 + (i - 1)$. Code that references variable x_i has one of these two forms:

$$x_i \qquad \Rightarrow \qquad \texttt{LOAD} \qquad \texttt{(ar)} + 2 + (i - 1), \texttt{rv}$$

$$\begin{aligned} \texttt{(set } x_i \texttt{ e)} \qquad \Rightarrow \qquad &\texttt{<code for e>}\\ &\texttt{STORE} \qquad \texttt{rv,(ar)} + 2 + (i - 1) \end{aligned}$$

Note that the quantity $2 + (i - 1)$ is a *static* value, i.e., a constant known at compile-time.

Function invocation has considerable work to do. It must establish the new AR for the called function and make sure ar points to it. Furthermore, it must store enough information in the new AR to allow the called function to restore ar at return time and to return to the right place. This is the purpose of the two extra slots. The actual form of an AR (for this language) is:

Return address	Dynamic link	Actual parameter 1	$\cdots$	Actual parameter n

The *return address* is the address to which the *calling* routine would like control to be returned when the *called* function is finished. The *dynamic link* is the address of the calling routine's AR, i.e., the old contents of ar. The called function will return its value in register rv.

We can now explain the actions involved in calling f (regardless of whether the call occurs from another function or as a recursive call from f itself):

```
(f e₁ ... eₙ)    ⇒     ALLOC   n+2              ; new AR addr. -> rv
                       PUSH    rv
                       <code for e₁ >
                       STORE   rv,((sp)-1)+2 ; first actual
                         ⋮
                       <code for eₙ >
                       STORE   rv,((sp)-1)+2 + (n − 1) ; nth actual
                       LOADL   l,rv
                       STORE   rv,((sp)-1)    ; return address
                       STORE   ar,((sp)-1)+1 ; dynamic link
                       POP     ar             ; new AR -> ar
                       JMP     l_f
                 l: LOAD   (ar)+1,ar       ; restore old AR
```

where $l_\mathbf{f}$ is the label on the code for function $\mathbf{f}$. The last LOAD instruction is executed after return from $\mathbf{f}$.

Finally, the definition of $\mathbf{f}$ itself compiles to the following code:

```
(define f (x₁...xₙ) e)    ⇒  lf:  <code for e>
                                JMP      ((ar))
```

We now have a complete translation from the language of Chapter 1 to "machine language." We could now proceed in one of two ways: (1) write a simulator for this machine language — taking pains to ensure the efficiency of the simulator — and compile programs exactly according to the translation just given; or (2) recast this translation in terms of the machine language for a real machine. The latter would, of course, lead to more efficient code, but the former would probably give us a more portable system. Both procedures are followed in practice.

We close this section by giving the translation of the exponentiation function:

```
(define exp (x y) (if (= y 0) 1 (* x (exp x (- y 1)))))
```

The translation is:

```
Lexp:  LOAD    (ar)+3,rv        ; y
       PUSH    rv
       LOADI   0,rv             ; 0
       CMPEQ                    ; (= y 0)
       JMPIFZ  L1               ; if (= y 0)
       LOADI   1,rv             ; true; return 1
       JMP     Lret
L1:    LOAD    (ar)+2,rv        ; x
       PUSH    rv
       ALLOC   4                ; begin recursive call
       PUSH    rv               ; push new AR
       LOAD    (ar)+2,rv        ; x
       STORE   rv,((sp)-1)+2    ; first actual -> new AR
       LOAD    (ar)+3,rv        ; y
       PUSH    rv
       LOADI   1,rv             ; 1
       SUB                      ; (- y 1)
       STORE   rv,((sp)-1)+3    ; second actual -> new AR
```

```
        LOADL    L2,rv              ; return address
        STORE    rv,((sp)-1)        ; -> new AR
        STORE    ar,((sp)-1)+1      ; dynamic link -> new AR
        POP      ar                 ; new AR
        JMP      Lexp
L2:     LOAD     (ar)+1,ar          ; restore old AR
        MULT                        ; (* x (exp x (- y 1)))
Lret:   JMP      ((ar))             ; return to caller
```

9.3 Translation of SCHEME

The code given above for control operations and value-op's is generally still valid in SCHEME. However, SCHEME presents two features that make its compilation more interesting: nested scopes and function values. Nested scope is especially interesting, because it changes the way variables are referenced, incident to a change in the format of AR's.

Before discussing that, we can dispose of the processing of lambda's. lambda's create closures. A closure consists of two words, just as it did in the interpreter:

| Address | Address |
| of code | of AR |

The major difference from the interpreter is that these closures contain pointers to *code* rather than to expressions. The AR pointer is analogous to the *ENV* pointer. A lambda expression is translated to code that creates a closure and places its address into rv as with any value (recall that scr is just an extra general-purpose register):

(lambda (x$_1$...x$_n$) e) $\Rightarrow$	ALLOC	2	; two words for closure
	LOADL	l_e,scr	; address of body
	STORE	scr,(rv)	; -> closure
	STORE	ar,(rv)+1	; AR pointer -> closure

where l_e is the label of the code generated for the body of this lambda, as follows:

e as body of lambda $\Rightarrow$ l_e:	< code for e >
	JMP ((ar))

To understand the new format of AR's, recall how SCHEME environments in our interpreter differed from the environments of Chapter 1: There was an extra field, called *enclosing*, linking environments together. Variables were referenced by following back *enclosing* links until the enclosing environment containing the variable in question was reached (see function *findVar*). SCHEME activation records contain an analogous field, called the *static link*:

Return address	Dynamic link	Static link	Actual parameter 1	$\cdots$	Actual parameter n

Again, the register `ar` will always point to the AR for the currently executing `lambda` body. Suppose we have the expression:

$$(\text{lambda } (x_1^{(k)} \ldots x_{n_k}^{(k)})$$

$$\cdot \cdot \cdot$$

$$(\text{lambda } (x_1^{(1)} \ldots x_{n_1}^{(1)})$$
$$(\text{lambda } (x_1^{(0)} \ldots x_{n_0}^{(0)}) \text{ e})) \ldots).$$

and are currently executing within e. A reference to a variable x_i^j is processed by following static links back j times, then finding the ith actual parameter in that AR. More precisely, its address is determined by the following code, which places that address in register `scr`:

$$j \text{ times} \begin{cases} \text{MOVE} & \text{ar,scr} \\ \text{LOAD} & \text{(scr)+2,scr} \\ \vdots & \\ \text{LOAD} & \text{(scr)+2,scr} \end{cases}$$
$$\text{ADDI} \quad i+2,\text{scr}$$

Note that both i and j are static values. j is called the *lexical distance* (of the variable from its declaration), and i is the *offset*. (If $j = 0$ — so the variable is local — this computes the address by:

$$\text{MOVE} \quad \text{ar,scr}$$
$$\text{ADDI} \quad i+2,\text{scr}$$

which is the same as in the previous section except that the $i+2$ was $i+1$.)

A variable reference or `set` occurring in e for a `lambda`-bound (as opposed to global) variable is translated as follows:

x_i^j	$\Rightarrow$	< code given above >
		LOAD (scr),rv

(set x_i^j e)	$\Rightarrow$	< code for e >
		< code given above >
		STORE rv,(scr)

We now have only to show how to compile applications. In the application that follows, e_0 is not a **value-op**. Moreover, we make the following simplifying language restriction: If e_0 is not a **value-op** or control operation, it must necessarily evaluate to a closure. (In effect, this restriction amounts to decreeing that **value-op**'s are no longer assignable.)

```
(e₀ e₁ ... eₙ)    ⇒       < code for e₀ >
                          PUSH   rv            ; closure
                          ALLOC  n + 3         ; rv := addr. of new AR
                          PUSH   rv
                          <code for e₁ >
                          STORE rv,((sp)-1)+3 ; first actual
                            ⋮
                          < code for eₙ >
                          STORE rv,((sp)-1)+3 + (n − 1) ; nth actual
                          LOADL l,rv           ; return address
                          STORE rv,((sp)-1)    ; -> new AR
                          STORE ar,((sp)-1)+1  ; dynamic link
                          POP    ar            ; new AR
                          POP    rv            ; closure
                          LOAD   (rv)+1,scr    ; AR from closure is
                          STORE scr,(ar)+2     ; static link of new AR
                          JMP    ((rv))        ; code addr. from closure
                       l: LOAD  (ar)+1,ar      ; restore old AR
```

Here is an example; the subexpressions are labeled for later reference:

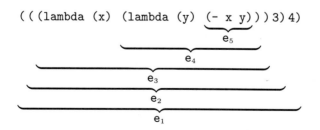

and here is the code we produce:

```
              ; begin code for e₁ (an application)
              ;    begin code for e₂ (an application)


;      begin code for e₃ (a lambda)
       ALLOC    2              ; closure
       LOADL    Le4,scr        ; body
       STORE    scr,(rv)
       STORE    ar,(rv)+1      ; static link
;      end code for e₃
;    continue code for e₂, applying e₃ to 3
       PUSH     rv             ; closure of e₃
       ALLOC    4
       PUSH     rv             ; new AR
       LOADI    3,rv           ; actual parameter
       STORE    rv,((sp)-1)+3  ; -> new AR
       LOADL    L1,rv
       STORE    rv,((sp)-1)    ; return addr. -> new AR
       STORE    ar,((sp)-1)+1  ; dyn. link -> new AR
       POP      ar             ; new AR
       POP      rv             ; closure
       LOAD     (rv)+1,scr     ; AR from closure
       STORE    scr,(ar)+2     ; static link
       JMP      ((rv))         ; code addr. from closure
L1:    LOAD     (ar)+1,ar      ; restore old AR
;    end code for e₂
; continue code for e₁, applying e₂ to 4
       PUSH     rv             ; closure of e₂
       ALLOC    4
       PUSH     rv             ; new AR
       LOADI    4,rv           ; actual parameter
       STORE    rv,((sp)-1)+3  ; -> new AR
       LOADL    L2,rv
       STORE    rv,((sp)-1)    ; return addr. -> new AR
       STORE    ar,((sp)-1)+1  ; dyn. link -> new AR
       POP      ar             ; new AR
       POP      rv             ; closure
       LOAD     (rv)+1,scr     ; AR from closure
       STORE    scr,(ar)+2     ; static link
       JMP      ((rv))         ; code addr. from closure
L2:    LOAD     (ar)+1,ar      ; restore old AR ; end code for e₁
```

The code for the body of e_3, i.e., e_4 (a `lambda`), follows:

```
Le4:   ALLOC    2                ; allocate closure
       LOADL    Le5,scr          ; code address
       STORE    scr,(rv)         ; -> closure
       STORE    ar,(rv)+1        ; env pointer -> closure
       JMP      ((ar))           ; return to caller
```

The body of e_4, i.e., e_5, is an application of a **value-op**:

```
Le5:   MOVE     ar,scr           ; compute addr. of x
       LOAD     (scr)+2,scr
       ADDI     3,scr
       LOAD     (scr),rv         ; and fetch
       PUSH     rv
       MOVE     ar,scr           ; compute addr. of y
       ADDI     3,scr
       LOAD     (scr),rv         ; and fetch
       SUB                       ; (- x y)
       JMP      ((ar))           ; return to caller
```

To make sure we're together on this, here is how e_1 would be evaluated in the interpreter:

- Since e_1 is an application, we first evaluate its operator position, e_2.

  - Since e_2 is an application, we first evaluate its operator position, e_3. It evaluates to the closure

  $$\kappa_1 = \langle\!\langle e_3, \{\} \rangle\!\rangle.$$

  - Proceed with the evaluation of e_2 by applying κ_1 to argument 3, which is to say, evaluate e_4 in environment

  $$\rho_1 = \{x \mapsto 3\}.$$

  Since e_4 is a `lambda`, return

  $$\kappa_2 = \langle\!\langle e_4, \rho_1 \rangle\!\rangle.$$

- Proceed with the evaluation of e_1 by applying κ_2 to argument 4, which is to say, evaluate e_5 in environment

$$\rho_2 = \{y \mapsto 4, x \mapsto 3\}.$$

The value -1 is returned.

Now, we trace through the code:

1. At the start, **ar** is nil.

2. Allocate a closure for e_3 and fill it in:

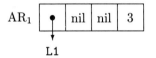

This corresponds to κ_1.

3. Allocate an AR for e_2, and fill it in with the actual parameter (3) of e_2, the return address (L1), the dynamic link from **ar** (nil), and the static link obtained from CLO_1:

$$AR_1 \quad \boxed{\;\bullet\;|\;\text{nil}\;|\;\text{nil}\;|\;3\;}$$

$$L1$$

This corresponds to ρ_1. **ar** is set to point to AR_1, and control goes to **Le4**.

4. At **Le4**, allocate the closure for e_3 and fill it in:

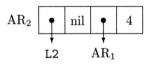

This corresponds to κ_2.

5. Return control to **L1**, where **ar** is reset to nil. **rv** points to CLO_2, the value returned from the call to **Le4**.

6. At **L1**, allocate an AR for e_1 and fill it in with the actual parameter (4) of e_1, return address L2, dynamic link (nil), and static link obtained from CLO_2:

$$AR_2 \quad \boxed{\;\bullet\;|\;\text{nil}\;|\;\bullet\;|\;4\;}$$

$$L2 \qquad AR_1$$

This corresponds to ρ_2. **ar** is set to point to AR_2, and control goes to **Le5**.

7. At Le5, the value of x (3) is loaded into rv by following the static link of AR_2 back to AR_1. The value of y (4) is loaded from AR_2 into rv. The value $3 - 4$ is placed into rv, and control returns to L2.

9.4   Stack-Allocation of AR's for the Language of Chapter 1

The mysterious ALLOC instruction can be eliminated by giving a specific scheme for allocating memory for AR's. It turns out that for Chapter 1 (and this holds also for LISP, APL, CLU, and SMALLTALK), AR's can be allocated on the stack.

The change in the code that is generated is fairly small. In the code for function application, just change the ALLOC instruction to:

```
MOVE      sp,rv
ADDI      n + 2,sp
```

Thus, rv points to the new activation record, and sp continues to point to the top of the stack (which is now just above that activation record).

Similarly, function return has an extra instruction added, which "deallocates" the activation record:

```
(define f (x₁ ... xₙ) e) ⇒  l_f:    <code for e>
                                     SUBI  n + 2,sp ; de-allocate AR
                                     JMP   ((ar))
```

Note that the dynamic link of each AR always points to the previous AR on the stack.

As an example, we illustrate the stack configurations that occur during the execution of the call (exp 3 2) after the translation to stack code has been made. As execution begins, sp points to the top of the stack, and **ar** is nil (or, at least, of no interest to us):

Immediately after the call (**exp 3 2**), it looks like this (**Lr** is the label to return to when this call is done):

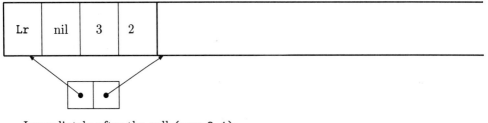

Immediately after the call (**exp 3 1**):

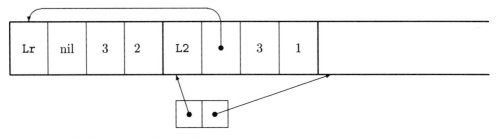

Immediately after call (**exp 3 0**):

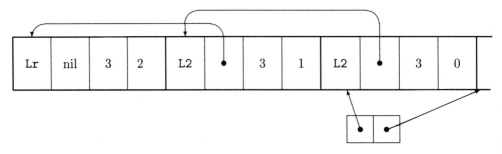

After return from (**exp 3 0**):

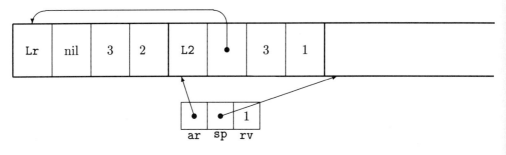

After return from (**exp 3 1**):

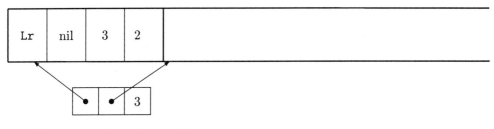

After return from (**exp 3 0**):

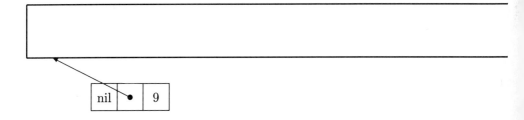

9.5 Stack-Allocation of AR's for PASCAL

PASCAL activation records look just like SCHEME's. Because PASCAL has nested scopes, a function invocation must have its own AR for its formal parameters (and local variables) and a static link to access nonlocal variables. (In PASCAL, global variables do not need to be treated specially, but they can just be regarded as local variables of the outermost scope. This would work in SCHEME as well, if global variables were all predeclared, since each could be assigned an offset in the global AR. In other words, it would be as if all the global variables were bound in a big surrounding `lambda`.)

Unlike SCHEME, on the other hand, PASCAL lacks upward function values, a significant restriction on the language's semantics which permits a significant simplification of its implementation. The problem with upward funargs is that they "capture" environments — i.e., AR's — for use at some indeterminate later time. Thus, in SCHEME, *an AR can survive the function invocation for which it was created.* This makes the use of a stack in SCHEME inappropriate, since, by definition, AR's placed on a stack are subject to destruction (the space they occupy is considered free) as soon as the call for which they were created is complete.[2] In PASCAL, an AR can never survive the call for which it was created.

To illustrate compilation of PASCAL, we define a new language with nested scopes but no function values, something between the language of Chapter 1 and SCHEME. Here is its syntax; refer to Chapter 1 for the definitions of all undefined nonterminals:

input	$\longrightarrow$	expression | fundef
fundef	$\longrightarrow$	(define function arglist local-functions body)
local-functions	$\longrightarrow$	fundef*
body	$\longrightarrow$	expression

---

[2]An obvious solution is to *copy* the AR from the stack to the closure at the time the closure is constructed. However, this solution has two drawbacks: (1) Both the AR itself and all AR's on its static link chain must be copied; this could entail considerable expense. (2) The value of a variable could be modified *after* the AR containing that variable has already been captured in a closure. For example, the following expression should print "**4**":

```
((lambda (x)
    (begin
      (set f (lambda () (print x)))
      (set x (+1 x))
      (f)))
  3)
```

Since copying AR's when forming closures results in two copies of each variable (the one in the closure and the one on the stack), assignment becomes very difficult.

In fact, SCHEME is always compiled using a stack for activation records but only after changing the definition of "activation record." Specifically, static links and values of actual parameters — the data needed to reference variables — are still placed in the heap, but "control" information — return address and dynamic link — are placed on the stack. See the exercises for more details.

As an illustration we use a program for the **fib** function, based on the well-known linear-time algorithm:

function *iterfib* (*x*: *integer*): *integer*;
var *prev, next, newnext*: *integer*;
     i: *integer*;
begin
    if *x* < 2
    then *iterfib* := *x*
    else begin
        prev := 1;
        next := 1;
        for *i* := 3 **to** *x* **do begin**
            newnext := *prev+next*;
            prev := *next*;
            next := *newnext*
            end;
        iterfib := *next*
        end
end; (* *iterfib* *)

That's the easy way to write the function, but to illustrate the scope issues that interest us, we need a convoluted version:[3]

function *fib* (*x*: *integer*): *integer*;

    function *fib1* (*prev, next*: *integer*): *integer*;

        function *fib2* (*newnext*: *integer*): *integer*;
        begin *fib2* := *fib1* (*next, newnext*) **end**; (* *fib2* *)

    begin (* *fib1* *)
        if *x* = 2 **then** *fib1* := *next*
        else begin *x* := *x*−1; *fib1* := *fib2*(*prev+next*) **end**
    end; (* *fib1* *)

    begin
        if *x* < 2 **then** *fib* := *x* **else** *fib* := *fib1*(1, 1)
    end; (* *fib* *)

Note that the values of *prev* and *next* on successive calls of *fib1* are the same as in successive iterations of the **for** loop.

---

[3] For a more natural function illustrating the same kind of complexity with the respect to scope, just consider our interpreter function *eval*.

In the language we just defined, this is:

```
(define fib (x)
      (define fib1 (prev next)
            (define fib2 (newnext)
                  (fib1 next newnext))
            (if (= x 2) next
                (begin
                    (set x (- x 1))
                    (fib2 (+ prev next)))))
      (if (< x 2) x (fib1 1 1)))
```

Consider now the evaluation of (fib 5). We will show the state of the stack through several function calls, including in each picture the actual parameter values and the static link of every AR on the stack; the empty spaces are for the return addresses (which we don't know) and the dynamic links, which simply point back to the previous AR on the stack. Our first stack configuration is just after the call (fib 5):

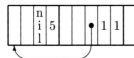

This calls (fib1 1 1):

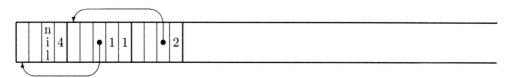

which calls (fib2 2):

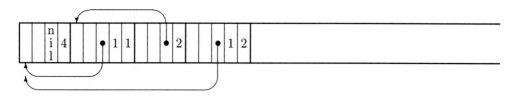

So far, the static links have been no different from the dynamic links. However, fib2 now calls (fib1 1 2). The enclosing environment of fib1 is still the AR of the original call to fib. To put it another way, to reference x, fib1 should follow its static link back once. Thus, the call (fib1 1 2) produces:

Here are the next four stack configurations and the calls that lead to them:

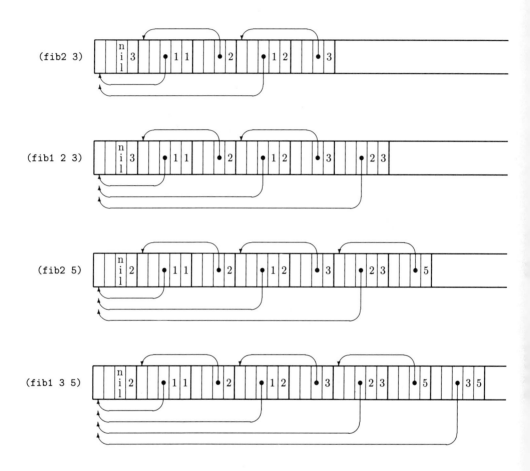

At this point, x is 2, so fib1 returns next, which is 5. The entire stack empties with no further computation taking place (since all these function calls are the last function calls in their respective function bodies), and 5 is returned from the original call.

How is this language compiled? Not surprisingly, the compilation of value-op's and control operations (except assignment to formal parameters) is the same as in previous sections. Furthermore, formal parameter referencing and assignment are the same as for SCHEME, given an analogous definition of *lexical distance* (left to the reader).

Function return is virtually the same as in the previous section. If f is a function with n formal parameters:

e as body of f	$\Rightarrow l_f$:	$<$code for e$>$	
		SUBI	$n + 3$,sp	; de-allocate AR
		JMP	((ar))	

What has changed significantly is function invocation, because, unlike the Chapter 1 language, the AR's in this language have static links, and unlike SCHEME, those static links are not obtained from closures that have been previously constructed. Rather, the static link for a call of function f depends upon the *lexical distance* between the call and the declaration of f. Suppose the call occurs in the body of a function g, and consider the possibilities:

- f is local to g; i.e., the definition of g has the form:

$$\text{(define g } (y_1 \ \dots \ y_m)$$
$$\vdots$$
$$\text{(define f } (x_1 \ \dots \ x_n) \ \cdots)$$
$$\vdots$$
$$(\cdots \ (f \ e_1 \ \dots \ e_n) \ \cdots))$$

Then the static link for the call is the current AR (the one created for the invocation of g). That is, references to y_i within the body of f should be resolved by following the static link back once.

- f is g; i.e., this is a recursive call. Then the new AR will contain new values for $y_1, \dots, y_m$, but any references to variables in outer scopes (global to g) should be resolved by looking in the same AR as would be used for the current call. Thus, the static link of the new AR is the same as the static link of the current AR.

- f is a "sibling" of g, as in:

$$\text{(define h } (\cdots)$$
$$\vdots$$
$$\text{(define f } (x_1 \ \dots \ x_n) \ \cdots)$$
$$\vdots$$
$$\text{(define g } (y_1 \ \dots \ y_m)$$
$$\vdots \ \text{(local function declarations of g)}$$
$$(\cdots \ (f \ e_1 \ \dots \ e_n) \ \cdots)) \ ; \text{ body of g}$$
$$\vdots$$
$$(\cdots)) \ ; \text{ body of h}$$

Then the same reasoning applies as in the previous case.

- f is the "parent" of g (h in the above). Then the static link of the new AR is found by following the current static link back once and using the static link from *that* AR (which was created for a call to h). Similarly if f is a sibling of g's parent.

So, define the *lexical distance* from a function call (f e_1 ... e_n) contained in the body of function g to the declaration of f to be: 0, if f is local to g; 1, if f is g or a sibling of g; 2, if f is the parent of g or a sibling thereof; and so on. Then, the static link for the call is placed into register scr by this code:

$$j \text{ times} \begin{cases} \text{MOVE} & \text{ar,scr} \\ \text{LOAD} & \text{(scr)+2,scr} \\ \vdots \\ \text{LOAD} & \text{(scr)+2,scr} \end{cases}$$

where j is the lexical distance.

Given this, the entire call is compiled as follows:

```
(f e₁ ... eₙ)    ⇒    MOVE  sp,rv              ; new AR
                      ADDI  n + 3,sp
                      PUSH  rv
                      <code for e₁ >
                      STORE rv,((sp)-1)+3      ; first actual

                        ⋮

                      < code for eₙ >
                      STORE rv,((sp)-1)+3 + (n − 1) ; nth actual
                      LOADL l,rv
                      STORE rv,((sp)-1)        ; return addr. -> new AR
                      STORE ar,((sp)-1)+1      ; dyn. link -> new AR
                      < code to compute new static link >
                      STORE scr,((sp)-1)+2     ; static link -> new AR
                      POP   ar                 ; new AR
                      JMP   lf
                  l:  LOAD  (ar)+1,ar          ; restore old AR
```

9.5.1 DISPLAYS

What was presented in the previous section is not quite the scheme ordinarily used to handle nested scopes, because it has the disadvantage that references to nonlocal variables take extra time. A simple change of representation can solve that problem.

At any given time, only a small number of AR's can be reached by static links from the current AR, namely one AR for each function enclosing the one currently executing. In this section, the address of each of these currently accessible AR's will be kept in a global array, called the *display*. Variable referencing will be accomplished by using the lexical depth of a variable's declaration as an index into the display, so that all variable references will take the same amount of time. The tricky part is maintaining the display at a reasonable cost.

For example, here is how the display would look at various points in the execution of (fib 5):

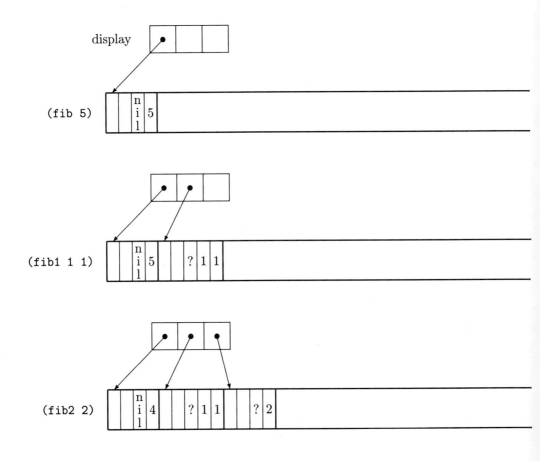

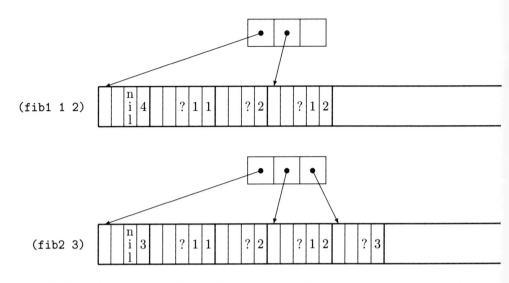

All the fields in each AR are the same as in the previous section, except the static link. Static links are no longer needed for variable referencing, but the space they formerly occupied will be needed for display maintenance, as we will see shortly.

From now on, assume the register **ds** points to the display. The display itself is allocated as soon as the program starts, and it never moves; so the contents of **ds** do not change, even as the contents of the display are changed.

To be specific about variable referencing: The *lexical depth* of a variable declaration is its distance from the *outermost* scope: 0 for parameters of top-level functions;[4] 1 for parameters of functions declared immediately within a top-level function; and so on. (The important point to note is that we are counting from the outer scope to the variable declaration, where we had previously counted from the reference itself toward outer scopes. One consequence is that, using displays, references to a particular variable look the same regardless of where they occur.) Referencing of, and assignment to, formal parameters are compiled as follows:

x_i	$\Rightarrow$	LOAD	(ds)+j,scr
		LOAD	(scr)+$i+2$,scr

(set x_i e)	$\Rightarrow$	<code for e>	
		LOAD	(ds)+j,scr
		STORE	rv,(scr)+$i+2$

where j is the lexical depth of the declaration of x_i, and i is its offset.

---

[4]In PASCAL, we might put global variables in the first AR, in which case they would be at depth 0.

Ensuring that the display contains the proper pointers is the responsibility of the function call and return code. The key to understanding display maintenance is the observation that when invoking a function defined at depth j (counting top-level functions as being at level 0), the first j items in the display are still valid. Thus, only *one pointer* in the display needs to be changed when calling a function. Display maintenance involves the modification of one slot of the display when a function is called and the restoration of the previous value of that slot when the function returns. Assume f is declared at lexical depth j:

```
(f e₁ ... eₙ)        ⇒      MOVE   sp,rv              ; new AR
                            ADDI   n + 3,sp
                            PUSH   rv
                            <code for e₁ >
                            STORE  rv,((sp)-1)+3 ; first actual
                              ⋮
                            < code for eₙ >
                            STORE  rv,((sp)-1)+3 + (n − 1) ; nth actual
                            LOADL  l,rv
                            STORE  rv,((sp)-1)     ; return addr. -> new AR
                            STORE  ar,((sp)-1)+1 ; dyn. link -> new AR
                            LOAD   (ds)+j,rv       ; old contents
                            STORE  rv,((sp)-1)+2 ; of display slot
                            POP    ar
                            STORE  ar,(ds)+j       ; new contents
                            JMP    l_f
                      l: LOAD   (ar)+2,scr       ; saved from display
                            STORE  scr,(ds)+j      ; -> display slot
```

The code for function return is identical to that in the previous section.

The reader can compile and trace the fib function and see that the display values are as we pictured them. Our illustration was incomplete, however. In the picture of the display for the call (fib1 1 2), the last entry in the display appears to be blank; in fact, it still contains the pointer it had from the previous call. Also, the AR slots formerly used for the static link now contain pointers saved from the display. Thus, the picture should have been:

| (fib1 1 2) | | n i l | 4 | | n i l | 1 | 1 | | n i l | 2 | | • | 1 | 2 |

9.5.2 DOWNWARD FUNARGS

We earlier stated that PASCAL does not create closures, but that is false. What is true is that, because PASCAL has only "downward funargs" — functions passed as arguments but not returned as results — any closure created necessarily points to an AR that is below it on the stack, and therefore the closure itself becomes obsolete before the AR it contains is popped from the stack. Therefore, AR's still can safely be placed on the stack.

As a concrete example of passing procedures as parameters and of the stack structure that results, consider this function, a continuation-passing version of factorial:

function *id* (*x*: *integer*): *integer*;
begin *id* := *x* **end**; (* *id* *)

function *fac* (*x*: *integer*): *integer*;

    function *fac1* (*x*: *integer*; **function** *f* (*i*: *integer*): *integer*): *integer*;

        function *fac2* (*y*: *integer*): *integer*;
        begin *fac2* := *f*(*x**y) **end**; (* *fac2* *)

    begin
      if *x* <= 1 **then** *fac1* := *f*(1)
          else *fac1* := *fac1*(*x*−1, *fac2*)
    end; (* *fac1* *)

begin (* *fac* *)
    fac := *fac1*(*x*, *id*)
end; (* *fac* *)

This function actually computes the factorial correctly, believe it or not. Generalizing our new language to permit function names to be passed as parameters, we would write it as:

```
(define id (x) x)
(define fac (x)
      (define fac1 (x f)
            (define fac2 (y) (f (* x y)))
            (if (<= x 1) (f 1) (fac1 (- x 1) fac2)))
      (fac1 x id))
```

Again, we will start by tracing the stack configurations resulting from a call to this function, and then we will consider how to compile the function to achieve these configurations. *We go back to using static links rather than displays.* The function call being traced is (`fac 3`). Again, return addresses and dynamic links are omitted. Here is the stack after that call *and* the subsequent call (`fac1 3 id`):

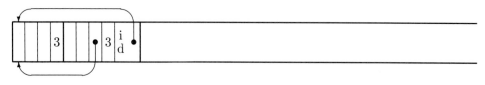

The double box contains a closure, which, of course, contains two pointers, one to code and the other to an AR. This closure is created when `id` is passed as a parameter. (In this example, arrows below the stack are static links and those above are closure pointers.) The next call is (`fac1 2 fac2`); `fac2` being a local function of `fac1`, its static link is the current AR:

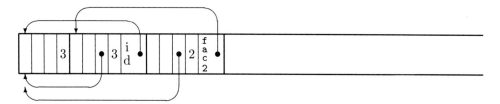

`fac1` again calls itself recursively, as (`fac1 1 fac2`):

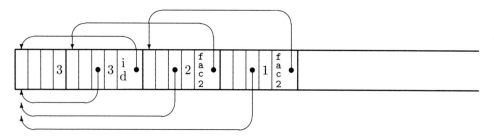

x being 1, `fac1` now undertakes to call its function argument, `f`, with argument 1. It looks in the actual parameter for `f` — a closure — for the new static link and code address, and so it calls `fac2` in this configuration:

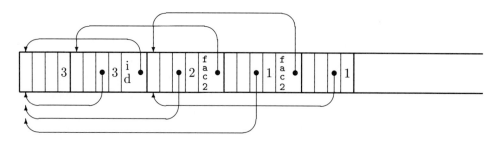

Now, `fac2` wants to evaluate `(f (* x y))`. `y` is a local variable (with value 1), and `x` *and* `f` are found by following the static link back once. `x` is bound to 2 and `f` to a closure. Again, the static link for the new AR is obtained from this closure, as is the code address to jump to; so `fac2` is called in this configuration:

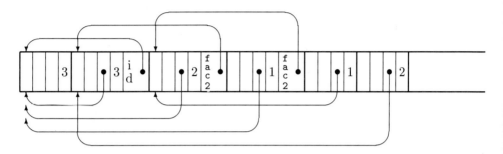

`fac2` again evaluates `(f (* x y))`, this time with y=2, x=3, and f=id. So `id` is called:

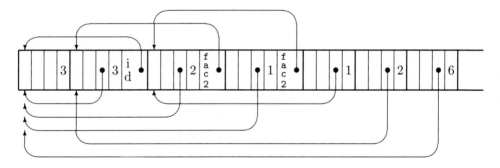

`id` returns 6, and this value is passed out of all these calls and returned as the value of `(fac 3)`.

Compilation of this language is quite straightforward, so long as we know which arguments represent functions; we will assume that, in fact, normal arguments and function arguments are in some way syntactically distinguished (as they are in PASCAL by declarations). Another minor problem, really just an annoyance, is that closures naturally occupy two words, whereas we have assumed all arguments occupy a single word. As mentioned in a footnote earlier in this chapter, this is not a problem in principle, assuming, again, that it is known which arguments are closures (or, in general, how many words each parameter occupies). We will just assume that the offsets of all parameters have been correctly computed.

There are two new aspects to compilation: (1) creating closures when functions are passed as arguments, and (2) calling functions that have been passed as arguments. One thing that is *not* a problem is passing function parameters to other functions. That is, if **g** has a formal parameter **f** that represents a function, and **g** calls **h** passing **f** as an argument, then **g** just obtains the value of **f** from its AR as it would for any other variable (modulo the double-word issue) and places it in the new AR. In other words, the only case that involves anything new from the point of view of compilation is when a function name is passed as a parameter — for this is when a closure is built — and when a closure is applied.

The question involved in closure construction is this: Which AR should be placed in the closure? The answer is that it should be the same AR that would have been the static link if the function being passed were simply being called. Recall the code to find the static link for a call to a function **f**, when the lexical distance between the call and the declaration is j (from page 431):

$$j \text{ times} \left\{ \begin{array}{ll} \texttt{MOVE} & \texttt{ar,scr} \\ \texttt{LOAD} & \texttt{(scr)+2,scr} \\ \vdots & \\ \texttt{LOAD} & \texttt{(scr)+2,scr} \end{array} \right.$$

and the code to find the address of a variable and place it into **scr** (from page 418):

$$j \text{ times} \left\{ \begin{array}{ll} \texttt{MOVE} & \texttt{ar,scr} \\ \texttt{LOAD} & \texttt{(scr)+2,scr} \\ \vdots & \\ \texttt{LOAD} & \texttt{(scr)+2,scr} \\ \texttt{ADDI} & i+2\texttt{,scr} \end{array} \right.$$

Given this, **f**, when passed as a procedure parameter, would be compiled as:

f, as ith actual parameter $\Rightarrow$	$\begin{array}{ll} \texttt{LOADL} & l_{\texttt{f}}\texttt{,rv} \\ \texttt{STORE} & \texttt{rv,((sp)-1)+3} + (i-1) \\ \texttt{< code to compute static link >} \\ \texttt{STORE} & \texttt{scr,((sp)-1)+3} + i \end{array}$

A call to the *i*th parameter would be compiled as:

```
(xᵢ e₁ ... eₙ)    ⇒    < code for address of xᵢ >
                       PUSH   scr              ; closure
                       MOVE   sp,rv            ; addr. of new AR
                       ADDI   n + 3,sp
                       PUSH   rv
                       <code for e₁ >
                       STORE  rv,((sp)-1)+3    ; first actual
                         ⋮
                       < code for eₙ >
                       STORE  rv,((sp)-1)+3 + (n − 1)    ; nth actual
                       LOADL  l,rv             ; return address
                       STORE  rv,((sp)-1)      ; -> new AR
                       STORE  ar,((sp)-1)+1    ; dyn. link -> new AR
                       POP    ar               ; new AR
                       POP    rv               ; closure
                       LOAD   (rv)+1,scr       ; AR from closure is
                       STORE  scr,(ar)+2       ; static link of new AR
                       JMP    ((rv))           ; code addr. from closure
                   l:  LOAD   (ar)+1,ar        ; restore old AR
```

This code is nearly identical to that for application in SCHEME, except for the stack-allocation of AR's. The main difference is that here the closure is necessarily bound to a variable, whereas there it was computed as the value of an arbitrary expression.

Finally, we mention that it is possible to use a display when treating functions as parameters, but in that case the entire display must be stored in the closure, incurring a greater expense than in the scheme just presented. Because this feature is usually not heavily used in imperative languages like PASCAL, most compiler-writers prefer to use a display and accept this inefficiency in closure creation.

9.6 Summary

Compilation is the process of translating high-level language programs to machine language. Besides eliminating the run-time cost of interpretation *per se* — that is, the cost of testing the types of expressions, decomposing them, and dispatching — compilation replaces variable look-up by direct access to the memory location that holds the value of the variable. The key step is to replace association-list-like structures (*ENV*'s) by single chunks of memory, called *activation records*. A further optimization, applicable to languages that don't have upward function values, is to store all AR's on a run-time stack.

9.6.1 GLOSSARY

activation record. The memory area containing all information relevant to
a single invocation of a function, namely the return address, dynamic
link, static link (or pointer saved from the display), and values of actual
parameters and local variables.

display. An array of pointers to all activation records relevant to the execution
of the current function. Variable referencing is accomplished by indexing
into this array, at a position determined at compile time according to the
lexical depth at which the variable was declared.

dynamic link. Pointer to the activation record of the calling function.

static link. Pointer to the activation record of the lexically enclosing function.
Variable referencing is accomplished by following static links; the distance
to travel on this chain is determined at compile time according to the
lexical distance of the reference from the declaration of the variable.

9.6.2 FURTHER READING

Most of what has been discussed here can be found in any textbook on programming languages or compilation; see the end of Chapter 4 for references.
SCHEME compilation is not covered in those books; see Abelson and Sussman
[1985, Chapter 5], Bartley and Jensen [1986], and Kranz, et al. [1986].

Some of the other languages we have covered present special compilation
problems. SASL compilation is discussed in the SASL chapter and the references
given there (some of which are also applicable to SCHEME). SMALLTALK can
be compiled using the methods presented in this chapter, but a compilation
problem peculiar to it is reducing the cost of the method search; see Johnson,
et al. [1988] for a sample of research on this. PROLOG compilation is quite a
specialized topic, for which the techniques described in this chapter have little
relevance; see Maier and Warren [1988] and references cited there.

9.7 Exercises

1. Implement one of the compilation methods described in this chapter.
   Then write an emulator for our machine language. What kind of speed-
   up do you get over interpreted code? Can you explain where the savings
   are coming from?

2. How can the restriction on SCHEME programs — that `value-op`'s cannot
   be assigned — be lifted? Give the corrected compilation scheme.

3. Show that, according to our compilation methods, a top-level `lambda` in
   SCHEME, with no enclosed `lambda`'s, works the same as `define` in LISP.

4. Implement an interpreter for the language defined in Section 9.5.

5. A problem with the compilation of CLU is that in CLU, as in SCHEME, environments can be captured in values. Namely, whenever a constructor is applied in CLU, it forms a value which contains the environment that was created for that application. However, unlike SCHEME, there is no difficulty here in copying the environment. Give a compilation scheme for CLU that uses a run-time stack and copies the AR when a constructor is applied. Make sure you describe how to compile selectors and settors as well.

6. Even in SCHEME, function call/return is inherently stack-like. From the point of view of our compilation algorithm, this stack is made up of those AR's encountered by following dynamic links back from the current AR. This *control stack* can actually be separated from the data and implemented as a true stack, with only the data portions of the AR going into the heap, as follows: AR's, allocated on a stack, have this form:

Return address	Dynamic link	Data pointer

The "data pointer" points to a data record stored in the heap, having this form:

Static link	Actual parameter 1	$\cdots$	Actual parameter n

This static link is a pointer to another such data record in the heap. A closure contains a code pointer and a pointer to a data record (rather than to an AR). Referencing of variables is compiled in essentially the same way, with just an extra indirection off the data pointer of the current AR (or, more aptly, the use of a register to hold that data pointer). Give a compilation scheme using this approach.

7. Starting from the compilation method of the previous problem, consider this: Suppose h calls f, and the *last action* taken by f is to call g. Then, after g terminates, it will return to f, which will *immediately* return to h. Why not eliminate the middle-man, and simply re-use f's AR for g (changing only the data pointer)? Such a call from f to g is called a *tail-recursive* call, and the advantage of following this idea is that tail-recursive calls are implemented *without growth of the control stack*. As an example, a function that calls itself tail-recursively, such as:

```
(set countones (lambda (l i)
       (if (null? l) 0
          (countones (cdr l) (if (= (car l) 1) (+1 i) i)))))
```

executes within a small amount of stack space: the stack grows only to the extent required to evaluate arguments, not for the recursive calls. This brings the cost of recursion more in line with the cost of iteration. It is actually stated in the SCHEME definition that implementations must apply this optimization.[5] Modify the previous compilation algorithm to be "properly tail-recursive."

8. Discuss the compilation of SASL. This is a straightforward adaptation of SCHEME compilation along the same lines as were used to obtain the SASL interpreter. If you have read section 5.9, compare the compilation algorithm to the graph reduction approach. Which do you think will be more efficient, if either?

9. Consider further the compilation of SASL. An important method to obtain better code is to avoid the construction of thunks where possible. As noted in Exercise 6 of Chapter 5, their construction is necessary only when the expression whose evaluation is being delayed is an application; your compilation method should certainly take this into account. However, even for applications the delay may be needless. There is no need to delay evaluation of the arguments of arithmetic operations, because these operations are strict, meaning they are bound to evaluate their arguments anyway. Similarly, there is no need to delay evaluation of the first argument of `if`. Modify the compilation algorithm to apply this optimization. How much speed-up did you achieve?

In fact, we can go much further by analyzing the strictness of *user-defined* functions. `+1`, for instance, is clearly strict in its one argument. The process of discovering the arguments of user-defined functions with respect to which those functions are strict is called *strictness analysis*. It is, indeed, so important to the generation of high-quality code for lazy functional languages that its study has become something of a cottage industry. Devise

---

[5] "Implementations of SCHEME are required to be properly tail-recursive" (Rees and Clinger [1986, page 3]). *Digression:* An interesting observation (for which I am indebted to Luddy Harrison) is that this requirement is not so unexceptionable as it seems. Consider the SCHEME version of function `fac1`, given in PASCAL on page 435:

```
(set fac1 (lambda (x f)
    (if (<= x 1) (f 1)
        (fac1 (- x 1) (lambda (y) (f (* x y)))))))
```

It is tail-recursive so must be executed without net growth of the stack, according to the requirement. However, since it builds closures as it recurses, it will end up using approximately as much space in the heap for closures as would have been used on the stack. A clever compiler might well recognize this as a downward funarg and compile it using only stack and no heap, as in PASCAL. Since this is not "properly tail-recursive," it is against the law, even though trading heap space for stack is generally considered to be an optimization.

a scheme for evaluating the strictness of user-defined functions (but note that it is provably impossible to obtain perfect analyses), implement it, and measure the speed-up. Consult Peyton Jones [1987], and references cited there, for a full discussion.

Chapter 10

Memory Management

All of our interpreters allocate memory using the PASCAL procedure *new*. This dynamically allocated memory is never disposed. Thus, more and more memory is allocated, until no more can be had and the interpreter ignominiously aborts. In this chapter, we take the LISP interpreter and show how to eliminate this craving for memory. The reader should review the LISP interpreter (Appendices B and C) before proceeding.[1] Although the methods introduced in this chapter are widely applicable, specific references to other languages are mostly confined to the exercises.

There are three reasons for allocating memory in LISP:

1. *ENV* and *VALUELIST* records are allocated in *EVALUATION*. *VALUELIST*'s are allocated in *evalList* to hold the arguments to user-defined functions and value-op's; *ENV*'s are allocated in *applyUserFun*.

2. *SEXP* records are allocated in *applyValueOp* for the results of arithmetic operations and cons, as well as in *INPUT*.

3. *EXP*, *EXPLIST*, *NAMELIST*, and *FUNDEF* records are allocated in *INPUT*.

These various reasons for dynamic memory allocation call for different treatments:

1. We will eliminate uses of *ENV* and *VALUELIST* records for holding arguments of user-defined functions by adopting the stack-allocation strategy from Chapter 9. This is done in Section 10.1. (The code relating to

---

[1]Section 10.1 can be read as a modification to the Chapter 1 interpreter to eliminate dynamic allocation of *ENV* and *VALUELIST* records. The other sections are LISP-specific.

global variables will be left as is, thereby admitting the allocation of a single *ENV* record, plus one *VALUELIST* record for each global variable.)

2. Our main goal in this chapter is to eliminate dynamic allocation of *SEXP* records in favor of allocating a fixed number of such records at the start and managing them so as to have them last for the entire session. Various approaches to the problem of *heap management* will be taken in Sections 10.3–10.5.

3. We're going to ignore the dynamic allocation of *EXP*, *EXPLIST*, *NAMELIST*, and *FUNDEF* records. These get allocated so slowly — at the speed of human typing — that it is not worth the trouble of avoiding their dynamic allocation, for expository purposes. A real LISP system would deal with them by the same techniques we use for *SEXP* records.

The treatment of *ENV* and *VALUELIST* records really doesn't add anything to what was said in Chapter 9, except that here the presentation will be interpreter-based. Memory to hold actual parameters is inherently allocable according to a stack discipline, so it is easy to manage. The allocation of *SEXP* records is another matter entirely. It is not at all stack-like, but rather entirely random. This is why these records are allocated from a *heap*.

PASCAL programmers are familiar with the notion of a heap, a large area of memory from which records can be allocated at any time. The big difference between PASCAL and LISP (as well as the other languages covered in this book) is that in PASCAL the heap is entirely user-managed: the user explicitly requests a record from the heap (via *new*) and explicitly returns it to the heap (via *dispose*). *No primitive operation in* PASCAL *allocates memory from the heap.* In LISP, the opposite is true: Memory is allocated from the heap implicitly when primitive operations — in particular, arithmetic operations and cons — are performed.

This places *on the* LISP *system* the burden of proper management of the heap. Specifically, *the system must determine when to return unneeded memory to the heap for re-use.* It would be impossible ever to do this if all *SEXP* records previously allocated via *new* remained useful, but that is not the case; at any given time, many of the *SEXP* records that were allocated earlier have since become obsolete. More precisely, they have become *inaccessible* — there is no way to get to them from the interpreter by any chain of pointers. Here are some examples of how this happens:

- Consider the evaluation of (set x '(a b)) at the top level. Five *SEXP* records are allocated as well as a *VALUELIST* record. In this picture, records are labeled with their types; the unlabeled ones are *SEXP*'s. Note that the a, b, and () represent *SEXP* records:

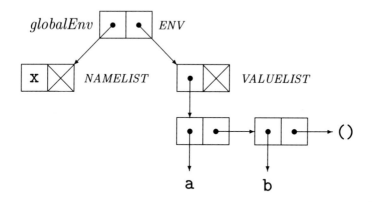

If the very next expression evaluated is (set x '()), we get:

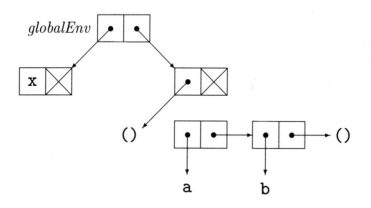

The records representing '(a b) are cut off — inaccessible — and can never again be relevant to the computation. They should be returned to the heap.

- Again suppose (set x '(a b)) is entered, immediately followed by (set x (cdr x)). The picture now is:

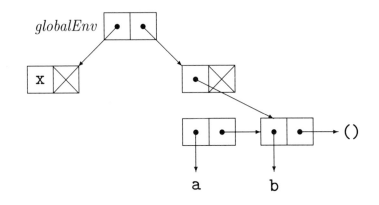

Two records have been made inaccessible and should be recycled to the heap.

- The biggest source of memory allocations and creation of inaccessible nodes is in the construction of temporary values during computation. For example, in the course of evaluating (length '(a b c)), *SEXP* records are allocated to hold the values 1, 2, and 3; the records containing 1 and 2 are inaccessible after 3 has been returned.

Inaccessible records are also called *garbage*. The job of heap management is to allow for the re-use of garbage memory. This limits the total memory requirement to the memory occupied by *accessible* records; even a computation that allocates an enormous number of records may have a relatively few accessible records at any given time. Thus, finding a way to recycle inaccessible records can dramatically reduce our use of memory. There are two general approaches to this:

Garbage collection: The interpreter allocates records from the heap until it runs out. The computation is halted while an attempt is made to discover the inaccessible records and make them available for reallocation. There are many methods of garbage collection, but all are essentially variants on the two methods we discuss: *mark-scan* and *semi-space*.

Reference-counting: Each *SEXP* record keeps a count of the number of pointers pointing to itself. Whenever a new reference is made to this record its *reference count* is incremented, and when a reference is removed the reference count is decremented. When the reference count goes to zero, the record is returned to the heap.

Though reference-counting is conceptually very simple, it is in practice rather tricky to implement and is also unable to deal with cyclic S-expressions, such as can arise from the use of `rplaca` and `rplacd`. Accordingly, garbage collection is the far more popular method of heap management.[2]

The plan for this chapter is as follows:

Section 10.1: Modify the LISP interpreter to allocate arguments on a stack, thereby eliminating almost all uses of *ENV* and *VALUELIST* records. This modification follows closely the discussion of stack allocation in Chapter 9, including the addressing of local variables by an offset in an "activation record." Besides saving considerable memory and time in itself, this modification has the crucial virtue of allowing us to find all the *accessible SEXP* records easily, something that cannot now be done.

Section 10.2: Sections 10.3–10.5 are introduced by a general discussion of heap management.

Section 10.3: The interpreter developed in Section 10.1 is modified by the addition of garbage collection using the mark-scan method.

Section 10.4: The interpreter developed in Section 10.1 is modified by the addition of garbage collection using the semi-space method.

Section 10.5: The interpreter developed in Section 10.1 is modified to use reference-counting.

The code for the stack-based interpreter of Section 10.1 and the reference-counting interpreter of Section 10.5 will be found in Appendix J. For the garbage-collecting interpreters, all the code will be given in the text.

10.1 Stacking Arguments

In this section, the use of a stack in compiling Chapter 1 code, as discussed in Chapter 9, will be adapted to the LISP interpreter. This entails placing all arguments — whether to user-defined or primitive functions — on a stack and referencing formal parameters via a small integer offset in the stack. The upshot of this modification is to obtain two very desirable benefits:

- Almost all uses of *ENV* and *VALUELIST* records are eliminated. (Only those used in *globalEnv* are retained, and those could be eliminated as well; see Exercise 1.) The result is less total memory usage and faster evaluation.

---

[2]In fact, no LISP implementation uses reference-counting. However, implementations of some of the other languages in this book, most notably SMALLTALK, do.

- All accessible *SEXP* records can now be found by looking in the stack and a few other places, such as *globalEnv*. This is vital to allow for management of *SEXP* records in later sections. The precise definition of accessibility is given in the next section.

In overview, the modifications of this section are:

- *evalList* pushes values onto the run-time stack rather than placing them into a list.

- *applyValueOp* pops its arguments from this stack.

- *applyUserFun* also accesses its arguments on the stack. How does a user-defined function know where to get the values of its actual parameters? A parameter of *eval*, called *AR*, gives the index in the stack of the first argument of the current function. By adding a variable's position in the formal parameter list to *AR*, its address on the stack is found. Whenever a user-defined function is called or returns, *AR* must be adjusted appropriately.

In presenting the details, those related to pushing and popping of arguments are given first, and those concerning referencing of formal parameters follow:

- The stack is an array of *SEXP*'s. *stacktop* gives the *next available* location:

$$argStack: \textbf{array } [1..STACKSIZE] \textbf{ of } SEXP;$$
$$stacktop: integer; (* \text{ range is } 1..STACKSIZE+1 *)$$

The following functions are included in a new code section, immediately following the declarations of global variables, called *MEMORY MANAGEMENT*. *initStack* is called from the top level before calling *eval*.

```
(* initStack - initialize environment stack *)
procedure initStack;
begin
    stacktop := 1
end; (* initStack *)

(* pushArg - push a single argument onto argStack *)
procedure pushArg (s: SEXP);
begin
    if stacktop > STACKSIZE
    then begin
            writeln('Stack overflow');
            stacktop := 1;
            goto 99
        end;
    argStack[stacktop] := s;
    stacktop := stacktop + 1
end; (* pushArg *)
```

```
(* topArg - return top item in stack *)
function topArg: SEXP;
begin
        topArg := argStack[stacktop−1]
end; (* topArg *)


(* popArgs - pop argument list from top of argStack *)
procedure popArgs (l: integer);
begin
        stacktop := stacktop−l
end; (* popArgs *)
```

(The stack is not quite identical to that in Chapter 9, since it is not divided into activation records, each containing a return address and dynamic link. The latter turn out to be unnecessary, since they are, in effect, stored in the PASCAL run-time stack of the interpreter.)

- Any expression contained in a function definition is evaluated with respect to a set of arguments. These arguments are, of course, held in successive locations on the stack. This segment of the stack constitutes the "activation record" of the function and takes the place of the *ENV* record that was used before. Therefore, the *rho*: *ENV* argument to *eval* is replaced by *AR*: *integer*, and all recursive calls to *eval* are changed accordingly.

- *evalList* pushes its values on the stack. It is now a procedure instead of a function.

- In the *APEXP* — function application — case of *eval*, calls to *apply-ValueOp* and *applyUserFun* are modified to reflect the fact that *evalList* is no longer a function. The call to *applyUserFun* has another, more interesting, change to:

```
            newAR := stacktop;
            evalList(args);
            eval := applyUserFun(optr, newAR)
```

The idea is that the beginning of the activation record for *optr* is just where the stack top was before its arguments were pushed on the stack.

- *applyValueOp* starts by popping its arguments off the stack:

```
            s1 := topArg; (* 1st actual *)
            popArgs(1);
            if arity(op) = 2
            then begin
                    s2 := s1; (* 1st actual was really 2nd actual *)
                    s1 := topArg; (* 1st actual *)
                    popArgs(1)
                end;
```

Note that it is no longer possible to check that the number of arguments to the value-op is correct.

- *applyUserFun* cannot check for the correct number of arguments either. It calls *eval* recursively, giving the new stack location as the *AR* argument, and pops its arguments when it is done:

```
function applyUserFun (nm: NAME; newAR: integer): SEXP;
var f: FUNDEF;
begin
    f := fetchFun(nm);
    if f = nil
    then ... undefined function error ...
    with f↑ do begin
        applyUserFun := eval(body, newAR);
        popArgs(lengthNL(formals))
        end
end; (* applyUserFun *)
```

Variable referencing for formal parameters is based on position within the formal parameter list. The representation for variables is changed:

```
EXPREC = record
        case etype: EXPTYPE of
            ⋮
            VAREXP: (varble: NAME; offset: integer); (* 0 for global *)
            ⋮
    end;
```

The *offset* field is set to zero — indicating a global variable — by *mkVAREXP* but is then modified if the variable is a formal parameter. This is accomplished by having *parseDef* call a new procedure, *processExpVars*. Offsets of formal parameters begin at 1. *processExpVars* is listed in Appendix J.1.

Referencing of formal parameters occurs in the *VAREXP* case of *eval* and the *SETOP* case of *applyCtrlOp*. The former is now:

```
VAREXP:
        if offset > 0
        then eval := argStack[AR+offset−1]
        else ... no change ...
```

See Appendix J.1 for the code for set.

It turns out that it makes no difference what number is passed to *eval* from the top level for its *AR* argument (why?); we arbitrarily choose zero.

In summary, we have eliminated almost all uses of *ENV* and *VALUELIST* records, resulting in significant savings in both memory and execution time. Moreover, it is now possible to give a precise definition of *accessible*, as we will see next.

10.2 Heap Management

The *SEXP* records allocated during the running of a program can become inactive, as we have seen. Moreover, they do not do so in a predictable manner or at predictable times. A value may be used as soon as it is returned and never needed again, or it may be stored in *globalEnv* and used for the rest of the session.

The only way to know that a record is active is if it is *accessible*. Based upon the stack-based evaluator of the previous section, we can define:

Definition 10.1 An *SEXP* record is *accessible* if there is a reference to it from one of the following:

- *globalEnv*.

- *currentExp* (i.e., from a *VALEXP*-type *EXP* record contained in *currentExp*).

- The body of a function definition in *fundefs*.

- *nilValue* or *trueValue*.

- *argStack*.

- Another *accessible SEXP* record.

Otherwise, it is *inaccessible*.

An inaccessible record cannot possibly have an effect on the future of the computation, so it can be recycled. All the work that follows in this chapter is aimed at recycling inaccessible records.

In recycling records, our memory management scheme should have two properties: First, it should never recycle a record that is still accessible, and second, it should recover every inaccessible record. The affect of premature deallocation will usually be that the accessible record will be allocated to another purpose and will then have its value changed; in other words, an active value will appear to change for no reason. This can make memory management bugs appear very mysterious, especially since the error may not show up until long after the mistaken deallocation. On the other hand, a failure to recover some inaccessible records — what is called a *memory leak* — may not even be noticed for some time. Its only symptom is to cause some programs to run out of memory earlier than they should have, and it is usually hard to determine

when they "should have." Thus, memory management schemes — and the
reader should bear this in mind when doing the exercises — can be extremely
difficult to debug.

The two basic approaches to recovering inaccessible records are *garbage-collection* and *reference-counting.*

- In garbage-collection, no records are recovered until the system runs out
  of memory. At that time, the system suspends the computation and
  undertakes to round up all the inaccessible records — the garbage — in
  one shot.

- In reference-counting, a record is recovered and made available for re-use
  as soon as it becomes inaccessible.

10.3   Mark-Scan Garbage Collection

The oldest method of garbage collection is called *mark-scan*, or *mark-and-sweep.*
Every record has a Boolean-valued field called the *mark.* All available cons cells
in the heap are kept on a linked list called the *free list.* When all the cells on
the free list have been allocated, the garbage collector is called. The algorithm
proceeds in three steps:

1. Unmark (i.e., set the *mark* field to false) *all records* in memory (whether
   accessible or not).

2. Mark (i.e., set the *mark* field to true) all accessible records. This involves
   a recursive traversal of these lists, starting from those directly referenced
   from *globalEnv*, *argStack*, and so on.

3. Scan all of memory, placing unmarked nodes on the free list.

The principal change in the interpreter (starting from the stack-based interpreter of Section 10.1) is the addition of the procedure *gc* itself (about 90
lines). Beside that, there are about 50 lines of new or altered code. The following changes apply as well to the semi-space garbage collector of the next
section:

- All calls to *mkSExp* are replaced by calls to *allocSExp*, the function to
  allocate a record from the free list.

- In *applyValueOp*, any memory allocations that are to be done should
  be done before popping the arguments from the stack. Otherwise, a
  garbage collection might be done, for example, after popping the two
  arguments of cons but before setting the fields of the new cons cell.
  Since those arguments are off the stack, they may be inaccessible. If they
  are, the garbage collector will feel free to mangle them in any way it sees

fit. When the `cons` is finally performed, there is no guarantee that the original arguments will be intact. Therefore, the calls to *allocSExp* in *applyValueOp* are moved to the beginning of the body of *applyValueOp*, as follows:

> **if** *op* **in** [*PLUSOP .. DIVOP*]
> **then** *result* := *allocSExp*(*NUMSXP*)
> **else if** *op* = *CONSOP*
>   **then** *result* := *allocSExp*(*LISTSXP*);

The remaining changes are almost entirely confined to the *MEMORY MAN-AGEMENT* section. In particular, *EVALUATION* is not altered one bit. There are two changes outside of *MEMORY MANAGEMENT*:

- *memory* and *freeSEXP* are declared as global variables, and *MEMSIZE* is declared as an integer constant. *memory* holds all the *SEXP* records in the heap, and *freeSEXP* is the beginning of the free list:

> *MEMSIZE* = 500;
> *memory*: **array** [1..*MEMSIZE*] **of** *SEXP*;
> *freeSEXP*: *SEXP*;

- *initMemory* is called from the top level.

In *MEMORY MANAGEMENT*, function *allocSExp* and procedures *initMemory* and *gc* are defined, and our present purpose is to explain these.

In a real LISP implementation, the heap would simply consist of a large area of memory, and the allocator would return a pointer into it whenever it was called. By analogy, we would like to define a fixed array of *SEXPREC*'s and return pointers to them. However, this is impossible in PASCAL. Instead, memory is an array of *SEXP*'s, and we start by allocating (via *new*) an *SEXPREC* for each one.

It is a property of the mark-scan approach to garbage collection that all free memory is placed on a free list and allocated from there. This free list is established at memory initialization time (using the *carval* field for the link) and restored by each garbage collection. *gc* is called by *allocSExp* when the free list is empty. Thus, we arrive at *initMemory* and *allocSExp*:

```
(* initMemory - initialize memory *)
procedure initMemory;
var i: integer;
begin
    for i:=1 to MEMSIZE do new(memory[i]);
    for i:=1 to MEMSIZE−1 do memory[i]↑.carval := memory[i+1];
    memory[MEMSIZE]↑.carval := nil;
    freeSEXP := memory[1]
end; (* initMemory *)
```

```
(* allocSExp - get SEXPREC from free list; call gc if necessary *)
function allocSExp (t: SEXPTYPE): SEXP;
var s: SEXP;
begin
      if freeSEXP = nil
      then begin
              gc;
              if freeSEXP = nil (* garbage collection didn't help *)
              then begin
                      writeln('Memory overflow');
                      goto 99
                  end;
              if currentExp = nil
              then begin
                      writeln('Called gc during parsing.  ',
                          'Parse aborted; reenter input');
                      goto 99
                  end
          end;
      s := freeSEXP;
      freeSEXP := s↑.carval;
      s↑.sxptype := t;
      allocSExp := s
  end; (* allocSExp *)
```

Recall that all functions that previously called *mkSExp* now call *allocSExp* instead. After the initial call to *initMemory*, no more *SEXP* records are ever obtained via *new*. The "gc during parsing" problem will be explained after the presentation of *gc*; the reader should ignore it for now.

We can now present *gc*, the mark-scan garbage collection procedure. First note that, for its use, a new field has been added to *SEXPREC*, the *mark*:

```
SEXPREC = record
              mark: Boolean;
              case sxptype: SEXPTYPE of
                  ... no change ...
          end;
```

As discussed earlier, *gc* has three phases, so its overall structure is:

```
(* gc - mark-scan garbage collector *)
procedure gc;

var collected: integer;
```

```
    procedure unmarkPhase;

    procedure markPhase;

    procedure scanPhase;

begin (* gc *)
    write('Garbage collection ...');
    unmarkPhase;
    markPhase;
    scanPhase;
    writeln('collected ', collected:1,
        '(', round(100*collected/MEMSIZE):1, '%) records')
end; (* gc *)
```

Unmarking is very simple:

```
(* unmarkPhase - reset mark in ALL cons cells *)
procedure unmarkPhase;
var i: integer;
begin
    for i := 1 to MEMSIZE do memory[i]↑.mark := false
end; (* unmarkPhase *)
```

mark is the most complicated phase. Before reading on, reread the definition of "accessible" (page 453), which is central to its operation. The idea is to mark all records directly accessible from *globalEnv*, *currentExp*, *argStack*, and so on, and recursively mark all records accessible from those. The function *markSExp* checks if its argument already has its *mark* set; if so, it means that record has already been visited in the traversal. This check not only avoids extra work but also allows the algorithm to handle circular list structures.

```
(* markPhase - set mark in all accessible cons cells *)
procedure markPhase;
var
    i: integer;
    fd: FUNDEF;

(* markSExp - set mark in s and all cells accessible from it *)
    procedure markSExp (s: SEXP);
    begin
        if not s↑.mark
        then begin
```

```
                        s↑.mark := true;
                        if s↑.sxptype = LISTSXP
                        then begin
                                markSExp(s↑.carval);
                                markSExp(s↑.cdrval)
                            end
                    end
            end; (* markSExp *)


(* markValuelist - set mark in all cells accessible from vl *)
    procedure markValuelist (vl: VALUELIST);
    begin
        while vl <> nil do begin
            markSExp(vl↑.head);
            vl := vl↑.tail
            end
    end; (* markValuelist *)


(* markEnv - set mark in all cells accessible from rho *)
    procedure markEnv (rho: ENV);
    begin
        markValuelist(rho↑.values)
    end; (* markEnv *)


(* markExp - set mark in all cells accessible from e *)
    procedure markExp (e: EXP);

(* markExplist - set mark in all cells accessible from el *)
        procedure markExplist (el: EXPLIST);
        begin
            while el <> nil do begin
                markExp(el↑.head);
                el := el↑.tail
                end
        end; (* markExplist *)

    begin (* markExp *)
        case e↑.etype of
            VALEXP: markSExp(e↑.sxp);
            VAREXP: ;
            APEXP: markExplist(e↑.args)
        end
    end; (* markExp *)
```

```
begin (* markPhase *)
    markSExp(nilValue);
    markSExp(trueValue);
    markEnv(globalEnv);
    if currentExp <> nil then markExp(currentExp);
    fd := fundefs;
    while fd <> nil do begin
        markExp(fd↑.body);
        fd := fd↑.nextfundef
        end;
    for i := 1 to stacktop−1 do markSExp(argStack[i])
end; (* markPhase *)
```

(The reader should ignore the "*currentExp <> nil*" test for the moment.)

scanPhase simply runs over all of memory again, constructing the free list from the unmarked nodes. *collected* is a count of the number of records recycled, computed only so that *gc* can report it to the user:

```
(* scanPhase - reconstruct free list from cells not marked *)
procedure scanPhase;
var i : integer:
begin
    freeSEXP := nil;
    collected := 0;
    for i := 1 to MEMSIZE do
        if not memory[i]↑.mark (* memory[i] inaccessible *)
        then begin
            memory[i]↑.carval := freeSEXP;
            freeSEXP := memory[i];
            collected := collected+1
            end
end; (* scanPhase *)
```

There is a glitch to which we have alluded, having to do with the relation of garbage-collecting and parsing. Suppose *gc* is called during parsing. Cons cells may have been allocated, but nothing in our definition of *accessible* accounts for these nodes; they will just be collected and the parsing process resumed, with obviously disastrous results. Unfortunately, fixing the definition of accessibility turns out to be quite tricky. Rather than be diverted to a discussion of this problem, we have adopted the simple expedient of "forbidding" calls to *gc* during parsing. That is, if such a call happens to occur, we do the garbage collection, then inform the user that we are unable to continue parsing and jump to the top level. *gc* tests whether it was called from a parsing routine by checking if *currentExp* is **nil**. *markExp* must also check this to ensure that it doesn't attempt to dereference *currentExp* when it is **nil**. To guarantee that

currentExp is indeed **nil** during parsing, it is always set to **nil** at the top level
before calling *parseDef* or *parseExp*. Thus, the top-level call to *eval* becomes:

$$currentExp := \textbf{nil};$$
$$currentExp := parseExp;$$
$$initStack;$$
$$prValue(eval(currentExp, 0));$$

10.3.1 SUMMARY

Mark-scan garbage collection requires a scan over all of memory. Since the
idea is to return all *inaccessible* nodes to the free list, this is unavoidable. It
does make this method rather slow, especially when the heap is very large and
virtual memory is used.

Another significant measure of memory management systems is the amount
of additional memory they require. Mark-scan uses additional memory in two
ways: First, the *mark* field must be added to each record; but this is only one
bit, and it can usually be squeezed into the address fields (car and cdr) of the
cons cell. For example, on 32-bit machines, a cons cell will usually occupy two
32-bit words, each containing an address; since 28 bits are sufficient to address
a quarter of a gigabyte (about 268 megabytes) of memory, it is fair to say that
at least the four higher-order bits of each address are not needed. One of these
can be used for the mark. Another, hidden, usage of memory in the mark-
scan approach is the stack required to support the recursive traversal of active
cells. Our implementation relied on the PASCAL stack, but in real systems,
garbage collection is usually invoked only when memory is genuinely used up.
Fortunately, there is a way to do tree traversals without a stack; the references
under "Further Reading" should be consulted.

10.4   The Semi-Space Method

The semi-space, or *stop-and-copy*, method of garbage collection represents a
dramatic trade-off of space for time. Using only one half of memory at a time
— sacrificing, in other words, half of memory — the garbage collector is able
to run in time proportional to the amount of *accessible* memory, usually much
smaller than the total memory. The idea is this:

- Use one half of memory at a time. The half in use is divided into two parts,
  the first part containing cells that have been allocated and the second
  containing cells that are available for allocation. Thus, new memory is
  allocated sequentially from the available part until it runs out. There is
  no free list.

- When the available memory in the current half is used up, switch to the
  other half, *copying* only the *accessible* cells from the current half to the

beginning of the other half. All activity now switches to the other half; new memory is allocated starting from the first location above the copied records. Note that the copying process touches only accessible records.

We return to the stack-based interpreter of Section 10.1. The changes in *applyValueOp* and the replacement of *mkSExp* by *allocSExp* are exactly as in the mark-scan code. *initMemory* is again called from the top level. *currentExp* is again set to **nil** before calling any parsing routine, and garbage collection during parsing again causes the parse to be aborted. Our job is to explain the new global variable declarations, the new versions of *initMemory* and *allocSExp*, and finally the garbage collection procedure, *switchMem*.

The new variables are:

> *memory*: **array** [1..2] **of array** [1..*HALFMEMSIZE*] **of** *SEXP*;
> *nextloc*: *integer*; (* range is 1..*HALFMEMSIZE*+1 *)
> *halfinuse*: 1..2;

Records are allocated sequentially in the memory half currently in use. *nextloc* gives the index of the next free record. The meaning of *halfinuse* is self-evident. As in the previous version of *initMemory*, all *SEXPREC*'s are allocated "statically," that is to say, before actual computation begins. Here, then, are *initMemory* and *allocSExp*:

```
(* initMemory - initialize both halves of memory *)
procedure initMemory;
var i: integer;
begin
    for i := 1 to HALFMEMSIZE do begin
        new(memory[1][i]);
        new(memory[2][i])
        end;
    nextloc := 1;
    halfinuse := 1
end; (* initMemory *)
```

```
(* allocSExp - get SEXPREC, call switchMem if necessary *)
function allocSExp (t: SEXPTYPE): SEXP;
var s: SEXP;
begin
    if nextloc > HALFMEMSIZE
    then begin
        switchMem;
```

```
        if nextloc > HALFMEMSIZE (* switchMem didn't help *)
        then begin
                writeln('Memory overflow');
                nextloc := 1;
                goto 99
            end;
        if currentExp = nil
        then begin
                writeln('Called gc during parsing.   ',
                    'Parse aborted; reenter input');
                goto 99
            end
    end;
    s := memory[halfinuse][nextloc];
    nextloc := nextloc+1;
    s↑.sxptype := t;
    s↑.moved := false;
    allocSExp := s
end; (* allocSExp *)
```

(The reader will note the addition of a *moved* field to *SEXPREC*'s. It will be explained along with the procedure *moveSExp*.)

The procedure *switchMem* is a very neat, but somewhat tricky, piece of code. The algorithm it uses can be described as a *level-order* traversal and copy of the accessible S-expressions from *halfinuse* to the other half, with the records already copied playing the role of the queue. Some subtlety arises from the fact that the S-expressions are not trees but acyclic graphs — that is, there can be more than one pointer to a record — and the algorithm must avoid making duplicate copies of such a record. (In fact, even cyclic structures would be handled with no difficulty, though in our interpreter it is impossible to construct them.)

The overall structure of *switchMem* is this:

```
(* switchMem - move all SEXPREC's from halfinuse to other half *)
procedure switchMem;
var
    newhalf: 1..2;
    newnextloc: integer; (* range is 1..HALFMEMSIZE+1 *)

function moveSExp (s: SEXP): SEXP;

procedure initNewHalf;

procedure traverse;
```

```
begin (* switchMem *)
    write('Switching memories...');
    newhalf := 3−halfinuse;
    initNewHalf;
    traverse;
    writeln('recovered ', HALFMEMSIZE−newnextloc+1:1,
        '(', round(100*(HALFMEMSIZE−newnextloc+1)/HALFMEMSIZE):1,
        '%) cells');
    halfinuse := newhalf;
    nextloc := newnextloc
end; (* switchMem *)
```

"$3-halfinuse$" is just a fancy way to set *newhalf* to 1 if *halfinuse* is 2, and to 2 if it is 1. *newnextloc* is set by *traverse* to just above the last location into which a record was copied; thus, it becomes the new value of *nextloc*. *moveSExp* is called from both *traverse* and *initNewHalf*.

switchMem starts by calling *initNewHalf* to copy the records *directly* accessible from *globalEnv*, *fundefs*, *argStack*, and so on, into the new half. At the same time, all the references to such *SEXP* records are changed to point to their new locations (in the new half):

```
(* initNewHalf - move directly accessible SEXP's to new half *)
procedure initNewHalf;
var
    fd: FUNDEF;
    vl: VALUELIST;
    i: integer;

(* moveExp - move SEXP's in e from halfinuse to newhalf *)
    procedure moveExp (e: EXP);
    var el: EXPLIST;
    begin
        with e↑ do
            case etype of
                VALEXP: sxp := moveSExp(sxp);
                VAREXP: ;
                APEXP:
                    begin
                        el := args;
                        while el <> nil do begin
                            moveExp(el↑.head);
                            el := el↑.tail
                        end
                    end
            end (* case and with *)
    end; (* moveExp *)
```

```
begin (* initNewHalf *)
    newnextloc := 1;
    nilValue := moveSExp(nilValue);
    trueValue := moveSExp(trueValue);
    vl := globalEnv↑.values;
    while vl <> nil do begin
        vl↑.head := moveSExp(vl↑.head);
        vl := vl↑.tail
        end;
    for i := 1 to stacktop−1 do
        argStack[i] := moveSExp(argStack[i]);
    if currentExp <> nil then moveExp(currentExp);
    fd := fundefs;
    while fd <> nil do begin
        moveExp(fd↑.body);
        fd := fd↑.nextfundef
        end
end; (* initNewHalf *)
```

The procedure *traversal* does a level-order traversal (see page 37 for a review), the queue consisting of the *SEXP*'s located in *memory*[*newhalf*][*queueptr*] ... *memory*[*newhalf*][*newnextloc*−1]:

```
(* traverse - level-order traversal and copying of all SEXP's *)
procedure traverse;
var queueptr: integer; (* range is 1..HALFMEMSIZE+1 *)
begin
    queueptr := 1;
    while queueptr < newnextloc do begin
        with memory[newhalf][queueptr]↑ do
            if sxptype = LISTSXP
            then begin
                    carval := moveSExp(carval);
                    cdrval := moveSExp(cdrval)
                end;
        queueptr := queueptr + 1
        end (* while *)
end; (* traverse *)
```

The front of the queue (from which items are taken off) is at *queueptr*; thus, the incrementing of *queueptr* amounts to the dequeue (or **rm-front**) operation. The back of the queue is at *newnextloc*; the calls to *moveSExp* will (usually) cause records to be moved onto the queue and *newnextloc* to be incremented, giving the effect of the **enqueue** operation.

We have only to describe the function *moveSExp*. This is the trickiest part of the code. When an *SEXP* is of type *LISTSXP*, its two children are to be moved to the end of the queue, and its *carval* and *cdrval* fields are to be changed to point to their new locations. However, it is possible that the *carval* or *cdrval*, or both, have already been moved. The problem is, how do we know?

The answer is to use the new field in *SEXPREC*:

> *SEXPREC* = **record**
> > *moved*: *Boolean*;
> > **case** *sxptype*: *SEXPTYPE* **of**
> > > ... no change ...
>
> **end**;

The *moved* field is used only by *moveSExp*. It is always false in every record in *halfinuse* before *switchMem* is called; this is guaranteed by assignments in *allocSExp* and *moveSExp*. In *moveSExp* it has the following meaning: If an *SEXP* in the old half (*halfinuse*) has a true *moved* field, that means it has already been moved to *newhalf*, and its *carval* field contains its new location. The argument to *moveSExp* is a pointer into *memory[halfinuse]*, and it returns the new address of that cell, which will be in *memory[newhalf]*. Here, then, is the code:

```
(* moveSExp - move SEXP s from halfinuse to newhalf *)
function moveSExp (s: SEXP): SEXP;
var target: SEXP;
begin
    if s↑.moved then moveSExp := s↑.carval
    else begin
            target := memory[newhalf][newnextloc];
            newnextloc := newnextloc+1;
            target↑.sxptype := s↑.sxptype;
            target↑.moved := false;
            case s↑.sxptype of
                NILSXP: ;
                NUMSXP: target↑.intval := s↑.intval;
                SYMSXP: target↑.symval := s↑.symval;
                LISTSXP:
```

$$\begin{aligned}
&\textbf{begin}\\
&\quad target\uparrow.carval := s\uparrow.carval;\\
&\quad target\uparrow.cdrval := s\uparrow.cdrval\\
&\textbf{end}\\
\textbf{end}&;\ (*\ \textbf{case}\ *)\\
s\uparrow.&carval := target;\\
s\uparrow.&moved := true;\\
moveSExp &:= target\\
\textbf{end}&\\
\textbf{end};\ (*\ &moveSExp\ *)
\end{aligned}$$

To illustrate, suppose *HALFMEMSIZE* were 10, *halfinuse*=1, and the memory looks like this:

1	2	3	4	5	6	7	8	9	10
a	b	5, 9	2, 3	c	d	()	e	6, 7	f

The letters represent *SEXP*'s of type *SYMSXP* (symbols), () an *SEXP* of type *NILSXP* (a nil list), and two numbers represent a pair with the given car and cdr. Of course, these point to other locations in this half of memory. The small arrows represent pointers from *globalEnv, argStack*, etc. Thus, the accessible S-expressions happen to all be part of one list:

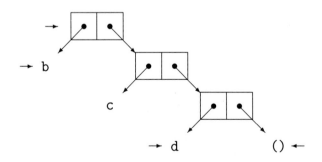

initNewHalf copies the four directly accessible records to the new half (which is represented here as a separate array with indices 11–20), changes the pointers from *globalEnv* and so on, and sets the forwarding pointers in those records (these are the arrows from the old half to the new):

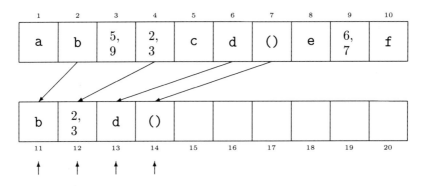

The traversal now begins. When the first *LISTSXP* record is encountered, *moveSExp* is called for its car and cdr. It so happens that the car field has already been moved (as can be seen by the fact that it has a forwarding pointer); its new address is filled in. However, the cdr has not been moved, so it is moved now and given a forwarding address, and its new address is filled in:

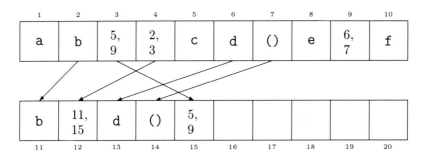

The next cons cell is at location 15. Neither its car nor its cdr has been moved, so they are now:

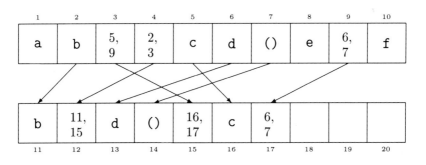

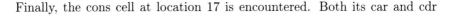

Finally, the cons cell at location 17 is encountered. Both its car and cdr fields have been moved already, so their new addresses are filled in from their forwarding addresses:

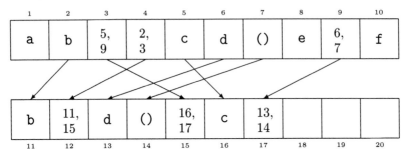

switchMem is now done, having recovered three cons cells.

10.4.1 SUMMARY

The semi-space garbage collection method was originally designed for use in virtual memory systems. Because it is inherently a *compacting* method — one which squeezes the accessible cons cells into the smallest possible space — it is particularly helpful when a penalty is paid for having active cells spread across memory, as in a virtual memory system. However, it can be enormously more efficient than mark-scan even when the heap is entirely contained in real memory. The number of accessible cells is often a small fraction of the size of memory. Moreover, since the number of accessible cells is solely a function of the computation, the cost of doing semi-space garbage collection is independent of the size of memory; it follows that the *per cell* cost of memory allocation decreases as memory size increases. In these days of large memories, this is a very compelling property.

10.5   Reference-Counting

An *SEXP* record is inaccessible if there are no references to it. An obvious idea is to have each record keep track of the references to itself; when there are none, the record is recycled.

Note that a record may have more than one reference. For example, in this session:

```
-> (set x '(a b))

-> (set y x)
```

the *SEXP* record for the list '(a b) has two references to it. If x were reassigned, it would be wrong to deallocate that record. The effect of such premature deallocation would be that the record could be reused, causing y to obtain a new value rather mysteriously.

Thus, we must keep track not only of *whether or not* there are references to a record, but *how many* references there are. This number is called the record's *reference count.* So, we start by changing the declaration of *SEXPREC*:

$$SEXPREC = \textbf{record}$$
$$refcnt\text{: } integer;$$
$$\textbf{case } sxptype\text{: } SEXPTYPE \textbf{ of}$$
$$\ldots \text{no change} \ldots$$
$$\textbf{end};$$

Allocation is from a free list, as in the mark-scan garbage-collection method. The general principle of reference-counting is to increment the *refcnt* fields when a new reference is made to a record, decrement it when a reference is removed, and return the record to the free list when the *refcnt* becomes zero. Here are some examples of where *refcnt*'s are incremented and decremented:

- A record has its *refcnt* incremented when it is pushed on the stack and decremented when it is popped.

- In *assign*, the newly assigned value has its *refcnt* incremented, and the previous value has its *refcnt* decremented.

- In the *CONSOP* case of *applyValueOp*, the *SEXP*'s being `cons`'ed both have their *refcnt*'s incremented.

There are many other cases where *refcnt*'s are incremented and decremented. In fact, the changes in the interpreter here are quite extensive — so extensive that we will not be describing them in detail. Instead, we cover the highlights and refer the reader to Appendix J.2.

To give the reader some idea of the problems that can arise with reference-counting, consider these cases:

- In *assign*, the *refcnt* of the newly assigned value must be incremented *before* the *refcnt* of the old value is decremented. Otherwise, in this case:

```
-> (set y 20)
20
-> (set y y)
```

here is what would happen: After the first assignment, the value 20 has a *refcnt* of 1 because y is bound to it. Evaluation of the expression y in the second assignment returns the same record, its *refcnt* still 1. We decrement this *refcnt*, resulting in deallocation of the record (placement on the free list). The *refcnt* is then incremented back to 1, but it is too late — the record is already on the free list; it will soon be allocated and its contents changed.

- Similarly, in *applyValueOp* it is no longer safe to pop the arguments to cons before actually doing the cons. Popping them may result in their immediate return to the free list. The new cons cell would then contain two pointers to records on the free list; such pointers are not very valuable.

- Perhaps the most serious problem — in that its solution requires significant changes in the interpreter — is illustrated by this session:

```
-> (define f (x y) y)
-> (+ (f (+ 1 2) (+ 3 4)) (+ 5 6))
```

When (f (+ 1 2) (+ 3 4)) is to be evaluated, 3 and 7 are pushed on the stack (giving them each a *refcnt* of 1) and then y is evaluated, returning 7. 3 and 7 are now popped from the stack, causing their *refcnt*'s to go to zero and their return to the free list. Thus, the *SEXP* returned from the application of f is now on the free list. When (+ 5 6) is evaluated, it will call *allocSExp* and obtain that very record, placing 11 into it. The outer addition will then return 22.

This last problem induces us to make a major change in the evaluation process: Results of *eval* will be *stacked* rather than returned. Thus, *eval* and its local functions *applyUserFun* and *applyCtrlOp*, plus *applyValueOp*, become procedures instead of functions.

With that we leave the reader to study the code in Appendix J.2.

Summary.   Reference counting is a very natural approach to recovering inaccessible memory for re-use. It is certainly used in real-world systems, but not very often. It has some disadvantages in the areas of efficiency, simplicity, and most of all, generality:

- *Efficiency* — Maintaining reference counts is an on-going cost of computations, which can be a considerable percentage of total cost when the code is compiled into an otherwise efficient form. On the other hand, garbage collection methods have their own efficiency problems, so this disadvantage cannot be easily assessed.

- *Simplicity* — Though simple in concept, reference counting can be very tricky to implement. It is dangerous to draw any general conclusions from the complexity of our implementation, but what can be said about reference-counting in general is that it requires pervasive changes in the evaluation process. Garbage collection, as we have seen, can be very cleanly separated from evaluation *per se*.

- *Generality* — The major problem with reference counting is that it cannot deal with circular data structures, such as those that can be created by rplaca and rplacd. To see this, consider a circular list with one outside reference (say, from *globalEnv*), like so:

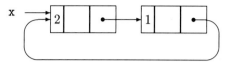

The first cons cell of the list has two direct references, so it has a *refcnt* of 2, and the second cell has one. Now suppose the reference from x is removed. The situation is this:

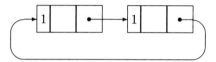

Neither cons cell was returned to the free list, and *neither ever will be*. Since there are no outside references to this list, there is no possibility of removing a reference, so the *refcnt* fields will never go to zero. These two cons cells will forever be in limbo, neither accessible nor reusable. This is an example of a memory leak. By contrast, the garbage collection methods we have studied have no trouble with circular data structures.

10.6 Summary

No memory management technique can help when the legitimate memory needs of a program exceed the memory available. The techniques of this chapter, however, can be used to limit the use of memory to just those legitimate needs, avoiding spurious memory overflows.

Memory management can be quite expensive. In the benchmarks given by Gabriel [1985], for example, it is not uncommon to see garbage collection times equaling more than half the total computation time. Steele [1975] claims that garbage collection times typically run from 10 to 40 percent of the total. There is every reason to charge reference counting with similar cost, though, being spread through the computation, it is more difficult to measure.

Since the time to perform any operation that requires memory allocation — cons in LISP, new in SMALLTALK, etc. — must be calculated as the sum of allocation time, operation time, and (its share of) deallocation (garbage collection) time, these are generally reckoned as particularly expensive operations. Accordingly, programmers will go to great lengths to minimize such operations; LISP programmers, for example, often use rplaca and rplacd to avoid cons'es. Such tricks tend to render code obscure and brittle, an effect which may be deemed a hidden cost of memory management. Perhaps the combination of larger memories and more advanced garbage collection methods will render such coding practices a thing of the past.

There are many topics in memory management which we have not even touched upon. Consider these questions:

- Can the mark-scan method operate without the stack which was used, implicitly, in the mark phase?

- Can garbage collection be done incrementally, avoiding the need to suspend computation for several seconds? This is a particularly crucial question, as much real-world programming involves timing constraints that preclude such pauses.

- Computation and garbage collection seem to be a natural for dual-processor implementation; can these two jobs in fact be neatly separated, with garbage collection being done on a separate processor and thereby appearing to be free?

- Can garbage collection be done when memory is allocated in chunks of varying size?

- Can reference counting be fixed to handle cyclic structures?

The answer to each of these questions is yes, more or less qualified; see the references listed under "Further Reading."

10.6.1 GLOSSARY

compacting garbage collection. Any method of garbage collection in which active cells are moved to contiguous memory locations. These methods generally have the property of improving performance in virtual memory systems.

garbage collection. An approach to memory management in which inaccessible, or garbage, cells are not recovered as they become inaccessible, but rather in a separate phase of computation.

heap-based memory allocation. When the order of allocation of chunks of memory cannot be related to the order of their *de*-allocation, a heap must be used. It is in this case that memory management techniques like reference counting and garbage collection are called for.

mark-scan garbage collection. In this method, the active records in memory are marked during a recursive traversal, followed by a scan of all of memory, reconstructing the free list from the unmarked cells. The method is also known as **mark-and-sweep**.

reference counting. A memory management technique in which each chunk of allocated memory contains a *refcnt* field which holds the number of references to that chunk. By incrementing and decrementing that field as references are added and removed, and deallocating the memory when the *refcnt* goes to zero, inaccessible memory can be recycled as soon as it becomes inaccessible.

semi-space garbage collection. In this method, one half of memory is used at a time. When it is exhausted, all active cells are moved to the other half and compacted into the beginning of that half. This is also called **stop-and-copy** garbage collection.

stack-based memory allocation. When the last chunk of memory to be allocated is always the first to be deallocated, memory can be allocated from a stack. The standard example is the allocation of memory for the formal parameters and local variables of a procedure or function (whether in our interpreters or in conventional languages like PASCAL).

10.6.2   FURTHER READING

The books by Knuth [1973] and Standish [1980] go into detail on a variety of memory management techniques; the survey paper by Cohen [1981] is also excellent. All have extensive lists of references.

The mark-scan method was outlined in McCarthy [1960]; the important technique of marking nodes without an additional stack is credited to Deutsch and, independently, to Schorr and Waite [1967] (see also the books by Knuth and Standish). A compacting method that uses secondary memory was described by Minsky [1963]. Fenichel and Yochelsen [1969] first described the semi-space method; Baker [1978] developed a well-known variant, which avoids the need to stop the computation to do garbage collection. More recent garbage collection methods are reported in Lieberman and Hewitt [1983] and Ungar [1984].

Stack-based memory is generally thought to be far more efficient than heap memory, for reasons that must be evident from our treatment of both in this chapter, but Appel [1987] presents an interesting dissenting argument.

10.7 Exercises

1. Eliminate *ENV* and *VALUELIST* records altogether by placing global variables in the stack. You may impose some language restrictions, such as requiring that all global variables be assigned at the top level before their first use inside a function.

2. The unmarking phase in the mark-scan algorithm can be easily eliminated by ensuring that all *mark* fields are set to false whenever *gc* is called. Implement this change.

3. Modify the mark-scan garbage collector to use the Deutsch-Schorr-Waite tree-traversal algorithm. (Consult the references for its description.)

4. For the mark-scan version of LISP, consider the following perturbations of the body of *markPhase*. For each one, give an example of a LISP program which works before doing the perturbation, but not after, and explain why it fails. To allow for smaller examples, you may decrease *MEMSIZE*, but be sure your example works with the decreased value before the perturbation.

    (a) Remove the statement *markSExp(nilValue)*.

    (b) Remove the statement *markEnv(globalEnv)*.

    (c) Remove the statement *markExp(currentExp)*.

    (d) Remove the loop containing the call *markSExp(argStack[i])*.

5. For the semi-space version of LISP, do the same as for the previous problem, using the following perturbations of *initNewHalf*. Again, you may decrease *HALFMEMSIZE*.

    (a) Remove the statement *nilValue := moveSExp(nilValue)*.

    (b) Remove the loop containing $vl\uparrow.head := moveSExp(vl\uparrow.head)$;

    (c) Remove the statement *currentExp := moveExp(currentExp)*.

    (d) Remove the loop containing *argStack[i] := moveSExp(argStack[i])*.

6. For the reference-counting interpreter, do the same as for the previous problem. The perturbations are:

    (a) Remove both calls to *increfcnt* from *parseList*.

    (b) Remove the call to *increfcnt* from *bindVar*.

    (c) Remove the call to *decrefcnt* from *assign*.

    (d) In *applyUserFun*, replace the statement "*stacktop := stacktop−1*" by "*popArgs(1)*".

    (e) Remove the call to *increfcnt* in the *SETOP* case of *applyCtrlOp*.

7. Modify the APL interpreter as follows:

    (a) Stack arguments. (This is an easy exercise because the changes are exactly as in Section 10.1.)

    (b) Add mark-scan garbage collection.

    (c) Add semi-space garbage collection.

In adding garbage collection, you must manage both *APLVALUE*'s and *INTLIST*'s.

8. Add stack allocation to CLU. Note that environments must be created by constructor operations. Then add either form of garbage collection; you should collect both *CLUVALUE*'s and the *ENV* records that are used to represent cluster instances.

9. Add garbage collection (either type) to SCHEME. You will need to start by modifying the interpreter to use a control stack, as suggested in the Exercises of Chapter 9. The heap will contain not only *SEXP*'s, but also the *ENV*'s pointed to by closures, and *VALUELIST*'s contained in those *ENV*'s. All will have to be allocated in separate *memory* arrays (or perhaps in one array of variant records), and all should be subject to garbage collection.

Appendix A

BNF

Context-free grammars — often called by computer scientists Backus-Naur Form, or BNF, grammars — are a method of describing the syntax of programming languages.

A BNF grammar consists of a list of grammar *rules*. Each rule has the form:

$$\mathsf{A} \longrightarrow \alpha,$$

where A is a *nonterminal symbol* (set in a sans-serif font), and α is a sequence of nonterminal and *terminal* symbols (set in a typewriter font).

A nonterminal symbol represents all the phrases in a syntactic category. Thus, input represents all legal inputs, expression all legal expressions, and name all legal names. A terminal symbol, on the other hand, represents characters that appear *as is* in syntactic phrases.

We refer to the syntax of Chapter 1 (page 3) for our examples in this Appendix. Consider the rules for input and fundef:

input	$\longrightarrow$	expression | fundef
fundef	$\longrightarrow$	(`define` function arglist expression)

These rules can be read as making the following assertions:

- A legal input is either a legal expression or a legal fundef.

- A legal fundef is a left parenthesis followed by the word `define`, then a function, an arglist, and an expression, and then a right parenthesis.

Thus, a *context-free grammar*, being a set of such rules, describes how the phrases of a syntactic category are formed, in one or more ways, by combining phrases of other categories and specific characters in a specified order.

For another example, the phrase

```
(set x 10)
```

is an input by the following reasoning:

- An input can be an expression.

- An expression can be a left parenthesis and the word set, followed by a variable and an expression, followed by a right parenthesis.

- A variable is a name, and a name is a sequence of characters which may be the sequence "x" (we appeal to the English description of this category).

- An expression can be a value, a value is an integer, and 10 is an integer.

The special symbols * and + must be explained. If A is a nonterminal, then A* represents *zero or more* occurrences of phrases in category A. For example, the phrase (x y z) is in category arglist, as are (x) and (). A⁺ is similar, representing *one or more* occurrences of phrases in category A. Thus, (begin (set x y) x) and (begin 4) are expression's, but (begin) is not.

The topic of context-free grammars is an important one in computer science. It will be covered in depth in almost any introductory theory or compiler construction book. Good sources are Aho, et al. [1986], Barrett, et al. [1986], and Hopcroft and Ullman [1979].

Appendix B

Interpreter for Chapter 1

This appendix contains, in full, the code for the interpreter described in Chapter 1. We include a table of contents for the code sections:

```
(****************************************************************
 *                     DECLARATIONS                            *
 ****************************************************************)
program chapter1 (input, output);

label 99;

const
    NAMELENG = 20;      (* Maximum length of a name *)
    MAXNAMES = 100;     (* Maximum number of different names *)
    MAXINPUT = 500;     (* Maximum length of an input *)
    PROMPT = '-> ';
    PROMPT2 = '> ';
    COMMENTCHAR = ';';
    TABCODE = 9;        (* in ASCII *)

type
    NAMESIZE = 0..NAMELENG;
    NAMESTRING = packed array [1..NAMELENG] of char;
```

479

```
NUMBER = integer;
NAME = 1 .. MAXNAMES; (* a NAME is an index in printNames *)

BUILTINOP = (IFOP,WHILEOP,SETOP,BEGINOP,PLUSOP,MINUSOP,
             TIMESOP,DIVOP,EQOP,LTOP,GTOP,PRINTOP);
VALUEOP = PLUSOP .. PRINTOP;
CONTROLOP = IFOP .. BEGINOP;


EXP = ^EXPREC;
EXPLIST = ^EXPLISTREC;
ENV = ^ENVREC;
VALUELIST = ^VALUELISTREC;
NAMELIST = ^NAMELISTREC;
FUNDEF = ^FUNDEFREC;


EXPTYPE = (VALEXP,VAREXP,APEXP);
EXPREC = record
             case etype: EXPTYPE of
                 VALEXP: (num: NUMBER);
                 VAREXP: (varble: NAME);
                 APEXP: (optr: NAME; args: EXPLIST)
         end;

EXPLISTREC = record
             head: EXP;
             tail: EXPLIST
         end;

VALUELISTREC = record
             head: NUMBER;
             tail: VALUELIST
         end;

NAMELISTREC = record
             head: NAME;
             tail: NAMELIST
         end;

ENVREC = record
             vars: NAMELIST;
             values: VALUELIST
         end;

FUNDEFREC = record
             funname: NAME;
             formals: NAMELIST;
             body: EXP;
             nextfundef: FUNDEF
         end;
```

```
var
   fundefs: FUNDEF;

   globalEnv: ENV;

   currentExp: EXP;

   userinput: array [1..MAXINPUT] of char;
   inputleng, pos: 0..MAXINPUT;

   printNames: array [NAME] of NAMESTRING;
   numNames, numBuiltins: NAME;

   quittingtime: Boolean;


(*****************************************************************
 *                    DATA STRUCTURE OP'S                       *
 *****************************************************************)
(* mkVALEXP - return an EXP of type VALEXP with num n          *)
function mkVALEXP (n: NUMBER): EXP;
var e: EXP;
begin
   new(e);
   e^.etype := VALEXP;
   e^.num := n;
   mkVALEXP := e
end; (* mkVALEXP *)

(* mkVAREXP - return an EXP of type VAREXP with varble nm      *)
function mkVAREXP (nm: NAME): EXP;
var e: EXP;
begin
   new(e);
   e^.etype := VAREXP;
   e^.varble := nm;
   mkVAREXP := e
end; (* mkVAREXP *)

(* mkAPEXP - return EXP of type APEXP w/ optr op and args el   *)
function mkAPEXP (op: NAME; el: EXPLIST): EXP;
var e: EXP;
begin
   new(e);
   e^.etype := APEXP;
   e^.optr := op;
   e^.args := el;
```

```
   mkAPEXP := e
end; (* mkAPEXP *)

(* mkExplist - return an EXPLIST with head e and tail el        *)
function mkExplist (e: EXP; el: EXPLIST): EXPLIST;
var newel: EXPLIST;
begin
   new(newel);
   newel^.head := e;
   newel^.tail := el;
   mkExplist := newel
end; (* mkExplist *)

(* mkNamelist - return a NAMELIST with head n and tail nl       *)
function mkNamelist (nm: NAME; nl: NAMELIST): NAMELIST;
var newnl: NAMELIST;
begin
   new(newnl);
   newnl´.head := nm;
   newnl^.tail := nl;
   mkNamelist := newnl
end; (* mkNamelist *)

(* mkValuelist - return an VALUELIST with head n and tail vl    *)
function mkValuelist (n: NUMBER; vl: VALUELIST): VALUELIST;
var newvl: VALUELIST;
begin
   new(newvl);
   newvl^.head := n;
   newvl^.tail := vl;
   mkValuelist := newvl
end; (* mkValuelist *)

(* mkEnv - return an ENV with vars nl and values vl             *)
function mkEnv (nl: NAMELIST; vl: VALUELIST): ENV;
var rho: ENV;
begin
   new(rho);
   rho^.vars := nl;
   rho^.values := vl;
   mkEnv := rho
end; (* mkEnv *)

(* lengthVL - return length of VALUELIST vl                     *)
function lengthVL (vl: VALUELIST): integer;
var i: integer;
begin
   i := 0;
   while vl <> nil do begin
     i := i+1;
```

```
      vl := vl^.tail
      end;
   lengthVL := i
end; (* lengthVL *)

(* lengthNL - return length of NAMELIST nl                    *)
function lengthNL (nl: NAMELIST): integer;
var i: integer;
begin
   i := 0;
   while nl <> nil do begin
      i := i+1;
      nl := nl^.tail
      end;
   lengthNL := i
end; (* lengthNL *)


(***************************************************************
 *                    NAME MANAGEMENT                         *
 ***************************************************************)

(* fetchFun - get function definition of fname from fundefs   *)
function fetchFun (fname: NAME): FUNDEF;
var
   f: FUNDEF;
   found: Boolean;
begin
   found := false;
   f := fundefs;
   while (f <> nil) and not found do
      if f^.funname = fname
      then found := true
      else f := f^.nextfundef;
   fetchFun := f
end; (* fetchFun *)

(* newFunDef - add new function fname w/ parameters nl, body e *)
procedure newFunDef (fname: NAME; nl: NAMELIST; e: EXP);
var f: FUNDEF;
begin
   f := fetchFun(fname);
   if f = nil (* fname not yet defined as a function *)
   then begin
           new(f);
           f^.nextfundef := fundefs; (* place new FUNDEFREC *)
           fundefs := f             (* on fundefs list *)
        end;
   f^.funname := fname;
   f^.formals := nl;
```

```
      f^.body := e
end; (* newFunDef *)

(* initNames - place all pre-defined names into printNames        *)
procedure initNames;
var i: integer;
begin
   fundefs := nil;
   i := 1;
   printNames[i] := 'if                 '; i := i+1;
   printNames[i] := 'while              '; i := i+1;
   printNames[i] := 'set                '; i := i+1;
   printNames[i] := 'begin              '; i := i+1;
   printNames[i] := '+                  '; i := i+1;
   printNames[i] := '-                  '; i := i+1;
   printNames[i] := '*                  '; i := i+1;
   printNames[i] := '/                  '; i := i+1;
   printNames[i] := '=                  '; i := i+1;
   printNames[i] := '<                  '; i := i+1;
   printNames[i] := '>                  '; i := i+1;
   printNames[i] := 'print              ';
   numNames := i;
   numBuiltins := i
end; (* initNames *)

(* install - insert new name into printNames                       *)
function install (nm: NAMESTRING): NAME;
var
   i: integer;
   found: Boolean;
begin
   i := 1; found := false;
   while (i <= numNames) and not found
   do if nm = printNames[i]
      then found := true
      else i := i+1;
   if not found
   then begin
           if i > MAXNAMES
           then begin
                   writeln('No more room for names');
                   goto 99
                end;
           numNames := i;
           printNames[i] := nm
        end;
   install := i
end; (* install *)

(* prName - print name nm                                          *)
```

```
procedure prName (nm: NAME);
var i: integer;
begin
   i := 1;
   while i <= NAMELENG
   do if printNames[nm][i] <> ' '
      then begin
              write(printNames[nm][i]);
              i := i+1
           end
      else i := NAMELENG+1
end; (* prName *)

(* primOp - translate NAME optr to corresponding BUILTINOP      *)
function primOp (optr: NAME): BUILTINOP;
var
   op: BUILTINOP;
   i: integer;
begin
   op := IFOP; (* N.B. IFOP is first value in BUILTINOPS *)
   for i := 1 to optr-1 do op := succ(op);
   primOp := op
end; (* primOp *)


(******************************************************************
 *                          INPUT                                 *
 ******************************************************************)

(* isDelim - check if c is a delimiter                          *)
function isDelim (c: char): Boolean;
begin
   isDelim := c in ['(', ')', ' ', COMMENTCHAR]
end; (* isDelim *)

(* skipblanks - return next non-blank position in userinput     *)
function skipblanks (p: integer): integer;
begin
   while userinput[p] = ' ' do p := p+1;
   skipblanks := p
end; (* skipblanks *)

(* matches - check if string nm matches userinput[s .. s+leng]  *)
function matches (s: integer; leng: NAMESIZE;
                  nm: NAMESTRING): Boolean;
var
   match: Boolean;
   i: integer;
begin
   match := true; i := 1;
```

```
  while match and (i <= leng) do begin
     if userinput[s] <> nm[i] then match := false;
     i := i+1;
     s := s+1
     end;
  if not isDelim(userinput[s]) then match := false;
  matches := match
end; (* matches *)

(* reader - read char's into userinput; be sure input not blank  *)
procedure reader;

(* readInput - read char's into userinput                         *)
  procedure readInput;

  var c: char;

(* nextchar - read next char - filter tabs and comments           *)
    procedure nextchar (var c: char);
    begin
       read(c);
       if c = chr(TABCODE)
       then c := ' '
       else if c = COMMENTCHAR
            then begin while not eoln do read(c); c := ' ' end
    end; (* nextchar *)

(* readParens - read char's, ignoring newlines, to matching ')'  *)
    procedure readParens;
    var
       parencnt: integer; (* current depth of parentheses *)
       c: char;
    begin
       parencnt := 1; (* '(' just read *)
       repeat
          if eoln then write(PROMPT2);
          nextchar(c);
          pos := pos+1;
          if pos = MAXINPUT
          then begin
                   writeln('User input too long');
                   goto 99
               end;
          userinput[pos] := c;
          if c = '(' then parencnt := parencnt+1;
          if c = ')' then parencnt := parencnt-1
       until parencnt = 0
    end; (* readParens *)
```

```
   begin (* readInput *)
      write(PROMPT);
      pos := 0;
      repeat
         pos := pos+1;
         if pos = MAXINPUT
         then begin
                  writeln('User input too long');
                  goto 99
              end;
         nextchar(c);
         userinput[pos] := c;
         if userinput[pos] = '(' then readParens
      until eoln;
      inputleng := pos;
      userinput[pos+1] := COMMENTCHAR (* sentinel *)
   end; (* readInput *)

begin (* reader *)
   repeat
      readInput;
      pos := skipblanks(1);
   until pos <= inputleng (* ignore blank lines *)
end; (* reader *)

(* parseName - return (installed) NAME starting at userinput[pos]*)
function parseName: NAME;
var
   nm: NAMESTRING; (* array to accumulate characters *)
   leng: NAMESIZE; (* length of name *)
begin
   leng := 0;
   while (pos <= inputleng) and not isDelim(userinput[pos])
   do begin
         if leng = NAMELENG
         then begin
                  writeln('Name too long, begins: ', nm);
                  goto 99
              end;
         leng := leng+1;
         nm[leng] := userinput[pos];
         pos := pos+1
      end;
   if leng = 0
   then begin
         writeln('Error: expected name, instead read: ',
                  userinput[pos]);
         goto 99
      end;
```

```
      for leng := leng+1 to NAMELENG do nm[leng] := ' ';
      pos := skipblanks(pos); (* skip blanks after name *)
      parseName := install(nm)
   end; (* parseName *)

(* isNumber - check if a number begins at pos                    *)
   function isNumber (pos: integer): Boolean;

(* isDigits - check if sequence of digits begins at pos          *)
      function isDigits (pos: integer): Boolean;
      begin
         if not (userinput[pos] in ['0'..'9'])
         then isDigits := false
         else begin
                 isDigits := true;
                 while userinput[pos] in ['0'..'9'] do pos := pos+1;
                 if not isDelim(userinput[pos])
                 then isDigits := false
              end
      end; (* isDigits *)

begin (* isNumber *)
   isNumber := isDigits(pos) or
                ((userinput[pos] = '-') and isDigits(pos+1))
end; (* isNumber *)

(* parseVal - return number starting at userinput[pos]           *)
function parseVal: NUMBER;
var n, sign: integer;
begin
   n := 0; sign := 1;
   if userinput[pos] = '-'
   then begin
           sign := -1;
           pos := pos+1
        end;
   while userinput[pos] in ['0'..'9'] do
      begin
         n := 10*n + (ord(userinput[pos]) - ord('0'));
         pos := pos+1
      end;
   pos := skipblanks(pos); (* skip blanks after number *)
   parseVal := n*sign
end; (* parseVal *)

function parseEL: EXPLIST; forward;

(* parseExp - return EXP starting at userinput[pos]              *)
function parseExp: EXP;
var
```

```
      nm: NAME;
      el: EXPLIST;
begin
   if userinput[pos] = '('
   then begin    (* APEXP *)
           pos := skipblanks(pos+1); (* skip '( ..' *)
           nm := parseName;
           el := parseEL;
           parseExp := mkAPEXP(nm, el)
        end
   else if isNumber(pos)
        then parseExp := mkVALEXP(parseVal)    (* VALEXP *)
        else parseExp := mkVAREXP(parseName)   (* VAREXP *)
end; (* parseExp *)

(* parseEL - return EXPLIST starting at userinput[pos]          *)
function parseEL;
var
   e: EXP;
   el: EXPLIST;
begin
   if userinput[pos] = ')'
   then begin
           pos := skipblanks(pos+1); (* skip ') ..' *)
           parseEL := nil
        end
   else begin
           e := parseExp;
           el := parseEL;
           parseEL := mkExplist(e, el)
        end
end; (* parseEL *)

(* parseNL - return NAMELIST starting at userinput[pos]          *)
function parseNL: NAMELIST;
var
   nm: NAME;
   nl: NAMELIST;
begin
   if userinput[pos] = ')'
   then begin
           pos := skipblanks(pos+1); (* skip ') ..' *)
           parseNL := nil
        end
   else begin
           nm := parseName;
           nl := parseNL;
           parseNL := mkNamelist(nm, nl)
        end
```

```
end; (* parseNL *)

(* parseDef - parse function definition at userinput[pos]          *)
function parseDef: NAME;
var
   fname: NAME;          (* function name *)
   nl: NAMELIST;         (* formal parameters *)
   e: EXP;               (* body *)
begin
   pos := skipblanks(pos+1); (* skip '( ..' *)
   pos := skipblanks(pos+6); (* skip 'define ..' *)
   fname := parseName;
   pos := skipblanks(pos+1); (* skip '( ..' *)
   nl := parseNL;
   e := parseExp;
   pos := skipblanks(pos+1); (* skip ') ..' *)
   newFunDef(fname, nl, e);
   parseDef := fname
end; (* parseDef *)


(*****************************************************************
 *                      ENVIRONMENTS                           *
 *****************************************************************)

(* emptyEnv - return an environment with no bindings              *)
function emptyEnv: ENV;
begin
   emptyEnv := mkEnv(nil, nil)
end; (* emptyEnv *)

(* bindVar - bind variable nm to value n in environment rho       *)
procedure bindVar (nm: NAME; n: NUMBER; rho: ENV);
begin
   rho^.vars := mkNamelist(nm, rho^.vars);
   rho^.values := mkValuelist(n, rho^.values)
end; (* bindVar *)

(* findVar - look up nm in rho                                    *)
function findVar (nm: NAME; rho: ENV): VALUELIST;
var
   nl: NAMELIST;
   vl: VALUELIST;
   found: Boolean;
begin
   found := false;
   nl := rho^.vars;
   vl := rho^.values;
   while (nl <> nil) and not found do
      if nl^.head = nm
```

```
      then found := true
      else begin
              nl := nl^.tail;
              vl := vl^.tail
          end;
  findVar := vl
end; (* findVar *)

(* assign - assign value n to variable nm in rho              *)
procedure assign (nm: NAME; n: NUMBER; rho: ENV);
var varloc: VALUELIST;
begin
  varloc := findVar(nm, rho);
  varloc^.head := n
end; (* assign *)

(* fetch - return number bound to nm in rho                   *)
function fetch (nm: NAME; rho: ENV): NUMBER;
var vl: VALUELIST;
begin
  vl := findVar(nm, rho);
  fetch := vl^.head
end; (* fetch *)

(* isBound - check if nm is bound in rho                      *)
function isBound (nm: NAME; rho: ENV): Boolean;
begin
  isBound := findVar(nm, rho) <> nil
end; (* isBound *)


(******************************************************************
 *                        NUMBERS                               *
 ******************************************************************)

(* prValue - print number n                                   *)
procedure prValue (n: NUMBER);
begin
  write(n:1)
end; (* prValue *)

(* isTrueVal - return true if n is a true (non-zero) value    *)
function isTrueVal (n: NUMBER): Boolean;
begin
  isTrueVal := n <> 0
end; (* isTrueVal *)

(* applyValueOp - apply VALUEOP op to arguments in VALUELIST vl *)
function applyValueOp (op: VALUEOP; vl: VALUELIST): NUMBER;

var n, n1, n2: NUMBER;
```

```
(* arity - return number of arguments expected by op          *)
   function arity (op: VALUEOP): integer;
   begin
      if op in [PLUSOP .. GTOP] then arity := 2 else arity := 1
   end; (* arity *)

begin (* applyValueOp *)
   if arity(op) <> lengthVL(vl)
   then begin
           write('Wrong number of arguments to ');
           prName(ord(op)+1);
           writeln;
           goto 99
        end;
   n1 := vl^.head; (* 1st actual *)
   if arity(op) = 2 then n2 := vl^.tail^.head; (* 2nd actual *)
   case op of
      PLUSOP: n := n1+n2;
      MINUSOP: n := n1-n2;
      TIMESOP: n := n1*n2;
      DIVOP: n := n1 div n2;
      EQOP: if n1 = n2 then n := 1 else n := 0;
      LTOP: if n1 < n2 then n := 1 else n := 0;
      GTOP: if n1 > n2 then n := 1 else n := 0;
      PRINTOP:
         begin prValue(n1); writeln; n := n1 end
   end; (* case *)
   applyValueOp := n
end; (* applyValueOp *)


(*****************************************************************
 *                       EVALUATION                             *
 *****************************************************************)

(* eval - return value of expression e in local environment rho  *)
function eval (e: EXP; rho: ENV): NUMBER;

var op: BUILTINOP;

(* evalList - evaluate each expression in el                   *)
   function evalList (el: EXPLIST): VALUELIST;
   var
      h: NUMBER;
      t: VALUELIST;
   begin
      if el = nil then evalList := nil
      else begin
              h := eval(el^.head, rho);
              t := evalList(el^.tail);
```

```
                  evalList := mkValuelist(h, t)
               end
    end; (* evalList *)

(* applyUserFun - look up definition of nm and apply to actuals  *)
    function applyUserFun (nm: NAME; actuals: VALUELIST): NUMBER;
    var
       f: FUNDEF;
       rho: ENV;
    begin
       f := fetchFun(nm);
       if f = nil
       then begin
               write('Undefined function: ');
               prName(nm);
               writeln;
               goto 99
            end;
       with f^ do begin
          if lengthNL(formals) <> lengthVL(actuals)
          then begin
                  write('Wrong number of arguments to: ');
                  prName(nm);
                  writeln;
                  goto 99
               end;
          rho := mkEnv(formals, actuals);
          applyUserFun := eval(body, rho)
          end
    end; (* applyUserFun *)

(* applyCtrlOp - apply CONTROLOP op to args in rho                *)
    function applyCtrlOp (op: CONTROLOP;
                          args: EXPLIST): NUMBER;
    var n: NUMBER;
    begin
       with args^ do
          case op of
            IFOP:
               if isTrueVal(eval(head, rho))
               then applyCtrlOp := eval(tail^.head, rho)
               else applyCtrlOp := eval(tail^.tail^.head, rho);
            WHILEOP:
               begin
                 n := eval(head, rho);
                 while isTrueVal(n)
                 do begin
                        n := eval(tail^.head, rho);
                        n := eval(head, rho)
```

```
                        end;
                    applyCtrlOp := n
                end;
            SETOP:
                begin
                    n := eval(tail^.head, rho);
                    if isBound(head^.varble, rho)
                    then assign(head^.varble, n, rho)
                    else if isBound(head^.varble, globalEnv)
                            then assign(head^.varble, n, globalEnv)
                            else bindVar(head^.varble, n, globalEnv);
                    applyCtrlOp := n
                end;
            BEGINOP:
                begin
                    while args^.tail <> nil do
                        begin
                            n := eval(args^.head, rho);
                            args := args^.tail
                        end;
                    applyCtrlOp := eval(args^.head, rho)
                end
        end (* case and with *)
    end; (* applyCtrlOp *)

begin (* eval *)
    with e^ do
        case etype of
            VALEXP:
                eval := num;
            VAREXP:
                if isBound(varble, rho)
                then eval := fetch(varble, rho)
                else if isBound(varble, globalEnv)
                        then eval := fetch(varble, globalEnv)
                        else begin
                                write('Undefined variable: ');
                                prName(varble);
                                writeln;
                                goto 99
                            end;
            APEXP:
                if optr > numBuiltins
                then eval := applyUserFun(optr, evalList(args))
                else begin
                        op := primOp(optr);
                        if op in [IFOP .. BEGINOP]
                        then eval := applyCtrlOp(op, args)
                        else eval := applyValueOp(op,
```

```
                                    evalList(args))
                   end
         end (* case and with *)
end; (* eval *)


(****************************************************************
 *                    READ-EVAL-PRINT LOOP                     *
 ****************************************************************)

begin (* chapter1 main *)
   initNames;
   globalEnv := emptyEnv;

   quittingtime := false;
99:
   while not quittingtime do begin
      reader;
      if matches(pos, 4, 'quit                  ')
      then quittingtime := true
      else if (userinput[pos] = '(') and
              matches(skipblanks(pos+1), 6, 'define                  ')
           then begin
                    prName(parseDef);
                    writeln
                 end
           else begin
                    currentExp := parseExp;
                    prValue(eval(currentExp, emptyEnv));
                    writeln;
                    writeln
                 end
      end (* while *)
end. (* chapter1 *)
```

Appendix C

Interpreter for LISP

This appendix contains the code for the LISP interpreter, insofar as it differs from the code in Appendix B. Thus, when we say "such-and-such has not changed," we mean "has not changed from Appendix B."

```
(****************************************************************
*                       DECLARATIONS                          *
****************************************************************)
```

The following changes were discussed in Section 2.2. The declaration of type `NUMBER` is removed. There are also the declarations, not shown here, of variable `nilValue` and `trueValue` of type SEXP. There are no other changes of importance.

```
BUILTINOP = (IFOP,WHILEOP,SETOP,BEGINOP,PLUSOP,MINUSOP,
             TIMESOP,DIVOP,EQOP,LTOP,GTOP,CONSOP,
             CAROP,CDROP,NUMBERPOP,SYMBOLPOP,
             LISTPOP,NULLPOP,PRINTOP);
VALUEOP = PLUSOP .. PRINTOP;
CONTROLOP = IFOP .. BEGINOP;

SEXP = ^SEXPREC;
SEXPTYPE = (NILSXP,NUMSXP,SYMSXP,LISTSXP);
SEXPREC = record
            case sxptype: SEXPTYPE of
```

```
                  NILSXP: ();
                  NUMSXP: (intval: integer);
                  SYMSXP: (symval: NAME);
                  LISTSXP: (carval, cdrval: SEXP)
           end;

   EXPTYPE = (VALEXP,VAREXP,APEXP);
   EXPREC = record
                case etype: EXPTYPE of
                    VALEXP: (sxp: SEXP);
                    VAREXP: (varble: NAME);
                    APEXP: (optr: NAME; args: EXPLIST)
           end;

   VALUELISTREC = record
                head: SEXP;
                tail: VALUELIST
           end;
```

```
(****************************************************************
*                     DATA STRUCTURE OP'S                      *
****************************************************************)
```

The only significant change here is the addition of a new function:

```
(* mkSExp - return SEXP of type t (but no value)             *)
function mkSExp (t: SEXPTYPE): SEXP;
var s: SEXP;
begin
   new(s);
   s^.sxptype := t;
   mkSExp := s
end; (* mkSExp *)
```

```
(****************************************************************
*                     NAME MANAGEMENT                          *
****************************************************************)
```

Only initNames is changed in this section.

```
(* initNames - place all pre-defined names into printNames    *)
procedure initNames;
var i: integer;
begin
   fundefs := nil;
   i := 1;
   printNames[i] := 'if                    '; i := i+1;
   printNames[i] := 'while                 '; i := i+1;
```

```
      printNames[i] := 'set              '; i := i+1;
      printNames[i] := 'begin            '; i := i+1;
      printNames[i] := '+                '; i := i+1;
      printNames[i] := '-                '; i := i+1;
      printNames[i] := '*                '; i := i+1;
      printNames[i] := '/                '; i := i+1;
      printNames[i] := '=                '; i := i+1;
      printNames[i] := '<                '; i := i+1;
      printNames[i] := '>                '; i := i+1;
      printNames[i] := 'cons             '; i := i+1;
      printNames[i] := 'car              '; i := i+1;
      printNames[i] := 'cdr              '; i := i+1;
      printNames[i] := 'number?          '; i := i+1;
      printNames[i] := 'symbol?          '; i := i+1;
      printNames[i] := 'list?            '; i := i+1;
      printNames[i] := 'null?            '; i := i+1;
      printNames[i] := 'print            '; i := i+1;
      printNames[i] := 'T                ';
      numNames := i;
      numBuiltins := i
end; (* initNames *)



(******************************************************************
 *                         INPUT                                  *
 ******************************************************************)
```

The only change here is in the parsing of constants. (The character input routine, **reader**, is not changed, nor are the other parsing routines, like **parseExp** and **parseDef**.) **isValue** is called by **parseExp** to determine if the expression is a constant or a variable; this is in contrast to Appendix B, where **isNumber** was used for this purpose.

```
(* isValue - check if a number or quoted const begins at pos      *)
function isValue (pos: integer): Boolean;
begin
    isValue:= (userinput[pos] = '''') or isNumber(pos)
end; (* isValue *)

(* parseVal - return S-expression starting at userinput[pos]      *)
function parseVal: SEXP;

(* parseSExp - return quoted S-expr starting at userinput[pos]    *)
   function parseSExp: SEXP;

   var s: SEXP;

(* parseInt - return number starting at userinput[pos]            *)
      function parseInt: SEXP;
      var sum, sign: integer;
```

```
    begin
      s := mkSExp(NUMSXP);
      sum := 0; sign := 1;
      if userinput[pos] = '-'
      then begin
              sign := -1;
              pos := pos+1
           end;
      while userinput[pos] in ['0'..'9'] do begin
         sum := 10*sum + (ord(userinput[pos]) - ord('0'));
         pos := pos+1
         end;
      s^.intval := sum * sign;
      pos := skipblanks(pos); (* skip blanks after number *)
      parseInt := s
    end; (* parseInt *)

(* parseSym - return symbol starting at userinput[pos]             *)
    function parseSym: SEXP;
    begin
      s := mkSExp(SYMSXP);
      s^.symval := parseName;
      parseSym := s
    end; (* parseSym *)

(* parseList - return list starting at userinput[pos]              *)
    function parseList: SEXP;
    var car, cdr: SEXP;
    begin
      if userinput[pos] = ')'
      then begin
              parseList := mkSExp(NILSXP);
              pos := skipblanks(pos+1)
           end
      else begin
              car := parseSExp;
              cdr := parseList;
              s := mkSExp(LISTSXP);
              s^.carval := car;
              s^.cdrval := cdr;
              parseList := s
           end
    end; (* parseList *)

  begin (* parseSExp *)
    if isNumber(pos)
    then parseSExp := parseInt
    else if userinput[pos] = '('
        then begin
```

```
                    pos := skipblanks(pos+1);
                    parseSExp := parseList
                  end
            else parseSExp := parseSym
   end; (* parseSExp *)

begin (* parseVal *)
   if userinput[pos] = '''' then pos := pos+1;
   parseVal := parseSExp
end; (* parseVal *)


(****************************************************************
*                      ENVIRONMENTS                           *
****************************************************************)

   No changes here.

(****************************************************************
*                      S-EXPRESSIONS                          *
****************************************************************)
(* prValue - print S-expression s                             *)
procedure prValue (s: SEXP);
var s1: SEXP;
begin
   with s^ do
      case sxptype of
         NILSXP: write('()');
         NUMSXP: write(intval:1);
         SYMSXP: prName(symval);
         LISTSXP:
            begin
               write('(');
               prValue(carval);
               s1 := cdrval;
               while s1^.sxptype = LISTSXP do begin
                  write(' ');
                  prValue(s1^.carval);
                  s1 := s1^.cdrval
                  end;
               write(')')
            end
      end (* case and with *)
end; (* prValue *)

(* isTrueVal - return true if s is true (non-NIL) value       *)
function isTrueVal (s: SEXP): Boolean;
begin
   isTrueVal := s^.sxptype <> NILSXP
end; (* isTrueVal *)
```

```
(* applyValueOp - apply VALUEOP op to arguments in VALUELIST vl  *)
function applyValueOp (op: VALUEOP; vl: VALUELIST): SEXP;

var
   result: SEXP;
   s1, s2: SEXP;

(* applyArithOp - apply binary, arithmetic VALUEOP to arguments  *)
   procedure applyArithOp (n1, n2: integer);
   begin
      result := mkSExp(NUMSXP);
      with result^ do
         case op of
            PLUSOP: intval := n1+n2;
            MINUSOP: intval := n1-n2;
            TIMESOP: intval := n1*n2;
            DIVOP: intval := n1 div n2
         end
   end; (* applyArithOp *)

(* applyRelOp - apply binary, relational VALUEOP to arguments    *)
   procedure applyRelOp (n1, n2: integer) ;
   begin
      case op of
         LTOP: if n1 < n2 then result := trueValue;
         GTOP: if n1 > n2 then result := trueValue
      end
   end; (* applyRelOp *)

(* arity - return number of arguments expected by op             *)
   function arity (op: VALUEOP): integer;
   begin
      if op in [PLUSOP .. CONSOP] then arity := 2 else arity := 1
   end; (* arity *)

begin (* applyValueOp *)
   if arity(op) <> lengthVL(vl)
   then begin
           write('Wrong number of arguments to ');
           prName(ord(op)+1);
           writeln;
           goto 99
        end;
   result := nilValue;
   s1 := vl^.head; (* 1st actual *)
   if arity(op) = 2 then s2 := vl^.tail^.head; (* 2nd actual *)
   if op in [PLUSOP .. DIVOP, LTOP .. GTOP]
   then if (s1^.sxptype = NUMSXP)
           and (s2^.sxptype = NUMSXP)
```

```
        then if op in [PLUSOP .. DIVOP]
            then applyArithOp(s1^.intval, s2^.intval)
            else applyRelOp(s1^.intval, s2^.intval)
        else begin
            write('Non-arithmetic arguments to ');
            prName(ord(op)+1);
            writeln;
            goto 99
          end
    else with s1^ do
        case op of
          EQOP:
            if (sxptype = NILSXP)
                and (s2^.sxptype = NILSXP)
            then result := trueValue
            else if (sxptype = NUMSXP)
                    and (s2^.sxptype = NUMSXP)
                    and (intval = s2^.intval)
                then result := trueValue
                else if (sxptype = SYMSXP)
                        and (s2^.sxptype = SYMSXP)
                        and (symval = s2^.symval)
                    then result := trueValue;
          CONSOP:
            begin
              result := mkSExp(LISTSXP);
              with result^ do begin
                carval := s1;
                cdrval := s2
                end
            end;
          CAROP:
            if sxptype <> LISTSXP
            then begin
                write('Error: car applied to non-list: ');
                prValue(s1);
                writeln
              end
            else result := carval;
          CDROP:
            if sxptype <> LISTSXP
            then begin
                write('Error: cdr applied to non-list: ');
                prValue(s1);
                writeln
              end
            else result := cdrval;
          NUMBERPOP:
            if sxptype = NUMSXP then result := trueValue;
```

```
        SYMBOLPOP:
            if sxptype = SYMSXP then result := trueValue;
        LISTPOP:
            if sxptype = LISTSXP then result := trueValue;
        NULLPOP:
            if sxptype = NILSXP then result := trueValue;
        PRINTOP:
            begin prValue(s1); writeln; result := s1 end
        end; (* case and with *)
    applyValueOp := result
end; (* applyValueOp *)
```

```
(****************************************************************
*                      EVALUATION                             *
****************************************************************)
```

The only changes here are: Use SEXP instead of NUMBERS; use local variable s instead of n.

```
(****************************************************************
*                  READ-EVAL-PRINT LOOP                       *
****************************************************************)
```

Variables nilValue and trueValue are initialized; after this, the top-level loop is unchanged.

```
begin (* lisp main *)
    initNames;

    nilValue := mkSExp(NILSXP);
    trueValue := mkSExp(SYMSXP); trueValue^.symval := numNames;


        : (as in Chapter 1 main)

end. (* lisp *)
```

Appendix D

Interpreter for APL

This appendix contains the code for the APL interpreter, insofar as it differs from the code in Appendix B. Thus, when we say "such-and-such has not changed," we mean "has not changed from Appendix B."

```
(*****************************************************************
*                      DECLARATIONS                            *
*****************************************************************)
```

The following changes were discussed in Section 3.2. NUMBER is replaced by APLVALUE, and the new type INTLIST is declared. The declarations of EXPREC and VALUELISTREC are changed only in that the components formerly of type NUMBER now have type APLVALUE (and in EXPREC that component's name is changed to be more descriptive).

```
BUILTINOP = (IFOP,WHILEOP,SETOP,BEGINOP,
             PLUSOP,MINUSOP,TIMESOP,DIVOP,MAXOP,
             OROP,ANDOP,EQOP,LTOP,GTOP,
             REDPLUSOP,REDMINUSOP,REDTIMESOP,
             REDDIVOP,REDMAXOP,REDOROP,REDANDOP,
             COMPRESSOP,SHAPEOP,RAVELOP,RESTRUCTOP,
             CATOP,INDXOP,TRANSOP,SUBOP,PRINTOP);
VALUEOP = PLUSOP .. PRINTOP;
CONTROLOP = IFOP .. BEGINOP;
```

```
REDOP = REDPLUSOP .. REDANDOP;

APLVALUE = ^APLVALUEREC;
INTLIST = ^INTLISTREC;

RANK = (SCALAR,VECTOR,MATRIX);
APLVALUEREC = record
                intvals: INTLIST;
                case rnk: RANK of
                    SCALAR: ();
                    VECTOR: (leng: integer);
                    MATRIX: (rows, cols: integer)
            end;

INTLISTREC = record
                int: integer;
                nextint: INTLIST
            end;

EXPTYPE = (VALEXP,VAREXP,APEXP);
EXPREC = record
                case etype: EXPTYPE of
                    VALEXP: (aplval: APLVALUE);
                    VAREXP: (varble: NAME);
                    APEXP: (optr: NAME; args: EXPLIST)
            end;

VALUELISTREC = record
                head: APLVALUE;
                tail: VALUELIST
            end;
```

```
(****************************************************************
*                   DATA STRUCTURE OP'S                        *
****************************************************************)
```

The only significant change here is the inclusion of function `lengthIL`, analogous to `lengthVL`, but for `INTLIST`'s. In addition, some occurrences of `NUMBER` are changed to `APLVALUE`.

```
(****************************************************************
*                   NAME MANAGEMENT                            *
****************************************************************)
```

`initNames` is changed to add the new operations.

```
(* initNames - place all pre-defined names into printNames       *)
procedure initNames;
var i: integer;
```

```
begin
   fundefs := nil;
   i := 1;
   printNames[i] := 'if            '; i := i+1;
   printNames[i] := 'while         '; i := i+1;
   printNames[i] := 'set           '; i := i+1;
   printNames[i] := 'begin         '; i := i+1;
   printNames[i] := '+             '; i := i+1;
   printNames[i] := '-             '; i := i+1;
   printNames[i] := '*             '; i := i+1;
   printNames[i] := '/             '; i := i+1;
   printNames[i] := 'max           '; i := i+1;
   printNames[i] := 'or            '; i := i+1;
   printNames[i] := 'and           '; i := i+1;
   printNames[i] := '=             '; i := i+1;
   printNames[i] := '<             '; i := i+1;
   printNames[i] := '>             '; i := i+1;
   printNames[i] := '+/            '; i := i+1;
   printNames[i] := '-/            '; i := i+1;
   printNames[i] := '*/            '; i := i+1;
   printNames[i] := '//            '; i := i+1;
   printNames[i] := 'max/          '; i := i+1;
   printNames[i] := 'or/           '; i := i+1;
   printNames[i] := 'and/          '; i := i+1;
   printNames[i] := 'compress      '; i := i+1;
   printNames[i] := 'shape         '; i := i+1;
   printNames[i] := 'ravel         '; i := i+1;
   printNames[i] := 'restruct      '; i := i+1;
   printNames[i] := 'cat           '; i := i+1;
   printNames[i] := 'indx          '; i := i+1;
   printNames[i] := 'trans         '; i := i+1;
   printNames[i] := '[]            '; i := i+1;
   printNames[i] := 'print         ';
   numNames := i;
   numBuiltins := i
end; (* initNames *)


(***************************************************************
 *                        INPUT                               *
 ***************************************************************)
```

As in LISP, the only change here is in the handling of constants. isValue is called from parseExp to determine whether the next expression is a constant or a variable; in Appendix B, when numbers were the only constants, isNumber was called for this purpose; isNumber is unchanged.

```
(* isValue - check if a number or vector const begins at pos   *)
function isValue (pos: integer): Boolean;
begin
```

```
   isValue:= (userinput[pos] = '''') or isNumber(pos)
end; (* isValue *)

(* parseVal - return APL value starting at userinput[pos]          *)
function parseVal: APLVALUE;

var result: APLVALUE;

(* parseInt - return number starting at userinput[pos]             *)
   function parseInt: integer;
   var n, sign: integer;
   begin
      n := 0;
      sign := 1;
      if userinput[pos] = '-'
      then begin
              sign := -1;
              pos := pos+1
           end;
      while userinput[pos] in ['0'..'9'] do
         begin
            n := 10*n + (ord(userinput[pos]) - ord('0'));
            pos := pos+1
         end;
      pos := skipblanks(pos); (* skip blanks after number *)
      parseInt := n*sign
   end; (* parseInt *)

(* parseVec - return INTLIST starting at userinput[pos]            *)
   function parseVec: INTLIST;
   var il: INTLIST;
   begin
      if userinput[pos] = ')'
      then begin
              pos := skipblanks(pos+1); (* skip ') ...' *)
              il := nil
           end
      else begin
              new(il);
              il^.int := parseInt;
              il^.nextint := parseVec
           end;
      parseVec := il
   end; (* parseVec *)

begin (* parseVal *)
   new(result);
   with result^ do
      if userinput[pos] = ''''
```

```
        then begin
                rnk := VECTOR;
                pos := skipblanks(pos+2); (* skip ''(...' *)
                intvals := parseVec;
                leng := lengthIL(intvals)
            end
        else begin
                rnk := SCALAR;
                new(intvals);
                intvals^.int := parseInt;
                intvals^.nextint := nil
            end;
    parseVal := result
end; (* parseVal *)
```

```
(****************************************************************
*                        ENVIRONMENTS                         *
****************************************************************)
```

No changes here, except changing some occurrences of **NUMBER** to **APLVALUE**.

```
(****************************************************************
*                        APL VALUES                           *
****************************************************************)
```

This section is, of course, entirely new. As always, it defines prValue, isTrueVal, and applyValueOp. applyValueOp is much longer than in any other interpreter, because the implementations of the operations are more complex; its overall structure is familiar.

```
(* prValue - print APL value a                                 *)
procedure prValue (a: APLVALUE);

(* prIntlist - print INTLIST il as dim1 x dim2 matrix          *)
    procedure prIntlist (il: INTLIST; dim1, dim2: integer);
    var i, j: integer;
    begin
        for i:= 1 to dim1 do begin
            for j:= 1 to dim2 do begin
                write(il^.int:6, ' ');
                il := il^.nextint
                end;
            writeln
            end
    end; (* prIntlist *)

begin (* prValue *)
    with a^ do
        case rnk of
```

```
              SCALAR: prIntlist(intvals, 1, 1);
              VECTOR: prIntlist(intvals, 1, leng);
              MATRIX: prIntlist(intvals, rows, cols);
          end
end; (* prValue *)

(* isTrueVal - return true if first value in a is one         *)
function isTrueVal (a: APLVALUE): Boolean;
begin
     with a^ do
        if intvals = nil
        then isTrueVal := false
        else isTrueVal := intvals^.int = 1
end; (* isTrueVal *)

(* applyValueOp - apply VALUEOP op to arguments in VALUELIST vl  *)
function applyValueOp (op: VALUEOP; vl: VALUELIST): APLVALUE;

var a1, a2, result: APLVALUE;

(* size - return number of elements in a                      *)
   function size (a: APLVALUE): integer;
   begin
      with a^ do
         case rnk of
            SCALAR: size := 1;
            VECTOR: size := leng;
            MATRIX: size := rows * cols
         end
   end; (* size *)

(* skipover - return pointer to nth record in il              *)
   function skipover (n: integer; il: INTLIST): INTLIST;
   begin
       while n > 0 do begin
          il := il^.nextint;
          n := n-1
          end;
       skipover := il
   end; (* skipover *)

(* applyArithOp - apply binary operator to a1 and a2          *)
   procedure applyArithOp (op: BUILTINOP; a1, a2: APLVALUE);

(* copyrank - copy rank and shape of a to r                   *)
      procedure copyrank (a, r: APLVALUE);
      begin
         with r^ do
            begin
               rnk := a^.rnk;
```

```
                  case rnk of
                     SCALAR: ;
                     VECTOR: leng := a^.leng;
                     MATRIX:
                        begin
                           rows := a^.rows;
                           cols := a^.cols;
                        end
                  end (* case *)
               end (* with *)
         end; (* copyrank *)


(* applyOp - apply VALUEOP op to integer arguments            *)
      function applyOp (op: BUILTINOP; i, j: integer): integer;
      begin
         case op of
            PLUSOP: applyOp := i+j;
            MINUSOP: applyOp := i-j;
            TIMESOP: applyOp := i*j;
            DIVOP: applyOp := i div j;
            MAXOP:
               if i > j then applyOp := i else applyOp := j;
            OROP:
               if (i = 1) or (j = 1) then applyOp := 1
                                     else applyOp := 0;
            ANDOP:
               if (i = 1) and (j = 1) then applyOp := 1
                                      else applyOp := 0;
            EQOP:
               if i = j then applyOp := 1 else applyOp := 0;
            LTOP:
               if i < j then applyOp := 1 else applyOp := 0;
            GTOP:
               if i > j then applyOp := 1 else applyOp := 0
         end (* case *)
      end; (* applyOp *)


(* applyIntlis - apply op to two lists, extending appropriately *)
      function applyIntlis (op: BUILTINOP; il1, il2: INTLIST;
                         il1leng, il2leng: integer): INTLIST;
      var il:INTLIST;
      begin
         if (il1 = nil) or (il2 = nil)
         then applyIntlis := nil
         else begin
                  new(il);
                  with il^ do begin
                     int := applyOp(op, il1^.int, il2^.int);
                     if il1leng = 1
```

```
            then nextint := applyIntlis(op, il1,
                        il2^.nextint, il1leng, il2leng)
            else if il2leng = 1
                then nextint :=
                        applyIntlis(op, il1^.nextint,
                                    il2, il1leng, il2leng)
                else nextint :=
                        applyIntlis(op, il1^.nextint,
                            il2^.nextint, il1leng, il2leng);
            applyIntlis := il
            end (* with *)
        end
  end; (* applyIntlis *)

begin  (* applyArithOp *)
    new(result);
    if (a1^.rnk = SCALAR)
    then copyrank(a2, result)
    else if (a2^.rnk = SCALAR)
        then copyrank(a1, result)
        else if size(a1) = 1
            then copyrank(a2, result)
            else copyrank(a1, result);
    result^.intvals := applyIntlis(op, a1^.intvals,
                        a2^.intvals, size(a1), size(a2))
  end; (* applyArithOp *)

(* applyRedOp - apply reduction operator                    *)
  procedure applyRedOp (op: REDOP; a: APLVALUE);

(* applyOp - apply base operator of reduction operator       *)
    function applyOp (op: BUILTINOP; i, j: integer): integer;
    begin
        case op of
            REDPLUSOP: applyOp := i+j;
            REDMINUSOP: applyOp := i-j;
            REDTIMESOP: applyOp := i*j;
            REDDIVOP: applyOp := i div j;
            REDMAXOP:
                if i > j then applyOp := i else applyOp := j;
            REDOROP:
                if (i = 1) or (j = 1) then applyOp := 1
                                    else applyOp := 0;
            REDANDOP:
                if (i = 1) and (j = 1) then applyOp := 1
                                    else applyOp := 0
        end (* case *)
    end; (* applyOp *)

(* redVec - reduce op (argument to applyRedOp) over list         *)
```

```
      function redVec (il: INTLIST; leng: integer): integer;
      begin
         if leng = 0
         then redVec := 0
         else if leng = 1
                 then redVec := il^.int
                 else redVec := applyOp(op, il^.int,
                                      redVec(il^.nextint, leng-1))
      end; (* redVec *)

(* redMat - reduce op (argument to applyRedOp) over matrix       *)
      function redMat (il: INTLIST; cols, rows: integer): INTLIST;
      var ilnew: INTLIST;
      begin
         if rows = 0 then redMat := nil
         else begin
                 new(ilnew);
                 ilnew^.int := redVec(il, cols);
                 ilnew^.nextint :=
                         redMat(skipover(cols, il), cols, rows-1);
                 redMat := ilnew
              end
      end; (* redmat *)

   begin (* applyRedOp *)
      new(result);
      case a^.rnk of
         SCALAR: result := a;
         VECTOR:
            with result^ do begin
               rnk := SCALAR;
               new(intvals);
               intvals^.int := redVec(a^.intvals, a^.leng);
               intvals^.nextint := nil
               end;
         MATRIX:
            with result^ do begin
               rnk := VECTOR;
               leng := a^.rows;
               intvals := redMat(a^.intvals, a^.cols, leng)
               end
      end (* case *)
   end; (* applyRedOp *)

(* append - append il2 to il1; il1 is altered                  *)
   function append (il1, il2: INTLIST): INTLIST;
   begin
      if il1 = nil
      then append := il2
```

```
        else begin
                append := il1;
                while il1^.nextint <> nil do il1 := il1^.nextint;
                il1^.nextint := il2
            end
    end; (* append *)


(* ncopy - copy elements of src until list has reps elements      *)
    function ncopy (src: INTLIST; reps: integer): INTLIST;
    var
        il, suffix: INTLIST;
        i: integer;
    begin
        if reps = 0
        then ncopy := nil
        else begin
                new(il);
                ncopy := il;
                il^.int := src^.int;
                suffix := src^.nextint;
                for i := 2 to reps do begin
                    if suffix = nil (* exhausted src *)
                    then suffix := src; (* start over *)
                    new(il^.nextint);
                    il := il^.nextint;
                    il^.int := suffix^.int;
                    suffix := suffix^.nextint
                end
            end
    end; (* ncopy *)


(* compress - compress a1 over a2                                  *)
    procedure compress (a1, a2: APLVALUE);

    var width: integer;

(* ilcompress - il1 over il2, taking il2 in chunks of size width *)
    function ilcompress (il1, il2: INTLIST;
                            width: integer): INTLIST;
    var il: INTLIST;
    begin
        if il1 = nil
        then ilcompress := nil
        else if il1^.int = 1
            then begin
                    il := ncopy(il2, width);
                    il := append(il, ilcompress(il1^.nextint,
                            skipover(width, il2), width));
                    ilcompress := il
```

```
                    end
            else ilcompress := ilcompress(il1^.nextint,
                                    skipover(width, il2), width)
      end; (* ilcompress *)

(* countones - count ones in il                              *)
      function countones (il: INTLIST): integer;
      var i: integer;
      begin
         i := 0;
         while il <> nil do begin
            if il^.int = 1 then i := i+1;
            il := il^.nextint
            end;
         countones := i
      end; (* countones *)

   begin (* compress *)
      with a2^ do
         if rnk = VECTOR then width := 1 else width := cols;
      new(result);
      with result^ do begin
         rnk := a2^.rnk;
         intvals := ilcompress(a1^.intvals,
                           a2^.intvals, width);
         if rnk = VECTOR
         then leng := countones(a1^.intvals)
         else begin
               cols := a2^.cols;
               rows := countones(a1^.intvals)
            end
         end (* with *)
   end; (* compress *)

(* shape - return vector giving dimensions of a              *)
   procedure shape (a: APLVALUE);
   var il: INTLIST;
   begin
      new(result);
      result^.rnk := VECTOR;
      with a^ do
         case rnk of
            SCALAR:
               begin
                  result^.leng := 0;
                  result^.intvals := nil
               end;
            VECTOR:
               begin
```

```
                    result^.leng := 1;
                    new(il);
                    result^.intvals := il;
                    il^.int := leng;
                    il^.nextint := nil
                  end;
              MATRIX:
                  begin
                    result^.leng := 2;
                    new(il);
                    result^.intvals := il;
                    il^.int := rows;
                    new(il^.nextint);
                    il := il^.nextint;
                    il^.int := cols;
                    il^.nextint := nil
                  end
            end (* case *)
        end; (* shape *)

(* ravel - transform a to a vector without changing elements    *)
    procedure ravel (a: APLVALUE);
    var size: integer;
    begin
       new(result);
       with a^ do
          case rnk of
             SCALAR: size := 1;
             VECTOR: size := leng;
             MATRIX: size := rows*cols
          end;
       with result^ do begin
          rnk := VECTOR;
          leng := size;
          intvals := a^.intvals
          end
    end; (* ravel *)

(* restruct - restructure valuevec according to shapevec        *)
    procedure restruct (shapevec, valuevec: APLVALUE);
    var
       newrank: RANK;
       dim1, dim2: integer;
    begin
       if (valuevec^.intvals = nil)
       then begin
               writeln('Cannot restructure null vector');
               goto 99
            end;
```

```
          with shapevec^ do
             if rnk = SCALAR
             then begin
                      newrank := VECTOR;
                      dim1 := intvals^.int;
                      dim2 := 1
                  end
             else if leng = 0
                  then begin
                           newrank := SCALAR;
                           dim1 := 1;
                           dim2 := 1
                       end
                  else if leng = 1
                       then begin
                                newrank := VECTOR;
                                dim1 := intvals^.int;
                                dim2 := 1
                            end
                       else begin
                                newrank := MATRIX;
                                dim1 := intvals^.int;
                                dim2 := intvals^.nextint^.int
                            end; (* with *)
          new(result);
          with result^ do begin
             rnk := newrank;
             if rnk = VECTOR
             then leng := dim1
             else if rnk = MATRIX
                  then begin
                           rows := dim1;
                           cols := dim2
                       end;
             intvals := ncopy(valuevec^.intvals, dim1*dim2)
             end (* with *)
       end; (* restruct *)

(* copyIntlis - make a fresh copy of il                        *)
   function copyIntlis (il: INTLIST): INTLIST;
   begin
      copyIntlis := ncopy(il, lengthIL(il))
   end; (* copyIntlis *)

(* cat - create a vector by joining ravels of a1 and a2        *)
   procedure cat (a1, a2: APLVALUE);
   begin
      new(result);
      with result^ do begin
```

```
                  rnk := VECTOR;
                  leng := size(a1) + size(a2);
                  intvals := copyIntlis(a1^.intvals);
                  intvals := append(intvals, a2^.intvals)
                  end
         end; (* cat *)

(* indx - perform index generation, using first value in a        *)
      procedure indx (a: APLVALUE);
      var
         i: integer;
         il: INTLIST;
      begin
         i := a^.intvals^.int;
         new(result);
         with result^ do begin
            rnk := VECTOR;
            intvals := nil;
            leng := i;
            while i > 0 do begin
               new(il);
               il^.int := i;
               il^.nextint := intvals;
               intvals := il;
               i := i-1
               end (* while *)
            end (* with *)
      end; (* indx *)

(* trans - perform "trans"                                         *)
      procedure trans (a: APLVALUE);
      var
         il, ilnew: INTLIST:
         i: integer;

(* skiplist - subscript il by cols and rows                        *)
         function skiplist (il: INTLIST;
                     cols, rows: integer): INTLIST;
         var ilnew: INTLIST;
         begin
            new(ilnew);
            if rows = 1
            then begin
                     ilnew^.int := il^.int;
                     ilnew^.nextint := nil
                  end
            else begin
                     ilnew^.int := il^.int;
                     ilnew^.nextint :=
```

```
                          skiplist(skipover(cols, il), cols, rows-1);
                end;
            skiplist := ilnew
      end; (* skiplist *)

   begin (* trans *)
      if (a^.rnk <> MATRIX) or (a^.intvals = nil)
      then result := a
      else begin
               new(result);
               with result^ do begin
                  rnk := MATRIX;
                  cols := a^.rows;
                  rows := a^.cols;
                  il := a^.intvals;
                  ilnew := nil;
                  for i:= 1 to rows do begin
                     ilnew := append(ilnew,
                                     skiplist(il, rows, cols));
                     il := il^.nextint
                     end;
                  intvals := ilnew
                  end (* with *)
            end
   end; (* trans *)

(* subscript - "[]" operation; a1 a vector or matrix, a2 vector  *)
   procedure subscript (a1, a2: APLVALUE);

   var width: integer;

(* sub - find nth chunk in il, each chunk having width elements  *)
      function sub (il: INTLIST; n, width: integer): INTLIST;
      var i, j: integer;
      begin
         for i:=1 to n-1 do
            for j:=1 to width do
               il := il^.nextint;
         sub := il
      end; (* sub *)

(* ilsub - subscript src by subs in chunks of size width         *)
      function ilsub (src, subs: INTLIST; width: integer): INTLIST;
      var il: INTLIST;
      begin
         if subs = nil
         then il := nil
         else begin
                  il := sub(src, subs^.int, width);
```

```
                           il := ncopy(il, width);
                           il := append(il, ilsub(src, subs^.nextint,
                                                       width))
                       end;
                   ilsub := il
               end; (* ilsub *)

       begin (* subscript *)
           new(result);
           with result^ do begin
               rnk := a1^.rnk;
               if rnk = VECTOR
               then begin
                       if a2^.rnk = SCALAR
                       then leng := 1
                       else leng := a2^.leng;
                       width := 1
                   end
               else begin
                       if a2^.rnk = SCALAR
                       then rows := 1
                       else rows := a2^.leng;
                       cols := a1^.cols;
                       width := cols
                   end;
               intvals := ilsub(a1^.intvals, a2^.intvals, width)
               end (* with *)
       end; (* subscript *)

   (* arity - return number of arguments expected by op          *)
       function arity (op: VALUEOP): integer;
       begin
           if op in [PLUSOP .. GTOP,COMPRESSOP,RESTRUCTOP,CATOP,SUBOP]
           then arity := 2 else arity := 1
       end; (* arity *)

   begin (* applyValueOp *)
       if arity(op) <> lengthVL(vl)
       then begin
               write('Wrong number of arguments to ');
               prName(ord(op)+1);
               writeln;
               goto 99
           end;
       a1 := vl^.head; (* 1st actual *)
       if arity(op) = 2 then a2 := vl^.tail^.head; (* 2nd actual *)
       case op of
           PLUSOP,MINUSOP,TIMESOP,DIVOP,MAXOP,OROP,ANDOP,
           EQOP,LTOP,GTOP:
```

```
                 applyArithOp(op, a1, a2);
            REDPLUSOP,REDMINUSOP,REDTIMESOP,REDDIVOP,REDMAXOP,
            REDOROP,REDANDOP:
                 applyRedOp(op, a1);
            COMPRESSOP:
                 compress(a1, a2);
            SHAPEOP:
                 shape(a1);
            RAVELOP:
                 ravel(a1);
            RESTRUCTOP:
                 restruct(a1, a2);
            CATOP:
                 cat(a1, a2);
            INDXOP:
                 indx(a1);
            TRANSOP:
                 trans(a1);
            SUBOP:
                 subscript(a1, a2);
            PRINTOP:
                 begin prValue(a1); result := a1 end
        end; (* case *)
        applyValueOp := result
end; (* applyValueOp *)


(*****************************************************************
 *                     EVALUATION                               *
 *****************************************************************)
```

The only changes here are: NUMBER is changed to APLVALUE; we use local variable a instead of n.

```
(*****************************************************************
 *                 READ-EVAL-PRINT LOOP                         *
 *****************************************************************)
```

The top-level loop is unchanged.

Appendix E

Interpreter for SCHEME

This appendix contains the code for the SCHEME interpreter, which is based upon the LISP interpreter of Appendix C.

```
(*****************************************************************
*                      DECLARATIONS                            *
*****************************************************************)
```

Two new built-in operations have been added (`primop?` and `closure?`), and the declarations for S-expressions, expressions, and environments have been changed as explained in the text. Also, declarations of FUNDEF and FUNDEFREC have been removed.

```
BUILTINOP = (IFOP,WHILEOP,SETOP,BEGINOP,PLUSOP,MINUSOP,
             TIMESOP,DIVOP,EQOP,LTOP,GTOP,CONSOP,
             CAROP,CDROP,NUMBERPOP,SYMBOLPOP,LISTPOP,
             NULLPOP,PRIMOPPOP,CLOSUREPOP,PRINTOP);
VALUEOP = PLUSOP .. PRINTOP;
CONTROLOP = IFOP .. BEGINOP;

SEXPTYPE = (NILSXP,NUMSXP,SYMSXP,LISTSXP,CLOSXP,PRIMSXP);
SEXPREC = record
            case sxptype: SEXPTYPE of
                NILSXP: ();
                NUMSXP: (intval: integer);
```

```
                SYMSXP: (symval: NAME);
                LISTSXP: (carval, cdrval: SEXP);
                CLOSXP: (clofun: EXP; cloenv: ENV);
                PRIMSXP: (primval: BUILTINOP)
            end;

    EXPTYPE = (VALEXP,VAREXP,APEXP,LAMEXP);
    EXPREC = record
                case etype: EXPTYPE of
                    VALEXP: (sxp: SEXP);
                    VAREXP: (varble: NAME);
                    APEXP: (optr: EXP; args: EXPLIST);
                    LAMEXP: (formals: NAMELIST; lambdabody: EXP)
            end;

    ENVREC = record
                vars: NAMELIST;
                values: VALUELIST;
                enclosing: ENV
            end;
```

```
(*****************************************************************
 *                   DATA STRUCTURE OP'S                        *
 *****************************************************************)
```

For mkAPEXP and mkEnv, the types and/or number of arguments have changed. The new functions in this section are mkLAMEXP, mkPRIMSXP, and mkCLOSXP.

```
(* mkAPEXP - return EXP of type APEXP w/ optr op and args el     *)
function mkAPEXP (op: EXP; el: EXPLIST): EXP;
var e: EXP;
begin
   new(e);
   e^.etype := APEXP;
   e^.optr := op;
   e^.args := el;
   mkAPEXP := e
end; (* mkAPEXP *)

(* mkLAMEXP - return EXP of type LAMEXP w/ formals f and body b  *)
function mkLAMEXP (f: NAMELIST; b: EXP): EXP;
var e: EXP;
begin
   new(e);
   e^.etype := LAMEXP;
   e^.formals := f;
   e^.lambdabody := b;
   mkLAMEXP := e
end; (* mkLAMEXP *)
```

```
(* mkPRIMSXP - return SEXP of type PRIMSXP w/ value op              *)
function mkPRIMSXP (op: BUILTINOP): SEXP;
var result: SEXP;
begin
   new(result);
   result^.sxptype := PRIMSXP;
   result^.primval := op;
   mkPRIMSXP := result
end; (* mkPRIMSXP *)

(* mkCLOSXP - return SEXP of type CLOSXP w/ expr e and env rho   *)
function mkCLOSXP (e: EXP; rho: ENV): SEXP;
var result: SEXP;
begin
   new(result);
   result^.sxptype := CLOSXP;
   result^.clofun := e;
   result^.cloenv := rho;
   mkCLOSXP := result
end; (* mkCLOSXP *)

(* mkEnv - return an ENV with vars nl, value vl, enclosing rho   *)
function mkEnv (nl: NAMELIST; vl: VALUELIST; rho: ENV): ENV;
var newrho: ENV;
begin
   new(newrho);
   newrho^.vars := nl;
   newrho^.values := vl;
   newrho^.enclosing := rho;
   mkEnv := newrho
end; (* mkEnv *)


(***************************************************************
*                    NAME MANAGEMENT                         *
***************************************************************)
```

Names closure? and primop? are added to *initNames*. fetchFun and newFunDef are removed, as is primOp (whose function is now served by initGlobalEnv).

```
(***************************************************************
*                       INPUT                                *
***************************************************************)
```

parseExp is modified to handle lambda expressions, and parseDef is removed.

```
(* parseExp - return EXP starting at userinput[pos]              *)
function parseExp: EXP;
var
   op, body: EXP;
```

```
      nl: NAMELIST;
      el: EXPLIST;
begin
   if userinput[pos] = '('
   then begin
            pos := skipblanks(pos+1); (* skip '( ..' *)
            if matches(pos, 6, 'lambda            ')
            then begin    (* LAMEXP *)
                    pos := skipblanks(pos+6);  (* skip 'lambda ..' *)
                    pos := skipblanks(pos+1); (* skip '( ..' *)
                    nl := parseNL;
                    body := parseExp;
                    pos := skipblanks(pos+1); (* skip ') ..' *)
                    parseExp := mkLAMEXP(nl, body)
                 end
            else begin    (* APEXP *)
                    op := parseExp;
                    el := parseEL;
                    parseExp := mkAPEXP(op, el)
                 end
         end
   else if isValue(pos)
        then parseExp := mkVALEXP(parseVal)    (* VALEXP *)
        else parseExp := mkVAREXP(parseName)   (* VAREXP *)
end; (* parseExp *)


(****************************************************************
 *                      ENVIRONMENTS                           *
 ****************************************************************)
```

The changes here are related to the change of representation of environments.

```
(* emptyEnv - return an environment with no bindings          *)
function emptyEnv: ENV;
begin
   emptyEnv := mkEnv(nil, nil, nil)
end; (* emptyEnv *)

(* bindVar - bind variable nm to value s in environment rho    *)
procedure bindVar (nm: NAME; s: SEXP; rho: ENV);
begin
   rho^.vars := mkNamelist(nm, rho^.vars);
   rho^.values := mkValuelist(s, rho^.values)
end; (* bindVar *)

(*  extendEnv - extend environment rho by binding vars to vals  *)
function extendEnv (rho: ENV;
                    vars: NAMELIST;
                    vals: VALUELIST): ENV;
```

```
begin
   extendEnv := mkEnv(vars, vals, rho)
end; (* extendEnv *)

(* findVar - look up nm in rho                              *)
function findVar (nm: NAME; rho: ENV): VALUELIST;

var vl: VALUELIST;

(* findVarInFrame - look up nm in one frame                 *)
   function findVarInFrame (nl: NAMELIST;
                            vl: VALUELIST): VALUELIST;
   var found: Boolean;
   begin
      found := false;
      while (nl <> nil) and not found do
         if nl^.head = nm
         then found := true
         else begin
                 nl := nl^.tail;
                 vl := vl^.tail
              end; (* while *)
      findVarInFrame := vl
   end; (* findVarInFrame *)

begin (* findVar *)
   repeat
      vl := findVarInFrame(rho^.vars, rho^.values);
      rho := rho^.enclosing
   until (vl <> nil) or (rho = nil);
   findVar := vl
end; (* findVar *)

(* assign - assign value s to variable nm in rho            *)
procedure assign (nm: NAME; s: SEXP; rho: ENV);
var varloc: VALUELIST;
begin
   varloc := findVar(nm, rho);
   varloc^.head := s
end; (* assign *)

(* fetch - return SEXP bound to nm in rho                   *)
function fetch (nm: NAME; rho: ENV): SEXP;
var vl: VALUELIST;
begin
   vl := findVar(nm, rho);
   fetch := vl^.head
end; (* fetch *)

(* isBound - check if nm is bound in rho                    *)
```

```
function isBound (nm: NAME; rho: ENV): Boolean;
begin
   isBound := findVar(nm, rho) <> nil
end; (* isBound *)


(*****************************************************************
 *                        S-EXPRESSIONS                         *
 *****************************************************************)
```

prValue is able to print the two new types of S-expressions (the other four cases are unchanged).

```
(* prValue - print S-expression s                              *)
procedure prValue (s: SEXP);
var s1: SEXP;
begin
   with s^ do
      case sxptype of
         NILSXP: write('()');
         NUMSXP: write(intval:1);
         SYMSXP: prName(symval);
         PRIMSXP:
            begin
               write('<primitive: ');
               prName(ord(primval)+1);
               write('>')
            end;
         CLOSXP: write('<closure>');
         LISTSXP:
            begin
               write('(');
               prValue(carval);
               s1 := cdrval;
               while s1^.sxptype = LISTSXP do begin
                  write(' ');
                  prValue(s1^.carval);
                  s1 := s1^.cdrval
                  end;
               write(')')
            end
      end (* case and with *)
end; (* prValue *)
```

isTrueVal is unchanged, and applyValueOp is changed only to the extent of adding cases for the two new operations:

```
                PRIMOPPOP:
                   if sxptype = PRIMSXP then result := trueValue;
                CLOSUREPOP:
                   if sxptype = CLOSXP then result := trueValue;
```

```
(*****************************************************************
*                       EVALUATION                             *
*****************************************************************)
```

evalList is not changed, but all other functions are listed here; applyUserFun is replaced by applyClosure. In applyCtrlOp, only the SETOP case has changed, and that only slightly. The body of eval has changed its treatment of VALEXP's slightly (analogously to the change in the treatment of SETOP), and its treatment of applications more significantly, and has added a case for LAMEXP's.

```
(* eval - return value of expression e in local environment rho  *)
function eval (e: EXP; rho: ENV): SEXP;

var
   op: SEXP;
   primname: BUILTINOP;

(* applyClosure - apply SEXP op of type CLOSXP to actuals        *)
   function applyClosure (op: SEXP; actuals: VALUELIST): SEXP;
   var
      fun, body: EXP;
      forms: NAMELIST;
      savedrho, newrho: ENV;
   begin
      fun := op^.clofun;
      savedrho := op^.cloenv;
      forms := fun^.formals;
      body := fun^.lambdabody;
      if lengthNL(forms) <> lengthVL(actuals)
      then begin
              writeln('Wrong number of arguments to closure');
              goto 99
           end;
      newrho := extendEnv(savedrho, forms, actuals);
      applyClosure := eval(body, newrho)
   end; (* applyClosure *)

(* applyCtrlOp - apply CONTROLOP op to args in rho               *)
   function applyCtrlOp (op: CONTROLOP;
                         args: EXPLIST): SEXP;
   var s: SEXP;
   begin
      with args^ do
         case op of
            IFOP:
               if isTrueVal(eval(head, rho))
               then applyCtrlOp := eval(tail^.head, rho)
               else applyCtrlOp := eval(tail^.tail^.head, rho);
            WHILEOP:
               begin
```

```
                 s := eval(head, rho);
                 while isTrueVal(s)
                 do begin
                         s := eval(tail^.head, rho);
                         s := eval(head, rho)
                     end;
                 applyCtrlOp := s
             end;
           SETOP:
             begin
                 s := eval(tail^.head, rho);
                 if isBound(head^.varble, rho)
                 then assign(head^.varble, s, rho)
                 else bindVar(head^.varble, s, globalEnv);
                 applyCtrlOp := s
             end;
           BEGINOP:
             begin
                 while args^.tail <> nil do
                     begin
                         s := eval(args^.head, rho);
                         args := args^.tail
                     end;
                 applyCtrlOp := eval(args^.head, rho)
             end
         end (* case and with *)
   end; (* applyCtrlOp *)

begin (* eval *)
   with e^ do
     case etype of
         VALEXP:
             eval := sxp;
         VAREXP:
             if isBound(varble, rho)
             then eval := fetch(varble, rho)
             else begin
                     write('Undefined variable: ');
                     prName(varble);
                     writeln;
                     goto 99
                 end;
         APEXP:
             begin
                 op := eval(optr, rho);
                 if op^.sxptype = PRIMSXP
                 then begin
                         primname := op^.primval;
                         if primname in [IFOP .. BEGINOP]
```

```
                              then eval :=
                                  applyCtrlOp(primname, args)
                         else eval := applyValueOp(primname,
                                            evalList(args))
                    end
              else eval :=
                    applyClosure(op, evalList(args))
           end;
        LAMEXP:
           eval := mkCLOSXP(e, rho)
      end (* case and with *)
end; (* eval *)


(*****************************************************************
 *                    READ-EVAL-PRINT LOOP                      *
 *****************************************************************)
```

    initGlobalEnv initializes the predefined names to have the corresponding built-
in operations as their values. The top level is simplified, in that it does not need to
recognize definitions as a special case.

```
(* initGlobalEnv - assign primitive function values to names    *)
procedure initGlobalEnv;
var op: BUILTINOP;
begin
    globalEnv := emptyEnv;
    for op := IFOP to PRINTOP do
       bindVar(ord(op)+1, mkPRIMSXP(op), globalEnv)
end; (* initGlobalEnv *)


begin (* scheme main *)
   initNames;

   nilValue := mkSExp(NILSXP);
   trueValue := mkSExp(SYMSXP); trueValue^.symval := numNames;

   initGlobalEnv;

   quittingtime := false;
99:
   while not quittingtime do begin
      reader;
      if matches(pos, 4, 'quit              ')
      then quittingtime := true
      else begin
              currentExp := parseExp;
              prValue(eval(currentExp, globalEnv));
              writeln;
              writeln
```

```
            end
       end (* while *)
end. (* scheme *)
```

Appendix F

Interpreter for SASL

This appendix contains the code for the SASL interpreter, insofar as it differs from the SCHEME interpreter of Appendix E.

```
(****************************************************************
*                       DECLARATIONS                          *
****************************************************************)
```

The changes listed here are the new declarations of BUILTINOP and SEXPREC, and two new variables used at the top level.

```
BUILTINOP = (IFOP,PLUSOP,MINUSOP,
             TIMESOP,DIVOP,EQOP,LTOP,GTOP,CONSOP,
             CAROP,CDROP,NUMBERPOP,SYMBOLPOP,LISTPOP,
             NULLPOP,PRIMOPPOP,CLOSUREPOP);
VALUEOP = PLUSOP .. CLOSUREPOP;
CONTROLOP = IFOP .. IFOP;

SEXPTYPE = (NILSXP,NUMSXP,SYMSXP,LISTSXP,CLOSXP,PRIMSXP,THUNK);
SEXPREC = record
            case sxptype: SEXPTYPE of
               NILSXP: ();
               NUMSXP: (intval: integer);
               SYMSXP: (symval: NAME);
```

```
                LISTSXP: (carval, cdrval: SEXP);
                CLOSXP, THUNK: (clofun: EXP; cloenv: ENV);
                PRIMSXP: (primval: BUILTINOP)
        end;

var
   setName: NAME;
   setVal: SEXP;
```

```
(*****************************************************************
 *                    DATA STRUCTURE OP'S                       *
 *****************************************************************)
```

There is one new operation in this section.

```
(* mkTHUNK - return SEXP of type THUNK w/ expr e and env rho    *)
function mkTHUNK (e: EXP; rho: ENV): SEXP;
var result: SEXP;
begin
   new(result);
   result^.sxptype := THUNK;
   result^.clofun := e;
   result^.cloenv := rho;
   mkTHUNK := result
end; (* mkTHUNK *)
```

```
(*****************************************************************
 *                    NAME MANAGEMENT                           *
 *****************************************************************)
```

The only change here is to remove the operator symbols while, set, begin, and print from initNames.

```
(*****************************************************************
 *                         INPUT                                *
 *****************************************************************)
```

The new function parseSet is added; it is called from the top level.

```
(* parseSet - read top-level definition                         *)
function parseSet: EXP;
var e: EXP;
begin
   pos := skipblanks(pos+1); (* skip '( ..' *)
   pos := skipblanks(pos+3); (* skip 'set ..' *)
   setName := parseName;
   e := parseExp;
   pos := skipblanks(pos+1); (* skip ') ..' *)
   parseSet := e
end; (* parseSet *)
```

```
(***************************************************************
*                     ENVIRONMENTS                            *
***************************************************************)
```

No changes here.

```
(***************************************************************
*                     S-EXPRESSIONS                           *
***************************************************************)
```

prValue changes to the extent of printing thunks as ellipses. In applyValueOp, the PRINTOP case is removed. More importantly, four calls to evalThunk are added; two are at the beginning, where it is called to evaluate thunks for strict operations (which includes all operations except cons), and the other two are in the CAROP and CDROP cases; all other cases are unchanged.

```
procedure evalThunk (s: SEXP); forward;

(* applyValueOp - apply VALUEOP op to arguments in VALUELIST vl  *)
function applyValueOp (op: VALUEOP; vl: VALUELIST): SEXP;

var
   result: SEXP;
   s1, s2: SEXP;

(* applyArithOp - apply binary, arithmetic VALUEOP to arguments  *)

     <unchanged>

(* applyRelOp - apply binary, relational VALUEOP to arguments    *)

     <unchanged>

(* arity - return number of arguments expected by op             *)

     <unchanged>

begin (* applyValueOp *)
   if arity(op) <> lengthVL(vl)
   then begin
           write('Wrong number of arguments to ');
           prName(ord(op)+1);
           writeln;
           goto 99
        end;
   result := nilValue;
   s1 := vl^.head; (* 1st actual *)
   if arity(op) = 2 then s2 := vl^.tail^.head; (* 2nd actual *)
   if op <> CONSOP then evalThunk(s1);
   if op in [PLUSOP .. GTOP] then evalThunk(s2);
```

```
      if op in [PLUSOP .. DIVOP, LTOP .. GTOP]
      then if (s1^.sxptype = NUMSXP)
              and (s2^.sxptype = NUMSXP)
           then if op in [PLUSOP .. DIVOP]
                then applyArithOp(s1^.intval, s2^.intval)
                else applyRelOp(s1^.intval, s2^.intval)
           else begin
                   write('Non-arithmetic arguments to ');
                   prName(ord(op)+1);
                   writeln;
                   goto 99
                end
      else with s1^ do
              case op of
                 EQOP:
                    if (sxptype = NILSXP)
                       and (s2^.sxptype = NILSXP)
                    then result := trueValue
                    else if (sxptype = NUMSXP)
                            and (s2^.sxptype = NUMSXP)
                            and (intval = s2^.intval)
                         then result := trueValue
                         else if (sxptype = SYMSXP)
                                 and (s2^.sxptype = SYMSXP)
                                 and (symval = s2^.symval)
                              then result := trueValue;
                 CONSOP:
                    begin
                       result := mkSExp(LISTSXP);
                       with result^ do begin
                          carval := s1;
                          cdrval := s2
                          end
                    end;
                 CAROP:
                    if sxptype <> LISTSXP
                    then begin
                            write('Error: car applied to non-list: ');
                            prValue(s1);
                            writeln
                         end
                    else begin
                            evalThunk(carval);
                            result := carval
                         end;
                 CDROP:
                    if sxptype <> LISTSXP
                    then begin
                            write('Error: cdr applied to non-list: ');
```

```
                        prValue(s1);
                        writeln
                    end
                else begin
                        evalThunk(cdrval);
                        result := cdrval
                    end;
            NUMBERPOP:
                if sxptype = NUMSXP then result := trueValue;
            SYMBOLPOP:
                if sxptype = SYMSXP then result := trueValue;
            LISTPOP:
                if sxptype = LISTSXP then result := trueValue;
            NULLPOP:
                if sxptype = NILSXP then result := trueValue;
            PRIMOPPOP:
                if sxptype = PRIMSXP then result := trueValue;
            CLOSUREPOP:
                if sxptype = CLOSXP then result := trueValue
            end; (* case and with *)
    applyValueOp := result
end; (* applyValueOp *)
```

```
(*****************************************************************
*                       EVALUATION                             *
*****************************************************************)
```

The changes to eval are as follows: evalList returns a list of thunks, never calling
eval recursively as in the past. applyClosure has no changes. applyCtrlOp retains
only the IFOP case; there is no change in its treatment of that case. The body of eval
includes a call to evalThunk in the VAREXP case. Finally, there is evalThunk itself,
which evaluates a thunk by calling eval, and then copies the value returned into its
argument.

```
(* eval - return value of expression e in local environment rho  *)
function eval (e: EXP; rho: ENV): SEXP;

var
    s: SEXP;
    op: SEXP;
    primname: BUILTINOP;

(* evalList - evaluate each expression in el                      *)
    function evalList (el: EXPLIST): VALUELIST;
    var
        h: SEXP;
        t: VALUELIST;
    begin
        if el = nil then evalList := nil
```

```
        else begin
                h := mkTHUNK(el^.head, rho);
                t := evalList(el^.tail);
                evalList := mkValuelist(h, t)
            end
    end; (* evalList *)


(* applyClosure - apply SEXP op of type CLOSXP to actuals        *)
    function applyClosure (op: SEXP; actuals: VALUELIST): SEXP;


    <unchanged>


(* applyCtrlOp - apply CONTROLOP op to args in rho               *)
    function applyCtrlOp (op: CONTROLOP;
                          args: EXPLIST): SEXP;
    begin
        with args^ do
            case op of
              IFOP:
                if isTrueVal(eval(head, rho))
                then applyCtrlOp := eval(tail^.head, rho)
                else applyCtrlOp := eval(tail^.tail^.head, rho)
            end (* case and with *)
    end; (* applyCtrlOp *)

begin (* eval *)
    with e^ do
        case etype of
          VALEXP:
                eval := sxp;
          VAREXP:
                begin
                  if isBound(varble, rho)
                  then s := fetch(varble, rho)
                  else begin
                          write('Undefined variable: ');
                          prName(varble);
                          writeln;
                          goto 99
                      end;
                  evalThunk(s);
                  eval := s
                end;
          APEXP:
                begin
                    op := eval(optr, rho);
                    if op^.sxptype = PRIMSXP
                    then begin
                            primname := op^.primval;
```

```
                              if primname = IFOP
                              then eval :=
                                      applyCtrlOp(primname, args)
                              else eval := applyValueOp(primname,
                                                   evalList(args))
                           end
                    else eval :=
                           applyClosure(op, evalList(args))
               end;
           LAMEXP:
               eval := mkCLOSXP(e, rho)
       end (* case and with *)
end; (* eval *)


(* evalThunk - evaluate thunk and replace it by its value        *)
procedure evalThunk;

var result: SEXP;

(* copyValue - copy SEXP s1 into s2                              *)
   procedure copyValue (s1, s2: SEXP);
   begin
      with s1^ do begin
         s2^.sxptype := sxptype;
         case sxptype of
            NILSXP: ;
            NUMSXP: s2^.intval := intval;
            SYMSXP: s2^.symval := symval;
            PRIMSXP: s2^.primval := primval;
            LISTSXP:
               begin
                  s2^.carval := carval;
                  s2^.cdrval := cdrval
               end;
            CLOSXP, THUNK:
               begin
                  s2^.clofun := clofun;
                  s2^.cloenv := cloenv
               end
         end (* case *)
      end (* with *)
   end; (* copyValue *)

begin (* evalThunk *)
   with s^ do
      if sxptype = THUNK
      then begin
              result := eval(clofun, cloenv);
              copyValue(result, s)
```

```
                end
end; (* evalThunk *)


(***************************************************************
 *                   READ-EVAL-PRINT LOOP                      *
 ***************************************************************)
```

initGlobalEnv is changed according to the new declaration of BUILTINOP. The top-level loop handles set.

```
(* initGlobalEnv - assign primitive function values to names    *)
procedure initGlobalEnv;
var op: BUILTINOP;
begin
    globalEnv := emptyEnv;
    for op := IFOP to CLOSUREPOP do
        bindVar(ord(op)+1, mkPRIMSXP(op), globalEnv)
end; (* initGlobalEnv *)


begin (* sasl main *)
    initNames;

    nilValue := mkSExp(NILSXP);
    trueValue := mkSExp(SYMSXP); trueValue^.symval := numNames;

    initGlobalEnv;

    quittingtime := false;
99:
    while not quittingtime do begin
        reader;
        if matches(pos, 4, 'quit              ')
        then quittingtime := true
        else if (userinput[pos]='(') and
                matches(skipblanks(pos+1), 3, 'set                ')
            then begin
                    currentExp := parseSet;
                    setVal := eval(currentExp, globalEnv);
                    if isBound(setName, globalEnv)
                    then assign(setName, setVal, globalEnv)
                    else bindVar(setName, setVal, globalEnv);
                    prValue(setVal);
                    writeln;
                    writeln
                end
            else begin
                    currentExp := parseExp;
                    prValue(eval(currentExp, globalEnv));
                    writeln;
```

```
            writeln
          end
      end (* while *)
end. (* sasl *)
```

Appendix G

Interpreter for CLU

This appendix contains the code for the CLU interpreter, insofar as it differs from that of Appendix B.

```
(****************************************************************
*                      DECLARATIONS                           *
****************************************************************)
```

This section gives the declaration of FUNNAME, for two-part names, the type CLU-VALUE, which replaces NUMBER, the new version of EXP, which has minor changes, the new version of FUNDEF (including the three new types of user-defined functions), the new type CLUSTER, and the variable clusters.

```
FNAMETYPE = (ONEPART,TWOPART);
FUNNAME = record
            funpart: NAME;
            case nametype: FNAMETYPE of
                ONEPART: ();
                TWOPART: (clpart: NAME)
          end;

CLUVALUE = ^CLUVALUEREC;
FUNDEF = ^FUNDEFREC;
CLUSTER = ^CLUSTERREC;
```

```
CLUVALUETYPE = (PRIM,USER);
CLUVALUEREC = record
              case vtype: CLUVALUETYPE of
                 PRIM: (intval: integer);
                 USER: (userval: ENV)
           end;

EXPTYPE = (VALEXP,VAREXP,APEXP);
EXPREC = record
              case etype: EXPTYPE of
                 VALEXP: (valu: CLUVALUE);
                 VAREXP: (varble: NAME);
                 APEXP: (optr: FUNNAME; args: EXPLIST)
           end;

FUNTYPE = (NORMAL,CONSTRUCTOR,SELECTOR,SETTOR);
FUNDEFREC = record
              funname: NAME;
              nextfundef: FUNDEF;
              case ftype : FUNTYPE of
                 NORMAL: (formals: NAMELIST; body: EXP);
                 CONSTRUCTOR, SELECTOR: ();
                 SETTOR: (selname: NAME)
           end;

CLUSTERREC = record
              clname: NAME;
              clrep: NAMELIST;
              exported: FUNDEF;
              nonexported: FUNDEF;
              nextcluster: CLUSTER
           end;

var
   clusters: CLUSTER;


(*****************************************************************
 *                    DATA STRUCTURE OP'S                       *
 *****************************************************************)
```

The function `mkAPEXP` is modified to allow for two-part names in applications. `mkPRIM` and `mkUSER`, which construct the two types of CLUVALUE's, are new.

```
(* mkAPEXP - return EXP of type APEXP w/ optr op or cl$op       *)
function mkAPEXP (ot: FNAMETYPE; op, cl: NAME; el: EXPLIST): EXP;
var e: EXP;
begin
   new(e);
```

```
      e^.etype := APEXP;
      e^.optr.funpart := op;
      e^.optr.nametype := ot;
      if ot = TWOPART then e^.optr.clpart := cl;
      e^.args := el;
      mkAPEXP := e
end; (* mkAPEXP *)

(* mkPRIM - return a CLUVALUE with integer value n              *)
function mkPRIM (n: integer): CLUVALUE;
var newval: CLUVALUE;
begin
   new(newval);
   newval^.vtype := PRIM;
   newval^.intval := n;
   mkPRIM := newval
end; (* mkPRIM *)

(* mkUSER - return a user-type CLUVALUE                         *)
function mkUSER (rho: ENV): CLUVALUE;
var newval: CLUVALUE;
begin
   new(newval);
   newval^.vtype := USER;
   newval^.userval := rho;
   mkUSER := newval
end; (* mkUSER *)



(****************************************************************
 *                    NAME MANAGEMENT                          *
 ****************************************************************)
```

Clusters are stored and fetched very much as function definitions were in Chapter 1; fetchCluster and newCluster are analogous to fetchFun and newFunDef. The definitions of the latter have been changed to allow for functions to be stored in different function environments.

```
(* fetchCluster - get cluster definition of cname from clusters *)
function fetchCluster (cname: NAME): CLUSTER;
var
   cl: CLUSTER;
   found: boolean;
begin
   found := false;
   cl := clusters;
   while (cl <> nil) and not found do
      if cl^.clname = cname
      then found := true
      else cl := cl^.nextcluster;
```

```
      fetchCluster := cl
end; (* fetchCluster *)



(* newCluster - add new cluster cname to clusters            *)
function newCluster (cname: NAME): CLUSTER;
var cl: CLUSTER;
begin
   cl := fetchCluster(cname);
   if cl = nil (* cname not yet defined as cluster *)
   then begin
           new(cl);
           cl^.clname := cname;
           cl^.nextcluster := clusters; (* place new CLUSTERREC *)
           clusters := cl               (* on clusters list *)
        end;
   newCluster := cl
end; (* newCluster *)



(* fetchFun - get function definition of NAME fname from fenv   *)
function fetchFun (fname: NAME; fenv: FUNDEF): FUNDEF;
var found: Boolean;
begin
   found := false;
   while (fenv <> nil) and not found do
      if fenv^.funname = fname
      then found := true
      else fenv := fenv^.nextfundef;
   fetchFun := fenv
end; (* fetchFun *)



(* newFunDef - add new function fname to fenv                *)
function newFunDef (fname: NAME; var fenv: FUNDEF): FUNDEF;
var f: FUNDEF;
begin
   f := fetchFun(fname, fenv);
   if f = nil (* fname not yet defined as a function *)
   then begin
           new(f);
           f^.funname := fname;
           f^.nextfundef := fenv; (* place new FUNDEFREC *)
           fenv := f              (* on fenv list *)
        end;
   newFunDef := f
end; (* newFunDef *)
```

```
(*******************************************************************
*                            INPUT                                *
*******************************************************************)
```

The major changes here are to allow for two-part names in expressions and to
read cluster definitions.

```
(* isDelim - check if c is a delimiter                          *)
function isDelim (c: char): Boolean;
begin
    isDelim := c in ['(', ')', ' ', '$', COMMENTCHAR]
end; (* isDelim *)

(* parseExp - return EXP starting at userinput[pos]             *)
function parseExp: EXP;
var
    fnm, cnm: NAME;
    el: EXPLIST;
    optrtype: FNAMETYPE;
begin
    if userinput[pos] = '('
    then begin    (* APEXP *)
            pos := skipblanks(pos+1); (* skip '( ..' *)
            optrtype := ONEPART;
            cnm := 1; (* arbitrary name *)
            fnm := parseName;
            if userinput[pos] = '$'
            then begin (* two-part name *)
                    pos := pos+1;
                    cnm := fnm;
                    optrtype := TWOPART;
                    fnm := parseName
                end;
            el := parseEL;
            parseExp := mkAPEXP(optrtype, fnm, cnm, el)
        end
    else if isNumber(pos)
        then parseExp := mkVALEXP(parseVal)    (* VALEXP *)
        else parseExp := mkVAREXP(parseName)   (* VAREXP *)
end; (* parseExp *)

(* parseDef - parse function definition at userinput[pos]       *)
function parseDef (var fenv: FUNDEF): NAME;
var
    fname: NAME;          (* function name *)
    newfun: FUNDEF;       (* new FUNDEFREC *)
begin
    pos := skipblanks(pos+1); (* skip '( ..' *)
    pos := skipblanks(pos+6); (* skip 'define ..' *)
    fname := parseName;
```

```
    newfun := newFunDef(fname, fenv);
    newfun^.ftype := NORMAL;
    pos := skipblanks(pos+1); (* skip '( ..' *)
    newfun^.formals := parseNL;
    newfun^.body := parseExp;
    pos := skipblanks(pos+1); (* skip ') ..' *)
    parseDef := fname
end; (* parseDef *)


(* parseCluster - parse cluster definition at userinput[pos]     *)
function parseCluster: NAME;

var
    cname, sel, fname: NAME;
    newclust: CLUSTER;
    rep: NAMELIST;
    cenv: FUNDEF;
    confun, selfun, setfun: FUNDEF;

(* mkSetName - make name of settor corresponding to selector nm *)
  function mkSetName (nm: NAME): NAME;
  var
      setname: NAMESTRING;
      i: integer;
  begin
      setname := 'set-                  ';
      if printNames[nm][NAMELENG-3] <> ' '
      then begin
              write('Selector name too long: ');
              prName(nm);
              writeln;
              goto 99
           end;
      for i:=1 to NAMELENG-4
          do setname[i+4] := printNames[nm][i];
      mkSetName := install(setname)
    end; (* mkSetName *)

begin (* parseCluster *)
    pos := skipblanks(pos+1); (* skip '( ..' *)
    pos := skipblanks(pos+7); (* skip 'cluster ...' *)
    cname := parseName;
    newclust := newCluster(cname);
    pos := skipblanks(pos+1); (* skip '( ...' *)
    pos := skipblanks(pos+3); (* skip 'rep ...' *)
    rep := parseNL; (* selector names *)
    newclust^.clrep := rep;
    cenv := nil;
    while userinput[pos]='(' do
```

```
      begin
         fname := parseDef(cenv);
         prName(fname);
         writeln
      end;
   newclust^.exported := cenv;
   cenv := nil;
   confun := newFunDef(cname, cenv);
   confun^.ftype := CONSTRUCTOR;
   while rep <> nil do
      begin
         sel := rep^.head;
         selfun := newFunDef(sel, cenv);
         selfun^.ftype := SELECTOR;
         setfun := newFunDef(mkSetName(sel), cenv);
         setfun^.ftype := SETTOR;
         setfun^.selname := sel;
         rep := rep^.tail
      end;
   newclust^.nonexported := cenv;
   pos := skipblanks(pos+1); (* skip ') ..' *)
   parseCluster := cname
end; (* parseCluster *)
```

```
(****************************************************************
*                      ENVIRONMENTS                           *
****************************************************************)
```

There are no changes in this section, except the replacement of occurrences of NUMBER by CLUVALUE.

```
(****************************************************************
*                        VALUES                               *
****************************************************************)
```

prValue may be called upon to print CLUVALUE's of type USER, which it does (albeit stupidly). isTrueVal checks that its argument is of type PRIM. applyValueOp is little changed, except that it must check that its arguments are of type PRIM for most operations.

```
(* prValue - print value v                                    *)
procedure prValue (v: CLUVALUE);
begin
   if v^.vtype = PRIM
   then write(v^.intval:1)
   else write('<userval>')
end; (* prValue *)

(* isTrueVal - return true if v is true (non-zero) value      *)
```

```
function isTrueVal (v: CLUVALUE): Boolean;
begin
  if v^.vtype = USER
  then isTrueVal := true
  else isTrueVal := v^.intval <> 0
end; (* isTrueVal *)

(* applyValueOp - apply VALUEOP op to arguments in VALUELIST vl  *)
function applyValueOp (op: VALUEOP; vl: VALUELIST): CLUVALUE;

var n, n1, n2: integer;

(* arity - return number of arguments expected by op            *)
   function arity (op: VALUEOP): integer;
   begin
      if op in [PLUSOP .. GTOP] then arity := 2 else arity := 1
   end; (* arity *)

begin (* applyValueOp *)
   if arity(op) <> lengthVL(vl)
   then begin
           write('Wrong number of arguments to ');
           prName(ord(op)+1);
           writeln;
           goto 99
        end;
   if op = PRINTOP
   then begin
           prValue(vl^.head);
           writeln;
           applyValueOp := vl^.head
        end
   else begin
           if (vl^.head^.vtype <> PRIM)
              or (vl^.tail^.head^.vtype <> PRIM)
           then begin
                   write('Arguments to primitive op not primitive: ');
                   prName(ord(op)+1);
                   writeln;
                   goto 99
                end;
           n1 := vl^.head^.intval; (* 1st actual *)
           n2 := vl^.tail^.head^.intval; (* 2nd actual *)
           case op of
              PLUSOP: n := n1+n2;
              MINUSOP: n := n1-n2;
              TIMESOP: n := n1*n2;
              DIVOP: n := n1 div n2;
              EQOP: if n1 = n2 then n := 1 else n := 0;
```

```
                LTOP: if n1 < n2 then n := 1 else n := 0;
                GTOP: if n1 > n2 then n := 1 else n := 0
            end; (* case *)
            applyValueOp := mkPRIM(n)
        end
end; (* applyValueOp *)



(*****************************************************************
*                        EVALUATION                            *
*****************************************************************)
```

   eval takes an additional argument, giving the cluster in which the expression e
occurs; this is necessary so that e can call cluster operations using their one-part
names. Aside from this, applyUserFun is considerably changed. First, it must determine where the function is defined; if it is given the two-part name, that is easy;
otherwise, it has to check the current cluster first and, if that fails, the global function
environment (fundefs). Second, it must process the three new types of user-defined
functions. The only changes in evalList and applyCtrlOp are to pass the third
argument in recursive calls of eval; these two functions are not given.

```
(* eval - return value of e in environment rho, cluster c        *)
function eval (e: EXP; rho: ENV; c: CLUSTER): CLUVALUE;

var op: BUILTINOP;

(* applyUserFun - look up definition of nm and apply to actuals  *)
   function applyUserFun (nm: FUNNAME;
                          actuals: VALUELIST): CLUVALUE;
   var
      f: FUNDEF;
      rho, valrho: ENV;
      v: CLUVALUE;
      cl: CLUSTER;

(* checkArgs - check number/type (as far as possible) of args    *)
      procedure checkArgs (nm: FUNNAME; f: FUNDEF; cl: CLUSTER);

(* arity - number of arguments expected by f                     *)
         function arity: integer;
         begin
            with f^ do
               case ftype of
                  NORMAL: arity := lengthNL(formals);
                  CONSTRUCTOR: arity := lengthNL(cl^.clrep);
                  SELECTOR: arity := 1;
                  SETTOR: arity := 2
               end (* case and with *)
         end; (* arity *)
```

```
(* typeError - print type error message                      *)
        procedure typeError;
        begin
            write('Wrong type argument to: ');
            prName(nm.funpart);
            writeln;
            goto 99
        end; (* typeError *)

    begin (* checkArgs *)
        if arity <> lengthVL(actuals)
        then begin
                write('Wrong number of arguments to: ');
                prName(nm.funpart);
                writeln;
                goto 99
            end;
        with f^ do
            begin
                if ftype in [SELECTOR, SETTOR]
                then if actuals^.head^.vtype = PRIM
                    then typeError;
                if ftype = SELECTOR
                then if not isBound(nm.funpart,
                                actuals^.head^.userval)
                    then typeError;
                if ftype = SETTOR
                then if not isBound(selname,
                                actuals^.head^.userval)
                    then typeError
            end
    end; (* checkArgs *)

  begin (* applyUserFun *)
    if nm.nametype = TWOPART
    then begin
            cl := fetchCluster(nm.clpart);
            if cl = nil
            then begin
                    write('Non-existent cluster: ');
                    prName(nm.clpart);
                    writeln;
                    goto 99
                end;
            f := fetchFun(nm.funpart, cl^.exported)
        end
    else begin (* one-part name *)
            cl := c;
            if cl = nil (* called from top level *)
```

```
               then f := fetchFun(nm.funpart, fundefs)
               else begin (* try exported function first *)
                       f := fetchFun(nm.funpart, cl^.exported);
                       if f = nil
                       then begin (* else non-exported *)
                               f := fetchFun(nm.funpart,
                                               cl^.nonexported);
                               if f = nil
                               then begin (* else top-level *)
                                       cl := nil;
                                       f := fetchFun(nm.funpart,
                                                       fundefs);
                                   end
                           end
                   end
           end;
       if f = nil
       then begin
               write('Undefined function: ');
               prName(nm.funpart);
               writeln;
               goto 99
           end;
       checkArgs(nm, f, cl);
       with f^ do
          case ftype of
             NORMAL:
                begin
                   rho := mkEnv(formals, actuals);
                   applyUserFun := eval(body, rho, cl)
                end;
             CONSTRUCTOR:
                applyUserFun := mkUSER(mkEnv(cl^.clrep, actuals));
             SELECTOR:
                begin
                   valrho := actuals^.head^.userval;
                   applyUserFun := fetch(nm.funpart, valrho)
                end;
             SETTOR:
                begin
                   valrho := actuals^.head^.userval;
                   v := actuals^.tail^.head;
                   assign(selname, v, valrho);
                   applyUserFun := v
                end
          end (* case and with *)
   end; (* applyUserFun *)

begin (* eval *)
```

```
    with e^ do
      case etype of
        VALEXP:
            eval := valu;
        VAREXP:
            if isBound(varble, rho)
            then eval := fetch(varble, rho)
            else if isBound(varble, globalEnv)
                    then eval := fetch(varble, globalEnv)
                    else begin
                            write('Undefined variable: ');
                            prName(varble);
                            writeln;
                            goto 99
                        end;
        APEXP:
            if optr.funpart > numBuiltins
            then eval := applyUserFun(optr, evalList(args))
            else begin
                    op := primOp(optr.funpart);
                    if op in [IFOP .. BEGINOP]
                    then eval := applyCtrlOp(op, args)
                    else eval := applyValueOp(op,
                                          evalList(args))
                end
      end (* case and with *)
end; (* eval *)
```

```
(*****************************************************************
*                    READ-EVAL-PRINT LOOP                       *
*****************************************************************)
```

The principal change here is to recognize and process cluster definitions.

```
begin (* clu main *)
   initNames;
   globalEnv := emptyEnv;

   quittingtime := false;
99:
   while not quittingtime do begin
      reader;
      if matches(pos, 4, 'quit              ')
      then quittingtime := true
      else if (userinput[pos] = '(') and
                matches(skipblanks(pos+1), 6, 'define              ')
             then begin
                    prName(parseDef(fundefs));
                    writeln
```

```
                    end
          else if (userinput[pos]=')' ) and
                   matches(skipblanks(pos+1),7,'cluster              ')
                   then begin
                           prName(parseCluster);
                           writeln
                        end
                   else begin
                           currentExp := parseExp;
                           prValue(eval(currentExp, emptyEnv, nil));
                           writeln;
                           writeln
                        end
        end (* while *)
end. (* clu *)
```

Appendix H

Interpreter for SMALLTALK

This appendix contains the code for the SMALLTALK interpreter, insofar as it differs from the code in Appendix G (that is, CLU). Thus, when we say "such-and-such has not changed," we mean "has not changed from Appendix G."

```
(****************************************************************
*                      DECLARATIONS                           *
****************************************************************)
```

The first change was made to accommodate the long names that are characteristic of SMALLTALK: increasing the `NAMELENG` constant. In various places (e.g., `initNames`) string constants have 10 extra blanks added.

```
NAMELENG = 30;       (* Maximum length of a name *)
```

The declaration of `FUNNAME` is removed. The following changes were discussed in Section 7.2:

```
BUILTINOP = (IFOP,WHILEOP,SETOP,BEGINOP,NEWOP,PLUSOP,
            MINUSOP,TIMESOP,DIVOP,EQOP,LTOP,GTOP,PRINTOP);
VALUEOP = PLUSOP .. PRINTOP;
CONTROLOP = IFOP .. NEWOP;

STVALUE = ^STVALUEREC;
```

```
FUNDEF = ^FUNDEFREC;
CLASS = ^CLASSREC;

STVALUETYPE = (INT,SYM,USER);
STVALUEREC = record
        owner: CLASS;
        case vtype: STVALUETYPE of
            INT: (intval: integer);
            SYM: (symval: NAME);
            USER: (userval: ENV)
        end;

FUNDEFREC = record
        funname: NAME;
        formals: NAMELIST;
        body: EXP;
        nextfundef: FUNDEF
        end;

CLASSREC = record
        clname: NAME;
        clsuper: CLASS;
        clrep: NAMELIST;
        exported: FUNDEF;
        nextclass: CLASS
        end;
```

Note the name change from "clusters" to "classes;" this entails various name changes throughout the interpreter, most of which we will not mention.

One of those changes is the replacement of the variable `clusters` by `classes`, having exactly the same function. The other new global variables were mentioned in Section 7.2.

```
classes: CLASS;

SELF: NAME;

OBJECTCLASS: CLASS;
objectInst: STVALUE;

trueValue, falseValue: STVALUE;
```

```
(****************************************************************
*                    DATA STRUCTURE OP'S                      *
****************************************************************)
```

The CLU interpreter had a `mkPRIM` function to create an integer `CLUVALUE`, but here we need two, one for integers and one for symbols. The only change in `mkUSER` is setting the `super` field. `mkAPEXP` returns to its previous form, since there are no longer two-part names. There are no other changes in this section.

```
(* mkINT - return an STVALUE with integer value n                *)
function mkINT (n: integer): STVALUE;
var newval: STVALUE;
begin
   new(newval);
   newval^.owner := OBJECTCLASS;
   newval^.vtype := INT;
   newval^.intval := n;
   mkINT := newval
end; (* mkINT *)

(* mkSYM - return an STVALUE with symbol value s                *)
function mkSYM (s: NAME): STVALUE;
var newval: STVALUE;
begin
   new(newval);
   newval^.owner := OBJECTCLASS;
   newval^.vtype := SYM;
   newval^.symval := s;
   mkSYM := newval
end; (* mkSYM *)

(* mkUSER - return a USER-type STVALUE                         *)
function mkUSER (rho: ENV; ownr: CLASS): STVALUE;
var newval: STVALUE;
begin
   new(newval);
   newval^.vtype := USER;
   newval^.userval := rho;
   newval^.owner := ownr;
   mkUSER := newval
end; (* mkUSER *)



(*****************************************************************
 *                     NAME MANAGEMENT                          *
 *****************************************************************)
```

fetchCluster and newCluster have their names changed to fetchClass and
newClass; also, newClass sets the super field (which it gets as an argument).

```
(* newClass - add new class cname to classes                   *)
function newClass (cname: NAME; super: CLASS): CLASS;
var cl: CLASS;
begin
   cl := fetchClass(cname);
   if cl = nil (* cname not yet defined as class *)
   then begin
           new(cl);
           cl^.clname := cname;
```

```
                cl^.nextclass := classes; (* place new CLASSREC *)
                classes := cl           (* on classes list *)
           end;
      cl^.clsuper := super;
      newClass := cl
end; (* newClass *)
```

initNames undergoes three minor changes: All string constants are now 30 characters long; the names "new" and "self" are added; and the new variables numCtrlOps
and SELF are set.

```
(*****************************************************************
*                          INPUT                               *
*****************************************************************)
```

isDelim is changed back to its old form ("$" is not a delimiter). isValue and
parseVal are changed to reflect the presence of symbol constants.

```
(* isValue - check if a number or quoted const begins at pos    *)
function isValue (pos: integer): Boolean;

(* isNumber - check if a number begins at pos                   *)
   function isNumber (pos: integer): Boolean;

   <as before>

begin (* isValue *)
   isValue:= (userinput[pos] = '#') or isNumber(pos)
end; (* isValue *)

(* parseVal - return primitive value starting at userinput[pos] *)
function parseVal: STVALUE;

(* parseInt - return number starting at userinput[pos]          *)
   function parseInt: integer;
   var n, sign: integer;
   begin
      n := 0; sign := 1;
      if userinput[pos] = '-'
      then begin
              sign := -1;
              pos := pos+1
           end;
      while userinput[pos] in ['0'..'9'] do
         begin
            n := 10*n + (ord(userinput[pos]) - ord('0'));
            pos := pos+1
         end;
      pos := skipblanks(pos); (* skip blanks after number *)
      parseInt := n*sign
```

```
    end; (* parseInt *)

begin (* parseVal *)
  if userinput[pos] = '#'
  then begin
           pos := pos+1;
           parseVal := mkSYM(parseName)
       end
  else parseVal := mkINT(parseInt)
end; (* parseVal *)
```

parseExp no longer needs to look for two-part names (it reverts to its pre-CLU form). parseClass (formerly parseCluster) has a number of changes:

```
(* parseClass - parse class definition at userinput[pos]        *)
function parseClass: NAME;

var
   cname, sname, fname: NAME;
   thisclass, superclass: CLASS;
   rep: NAMELIST;
   cenv: FUNDEF;

begin (* parseClass *)
   pos := skipblanks(pos+1); (* skip '( ..' *)
   pos := skipblanks(pos+5); (* skip 'class ...' *)
   cname := parseName;
   sname := parseName;
   superclass := fetchClass(sname);
   if superclass = nil
   then begin
           write('Undefined superclass: ');
           prName(sname);
           writeln;
           goto 99
        end;
   thisclass := newClass(cname,superclass);
   pos := skipblanks(pos+1); (* skip '( ...' *)
   rep := parseNL; (* component names *)
   cenv := nil;
   while userinput[pos]='(' do
      begin
         fname := parseDef(cenv);
         prName(fname);
         writeln
      end;
   thisclass^.exported := cenv;
   if rep = nil
   then thisclass^.clrep := superclass^.clrep
```

```
   else begin
          thisclass^.clrep := rep;
          while rep^.tail <> nil do rep := rep^.tail;
          rep^.tail := superclass^.clrep
      end;
   pos := skipblanks(pos+1); (* skip ' ..)' *)
   parseClass := cname
end; (* parseClass *)
```

```
(****************************************************************
*                        ENVIRONMENTS                         *
****************************************************************)
```

No changes here, except for replacing occurrences of CLUVALUE by STVALUE.

```
(****************************************************************
*                          VALUES                             *
****************************************************************)
```

```
(* prValue - print value v                                    *)
procedure prValue (v: STVALUE);
begin
   if v^.vtype = INT
   then write(v^.intval:1)
   else if v^.vtype = SYM
        then prName(v^.symval)
        else write('<userval>')
end; (* prValue *)
```

```
(* isTrueVal - return true if v is true (non-zero) value      *)
function isTrueVal (v: STVALUE): Boolean;
begin
  if (v^.vtype = USER) or (v^.vtype = SYM)
  then isTrueVal := true
  else isTrueVal := v^.intval <> 0
end; (* isTrueVal *)
```

```
(* applyValueOp - apply VALUEOP op to arguments in VALUELIST vl *)
function applyValueOp (op: VALUEOP; vl: VALUELIST): STVALUE;

var
   n, n1, n2: integer;
   s1, s2: STVALUE;
```

```
(* arity - return number of arguments expected by op          *)
   function arity (op: VALUEOP): integer;
   begin
      if op in [PLUSOP .. GTOP] then arity := 2 else arity := 1
   end; (* arity *)
```

```
begin (* applyValueOp *)
   if arity(op) <> lengthVL(vl)
   then begin
           write('Wrong number of arguments to ');
           prName(ord(op)+1);
           writeln;
           goto 99
        end;
   s1 := vl^.head; (* 1st actual *)
   if arity(op) = 2 then s2 := vl^.tail^.head; (* 2nd actual *)
   if op = PRINTOP
   then begin
           prValue(s1);
           writeln;
           applyValueOp := s1
        end
   else if op = EQOP
        then if s1^.vtype = s2^.vtype
             then if ((s1^.vtype = INT)
                         and (s1^.intval = s2^.intval))
                     or ((s1^.vtype = SYM)
                         and (s1^.symval = s2^.symval))
                  then applyValueOp := trueValue
                  else applyValueOp := falseValue
             else applyValueOp := falseValue
        else begin
                if (s1^.vtype <> INT)
                  or (s2^.vtype <> INT)
                then begin
                        write('Arguments to numeric op not integer: ');
                        prName(ord(op)+1);
                        writeln;
                        goto 99
                     end;
                n1 := s1^.intval;
                n2 := s2^.intval;
                case op of
                   PLUSOP: n := n1+n2;
                   MINUSOP: n := n1-n2;
                   TIMESOP: n := n1*n2;
                   DIVOP: n := n1 div n2;
                   LTOP: if n1 < n2 then n := 1 else n := 0;
                   GTOP: if n1 > n2 then n := 1 else n := 0
                end; (* case *)
                applyValueOp := mkINT(n)
             end
end; (* applyValueOp *)
```

```
(*****************************************************************
*                      EVALUATION                              *
*****************************************************************)
```

This section undergoes substantial changes. The only parts not materially changed are `evalList` and `applyCtrlOp`. (`applyGlobalFun` is the same as `applyUserFun` in Appendix B.)

```
(* eval - return value of e in environment rho, receiver rcvr    *)
function eval (e: EXP; rho: ENV; rcvr: STVALUE): STVALUE;

var
    vl: VALUELIST;
    f: FUNDEF;
```

The only change in `evalList` is to pass `rcvr` (instead of `c`) as the third argument in the recursive call of `eval`.

```
(* applyGlobalFun - apply function defined at top level          *)
    function applyGlobalFun (optr: NAME; actuals: VALUELIST): STVALUE;
    var
        f: FUNDEF;
        rho: ENV;

    begin (* applyGlobalFun *)
        f := fetchFun(optr, fundefs);
        if f = nil
        then begin
                write('Undefined function: ');
                prName(optr);
                writeln;
                goto 99
            end;
        with f^ do
            begin
                if lengthNL(formals) <> lengthVL(actuals)
                then begin
                        write('Wrong number of arguments to: ');
                        prName(funname);
                        writeln;
                        goto 99
                    end;
                rho := mkEnv(formals, actuals);
                applyGlobalFun := eval(body, rho, rcvr)
            end (* with *)
    end; (* applyGlobalFun *)

(* methodSearch - find class of optr, if any, starting at cl      *)
    function methodSearch (optr: NAME; cl: CLASS): FUNDEF;
    var f: FUNDEF;
```

```
begin
   f := nil;
   while (f = nil) and (cl <> nil) do begin
      f := fetchFun(optr, cl^.exported);
      if f = nil then cl := cl^.clsuper
      end;
   methodSearch := f
end; (* methodSearch *)
```

```
(* applyMethod - apply method f to actuals             *)
   function applyMethod (f: FUNDEF; actuals: VALUELIST): STVALUE;
   var rho: ENV;
   begin
      with f^ do begin
         if lengthNL(formals) <> lengthVL(actuals)-1
         then begin
                 write('Wrong number of arguments to: ');
                 prName(funname);
                 writeln;
                 goto 99
              end;
         rho := mkEnv(formals, actuals^.tail);
         applyMethod := eval(body, rho, actuals^.head)
         end
   end; (* applyMethod *)
```

`mkRepFor` is added as a local function of `applyCtrlOp`, used in the NEWOP case.
The SETOP case is modified to handle instance variables, and the NEWOP case is added.
The only other change is to pass `rcvr` (instead of `c`) as the third parameter in all
recursive calls of `eval`:

```
(* applyCtrlOp - apply CONTROLOP op to args in rho        *)
   function applyCtrlOp (op: CONTROLOP;
                        args: EXPLIST): STVALUE;
   var
      v: STVALUE;
      cl: CLASS;
      newval: STVALUE;
```

```
(* mkRepFor - make list of all zeros of same length as nl        *)
   function mkRepFor (nl: NAMELIST): VALUELIST;
   begin
      if nl = nil
      then mkRepFor := nil
      else mkRepFor := mkValuelist(falseValue,
                               mkRepFor(nl^.tail))
   end; (* mkRepFor *)

   begin (* applyCtrlOp *)
      with args^ do
```

```
case op of
   IFOP:
      if isTrueVal(eval(head, rho, rcvr))
      then applyCtrlOp := eval(tail^.head, rho, rcvr)
      else applyCtrlOp := eval(tail^.tail^.head, rho, rcvr);
   WHILEOP:
      begin
         v := eval(head, rho, rcvr);
         while isTrueVal(v)
         do begin
               v := eval(tail^.head, rho, rcvr);
               v := eval(head, rho, rcvr)
            end;
         applyCtrlOp := v
      end;
   SETOP:
      begin
         v := eval(tail^.head, rho, rcvr);
         if isBound(head^.varble, rho)
         then assign(head^.varble, v, rho)
         else if isBound(head^.varble, rcvr^.userval)
               then assign(head^.varble, v, rcvr^.userval)
               else if isBound(head^.varble, globalEnv)
                     then assign(head^.varble, v, globalEnv)
                     else bindVar(head^.varble, v, globalEnv);
         applyCtrlOp := v
      end;
   BEGINOP:
      begin
         while args^.tail <> nil do
            begin
               v := eval(args^.head, rho, rcvr);
               args := args^.tail
            end;
         applyCtrlOp := eval(args^.head, rho, rcvr)
      end;
   NEWOP:
      begin
         (* Argument is a VAREXP with the name of a class *)
         cl := fetchClass(args^.head^.varble);
         if cl = nil
         then begin
                 write('Undefined class: ');
                 prName(args^.head^.varble);
                 writeln;
                 goto 99
              end;
         newval :=
            mkUSER(mkEnv(cl^.clrep, mkRepFor(cl^.clrep)), cl);
```

```
                    assign(SELF, newval, newval^.userval);
                    applyCtrlOp := newval
               end
          end (* case and with *)
    end; (* applyCtrlOp *)
```

Finally, here is the body of **eval**:

```
begin (* eval *)
    with e^ do
       case etype of
          VALEXP:
             eval := valu;
          VAREXP:
             if isBound(varble, rho)
             then eval := fetch(varble, rho)
             else if isBound(varble, rcvr^.userval)
                    then eval := fetch(varble, rcvr^.userval)
                    else if isBound(varble, globalEnv)
                           then eval := fetch(varble, globalEnv)
                           else begin
                                   write('Undefined variable: ');
                                   prName(varble);
                                   writeln;
                                   goto 99
                                end;
          APEXP:
             if optr <= numCtrlOps
             then eval := applyCtrlOp(primOp(optr), args)
             else begin
                     vl := evalList(args);
                     if lengthVL(vl) = 0
                     then eval := applyGlobalFun(optr, vl)
                     else begin
                             f := methodSearch(optr, vl^.head^.owner);
                             if f <> nil
                             then eval := applyMethod(f, vl)
                             else if optr <= numBuiltins
                                    then eval := applyValueOp(primOp(optr), vl)
                                    else eval := applyGlobalFun(optr, vl)
                          end
                  end
       end (* case and with *)
end; (* eval *)
```

```
(****************************************************************
*                     READ-EVAL-PRINT LOOP                     *
****************************************************************)

(* initHierarchy - allocate class Object and create an instance  *)
procedure initHierarchy;
begin
    classes := nil;
    OBJECTCLASS :=
      newClass(install('Object                   '), nil);
    OBJECTCLASS^.exported := nil;
    OBJECTCLASS^.clrep := mkNamelist(SELF, nil);
    objectInst :=
        mkUSER(mkEnv(OBJECTCLASS^.clrep,
                     mkValuelist(mkINT(0), nil)),
                  OBJECTCLASS);
end; (* initHierarchy *)

begin (* smalltalk main *)
   initNames;
   initHierarchy;
   globalEnv := emptyEnv;

   trueValue := mkINT(1);
   falseValue := mkINT(0);

   quittingtime := false;
99:
   while not quittingtime do begin
      reader;
      if matches(pos, 4, 'quit                   ')
      then quittingtime := true
      else if (userinput[pos] = '(') and
              matches(skipblanks(pos+1), 6,
                    'define                 ')
           then begin
                   prName(parseDef(fundefs));
                   writeln
                end
           else if (userinput[pos]='(') and
                   matches(skipblanks(pos+1),5,
                         'class                  ')
                then begin
                        prName(parseClass);
                        writeln
                     end
                else begin
                        currentExp := parseExp;
                        prValue(eval(currentExp, emptyEnv, objectInst));
```

```
                         writeln;
                         writeln
                    end
       end (* while *)
end. (* smalltalk *)
```

Appendix I

Interpreter for PROLOG

This appendix contains the code for the PROLOG interpreter, in full, except for the following functions and procedures, whose definitions are exactly as in Appendix B: `install`, `prName`, `isDelim`, `matches`, `skipblanks`, `reader`, `parseName`, `isNumber`, and `parseInt`.

Code section	Page
DECLARATIONS	571
DATA STRUCTURE OP's	573
NAME MANAGEMENT	575
INPUT	576
OUTPUT	579
SUBSTITUTIONS	580
UNIFICATION	582
EVALUATION	584
READ-EVAL-PRINT LOOP	588

```
(****************************************************************
*                      DECLARATIONS                           *
****************************************************************)
program prolog (input, output);

label 99;

const
    NAMELENG = 20;      (* Maximum length of a name *)
    MAXNAMES = 300;     (* Maximum number of different names *)
    MAXINPUT = 2000;    (* Maximum length of an input *)
    PROMPT = '-> ';
    PROMPT2 = '> ';
    COMMENTCHAR = ';';
    TABCODE = 9;        (* in ASCII *)

type
```

```
NAMESIZE = O..NAMELENG;
NAMESTRING = packed array [1..NAMELENG] of char;

NAME = 1 .. MAXNAMES; (* a NAME is an index in printNames *)

CLAUSE = ^CLAUSEREC;
GOALLIST = ^GOALLISTREC;
GOAL = ^GOALREC;
EXP = ^EXPREC;
EXPLIST = ^EXPLISTREC;
VARIABLE = ^VARIABLEREC;
VARLIST = ^ VARLISTREC;
SUBST = ^SUBSTREC;

GOALREC = record
             pred: NAME;
             args: EXPLIST
          end;

GOALLISTREC = record
             head: GOAL;
             tail: GOALLIST;
          end;

VARIABLEREC = record
             varname: NAME;
             varindex: integer
          end;

VARLISTREC = record
             head: VARIABLE;
             tail: VARLIST;
          end;

EXPTYPE = (VAREXP,INTEXP,APEXP);
EXPREC = record
             case etype: EXPTYPE of
                VAREXP: (varble: VARIABLE);
                INTEXP: (intval: integer);
                APEXP: (optr: NAME; args: EXPLIST)
          end;

EXPLISTREC = record
             head: EXP;
             tail: EXPLIST;
          end;

CLAUSEREC = record
             lhs: GOAL;
```

```
                  rhs: GOALLIST;
                  nextclause: CLAUSE
            end;

   SUBSTREC = record
               domain: VARLIST;
               range: EXPLIST
            end;

var
   clauses, lastclause: CLAUSE;

   toplevelGoal: GOALLIST;

   userinput: array [1..MAXINPUT] of char;
   inputleng, pos: 0..MAXINPUT;

   printNames: array [NAME] of NAMESTRING;
   numNames, numBuiltins : NAME;

   quittingtime: Boolean;


(*****************************************************************
 *                    DATA STRUCTURE OP'S                       *
 *****************************************************************)
(* mkGoal - create a new GOAL with pred p and arguments a       *)
function mkGoal (p: NAME; a: EXPLIST): GOAL;
var newg: GOAL;
begin
   new(newg);
   newg^.pred := p;
   newg^.args := a;
   mkGoal := newg
end; (* mkGoal *)

(* mkVAREXP - create a new EXP of type VAREXP                   *)
function mkVAREXP (v: VARIABLE): EXP;
var newe: EXP;
begin
   new(newe);
   newe^.etype := VAREXP;
   newe^.varble := v;
   mkVAREXP := newe
end; (* mkVAREXP *)

(* mkINTEXP - create a new EXP of type INTEXP                   *)
function mkINTEXP (n: integer): EXP;
var newe: EXP;
```

```
begin
   new(newe);
   newe^.etype := INTEXP;
   newe^.intval := n;
   mkINTEXP := newe
end; (* mkINTEXP *)

(* mkAPEXP - create a new EXP of type APEXP                    *)
function mkAPEXP (o: NAME; a: EXPLIST): EXP;
var newe: EXP;
begin
   new(newe);
   newe^.etype := APEXP;
   newe^.optr := o;
   newe^.args := a;
   mkAPEXP := newe
end; (* mkAPEXP *)

(* mkVariable - create a new VARIABLE with name n and index i   *)
function mkVariable (n: NAME; i: integer): VARIABLE;
var newv: VARIABLE;
begin
   new(newv);
   newv^.varname := n;
   newv^.varindex := i;
   mkVariable := newv
end; (* mkVariable *)

(* mkVarlist - create a new VARLIST with head v and tail vl     *)
function mkVarlist (v: VARIABLE; vl: VARLIST): VARLIST;
var newvl: VARLIST;
begin
   new(newvl);
   newvl^.head := v;
   newvl^.tail := vl;
   mkVarlist := newvl
end; (* mkVarlist *)

(* mkGoallist - return a GOALLIST with head g and tail gl       *)
function mkGoallist (g: GOAL; gl: GOALLIST): GOALLIST;
var newgl: GOALLIST;
begin
   new(newgl);
   newgl^.head := g;
   newgl^.tail := gl;
   mkGoallist := newgl
end; (* mkGoallist *)

(* mkExplist - return an EXPLIST with head e and tail el        *)
function mkExplist (e: EXP; el: EXPLIST): EXPLIST;
```

```
var newel: EXPLIST;
begin
   new(newel);
   newel^.head := e;
   newel^.tail := el;
   mkExplist := newel
end; (* mkExplist *)

(* mkClause - create a new GOAL with lhs l and rhs r        *)
function mkClause (l: GOAL; r: GOALLIST): CLAUSE;
var c: CLAUSE;
begin
   new(c);
   c^.lhs := l;
   c^.rhs := r;
   c^.nextclause := nil;
   mkClause := c
end; (* mkClause *)

(* eqVar - compare two VARIABLE's for equality             *)
function eqVar (v1, v2: VARIABLE): Boolean;
begin
   eqVar := (v1^.varname = v2^.varname)
            and (v1^.varindex = v2^.varindex)
end; (* eqVar *)

(* lengthEL - return length of EXPLIST el                  *)
function lengthEL (el: EXPLIST): integer;
var i: integer;
begin
   i := 0;
   while el <> nil do begin
      i := i+1;
      el := el^.tail
      end;
   lengthEL := i
end; (* lengthEL *)


(***************************************************************
 *                    NAME MANAGEMENT                         *
 ***************************************************************)
```

Function install and procedure prName are as in Appendix B.

```
(* newClause - add new clause at end of clauses list       *)
procedure newClause (l: GOAL; r: GOALLIST);
begin
    if lastclause = nil
    then begin
```

```
              clauses := mkClause(l, r);
              lastclause := clauses
         end
    else begin
              lastclause^.nextclause := mkClause(l, r);
              lastclause := lastclause^.nextclause
         end
end; (* newClause *)

(* initNames - place all pre-defined names into printNames        *)
procedure initNames;
var i: integer;
begin
   clauses := nil;
   lastclause := nil;
   i := 1;
   printNames[i]:='plus                 '; i:=i+1;
   printNames[i]:='minus                '; i:=i+1;
   printNames[i]:='less                 '; i:=i+1;
   printNames[i]:='print                ';
   numBuiltins := i;
   numNames := i
end; (* initNames *)



(******************************************************************
 *                         INPUT                                  *
 ******************************************************************)
```

Functions isDelim, matches, skipblanks, parseName, isNumber, and parseInt, and procedure **reader**, are omitted.

```
(* isVar - check if first character of name n is upper-case       *)
function isVar (n: NAME): Boolean;
begin
   isVar := (printNames[n][1] >= 'A')
            and (printNames[n][1] <= 'Z')
end; (* isVar *)

function parseEL: EXPLIST; forward;

(* parseExp - return EXP starting at userinput[pos]               *)
function parseExp: EXP;
var
   n: NAME;
   el: EXPLIST;
begin
   if userinput[pos] = '('
   then begin
           pos := skipblanks(pos+1); (* skip '( ..' *)
```

```
                n := parseName;
                el := parseEL;
                parseExp := mkAPEXP(n, el)
           end
   else if isNumber(pos)
        then parseExp := mkINTEXP(parseInt)
        else begin
                 n := parseName;
                 if isVar(n)
                 then parseExp := mkVAREXP(mkVariable(n, 0))
                 else parseExp := mkAPEXP(n, nil)
             end
end; (* parseExp *)

(* parseEL - return EXPLIST starting at userinput[pos]                 *)
function parseEL;
var
   e: EXP;
   el: EXPLIST;
begin
   if userinput[pos] = ')'
   then begin
           pos := skipblanks(pos+1); (* skip ') ..' *)
           parseEL := nil
        end
   else begin
           e := parseExp;
           el := parseEL;
           parseEL := mkExplist(e, el)
        end
end; (* parseEL *)

(* parseGoal - return GOAL starting at userinput[pos]                 *)
function parseGoal: GOAL;
var
   pred: NAME;
   il: EXPLIST;
begin
   if userinput[pos] = '('
   then begin
           pos := skipblanks(pos+1); (* skip '( ...' *)
           pred := parseName;
           il := parseEL
        end
   else begin
           pred := parseName;
           il := nil
        end;
   parseGoal := mkGoal(pred, il)
```

```
end; (* parseGoal *)


(* parseGL - return GOALLIST starting at userinput[pos]          *)
function parseGL: GOALLIST;
var
   g: GOAL;
   gl: GOALLIST;
begin
   if userinput[pos] = ')'
   then begin
           pos := skipblanks(pos+1); (* skip ') ..' *)
           parseGL := nil
        end
   else begin
           g := parseGoal;
           gl := parseGL;
           parseGL := mkGoallist(g, gl)
        end
end; (* parseGL *)


(* parseClause - return CLAUSE at userinput[pos]                 *)
procedure parseClause;
var
   h: GOAL;
   g: GOALLIST;
begin
   pos := skipblanks(pos+1); (* skip '( ..' *)
   pos := skipblanks(pos+5); (* skip 'infer ..' *)
   h := parseGoal;
   if userinput[pos] = ')'
   then g := nil
   else begin
           pos := skipblanks(pos+4); (* skip 'from ..' *)
           g := parseGL
        end;
   pos := skipblanks(pos+1); (* skip ') ..' *)
   newClause(h, g)
end; (* parseClause *)


(* parseQuery - return GOALLIST starting at userinput[pos]       *)
function parseQuery: GOALLIST;
begin
   pos := skipblanks(pos+1); (* skip '( ..' *)
   pos := skipblanks(pos+6); (* skip 'infer? ..' *)
   parseQuery := parseGL;
   pos := skipblanks(pos+1) (* skip ') ..' *)
end; (* parseQuery *)
```

```
(****************************************************************
*                        OUTPUT                               *
****************************************************************)
(* prExplist - print an EXPLIST                               *)
procedure prExplist (el: EXPLIST);

(* prExp - print an EXP                                       *)
   procedure prExp (e: EXP);


(* prVariable - print variable, including index              *)
      procedure prVariable (v: VARIABLE);
      begin
         prName(v^.varname);
         if v^.varindex > 0
         then write(v^.varindex:1)
      end; (* prVariable *)

   begin (* prExp *)
      case e^.etype of
         INTEXP: write(e^.intval:1);
         VAREXP: prVariable(e^.varble);
         APEXP:
            if e^.args=nil
            then prName(e^.optr)
            else begin
                    write('(');
                    prName(e^.optr);
                    if e^.args <> nil
                    then begin
                            write(' ');
                            prExplist(e^.args)
                         end;
                    write(')')
                 end
      end (* case *)
   end; (* prExp *)

begin (* prExplist *)
   if el <> nil
   then begin
           prExp(el^.head);
           if el^.tail <> nil
           then begin
                   write(' ');
                   prExplist(el^.tail)
                end
        end
end; (* prExplist *)
```

```
(******************************************************************
*                      SUBSTITUTIONS                              *
******************************************************************)

(* emptySubst - create a substitution with no bindings          *)
function emptySubst: SUBST;
var s: SUBST;
begin
   new(s);
   s^.domain := nil;
   s^.range := nil;
   emptySubst := s
end; (* emptySubst *)

(* bindVar - bind variable v to expression e in sigma           *)
procedure bindVar (v: VARIABLE; e: EXP; sigma: SUBST);
begin
   sigma^.domain := mkVarlist(v, sigma^.domain);
   sigma^.range := mkExplist(e, sigma^.range)
end; (* bindVar *)

(* findVar - look up variable v in sigma                        *)
function findVar (v: VARIABLE; sigma: SUBST): EXPLIST;
var
   dl: VARLIST;
   rl: EXPLIST;
   found: Boolean;
begin
   found := false;
   dl := sigma^.domain;
   rl := sigma^.range;
   while (dl <> nil) and not found do
      if eqVar(dl^.head, v)
      then found := true
      else begin
              dl := dl^.tail;
              rl := rl^.tail
           end;
   findVar := rl
end; (* findVar *)

(* fetch - fetch binding of variable v in sigma                 *)
function fetch (v: VARIABLE; sigma: SUBST): EXP;
var el: EXPLIST;
begin
   el := findVar(v, sigma);
   fetch := el^.head
end; (* fetch *)

(* isBound - check if variable v is bound in sigma              *)
```

```pascal
function isBound (v: VARIABLE; sigma: SUBST): Boolean;
begin
   isBound := findVar(v, sigma) <> nil
end; (* isBound *)


procedure applyToExplist (s: SUBST; el: EXPLIST); forward;

(* applyToExp - apply substitution s to e, modifying e        *)
procedure applyToExp (s: SUBST; var e: EXP);
begin
   case e^.etype of
      INTEXP: ;
      VAREXP:
         if isBound(e^.varble, s)
         then e := fetch(e^.varble, s);
      APEXP: applyToExplist(s, e^.args)
   end
end; (* applyToExp *)

(* applyToExplist - apply substitution s to el, modifying el   *)
procedure applyToExplist;
begin
   while el <> nil do begin
      applyToExp(s, el^.head);
      el := el^.tail
      end
end; (* applyToExplist *)

(* applyToGoal - apply substitution s to g, modifying g        *)
procedure applyToGoal (s: SUBST; g: GOAL);
begin
   applyToExplist(s, g^.args)
end; (* applyToGoal *)

(* applyToGoallist - apply substitution s to gl, modifying gl  *)
procedure applyToGoallist (s: SUBST; gl: GOALLIST);
begin
   while gl <> nil do begin
      applyToGoal(s, gl^.head);
      gl := gl^.tail
      end
end; (* applyToGoallist *)

(* compose - change substitution s1 to composition of s1 and s2 *)
procedure compose (s1, s2: SUBST);
var
   dom: VARLIST;
   rng: EXPLIST;
begin
   applyToExplist(s2, s1^.range);
```

```
   if s1^.domain = nil
   then begin
           s1^.domain := s2^.domain;
           s1^.range := s2^.range
        end
   else begin
           dom := s1^.domain;
           rng := s1^.range;
           while dom^.tail <> nil do begin
              dom := dom^.tail;
              rng := rng^.tail
              end;
           dom^.tail := s2^.domain;
           rng^.tail := s2^.range
        end
end; (* compose *)


(*****************************************************************
 *                      UNIFICATION                             *
 *****************************************************************)

(* unify - unify g1 and g2; return unifying subst. (or nil)      *)
function unify (g1, g2: GOAL): SUBST;
var
   sigma, varsubst: SUBST;
   foundDiff: Boolean;
   diff1, diff2: EXP;

   function findExpDiff (e1, e2: EXP): Boolean;
      forward;

(* findELDiff - set diff1, diff2 to EXP's where el1, el2 differ *)
   function findELDiff (el1, el2: EXPLIST): Boolean;
   var foundDiff: Boolean;
   begin
      foundDiff := false;
      while (el1 <> nil) and not foundDiff do begin
         foundDiff := findExpDiff(el1^.head, el2^.head);
         el1 := el1^.tail;
         el2 := el2^.tail
         end;
      findELDiff := foundDiff
   end; (* findELDiff *)

(* findExpDiff - set diff1, diff2 to EXP's where e1, e2 differ   *)
   function findExpDiff;
   begin
      findExpDiff := true;
      diff1 := e1;
```

```
      diff2 := e2;
      if e1^.etype = e2^.etype
      then case e1^.etype of
              VAREXP:
                  if eqVar(e1^.varble, e2^.varble)
                  then findExpDiff := false;
              INTEXP:
                  if e1^.intval = e2^.intval
                  then findExpDiff := false;
              APEXP:
                  if e1^.optr = e2^.optr
                  then findExpDiff :=
                          findELDiff(e1^.args, e2^.args)
          end (* case *)
  end; (* findExpDiff *)


(* occursInExp - check whether variable v occurs in exp e       *)
   function occursInExp (v: VARIABLE; e: EXP): Boolean;
   var
      occurs: Boolean;
      el: EXPLIST;
   begin
      with e^ do
         case etype of
            INTEXP: occursInExp := false;
            VAREXP: occursInExp := eqVar(v, varble);
            APEXP:
               begin
                  occurs := false;
                  el := args;
                  while (el <> nil) and not occurs do
                     begin
                        occurs := occursInExp(v, el^.head);
                        el := el^.tail
                     end;
                  occursInExp := occurs
               end
         end (* case and with *)
   end; (* occursInExp *)


(* makeSubst - bind d1 to d2 in s, first checking if possible    *)
   procedure makeSubst (d1, d2: EXP; var s: SUBST);
   begin
      if d1^.etype <> VAREXP
      then s := nil
      else if occursInExp(d1^.varble, d2)
           then s := nil
           else bindVar(d1^.varble, d2, s)
   end; (* makeSubst *)
```

```
begin (* unify *)
   sigma := emptySubst;
   repeat
      foundDiff := findELDiff(g1^.args, g2^.args);
      varsubst := emptySubst;
      if foundDiff
      then if diff1^.etype = VAREXP
           then makeSubst(diff1, diff2, varsubst)
           else makeSubst(diff2, diff1, varsubst);
      if foundDiff and (varsubst <> nil)
      then begin
              applyToGoal(varsubst, g1);
              applyToGoal(varsubst, g2);
              compose(sigma, varsubst)
           end
   until (not foundDiff) (* done *)
        or (varsubst=nil); (* not unifiable *)
   if varsubst = nil
   then  unify := nil
   else unify := sigma
end; (* unify *)


(****************************************************************
 *                      EVALUATION                             *
 ****************************************************************)

(* applyPrim - apply primitive predicate, modifying sigma      *)
function applyPrim (g: GOAL; var sigma: SUBST): Boolean;

var
   arglist: EXPLIST;
   arg1, arg2, arg3: EXP;

   procedure applyArith (op: integer);
   var i: integer;
   begin
      arg3 := arglist^.tail^.tail^.head;
      if arg3^.etype = APEXP
      then applyPrim := false
      else begin
              case op of
                 1: i := arg1^.intval + arg2^.intval;
                 2: i := arg1^.intval - arg2^.intval
              end;
              if arg3^.etype = INTEXP
              then if arg3^.intval <> i
                   then applyPrim := false
                   else (* applyPrim already true *)
```

```
                    else bindVar(arg3^.varble, mkINTEXP(i), sigma)
                 end
       end; (* applyArith *)

begin
    sigma := emptySubst;
    applyPrim := true;
    arglist := g^.args;
    if g^.pred = 4 (* print *)
    then begin
                prExplist(arglist);
                writeln
            end
    else begin
                arg1 := arglist^.head;
                arg2 := arglist^.tail^.head;
                if (arg1^.etype <> INTEXP) or (arg2^.etype <> INTEXP)
                then applyPrim := false
                else case g^.pred of
                        1, 2: (* plus, minus *)
                            applyArith(g^.pred);
                        3: (* less *)
                            if arg1^.intval >= arg2^.intval
                            then applyPrim := false
                    end (* case *)
            end
end; (* applyPrim *)

function copyGoal (g: GOAL; id: integer): GOAL; forward;

(* copyGoallist - copy gl; rename variables if id<>0              *)
function copyGoallist (gl: GOALLIST; id: integer): GOALLIST;
begin
    if gl = nil
    then copyGoallist := nil
    else copyGoallist := mkGoallist(copyGoal(gl^.head, id),
                                    copyGoallist(gl^.tail, id))
end; (* copyGoallist *)

(* copyGoal - copy g; rename variables if id<>0                   *)
function copyGoal;

(* copyExplist - copy el; rename variables if id<>0              *)
    function copyExplist (el: EXPLIST): EXPLIST;

(* copyExp - copy e; rename variables if id<>0                   *)
        function copyExp (e: EXP): EXP;
        begin
            case e^.etype of
                INTEXP: copyExp := e;
```

```
                VAREXP:
                   if id = 0
                   then copyExp :=
                           mkVAREXP(mkVariable(e^.varble^.varname,
                                               e^.varble^.varindex))
                   else copyExp :=
                           mkVAREXP(mkVariable(e^.varble^.varname,
                                               id));
                APEXP: copyExp :=
                           mkAPEXP(e^.optr, copyExplist(e^.args))
            end (* case *)
         end; (* copyExp *)

      begin (* copyExplist *)
         if el = nil
         then copyExplist := nil
         else copyExplist :=
                    mkExplist(copyExp(el^.head),
                              copyExplist(el^.tail))
      end; (* copyExplist *)

   begin (* copyGoal *)
      copyGoal := mkGoal(g^.pred, copyExplist(g^.args))
   end; (* copyGoal *)

   (* append - append second to end of first, modifying first      *)
   function append (first, second: GOALLIST): GOALLIST;
   begin
      if first = nil
      then append := second
      else begin
              append := first;
              while first^.tail <> nil do first := first^.tail;
              first^.tail := second
           end
   end; (* append *)

   (* prove - prove goals gl; return subst; id used to rename var's *)
   function prove (gl: GOALLIST; id: integer): SUBST;

   var
      cl: CLAUSE;
      sigma0, sigma1: SUBST;

   (* tryClause - try to match goal g and clause head of c          *)
      function tryClause (clgoal, g: GOAL): SUBST;
      begin
         tryClause := nil;
         if (clgoal^.pred = g^.pred)
```

```
            and (lengthEL(clgoal^.args) = lengthEL(g^.args))
        then begin
                clgoal := copyGoal(clgoal, id);
                g := copyGoal(g, 0);
                tryClause := unify(clgoal, g)
            end
    end; (* tryClause *)


(* proveRest - add subgoals to restofgoals and prove            *)
    function proveRest (subgoals, restofgoals: GOALLIST): SUBST;
    begin
        subgoals := copyGoallist(subgoals, id);
        applyToGoallist(sigma0, subgoals);
        restofgoals := copyGoallist(restofgoals, 0);
        applyToGoallist(sigma0, restofgoals);
        proveRest := prove(append(subgoals, restofgoals), id+1)
    end; (* proveRest *)

begin (* prove *)
    if gl = nil
    then prove := emptySubst
    else begin
            if gl^.head^.pred <= numBuiltins
            then if applyPrim(gl^.head, sigma0)
                then begin
                        applyToGoallist(sigma0, gl^.tail);
                        sigma1 := prove(gl^.tail, id+1)
                    end
                else sigma1 := nil
            else begin
                sigma1 := nil;
                cl := clauses;
                while (cl <> nil) and (sigma1 = nil) do begin
                    sigma0 := tryClause(cl^.lhs, gl^.head);
                    if sigma0 <> nil
                    then sigma1 := proveRest(cl^.rhs, gl^.tail);
                    cl := cl^.nextclause
                    end (* while *)
                end;
            if sigma1 = nil
            then prove := nil
            else begin
                    compose(sigma0, sigma1);
                    prove := sigma0
                end
        end
end; (* prove *)
```

```
(***************************************************************
*                     READ-EVAL-PRINT LOOP                    *
***************************************************************)

begin (* prolog main *)
   initNames;

   quittingtime := false;
99:
   while not quittingtime do begin
      reader;
      if matches(pos, 4, 'quit              ')
      then quittingtime := true
      else if matches(skipblanks(pos+1), 5, 'infer                ')
           then begin
                   parseClause;
                   writeln
                end
           else begin
                   toplevelGoal := parseQuery;
                   writeln;
                   if prove(toplevelGoal, 1) = nil
                   then writeln('Not satisfied')
                   else writeln('Satisfied');
                   writeln
                end
      end
end. (* prolog *)
```

Appendix J

Interpreters from Chapter 10

This appendix contains the code for the stack-based and reference-counting interpreters of Chapter 10. The stack-based interpreter will be listed only insofar as it differs from the code in Appendix C, and the reference-counting interpreter only insofar as it differs from the stack-based interpreter.

J.1 Stack-Based Interpreter

```
(***************************************************************
*                      DECLARATIONS                           *
***************************************************************)
```

The only changes here are: The constant **STACKSIZE** is added, the **VAREXP** case in **EXPREC** is changed, and two variables representing the argument stack are declared:

```
STACKSIZE = 1000;

EXPREC = record
            case etype: EXPTYPE of
              VALEXP: (sxp: SEXP);
              VAREXP: (varble: NAME; offset: integer); (* 0 for global *)
```

```
                    APEXP: (optr: NAME; args: EXPLIST)
            end;

   argStack: array [1..STACKSIZE] of SEXP;
   stacktop: integer; (* range is 1..STACKSIZE+1 *)


(****************************************************************
*                    MEMORY MANAGEMENT                        *
****************************************************************)
```

This section is entirely new.

```
(* initStack - initialize environment stack                  *)
procedure initStack;
begin
   stacktop := 1
end; (* initStack *)

(* pushArg - push a single argument onto argStack            *)
procedure pushArg (s: SEXP);
begin
   if stacktop > STACKSIZE
   then begin
           writeln('Stack overflow');
           stacktop := 1;
           goto 99
        end;
   argStack[stacktop] := s;
   stacktop := stacktop + 1
end; (* pushArg *)

(* topArg - return top item in stack                         *)
function topArg: SEXP;
begin
   topArg := argStack[stacktop-1]
end; (* topArg *)

(* popArgs - pop argument list from top of argStack          *)
procedure popArgs (l: integer);
begin
   stacktop := stacktop - l
end; (* popArgs *)


(****************************************************************
*                    DATA STRUCTURE OP'S                      *
****************************************************************)
```

The only change here is that mkVAREXP sets the offset field to zero, indicating that a new variable is assumed to be global.

```
(* mkVAREXP - return an EXP of type VAREXP with varble nm          *)
function mkVAREXP (nm: NAME): EXP;
var e: EXP;
begin
   new(e);
   e^.etype := VAREXP;
   e^.varble := nm;
   e^.offset := 0;
   mkVAREXP := e
end; (* mkVAREXP *)


(****************************************************************
 *                      NAME MANAGEMENT                        *
 ****************************************************************)
```

   No changes.

```
(****************************************************************
 *                         INPUT                              *
 ****************************************************************)
```

Here, only `parseDef` is changed. It must set the `offset` field in each variable in the body of a function definition. (Note that `parseExp` assumes all variables are global, so that it works correctly when called from the top level; it therefore requires no changes.)

```
(* parseDef - parse function definition at userinput[pos]          *)
function parseDef: NAME;
var
   fname: NAME;          (* function name *)
   nl: NAMELIST;         (* formal parameters *)
   e: EXP;               (* body *)

(* processExpVars - insert offsets in all VAREXP's within e        *)
   procedure processExpVars (e: EXP);

(* offsetOfVar - return location of nm in nl, or zero              *)
     function offsetOfVar (nm: NAME; nl: NAMELIST): integer;
     var
        i: integer;
        found: Boolean;
     begin
        i := 1; found := false;
        while (nl <> nil) and not found do
           if nm = nl^.head
           then found := true
           else begin
                   i := i+1;
                   nl := nl^.tail
```

```
                  end;
           if not found then i := 0;
           offsetOfVar := i
       end; (* offsetOfVar *)

(* processELVars - apply processExpVars to each expression in el *)
     procedure processELVars (el: EXPLIST);
     begin
        while el <> nil do begin
           processExpVars(el^.head);
           el := el^.tail
           end
     end; (* processELVars *)

   begin (* processExpVars *)
     with e^ do
        case etype of
           VALEXP: ;
           VAREXP: offset := offsetOfVar(varble, nl);
           APEXP: processELVars(args)
        end
   end; (* processExpVars *)

begin (* parseDef *)
   pos := skipblanks(pos+1); (* skip '( ..' *)
   pos := skipblanks(pos+6); (* skip 'define ..' *)
   fname := parseName;
   pos := skipblanks(pos+1); (* skip '( ..' *)
   nl := parseNL;
   e := parseExp;
   pos := skipblanks(pos+1); (* skip ') ..' *)
   newFunDef(fname, nl, e);
   processExpVars(e);
   parseDef := fname
end; (* parseDef *)
```

```
(****************************************************************
*                       ENVIRONMENTS                          *
****************************************************************)
```

No changes.

```
(****************************************************************
*                      S-EXPRESSIONS                          *
****************************************************************)
```

The only change is in the declaration of applyValueOp and the first few lines of its body: Arguments are obtained from the stack, and no checking is done for the correct number of arguments.

```
(* applyValueOp - apply VALUEOP op to arguments on stop of stack *)
function applyValueOp (op: VALUEOP): SEXP;

begin (* applyValueOp *)
   result := nilValue;
   s1 := topArg; (* 1st actual *)
   popArgs(1);
   if arity(op) = 2
   then begin
           s2 := s1; (* 1st actual was really 2nd actual *)
           s1 := topArg; (* 1st actual *)
           popArgs(1)
        end;
   if op in [PLUSOP .. DIVOP, LTOP .. GTOP]
         :
      no changes here
         :
end; (* applyValueOp *)


(****************************************************************
 *                      EVALUATION                             *
 ****************************************************************)
```

Every function in this section undergoes significant changes, while retaining its basic purpose, as explained in the text.

```
(* eval - return value of e; param's start at argStack[AR]       *)
function eval (e: EXP; AR: integer): SEXP;

var
   op: BUILTINOP;
   newAR: integer;

(* evalList - evaluate each expression in el                     *)
   procedure evalList (el: EXPLIST);
   var h: SEXP;
   begin
      if el <> nil
      then begin
              h := eval(el^.head, AR);
              pushArg(h);
              evalList(el^.tail)
           end
   end; (* evalList *)

(* applyUserFun - apply nm; arg's start at argStack[newAR]       *)
   function applyUserFun (nm: NAME; newAR: integer): SEXP;
```

```
    var f: FUNDEF;
    begin
      f := fetchFun(nm);
      if f = nil
      then begin
              write('Undefined function: ');
              prName(nm);
              writeln;
              goto 99
          end;
      with f^ do begin
          applyUserFun := eval(body, newAR);
          popArgs(lengthNL(formals))
          end
    end; (* applyUserFun *)

(* applyCtrlOp - apply CONTROLOP op to args                    *)
    function applyCtrlOp (op: CONTROLOP;
                          args: EXPLIST): SEXP;
    var s: SEXP;
    begin
      with args^ do
        case op of
          IFOP:
              if isTrueVal(eval(head, AR))
              then applyCtrlOp := eval(tail^.head, AR)
              else applyCtrlOp := eval(tail^.tail^.head, AR);
          WHILEOP:
              begin
                s := eval(head, AR);
                while isTrueVal(s)
                do begin
                        s := eval(tail^.head, AR);
                        s := eval(head, AR)
                    end;
                applyCtrlOp := s
              end;
          SETOP:
              begin
                s := eval(tail^.head, AR);
                if head^.offset>0
                then argStack[AR+head^.offset-1] := s
                else if isBound(head^.varble, globalEnv)
                        then assign(head^.varble, s, globalEnv)
                        else bindVar(head^.varble, s, globalEnv);
                applyCtrlOp := s
              end;
          BEGINOP:
              begin
```

```
                        while args^.tail <> nil do
                           begin
                              s := eval(args^.head, AR);
                              args := args^.tail
                           end;
                        applyCtrlOp := eval(args^.head, AR)
                  end
            end (* case and with *)
      end; (* applyCtrlOp *)

begin (* eval *)
   with e^ do
      case etype of
         VALEXP:
            eval := sxp;
         VAREXP:
            if offset > 0
            then eval := argStack[AR+offset-1]
            else if isBound(varble, globalEnv)
                  then eval := fetch(varble, globalEnv)
                  else begin
                           write('Undefined variable: ');
                           prName(varble);
                           writeln;
                           goto 99
                        end;
         APEXP:
            if optr > numBuiltins
            then begin
                     newAR := stacktop;
                     evalList(args);
                     eval := applyUserFun(optr, newAR)
                  end
            else begin
                     op := primOp(optr);
                     if op in [IFOP .. BEGINOP]
                     then eval := applyCtrlOp(op, args)
                     else begin
                              evalList(args);
                              eval := applyValueOp(op)
                           end
                  end
      end (* case and with *)
end; (* eval *)
```

```
(***************************************************************
*                    READ-EVAL-PRINT LOOP                     *
***************************************************************)
```

The call to **eval** is changed to:

```
initStack;
prValue(eval(currentExp, 0));
```

J.2 Reference-Counting Interpreter

This interpreter is based on the stack-based one, and our presentation here notes differences with respect to that one.

```
(***************************************************************
*                       DECLARATIONS                          *
***************************************************************)
```

The only changes from the stack-based interpreter are: the constant **MEMSIZE** is added, a **refcnt** field is added to **SEXPREC**, and a global variable is declared to hold the free list:

```
MEMSIZE = 500;

SEXPREC = record
            refcnt: integer;
            case sxptype: SEXPTYPE of
                NILSXP: ();
                NUMSXP: (intval: integer);
                SYMSXP: (symval: NAME);
                LISTSXP: (carval, cdrval: SEXP)
          end;

freeSEXP: SEXP;
```

```
(******************************************************************
*                      MEMORY MANAGEMENT                         *
******************************************************************)
```

   initMemory, allocSExp, deallocSExp, increfcnt, decrefcnt, and rlsExp are
new. pushArg and popArgs have new calls to increfcnt and decrefcnt added; topArg
is unchanged; belowtopArg is new.

```
(* initMemory - allocate all SEXPREC's                          *)
procedure initMemory;
var
   i: integer;
   s: SEXP;
begin
   freeSEXP := nil;
   for i := 1 to MEMSIZE do begin
      s := freeSEXP;
      new(freeSEXP);
      freeSEXP^.carval := s
      end
end; (* initMemory *)

(* allocSExp - allocate SEXPREC from free list                  *)
function allocSExp (t: SEXPTYPE): SEXP;
var s: SEXP;
begin
   if freeSEXP = nil
   then begin
           writeln('Out of memory');
           goto 99
        end;
   s := freeSEXP;
   s^.sxptype := t;
   s^.refcnt := 0;
   allocSExp := s;
   freeSEXP := freeSEXP^.carval
end; (* allocSExp *)

(* deallocSExp - return SEXPREC to free list                    *)
procedure deallocSExp (s: SEXP);
begin
   s^.carval := freeSEXP;
   freeSEXP := s
end; (* deallocSExp *)

(* increfcnt - increment refcnt field of argument               *)
procedure increfcnt (s: SEXP);
begin
   s^.refcnt := s^.refcnt+1
end; (* increfcnt *)
```

```
(* decrefcnt - decrement refcnt field of argument and referents  *)
procedure decrefcnt (s: SEXP);
begin
   with s^ do begin
      refcnt := refcnt-1;
      if refcnt = 0
      then begin
              if sxptype = LISTSXP
              then begin
                      decrefcnt(carval);
                      decrefcnt(cdrval)
                   end;
              deallocSExp(s)
           end
      end
end; (* decrefcnt *)


(* rlsExp - decrement refcnt in all SEXP's within e              *)
procedure rlsExp (e: EXP);
var argl: EXPLIST;
begin
   case e^.etype of
      VALEXP: decrefcnt(e^.sxp);
      VAREXP: ;
      APEXP:
         begin
            argl := e^.args;
            while argl <> nil do begin
              rlsExp(argl^.head);
              argl := argl^.tail
              end
         end
   end
end; (* rlsExp *)


(* initStack - initialize argument stack                         *)
procedure initStack;
begin
   stacktop := 1
end; (* initStack *)


(* pushArg - push a single argument onto argStack                *)
procedure pushArg (s: SEXP);
begin
   if stacktop > STACKSIZE
   then begin
           writeln('stack overflow');
           stacktop := 1;
           goto 99
```

```
                end;
     argStack[stacktop] := s;
     stacktop := stacktop + 1;
     increfcnt(s)
end; (* pushArg *)


(* topArg - return top item in stack                               *)
function topArg: SEXP;
begin
     topArg := argStack[stacktop-1]
end; (* topArg *)


(* belowtopArg - return next-to-top item in stack                  *)
function belowtopArg: SEXP;
begin
     belowtopArg := argStack[stacktop-2]
end; (* belowtopArg *)


(* popArgs - pop argument list from top of stack                   *)
procedure popArgs (l: integer);
var i: integer;
begin
     for i := 1 to l do begin
        decrefcnt(argStack[stacktop-1]);
        stacktop := stacktop - 1
        end
end; (* popArgs *)




(*****************************************************************
 *                      DATA STRUCTURE OP'S                     *
 *****************************************************************)
```

The only change here is that mkVALEXP calls increfcnt:

```
(* mkVALEXP - return an EXP of type VALEXP with sxp s             *)
function mkVALEXP (s: SEXP): EXP;
var e: EXP;
begin
     new(e);
     e^.etype := VALEXP;
     e^.sxp := s;
     increfcnt(s);
     mkVALEXP := e
end; (* mkVALEXP *)
```

```
(****************************************************************
*                     NAME MANAGEMENT                          *
****************************************************************)
```

No changes.

```
(****************************************************************
*                          INPUT                               *
****************************************************************)
```

Here, as elsewhere, calls to `mkSExp` are changed to `allocSExp`; this change is not shown. The only other change is the calling of `increfcnt` from `parseList`. The `SEXP` record returned from `parseList` has a `refcnt` of 0 (incremented to 1 by `mkVALEXP`), but all `SEXP` records to which it points have a `refcnt` of 1.

```
(* parseList - return list starting at userinput[pos]          *)
      function parseList: SEXP;
      var car, cdr: SEXP;
      begin
         if userinput[pos] = ')'
         then begin
                 parseList := allocSExp(NILSXP);
                 pos := skipblanks(pos+1)
              end
         else begin
                 car := parseSExp;
                 cdr := parseList;
                 s  := allocSExp(LISTSXP);
                 s^.carval := car;
                 increfcnt(car);
                 s^.cdrval := cdr;
                 increfcnt(cdr);
                 parseList := s
              end
      end; (* parseList *)
```

```
(****************************************************************
*                      ENVIRONMENTS                            *
****************************************************************)
```

A call to `increfcnt` is made from `bindVar`, and calls to `increfcnt` and `decrefcnt` are made from `assign`.

```
(* bindVar - bind variable nm to value s in environment rho    *)
procedure bindVar (nm: NAME; s: SEXP; rho: ENV);
begin
   increfcnt(s);
   rho^.vars := mkNamelist(nm, rho^.vars);
   rho^.values := mkValuelist(s, rho^.values)
end; (* bindVar *)
```

```
(* assign - assign value s to variable nm in rho                *)
procedure assign (nm: NAME; s: SEXP; rho: ENV);
var varloc: VALUELIST;
begin
   increfcnt(s);
   varloc := findVar(nm, rho);
   decrefcnt(varloc^.head);
   varloc^.head := s
end; (* assign *)



(*****************************************************************
 *                       S-EXPRESSIONS                          *
 *****************************************************************)
```

applyValueOp becomes a procedure instead of a function; it places its result onto the stack. It is unsafe to pop its arguments off the stack until they have been consumed, so it postpones the popping until the end. The only other change is that increfcnt is called in the CONSOP case.

```
(* applyValueOp - apply VALUEOP op to arguments on stop of stack *)
procedure applyValueOp (op: VALUEOP);

begin (* applyValueOp *)
   result := nilValue;
   s1 := topArg; (* 1st actual *)
   if arity(op) = 2
   then begin
           s2 := s1; (* 1st actual was really 2nd actual *)
           s1 := belowtopArg (* 1st actual *)
        end;
   if op in [PLUSOP .. DIVOP, LTOP .. GTOP]
      :
      :
      no changes until CONSOP case
      :
      :
            CONSOP:
               begin
                  result := allocSExp(LISTSXP);
                  with result^ do begin
                     carval := s1;
                     increfcnt(s1);
                     cdrval := s2;
                     increfcnt(s2)
                     end
               end;
      :
      no changes until end
```

```
            :
   popArgs(arity(op));
   pushArg(result)
end; (* applyValueOp *)




(*****************************************************************
*                      EVALUATION                              *
*****************************************************************)
```

The changes here are quite extensive. We list the entire section.

```
(* eval - return value of e; param's start at argStack[AR]      *)
procedure eval (e: EXP; AR: integer);

var
   s: SEXP;
   op: BUILTINOP;
   newAR: integer;

(* evalList - evaluate each expression in el                    *)
   procedure evalList (el: EXPLIST);
   begin
      if el <> nil
      then begin
              eval(el^.head, AR);
              evalList(el^.tail)
           end
   end; (* evalList *)

(* applyUserFun - apply nm; arg's start at argStack[newAR]      *)
   procedure applyUserFun (nm: NAME; newAR: integer);
   var f: FUNDEF;
   begin
      f := fetchFun(nm);
      if f = nil
      then begin
              write('Undefined function: ');
              prName(nm);
              writeln;
              goto 99
           end;
      with f^ do begin
         eval(body, newAR);
         s := topArg;
         stacktop := stacktop-1;
         popArgs(lengthNL(formals));
         argStack[stacktop] := s ;
```

```
            stacktop := stacktop+1
            end
    end; (* applyUserFun *)

(* applyCtrlOp - apply CONTROLOP op to args                    *)
    procedure applyCtrlOp (op: CONTROLOP; args: EXPLIST);
    var s: SEXP;
    begin
        with args^ do
            case op of
                IFOP:
                    begin
                        eval(head,AR);
                        s := topArg;
                        if isTrueVal(s)
                        then begin popArgs(1); eval(tail^.head, AR) end
                        else begin popArgs(1); eval(tail^.tail^.head, AR) end
                    end;
                WHILEOP:
                    begin
                        pushArg(nilValue);
                        eval(head, AR);
                        s := topArg;
                        while isTrueVal(s) do begin
                            popArgs(2);
                            eval(tail^.head, AR);
                            eval(head, AR);
                            s := topArg
                            end;
                        popArgs(1)
                    end;
                SETOP:
                    begin
                        eval(tail^.head, AR);
                        s := topArg;
                        if head^.offset>0
                        then begin
                                increfcnt(s);
                                decrefcnt(argStack[AR+head^.offset-1]);
                                argStack[AR+head^.offset-1] := s
                            end
                        else if isBound(head^.varble, globalEnv)
                                then assign(head^.varble, s, globalEnv)
                                else bindVar(head^.varble, s, globalEnv)
                    end;
                BEGINOP:
                    begin
                        while args^.tail <> nil do
                            begin
```

```
                        eval(args^.head, AR);
                        popArgs(1);
                        args := args^.tail
                     end;
                  eval(args^.head, AR)
               end
         end (* case and with *)
    end; (* applyCtrlOp *)

begin (* eval *)
   with e^ do
      case etype of
         VALEXP:
            pushArg(sxp);
         VAREXP:
            begin
               if offset > 0
               then s := argStack[AR+offset-1]
               else if isBound(varble, globalEnv)
                     then s := fetch(varble, globalEnv)
                     else begin
                             write('Undefined variable: ');
                             prName(varble);
                             writeln;
                             goto 99
                          end;
               pushArg(s)
            end;
         APEXP:
            if optr > numBuiltins
            then begin
                    newAR := stacktop;
                    evalList(args);
                    applyUserFun(optr, newAR)
                 end
            else begin
                    op := primOp(optr);
                    if op in [IFOP .. BEGINOP]
                    then applyCtrlOp(op, args)
                    else begin
                            evalList(args);
                            applyValueOp(op)
                         end
                 end
      end (* case and with *)
   end; (* eval *)
```

```
(************************************************************
*                    READ-EVAL-PRINT LOOP                  *
************************************************************)
```

initMemory is called before beginning the read-eval-print loop. nilValue and trueValue start off with a reference count of 1; it can never go down to zero. When the input is an expression, its value must be printed before it is deallocated (because the process of deallocation can destroy its value). rlsExp decrements the reference counts of any SEXP records contained in the input expression.

```
begin (* lisp main *)
    initNames;
    initStack;
    initMemory;

    nilValue := allocSExp(NILSXP);
    increfcnt(nilValue);
    trueValue := allocSExp(SYMSXP); trueValue^.symval := numNames;
    increfcnt(trueValue);

    globalEnv := emptyEnv;

    quittingtime := false;
99:
    while not quittingtime do begin
        reader;
        if matches(pos, 4, 'quit                ')
        then quittingtime := true
        else if (userinput[pos] = '(') and
                matches(skipblanks(pos+1), 6, 'define                ')
            then begin
                    prName(parseDef);
                    writeln
                end
            else begin
                    currentExp := parseExp;
                    eval(currentExp, 0);
                    prValue(topArg);
                    popArgs(1);
                    rlsExp(currentExp);
                    writeln;
                    writeln
                end
        end (* while *)
end. (* lisp *)
```

Bibliography

[1985]   H. Abelson, G. J. Sussman, *Structure and Interpretation of Computer Programs*, MIT Press, Cambridge, Mass., 1985.

[1986]   A. Aho, R. Sethi, J. Ullman, *Compilers: Principles, Techniques, and Tools*, Addison-Wesley, Reading, Mass., 1986.

[1987]   A. W. Appel, "Garbage collection can be faster than stack allocation," *Info. Proc. Letters* **25**, 1987, pp. 275–279.

[1987]   A. W. Appel, D.B. MacQueen, *A Standard ML compiler*, Proc. Functional Programming Languages and Computer Architecture, G. Kahn (ed.), Portland, Oregon, Sept. 1987, published as *Lecture Notes in Computer Science* **274**, Springer-Verlag, New York, pp. 301–324.

[1979]   R. Austing, B. Barnes, D. Bonnette, G. Engel, G. Stokes (eds.), "Curriculum '78: Recommendations for the undergraduate program in Computer Science," *Comm. ACM* **22**(3), March 1979, pp. 147–166.

[1978]   J. Backus, "Can programming be liberated from the von Neumann style? A functional style and its algebra of programs," *Comm. ACM* **21**(8), Aug. 1978, pp. 613–641.

[1978]   H. G. Baker, "List-processing in real time on a serial computer," *Comm. ACM* **21**(4), April 1978, pp. 280–294.

[1981]   H. Barendregt, *The Lambda Calculus — Its Syntax and Semantics*, North-Holland, Amsterdam, 1981.

[1967]   W. Baring-Gould, *The Annotated Sherlock Holmes*, Clarkson N. Potter, Inc., New York, 1967.

[1983]   J. G. P. Barnes, *Programming in ADA*, 2nd ed., Addison-Wesley, Reading, Mass., 1983.

[1986]   W. Barrett, R. Bates, D. Gustafson, J. Couch, *Compiler Construction: Theory and Practice*, 2nd ed., SRA, Chicago, Illinois, 1986.

[1986]   D. H. Bartley, J. C. Jensen, "The implementation of PC Scheme,"
         Proc. ACM Symp. on Lisp and Functional Programming, Cambridge,
         Mass., August 1986, pp. 86–93.

[1973]   G. Birtwistle, O.-J. Dahl, B. Myhrhaug, K. Nygaard, *SIMULA BE-
         GIN*, Van Nostrand-Reinhold, New York, 1973.

[1986]   J. Bishop, *Data Abstraction in Programming Languages*, Addison-
         Wesley, Reading, Mass., 1986.

[1986]   D. Bobrow, K. Kahn, G. Kiczales, L. Masinter, M. Stefik, F. Zdybel,
         "CommonLoops: Merging Lisp and object-oriented programming,"
         Proc. ACM Conf. on Object-Oriented Programming Systems, Lan-
         guages and Applications (OOPSLA '86), Portland, Oregon, 1986, pp.
         17–29.

[1988]   D. Bobrow, L. G. DeMichiel, R. P. Gabriel, S. E. Keene, G. Kiczales,
         D. A. Moon, *Common Lisp Object System Specification, SIGPLAN
         Notices* **23**, Special Issue, Sept. 1988.

[1987]   T. Budd, *A Little Smalltalk*, Addison-Wesley, Reading, Mass., 1987.

[1983]   A. Bundy, *The Computer Modelling of Mathematical Reasoning*, Aca-
         demic Press, New York, 1983.

[1975]   W. H. Burge, *Recursive Programming Techniques*, Addison-Wesley,
         Reading, Mass., 1975.

[1971]   R. M. Burstall, J. S. Collins, R. J. Popplestone, *Programming in
         POP-2*, Edinburgh U. Press, Edinburgh, Scotland, 1971.

[1980]   R. M. Burstall, D. B. MacQueen, D. T. Sannella, "HOPE: an ex-
         perimental applicative language," 1980 LISP Conference, Stanford,
         Calif., 1980, pp. 136–143.

[1981]   *BYTE Magazine* **6**, Special Issue on SMALLTALK, August 1981.

[1973]   C.-L. Chang, R. C.-T. Lee, *Symbolic Logic and Mechanical Theorem
         Proving*, Academic Press, New York, 1973.

[1941]   A. Church, *The Calculi of Lambda Conversion*, Princeton Univ.
         Press, Princeton, New Jersey, 1941.

[1982]   K. L. Clark, S. A. Tarnlund (eds.), *Logic Programming*, Academic
         Press, New York, 1982.

[1987]   W. F. Clocksin, C. S. Mellish, *Programming in Prolog*, 3rd ed.,
         Springer-Verlag, New York, 1987. (First ed. 1981, 2nd ed. 1984.)

[1970]   E. F. Codd, "A relational model of data for large shared data banks,"
           Comm. ACM **13**(6), June 1970, pp. 377–387.

[1981]   J. Cohen, "Garbage collection of linked data structures," *ACM Com-
           puting Surveys,* **13**(3), 1981, pp. 341–368.

[1988]   J. Cohen, "A view of the origins and development of Prolog," *Comm.
           ACM* **31**(1), Jan. 1988, pp. 26–36.

[1986]   N. H. Cohen, *ADA as a Second Language*, McGraw-Hill, New York,
           1986.

[1973]   A. Colmerauer, H. Kanoui, P. Roussel, R. Pasero, *Un Système de
           Communication Homme-Machine en Francais*, Groupe de Recherche
           en Intelligence Artificielle, Université d'Aix-Marseille, 1973.

[1986]   B. J. Cox, *Object Oriented Programming: An Evolutionary Ap-
           proach*, Addison-Wesley, Reading, Mass., 1986.

[1972a]   O.-J. Dahl, E. W. Dijkstra, C. A. R. Hoare, *Structured Programming*,
           Academic Press, New York, 1972.

[1972b]   O.-J. Dahl, C. A. R. Hoare, "Hierarchical program structures," in
           Dahl et. al. [1972a], pp. 175–220.

[1986]   D. DeGroot, G. Lindstrom, *Logic Programming: Functions, Rela-
           tions, and Equations*, Prentice-Hall, Englewood Cliffs, New Jersey,
           1986.

[1983]   U.S. Department of Defense, *Reference Manual for the ADA Pro-
           gramming Language*, ANSI/MIL-STD-1815A, Jan. 1983.

[1985]   N. Dershowitz, "Computing with rewrite systems," *Information and
           Control* **65**(2/3), 1985, pp. 122–157.

[1988]   N. Dershowitz, J.-P. Jouannaud, "Rewrite systems," in J. van
           Leeuwen, (ed.), *Handbook of Theoretical Computer Science B: For-
           mal Methods and Semantics*, North-Holland, Amsterdam, 1990.

[1984]   L. P. Deutsch, A.M. Schiffman, "Efficient implementation of the
           Smalltalk-80 system," *11th Annual ACM Conf. on Principles of Pro-
           gramming Languages*, 1984, pp. 297–302.

[1987]   R. K. Dybvig, *The Scheme Programming Language*, Prentice-Hall,
           Englewood Cliffs, New Jersey, 1987.

[1969]   R. Fenichel, J. Yochelson, "A LISP garbage-collector for virtual-
           memory computer systems," *Comm. ACM* **12**(11), Nov. 1969,
           pp. 611–612.

[1967] R. W. Floyd, "Assigning meanings to programs," in J. T. Schwartz(ed.), "Mathematical Aspects of Computer Science," *Proc. Amer. Math. Soc.* **19**, 1967, pp. 19–32.

[1974] D. P. Friedman, *The Little LISPer*, SRA, Chicago, Illinois, 1974.

[1976] D. P. Friedman, D. Wise, "CONS should not evaluate its arguments," *3rd Intl. Colloq. on Automata, Languages, and Programming*, Edinburgh, 1976.

[1984] D. P. Friedman, C. T. Haynes, E. E. Kohlbecker, "Programming with continuations," in P. Pepper (ed.), *Program Transformations and Programming Environments*, Springer-Verlag, New York, 1984, pp. 263–274.

[1985] K. Futatsugi, J. Goguen, J.-P. Jouannaud, J. Meseguer, "Principles of OBJ2," *12th ACM Conf. on Princ. of Prog. Lang., New Orleans*, Jan. 1985, pp. 52–66.

[1985] R. Gabriel, *Performance and Evaluation of Lisp Systems*, The MIT Press, Cambridge, Mass., 1985.

[1986] J. Gallier, *Logic for Computer Science: Foundations of Automatic Theorem Proving*, Harper & Row, New York, 1986.

[1987] C. Ghezzi, M. Jazayeri, *Programming Language Concepts*, 2nd ed., Wiley, New York, 1987.

[1974] L. Gilman, A. Rose, *APL: An Interactive Approach*, 2nd ed., Wiley, New York, 1974.

[1979] J. Goguen, J. Thatcher, E. Wagner, "An initial algebra approach to the specification, correctness, and implementation of abstract data types," in Yeh [1979], pp. 80–149.

[1983] A. Goldberg, *Smalltalk-80: The Interactive Programming Environment*, Addison-Wesley, Reading, Mass., 1983.

[1983] A. Goldberg, D. Robson, *Smalltalk-80: The Language and its Implementation*, Addison-Wesley, Reading, Mass., 1983.

[1979] M. Gordon, *The Denotational Description of Programming Languages*, Springer-Verlag, New York, 1979.

[1978] M. Gordon, R. Milner, L. Morris, M. Newey, C. Wadsworth, "A metalanguage for interactive proof in LCF," *5th Annual ACM Conf. on Principles of Programming Languages*, 1978, pp. 119–130.

[1979b] M. Gordon, R. Milner, C. Wadsworth, *Edinburgh LCF, Lecture Notes in Computer Science* **78**, Springer-Verlag, New York, 1979.

[1987]   K. Gorlen, "An object-oriented class library for C++ programs,"
          Software — Practice and Experience **17**(12), Dec. 1987, pp. 899–922.

[1978]   D. Gries (ed.), *Programming Methodology, A Collection of Articles
          by Members of IFIP WG2.3*, Springer-Verlag, New York, 1978.

[1981]   D. Gries, *The Science of Programming*, Springer-Verlag, New York,
          1981.

[1978]   J. Guttag, E. Horowitz, D. Musser, "Abstract data types and soft-
          ware validation," *Comm. ACM* **21**, 1978, pp. 1048–1064.

[1976]   P. Henderson, J. M. Morris, "A lazy evaluator," *3rd Annual ACM
          Conf. on Principles of Programming Languages*, Atlanta, 1976,
          pp. 95–103.

[1980]   P. Henderson, *Functional Programming: Application and Implemen-
          tation*, Prentice-Hall International, Englewood Cliffs, New Jersey,
          1980.

[1969]   C. A. R. Hoare, "An axiomatic approach to computer programming,"
          Comm. ACM **12**, 1969, pp. 576–580, 583.

[1972]   C. A. R. Hoare, "Proof of correctness of data representations," *Acta
          Informatica* **1**(1), 1972, pp. 271–281. Reprinted in Gries [1978].

[1974]   C. A. R. Hoare, "Monitors: an operating system structuring con-
          cept," *Comm. ACM* **17**(10), October, 1974, pp. 549–557.

[1981]   C. A. R. Hoare, "The emperor's old clothes," 1980 Turing Award
          Lecture, *Comm. ACM* **24**(2), Feb. 1981, pp. 75–83.

[1985]   C. A. R. Hoare, J. C. Shepherdson, *Mathematical Logic and Pro-
          gramming Languages*, Prentice-Hall International, Englewood Cliffs,
          New Jersey, 1985.

[1984]   C. J. Hogger, *Introduction to Logic Programming*, Academic Press,
          London, 1984.

[1979]   J. Hopcroft, J. Ullman, *Introduction to Automata Theory, Lan-
          guages, and Computation*, Addison-Wesley, Reading, Mass., 1979.

[1983]   E. Horowitz, *Programming Languages: A Grand Tour*, Computer
          Science Press, Rockville, Md., 1983.

[1980]   G. Huet, D. C. Oppen, "Equations and rewrite rules: A survey," in
          Formal Language Theory: Perspectives and Open Problems, R. Book
          (ed.), Academic Press, New York, 1980, pp. 349–405.

[1984]   R. J. M. Hughes, "Why functional programming matters," Memo 40, Programming Methodology Group, Chalmers University of Technology, Göteborg, Sweden, 1984.

[1962]   K. Iverson, *A Programming Language*, Wiley, New York, 1962.

[1980]   K. Iverson, "Notation as a tool of thought," 1979 ACM Turing Award Lecture, *Comm. ACM* **23**, 8, August 1980, pp. 444–465.

[1979]   K. Iverson, "Operators," *ACM Trans. on Prog. Lang. and Sys.* **1**(2), 1979, pp. 161–176.

[1987]   K. Iverson, "A Dictionary of APL," *APL Quote Quad* **18**(1), Sept. 1987, pp. 5–37.

[1986]   M.A. Jenkins, J.I. Glasgow, C.D. McCrosky, "Programming styles in Nial," *IEEE Software* **3**(1), Jan. 1986, pp. 46–55.

[1988]   R. E. Johnson, J. O. Graver, L. W. Zurawski, "TS: an optimizing compiler for Smalltalk," *Proc. ACM Conf. on Objected-Oriented Programming Systems, Languages and Applications* (OOPSLA '88), San Diego, Calif., 1988, pp. 1–8.

[1971]   J. Johnston, "The contour model of block structured processes," in J. Tou, P. Wegner (eds.), *Proc. Symp. on Data Structures in Programming Languages, SIGPLAN Notices* **6**(2), June 1971, pp. 55–82.

[1985]   J.-P. Jouannaud (ed.), *Conf. on Functional Programming Languages and Computer Architecture*, Nancy, France, *Lecture Notes in Computer Science* **201**, Springer-Verlag, New York, 1985.

[1980]   C. B. Jones, *Software Development: A Rigorous Approach*, Prentice-Hall International, Englewood Cliffs, New Jersey, 1980.

[1986]   T. Kaehler, D. Patterson, *A Taste of Smalltalk*, Norton, New York, 1986.

[1977]   G. Kahn, D. B. MacQueen, "Coroutines and networks of parallel processes," *Info. Proc.* **77**, North-Holland, Amsterdam, 1977, pp. 993–998.

[1983]   S. Kamin, "Final Data Types and their Specification," *ACM Trans. on Prog. Lang. and Sys.* **5**(1), Jan. 1983, pp. 97–123.

[1969]   R. M. Karp, R. E. Miller, "Parallel Program Schemata," *J. of Comp. and Sys. Sci.* **3**, 1969, pp. 147-195.

[1978]   B. W. Kernighan, D. M. Ritchie, *The C Programming Language*, Prentice-Hall, Englewood Cliffs, New Jersey, 1978, 2nd Edition, 1988.

[1973]   D. E. Knuth, *The Art of Computer Programming*, Vol. 1, *Fundamental Algorithms*, 2nd Edition, Addison-Wesley, Reading, Mass., 1973.

[1974]   D. E. Knuth, "Computer programming as an art," 1974 ACM Turing Award Lecture, *Comm. ACM* **17**, 12, Dec. 1974, pp. 667–673.

[1981]   D. E. Knuth, *The Art of Computer Programming*, Vol. 2, *Seminumerical Algorithms*, 2nd Edition, Addison-Wesley, Reading, Mass., 1981.

[1974]   R. Kowalski, "Predicate logic as a programming language," *Proc. IFIP 74*, Stockholm, Sweden, North-Holland, Amsterdam, 1974, pp. 569–574.

[1979a]   R. Kowalski, "Algorithm = logic + control," *Comm. ACM* **22**(7), July 1979, pp. 424–436.

[1979b]   R. Kowalski, *Logic for Problem Solving*, Elsevier North-Holland, New York, 1979.

[1988]   R. Kowalski, "The early years of logic programming," *Comm. ACM* **31**(1), Jan. 1988, pp. 38–43.

[1986]   D. Kranz, R. Kelsey, J. Rees, P. Hudak, J. Philbin, N. Adams, "ORBIT: an optimizing compiler for Scheme," Proc. SIGPLAN '86 Symp. on Compiler Construction, Palo Alto, Calif., June 1986; published as *SIGPLAN Notices* **21**(7), July, 1986.

[1964]   P. J. Landin, "The mechanical evaluation of expressions," *Computer J.* **6**, 1964, pp. 308–320.

[1966]   P. J. Landin, "The next 700 programming languages," *Comm. ACM* **9**(3), March 1966, pp. 157–164.

[1983]   H. Lieberman, C. Hewitt, "A real-time garbage collector based on the lifetimes of objects," *Comm. ACM* **26**(6), June 1983, pp. 419–429.

[1975]   B. Liskov, S. Zilles, "Specification techniques for data abstractions," *IEEE Trans. on Software Eng.* **SE-1**(1), 1975, pp. 7–19.

[1977]   B. Liskov, R. Atkinson, C. Schaffert, "Abstraction mechanisms in CLU," *Comm. ACM* **20**(8), August 1977, pp. 564–576.

[1979]   B. Liskov, A. Snyder, "Exception Handling in CLU," *IEEE Trans. on Software Eng.* **SE-5**(6), 1979, pp. 547–558.

[1981]   B. Liskov, *CLU Reference Manual*, Lecture Notes in Computer Science 114, Springer-Verlag, New York, 1981.

[1986]   B. Liskov, J. Guttag, *Abstraction and Specification in Program Development*, The MIT Press, Cambridge, Mass., and McGraw-Hill, New York, 1986.

[1984]   J. W. Lloyd, *Foundations of Logic Programming*, Springer-Verlag, New York, 1984.

[1984]   J. J. C. Loeckx, K. Sieber, R. Stansifer, *The Foundations of Program Verification*, Wiley-Teubner, New York, 1984.

[1983]   D. Maier, *The Theory of Relational Databases*, Computer Science Press, Rockville, Md., 1983.

[1988]   D. Maier, D. S. Warren, *Computing with Logic*, Benjamin/Cummings, Menlo Park, Calif., 1988.

[1974]   Z. Manna, *Mathematical Theory of Computation*, McGraw-Hill, New York, 1974.

[1986]   M. Marcotty, H.F. Ledgard, *Programming Language Landscape*, 2nd ed., SRA, Chicago, Illinois, 1986.

[1960]   J. McCarthy, "Recursive functions of symbolic expressions and their computation by machine," *Comm. ACM* **3**(4), April 1960, pp. 184–195.

[1962]   J. McCarthy, *Lisp 1.5 Programmer's Manual*, The MIT Press, Cambridge, Mass., 1962 (reprinted in Horowitz [1983]).

[1987]   B. MacLennan, *Principles of Programming Languages*, 2nd ed., Holt, Rinehart, and Winston, New York, 1987.

[1982]   A. D. McGettrick, *Program Verification using ADA*, Cambridge Univ. Press, Cambridge, England, 1982.

[1987]   B. Meyer, "Eiffel: Programming for reusability and extendibility," *SIGPLAN Notices* **22**(2), Feb. 1987, pp. 85–94.

[1988]   B. Meyer, *Object-Oriented Software Construction*, Prentice-Hall International, Englewood Cliffs, New Jersey, 1988.

[1978]   R. Milner, "A theory of type polymorphism in programming," *J. of Comp. Systems and Science* **17**, 1978, pp. 348–375.

[1984]   R. Milner, "A proposal for Standard ML," *1984 ACM Symp. on LISP and Functional Programming*, pp. 184–197.

[1987]   R. Milner, "The Standard ML Core Language (revised version)," in Wikström [1987], pp. 378–408.

[1963]   M. L. Minsky, "A Lisp garbage collector algorithm using serial sec-
          ondary storage," Memo 58 (rev.), Project MAC, MIT, Cambridge,
          Mass., Dec. 1963.

[1986]   D. A. Moon, "Object-oriented programming with flavors," *Proc.
          ACM Conf. on Objected-Oriented Programming Systems, Languages
          and Applications* (OOPSLA '86), Portland, Oregon, 1986, pp. 1–8.

[1979]   T. More, "The nested rectangular array as a model of data," *Proc.
          APL 79, APL Quote Quad* **9**(4), June 1979, pp. 55–73.

[1980]   N. J. Nilsson, *Principles of Artificial Intelligence*, Tioga, Palo Alto,
          Calif., 1980.

[1972a]   D. Parnas, "A technique for software module specification with ex-
          amples," *Comm. ACM* **15**(5), 1972, pp. 330–336.

[1972b]   D. Parnas, "On the criteria to be used in decomposing systems into
          modules," *Comm. ACM* **15**(12), 1972, pp. 1053–1058.

[1982]   J. Payne, *Introduction to Simulation: Programming Techniques and
          Methods of Analysis*, McGraw-Hill, New York, 1982.

[1987]   S. L. Peyton Jones, *The Implementation of Functional Programming
          Languages*, Prentice-Hall International, Englewood Cliffs, New Jer-
          sey, 1987.

[1988]   L. J. Pinson, R. S. Wiener, *An Introduction to Object-Oriented Pro-
          gramming and Smalltalk*, Addison-Wesley, Reading, Mass., 1988.

[1975]   R. Polivka, S. Pakin, *APL: The Language and Its Usage*, Prentice-
          Hall, Englewood Cliffs, New Jersey, 1975.

[1986]   J. Rees, W. Clinger (eds.), "Revised[3] report on the algorithmic lan-
          guage SCHEME," *SIGPLAN Notices* **21**(12), Dec. 1986, pp. 37–79.

[1986]   E. Reingold, W. Hansen, *Data Structures in Pascal*, Little, Brown,
          Boston, Mass., 1986.

[1988]   E. Reingold, R. Reingold, *PascAlgorithms: An Introduction to Pro-
          gramming*, Scott, Foresman, Glenview, Ill., 1988.

[1981]   J. C. Reynolds, *The Craft of Programming*, Prentice-Hall Interna-
          tional, Englewood Cliffs, New Jersey, 1981.

[1988]   G. A. Ringwood, "Parlog86 and the dining logicians," *Comm. ACM*
          31(1), Jan. 1988, pp. 10–25.

[1986]   E. S. Roberts, *Thinking Recursively*, Wiley, New York, 1986.

[1965]   J. A. Robinson, "A machine-oriented logic based on the resolution principle," *JACM* **12**(1), Jan. 1965, 23–41.

[1983]   J. A. Robinson, "Logic programming — past, present, and future," *New Generation Computing* **1**, 1983, pp. 107–124.

[1984]   J. S. Rohl, *Recursion via Pascal*, Cambridge Univ. Press, Cambridge, England, 1984.

[1988]   N. C. Rowe, *Artificial Intelligence Through Prolog*, Prentice Hall, Englewood Cliffs, New Jersey, 1988.

[1986]   C. Schaffert, T. Cooper, B. Bullis, M. Kilian, C. Wilpolt, "An introduction to Trellis/Owl," *Proc. ACM Conf. on Object-Oriented Programming Systems, Languages and Applications* (OOPSLA '86), Portland, Oregon, 1986, pp. 9–16.

[1986]   D. Schmidt, *Denotational Semantics: A Methodology for Language Development*, Allyn and Bacon, Boston, Mass., 1986.

[1986]   K. Schmucker, *Object-Oriented Programming for the Macintosh*, Hayden Book Co., Hasbrouck Heights, New Jersey, 1986.

[1967]   H. Schorr, W. Waite, "An efficient machine-independent procedure for garbage collection in various list structures," *Comm. ACM* **10**(8), August 1967, pp. 501–506.

[1974]   T. Schriber, *Discrete System Simulation*, Wiley, New York, 1974.

[1989]   R. Sethi, *Programming Languages: Concepts and Constructs*, Addison-Wesley, Reading, Mass., 1988.

[1983]   J. Siekmann, G. Wrightson (eds.), *Automation of Reasoning: Classical Papers on Computational Logic*, volumes 1 (1957–1966) and 2 (1967–1970), Springer-Verlag, New York, 1983.

[1987]   S. Slade, *The T Programming Language*, Prentice-Hall, Englewood Cliffs, New Jersey, 1987.

[1980]   T. A. Standish, *Data Structure Techniques*, Addison-Wesley, Reading, Mass., 1980.

[1975]   G. L. Steele, Jr., "Multiprocessing compactifying garbage collection," *Comm. ACM* **18**, 9, Sept. 1975, pp. 495–508.

[1976]   G. L. Steele, Jr., G. J. Sussman, "LAMBDA: The ultimate imperative," MIT AI Memo No. 453, March, 1976.

[1978]   G. L. Steele, Jr., G. J. Sussman, "The art of the interpreter, or, The modularity complex (Parts zero, one, and two)," MIT AI Memo No. 453, May, 1978.

[1984]   G. L. Steele, Jr., *Common Lisp: The Language*, Digital Press, Burlington, Mass., 1984.

[1986]   L. Sterling, E. Shapiro, *The Art of Prolog*, The MIT Press, Cambridge, Mass., 1986.

[1977]   J. Stoy, *Denotational Semantics: The Scott-Strachey Approach to Programming Language Theory*, MIT Press, Cambridge, Mass., 1977.

[1986]   B. Stroustrup, *The C++ Programming Language*, Addison-Wesley, Reading, Mass., 1986.

[1988]   B. Stroustrup, "What is object-oriented programming?" *IEEE Software* **5**(3), May 1988, pp. 10–20.

[1975]   G. J. Sussman, G. L. Steele, Jr., "Scheme: An interpreter for an extended lambda calculus," MIT AI Memo No. 349, Dec. 1975.

[1985]   *TI SCHEME Language Reference Manual*, Computer Science Laboratory, Texas Instruments Inc., Dallas, Texas, 1985.

[1984]   D. Touretzky, *LISP: A Gentle Introduction to Symbolic Computation*, Harper-Row, New York, 1984.

[1979a] D. A. Turner, "A new implementation technique for applicative languages," *Software — Practice and Experience* **9**, 1979, pp. 31–49.

[1979b] D. A. Turner, "Another algorithm for bracket abstraction," J. of Symbolic Logic 44(2), June 1979, pp. 267–270.

[1983]   D. A. Turner, *SASL Language Manual*, Computer Laboratory, U. of Kent, Canterbury, England, originally dated 1976, revised 1979 and 1983.

[1985a] D. A. Turner, "Functional programs as executable specifications," in C. A. R. Hoare, J. C. Shepherdson [1985], 1985, pp. 29–54.

[1985b] D. A. Turner, "MIRANDA— a non-strict functional language with polymorphic types," in Jouannaud [1985], pp. 1–16.

[1985c] D. A. Turner, "An introduction to MIRANDA," in Peyton Jones [1987], pp. 431–438.

[1984]   D. Ungar, "Generation scavenging: a non-disruptive high performance storage reclamation algorithm," ACM SIGSOFT/SIGPLAN Conf. on Practical Software Development Environments, April 1984, pp. 157–167; published as *SIGPLAN Notices* **19**(5), May 1984.

[1968]   P. Wegner, *Programming Languages, Information Structures, and Machine Organization*, McGraw-Hill, New York, 1968.

[1981]   R. Wexelblat (ed.), *History of Programming Languages*, Academic Press, New York, 1981.

[1988]   R. S. Wiener, L. J. Pinson, *An Introduction to Object-Oriented Programming and C++*, Addison-Wesley, Reading, Mass., 1988.

[1987]   Å Wikström, *Functional Programming using Standard ML*, Prentice-Hall International, Englewood Cliffs, New Jersey, 1987.

[1986]   R. Wilensky, *Common LISPcraft*, Norton, New York, 1986.

[1972]   T. Winograd, *Understanding Natural Language*, Academic Press, New York, 1972.

[1977]   P. H. Winston, *Artificial Intelligence*, Addison-Wesley, Reading, Mass., 1977.

[1984]   P. H. Winston, B. K. Horn, *LISP*, 2nd ed., Addison-Wesley, Reading, Mass., 1984.

[1971]   N. Wirth, "The development of programs by stepwise refinement," *Comm. ACM* **14**, 1971, pp. 221–227.

[1982]   N. Wirth, *Programming in Modula-2*, 2nd ed., Springer-Verlag, New York, 1982.

[1984]   L. Wos, R. Overbeek, E. Lusk, J. Boyle, *Automated Reasoning: Introduction and Applications*, Prentice-Hall, Englewood Cliffs, New Jersey, 1984.

[1976]   W. Wulf, R. London, M. Shaw, "An introduction to the construction and verification of ALPHARD Programs," *IEEE Trans. on Software Eng.* **SE-2**(4), 1976, pp. 253–265.

[1979]   R. Yeh (ed.), *Current Trends in Programming Methodology IV: Data Structuring*, Prentice-Hall, Englewood Cliffs, New Jersey, 1979.

Index